AF379127

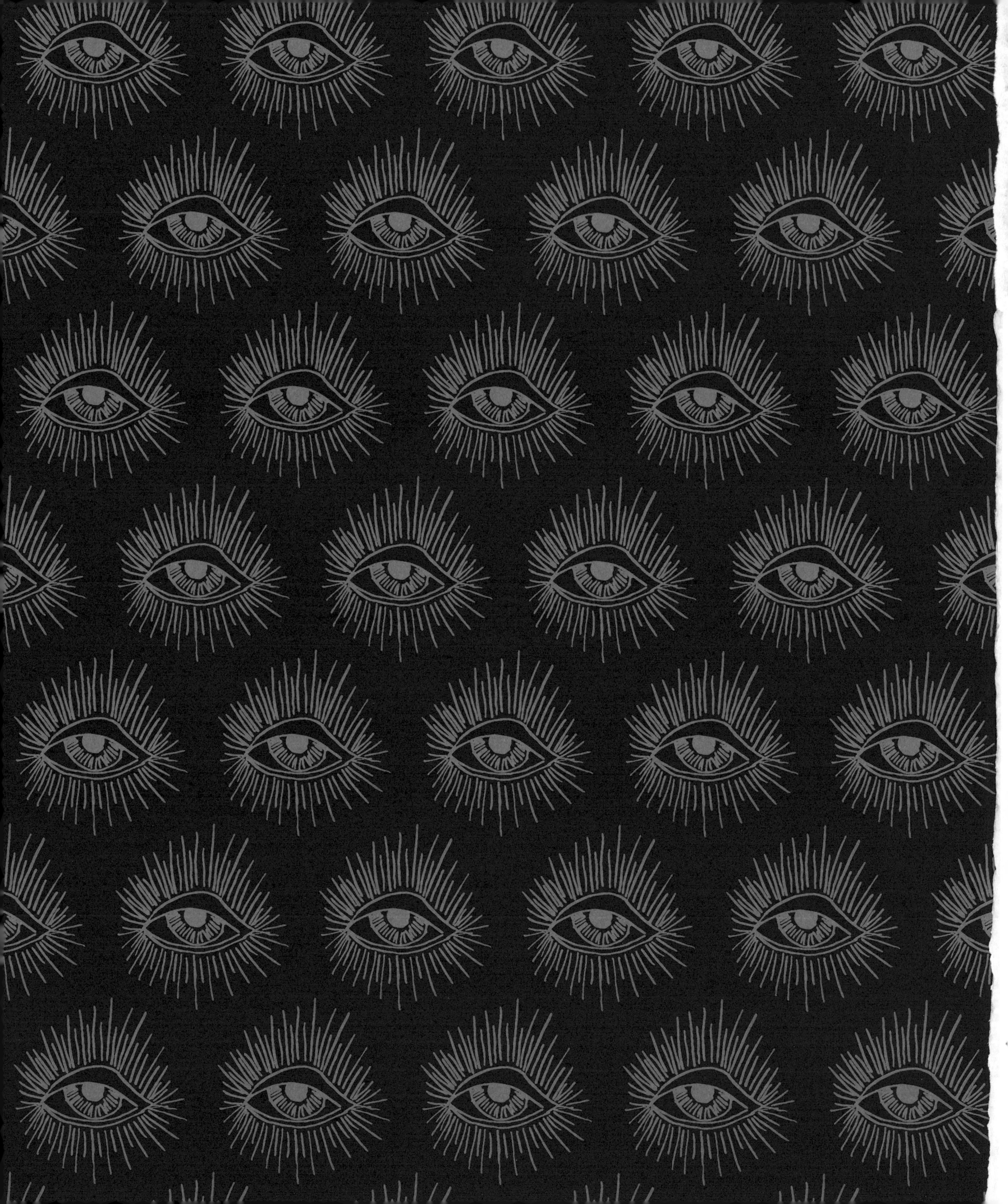

GAYFACE

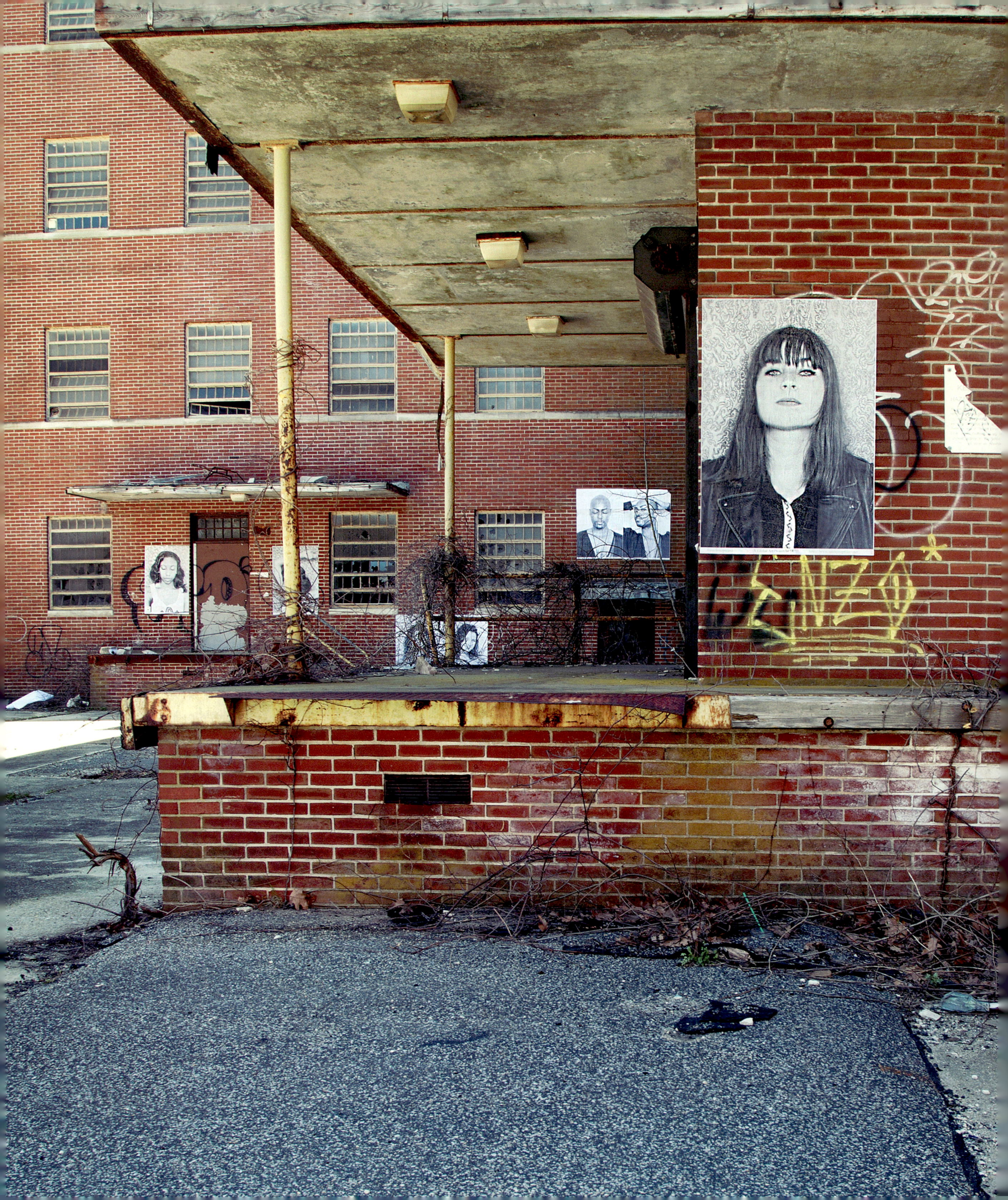
GANZO*

GAYFACE

— ASH KOLODNER —

WITH CONTRIBUTIONS FROM

Kimberly Peirce

Jordan Roth

RuPaul

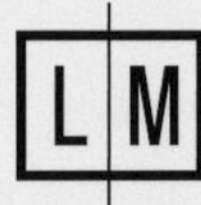

LUCIA | MARQUAND Seattle

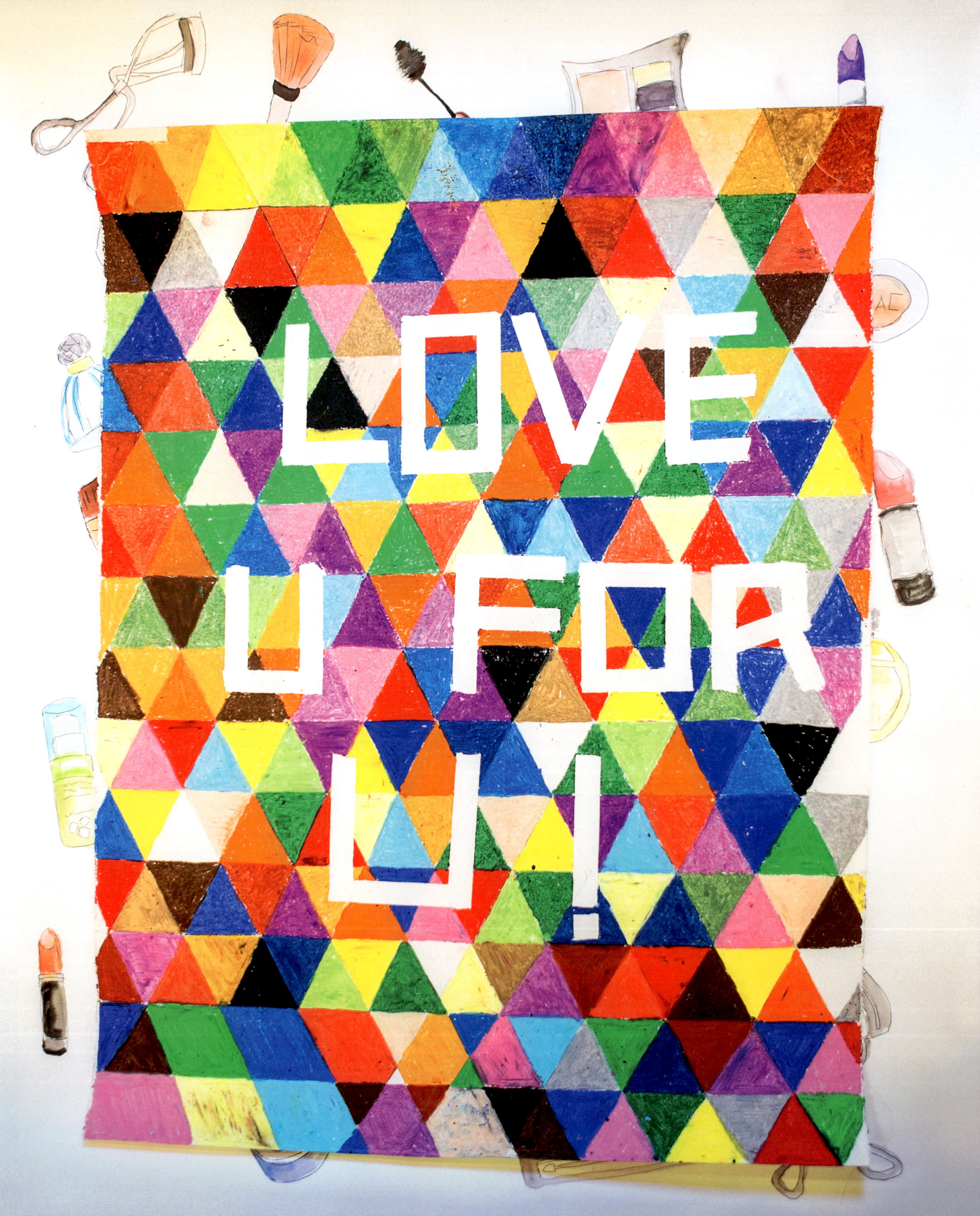

LOVE
U FOR
U !

CONTENTS

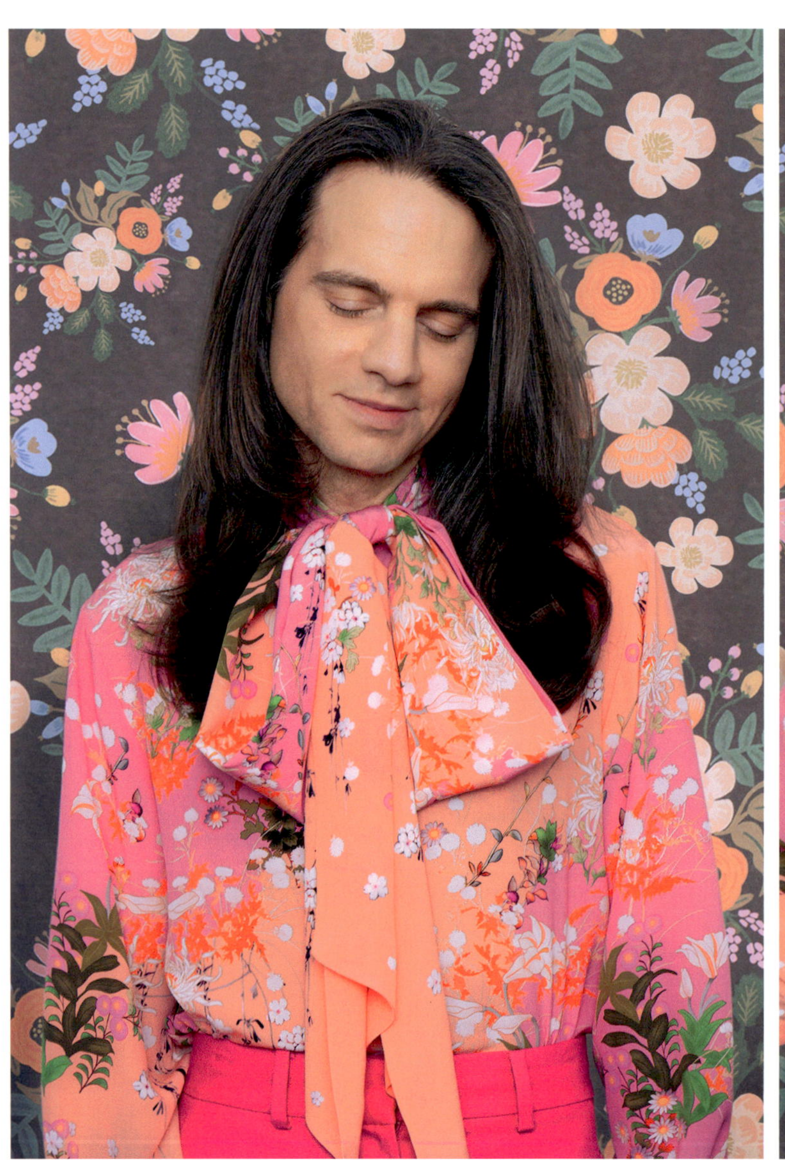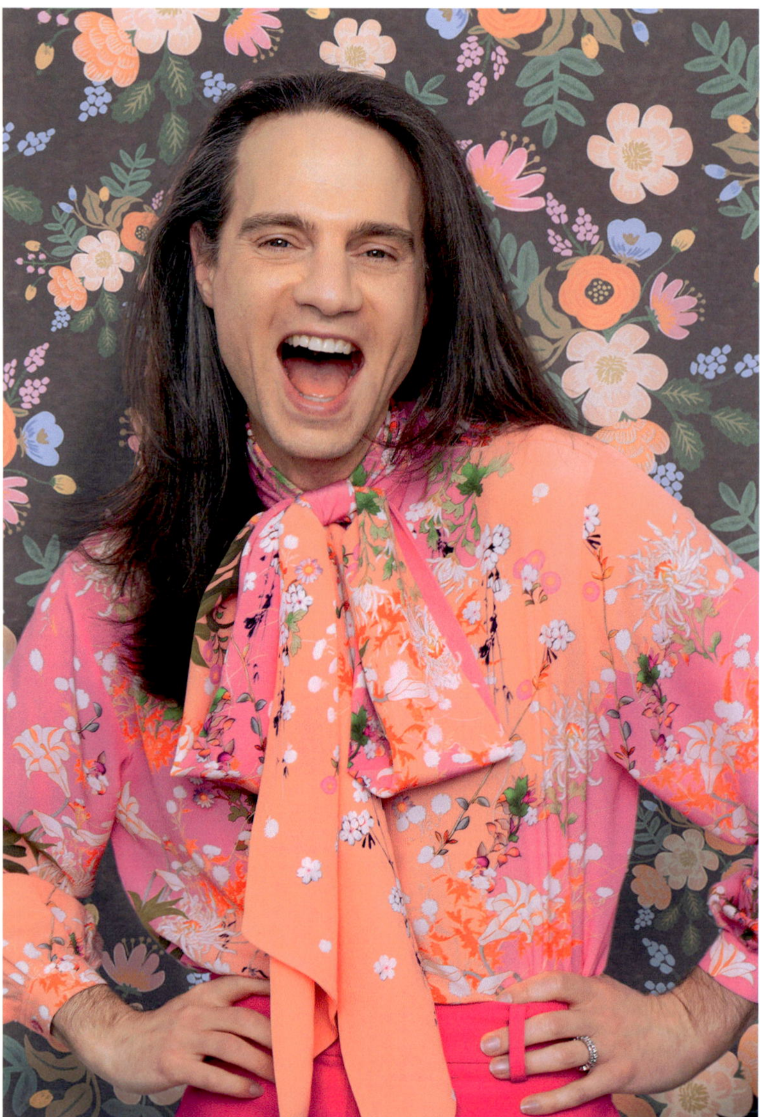

FOREWORD
JORDAN ROTH

Close your eyes.
What do you see?

Know you're being watched.
What do you feel?

This is the first experience of being photographed for Ash Kolodner's Gayface, and it's a lot like being in the closet. Closing our eyes to ourselves, but knowing others can still look in against our will. That constant dull ache of being watched, never seen.

Now open your eyes. First to yourself.

Open your eyes to all that is beautiful and holy within. And in seeing yourself, allow others to see you—on your own terms, of your own design, in your own vibrant colors and patterns. Show us the glorious gay face that is you. Only you.

Opening and closing our eyes is the simplest human act, really. A blink. We try it in the first moments of life, and as Kolodner shows us, we keep trying—but it gets harder. There is so much to see, so much to unsee, so many other eyes. But we keep trying to see, trying to be seen, trying to be known.

It's said that 80% of the body's stimuli comes in through the eyes, which is why the first step of meditation is to close them to achieve a natural calm. But different from the closed closet eyes, these eyes close to the outside in order for us to see all that is inside us, in order to reveal and revel in that great well of all that is within us, that makes us unique, and that connects us.

Close to open.

May we open our eyes to all, for all.

Welcome to Ash Kolodner's Gayface. What do you see?

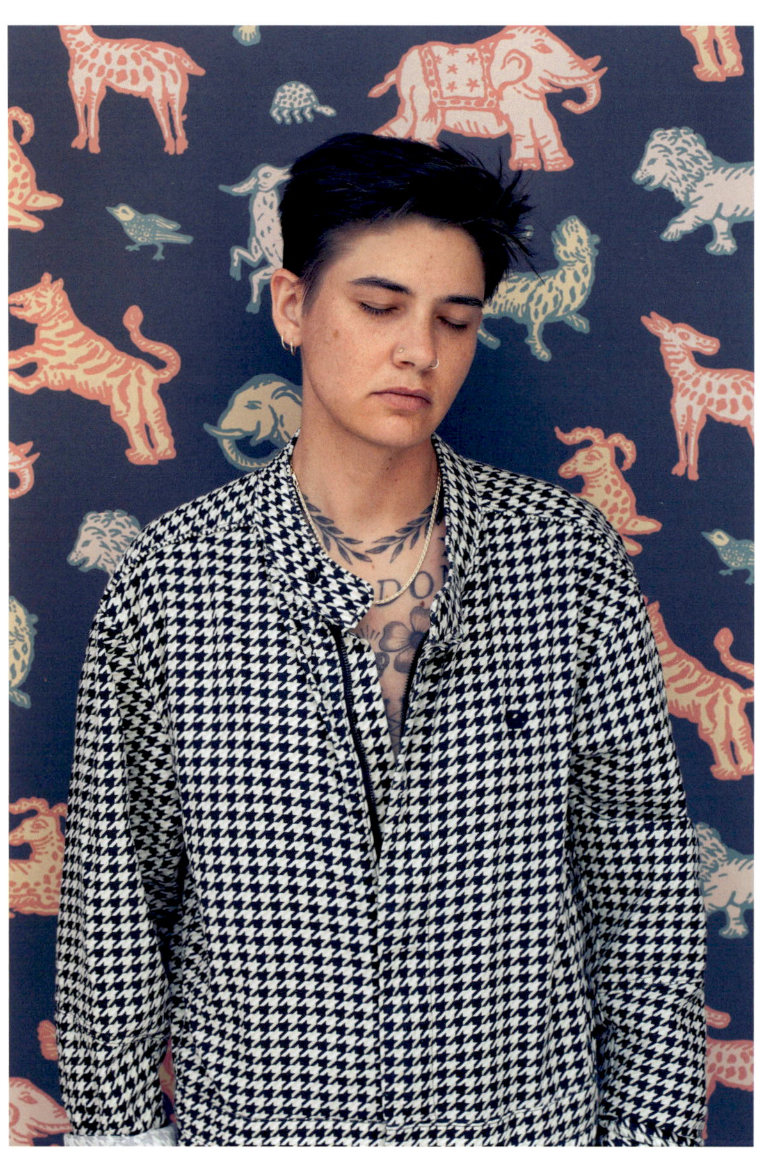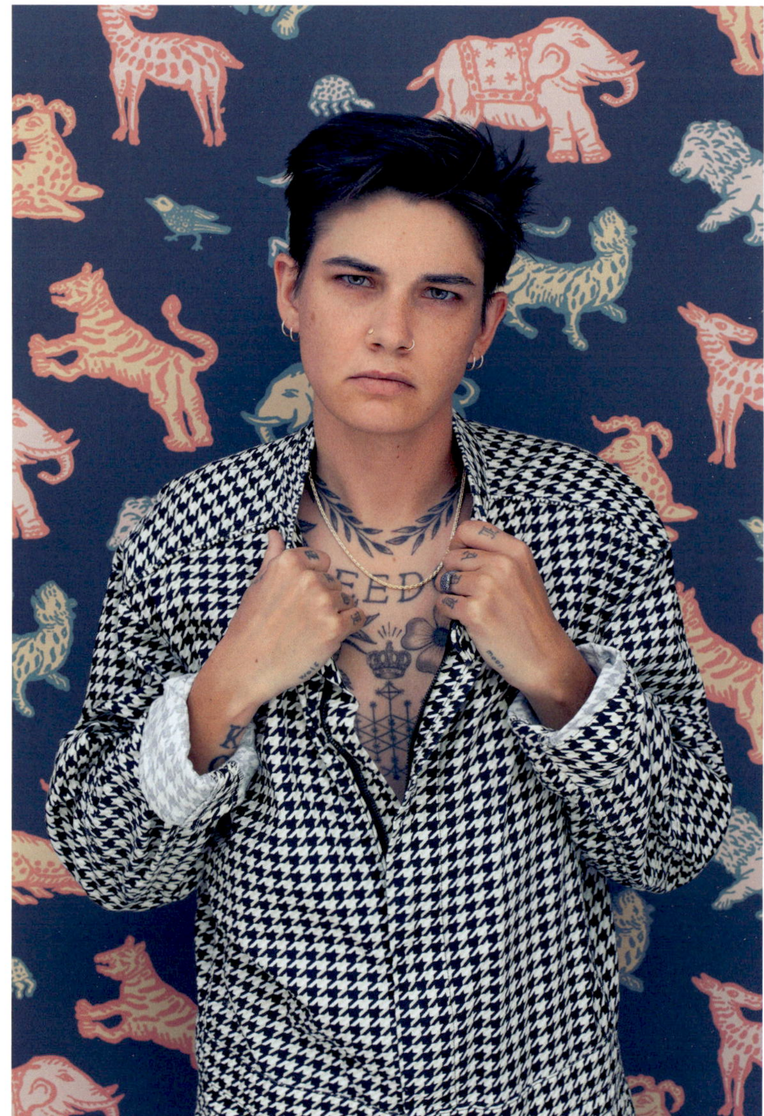

PREFACE

ASH KOLODNER

IFIRST sat down to write this preface in June of 2020. I did so against the backdrop of weeks of critical and long overdue protests against racial injustice and police brutality, as well as the first months of an unprecedented global pandemic. Like most people, I was feeling a mix of emotions: frustrated at the world of racial injustice we live in, inspired by the collective actions of many, and uncertain about what the future held.

And although we were facing what still feels like a constant and unrelenting battle, our LGBTQ+ community had also just experienced a hard-earned and critical milestone: in deciding the case of Bostock v. Clayton County, Georgia, the United States Supreme Court ruled to uphold the civil rights of LGBTQ+ workers: "An employer who fires an individual merely for being gay or transgender defies the law." At face value, this major decision ensured that the protection of gay and transgender rights is covered under the 1964 Civil Rights Act and was, indeed, a cause for joy. But, like so many things in life, not everything is as it appears on the surface. A closer look at the Court's majority opinion reveals escape hatch language that employers, citing religious freedom, may ultimately be able to use against us.

Fast forward two years: as I revisit this preface, the COVID-19 pandemic persists and the steady and sustained demand for change remains more crucial than ever. Since this book's inception, there have been a historic number of bills attempting to limit, if not completely erode, LGBTQ+ rights and dignity. We've seen proposals ranging from restricting healthcare services for transgender youth to legislation that dictates how we discuss, address, and interact with LGBTQ+ individuals in schools. These bills signal one undeniable fact: the fight for our humanity must continue, and we must grow stronger.

This project, this collection of portraits, feels all the more urgent to me now. And despite the enormity of that feeling, the initial idea to create these pictures came at an otherwise relatively routine moment. I'd long had a habit of keeping pen and paper and tape nearby, in case any insights or ideas occurred to me that I might write down and tape on the walls around me to consider, even while in the bath. And so it was, sometime around the end of 2011, while lost in thought and soaking in the bathtub, that the idea for Gayface first came to me. It seems as if it were just yesterday: the feeling of sinking down into the water, holding my breath, eyes closed, aware of my body, aware of being my Self suspended in a state of submerged vulnerability. Then the contrast of what came next: the obvious coming up for air with a feeling of emerging, surfacing, clearing the water away from my open eyes, suddenly back in the world and now aware not of internal vulnerability, but my external nakedness. (Despite any sense of security and warmth felt from the full embrace of the bath water, we know that if we stay under for too long, we drown.) It was just then that I quickly drew two squares with a human figure in each—one with eyes closed and one with eyes open.

It would be more than a year before the full concept came into focus, but as it evolved, I knew that I wanted to create a series of portraits that would attempt to capture the LGBTQ+ community that I knew and loved, in all its beautiful, raw and occasionally flamboyant, full-spectrum glory. I began to see this project as a way to get closer to my community— my own chosen queer family of friends and strangers.

Before long, I was traveling across the United States, photographing in homes, community centers, galleries, nightclubs—wherever I was invited or welcomed. What began with Craigslist ads seeking portrait subjects soon turned into dozens of people reaching out, inviting me to their cities after hearing about my project via word of mouth.

This project—and this journey—has been such a blessing in so many ways. One moment that stands out in particular was when I was invited by Philadelphia's Mural Arts to bring Gayface to help build cross-generational relationships within Philadelphia's queer community. We held a series of workshops that brought together residents of the John C. Anderson Apartments—Philadelphia's first housing project devoted to serving LGBTQ+ seniors—and young adults from the Attic Youth Center. Together, we explored everything from personal histories and shared freedoms to emotional vulnerabilities and aspirations. In those moments, we created a safe space, and in doing so we felt powerful.

When I first conceived of Gayface, I didn't anticipate that creating a series to highlight our community would become an act of community-building in itself. I've kept in touch with many of the people in this book, whether they were friends from the outset or became friends because of the project. For many, the shared experience of participating and subsequently seeing their images as part of a larger collective portrait created a shared bond with a community they had perhaps only partly known.

Because portraiture is always a collaboration and the resulting document is a record of that relationship, I want each interaction with my subjects to be as meaningful as possible. Sitting for a portrait, being portrayed in a photograph requires trust—a certain amount of giving of oneself by both subject and artist. My offering was to try to create an experience in which each individual would not only feel empowered, but more importantly, *seen*. Perhaps we could also simultaneously, and together, offer some kind of meaningful reflection back to the viewer.

And so I ask: Do *you* see yourself, maybe your reflection, here, anywhere within these pictures? Do you see a friend or family member? And those whose portraits are not present in these pages— are they here? What about those who are not part of your own immediate community? Can you see them? This book is about more than representation. It's about more than allyship. It is about accompliceship. For we are your mothers, fathers, grandparents, sisters, brothers, cousins, aunts, uncles, friends and acquaintances, and we will not

Kolodner working with a member of Philadelphia's Attic Youth Center to create their personal, one-of-a-kind Gayface wallpaper before taking their portrait.

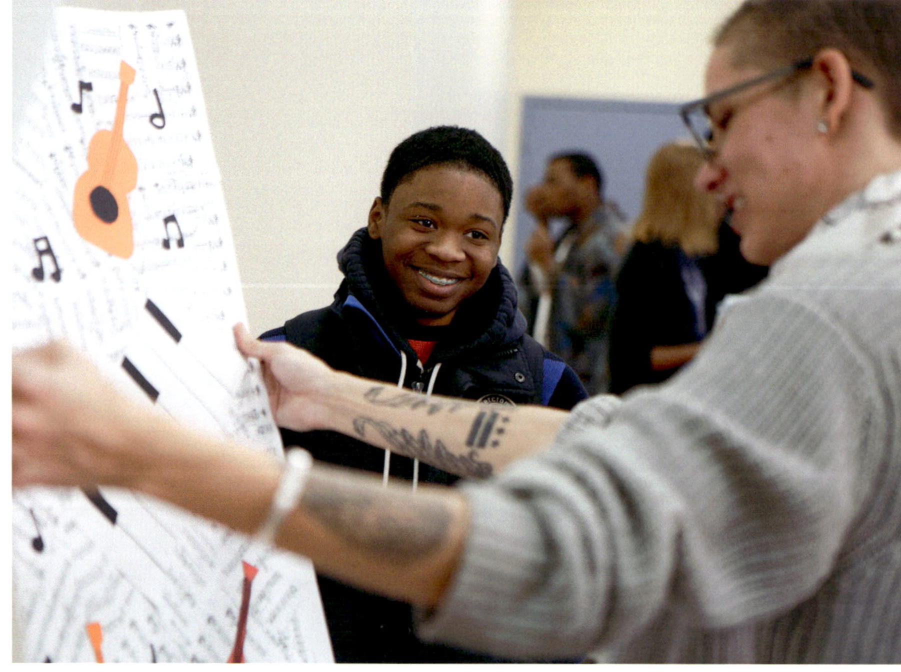

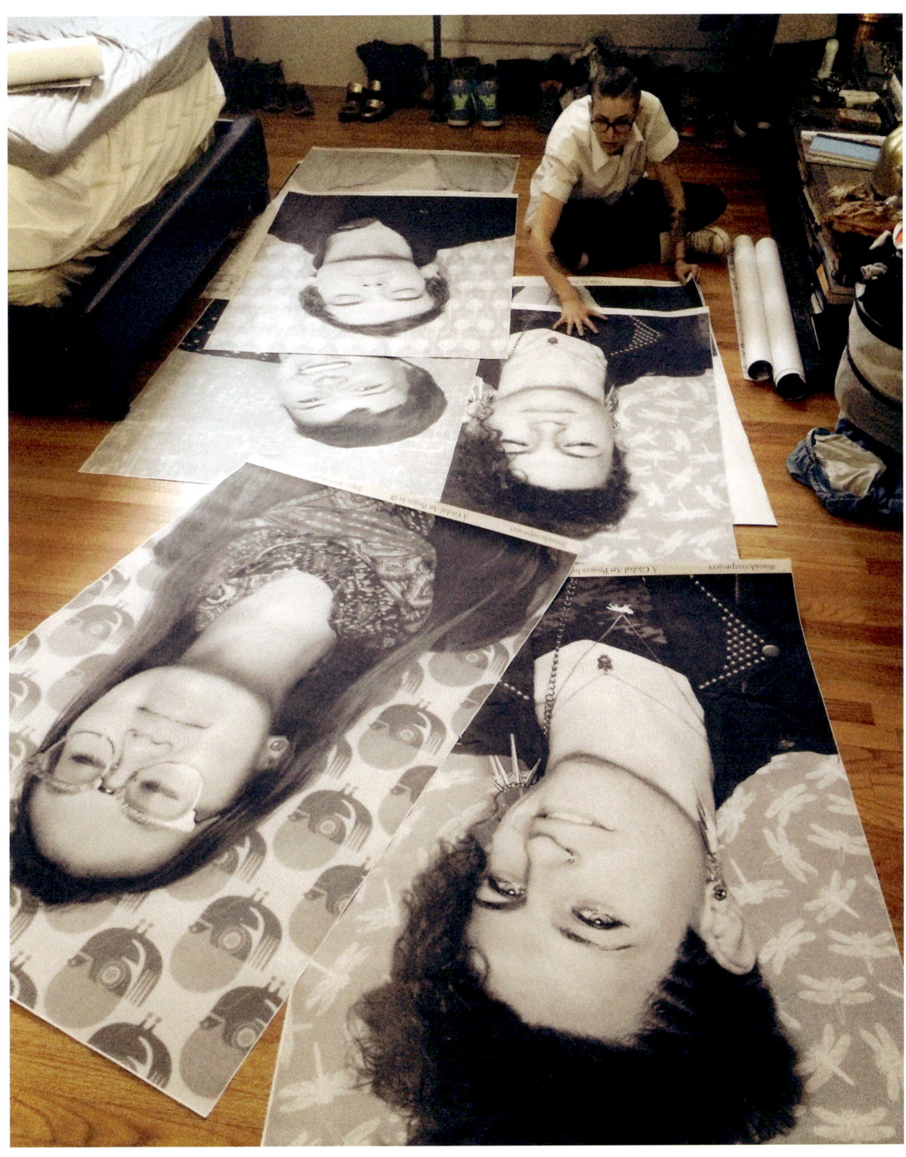

Kolodner printing large-format street pastings of Gayface portraits as part of photographer and street artist JR's Inside Out project. New York City, 2014.

be shamed into staying hidden in the shadows but rather will celebrate ourselves (and each other) for the beautiful, complex and wonderous human beings we are.

I hope this series will help educate—and inspire—every person who comes across it. I also hope it inspires many to become more involved, and to educate themselves about this incredibly important and diverse community. In the back of this book, you'll find a selected glossary of terms to help foster greater communication and understanding about the LGBTQ+ community. I sincerely hope you take the time to read through it. By doing so, you'll be taking a small—but essential—step toward creating greater visibility and raising up the power of our community.

Thank you to everyone who helped make this book possible—especially all the humans who willingly allowed themselves to be vulnerable sitting for their portraits. And for those who still quietly struggle with who they are: you are not alone.

Thank you to my wife, Sabrina, who encouraged me to follow my dream of turning this photo series into a book. Thank you to my parents and family who supported my coming out and stood by my queerness throughout the years, and still do so, as I continue my journey of self-discovery through gender and sexuality. Thank you to Jordan Roth, Kimberly Peirce, RuPaul, JR, Nicolas Newbold, Marc Jacobs, Dylan Coulter, Mo Flanagan, Chris Blue, Tzlil Hadass, Taylor Ballantyne, Susie Taylor, Lisa Markuson, Alex Gremillion, Taylor Forrest, BK Frankie, Joe Zohar, Herb Sosa, and Abigail Cardinal. Thank you to everyone who opened up their homes/studios/venues across the United States for me to photograph. Thank you to Philadelphia Mural Arts, Inside Out Project, Brooklyn Community Pride Project, Gay Men of African Descent, True Colors New Orleans, Lucky Pierre's, Betsy Hotel, the Betsy Writer's Room, Celebrate Orgullo Miami, The Dunes D.C., Hot Rabbit, The Monster, The DL Lounge, Q Night Club, Toshi's Living Room and Penthouse, The Madelyn NYC, Eiffel Society, The Peaceman Foundation, Moving Box Studios, the Attic Youth Center, the John C. Anderson Apartments, and Brooklyn Boihood. Thank you to the Paper Source for its incredible selection of art papers that provided the backgrounds for each portrait. Thank you to Lucia | Marquand and its team for championing this book.

April 2022
Light and love,
Ash Kolodner

GAYFACE

COAT OF ARMS

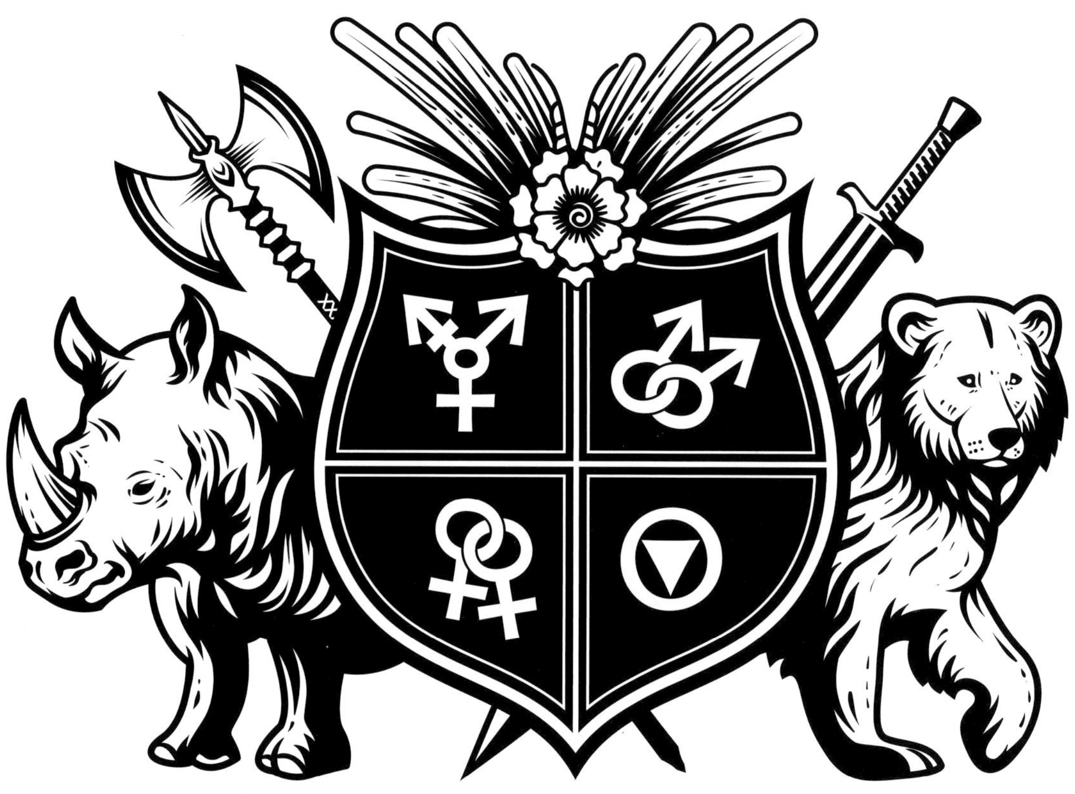

Coats of arms date back to the twelfth century when they were worn over armor in battle and in tournaments so that opponents could be readily identified. Eventually, coats of arms evolved to represent family descent, among other things, and became widely adopted by kings, princes, knights and other sources of power in Europe. Traditionally, to have a legal right to a coat of arms, a person must have had it granted to them by a ruling monarch, or they must be descended in the male line from a person to whom it was awarded.

I created a coat of arms for this project because so many people both within and outside of the LGBTQ+ community define "family" in ways that challenge the traditional definition of the word. For some of us, family is something that is self-defined or self-created as the result of discrimination or rejection by parents, siblings, or relatives. Coming out, whether it's at the age of five or eighty-five, is a unifying experience, and I wanted to honor that with a heraldry to confer honor upon a different kind of family, one that transcends individual ownership.

Coats of arms are devised according to a system of symbols often centered around a shield. Each of the elements is intended to have its own alluring meaning. The Gayface Coat of Arms imprinted on the back cover of this book consists of the following symbols.

—Ash Kolodner

Bear

The bear is a symbol for strength and confidence. Always ready to stand against adversity, it takes action and leadership to protect its clan. The spirit of the bear provides a strong grounding force. Like the bear, our community will stand strong against adversity so long as it is needed.

Rhinoceros

In 1974, Boston activists reimagined the purple rhinoceros as a symbol for the gay rights movement. Often a misunderstood animal, the rhino is docile and intelligent despite its ferocious abilities. Like the rhino, our community is not always what it seems.

Labrys

A labrys, or doubled-bladed battle axe, was used to symbolize the matriarchal tendencies of the ancient Minoan Crete civilization, representing feminist strength and self-sufficiency. For lesbians in the 1970s, the labrys was adopted as a symbol of women's empowerment, and since this time, it has often functioned as a more covert identifier of female homosexuality than the double Venus.

Sword

A sword is symbolic of the penetrating power of the mind, encouraging the wielding of intellect to bring about results. It is an emblem of both bravery and defense, slashing ignorance to reach the truth.

Calamus

Acorus calamus is a tall flowering wetland plant. It is also the name of a cluster of poems, written by iconic American poet Walt Whitman, celebrating romantic relationships between men.

Carnation

In ancient Rome, green indicated homosexual affiliations. In nineteenth-century England, the green carnation became a Victorian symbol of the gay community when men began pinning a green carnation on their lapel after it was popularized by Irish author and playwright Oscar Wilde.

Interlocking Mars Symbols

The pointed Mars symbol represents a male organism or man. In the 1970s, gay men began using two interlocking Mars symbols to symbolize male homosexuality. The two, of course, had to be slightly off-center to avoid the arrow of one intersecting the circle of the other.

Interlocking Venus Symbols

The Venus symbol represents a female organism or woman. Some lesbians started using two interlocking female symbols, also during the 1970s, to symbolize female homosexuality.

Transgender Symbol

Popular symbols used to identify transvestites, transsexuals, and other transgender people frequently consist of modified gender symbols combining elements from the male, female and genderqueer symbols.

Ally

In addition to the more recognizable symbols of the LGBTQ+ community, other symbols, such as a triangle inside a circle, have been used to represent unity, pride, shared values, and allegiance to one another both inside the community as well as with straight allies.

PORTRAITS

There is no one way to look, feel or *be* LGBTQ+. I created Gayface as a response to the stereotypes that the LGBTQ+ community is often reduced to, as well as the notion that a "gay face" exists. As you'll see in these portraits, the power—and beauty—of our community comes from the diversity of its members.

These photographs were taken from 2013 to 2016 and exist as moments of time. Not all the subjects identify today in the same way they did when their photo was originally taken. I hope that you will respect and appreciate that the portraits showcase the subjects as who they were then, but not always who they are now.

—Ash Kolodner

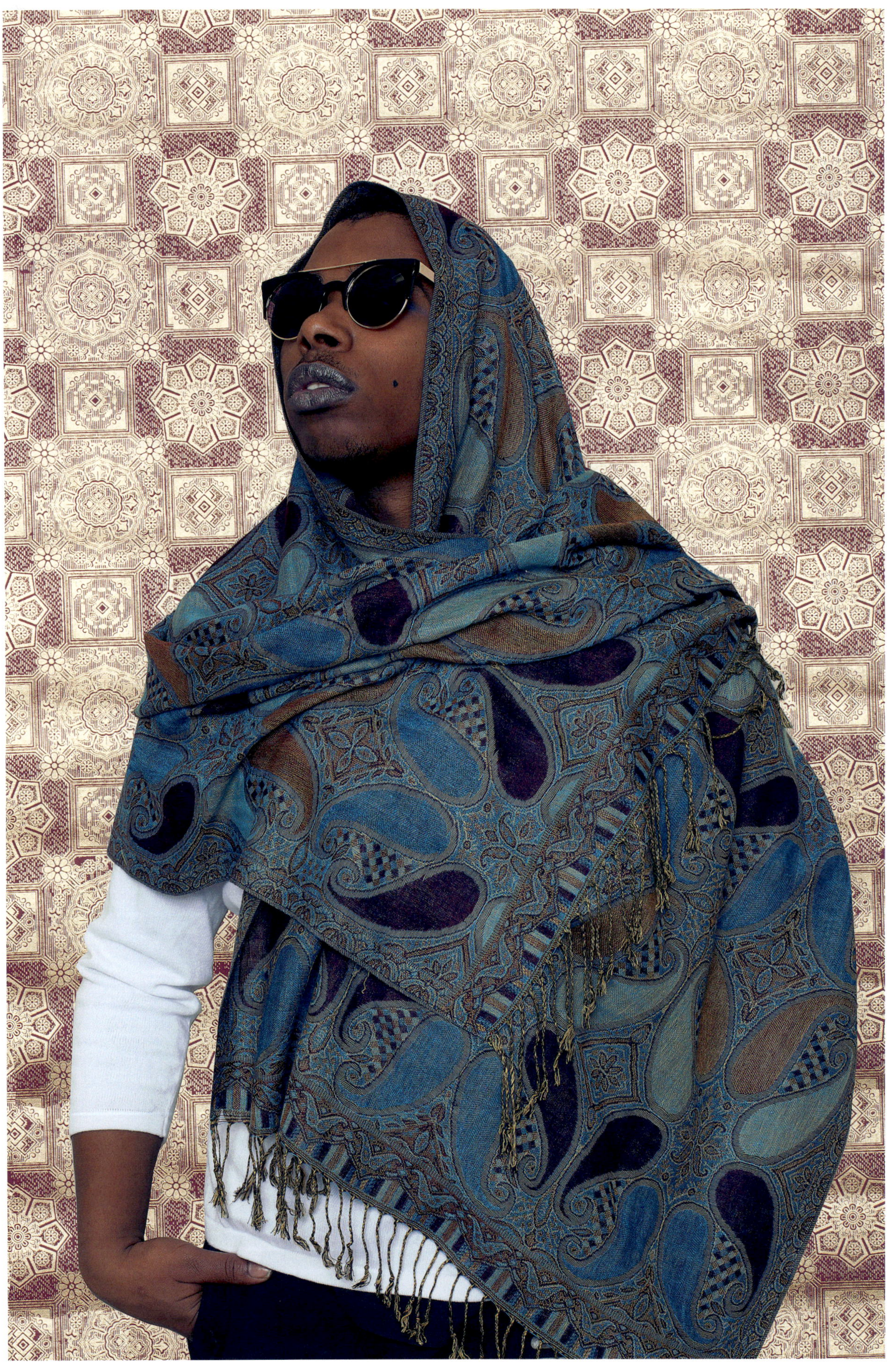

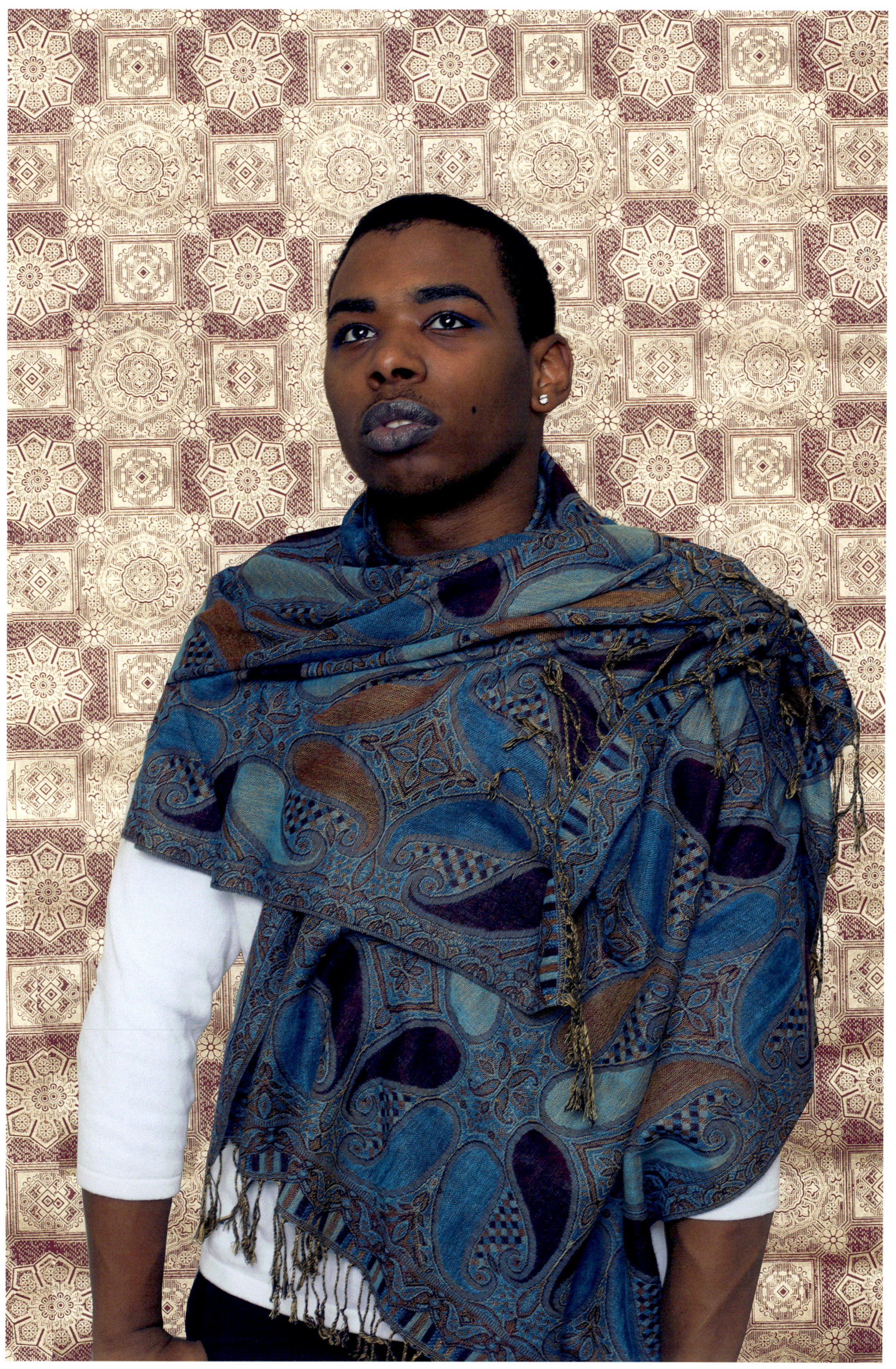

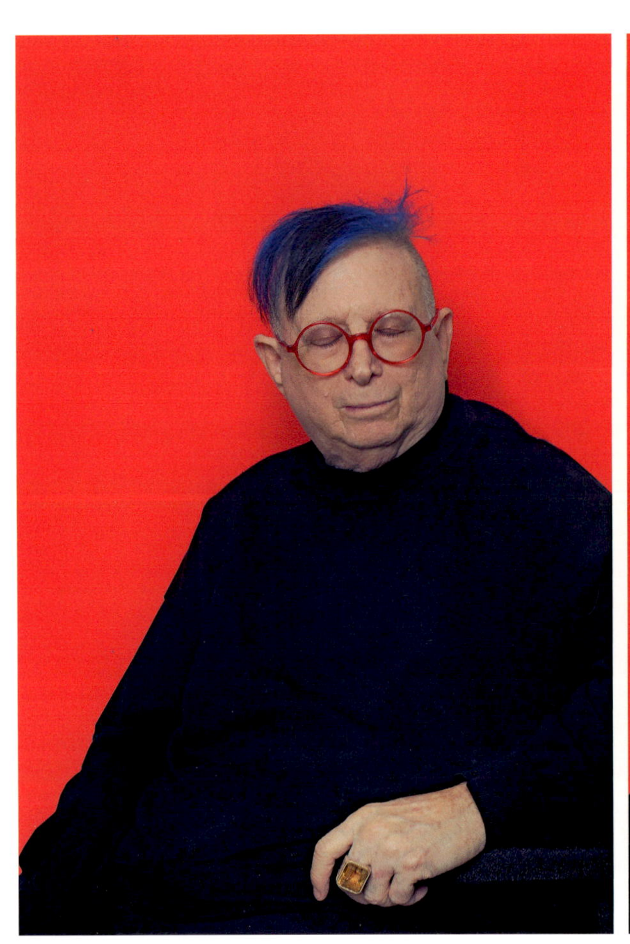
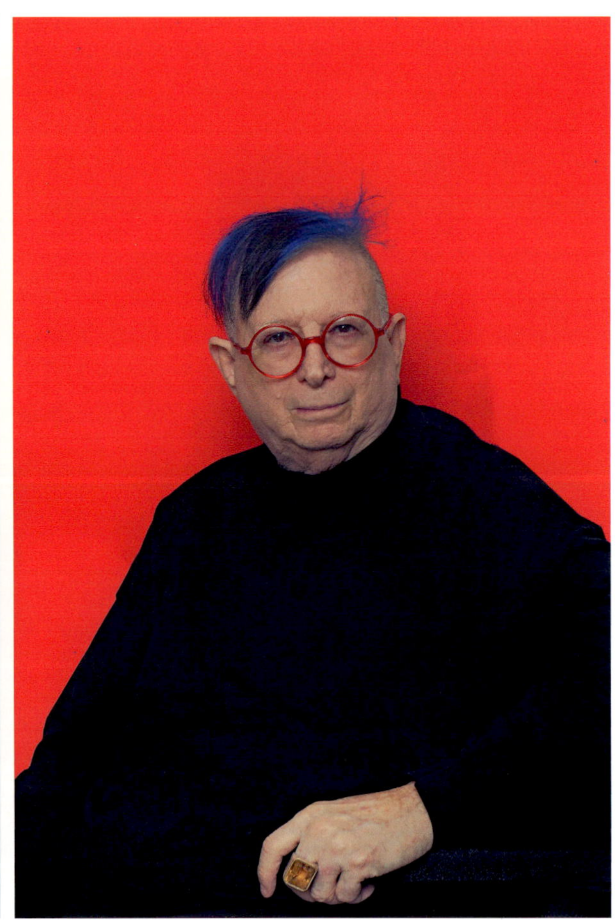
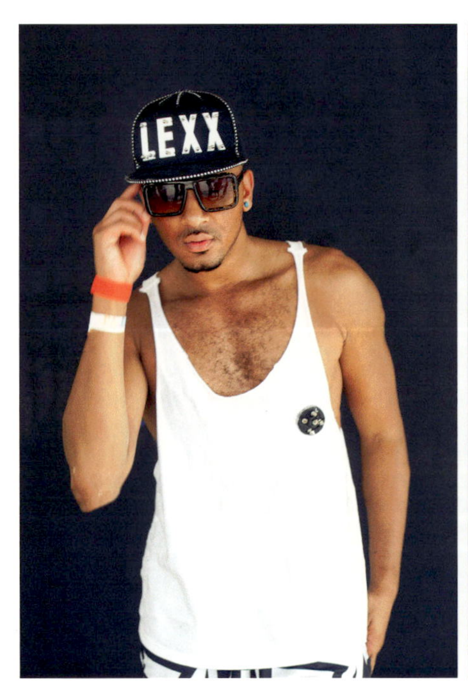
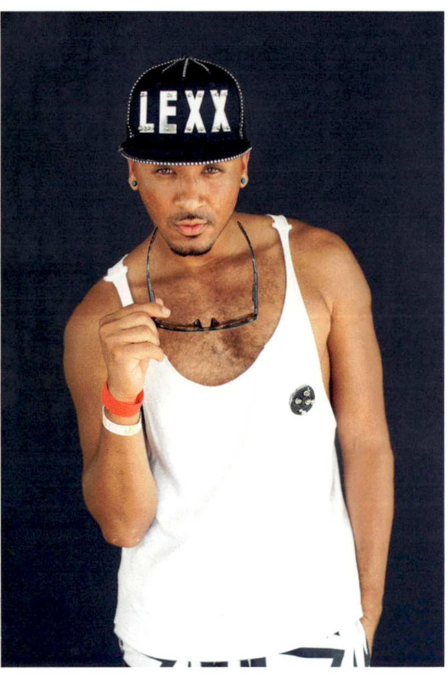

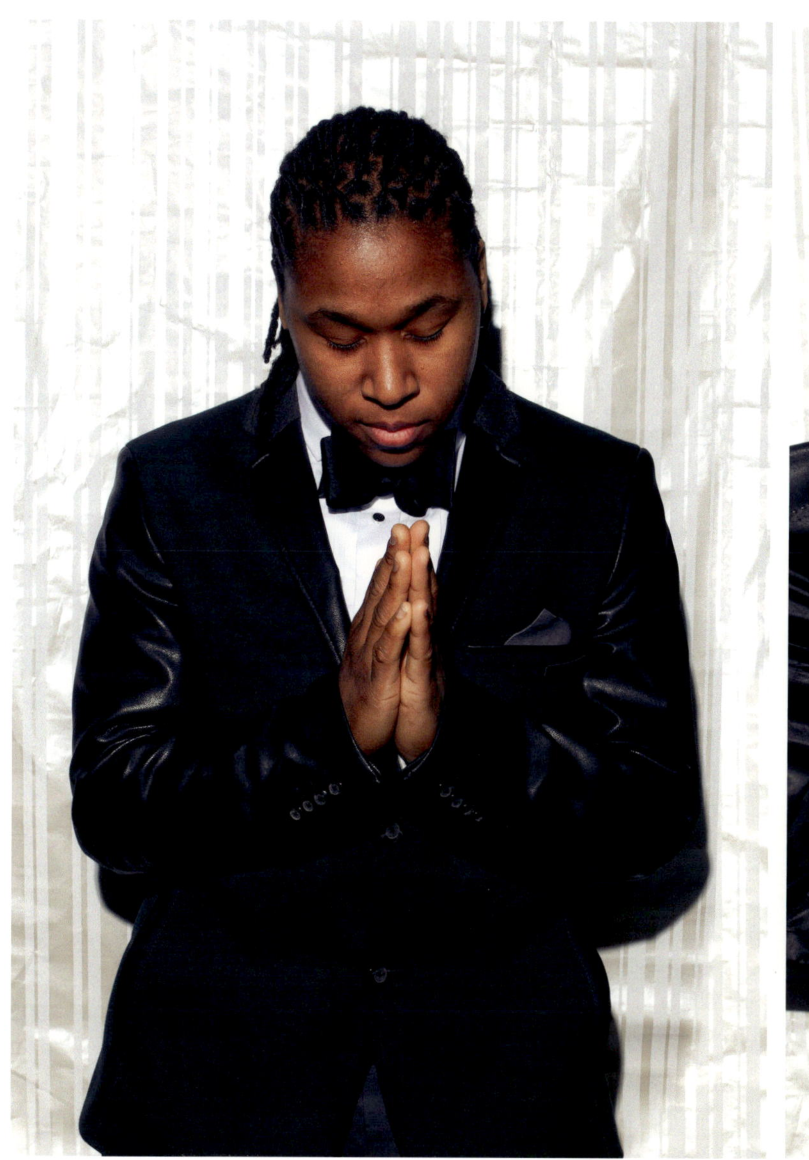
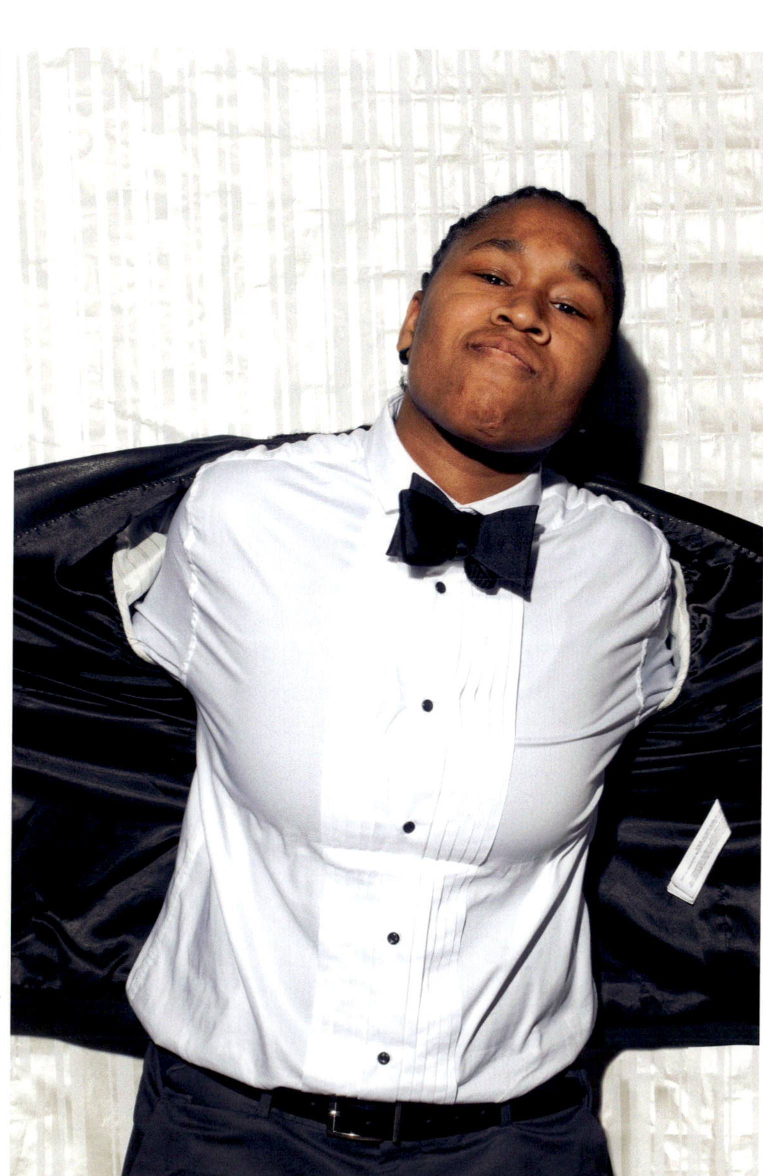

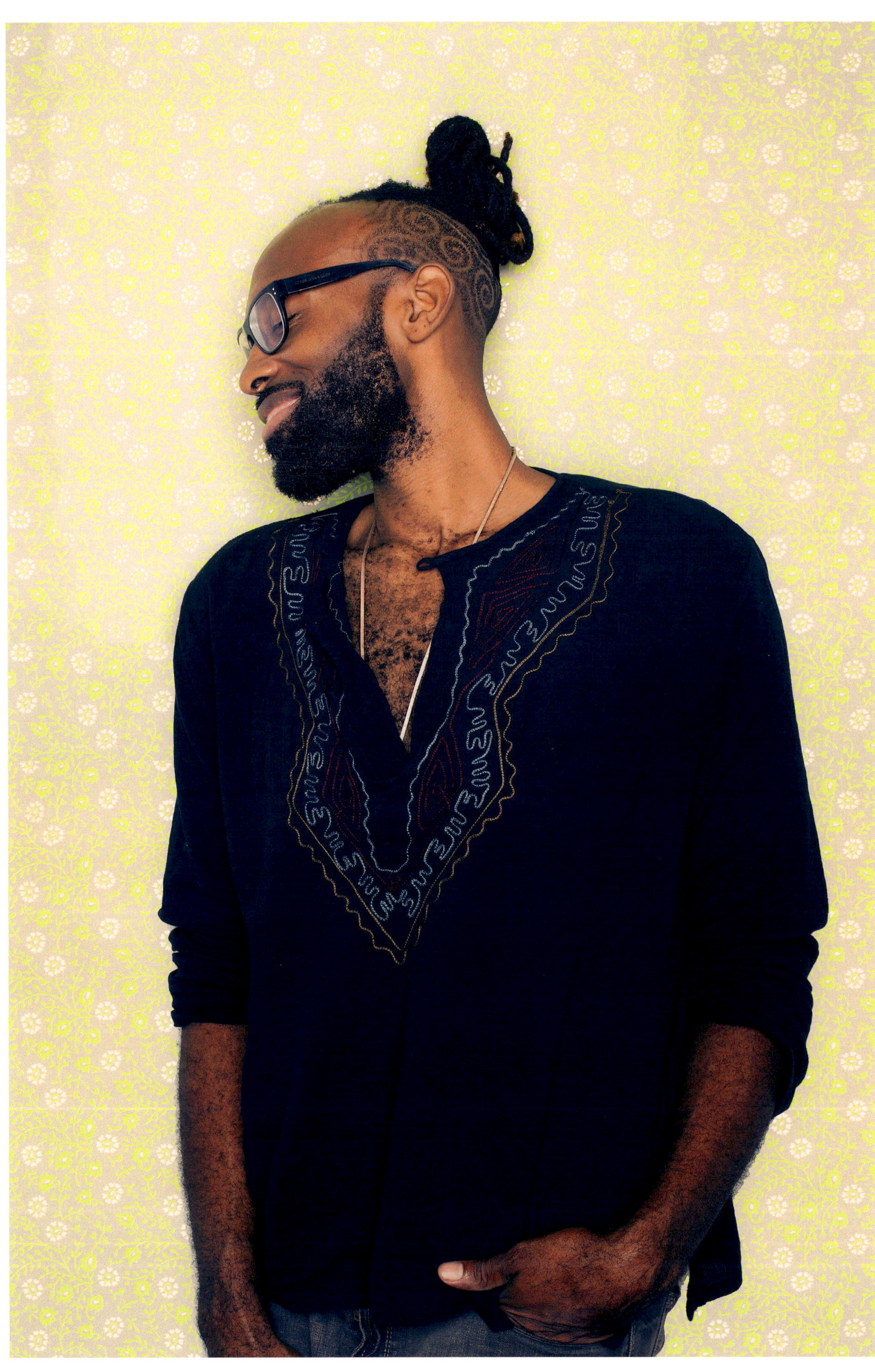

GAY | FACE

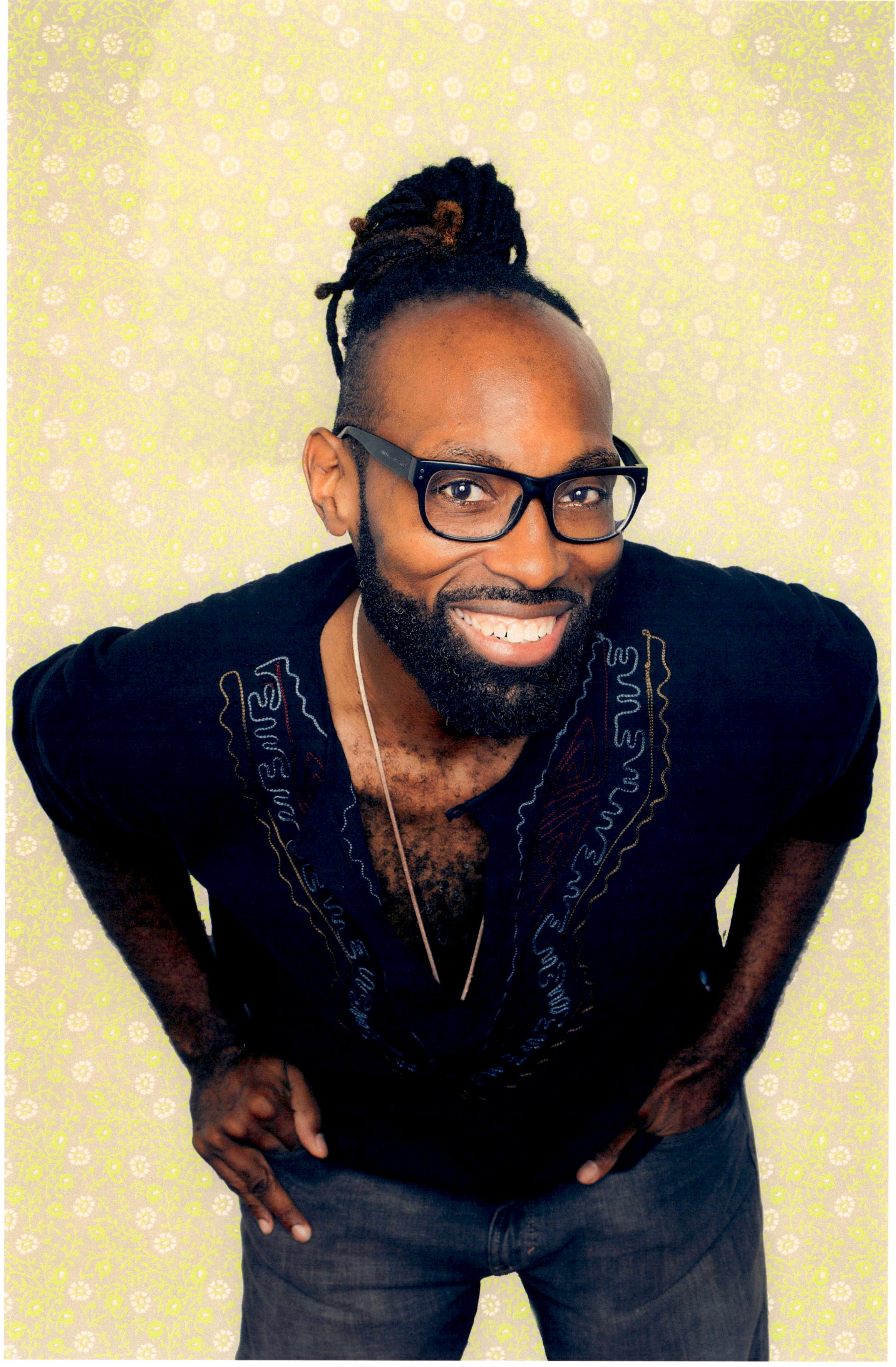

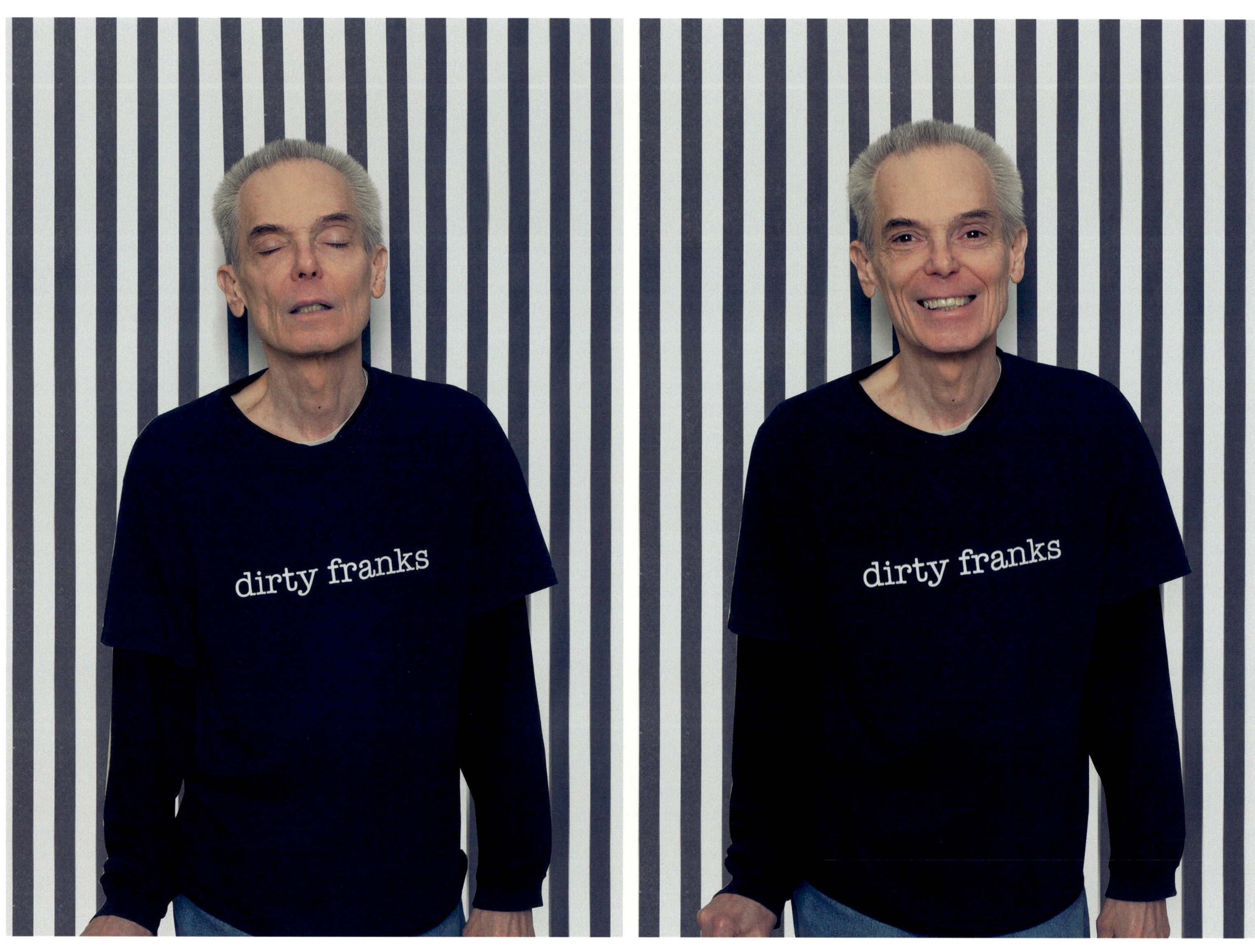

dirty franks
dirty franks

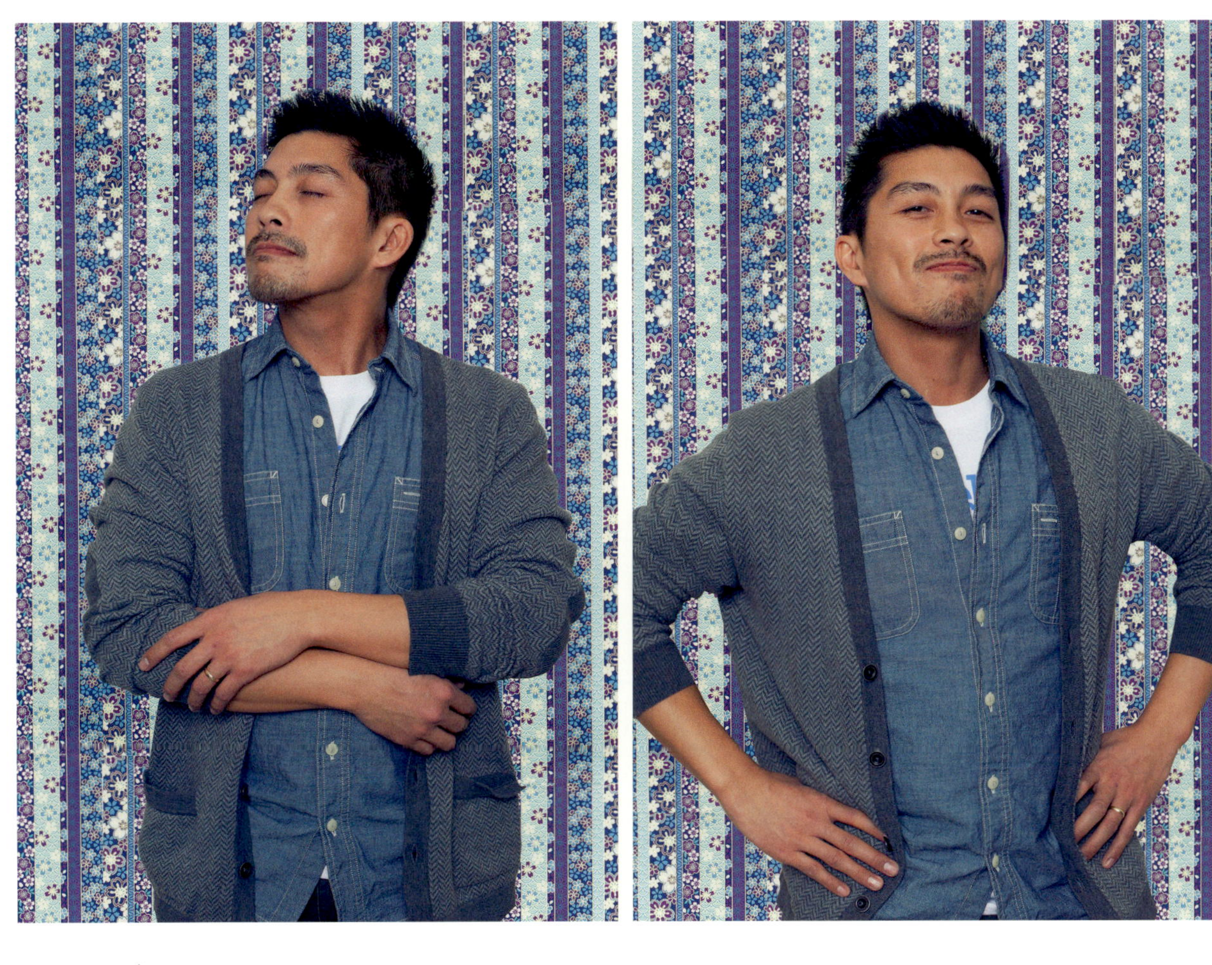

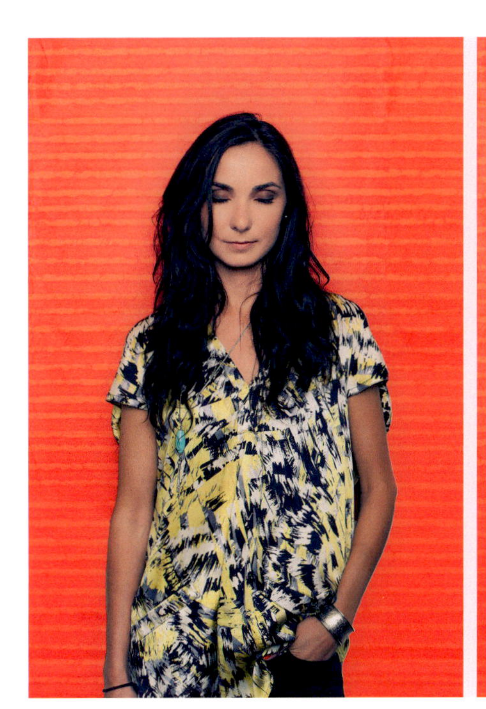

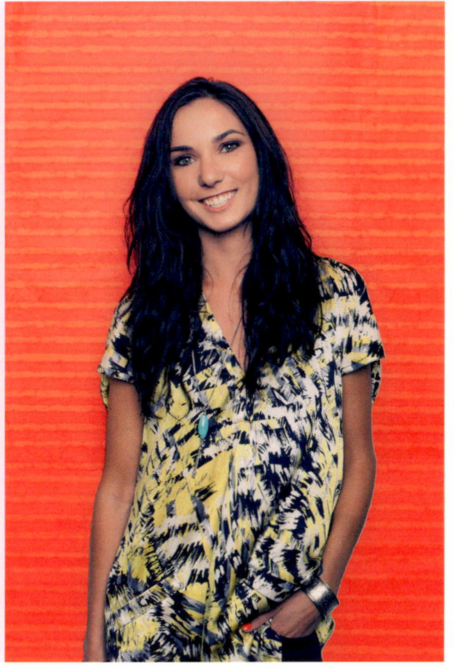

GAY | FACE

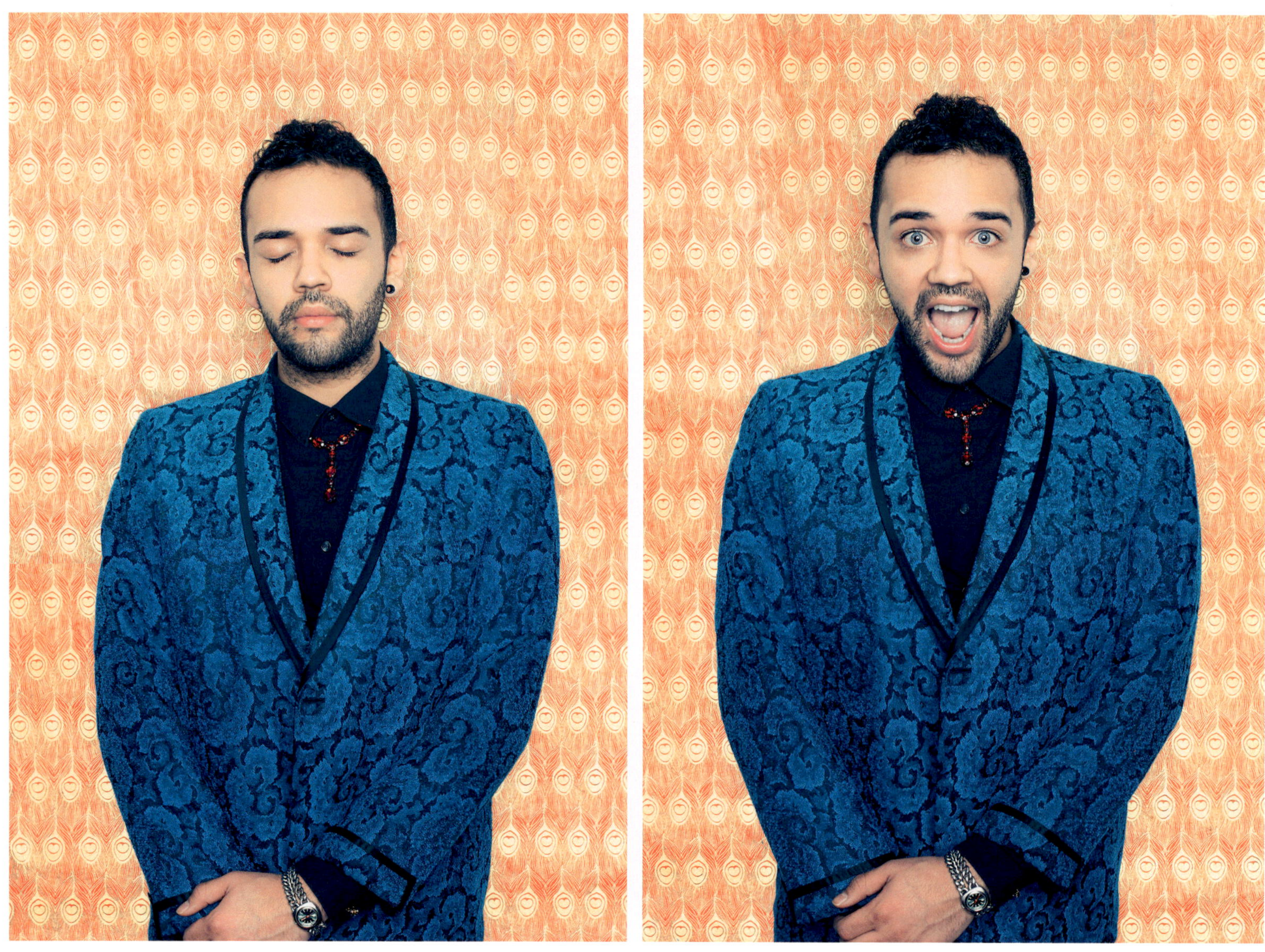

Paris R.

QUEENS, NEW YORK

How would you identify your sexuality?
Gay and proud!

Describe your coming out. Are you coming out in some way by participating in this project?
I was always feminine growing up, and I knew that I was different; it wasn't until I was a preteen that I understood what gay meant, and then I knew I was gay. Friends said I was gay in high school, but I wasn't ready to handle it yet. It wasn't till college, where I flung open the door and was able to say loud and proud, "I'm gay." I'm pretty sure my parents knew in the back of their minds after watching me singing songs by the Spice Girls covered in body glitter during the fourth grade talent show, but it was still shocking to hear me say it after twenty years.

If you could change one thing about mainstream society to improve the lives of LGBTQ+ people, what would it be?
There is a lot that I would love to see changed within society, but one issue that's been on my mind is the HIV epidemic in prisons.

Why should people support same-sex marriage?
I still don't understand why gay marriage is still even an issue. Homophobia is not part of the natural order, it's an arbitrary invention of this particular time and place. People, please: enough with the bullshit already!

Why did you want to be a part of this project?
I'm really grateful for the opportunity to be a part of Gayface. I'm proud to be a gay man, and grateful for a friend like Ash, who creates such beautiful works of art and has invited me to become part of it. The world can heal itself if the human race will let it!

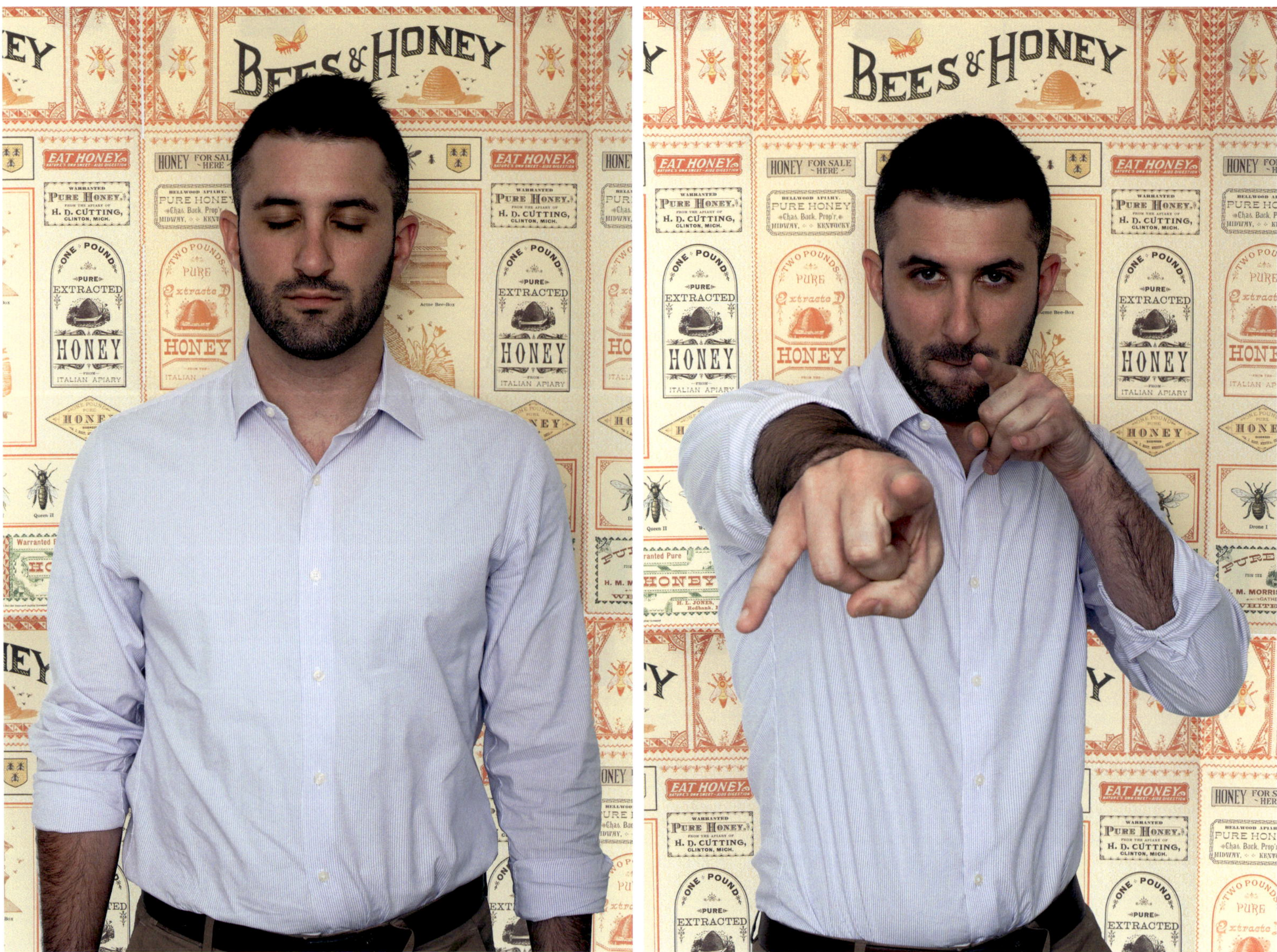

GAY | FACE

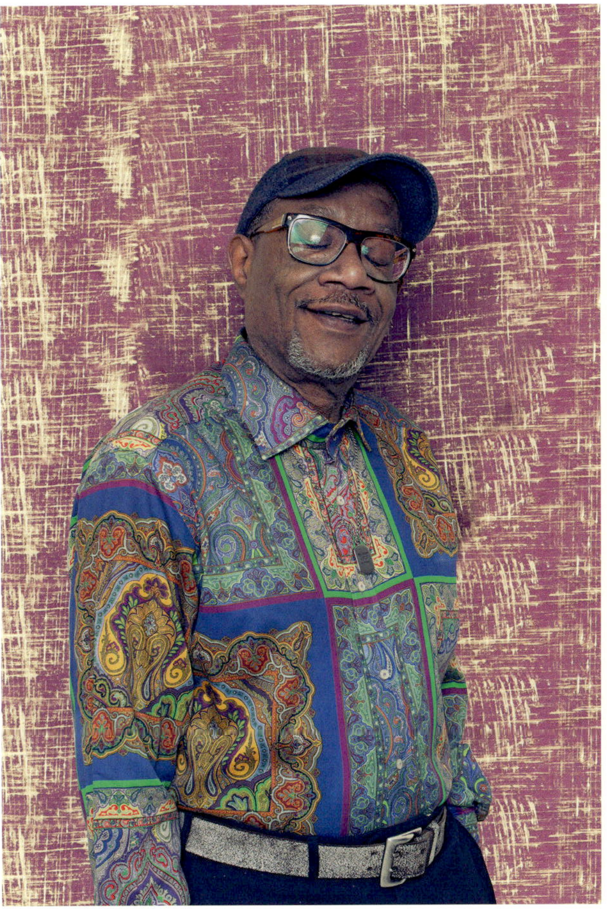
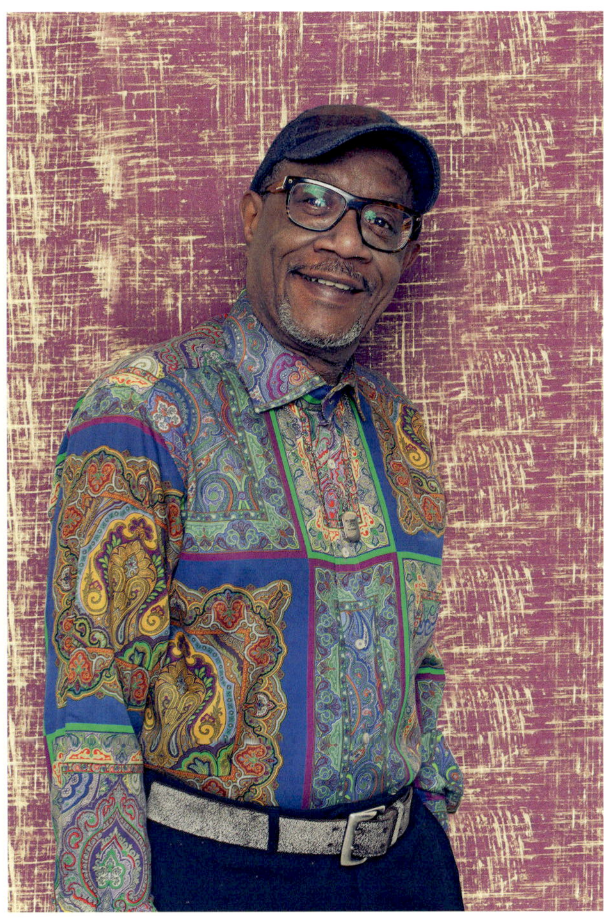
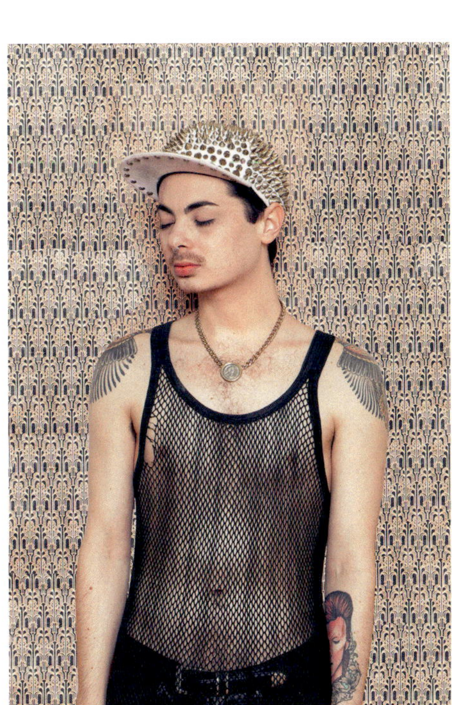
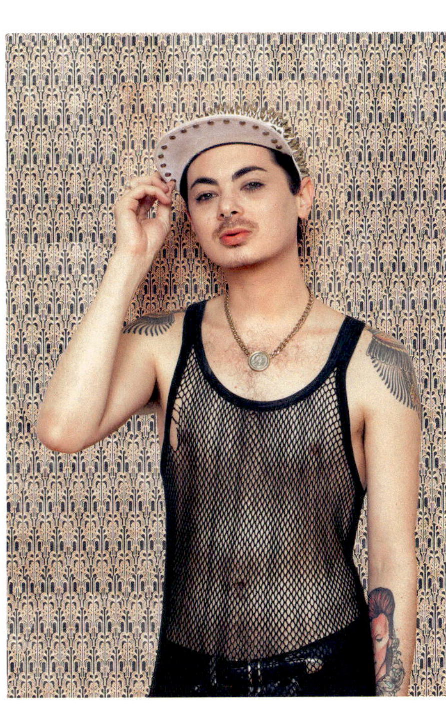

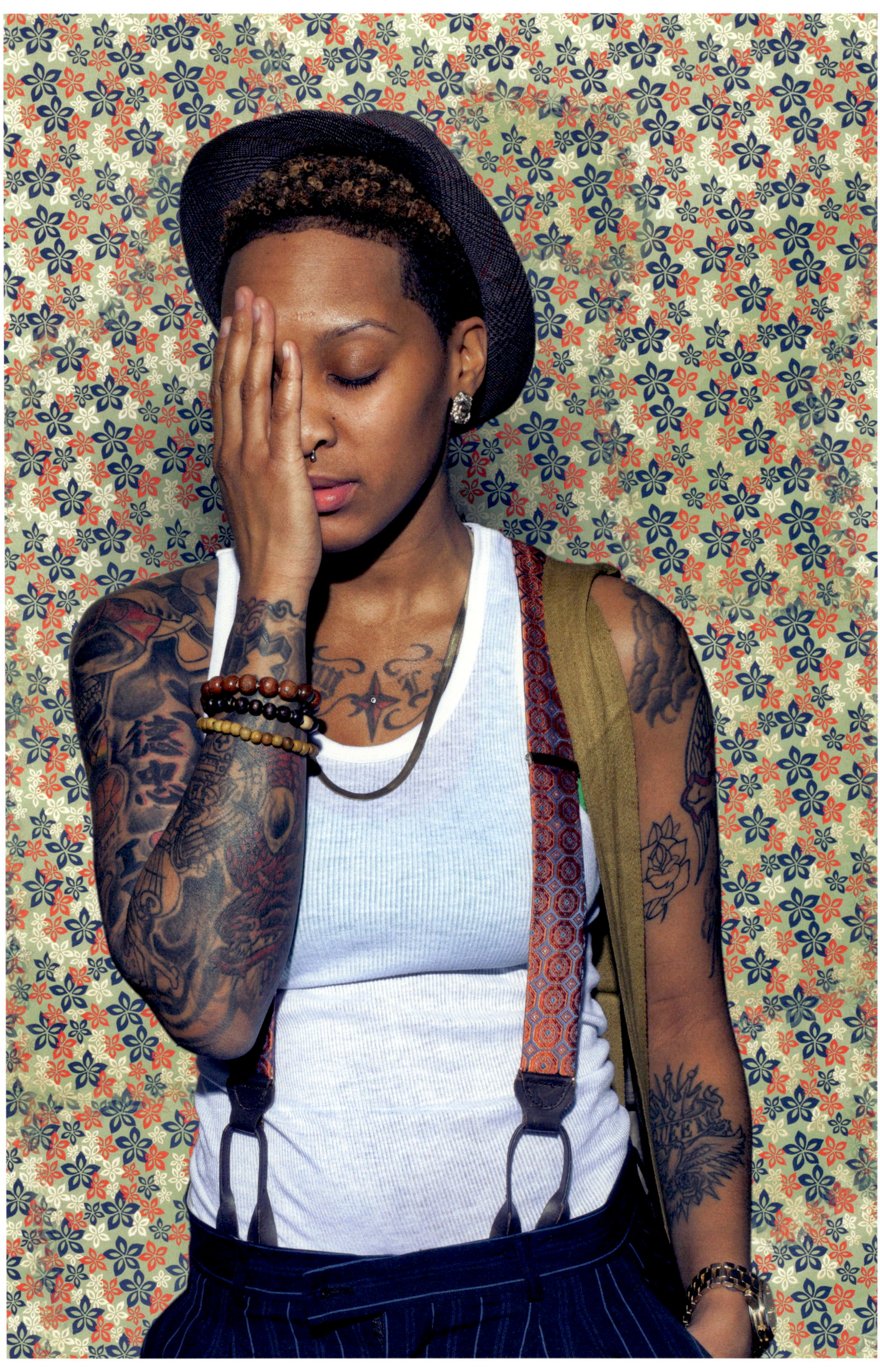

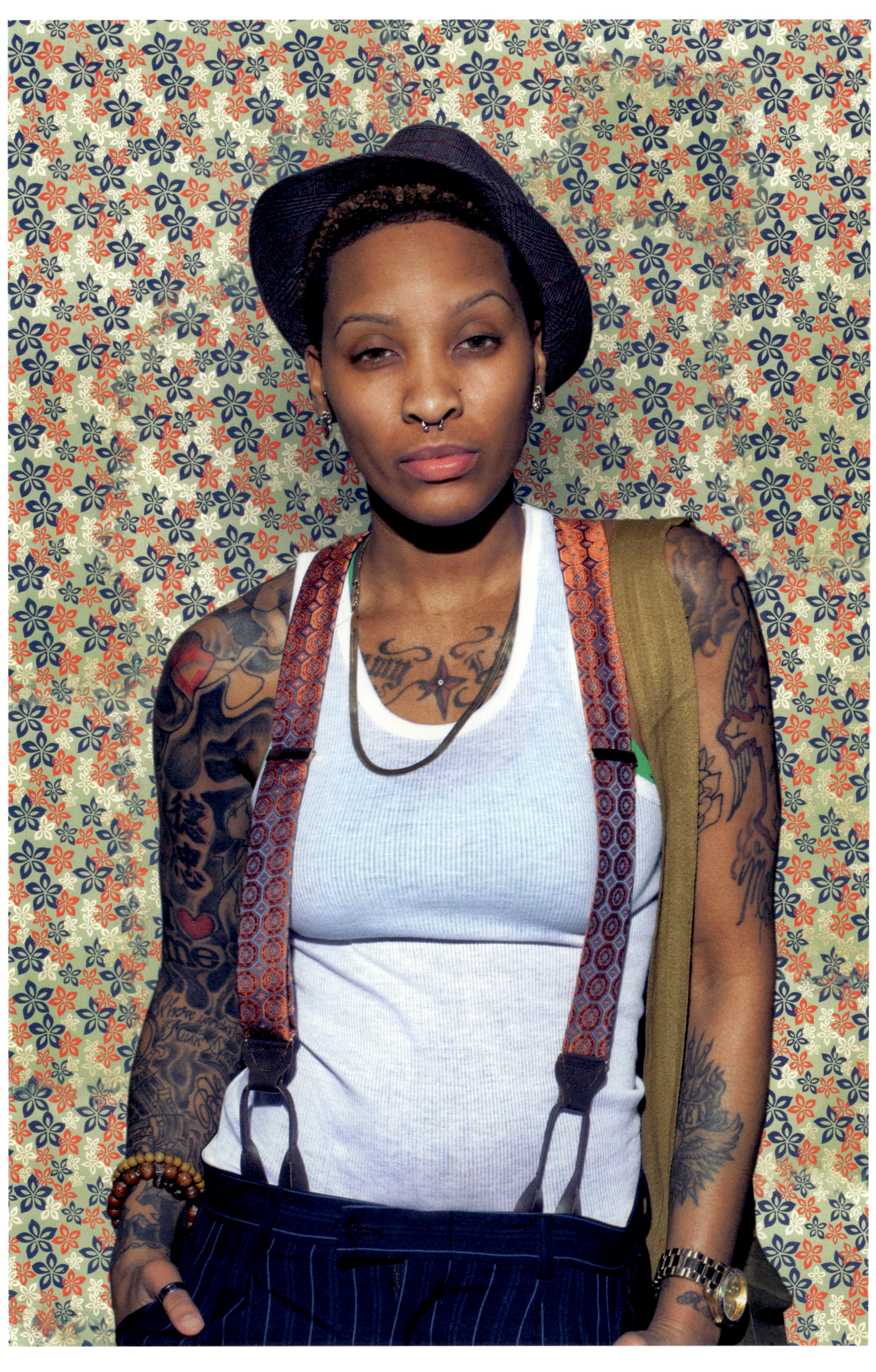

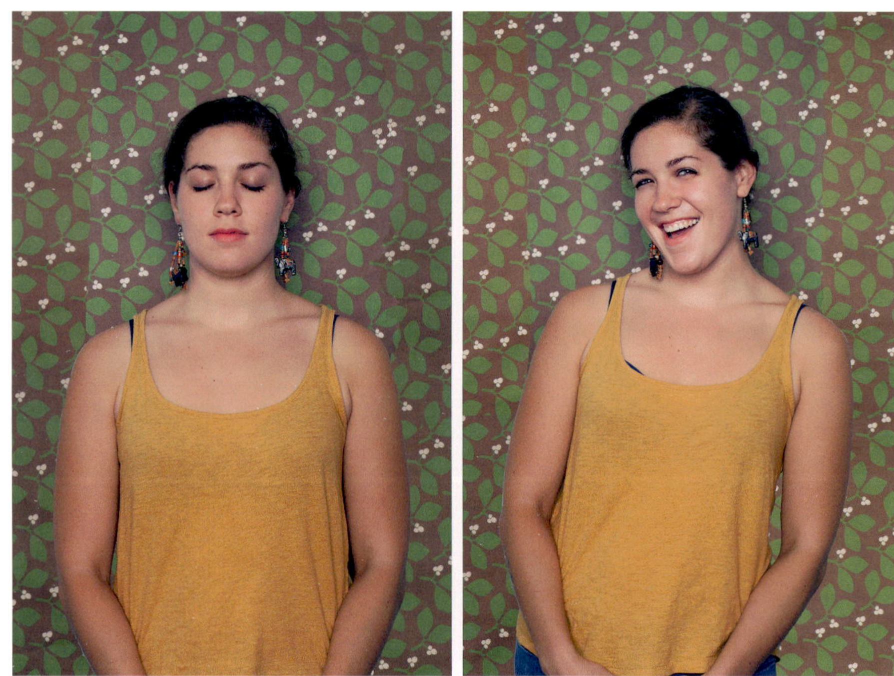

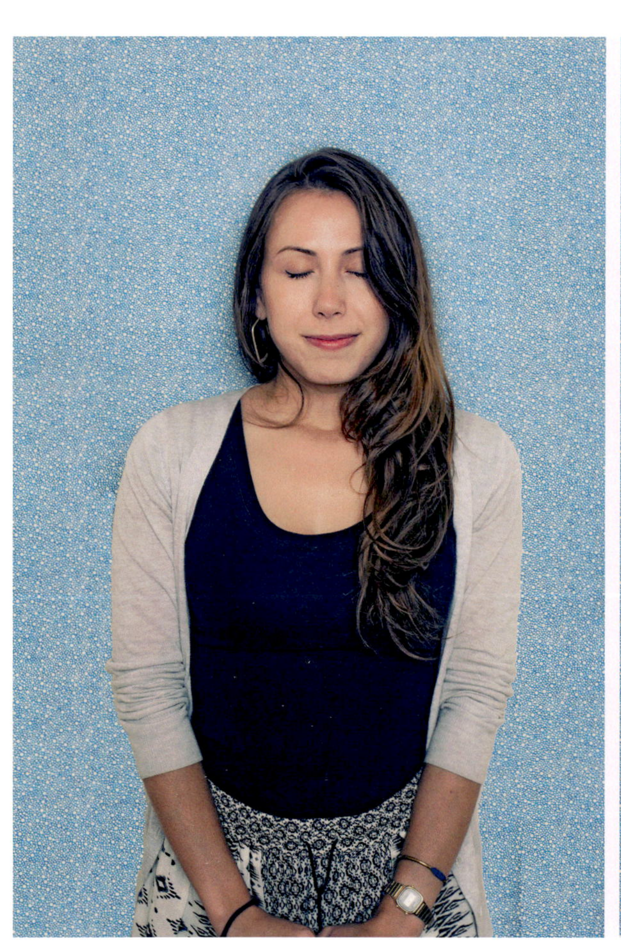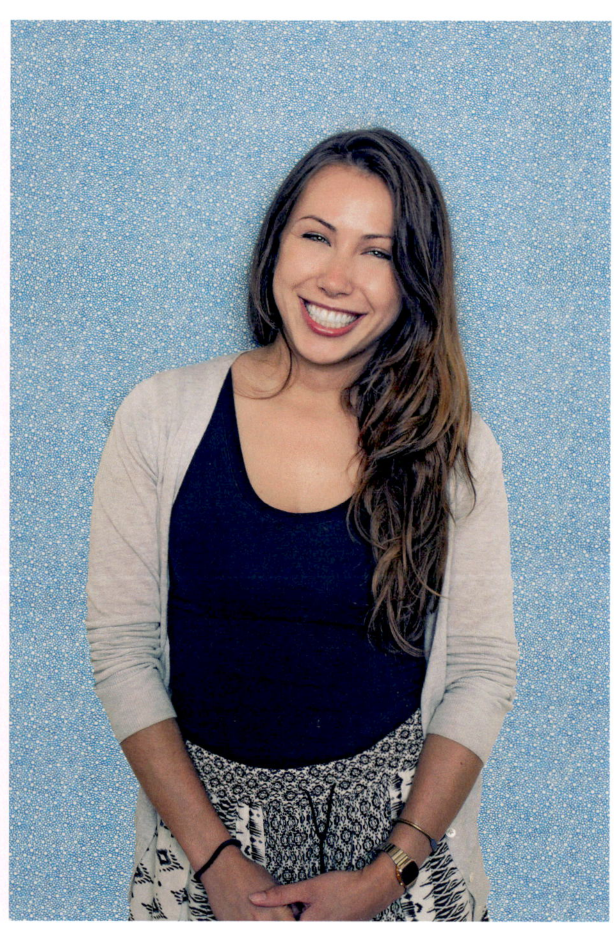

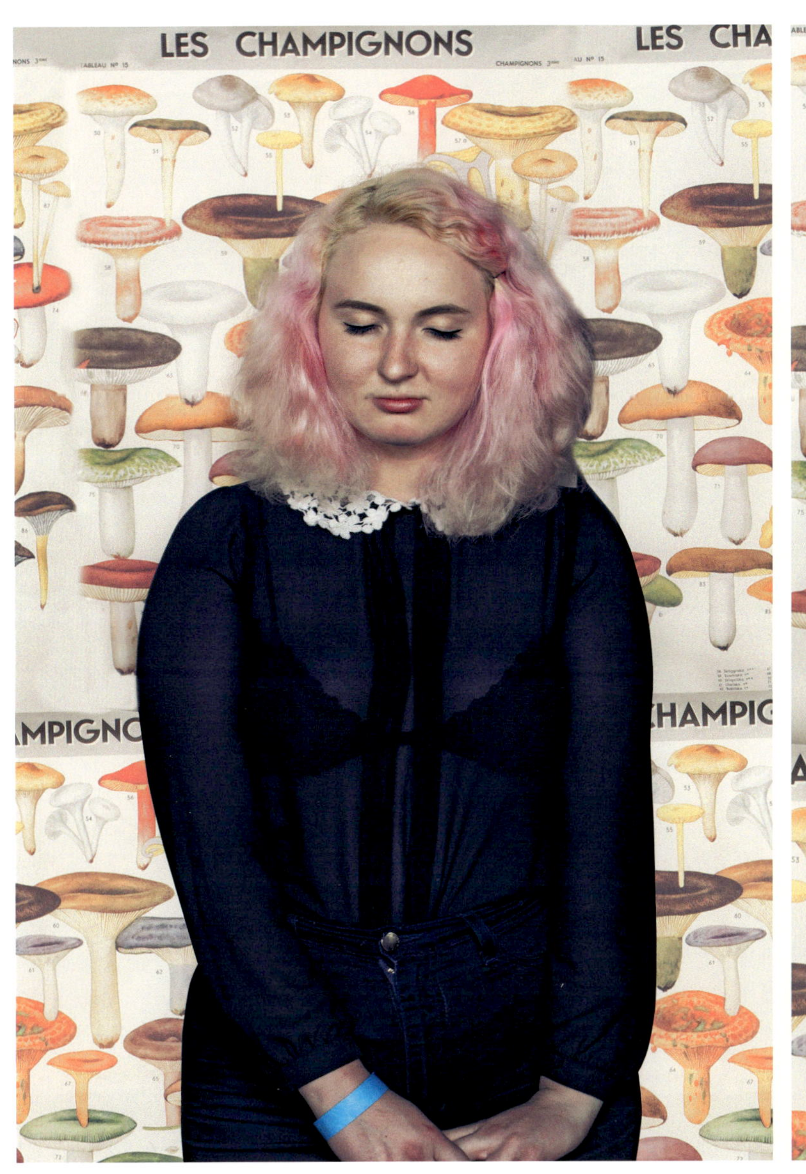
LES CHAMPIGNONS
LES CHA
CHAMPIGNO
AMPIGNON
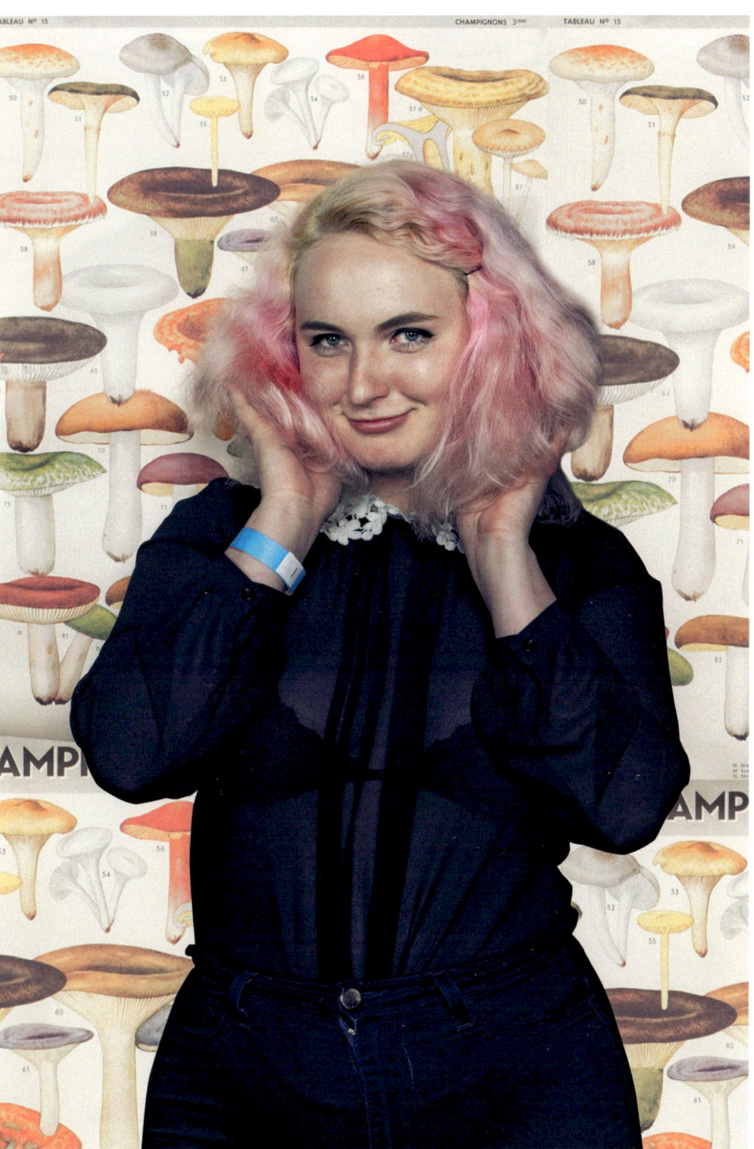
CHAMPIGNONS 3ème   TABLEAU Nº 15
AMP
AMPI

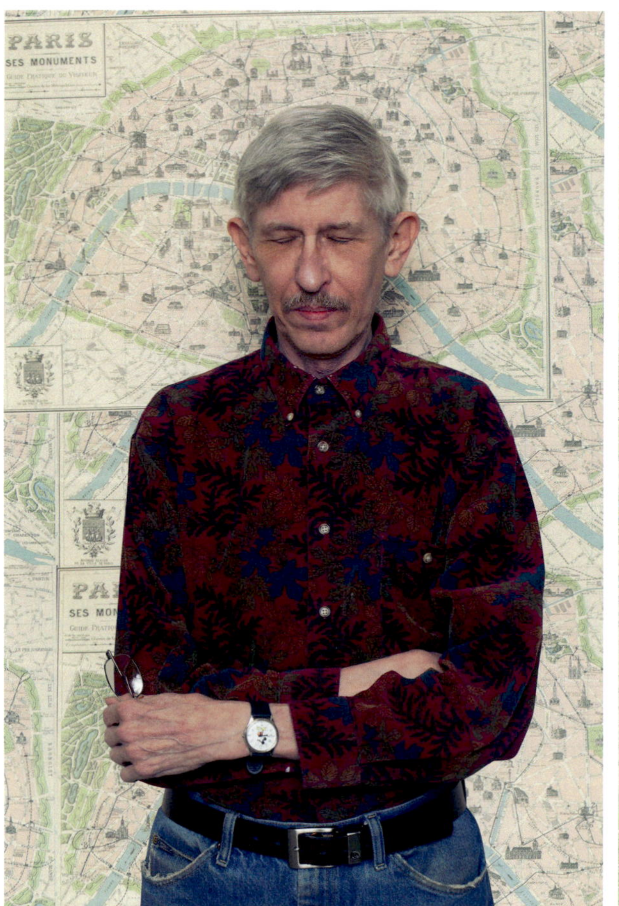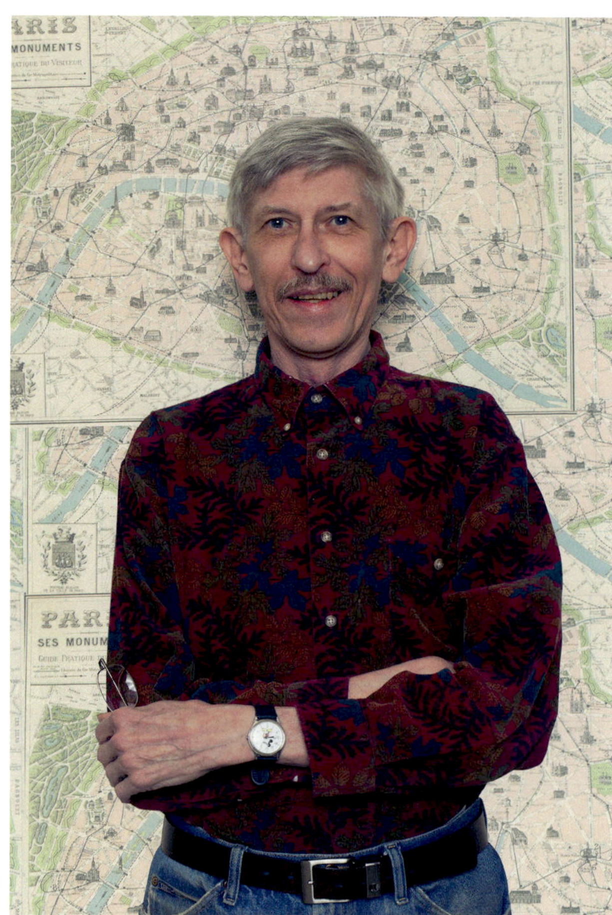

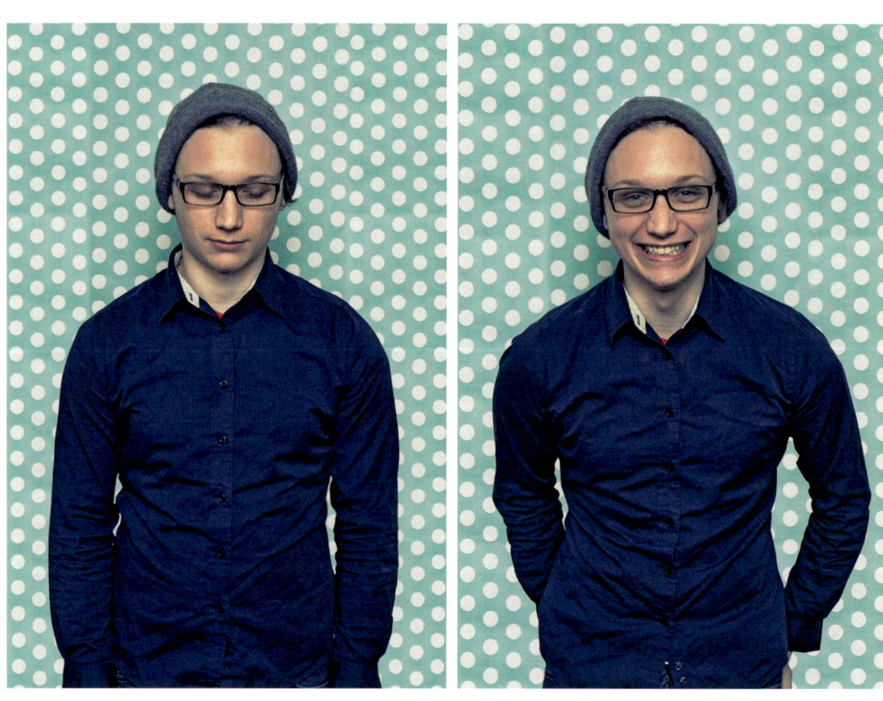

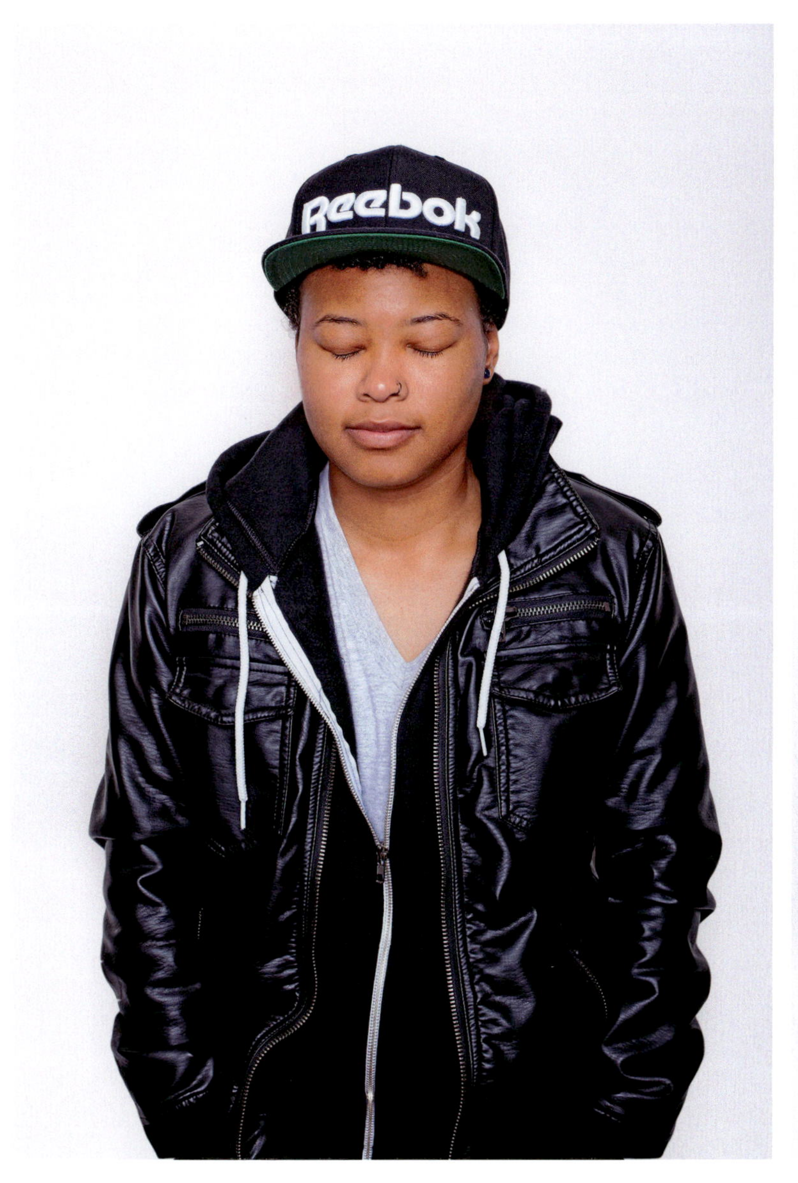
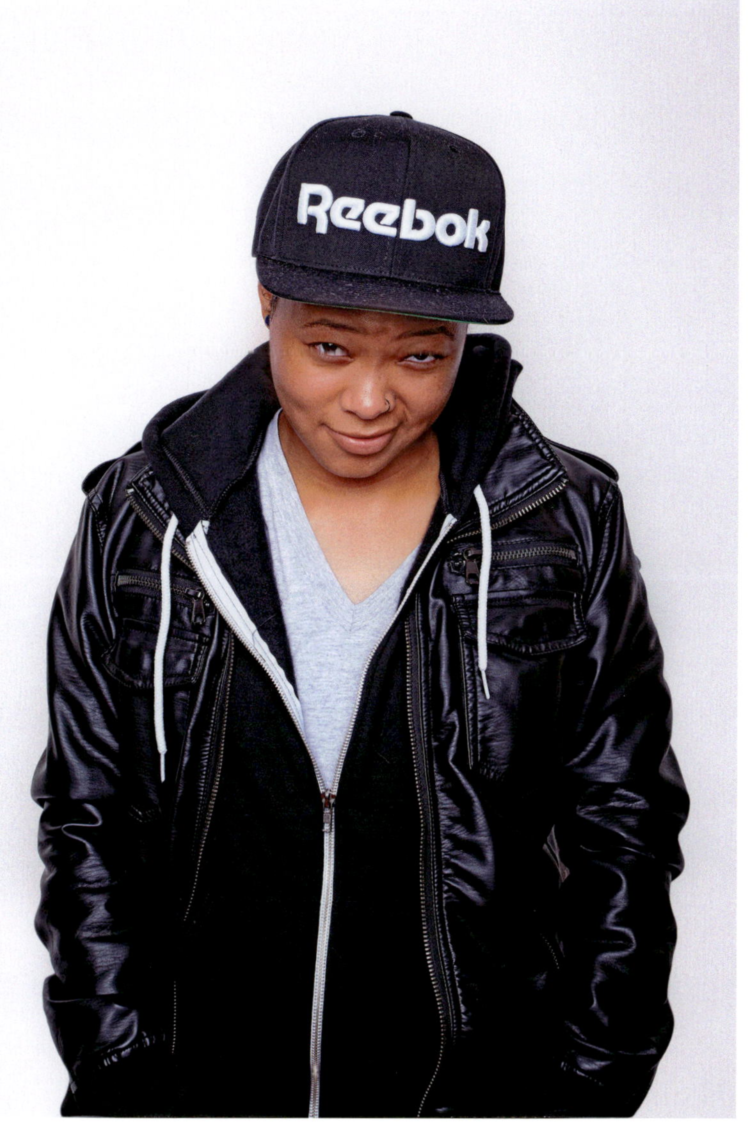

GAY | FACE

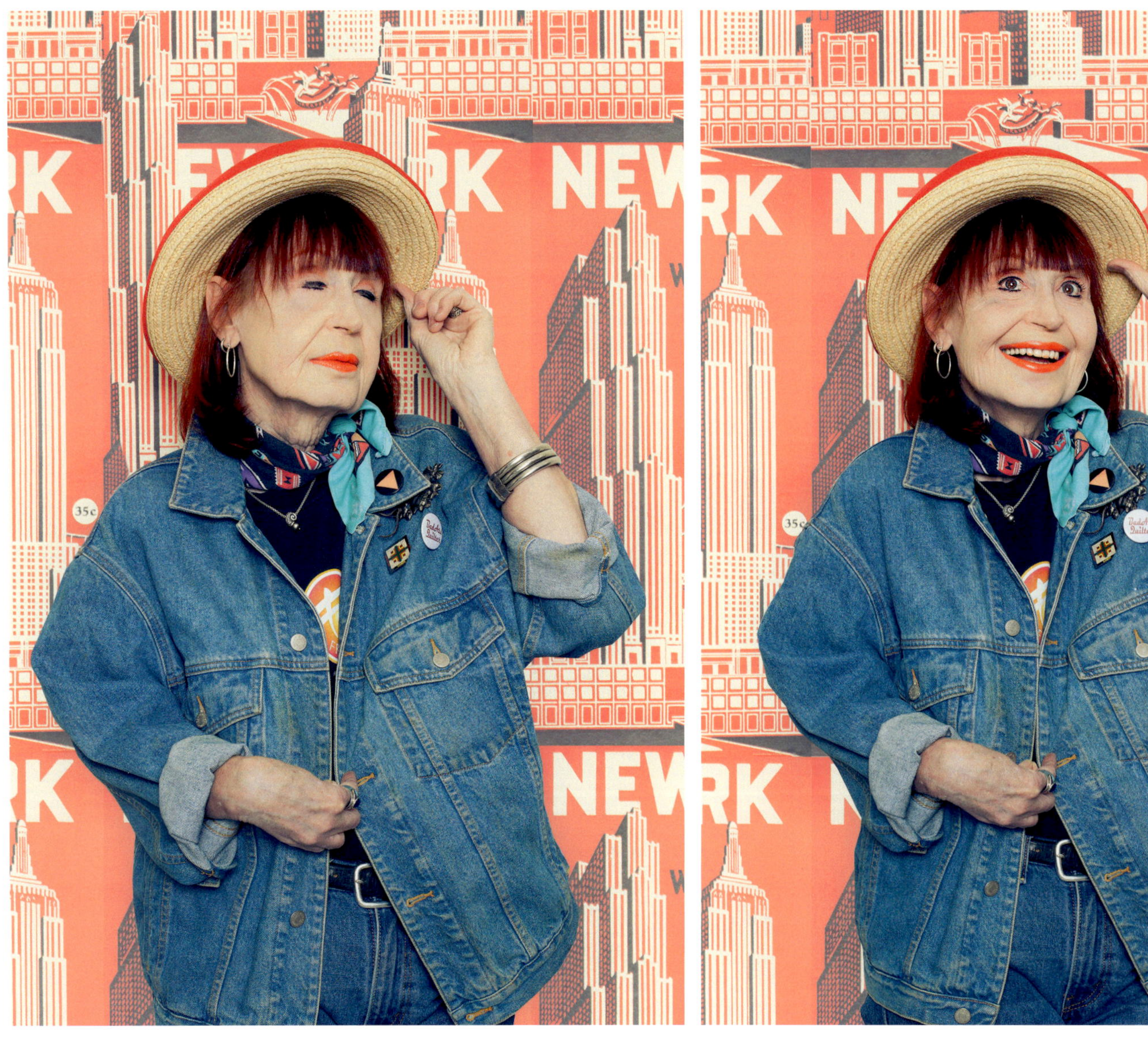

Elizabeth W.

BROOKLYN, NEW YORK

How would you identify your sexuality?
Queer gender-female with transgender history.

Why did you choose to be a part of this project?
Documenting the words, voices, and images of the LGBTQ+ community is very important. Too much of our history—visual, written, and verbal—has been lost over hundreds, and even thousands, of years. I'm glad to be a small part of documenting LGBTQ+ folks of this present era.

What do you think of your portrait?
I'm always terribly critical of images of myself. I don't love the picture with my eyes closed because I think I look sad. I actually love the photo with my eyes open because it reminds me of Marlo Thomas from *That Girl* and I think that's hysterical!

Describe your coming out. Are you coming out in some way by participating in this project?
I've been out for so long, I'm not sure if I was ever in. If there was any kind of coming out, it was so long ago that instead of coming out of a closet I probably came out of an armoire!

Have you ever experienced discrimination based on your gender or sexual orientation?
Of course I have, everyone has, but I never allowed it to affect the way I felt about myself. It's the haters, bigots, and morons that have to change, not me. I've been standing up for too long to even consider sitting down now.

If you could change one thing about mainstream society to improve the lives of LGBTQ+ people, what would it be?
If everyone would embrace a mindset of genuine inclusivity for all of our sisters, brothers, and others, that would be a dramatically positive shift in our society and the world.

Describe how this project has affected you, both personally and as a member of the LGBTQ+ community as a whole.
It has given me the opportunity to say, "I'm here, and I'm happy and proud of who I am."

What advice have you been given by another LGBTQ+ person, or that you might offer someone?
I'd like to pass on the best advice that was given to me, which is to be yourself and live authentically. Anything else is a sham, a tragic masquerade.

Who are your LGBTQ+ role models?
The defiant ones, the activists—too many to mention—who have stood up in the face of adversity and said, "We're queer, we're here, and we're not going away. Get over it." The artists and dreamers who, because of their contributions throughout history, our world is an immeasurably more interesting and beautiful place.

GAY | FACE

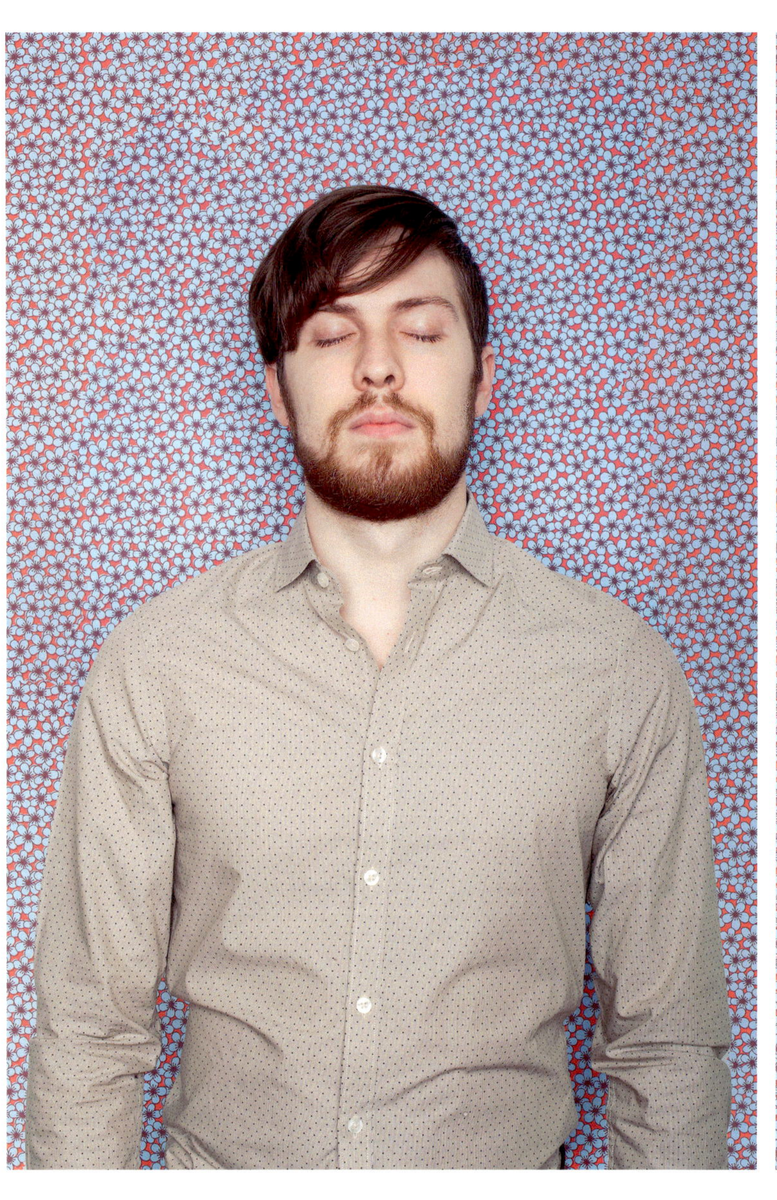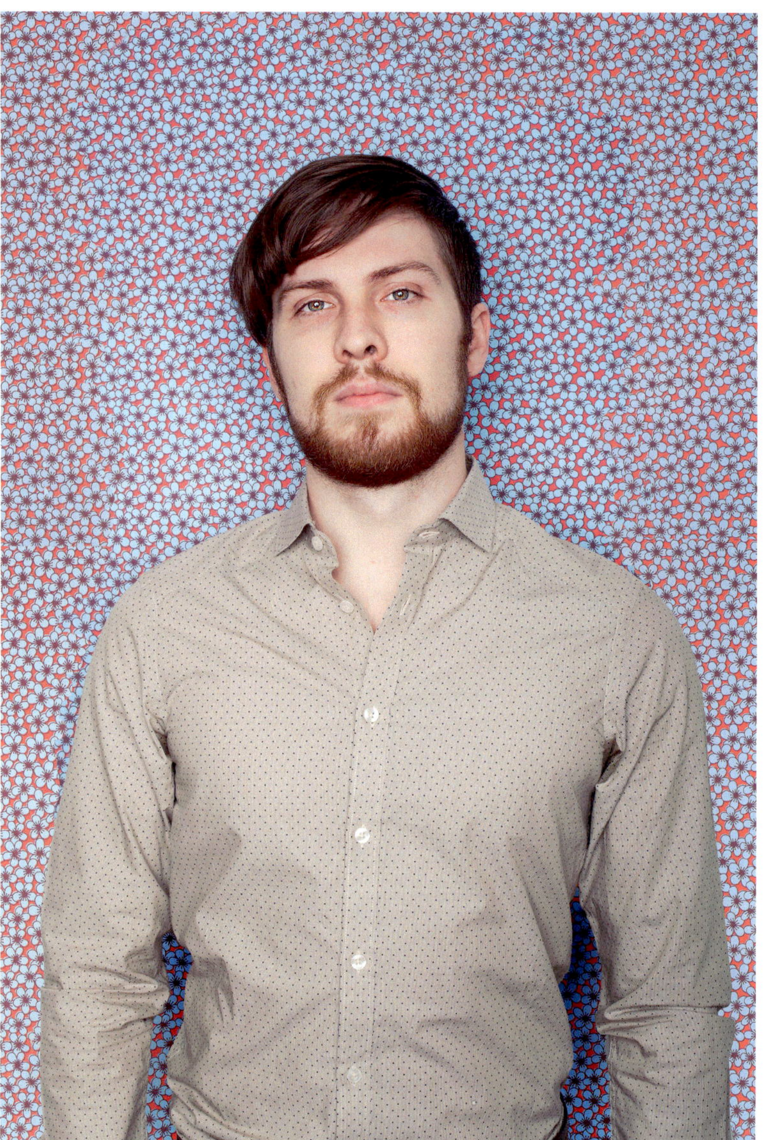

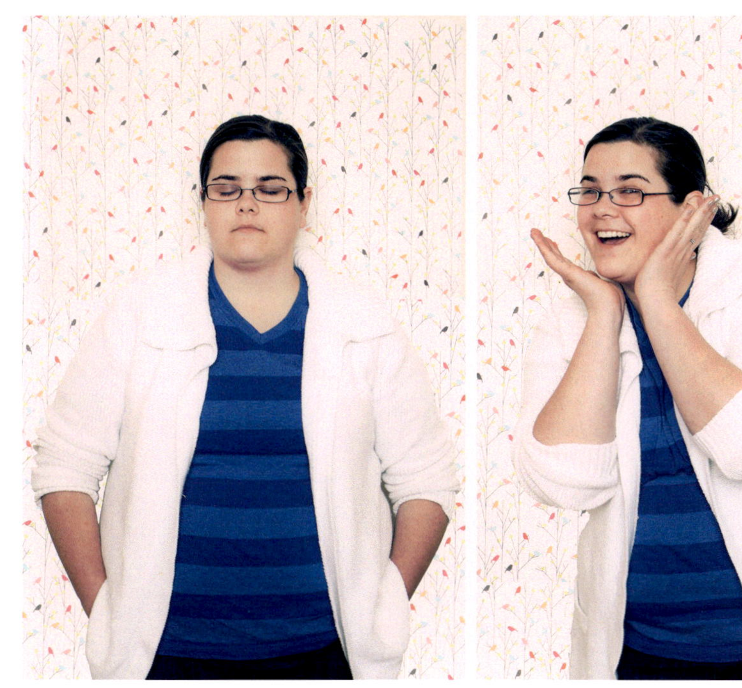

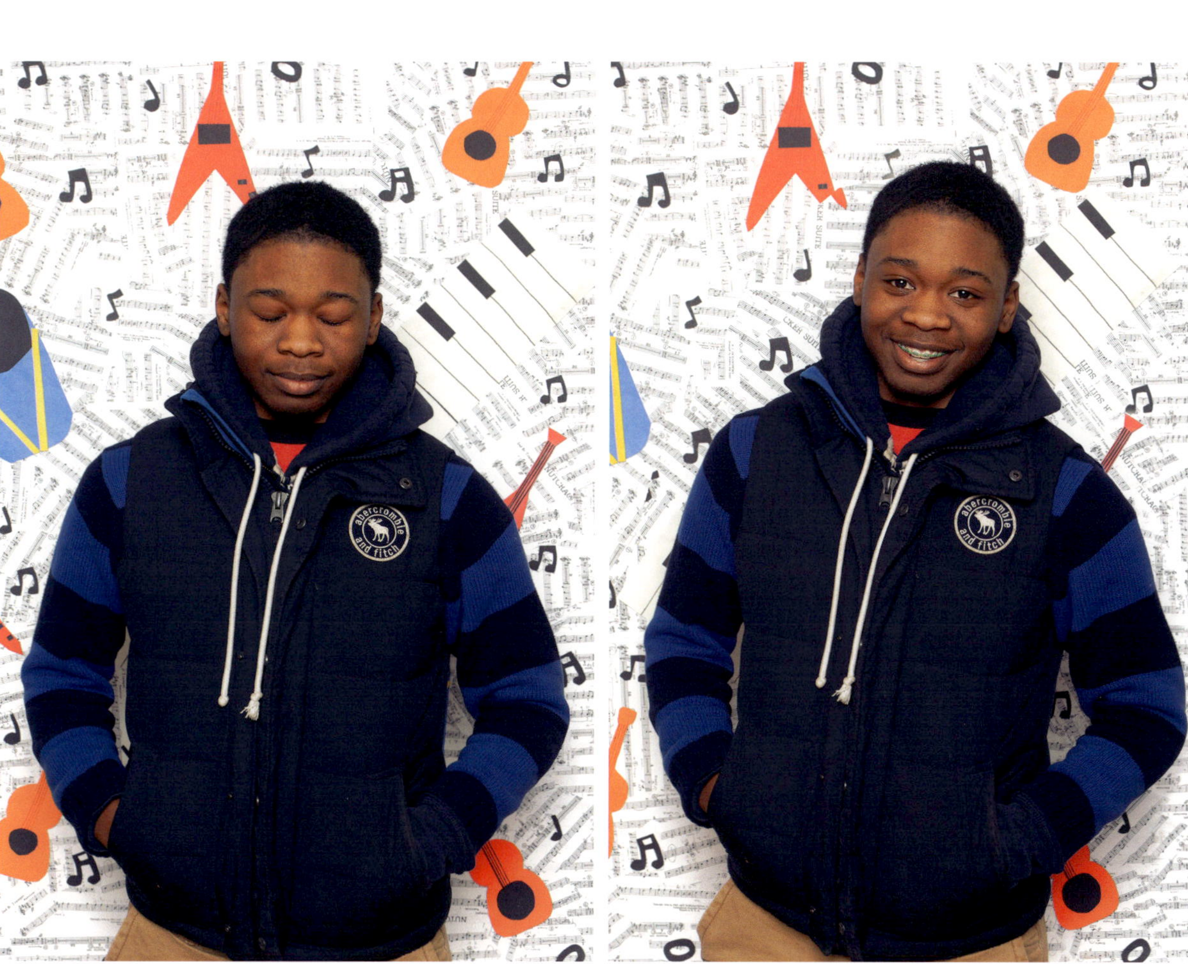

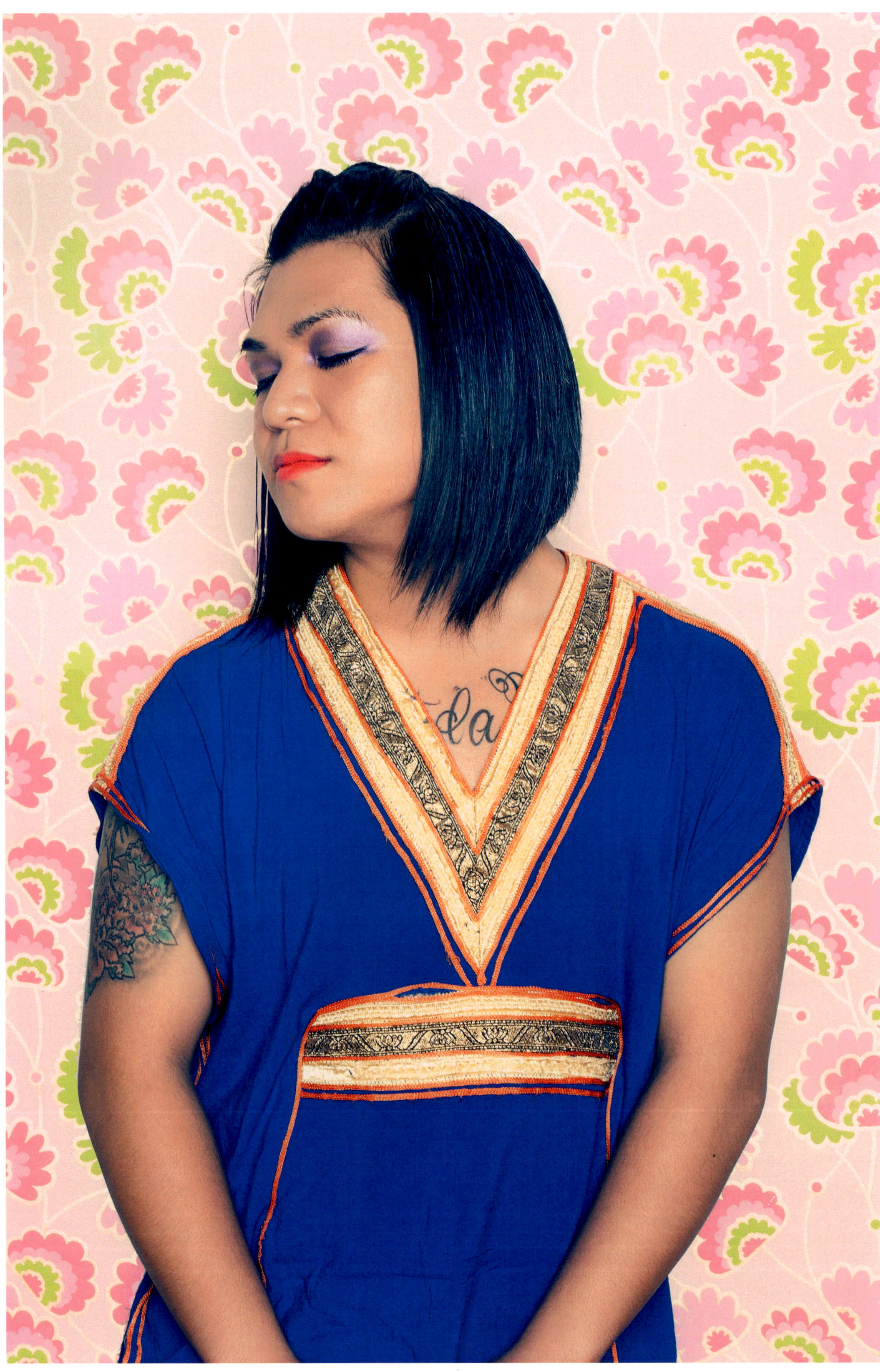

GAY | FACE

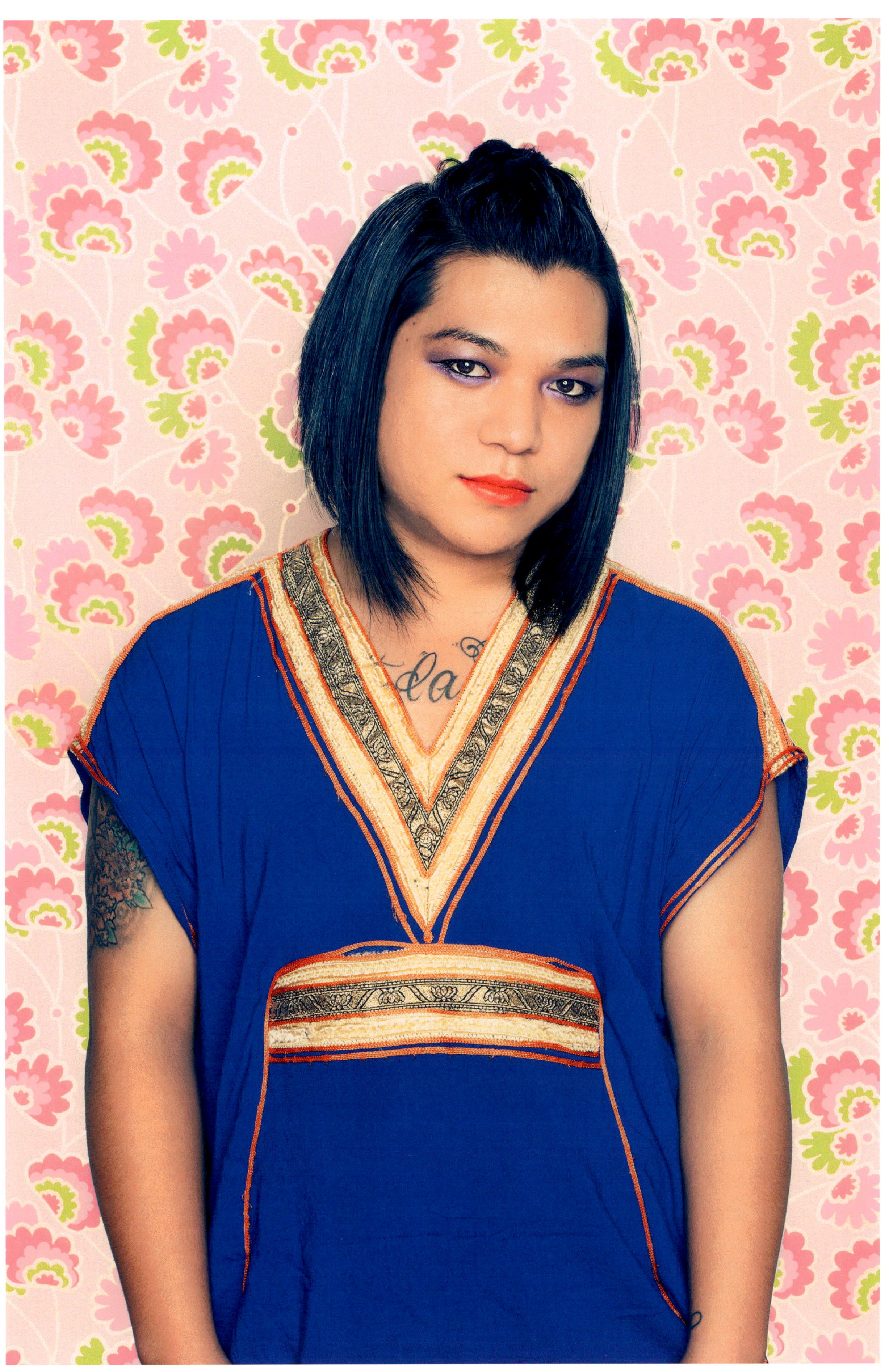

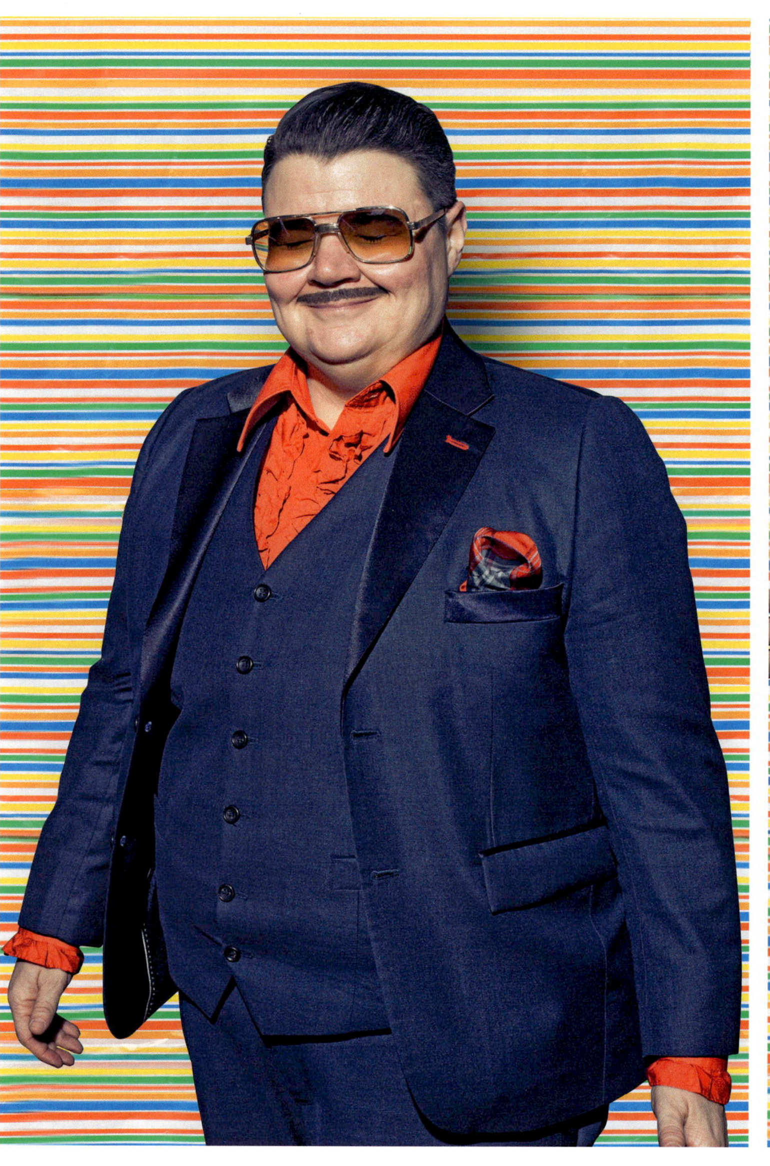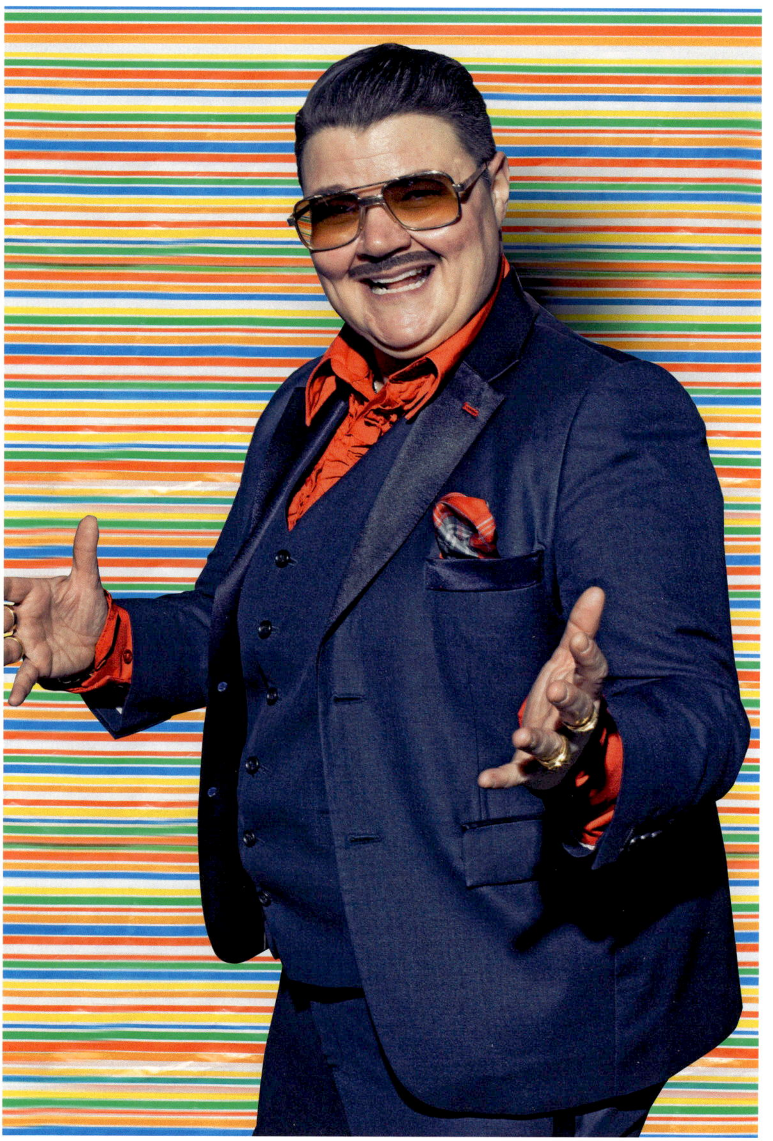

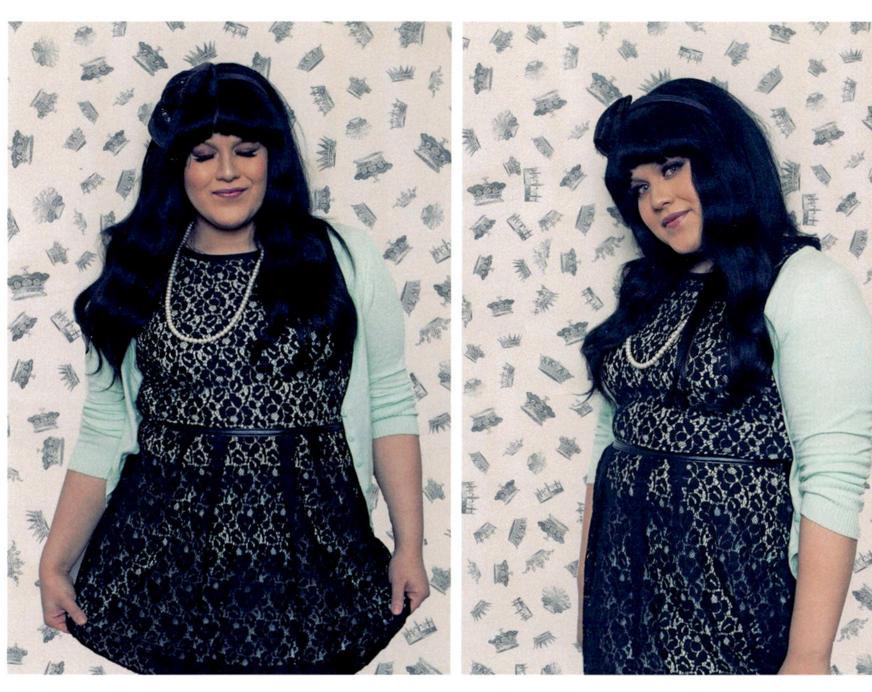

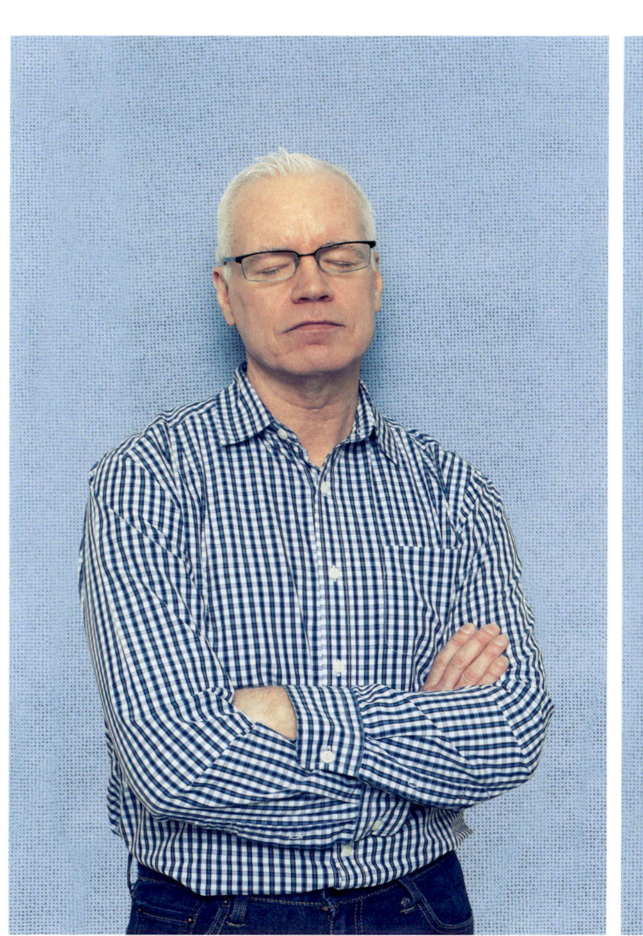

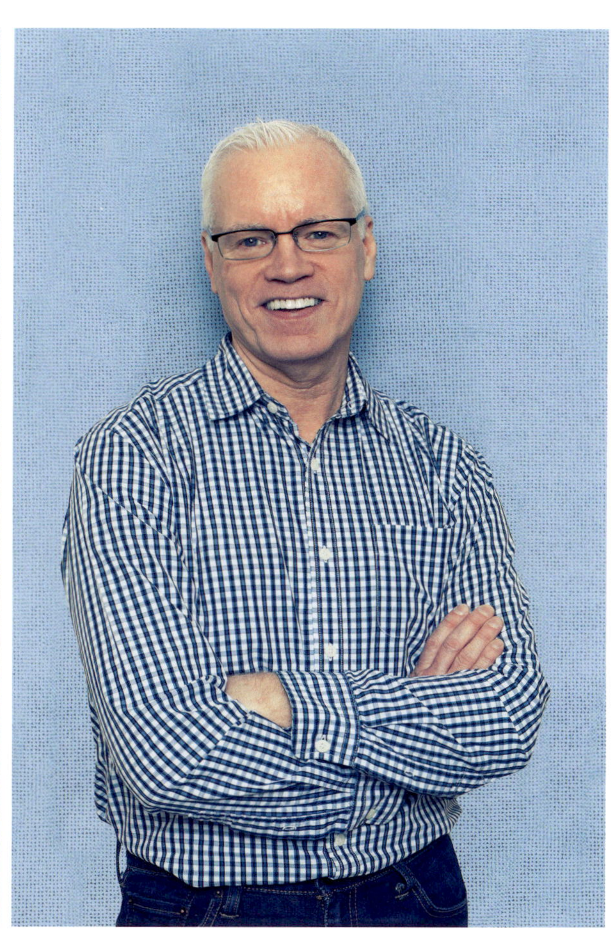

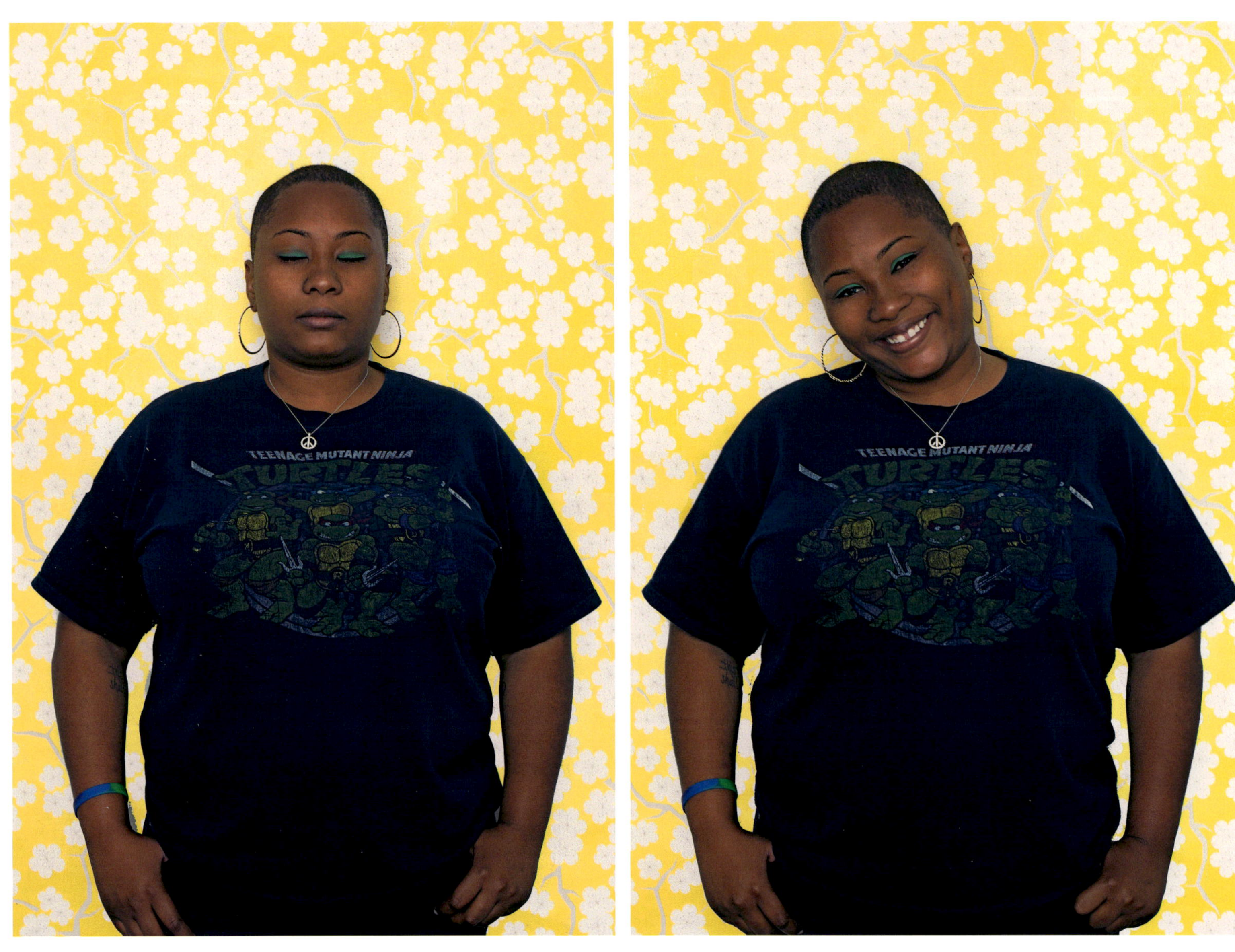

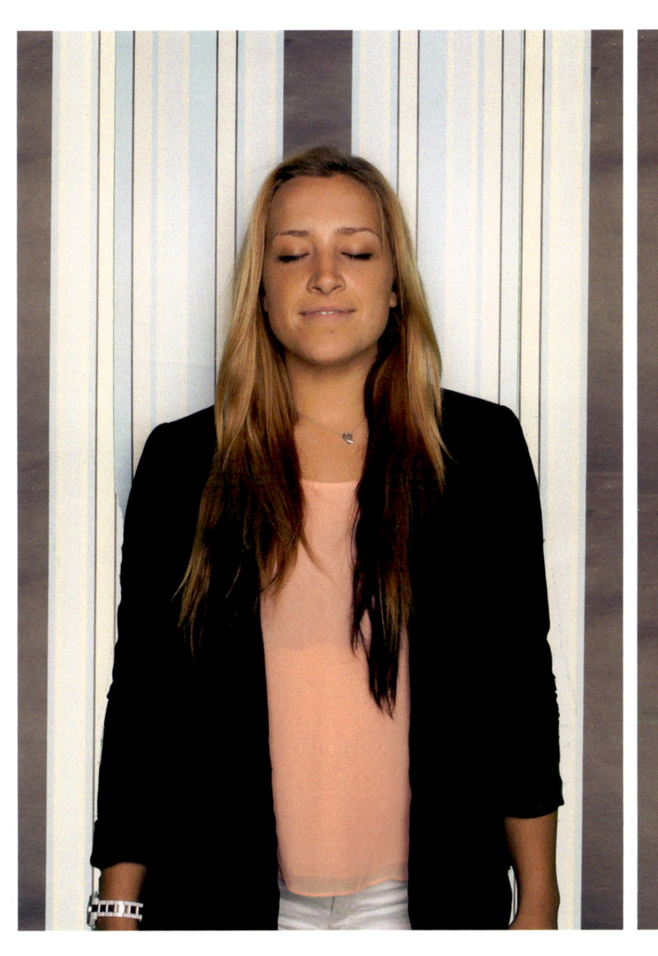
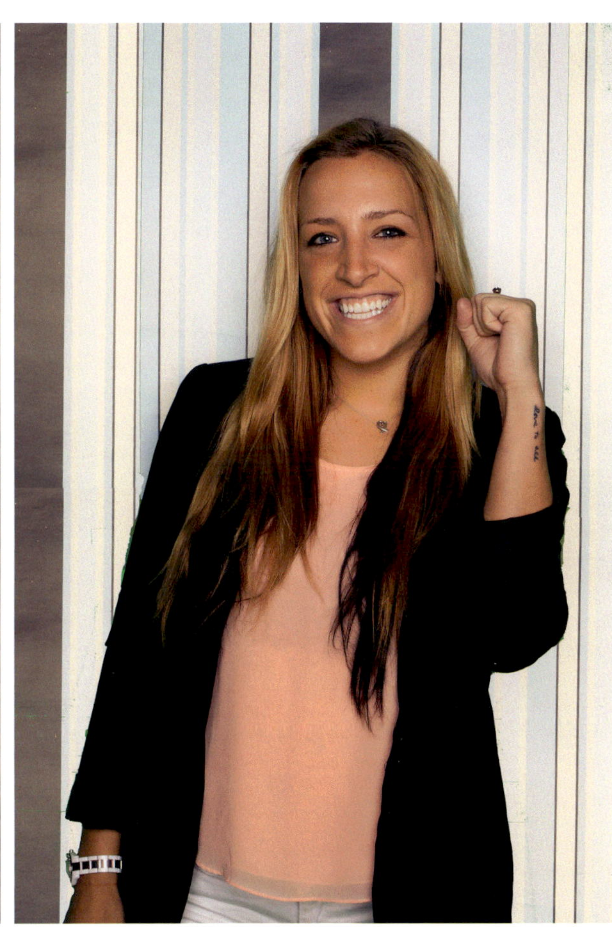

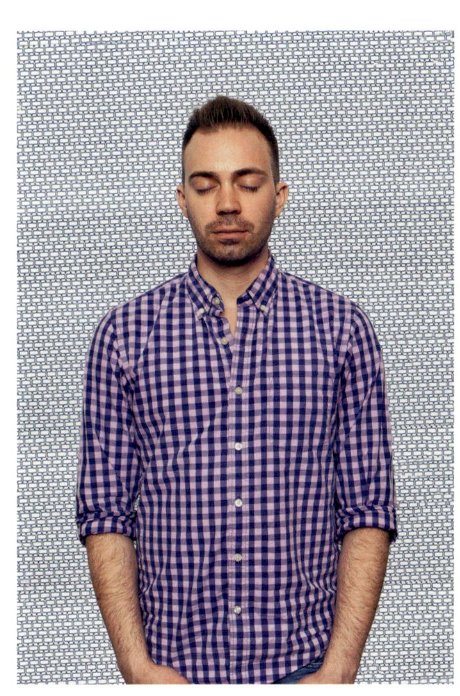
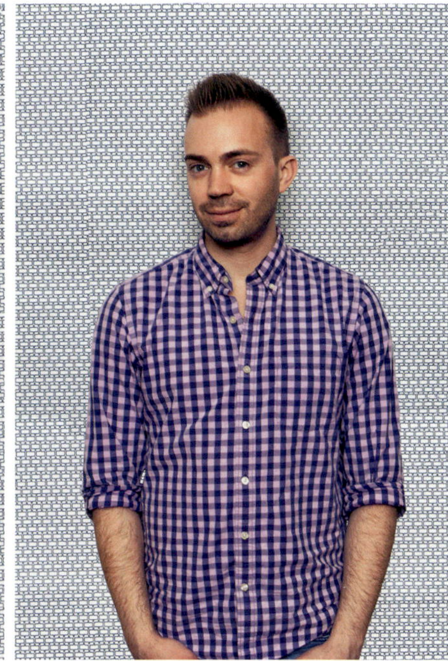

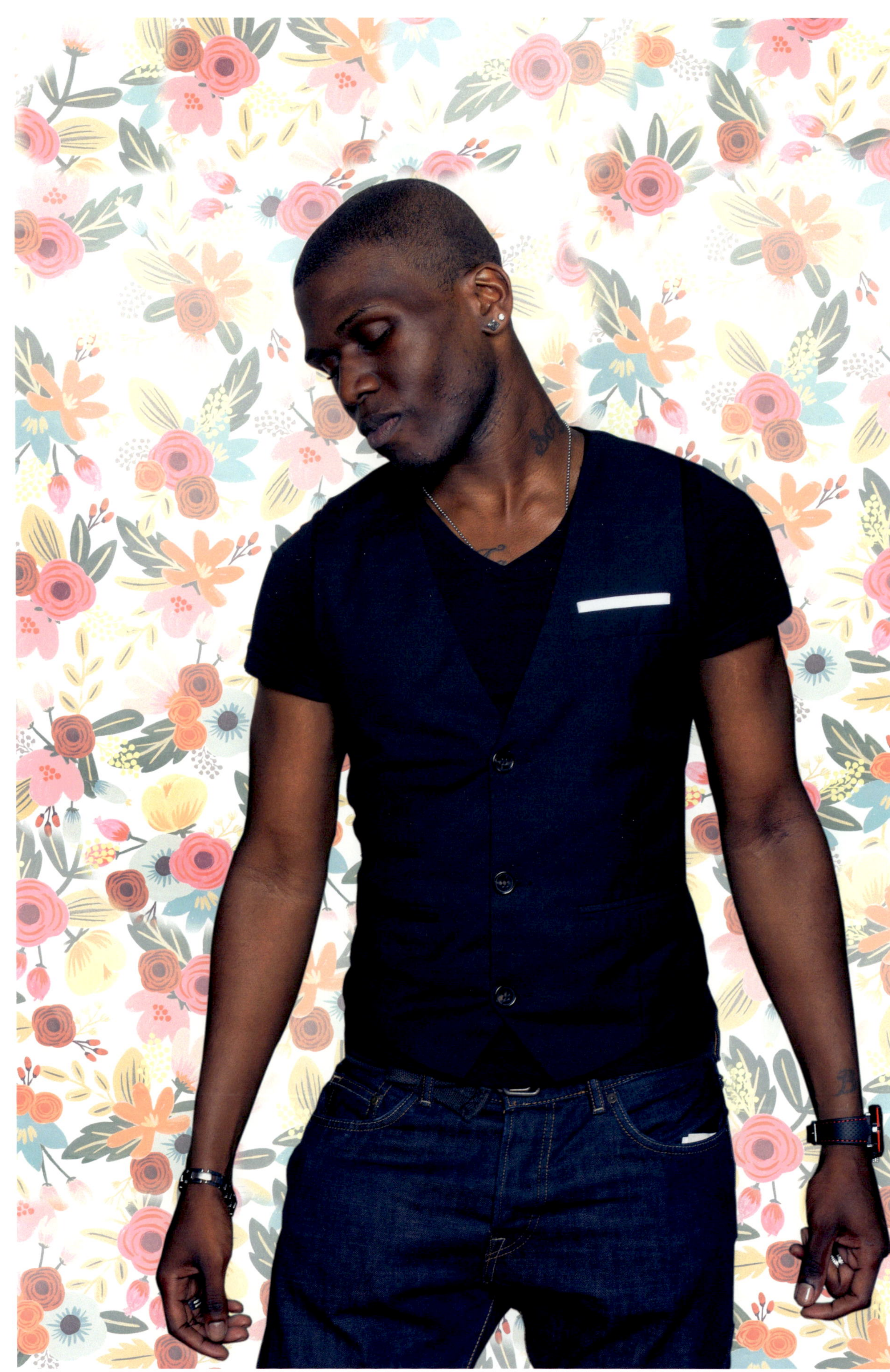

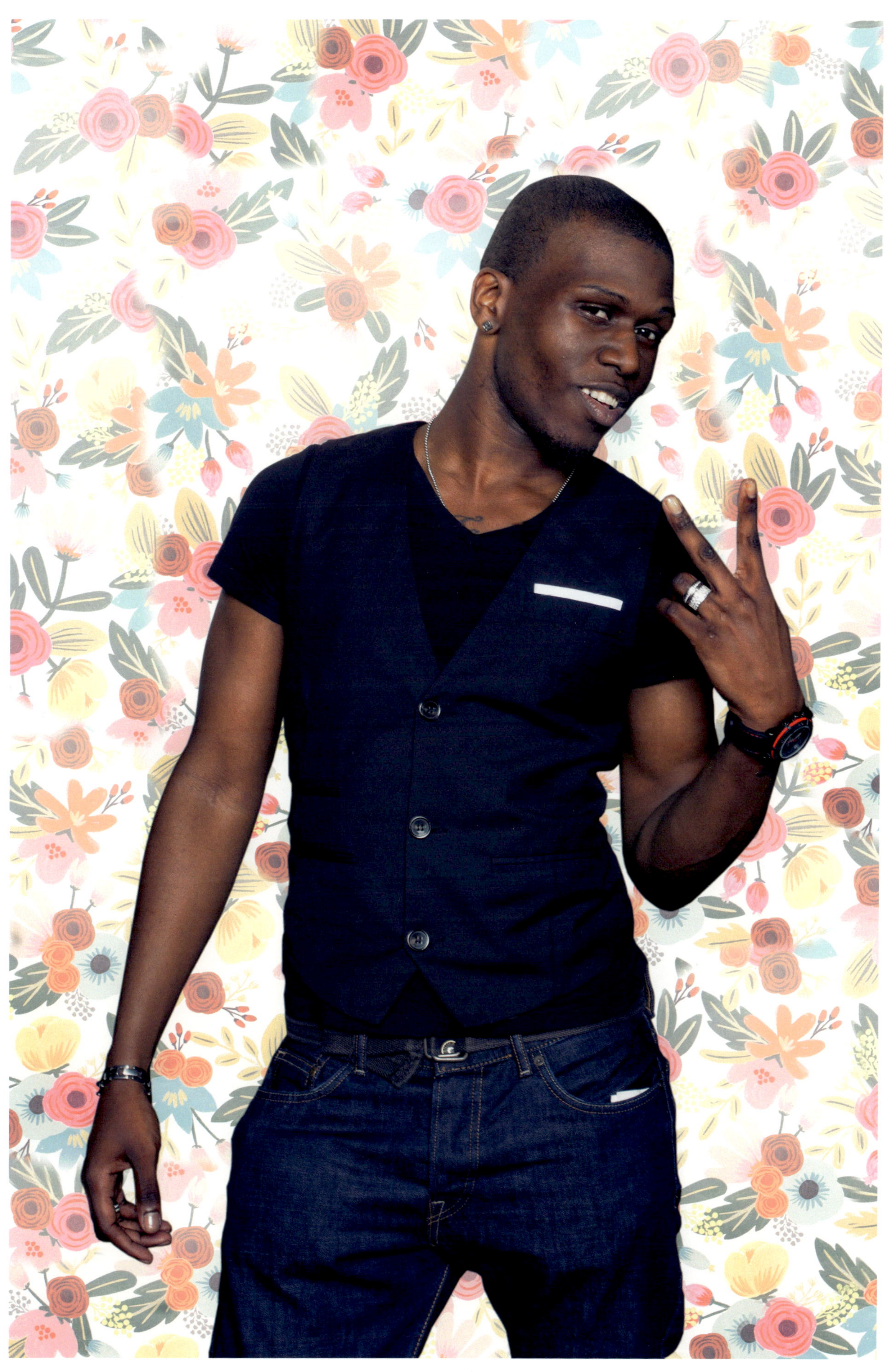

GAY | FACE

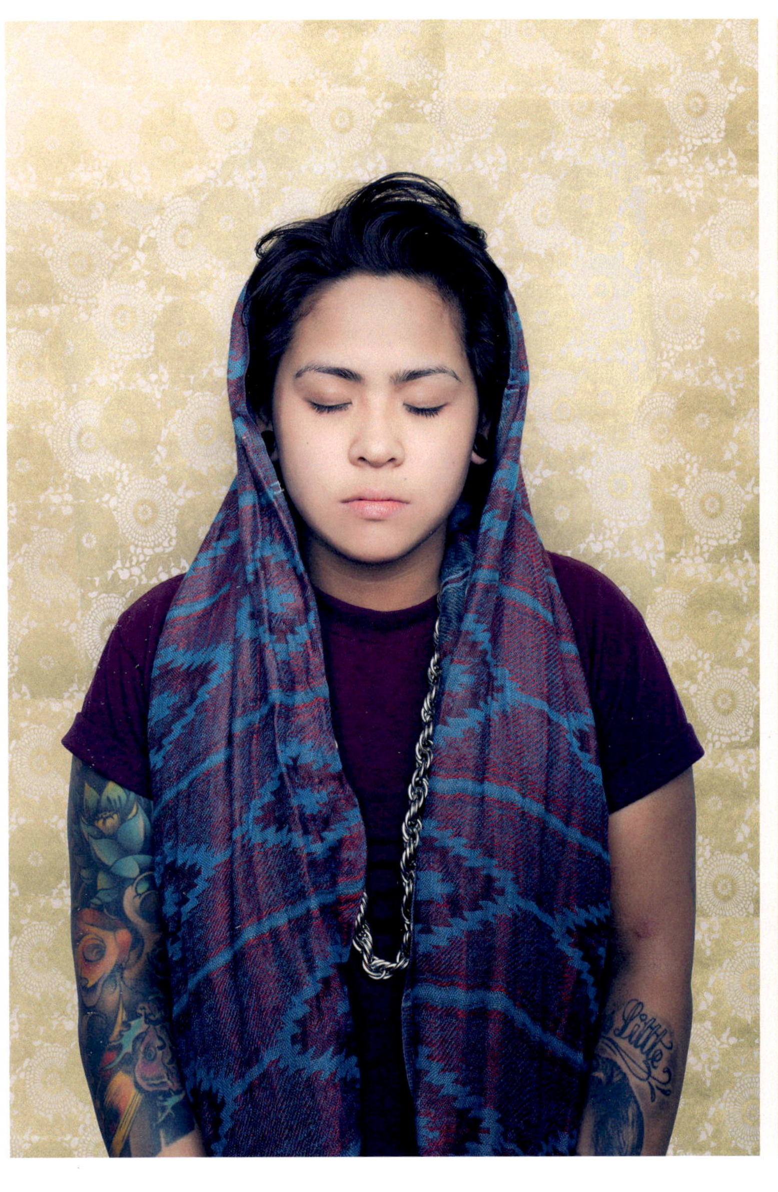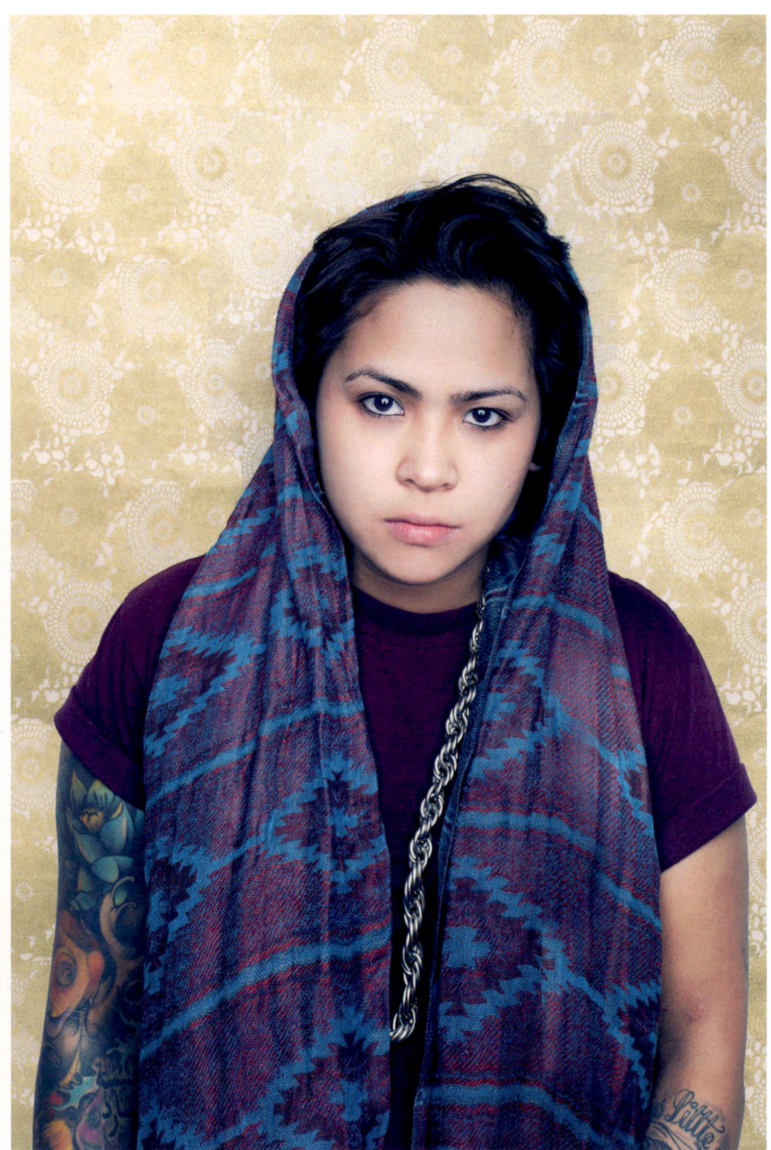

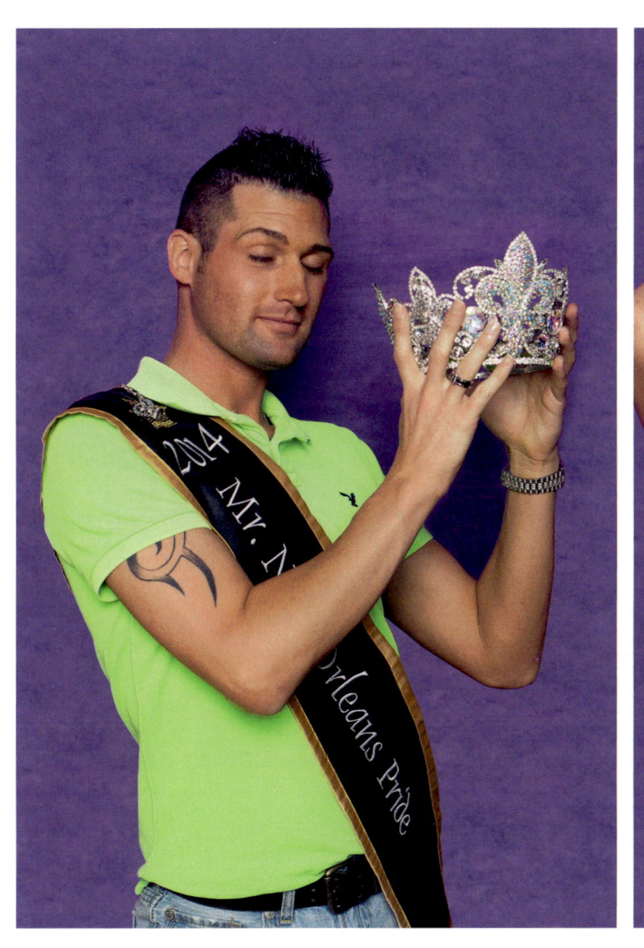

2014
Mr. New Orleans Pride

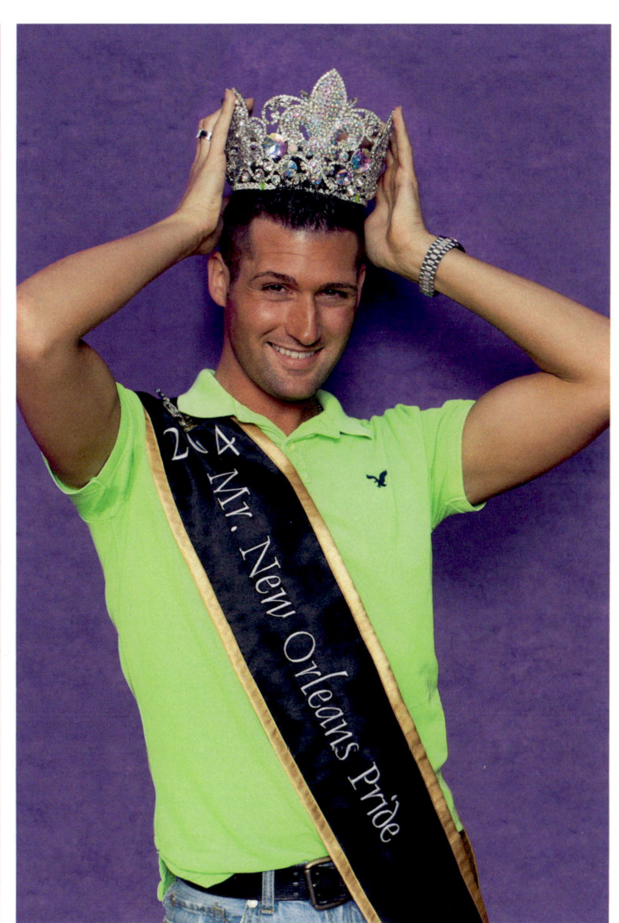

2014
Mr. New Orleans Pride

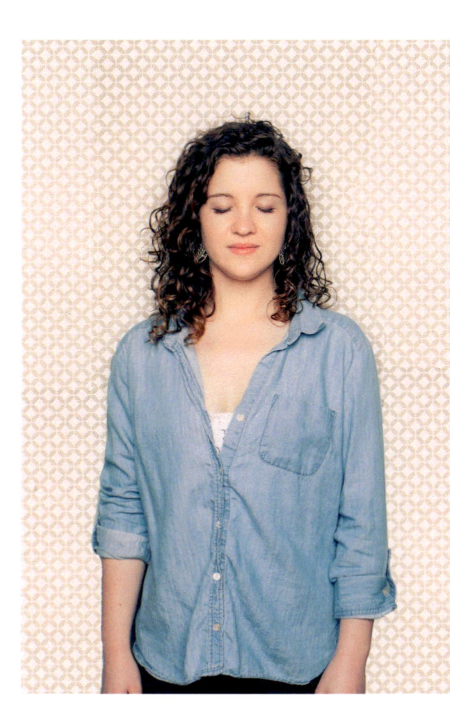

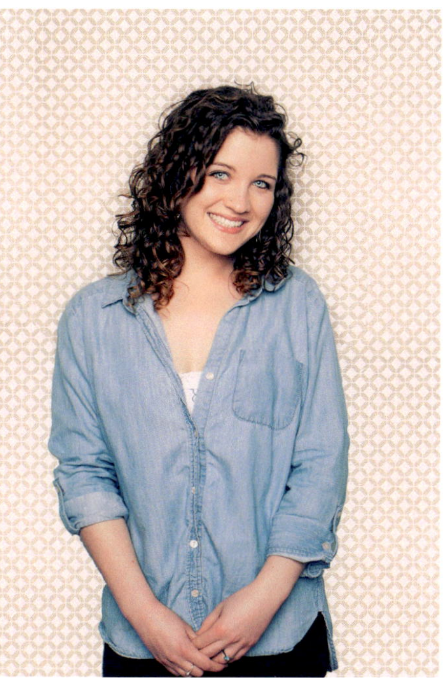

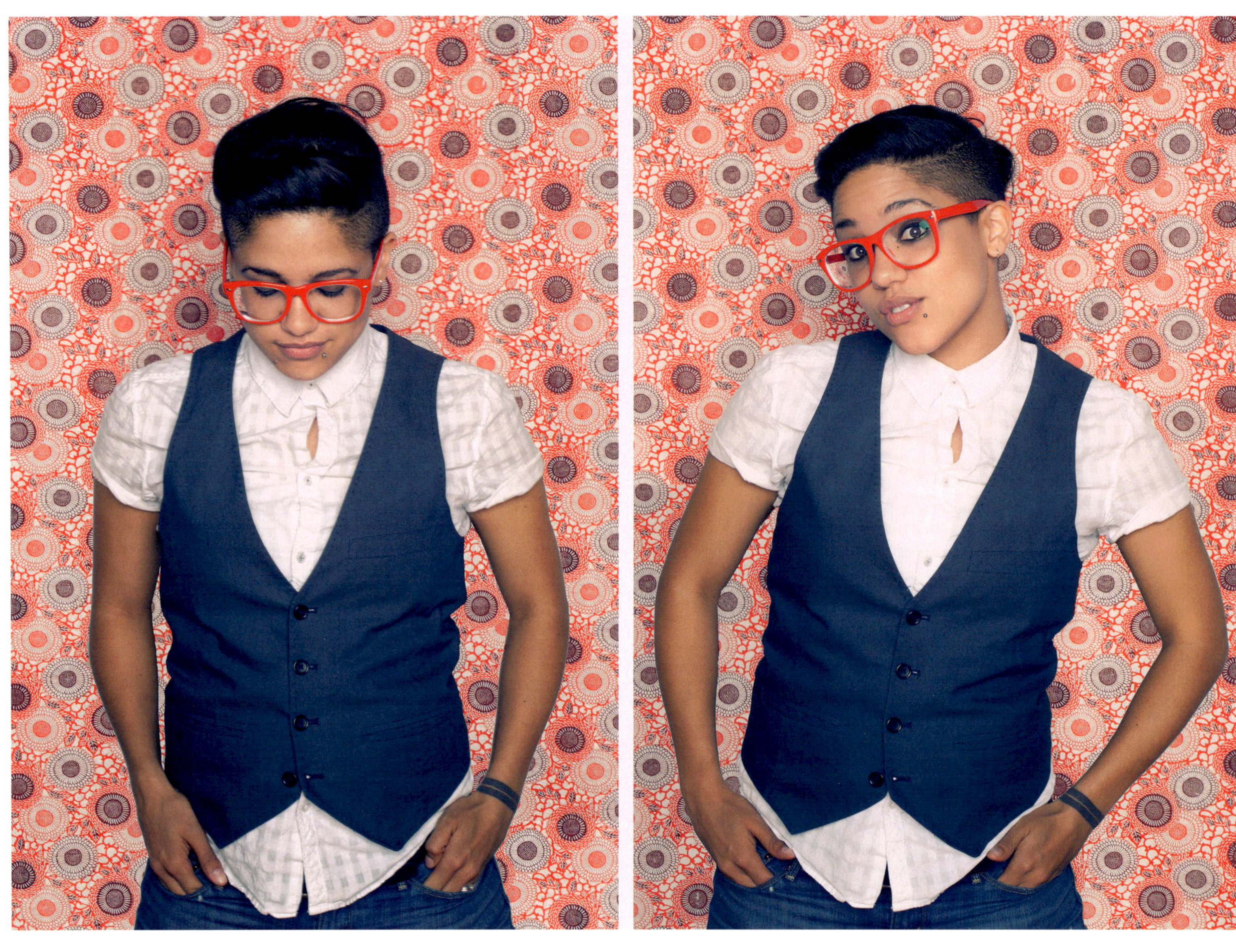

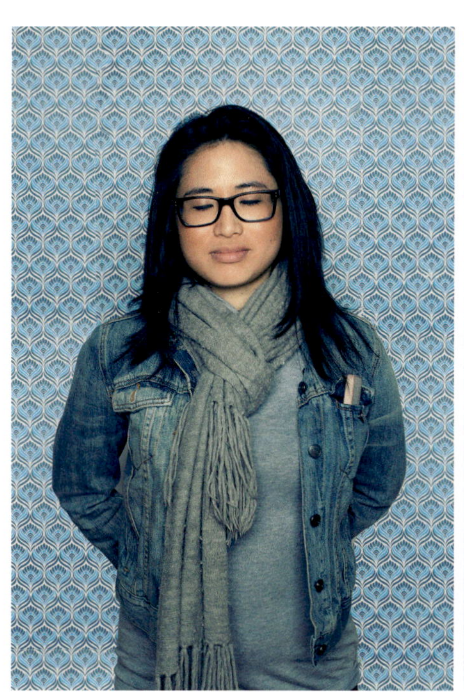
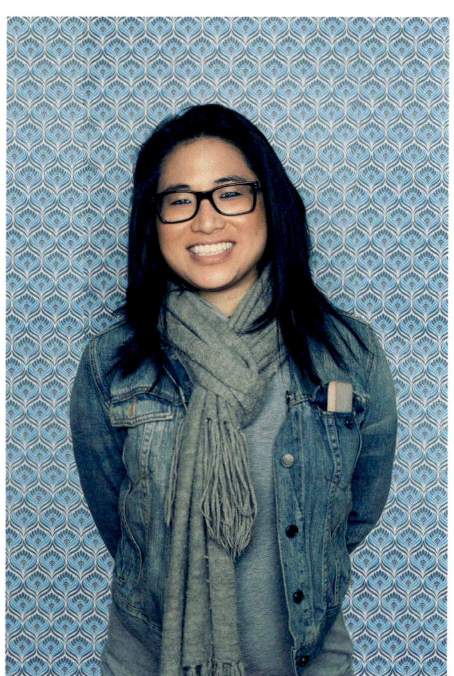

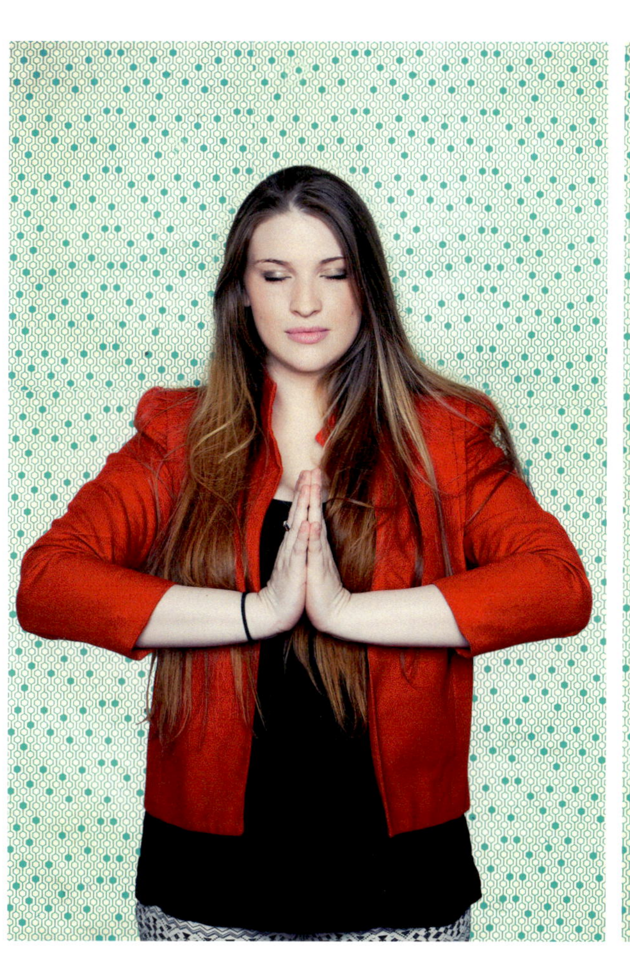
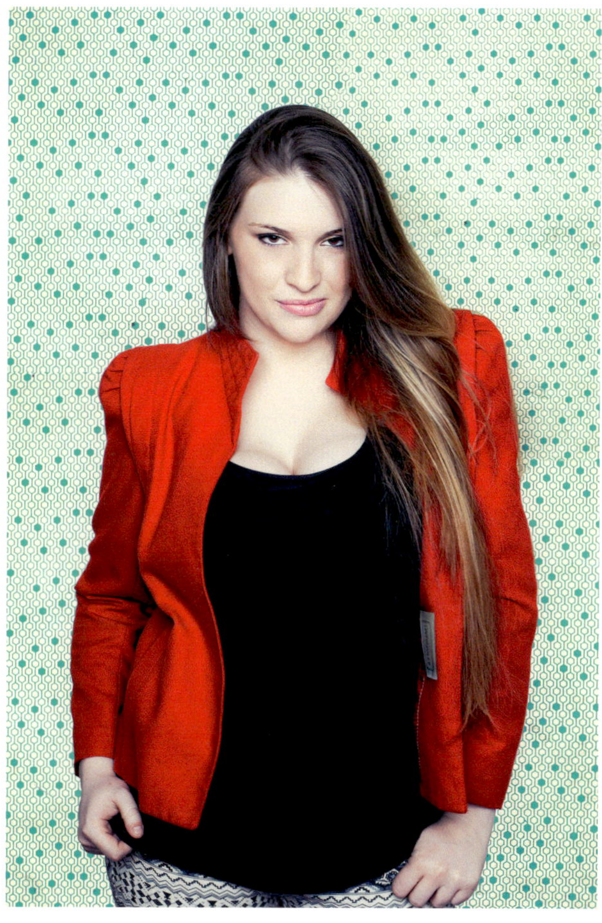

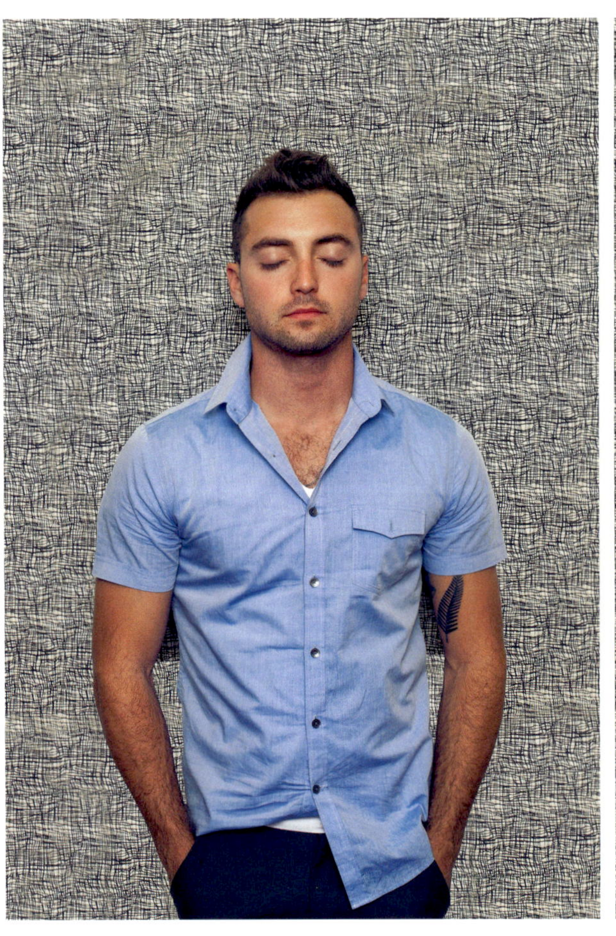

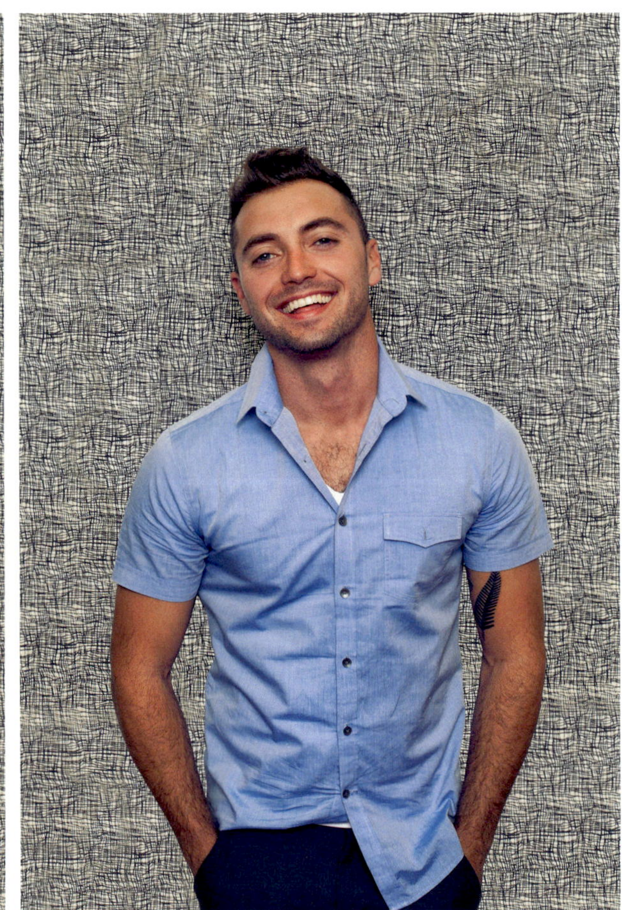

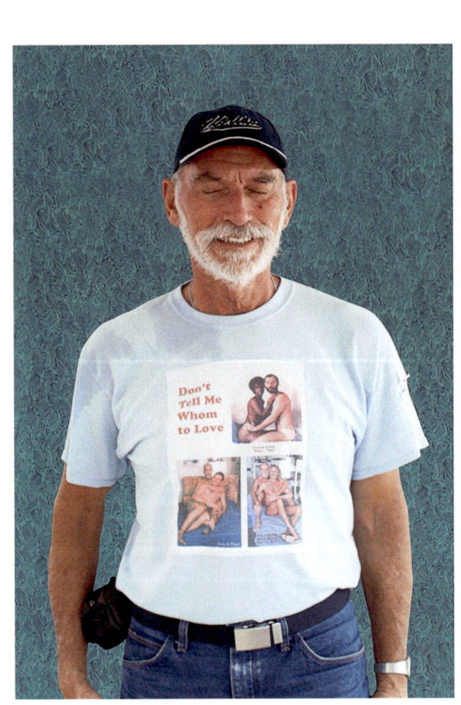
Don't
Tell Me
Whom
to Love

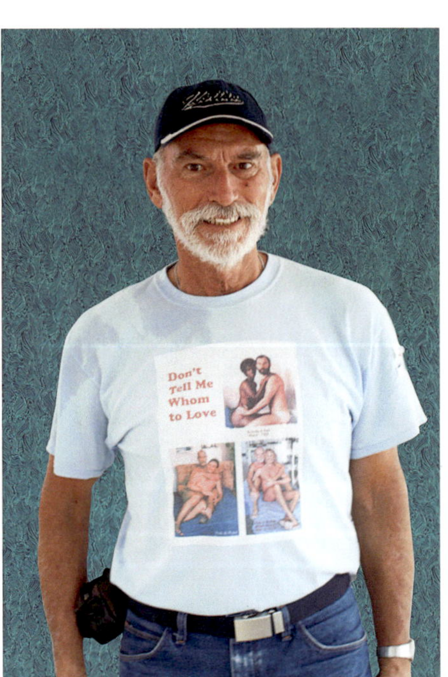
Don't
Tell Me
Whom
to Love

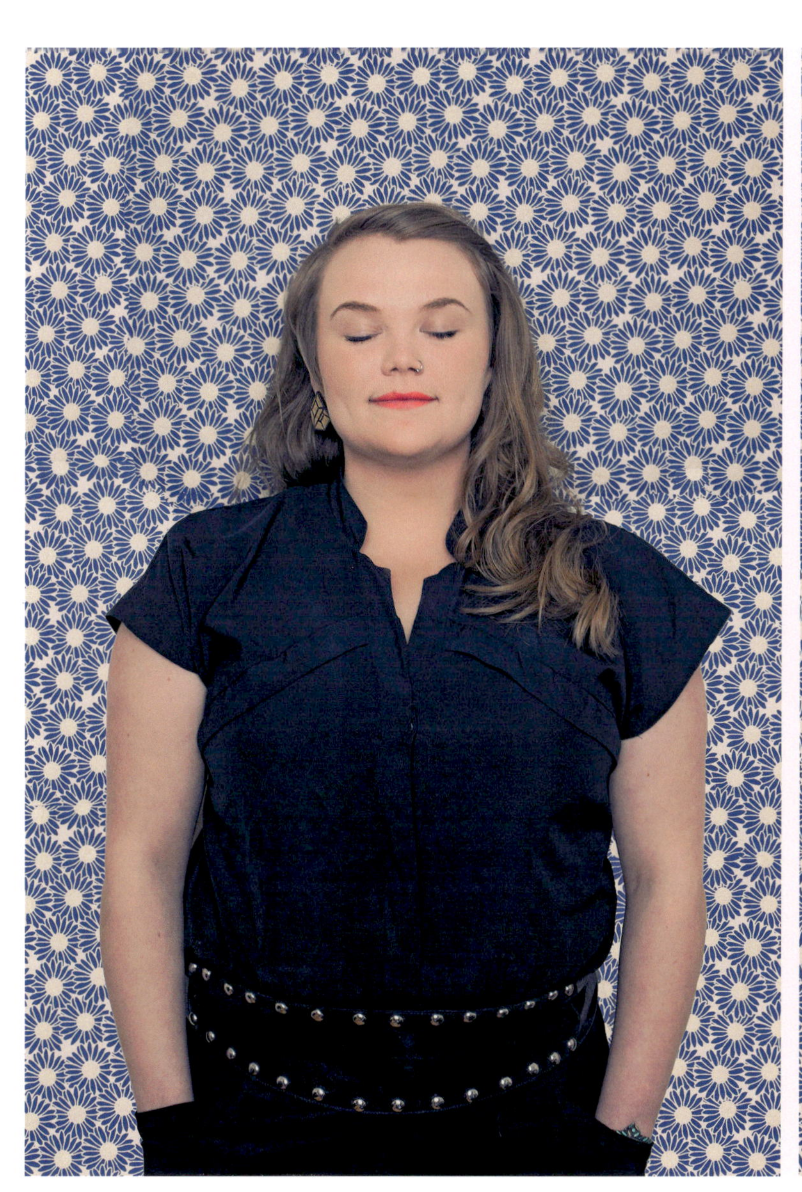
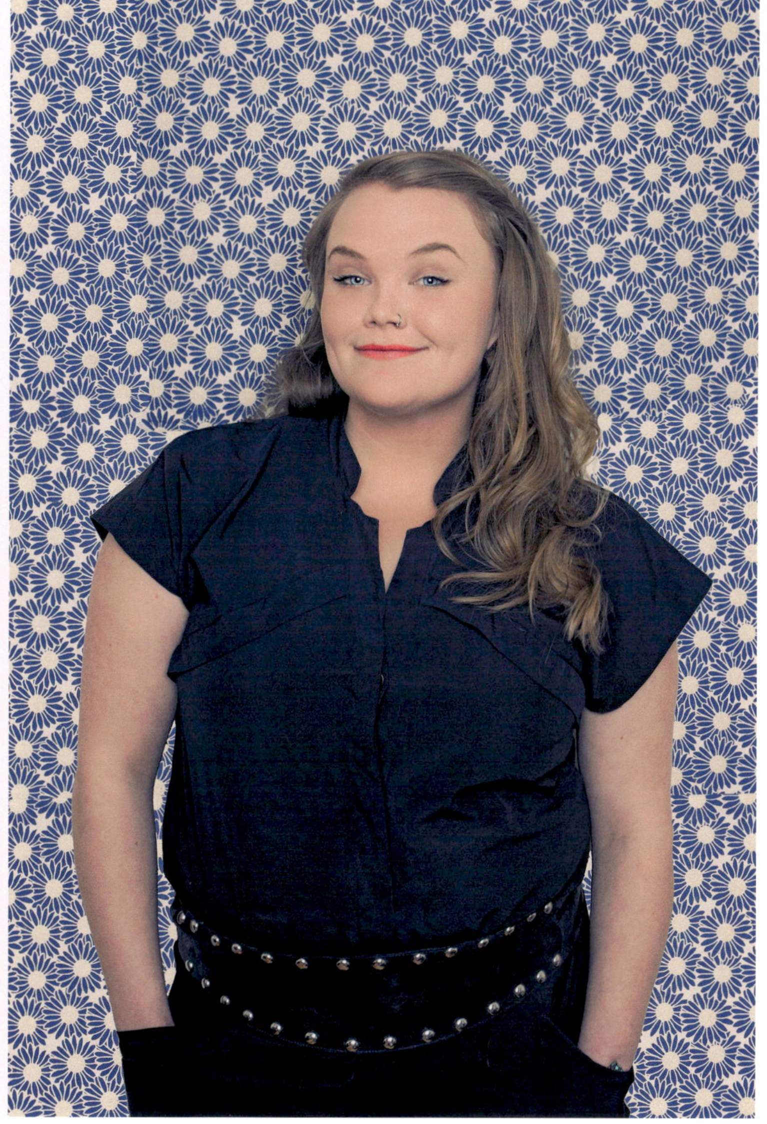

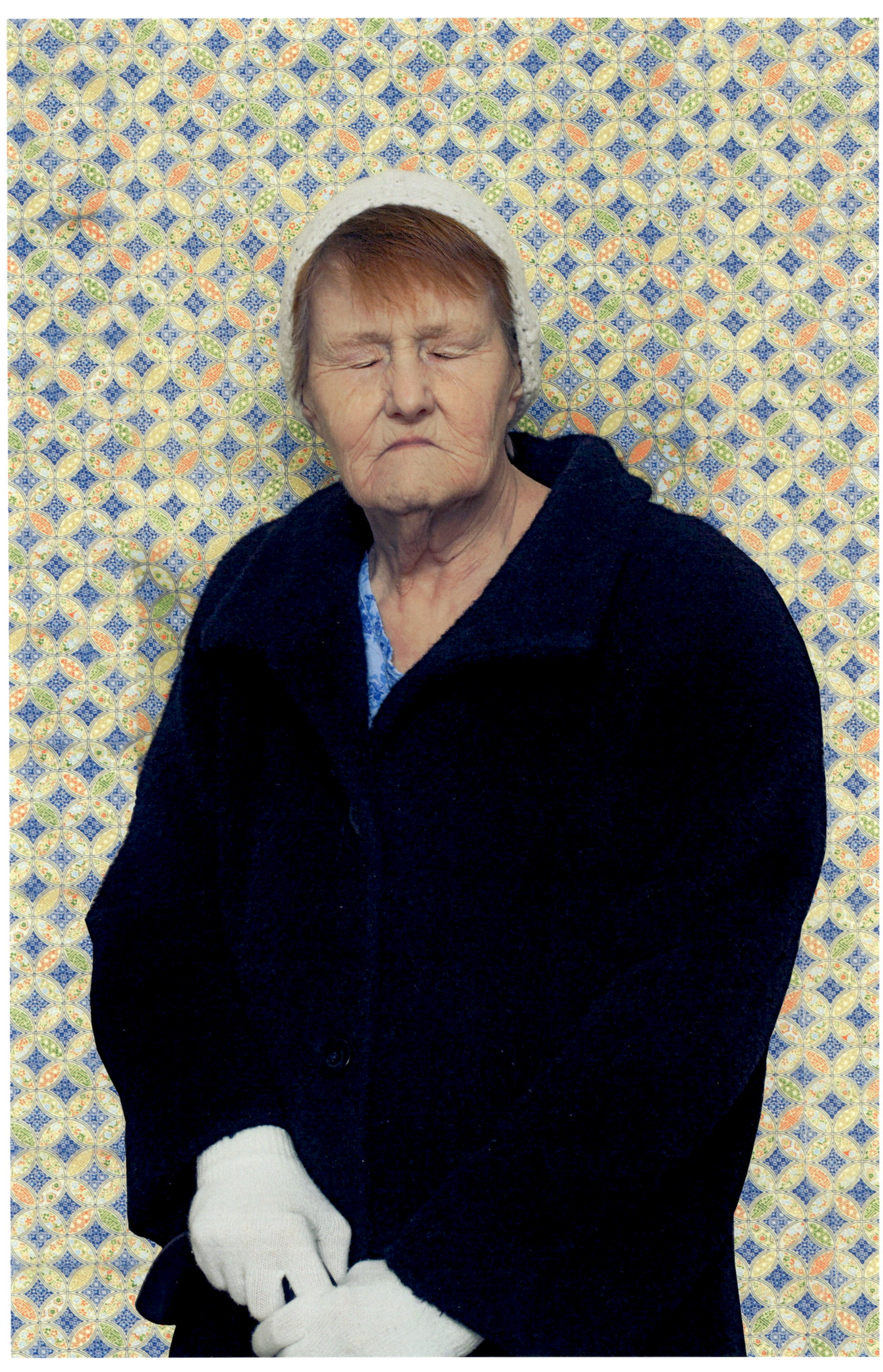

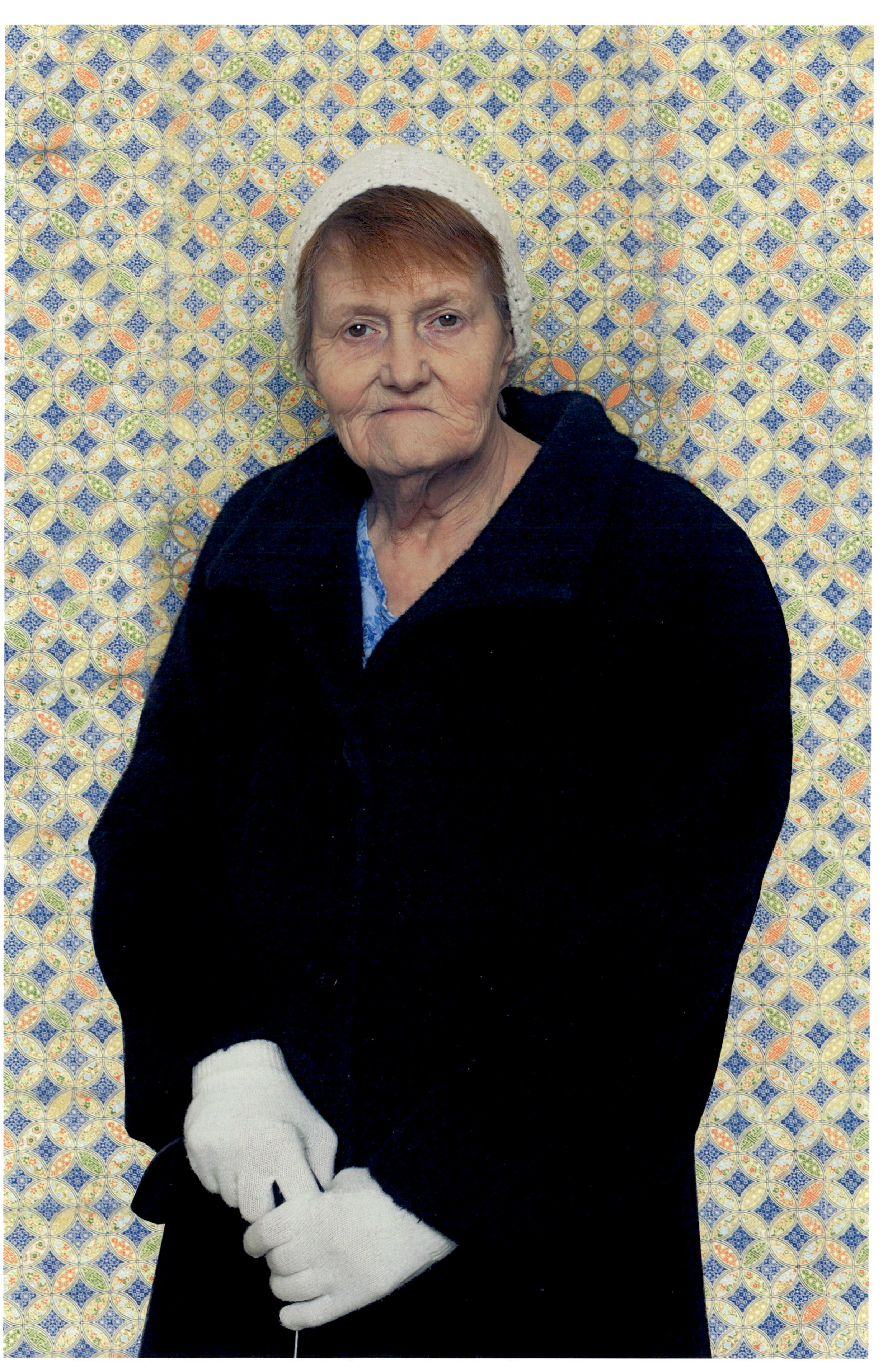

GAY | FACE

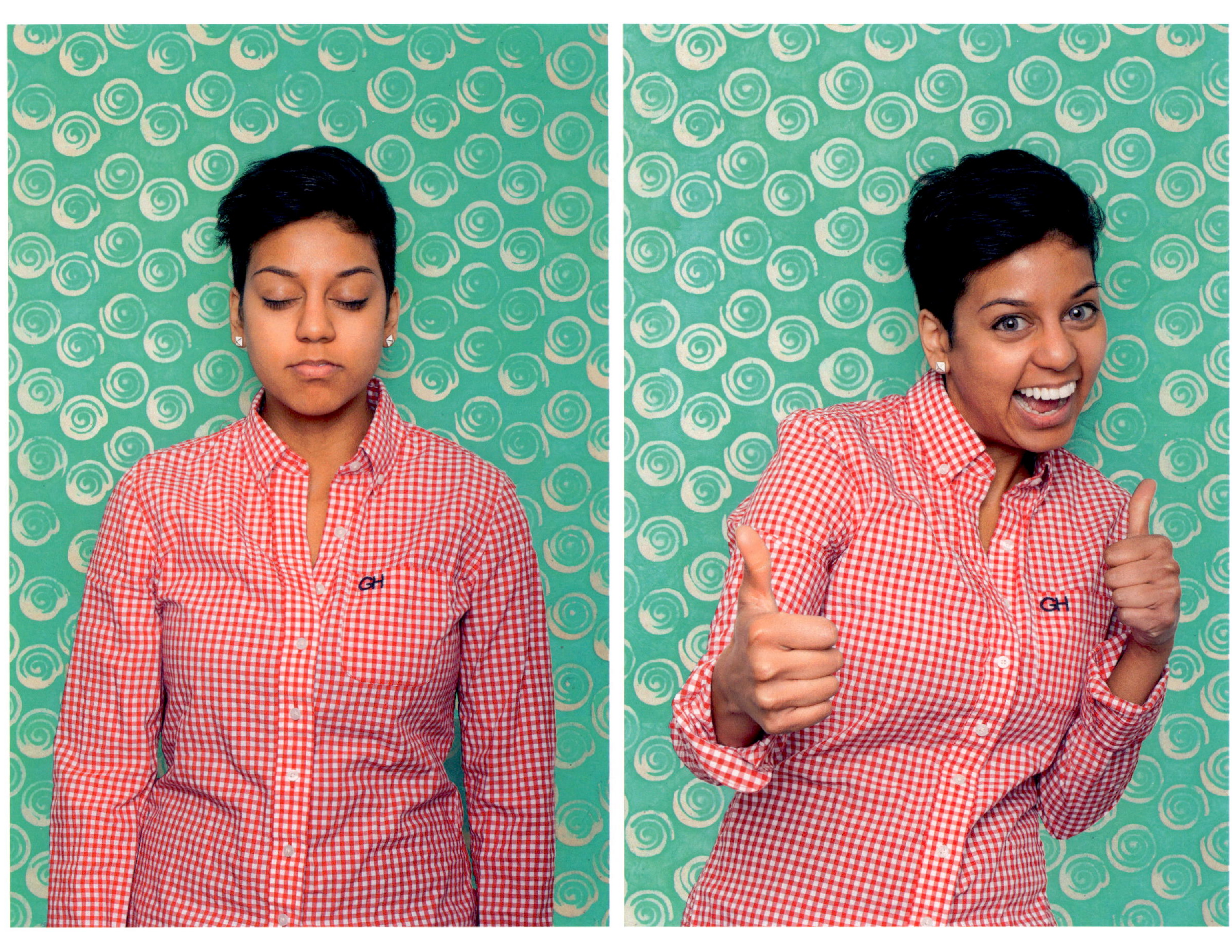

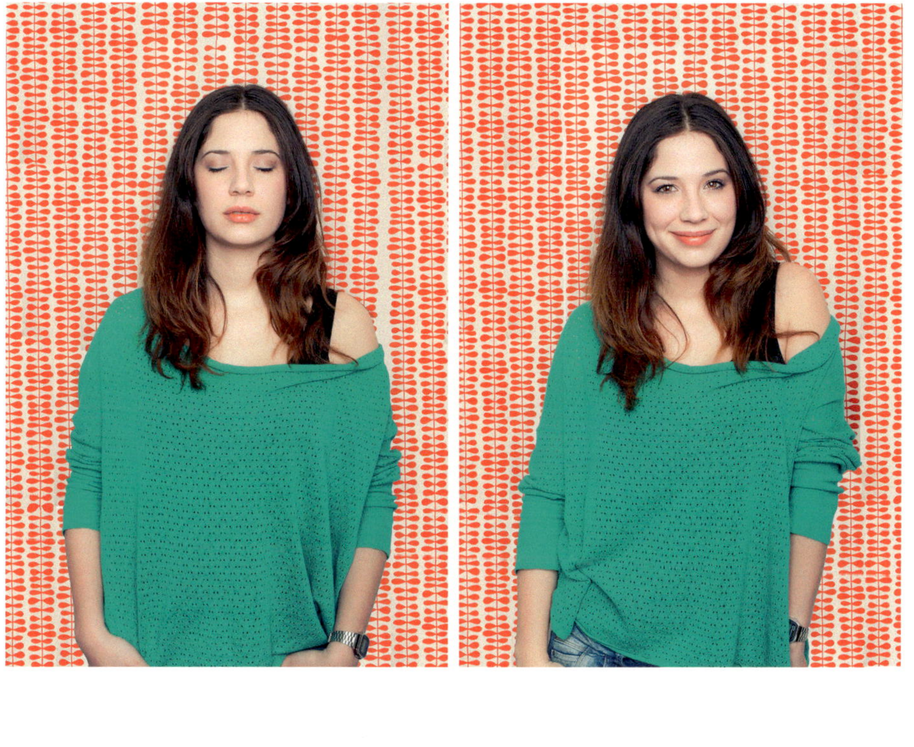

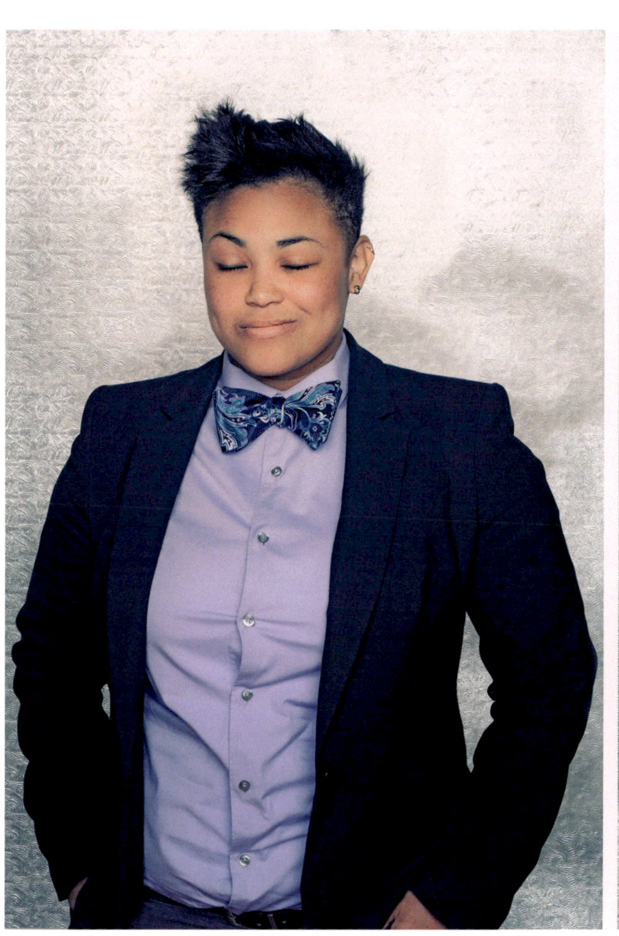
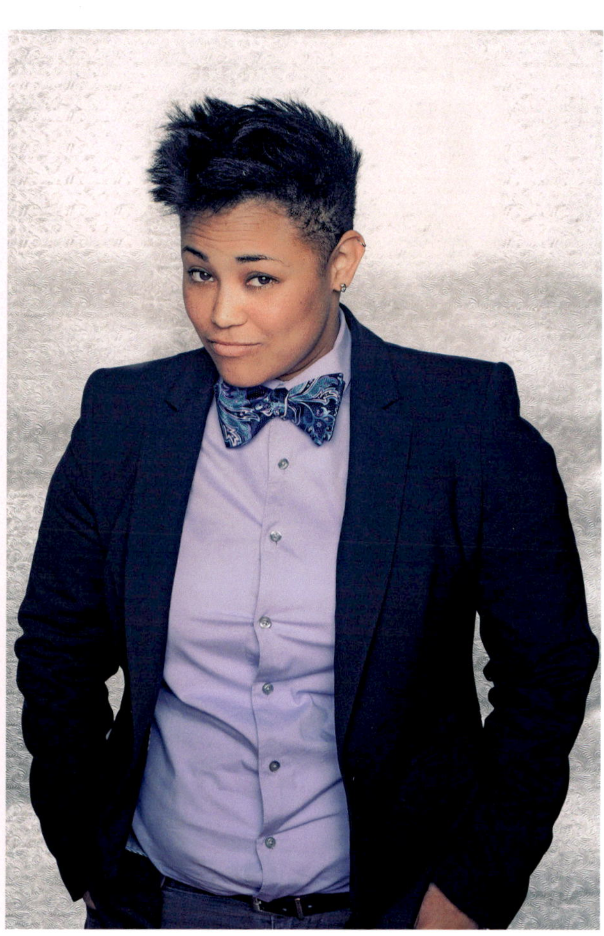

GAY | FACE

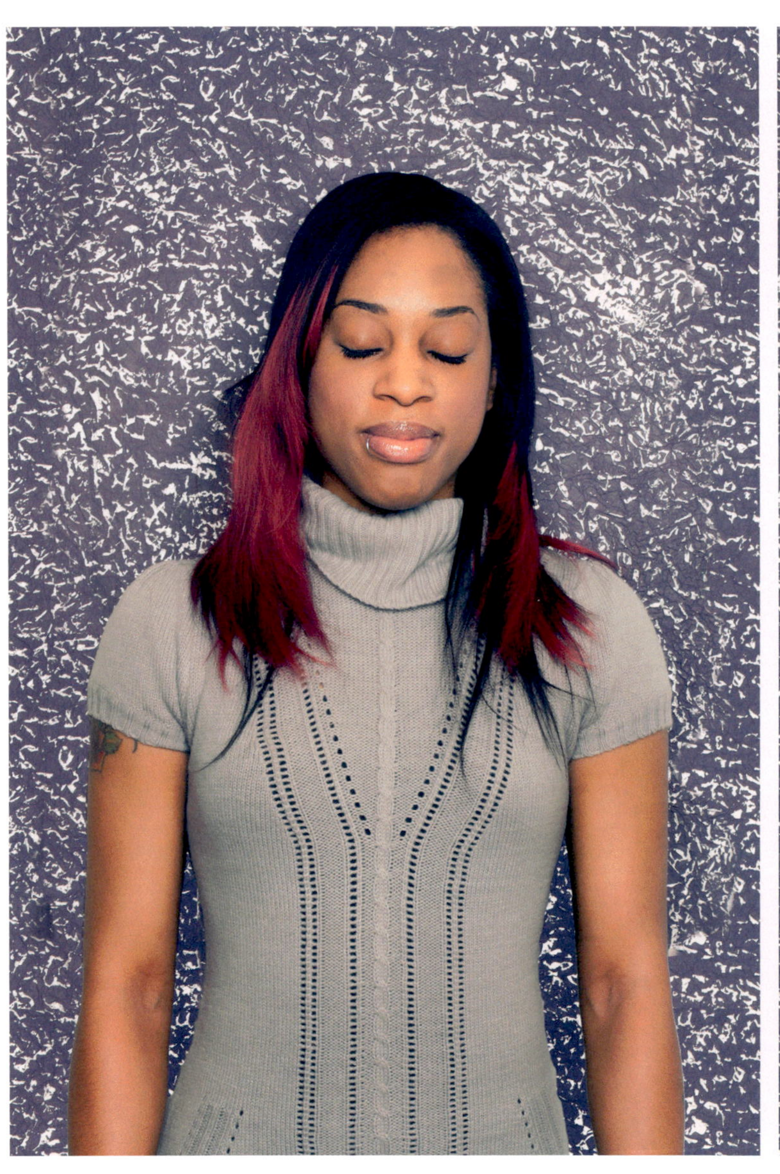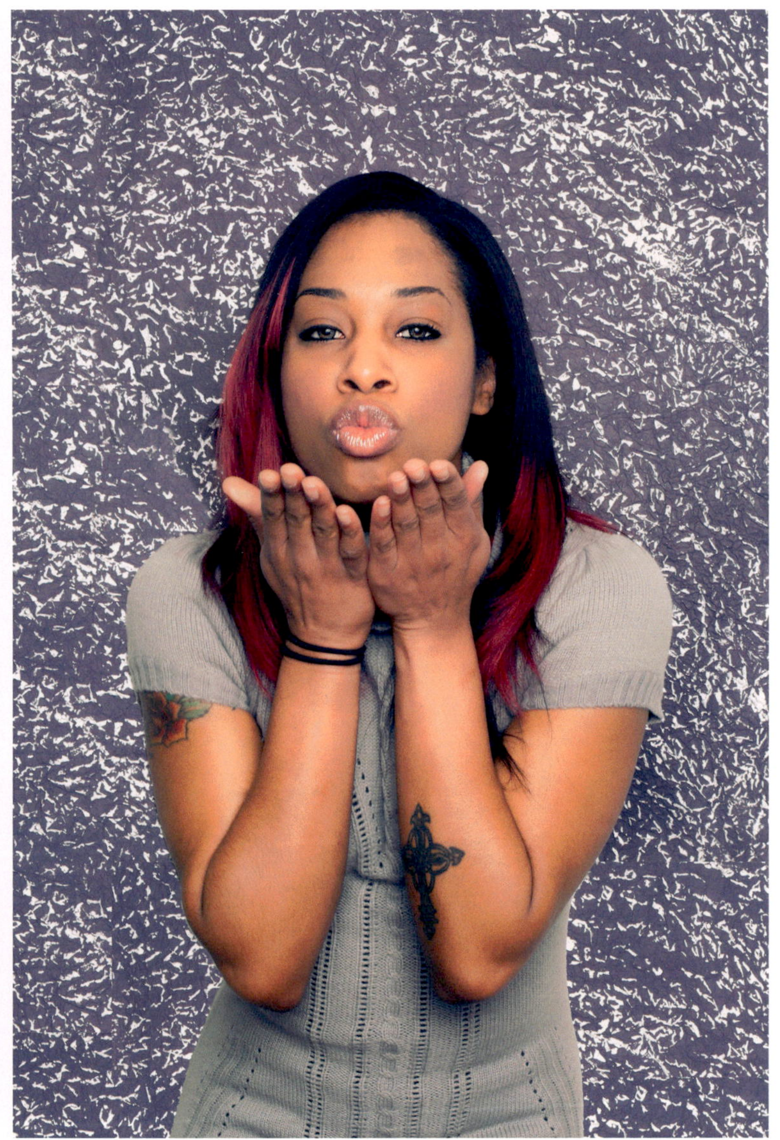

Kailey Y.

MONTEGO BAY, JAMAICA

How would you identify your sexuality?
Free love, man. I love people, and that's as real as it gets.

Describe your coming out. Are you coming out in some way by participating in this project?
I had the amazing opportunity to attend a small, quirky performing arts high school with a very accepting student body. As artists, we were all a little weird, and I was coming out at the same time a friend in my freshman music theory class—it was a really cute moment. After that, it was like telling people my shoe size. I was still a little hesitant about who I blatantly came out to, but there were a lot of girls of the same orientation, which made it more comfortable.

If you could change one thing about mainstream society to improve the lives of LGBTQ+ people, what would it be?
A priority could be eradicating stereotypes and archetypes, or simply the notion of any sort of "type" when it comes to gender and sexuality. Preconceived ideas function only as limitations.

Why should people support same-sex marriage?
Well, it's been said that if gays want to be as miserable as heterosexuals in marriage then why not let them! The main reason is very simple, yet we still have to fight for it despite all of our advancements as a society: equality. Everyone should have the same rights, period. It would be a considerable step forward in fighting the prevailing ignorance here in this country and elsewhere, which ultimately holds us back as human beings. Imagine how beautiful the world would be if we all opened our eyes.

Why did you want to be a part of this project?
I wanted to show my support and let my voice be heard, especially in light of all that's going on right now. I think that for every LGBTQ+ story there is out there, if one more person is empowered to be who they are and to become who they want to be, we all move forward.

Has this project helped you or changed your life in anyway?
I've met some of the most amicable, insightful, and inspiring people, and I've witnessed an amazing amount of support. I've learned that there is no longer a stigma associated with being part of the LGBTQ+ community: we are no longer ashamed and secretive, but proud and transparent. We are at a point in which our adversaries are the ones who now need to justify their misguided convictions.

GAY | FACE

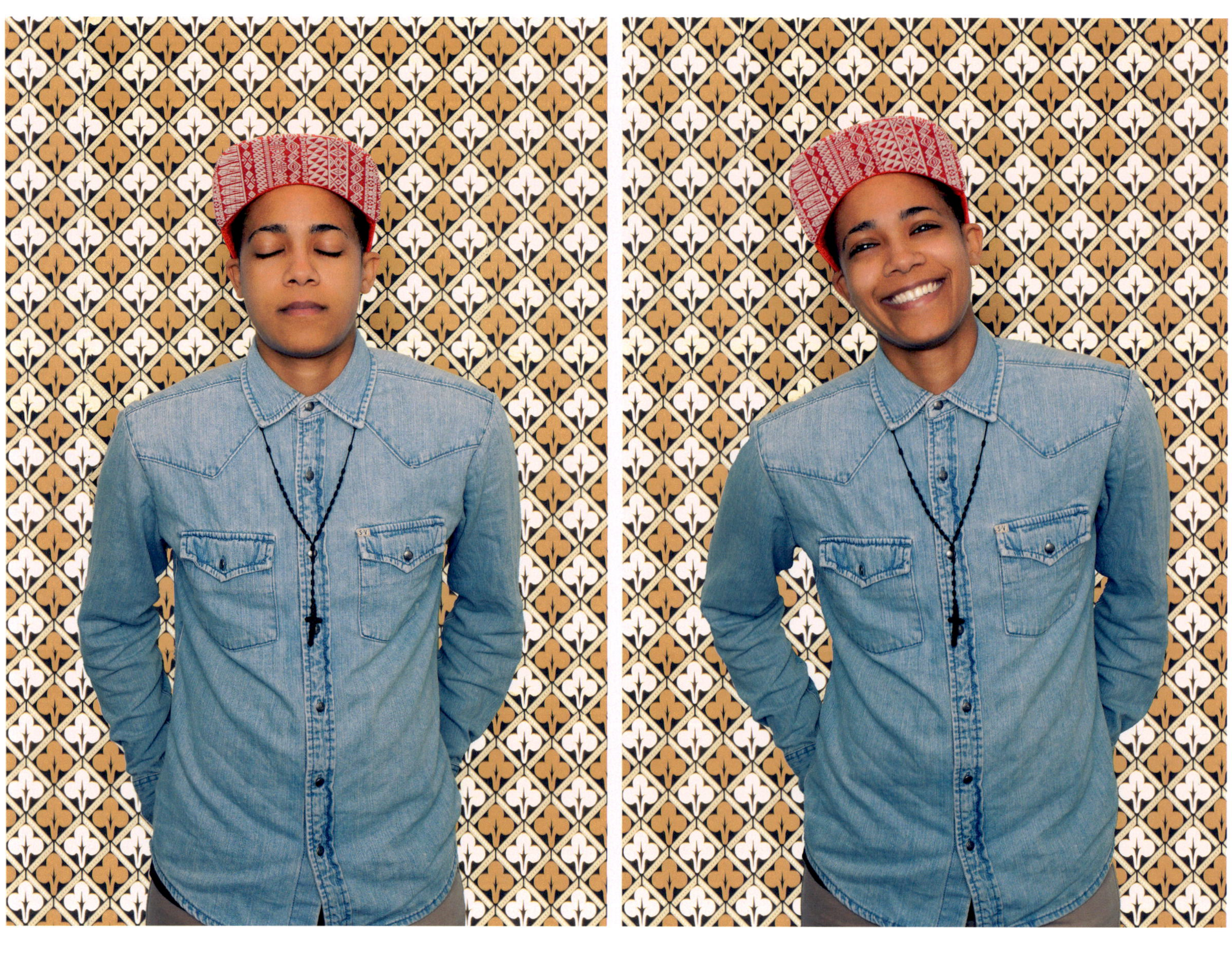

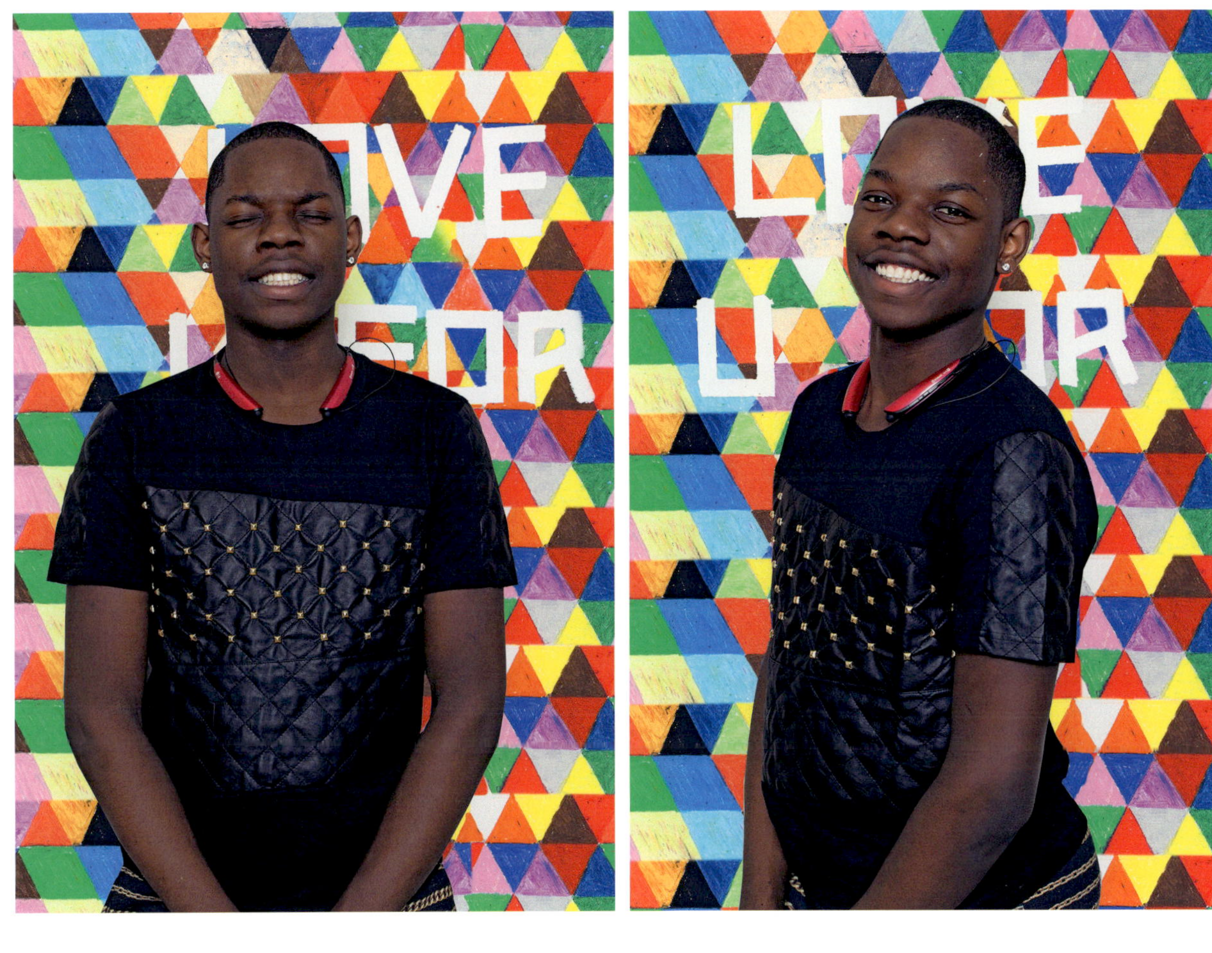

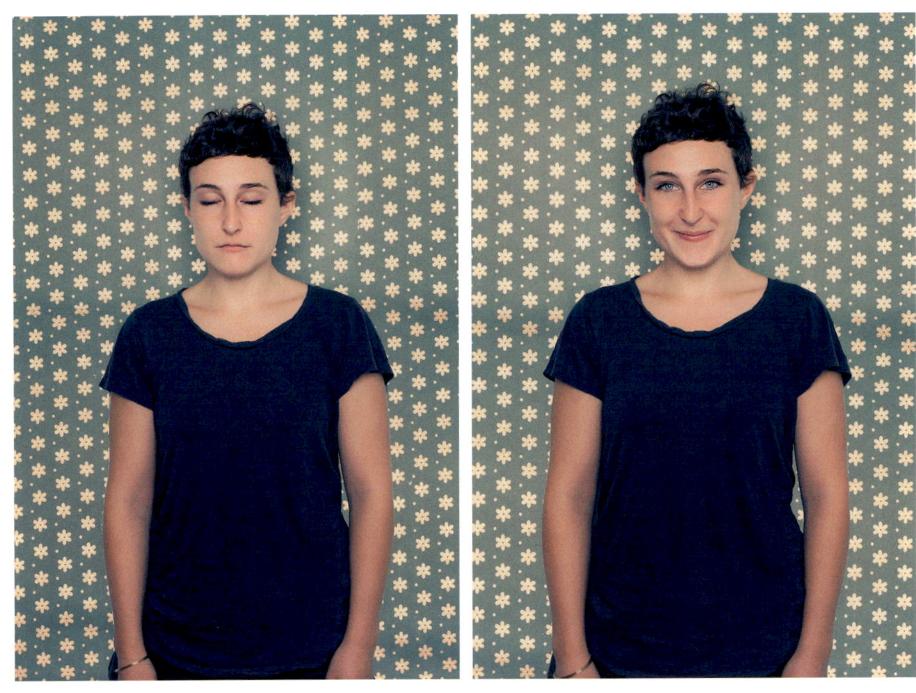

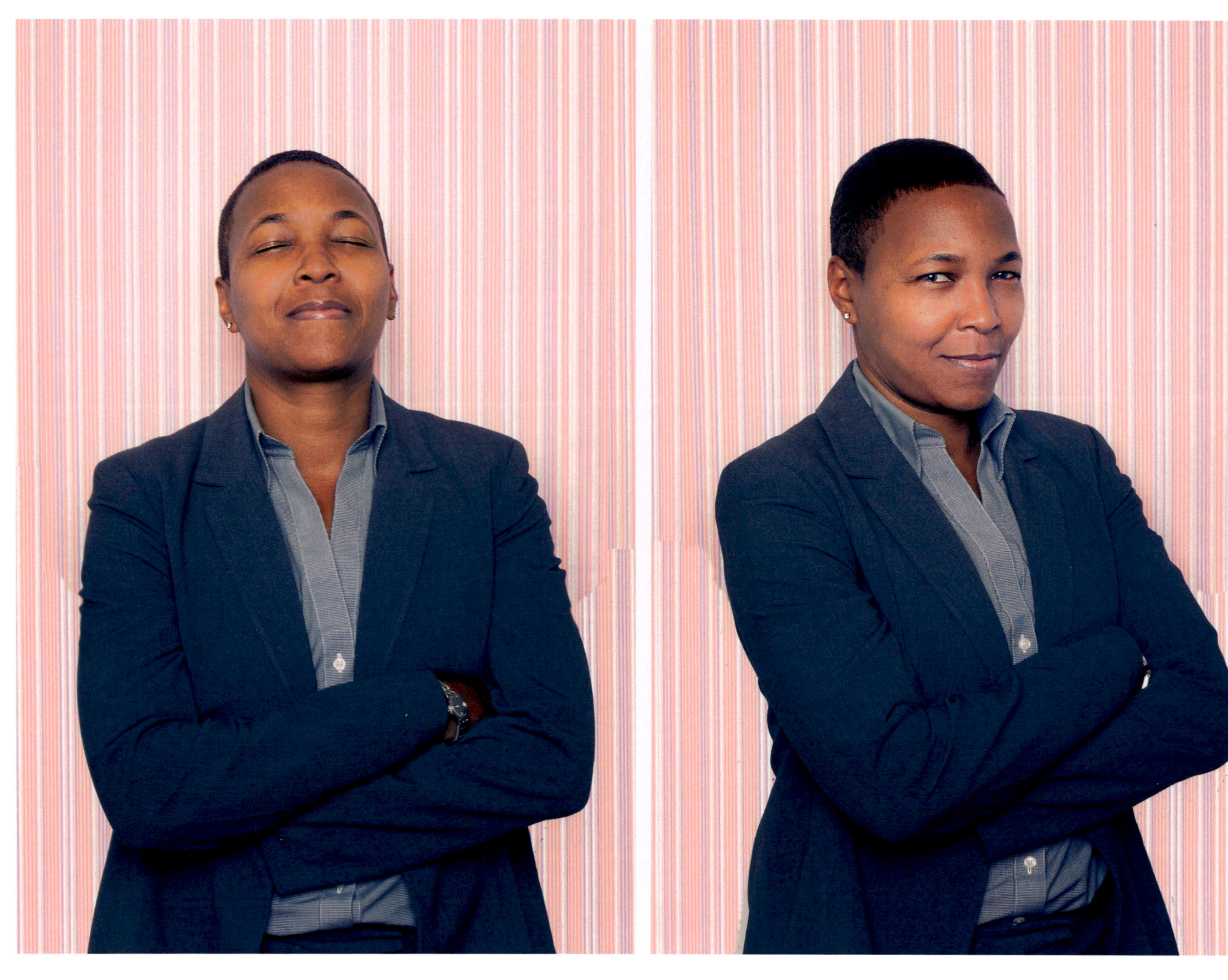

GAY | FACE

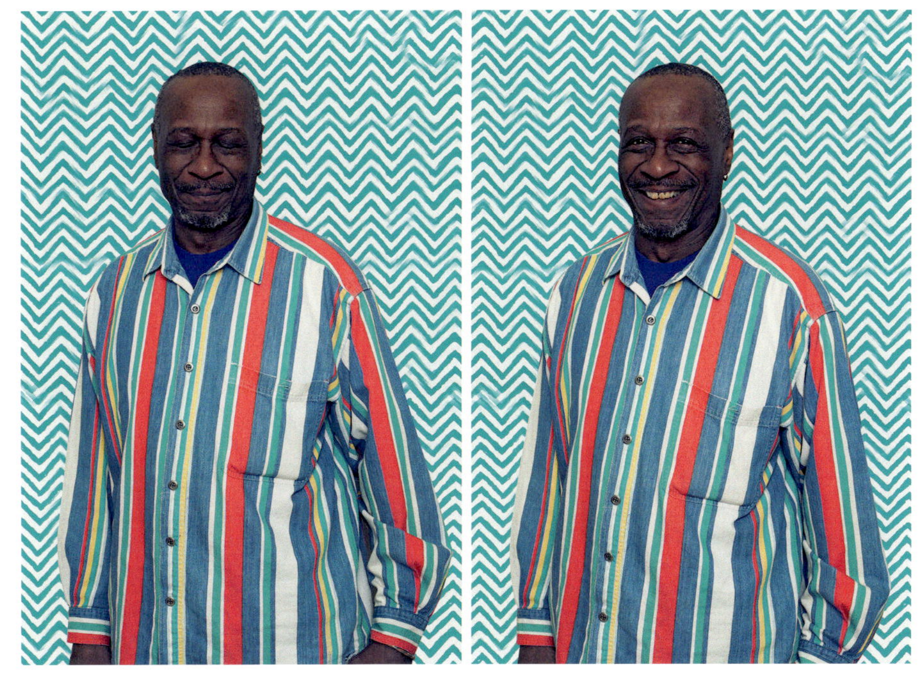

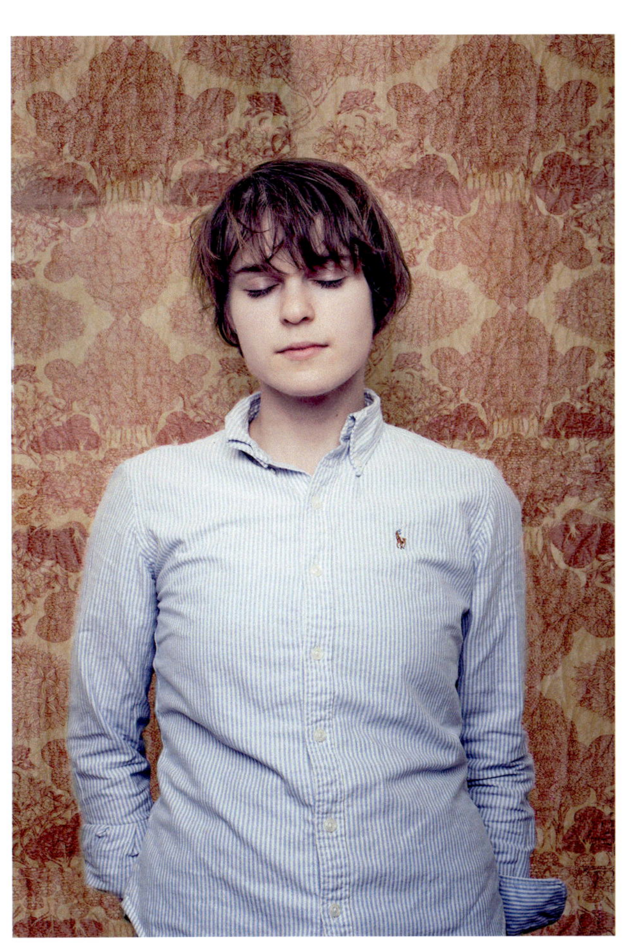

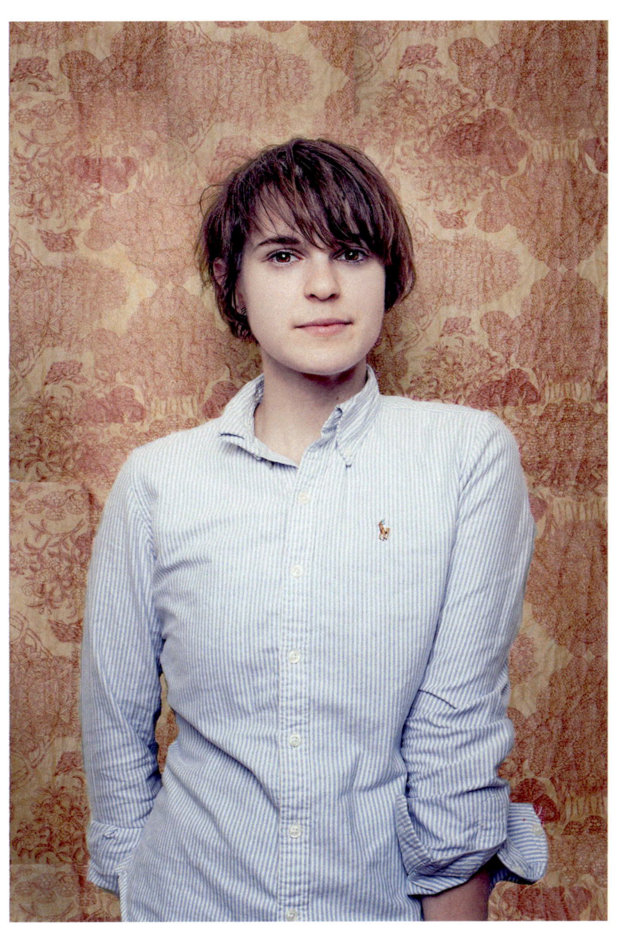

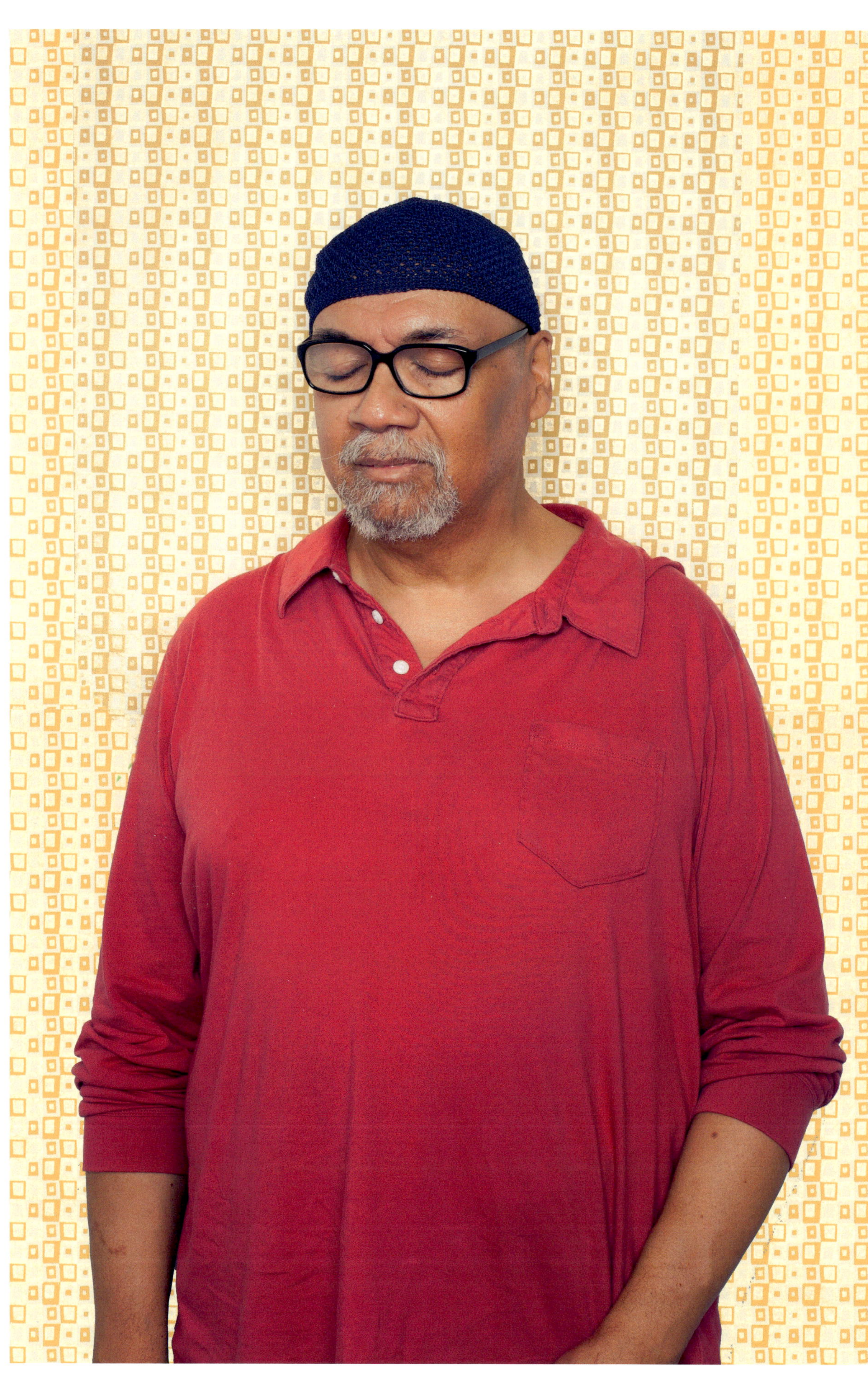

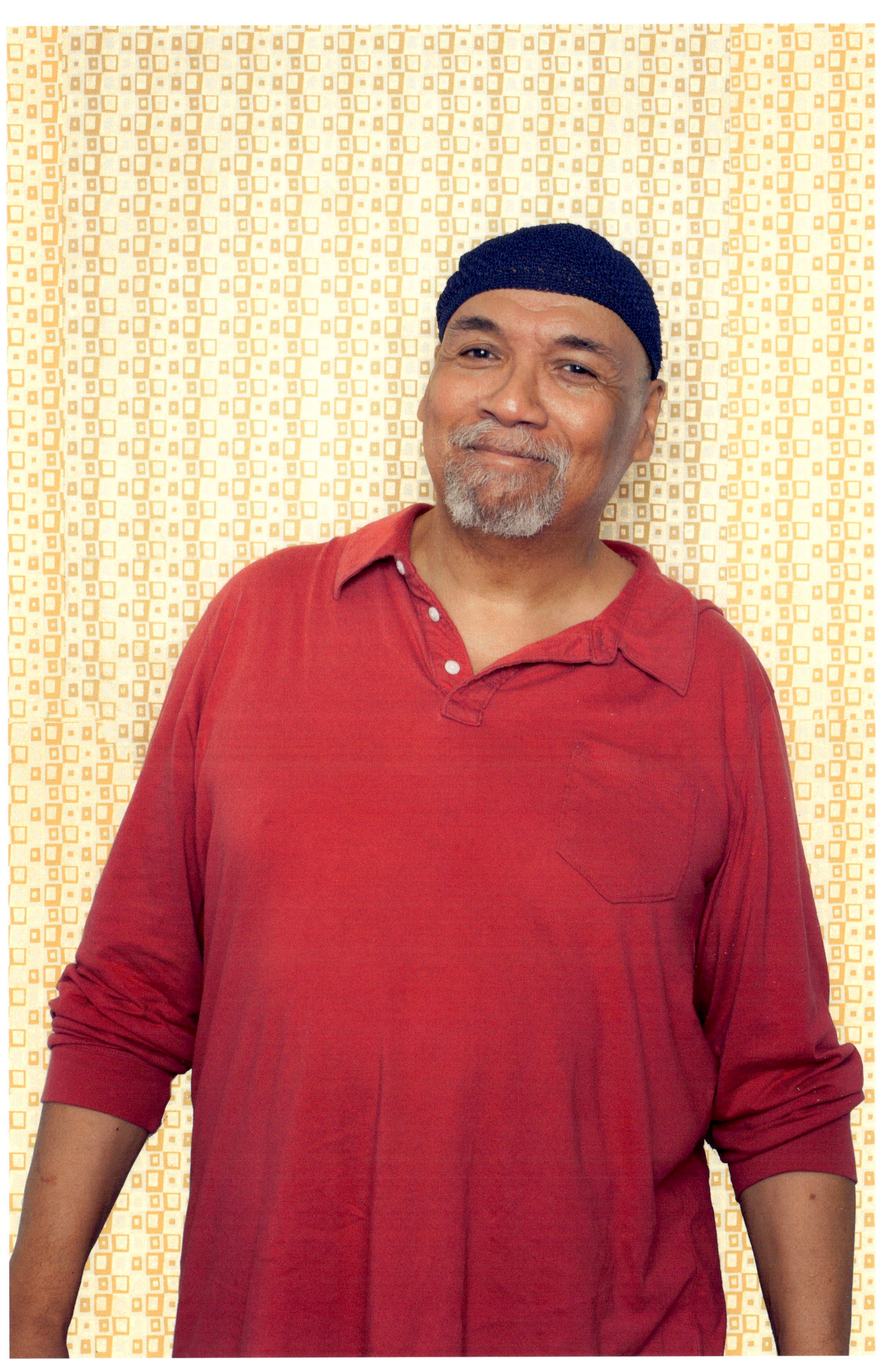

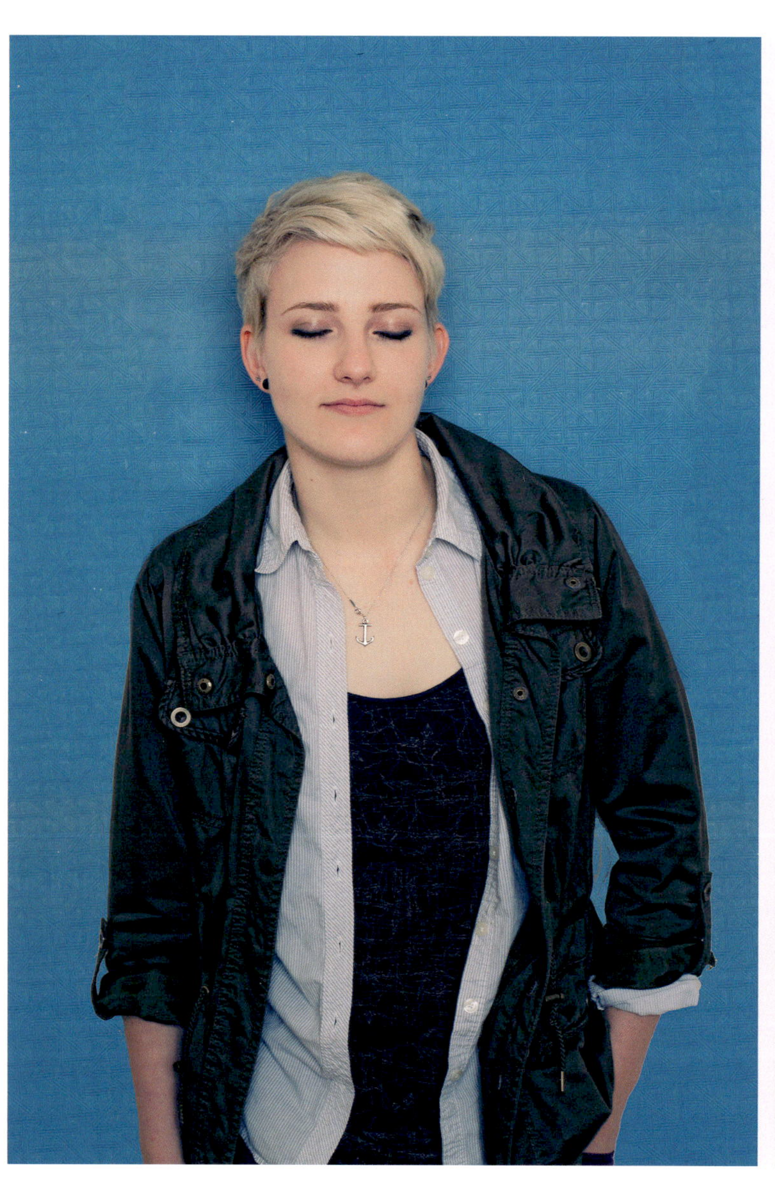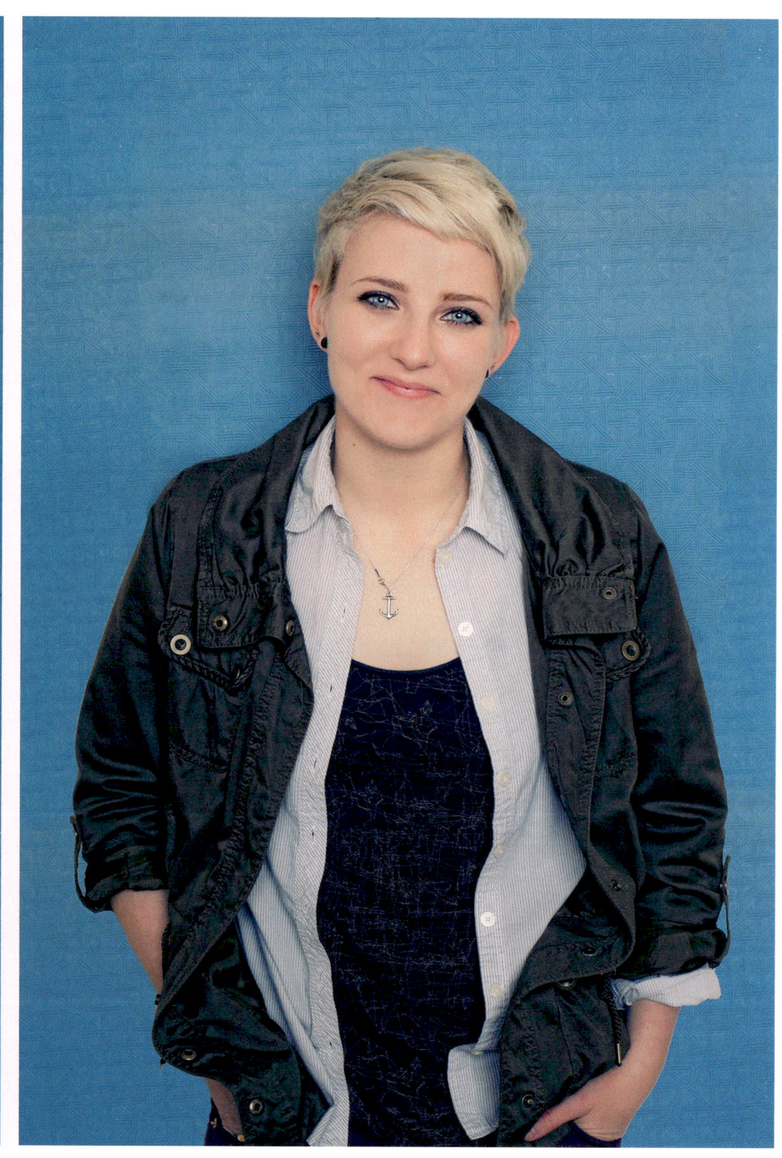

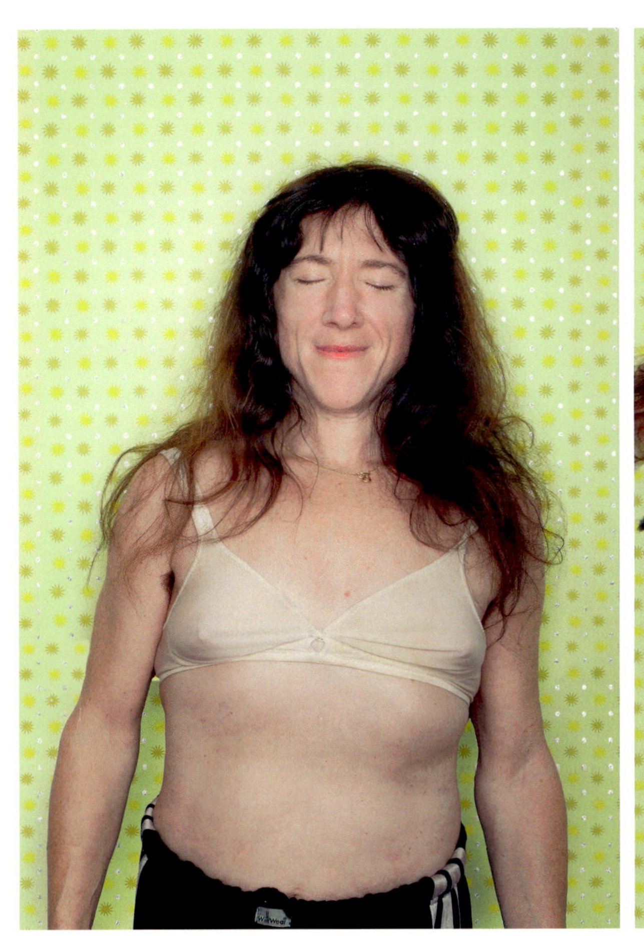
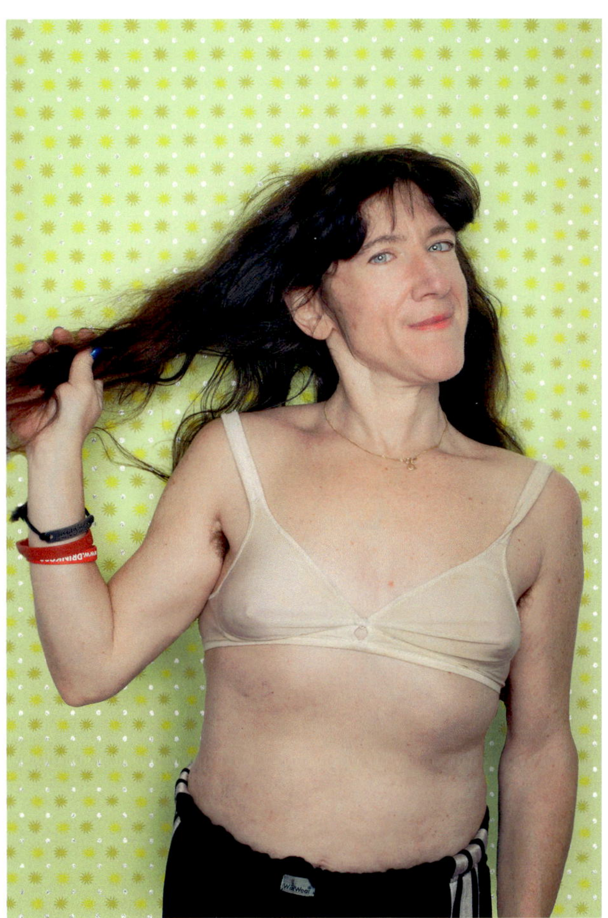

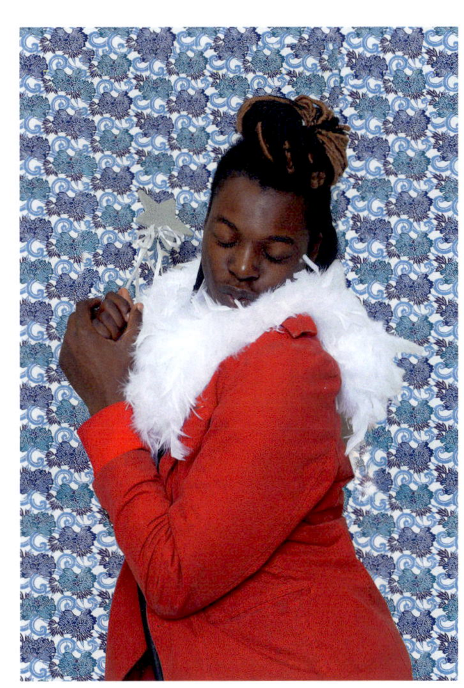
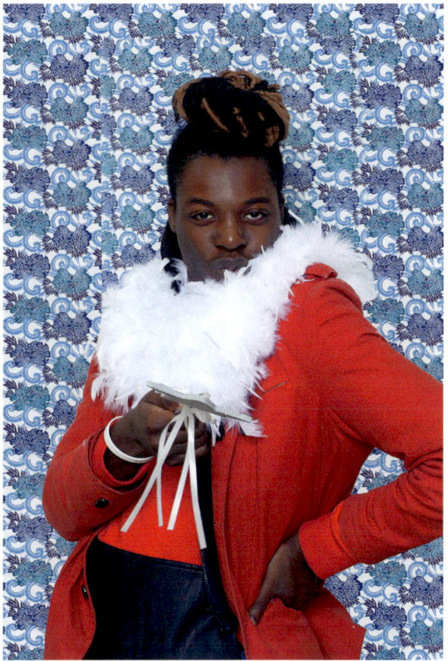

GAY | FACE

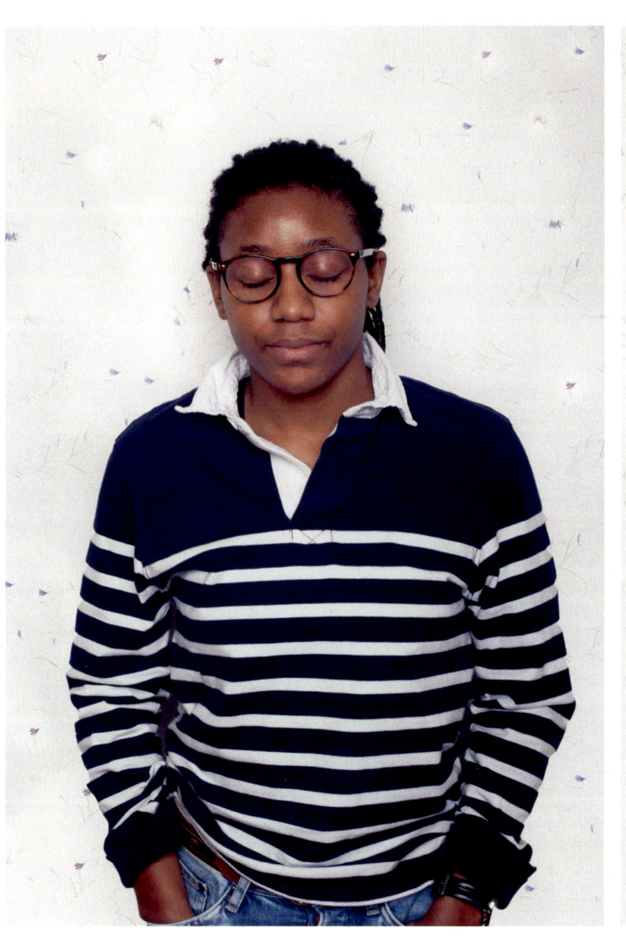 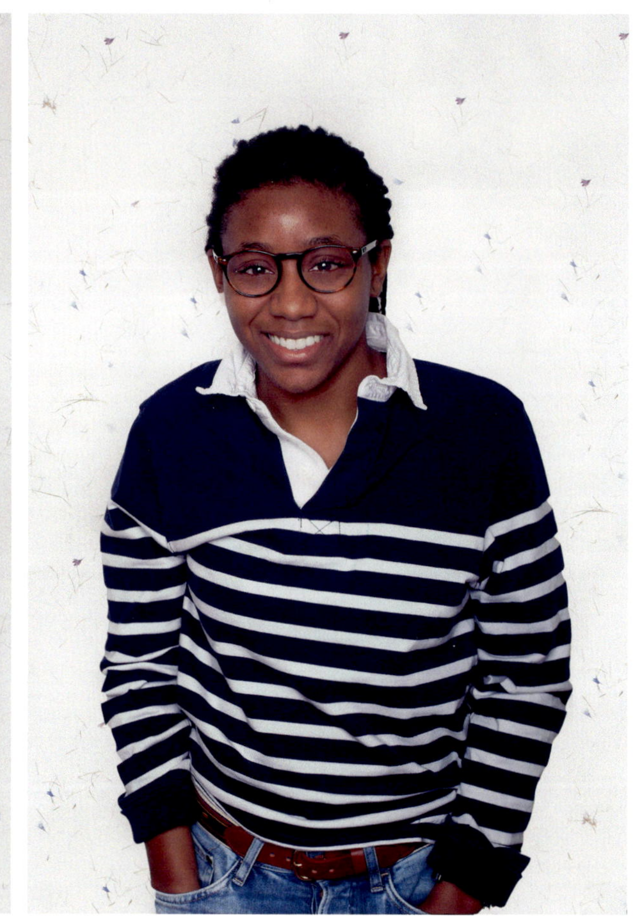

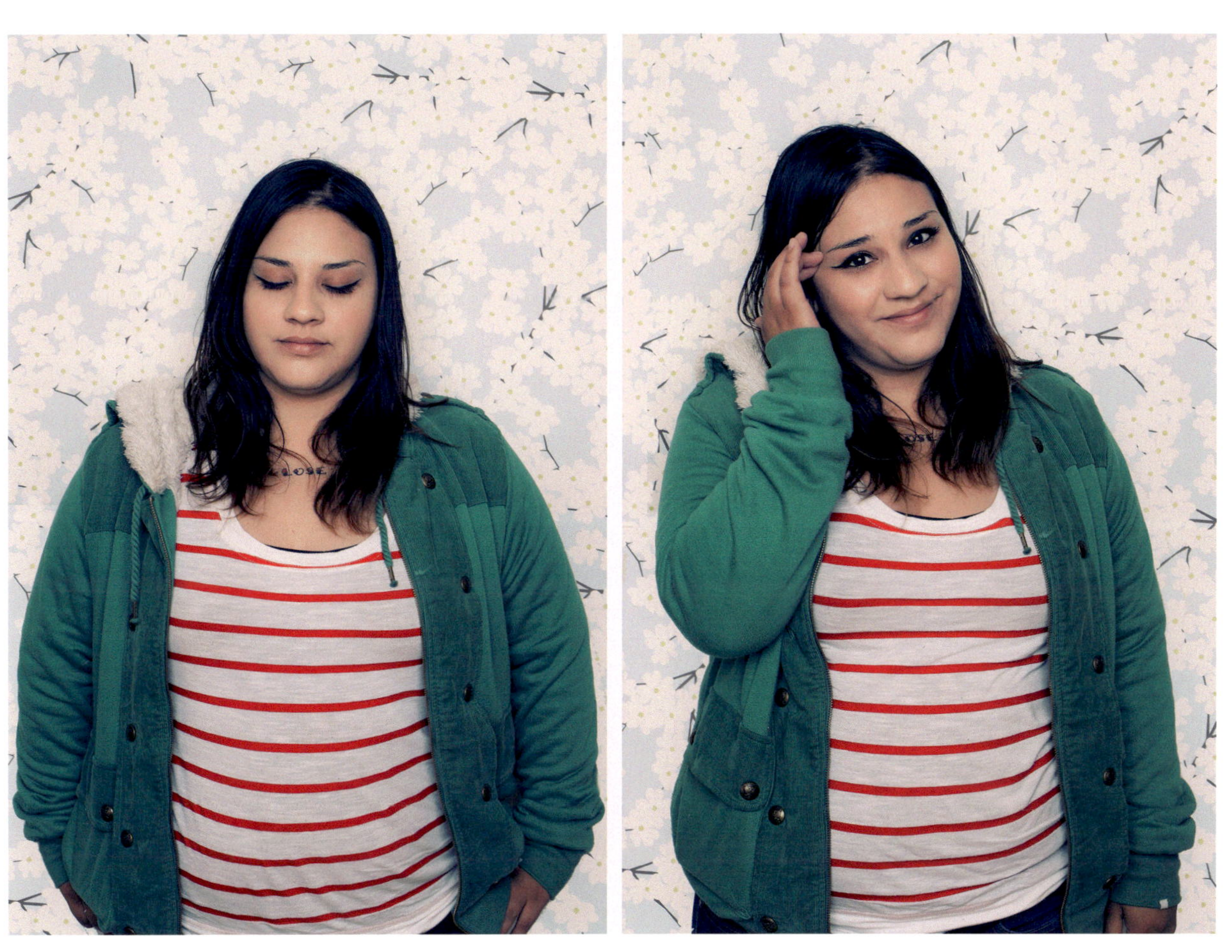

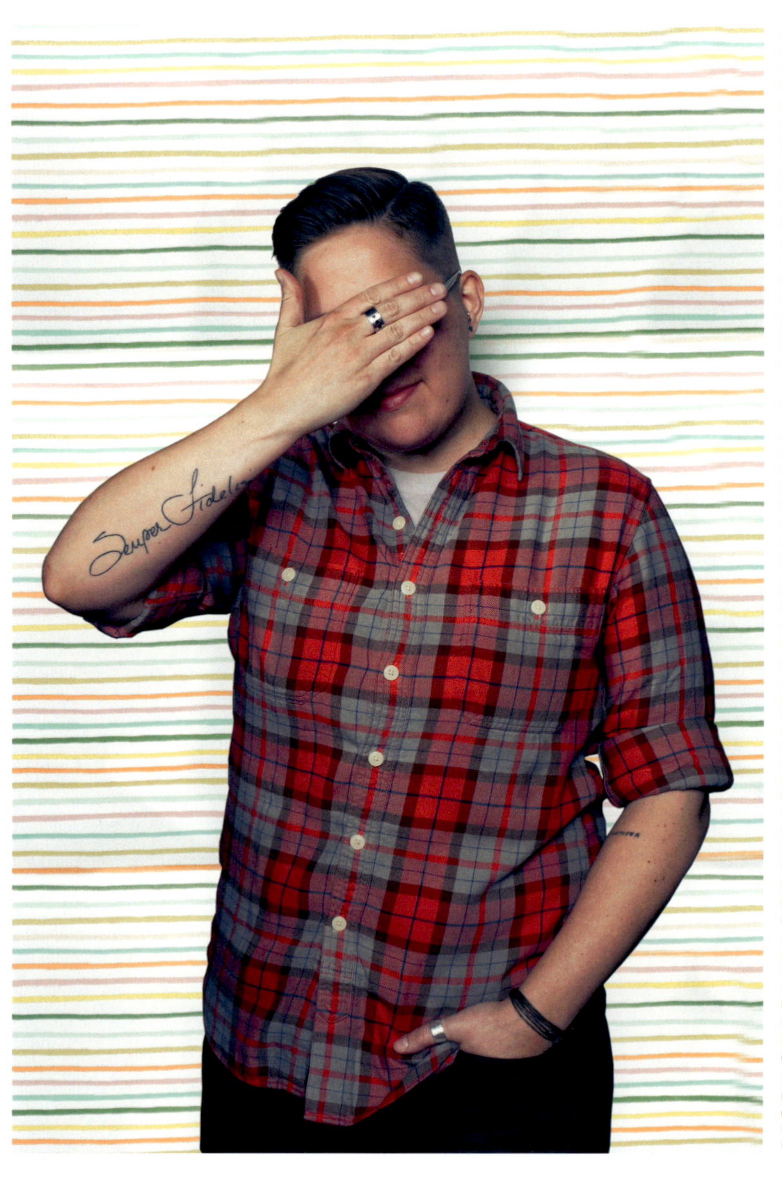 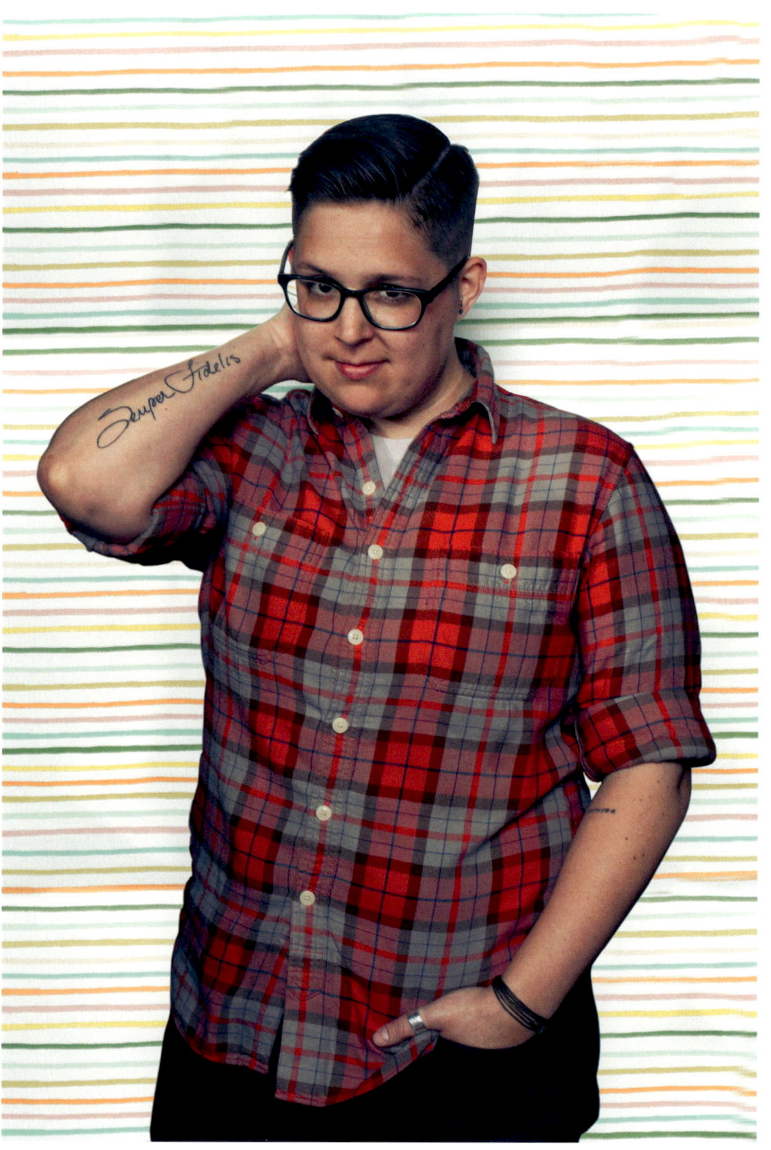

Emily H.
FARMINGTON, CONNECTICUT

How would you identify your sexuality?
Lesbi-queer.

Why did you choose to be a part of this project?
Documenting each queer time capsule moment in history is so important for our community. We are always evolving, and we have as much to learn from our past as we do from our future. It's exciting to think of future generations considering how we lived in this era and to consider how they might live.

What do you think of your portrait?
I love it! And I love that everyone was able to choose their own background, which lends an extra layer of individualism.

Describe your coming out. Are you coming out in some way by participating in this project?
When I was sixteen I cut all my hair off, started dressing how I wanted to, and came out to a few friends. But I struggled with my identity—how to talk about it, or not talk about it. There was homophobia in my school, church, and the community at large, and I was afraid to tell my family right away. I am lucky, though; they were supportive when I did. At that time summer camp was a refuge, a place where I could openly be myself. And then I went to a women's college, which was a place to thrive and build confidence. I finally moved to New York City, which is a queer utopia.

Have you ever experienced discrimination based on your gender or sexual orientation?
I think all women and queer people have experienced discrimination, some more than others. The most threatening situations have been related to transportation: subways, cabs, buses or gender-segregated bathrooms. I'm grateful for the movement to make bathrooms gender neutral in New York City. Sometimes it's more funny than threatening: more than once I've walked out of a women's room and caused a probably-straight cis man to waltz right in.

If you could change one thing about mainstream society to improve the lives of LGBTQ+ people, what would it be?
I would still like to see more representation of LGBTQ+ people in government, film, TV, music, business, and all positions of power, leadership, and the media. I think when you take away the "bogeyman" fear of queer people by seeing us, knowing us, and spending time with us, you destroy the underlying energy of othering that gives homophobia and transphobia their power.

What advice have you been given by another LGBTQ+ person, or that you might offer someone?
Always take the high road, you'll thank yourself for it. In your darkest moments, if you can take comfort in your own integrity, your honesty, your good will and good intentions, you'll always find comfort in those things.

Who are your LGBTQ+ role models?
I admire the activists who fought for us to have the rights we have now, and those who are still fighting. I admire the performers, artists, and creators of the night world that we have thrived in. Special recognition to Sarah Jenny, Tikka Masala, and Ellie Conant (RIP, my friend), who showed me how to create the pulsing, magical, glitter-covered organism that is a queer dance floor. There is nothing like it.

GAY | FACE

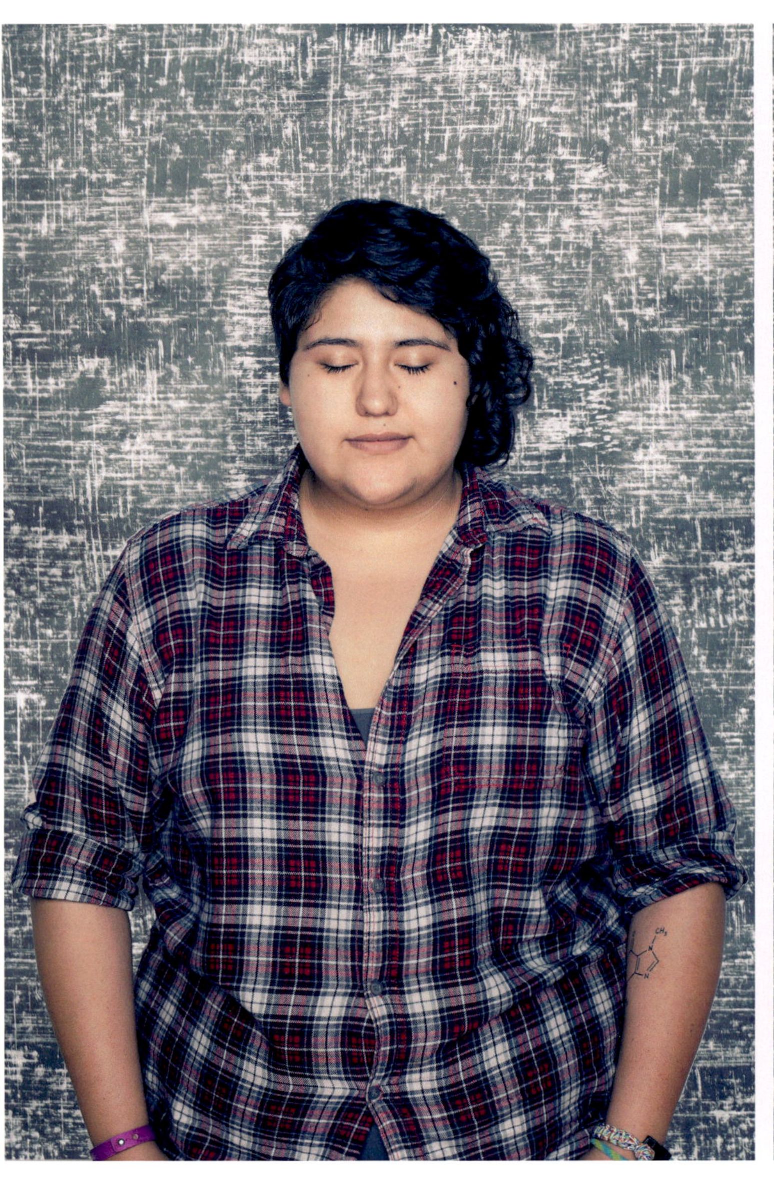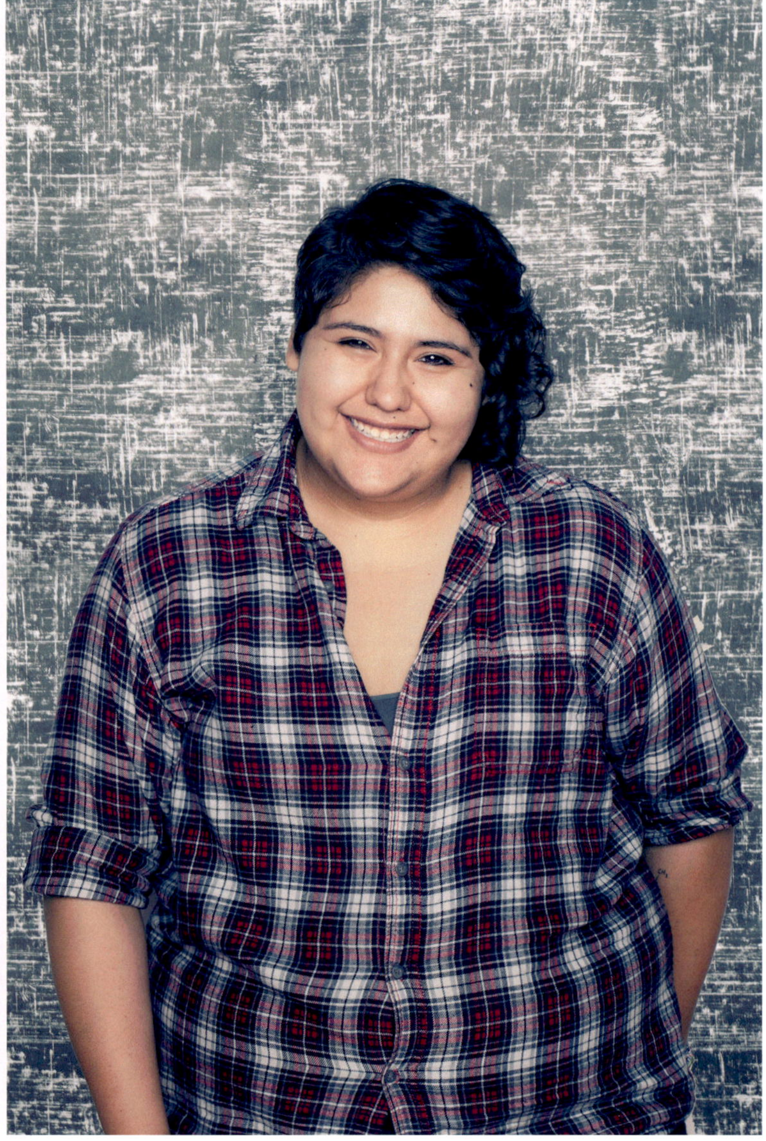

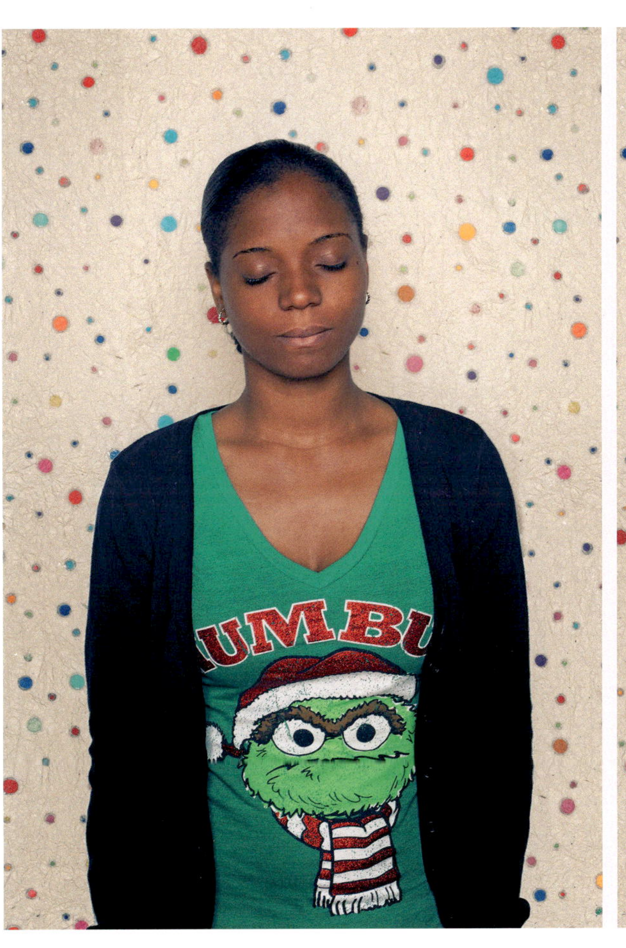
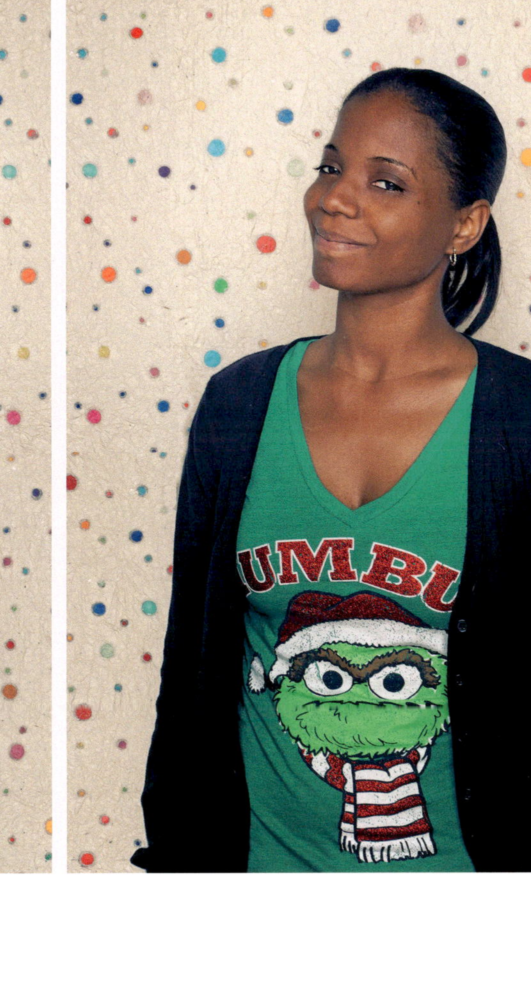
UMBU
UMBU

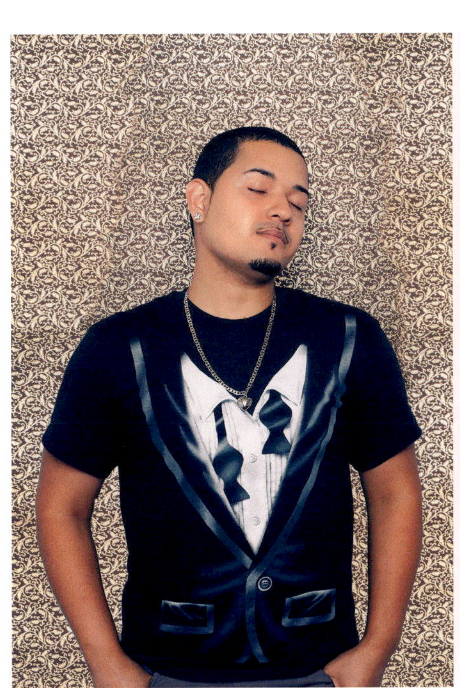
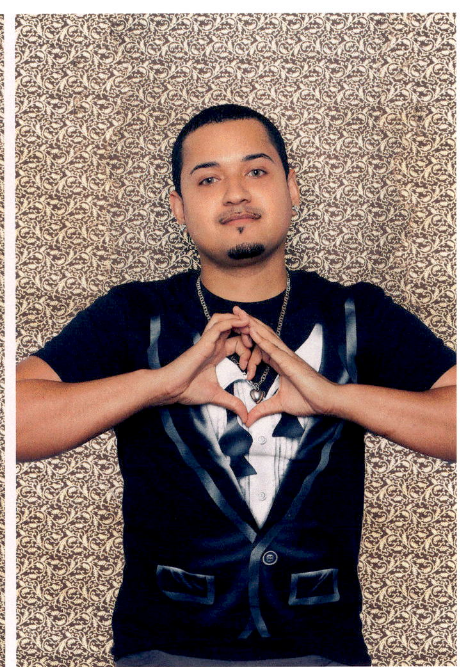

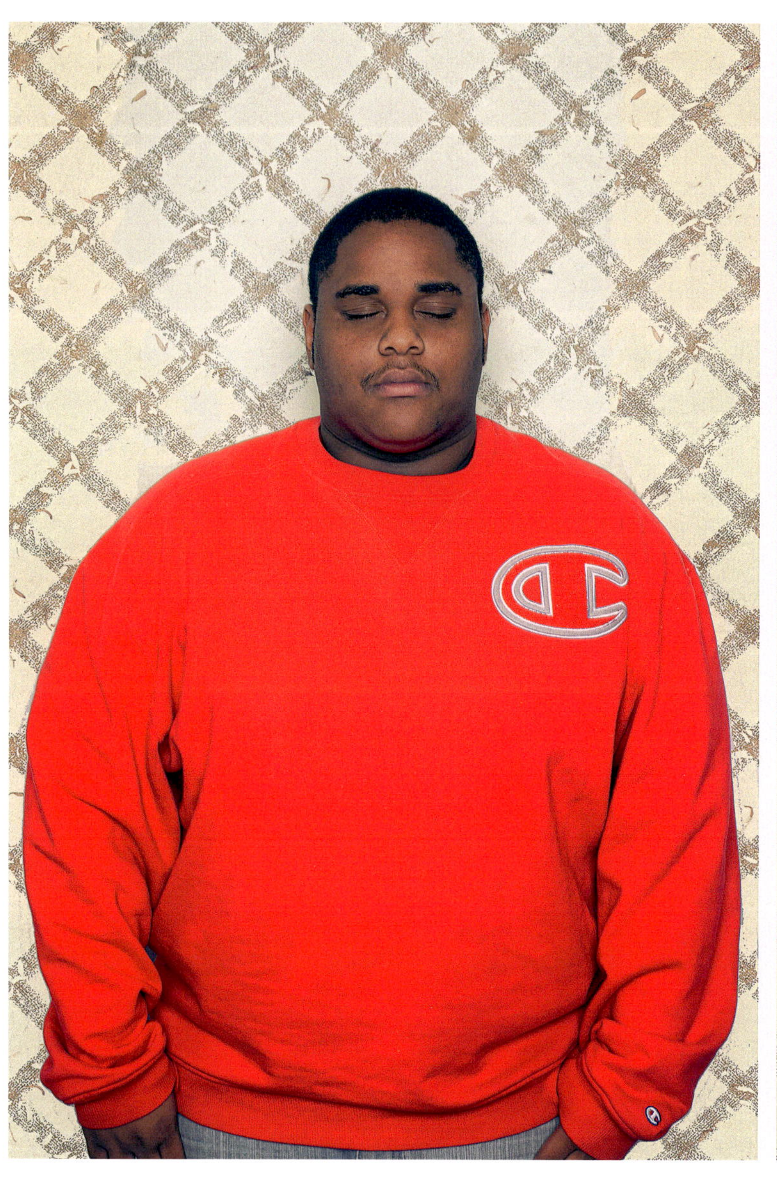
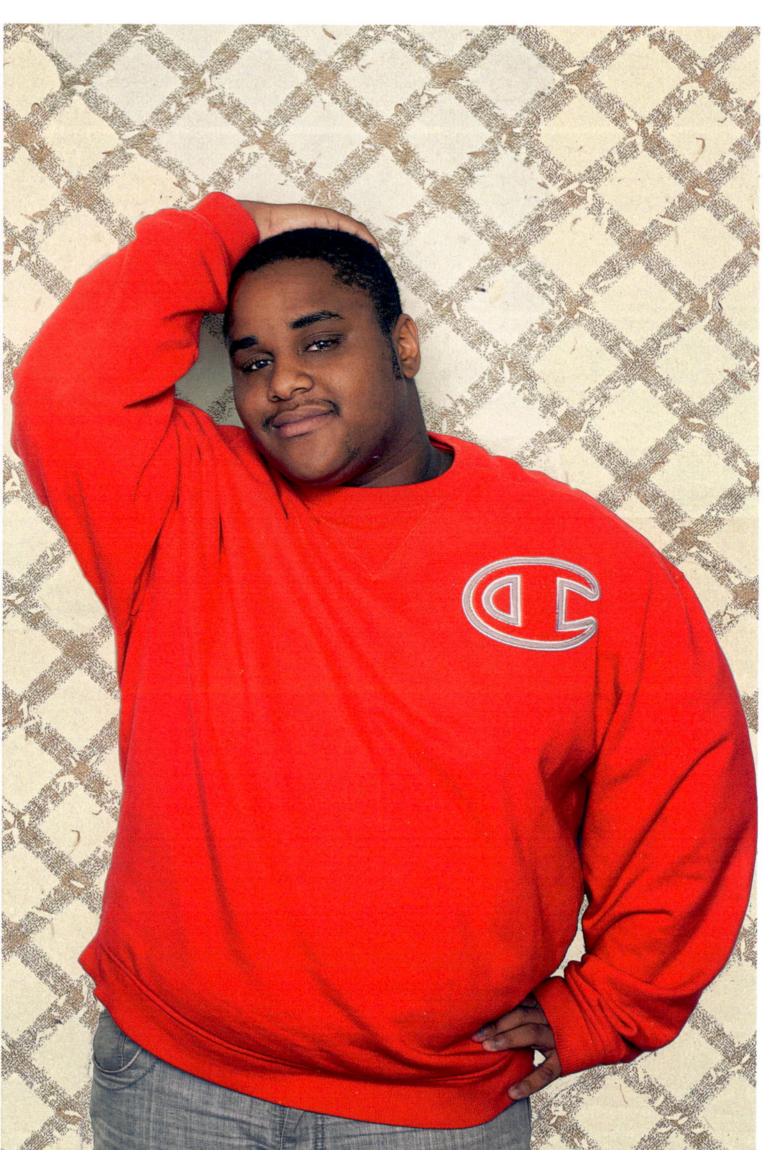

GAY | FACE

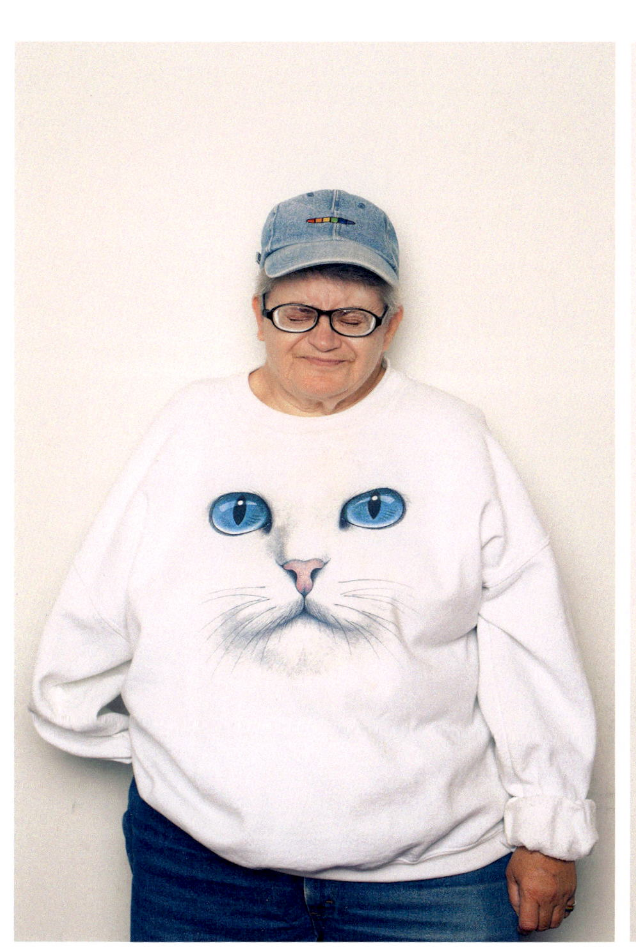
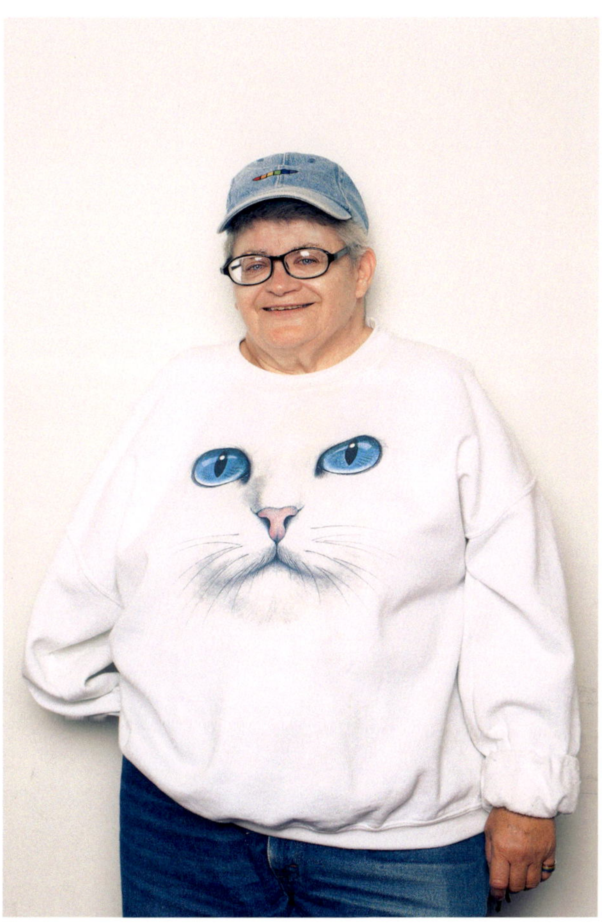
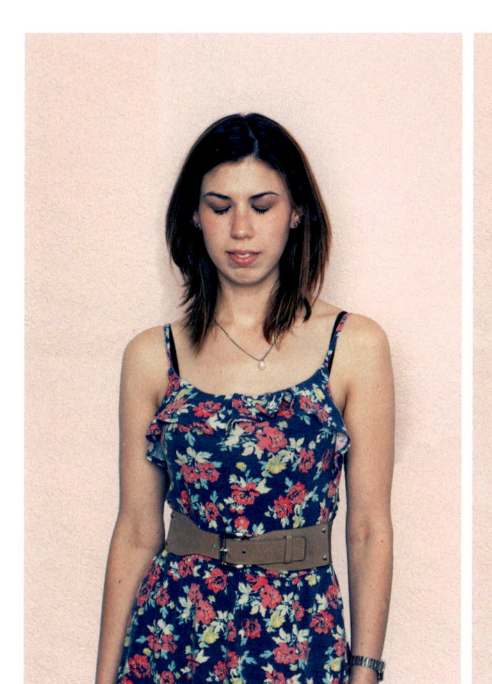
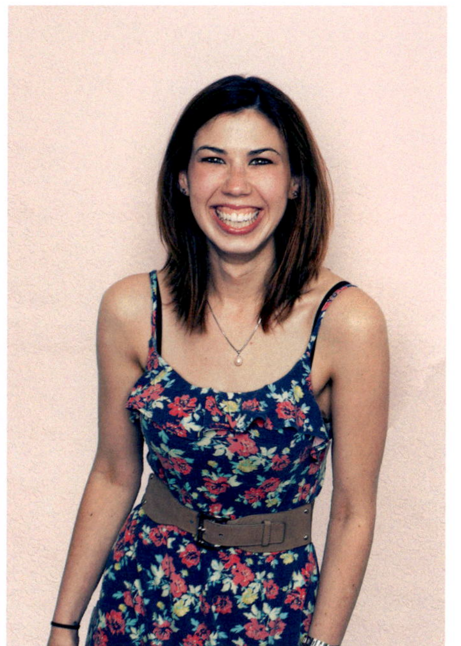

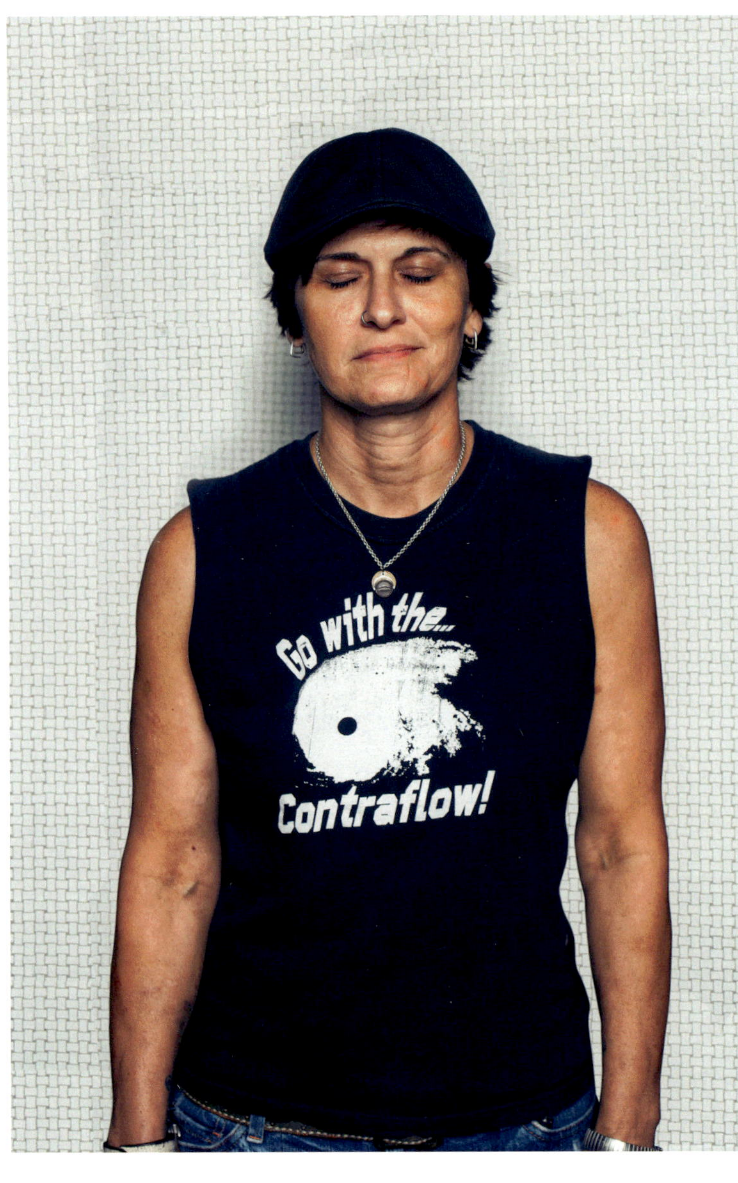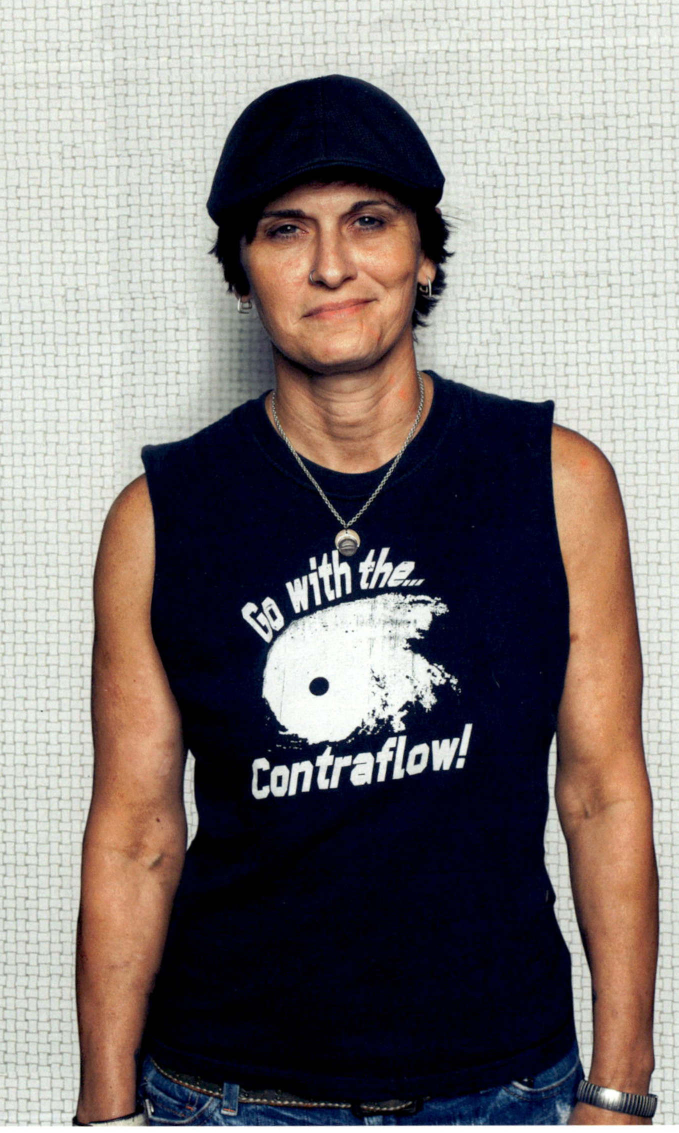
Go with the...
Contraflow!

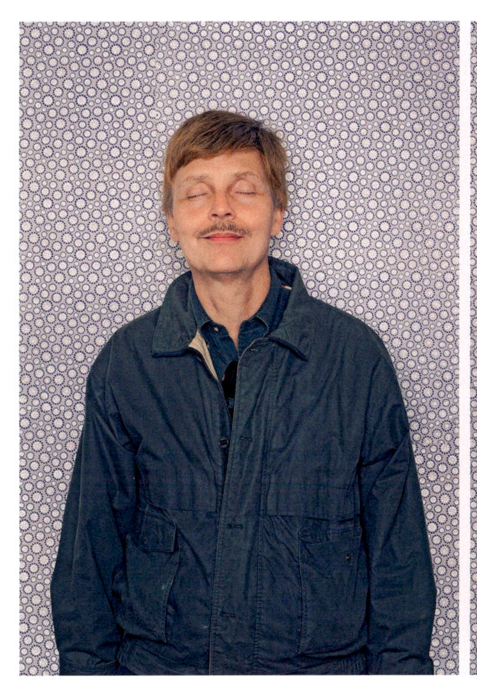
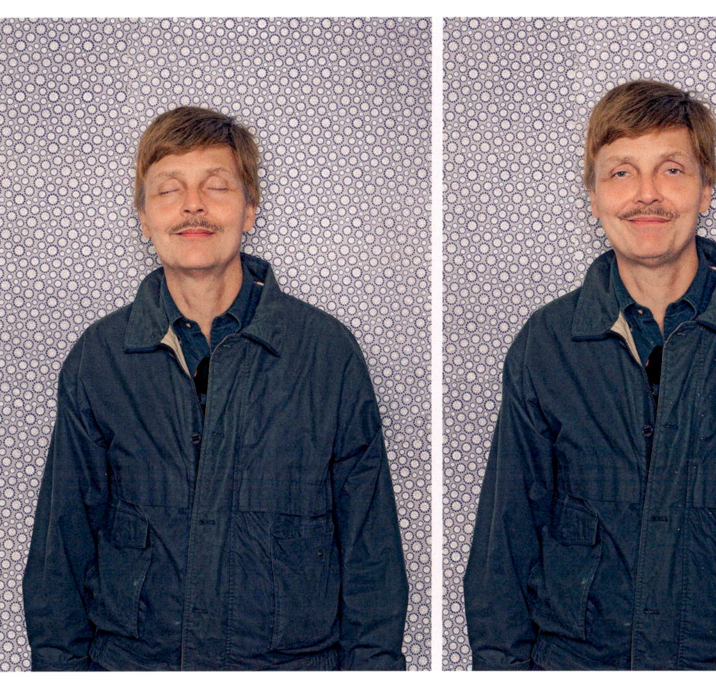

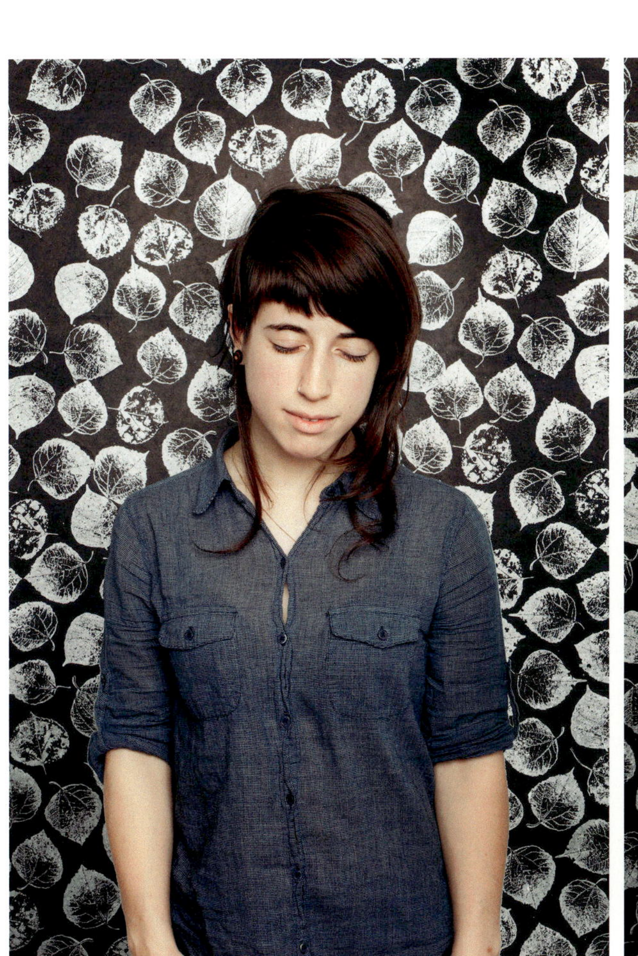
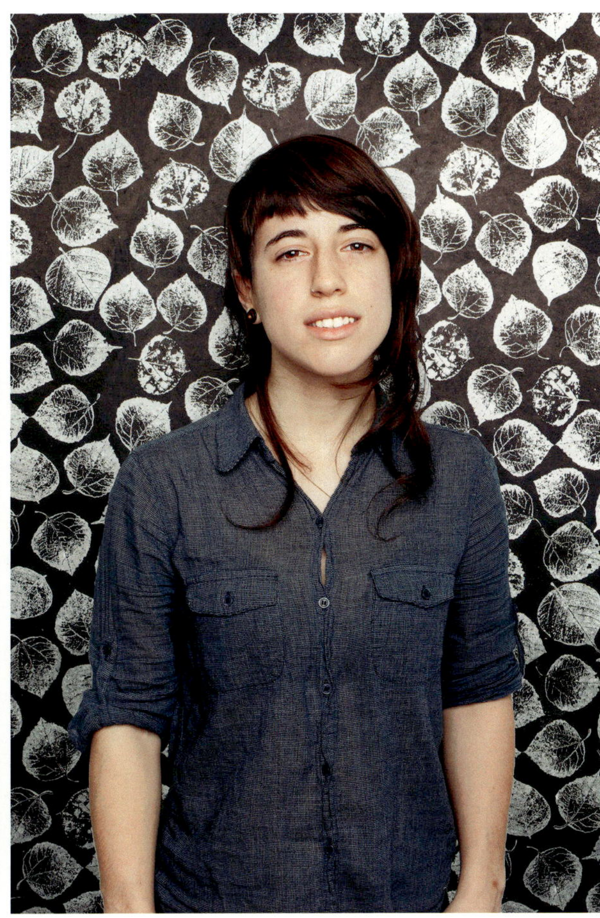

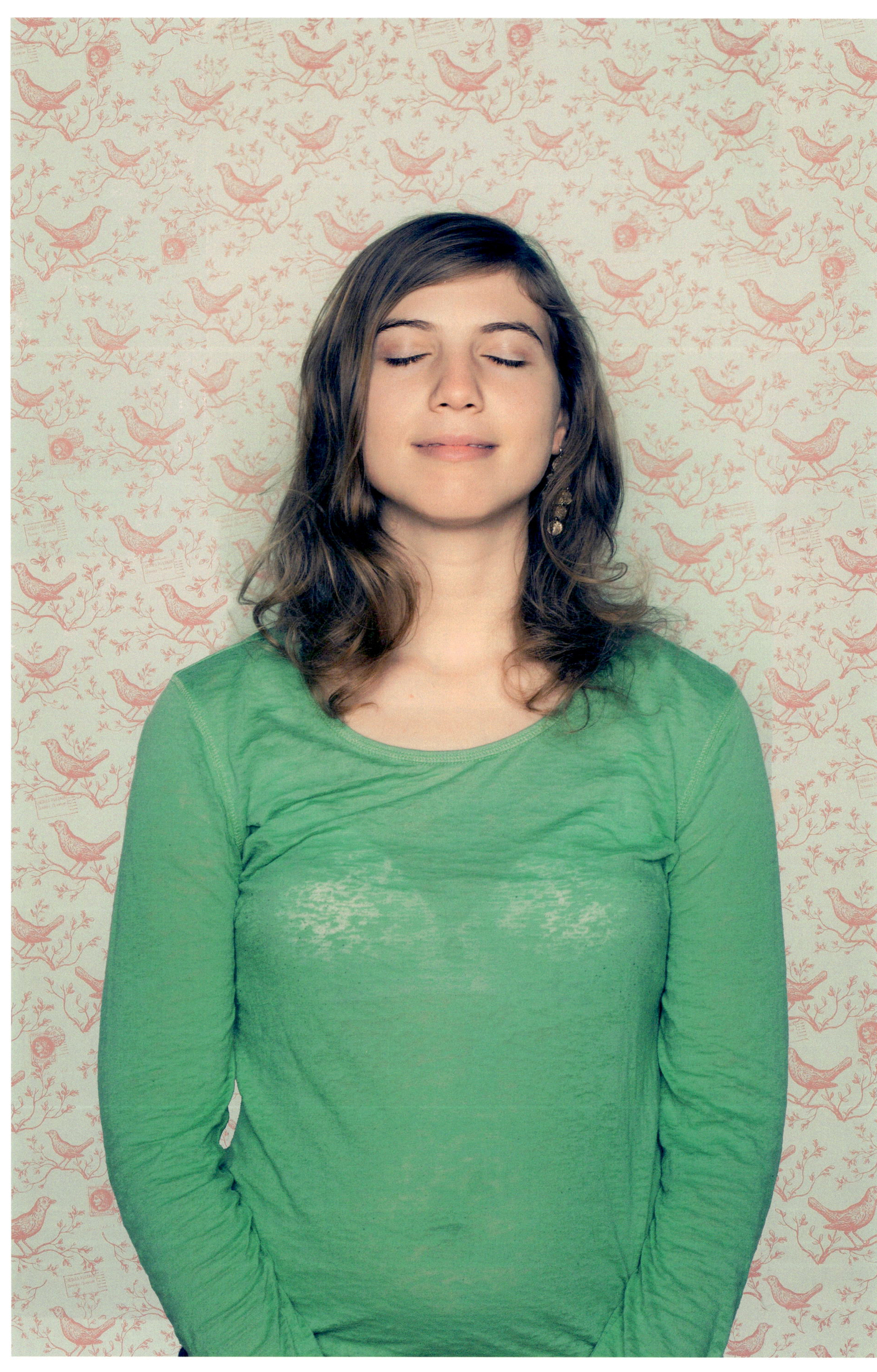
GAY | FACE

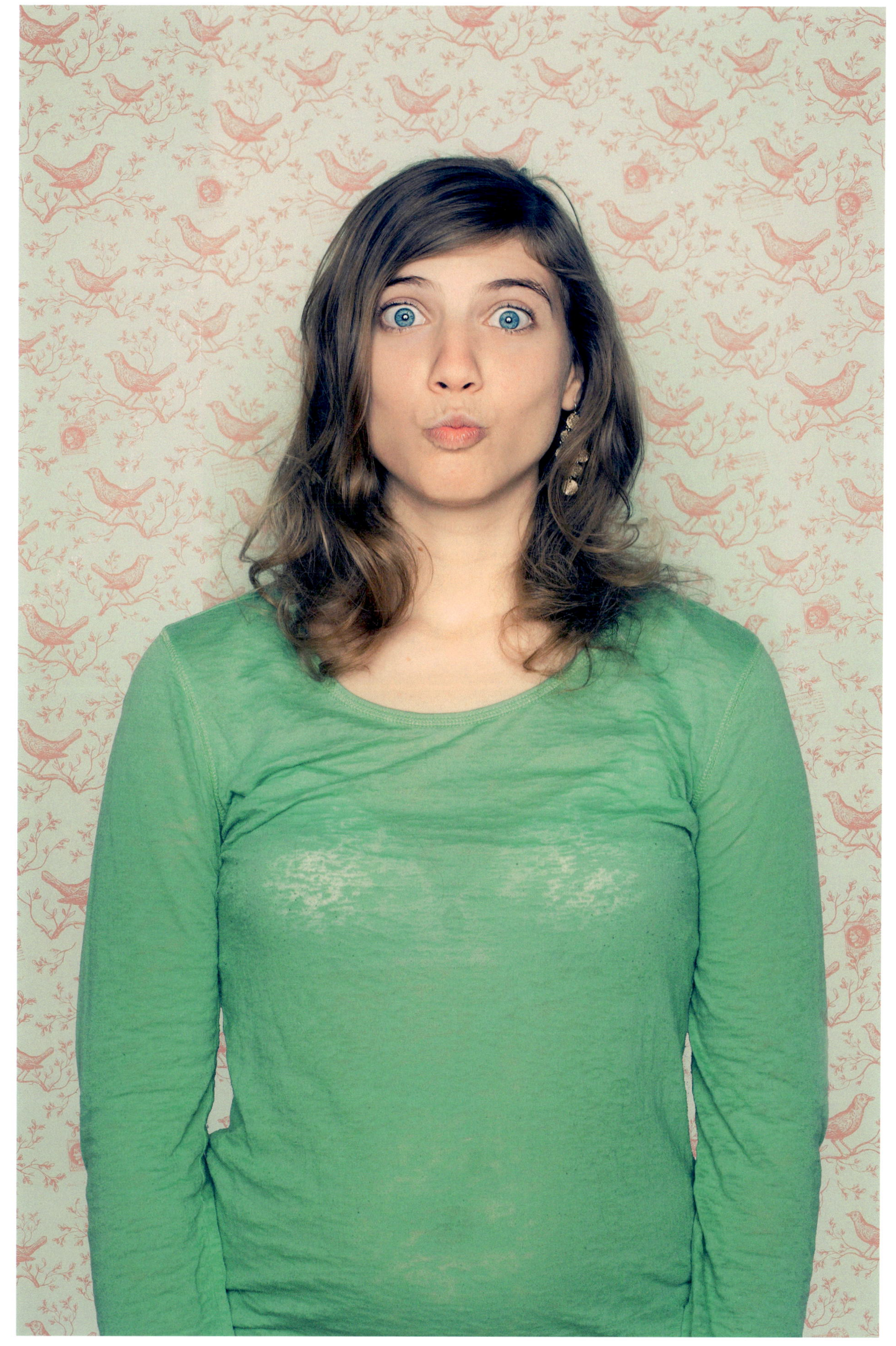

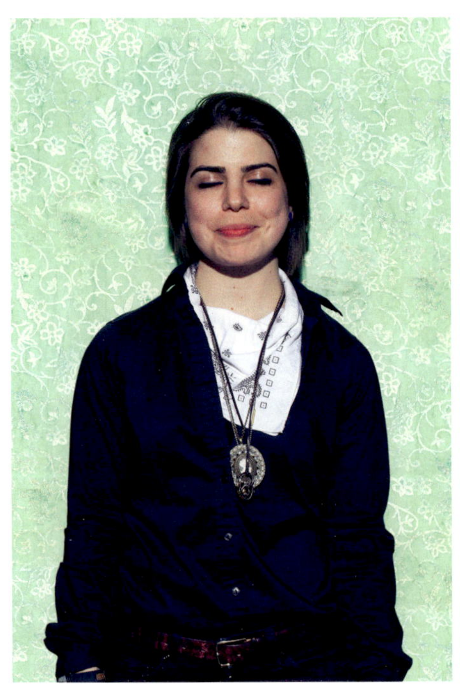
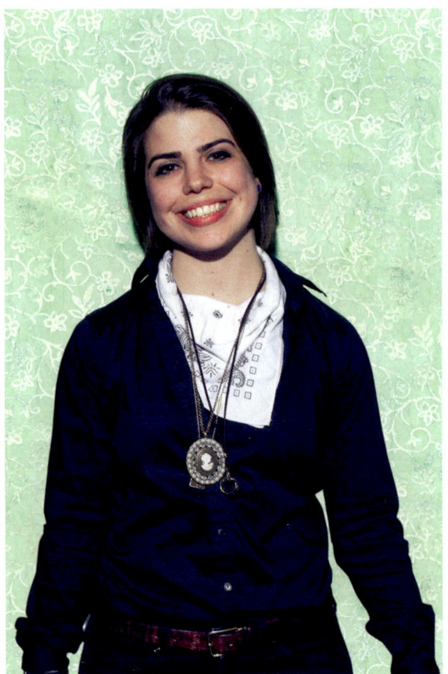
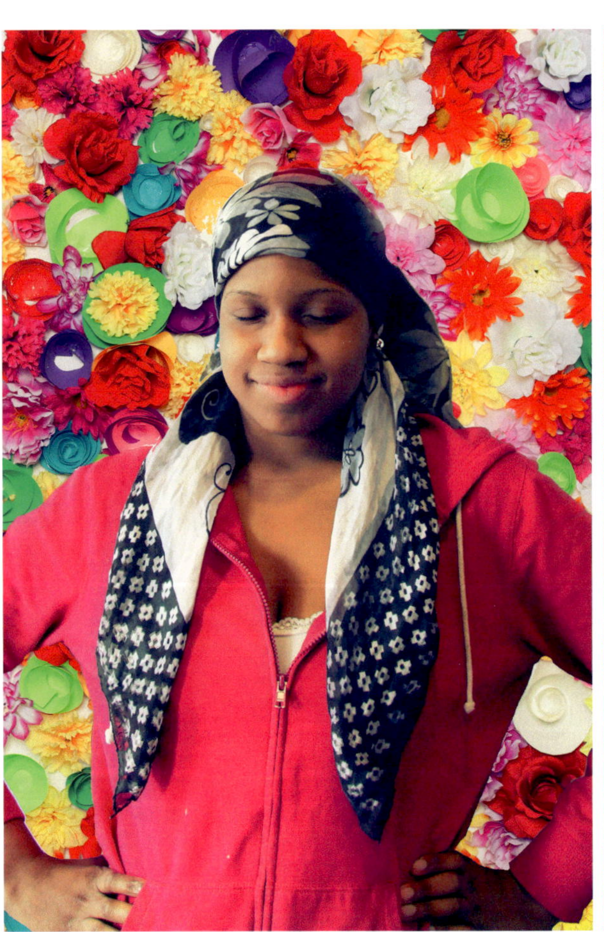
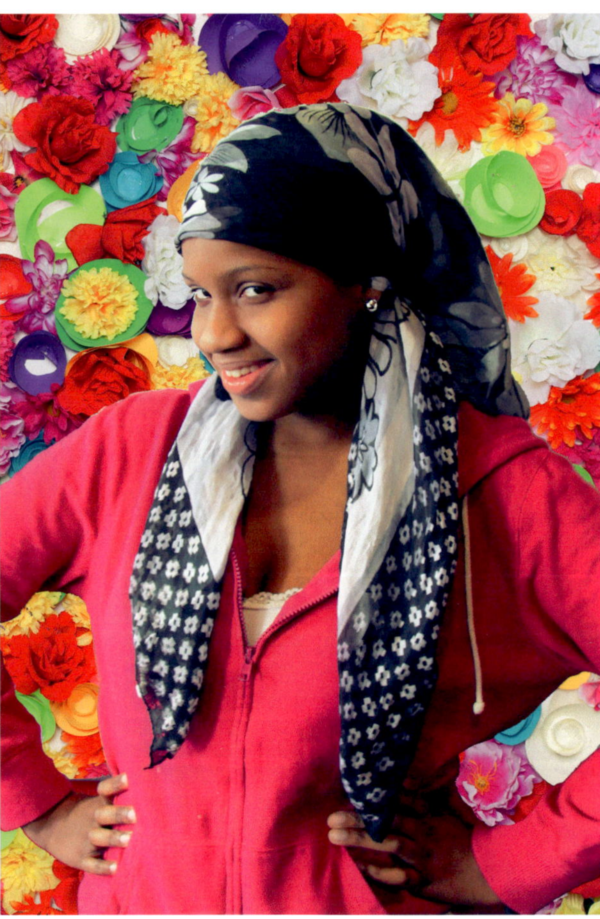

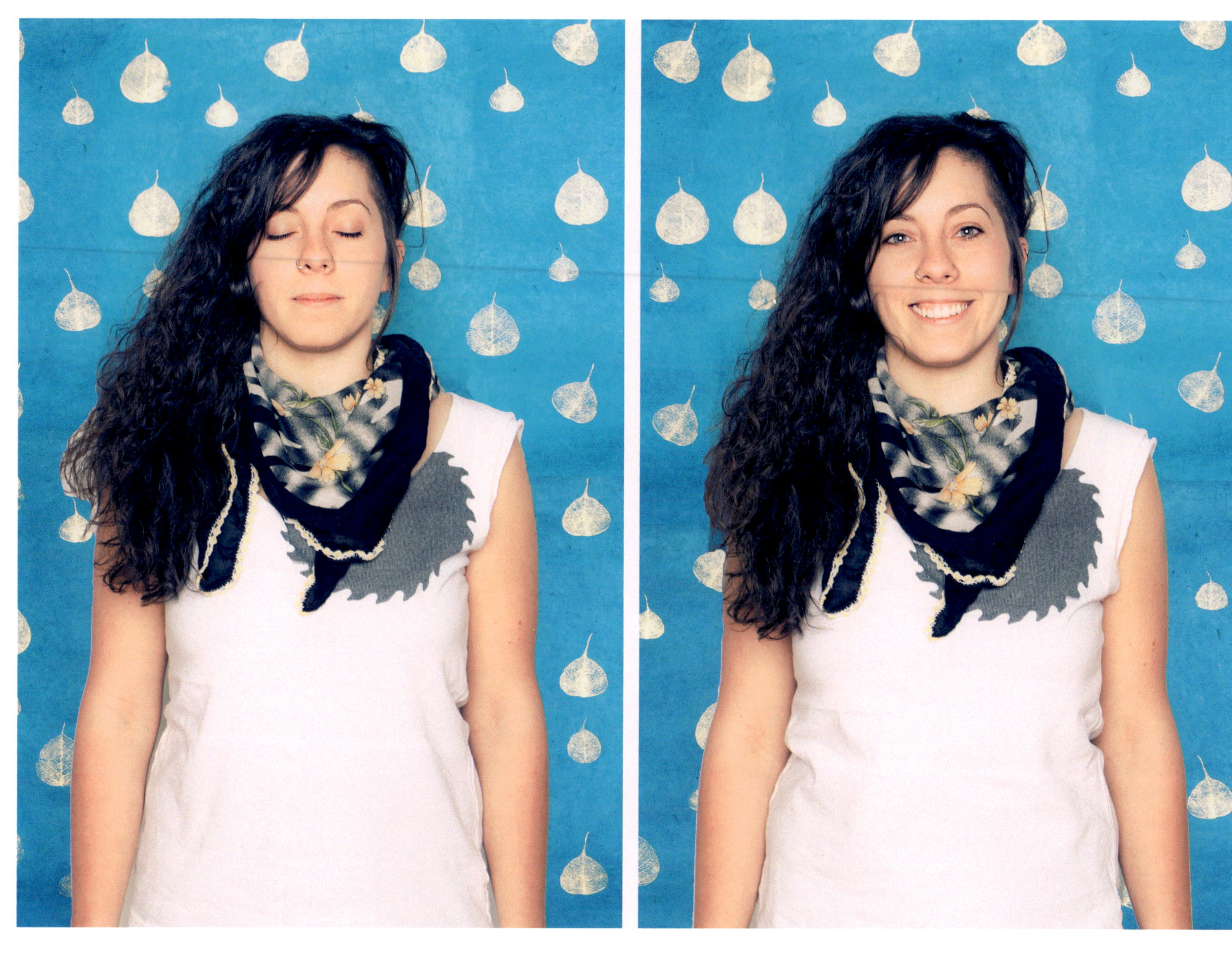

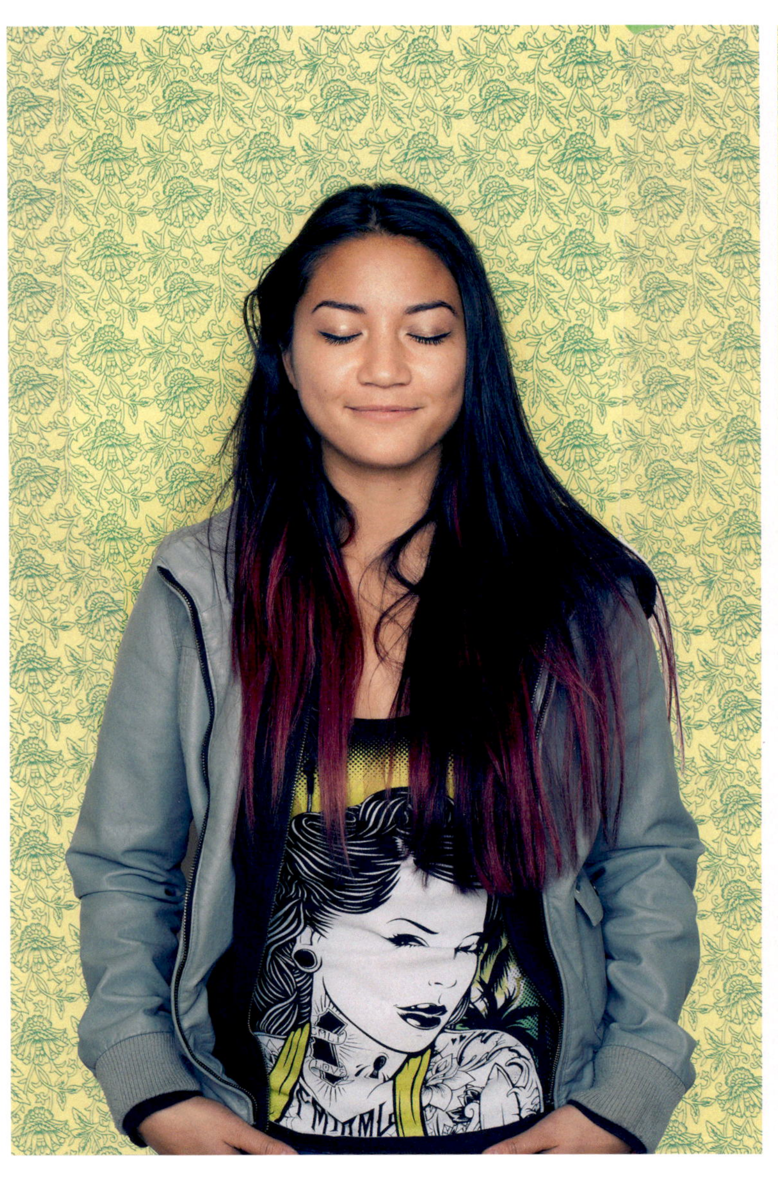
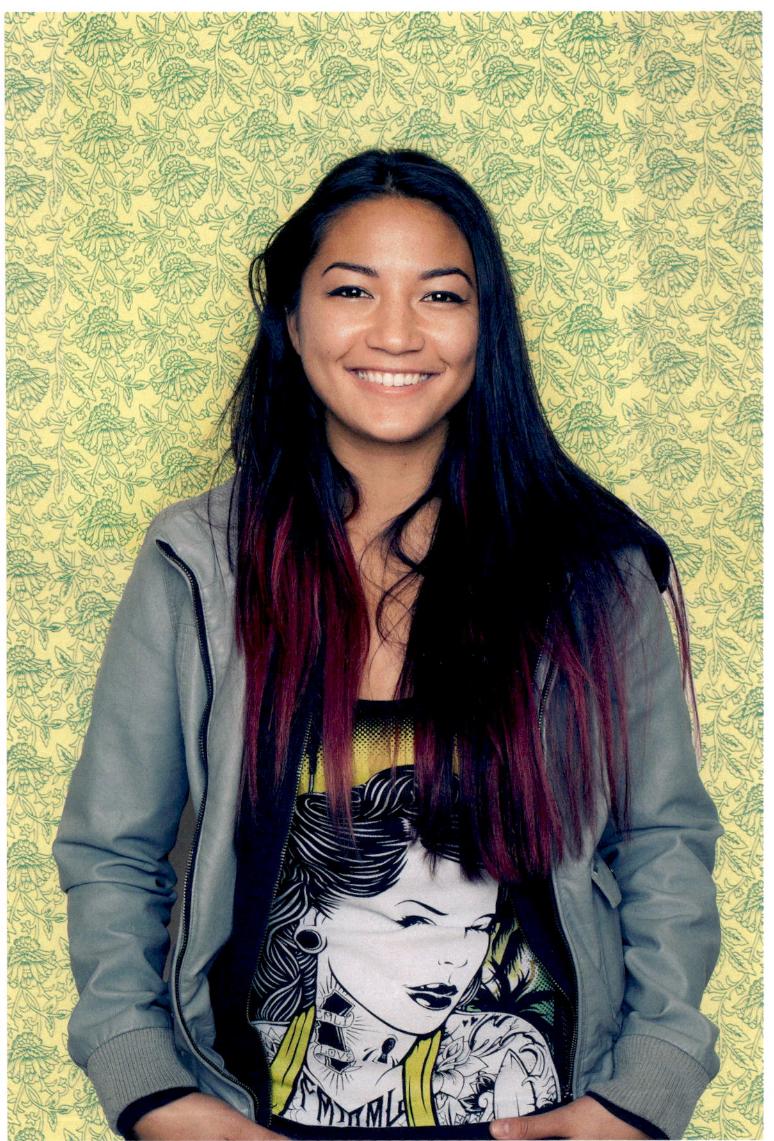

Coco M.

SAN MATEO, CALIFORNIA

How would you identify your sexuality?
A lover of ladies!

Why did you choose to be a part of this project?
My friend Jena said she had a friend in town work-ing on a photography project called Gayface. I didn't know exactly what it was, but I love to support the community and especially other artists and have been pleasantly surprised at how it's unfolded.

What do you think of your portrait?
It encapsulates my personality perfectly: shy and awkward, but happy.

Describe your coming out. Are you coming out in some way by participating in this project?
I was lucky, I to came out to a very open group of family and friends. I didn't explicitly say "hey, I'm gay," but there was a girl I hung out with every day, and when I started putting extra effort into my appearance, my family noticed and connected the dots. Having a conversation about labels or identity felt awkward because I really didn't know what was going on at the time—I just dove into this new gay world. I'm grateful to have had a positive experience and accepting family because I know many others have very serious struggles.

Have you ever experienced discrimination based on your gender or sexual orientation?
As a female, discrimination is inevitable, whether it's intentional or not. California is really open, which makes being open easy and comfortable. However, during a recent trip to Morocco, my girlfriend and I avoided physical contact because we feared being mistreated. Any time we take a trip, we *have* to take that extra step to know the laws around homosexu-ality, but also what's generally accepted by society.

If you could change one thing about mainstream society to improve the lives of LGBTQ+ people, what would it be?
Violence against others. People should never be abused because of their identity—it creates fear, inhibits people from living honestly, and perpet-uates a hostile environment. I understand that xcnophobia comes from confusion, or sometimes disappointment, but it's not okay to abuse others verbally, mentally, or physically.

Describe how this project has affected you, both per-sonally and as a member of the LGBTQ+ community as a whole.
Gayface has done an excellent job of showing all types of people within the community. The pro-ject has brought together strangers from across the country who may not have much in common aside from being a little different. When the giant posters were put up, it felt like I was waving hello to every-one in the community. I love how each personality is captured by the two photos; the closed eye version is just another person on the street, but the second image allows that person to really be seen—they remind us that people really just want to be happy and accepted as they are.

What advice have you been given by another LGBTQ+ person, or that you might offer someone?
The best thing you can do is be there for someone else —if you know someone who is going through similar struggles, support each other. Life is easier with a friend by your side and you never have to be alone.

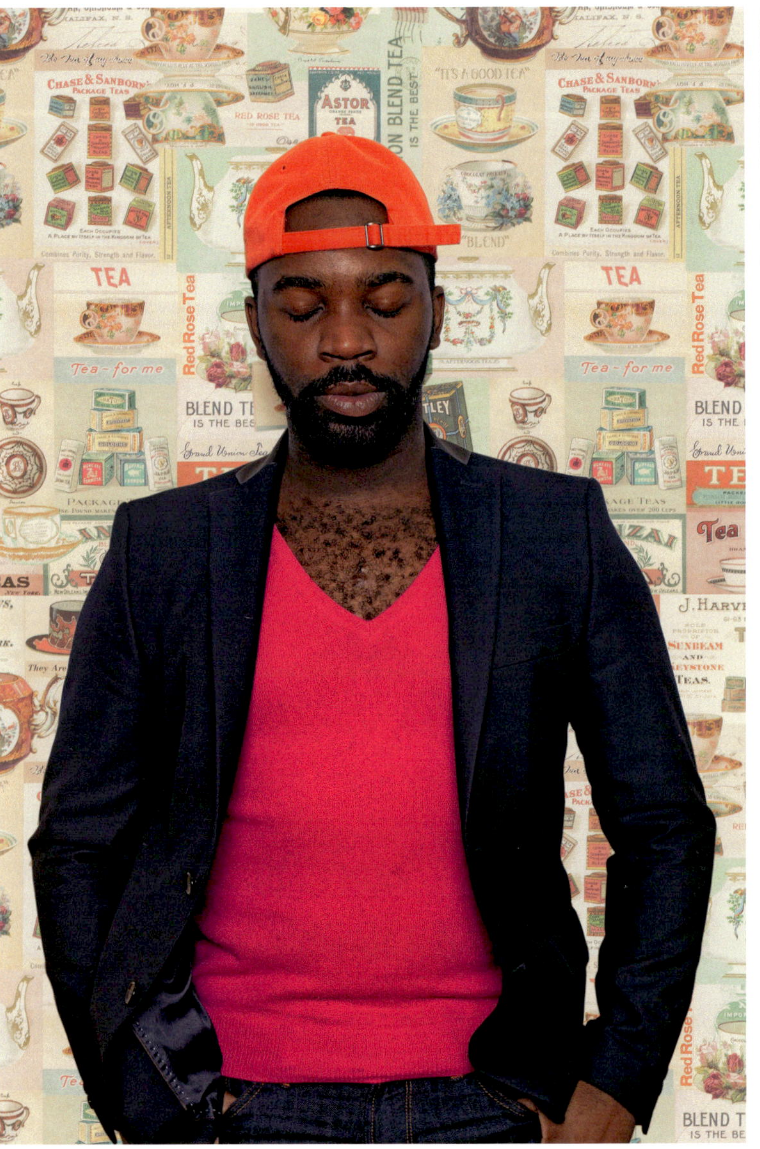
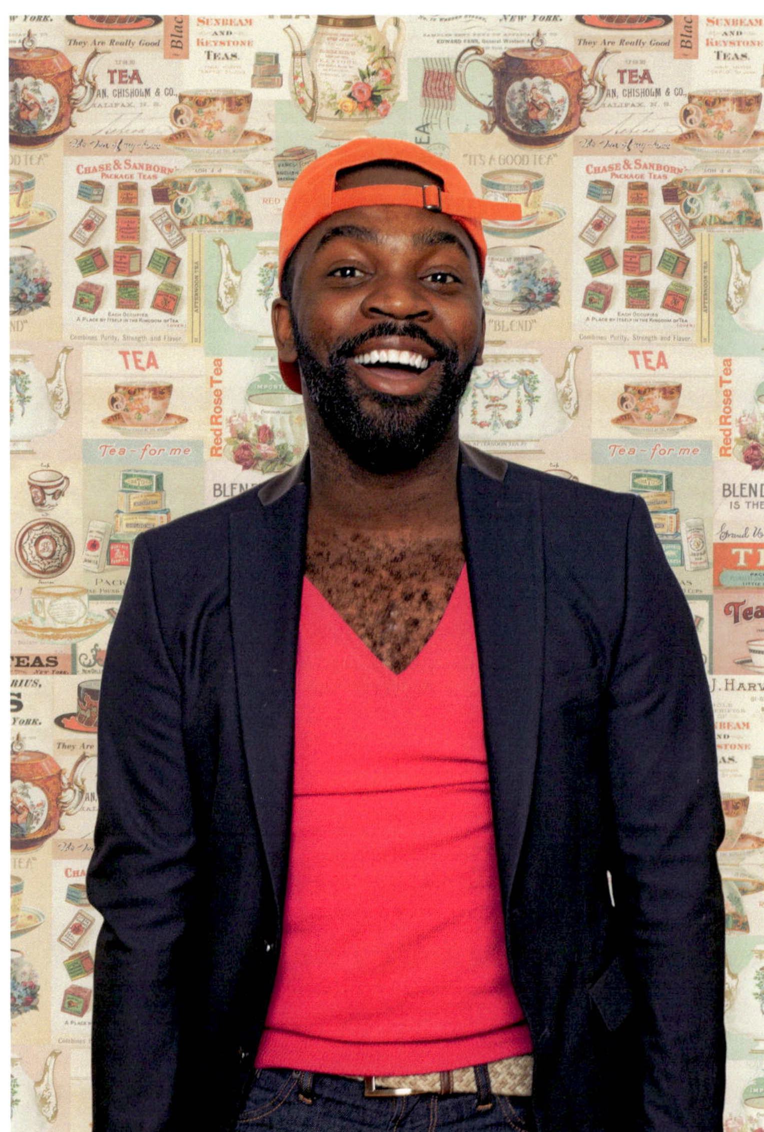

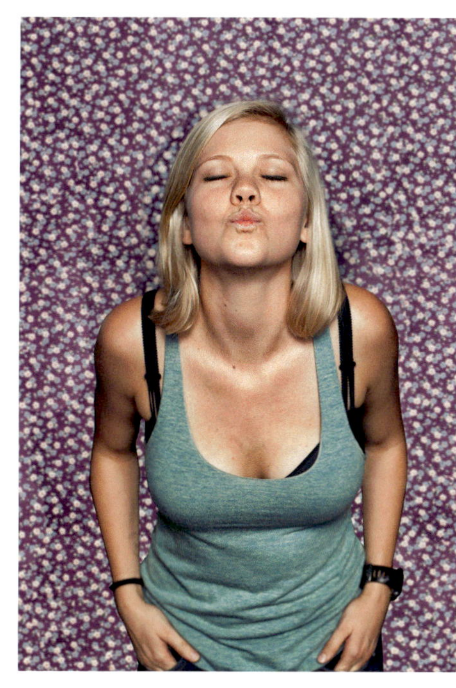
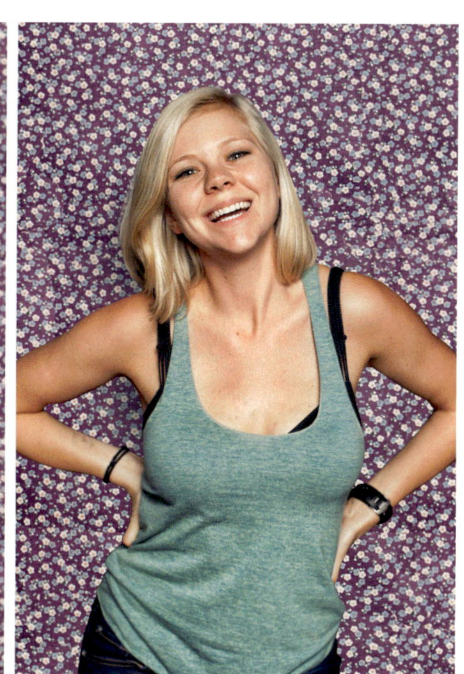

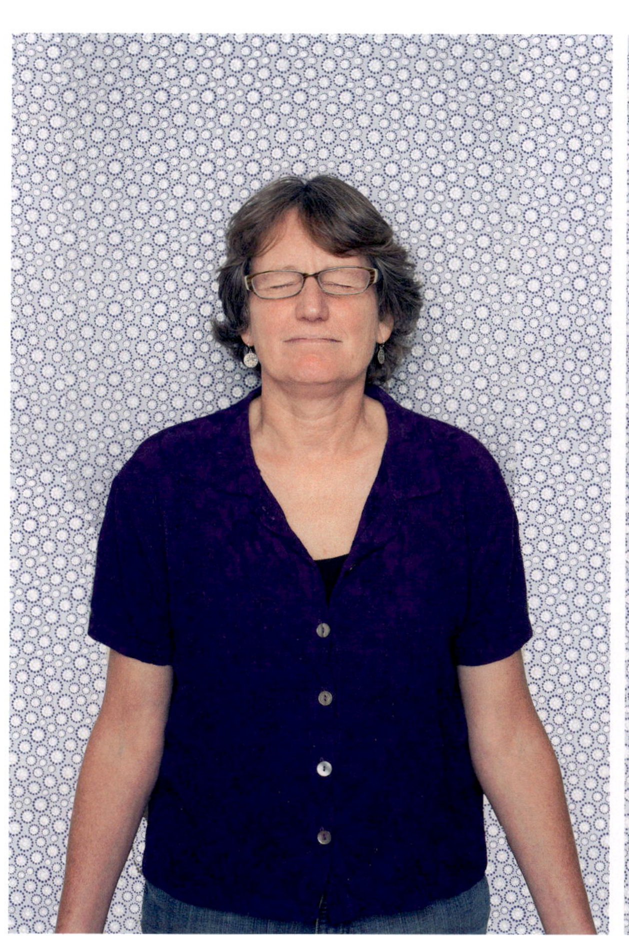
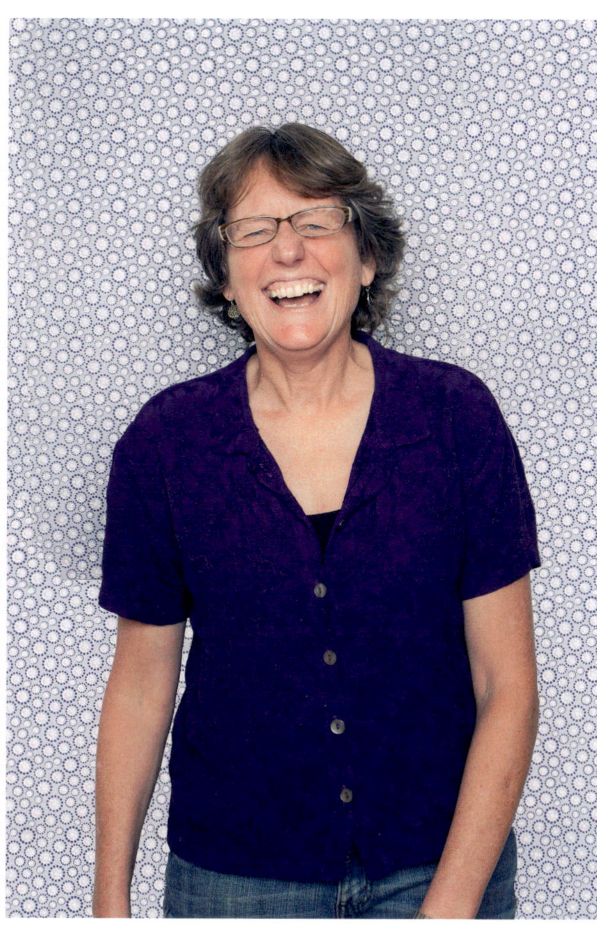

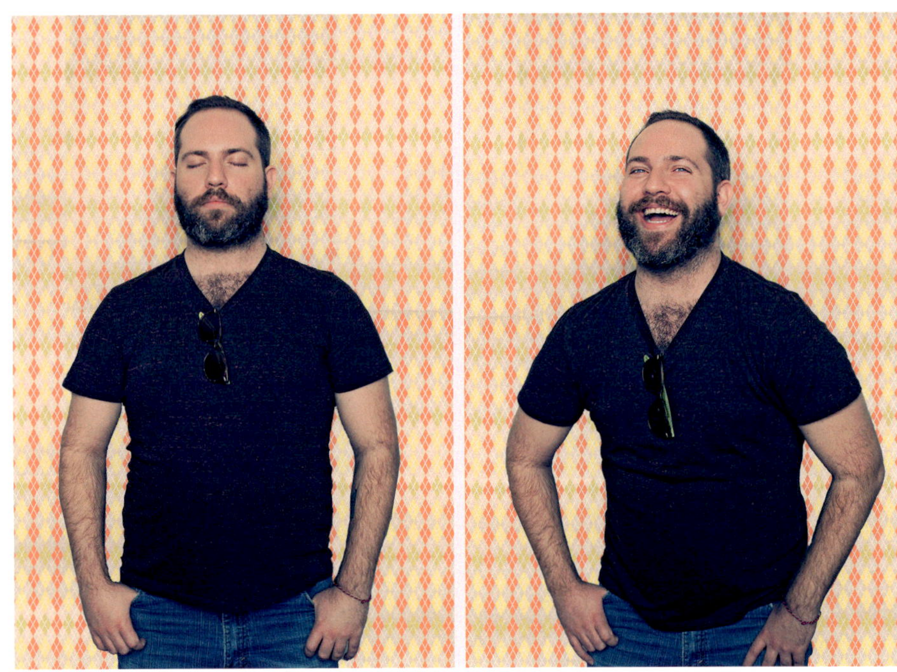

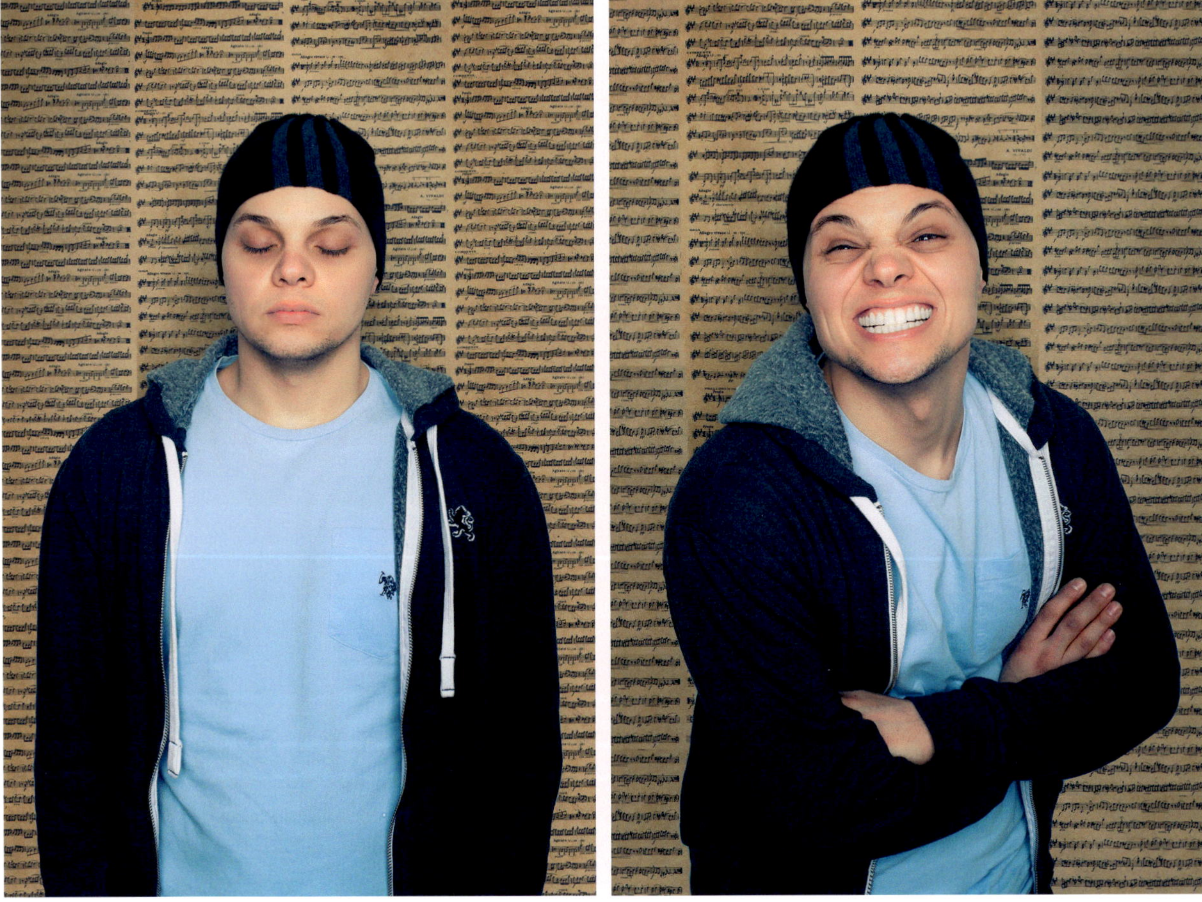

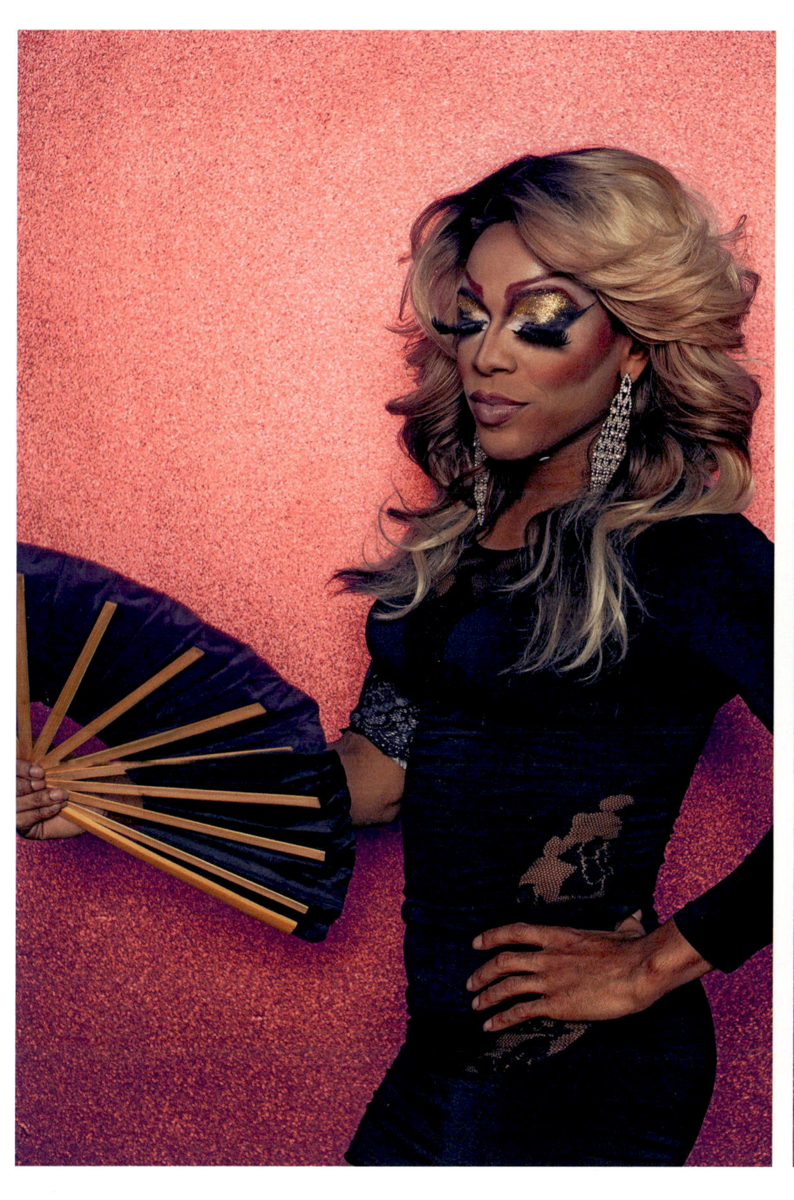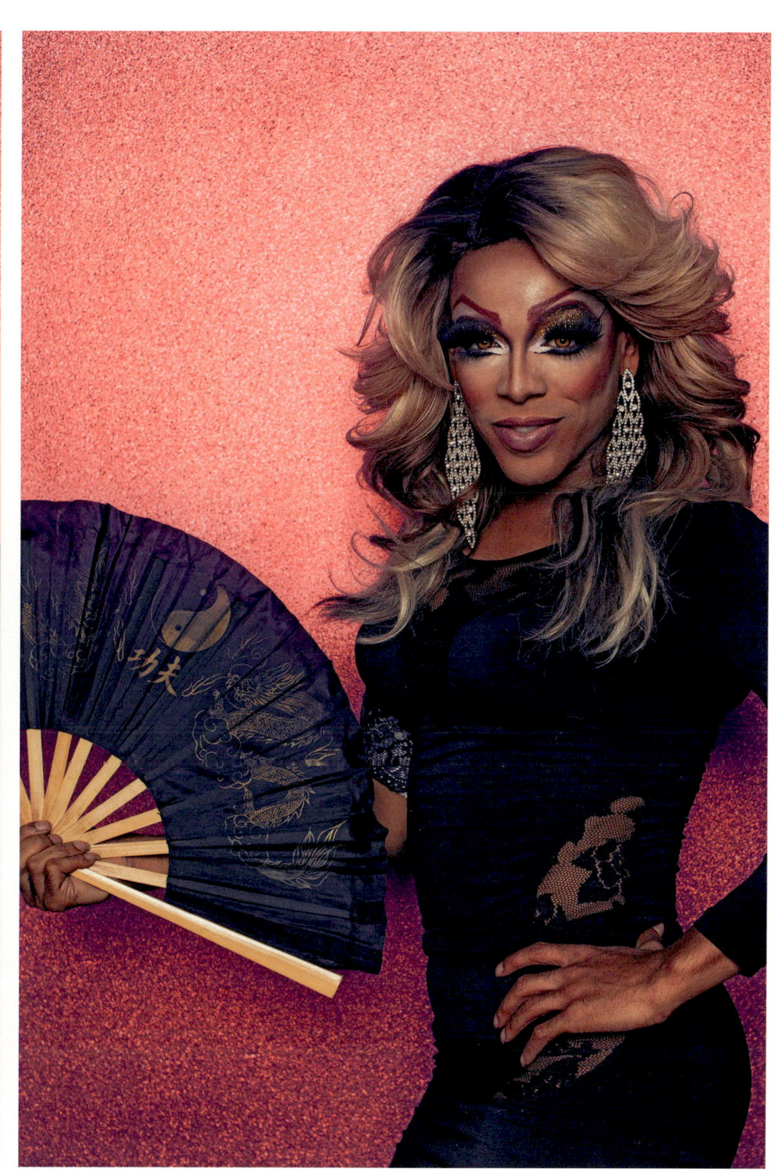

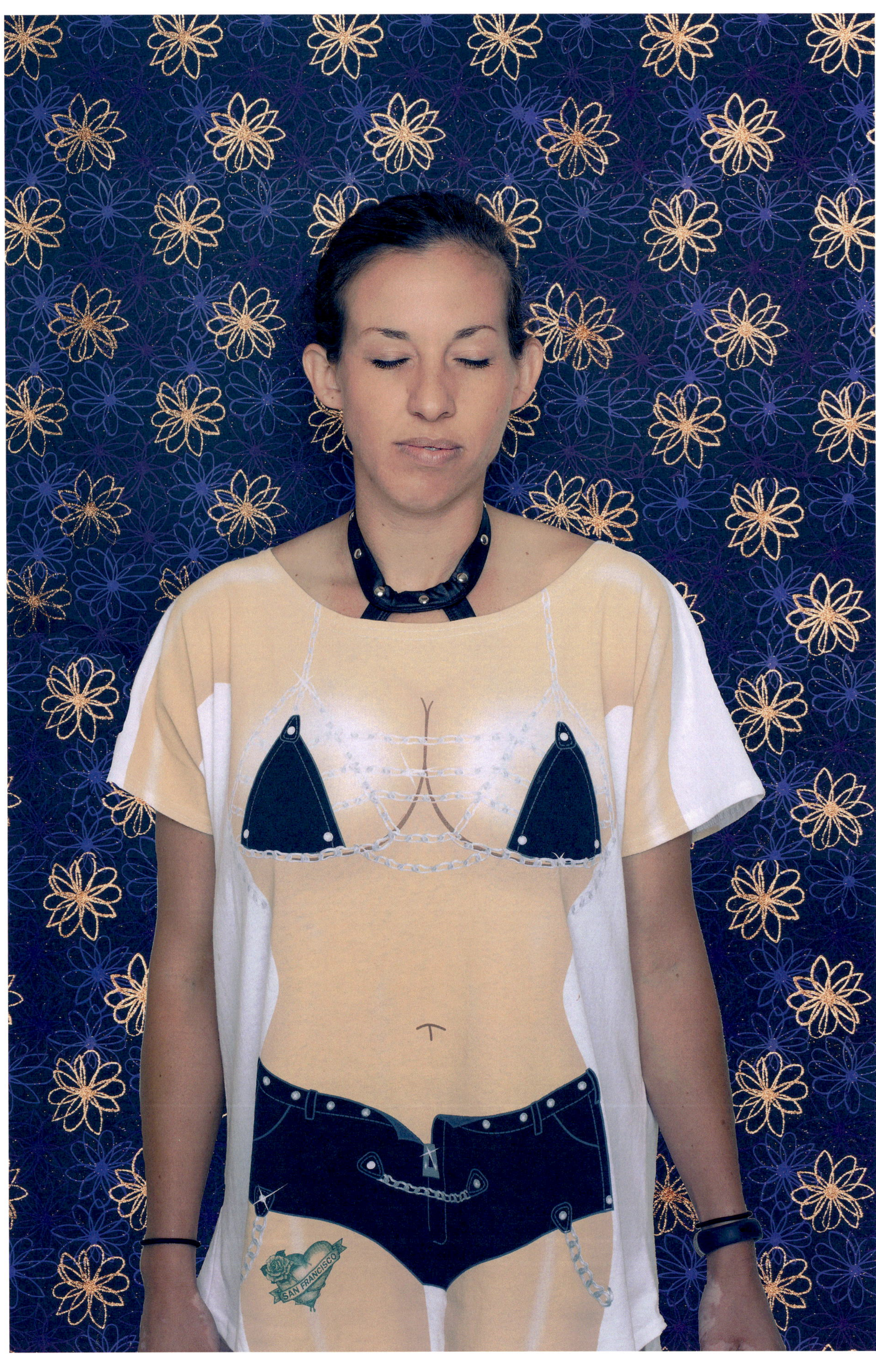

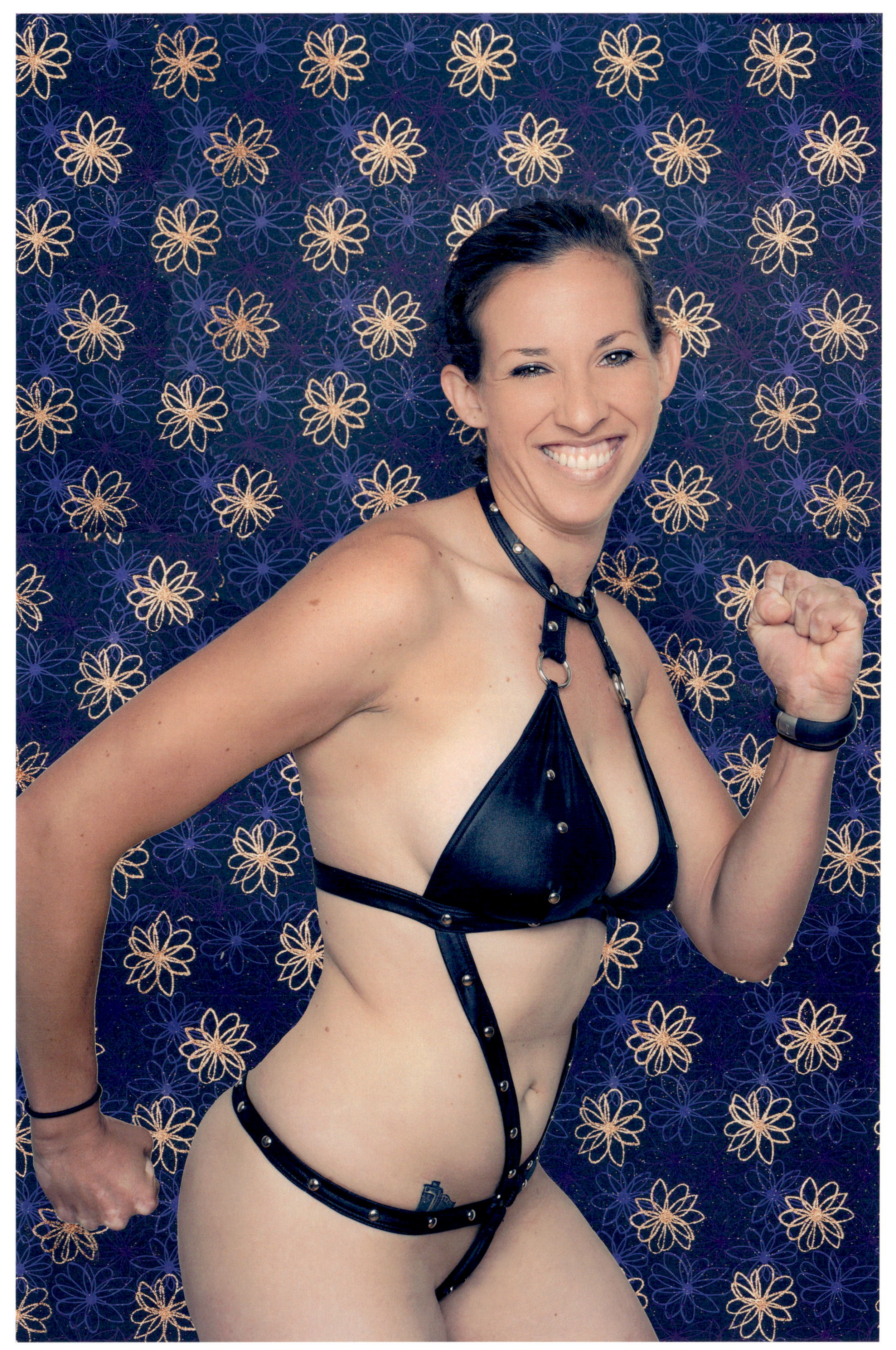

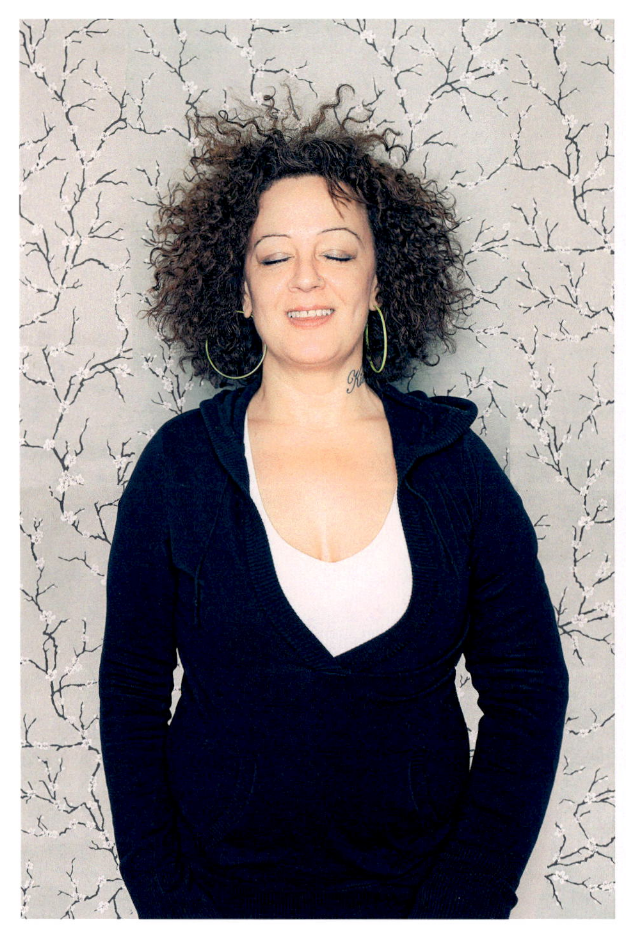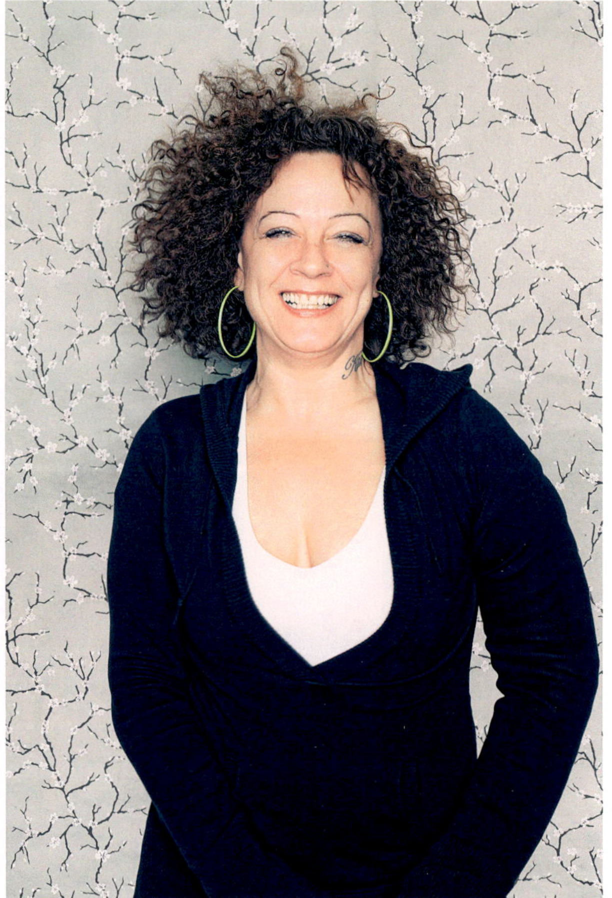

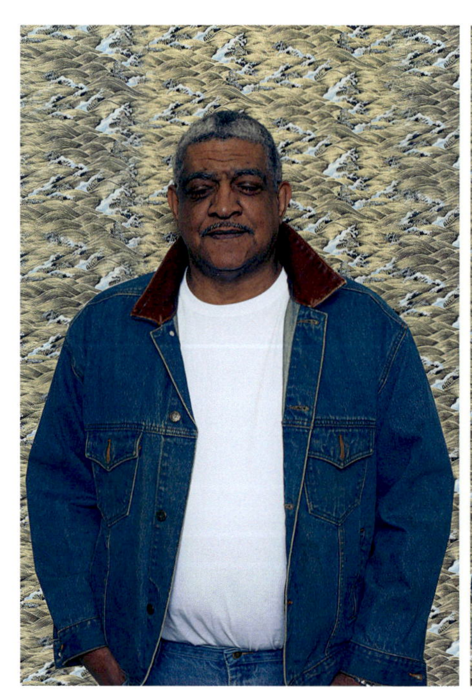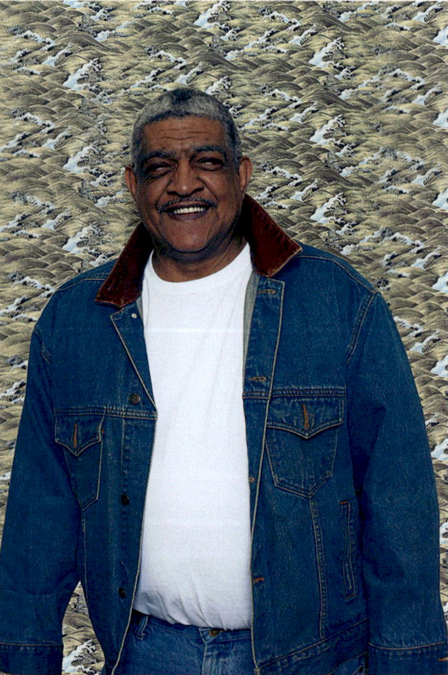

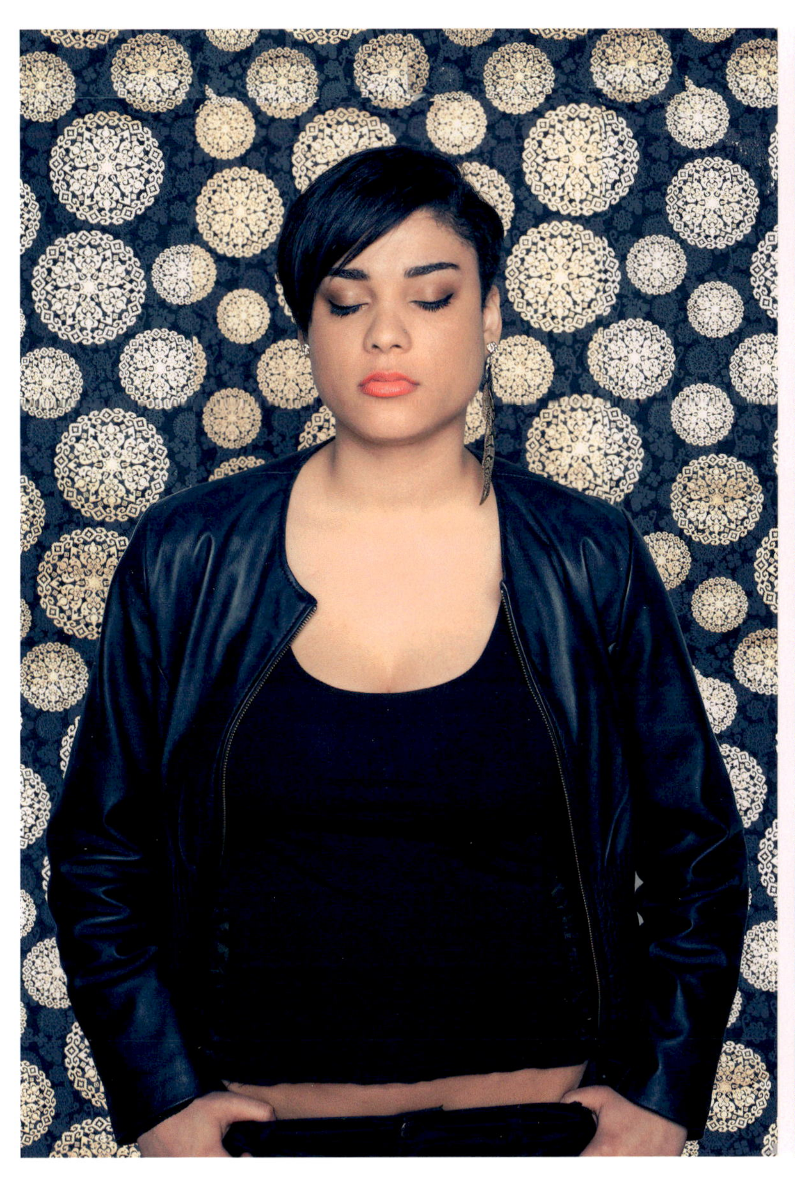
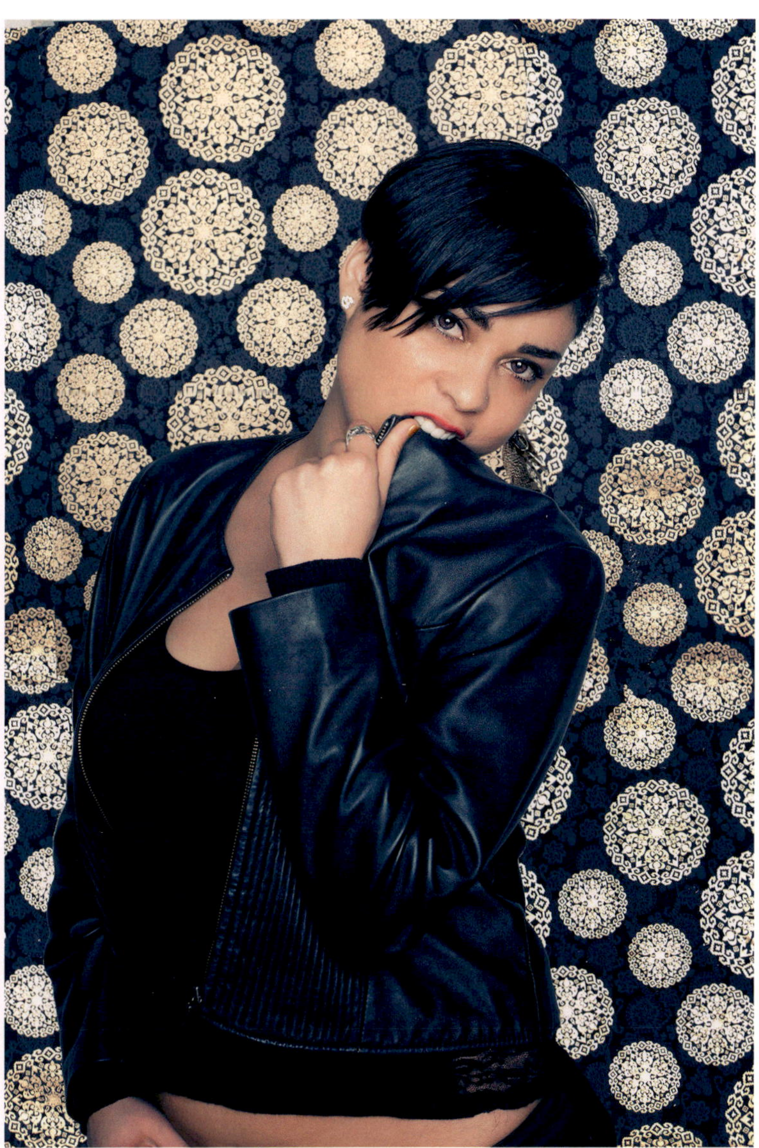

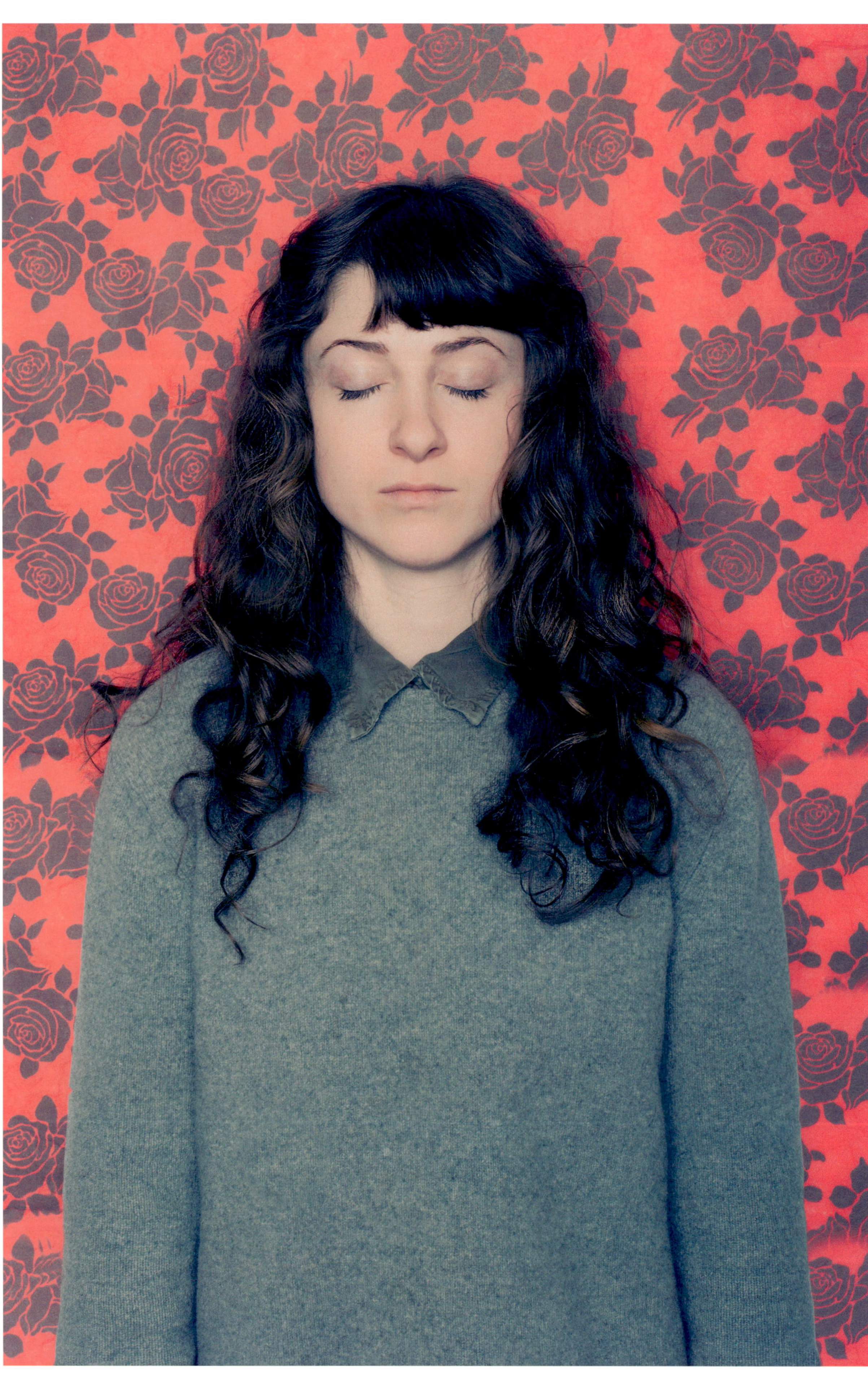

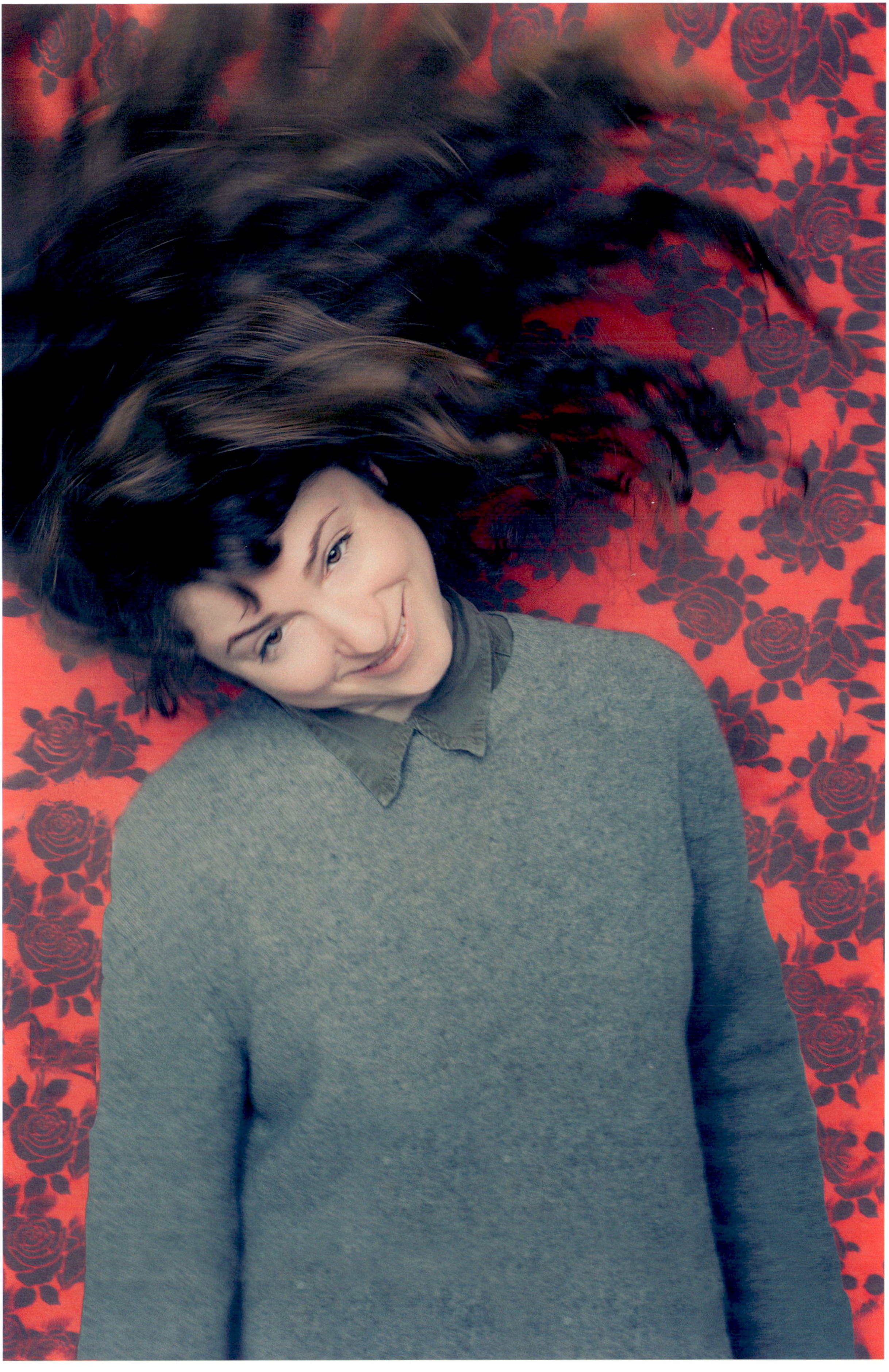

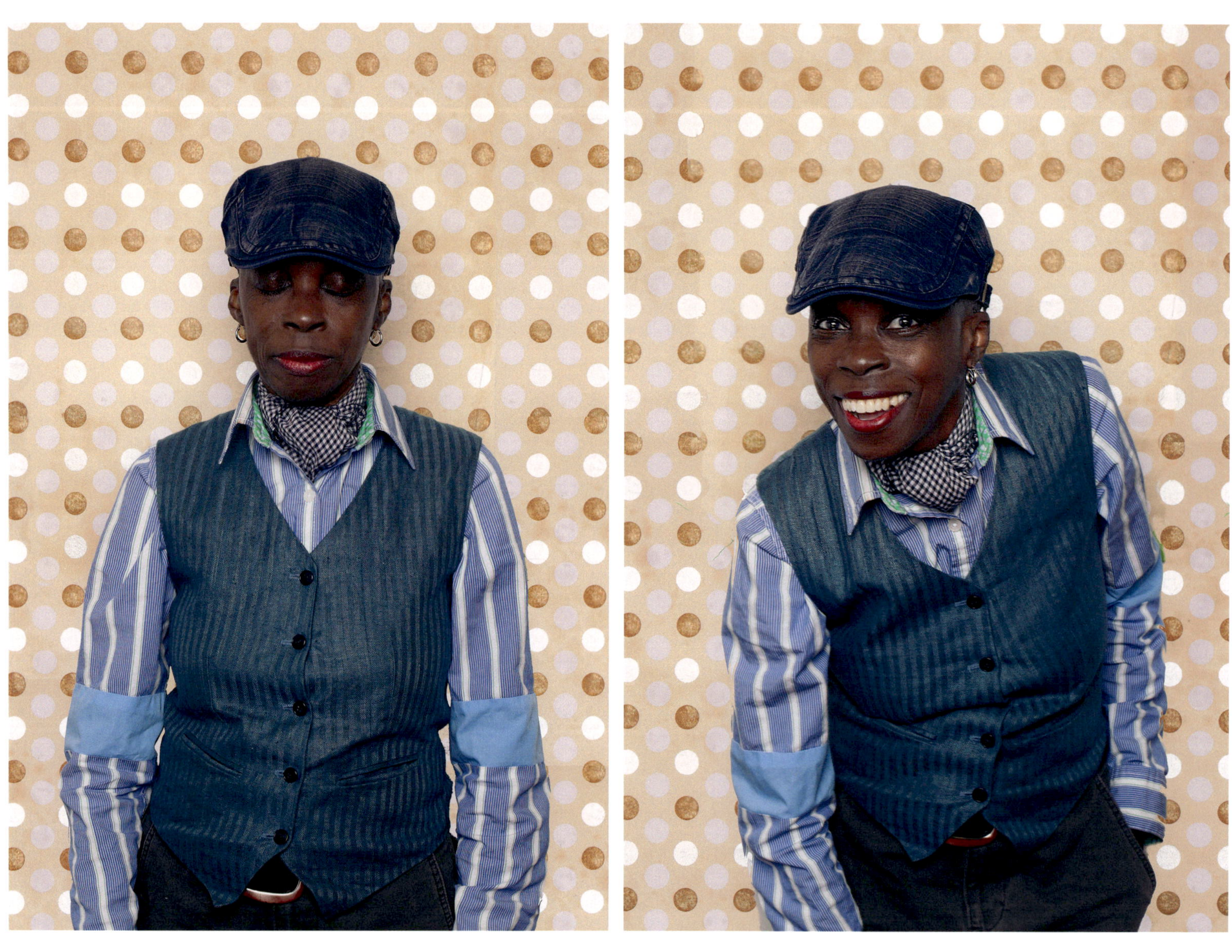

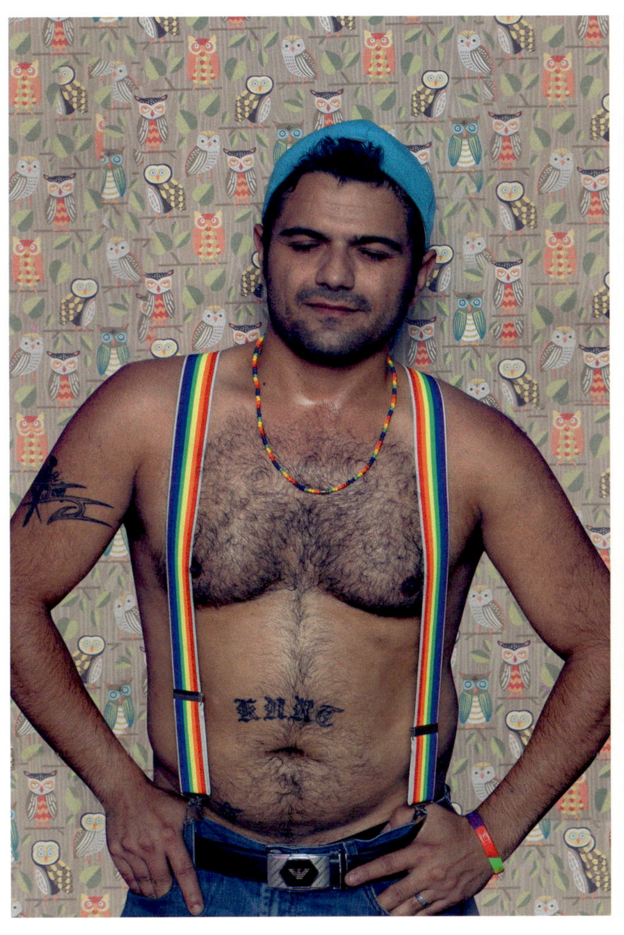
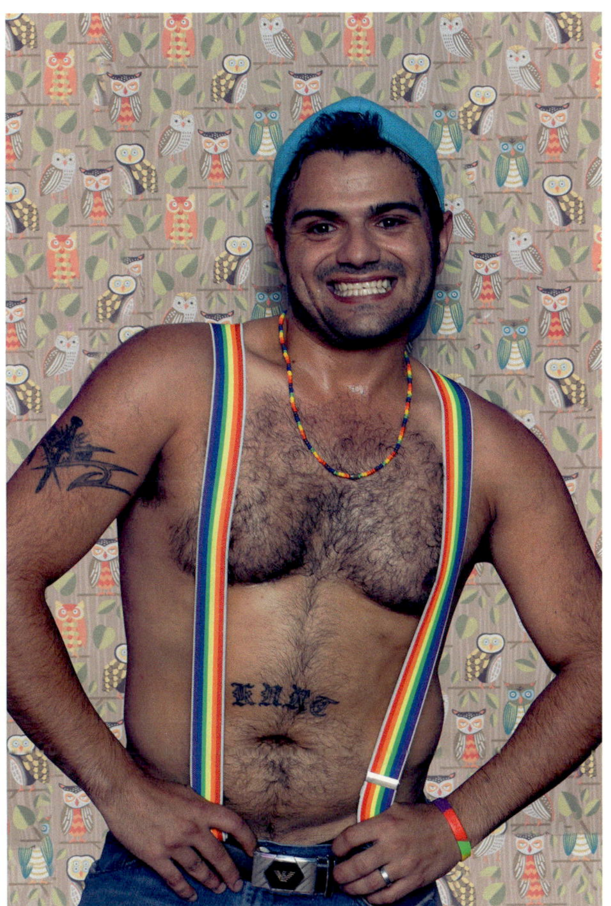

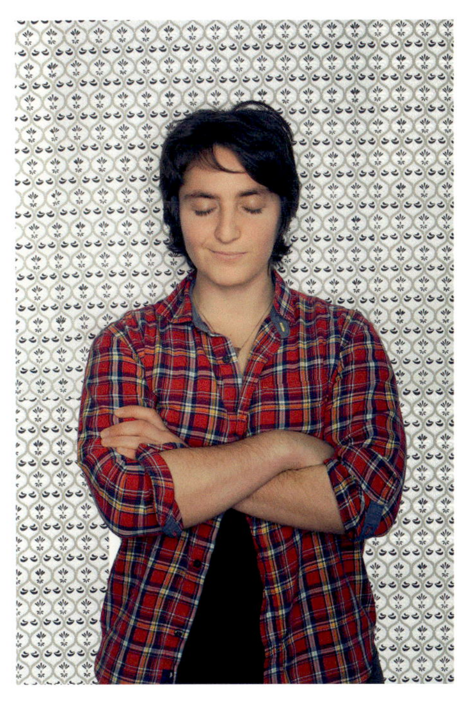
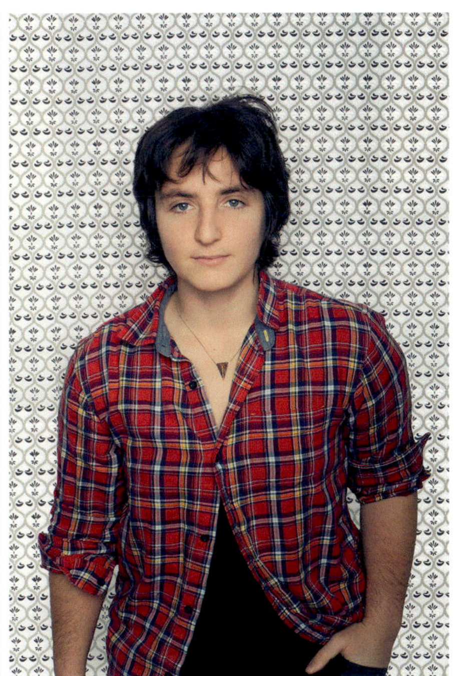

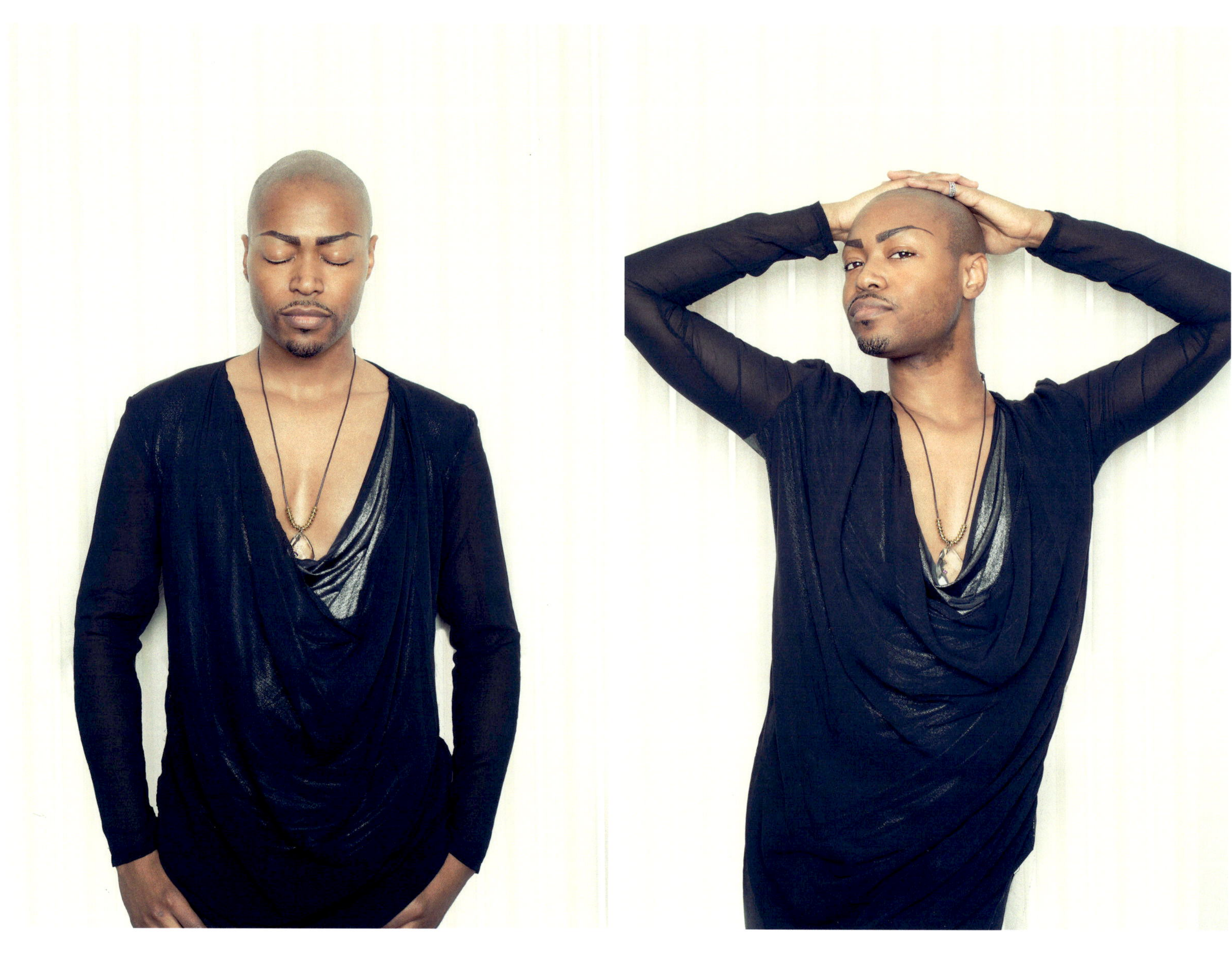

GAY | FACE

Kevin L.

QUEENS, NEW YORK

How would you identify your sexuality?
Gay.

What pronouns do you prefer?
I prefer to be known as being "male." I don't like "girl," "honey," or "sweetie" which is so common in the community, but these terms unnerve me. I don't get upset, but I do politely correct people.

Why did you choose to be a part of this project?
I hope younger generations will find this work inspiring, and perhaps avoid the years of coming to terms with their own sexuality. I think these portraits can help foster a generation of queer people who are at peace with themselves, and arrive at this place sooner than I did.

Describe your coming out. Are you coming out in some way by participating in this project?
My coming out experience was to one person, my grandmother. I was twenty-five. I had just returned to New York from about ten years in Alabama. I always felt uncomfortable around gay men so I chose to volunteer for GLAAD or HRC, I can't remember which right now. I marched in the gay pride parade that year, and as I looked at the many faces of queer people and supporters, I suddenly felt it was necessary to call my very religious Christian grandmother in Alabama and tell her I that was gay and confront the possibility that she would not want to be a part of my life anymore. She was silent for a few seconds but then she came around. She said that she loved me and that nothing changed. I was relieved and grateful, knowing that this response isn't the most common. She was the only person that mattered, so hers was the only opinion that weighed heavily on me.

Have you ever experienced discrimination based on your gender or sexual orientation?
The only discrimination I experienced was in my elementary to junior high school years. From high school onward, thankfully, no.

If you could change one thing about mainstream society to improve the lives of LGBTQ+ people, what would it be?
Gosh I don't know. The world today is such a different place than when I grew up. Mainstream American culture has changed so much and has become much more tolerant and accepting.

Describe how this project has affected you, both personally and as a member of the LGBTQ+ community as a whole.
I want to ease the suffering of others; I want to have an impact on the next generation.

What advice have you been given by another LGBTQ+ person, or that you might offer someone?
"If you can't love yourself, how in the hell are you gonna love somebody else?" RuPaul said it best, but it is a truth that has many layers and applications. Just chew on that for a little while. Give it a couple decades to sink in.

Who are your LGBTQ+ role models?
My queer heroes aren't famous (with the exception of RuPaul).

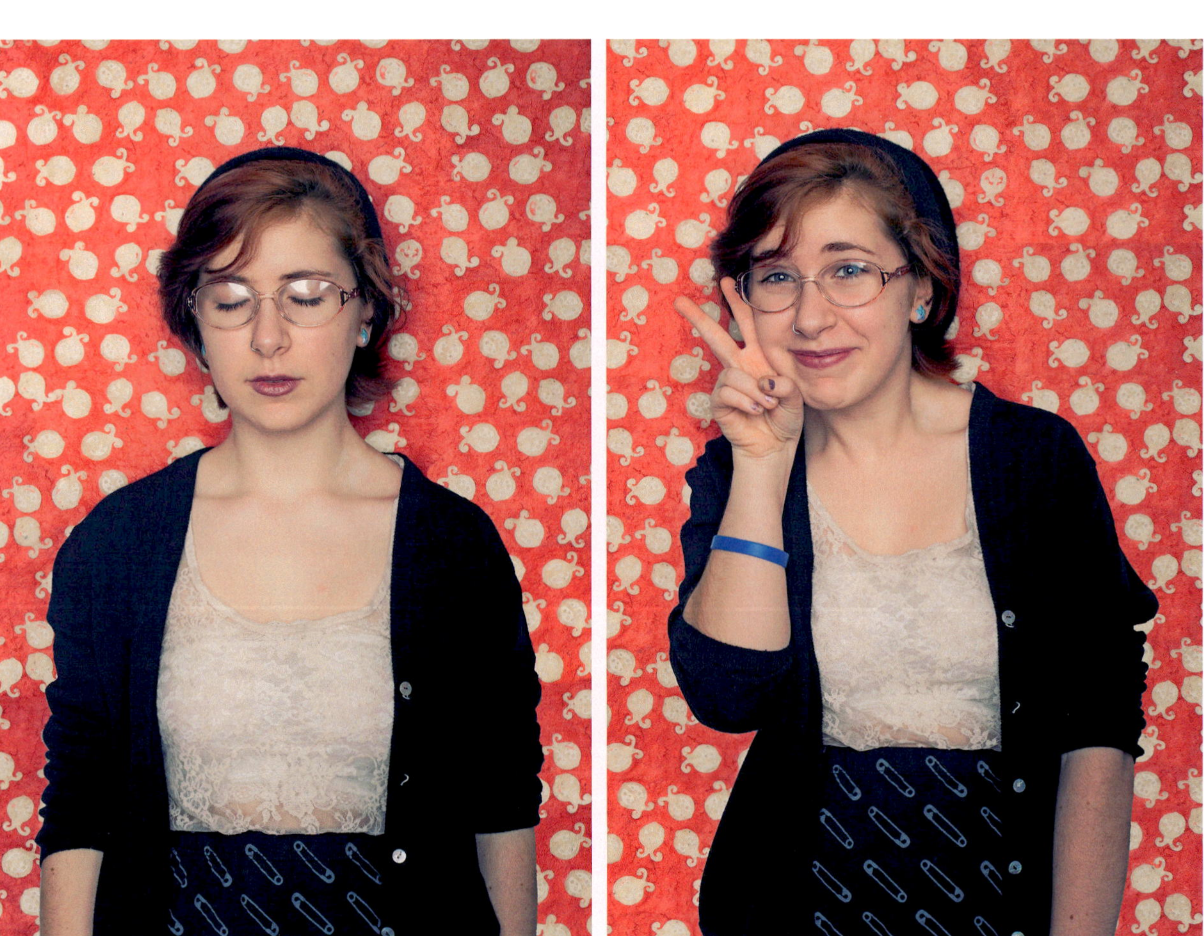

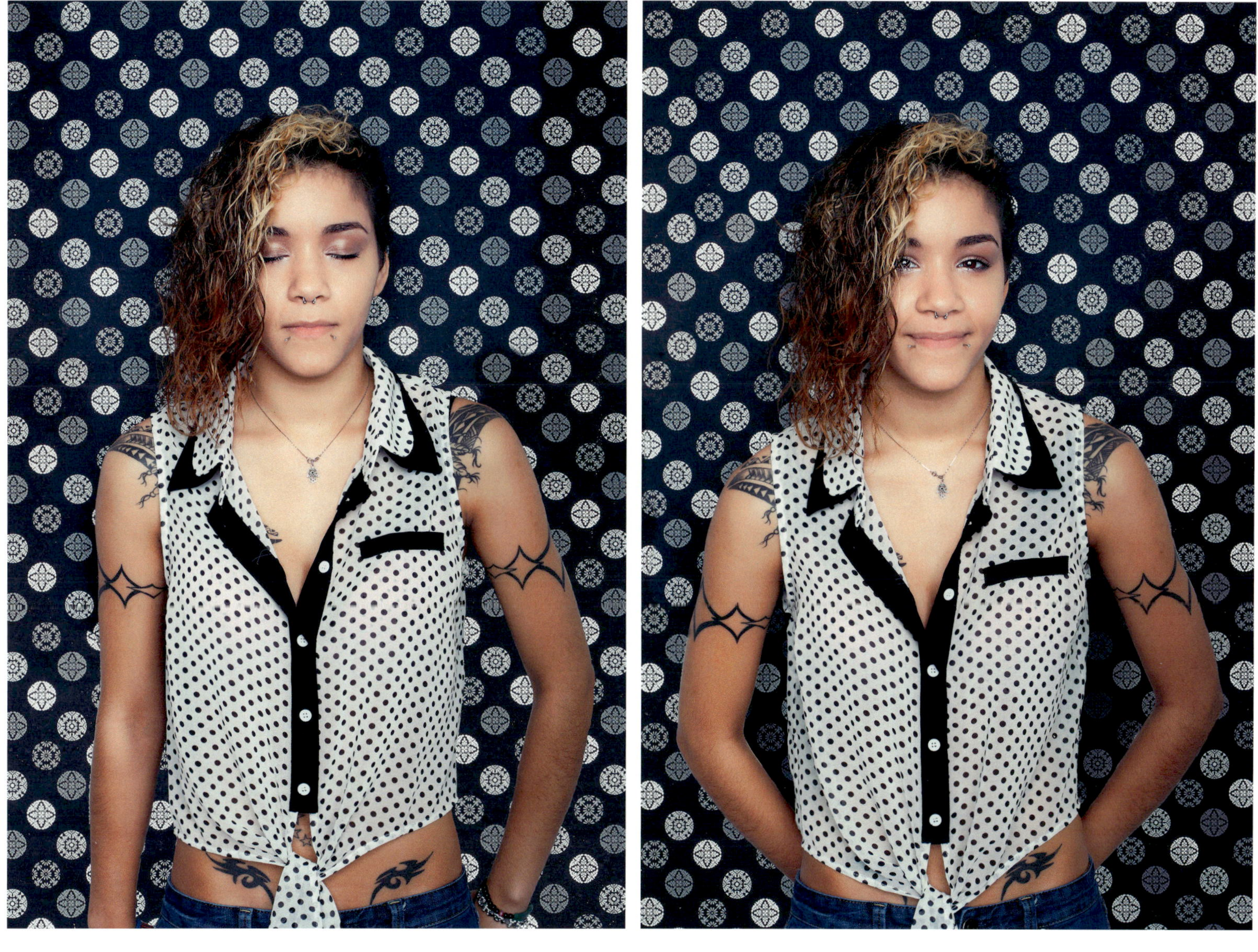

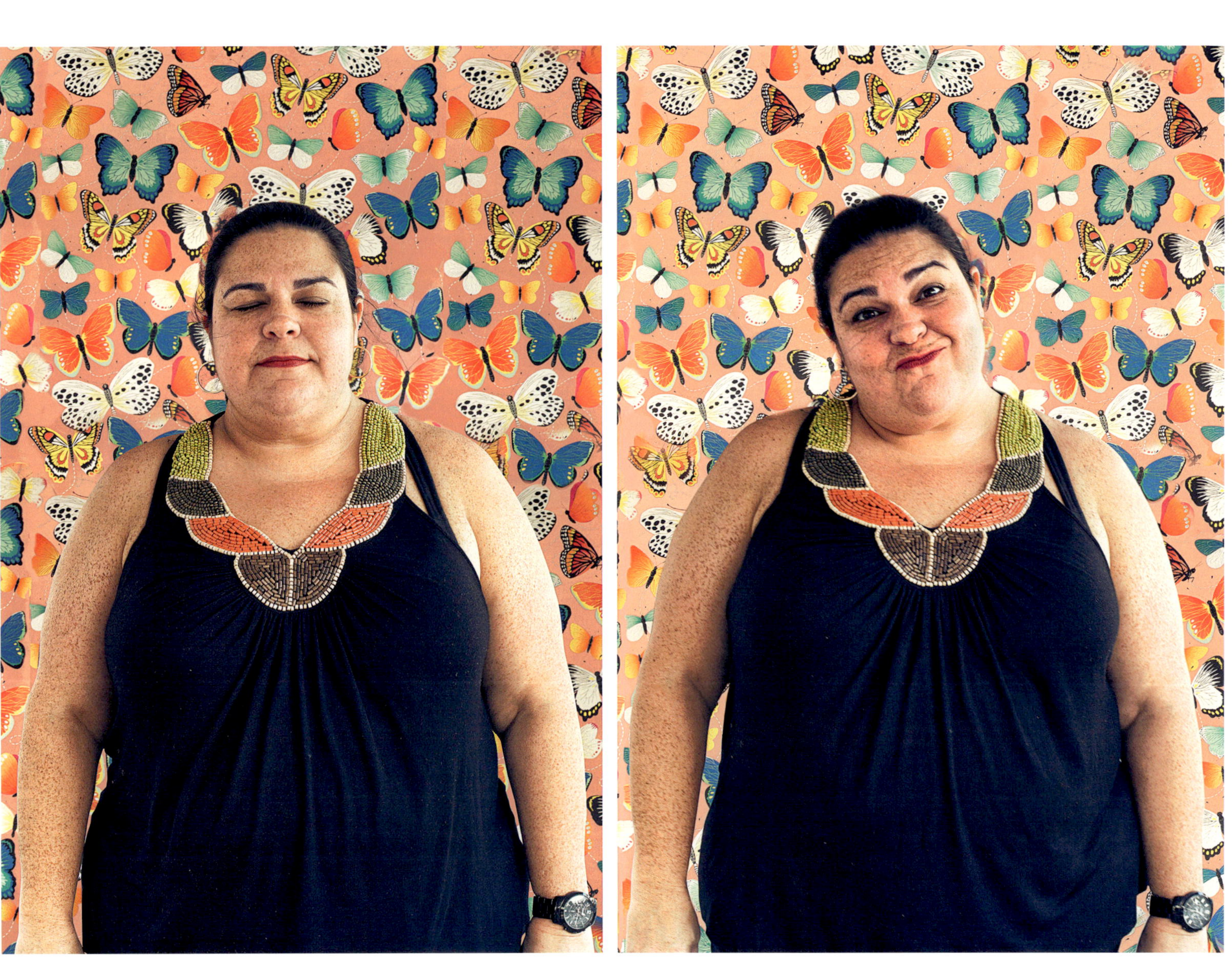

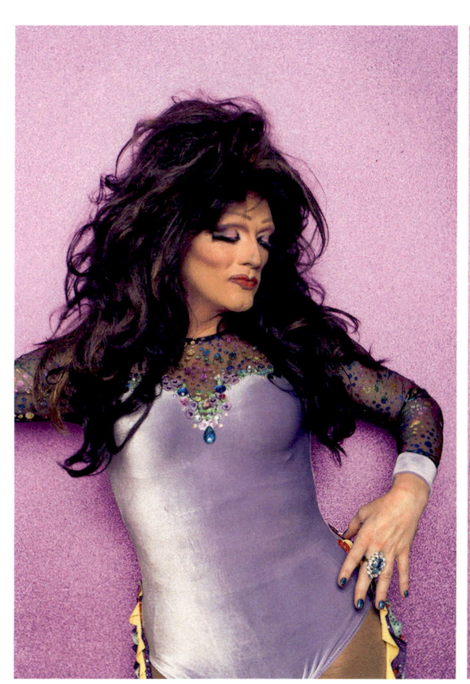 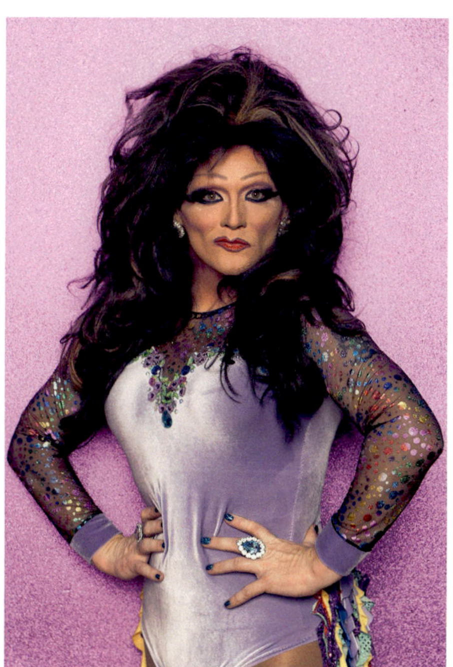

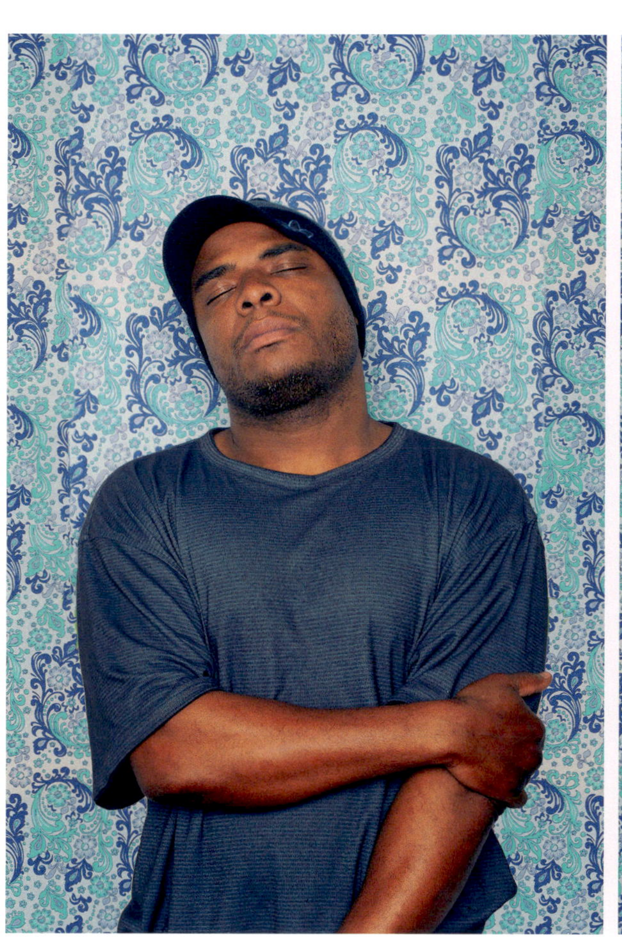 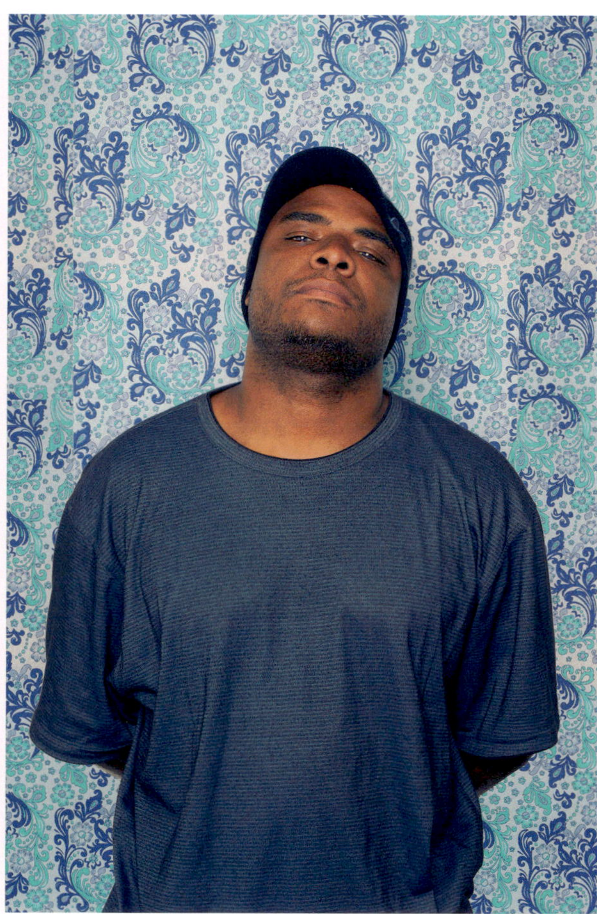

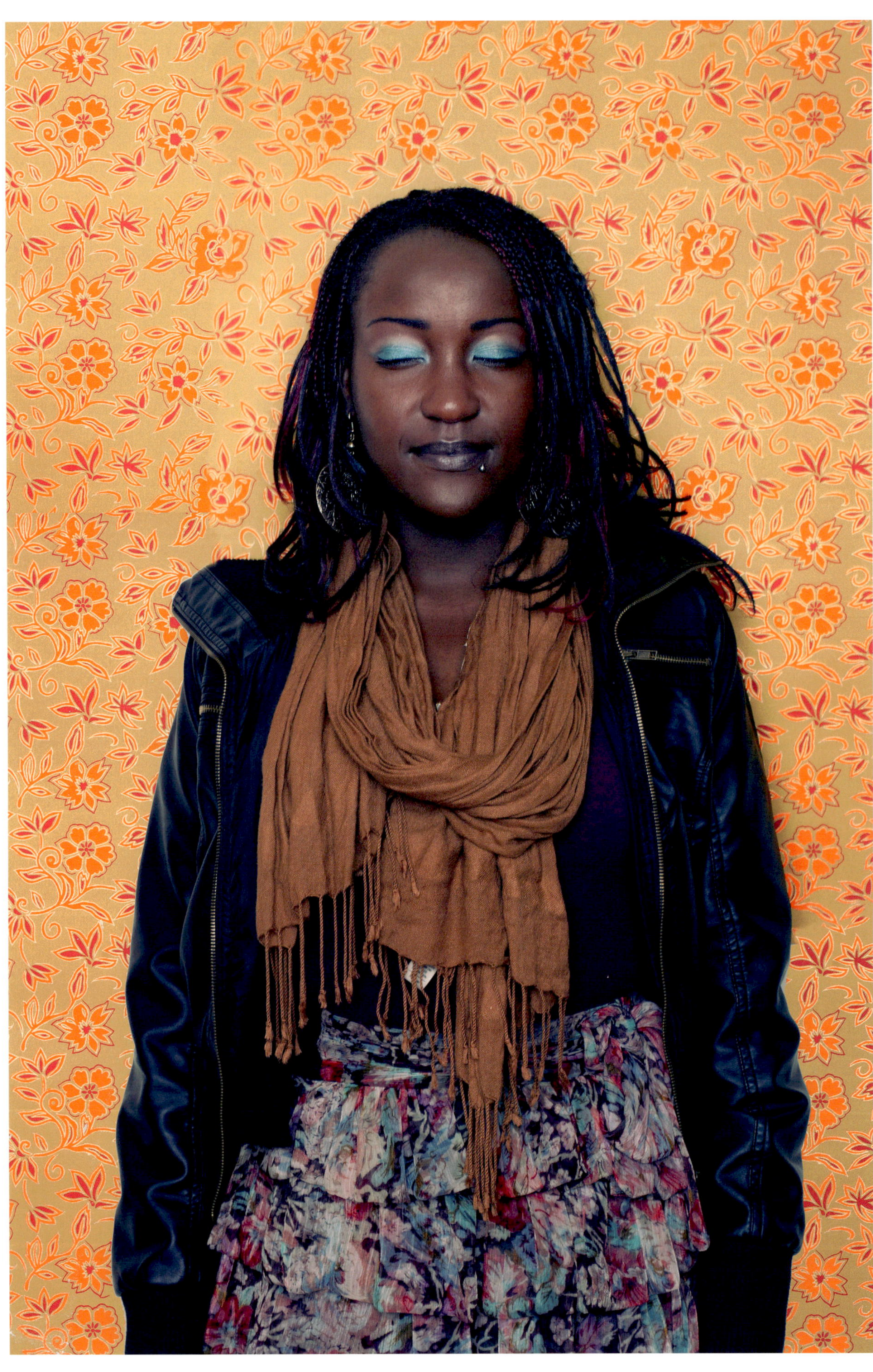

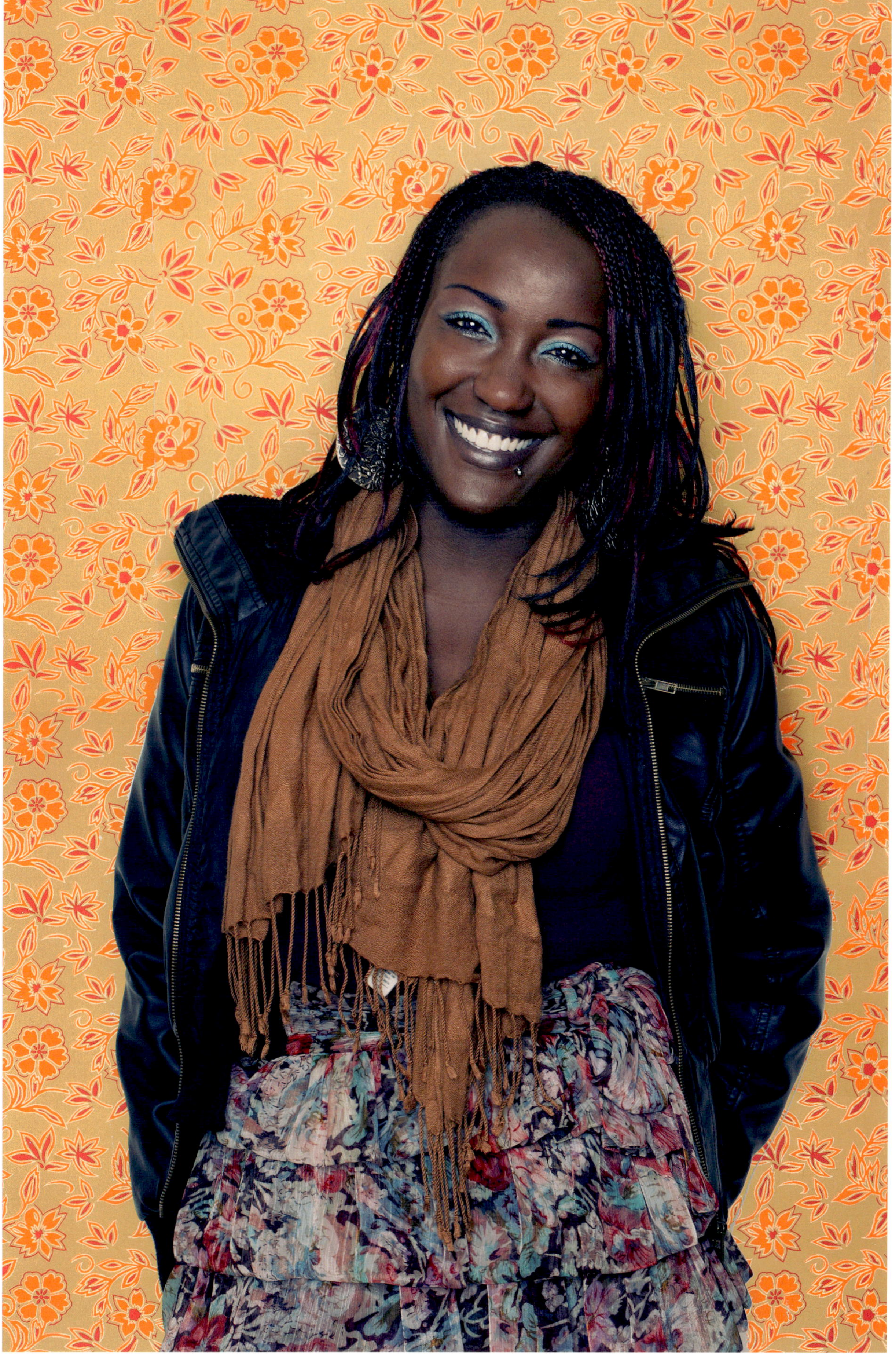

GAY | FACE

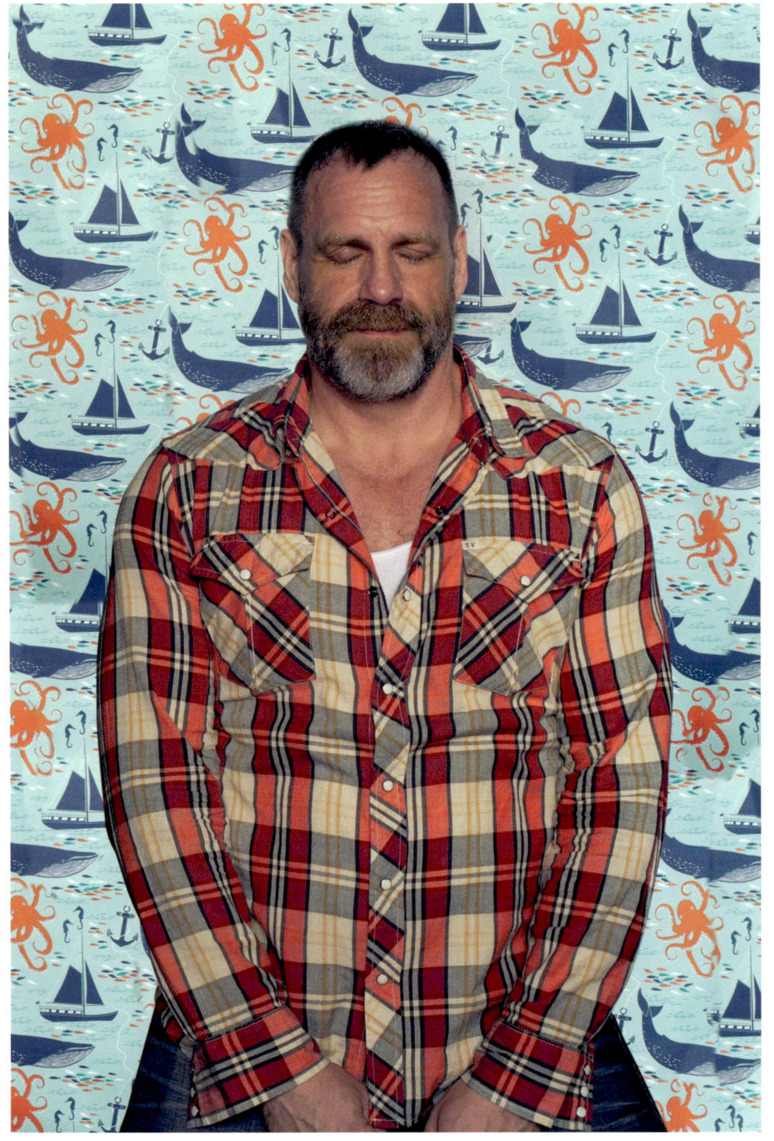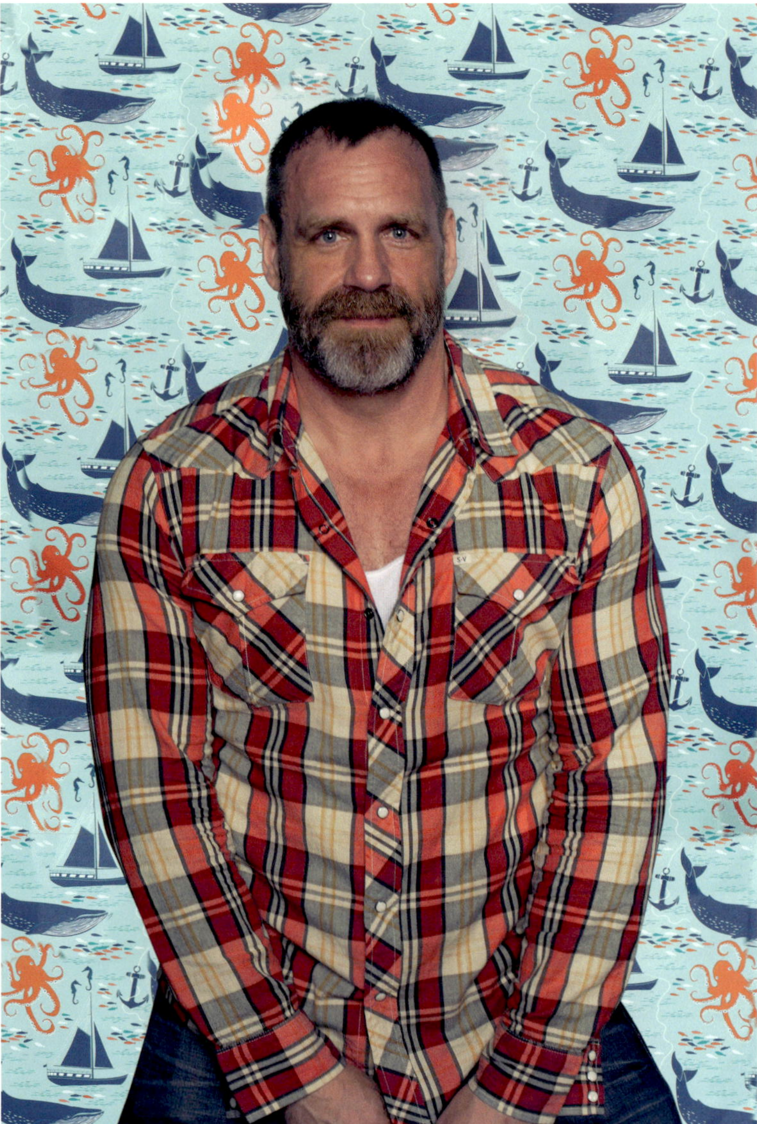

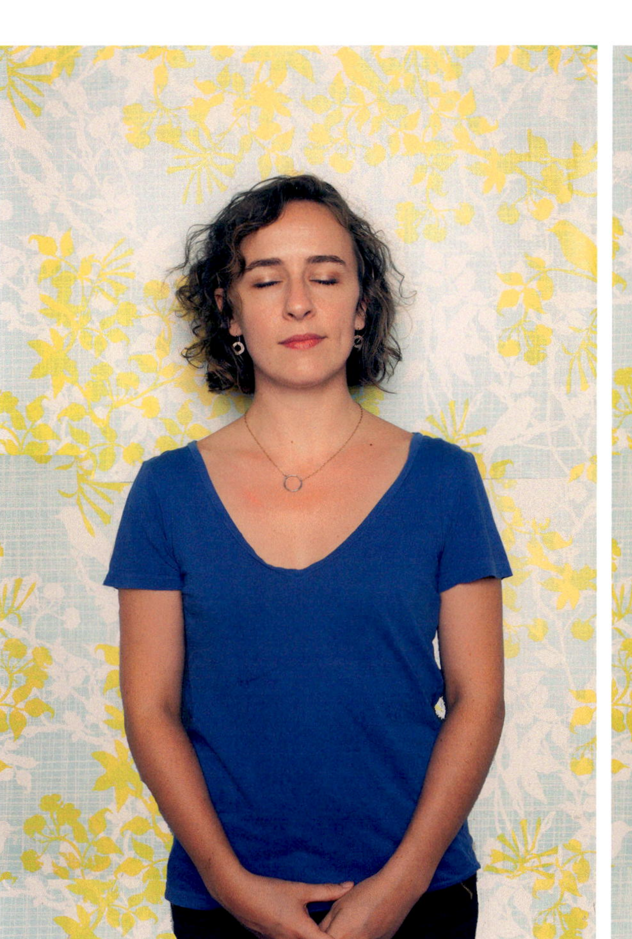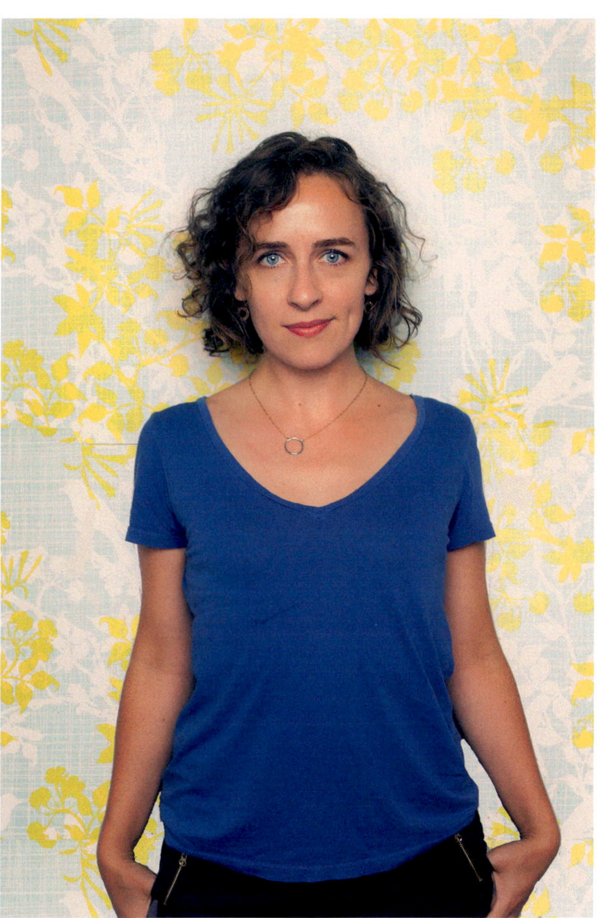

GAY | FACE

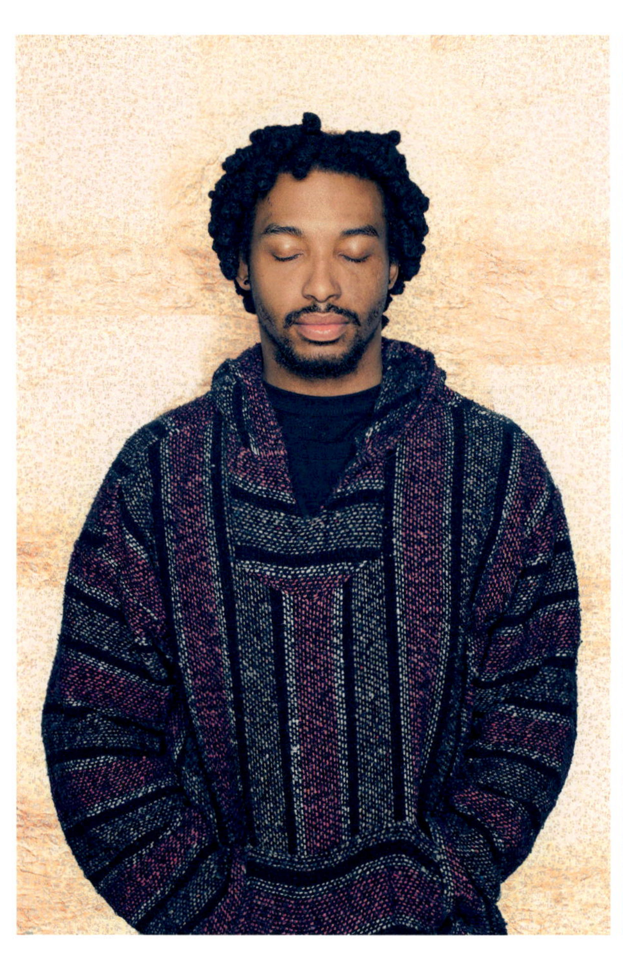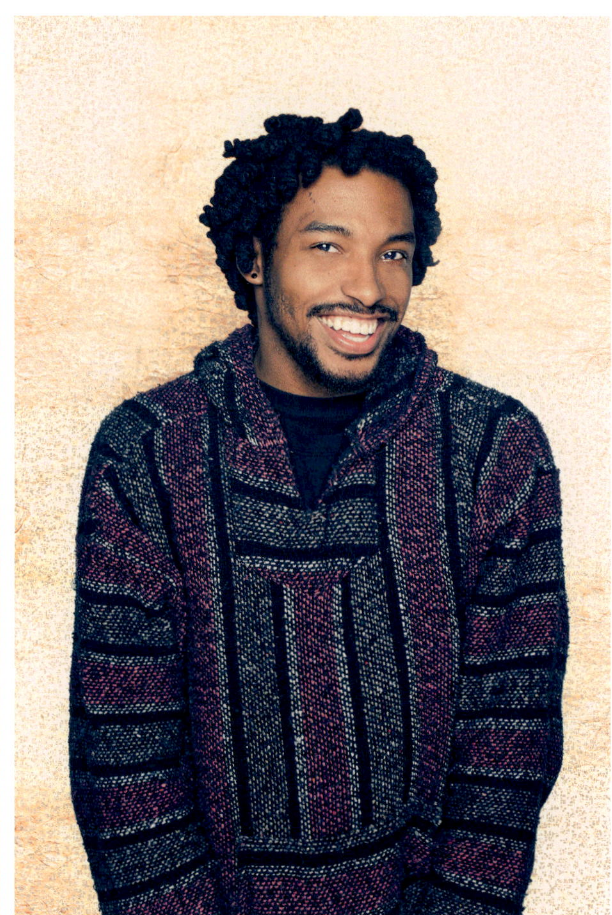

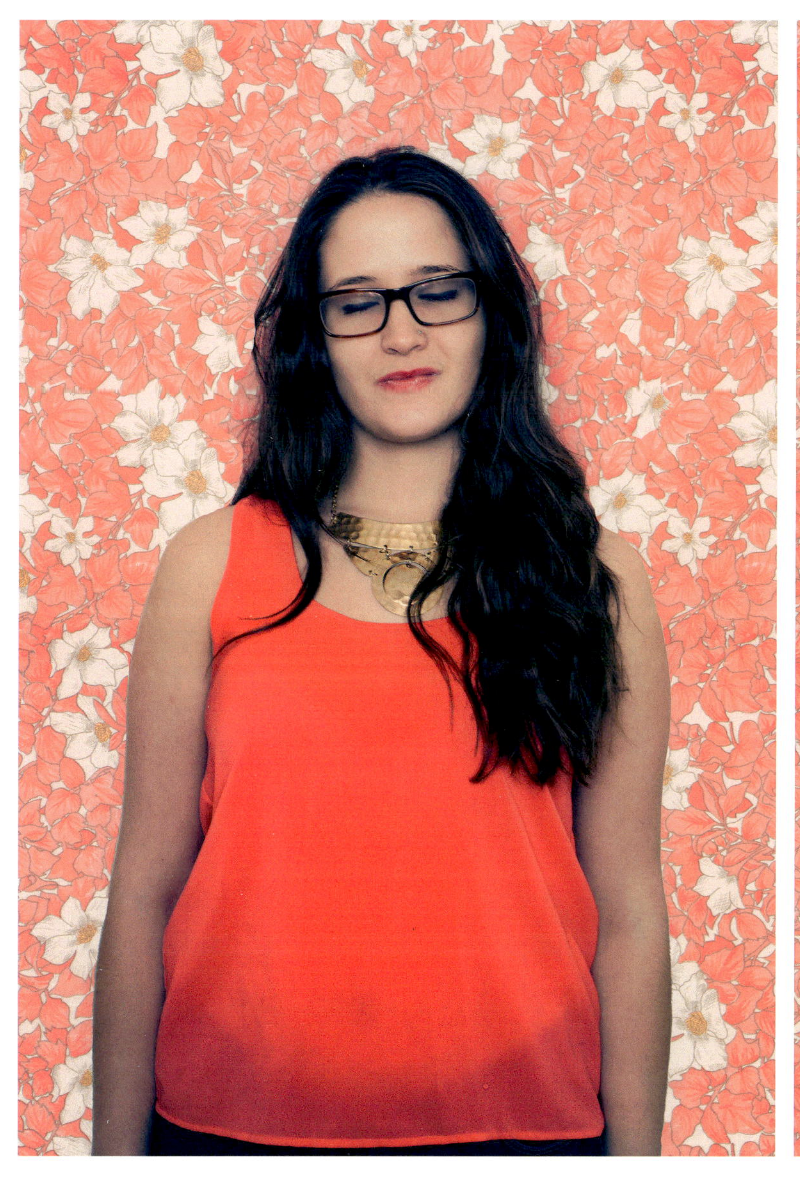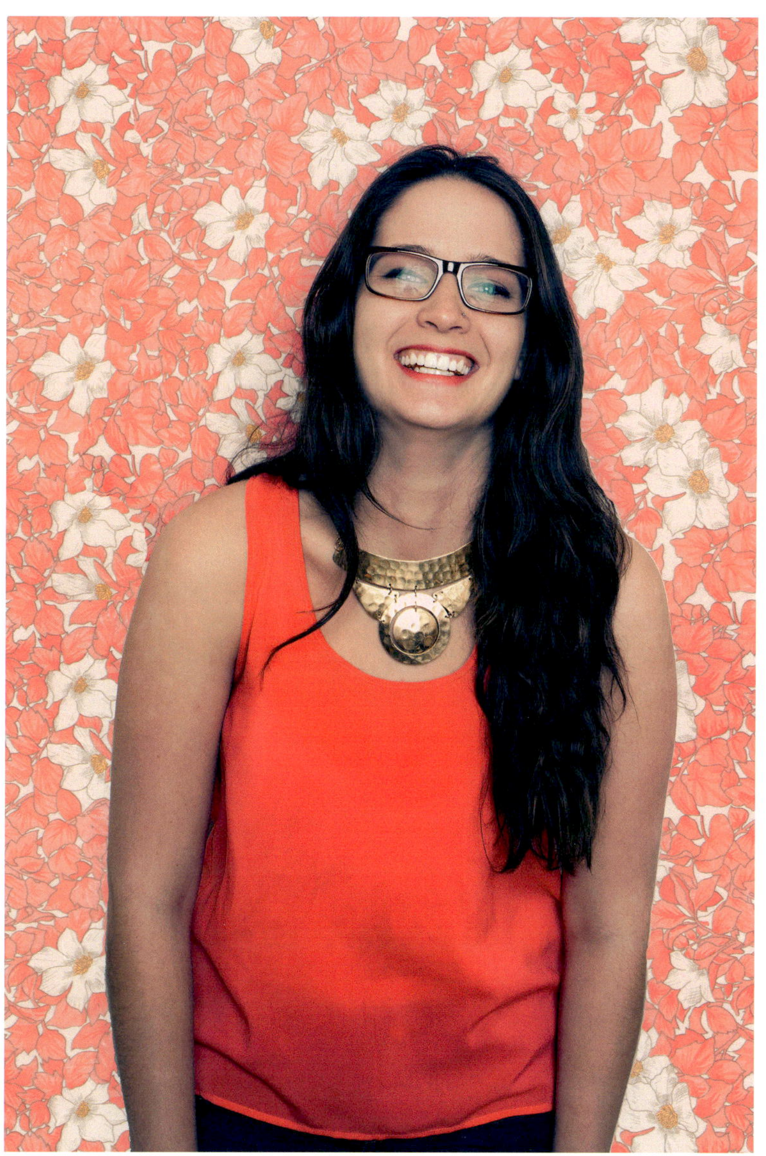

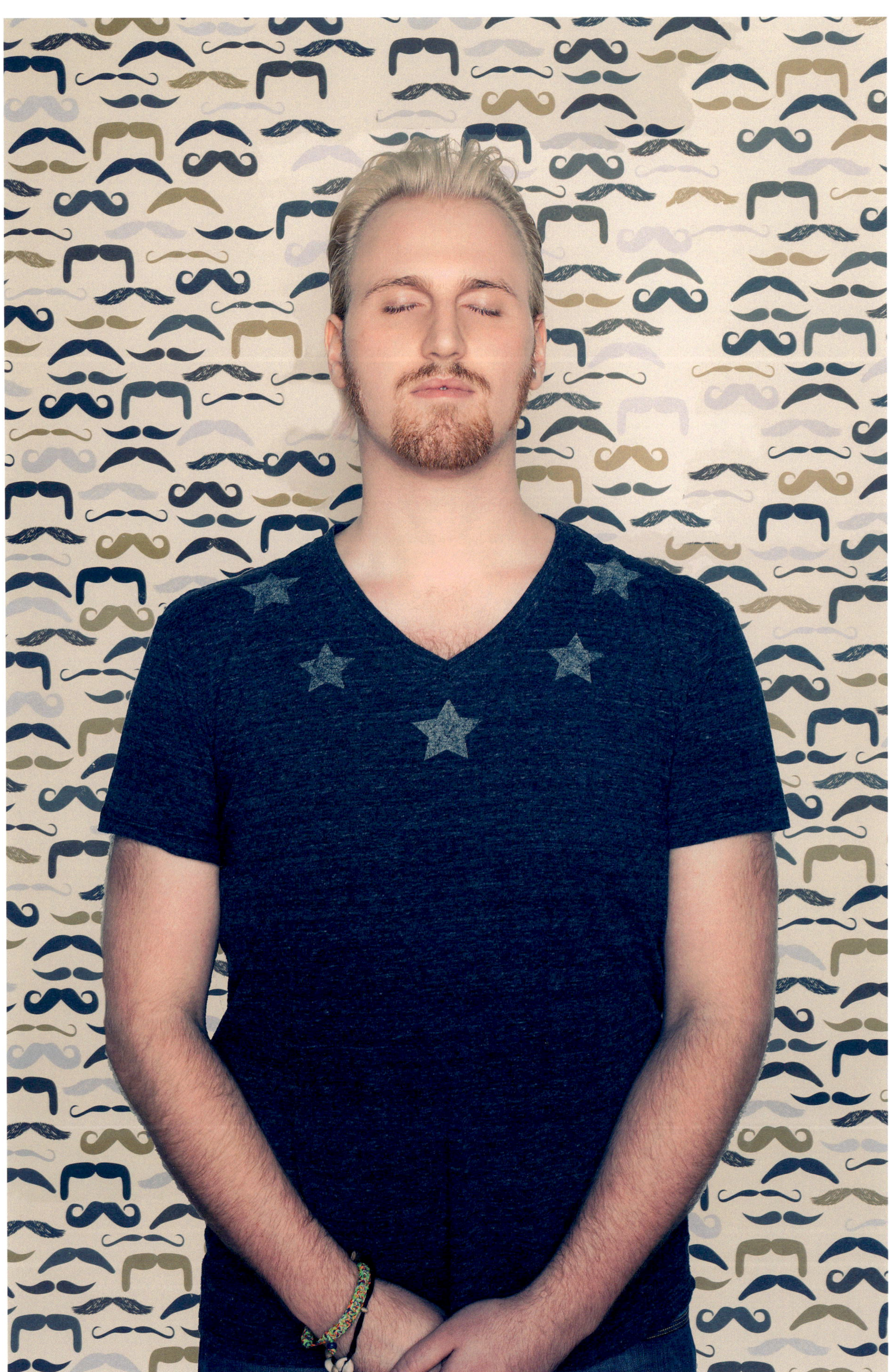

GAY | FACE

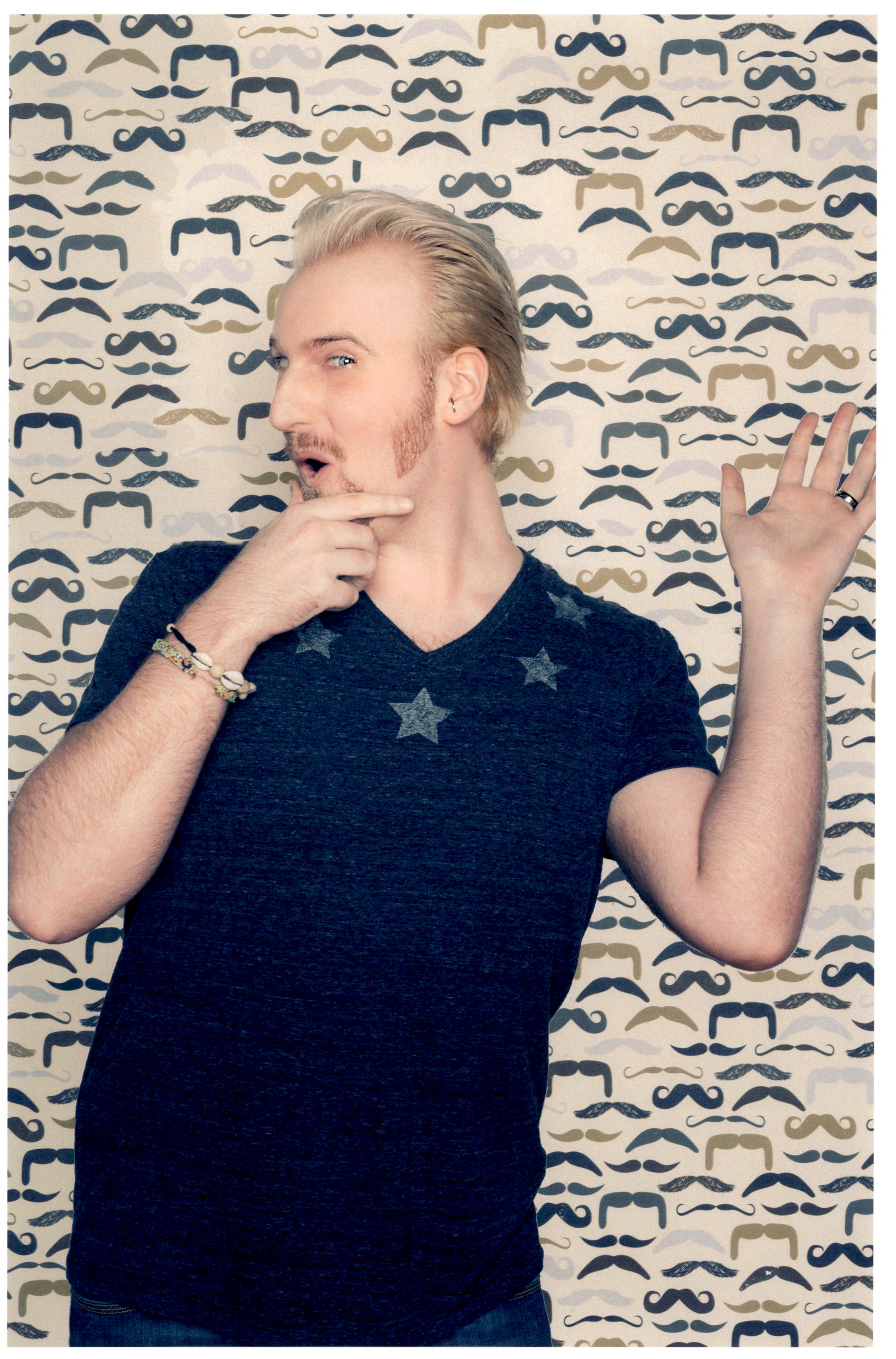

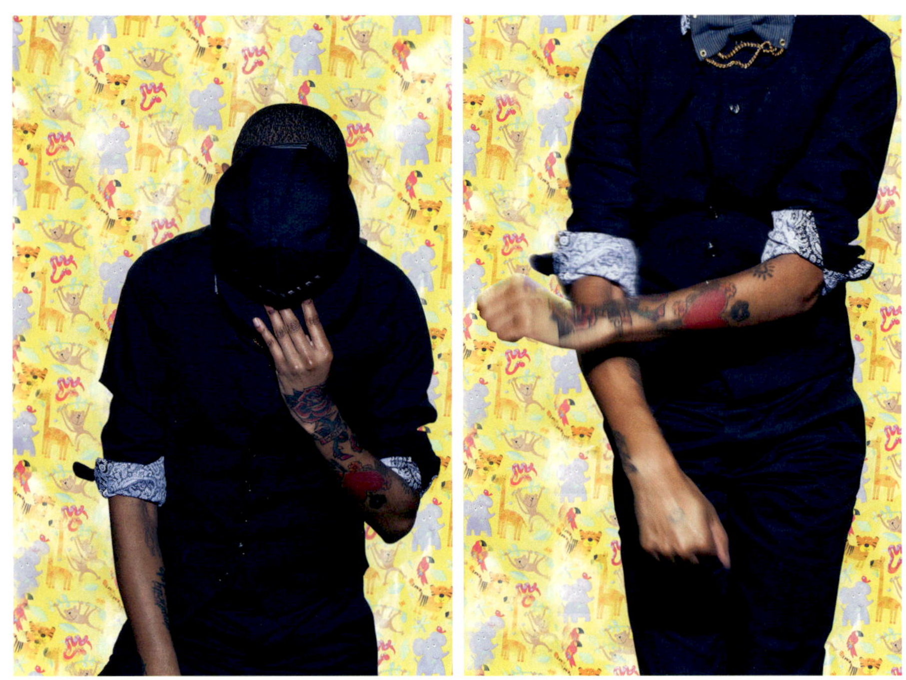

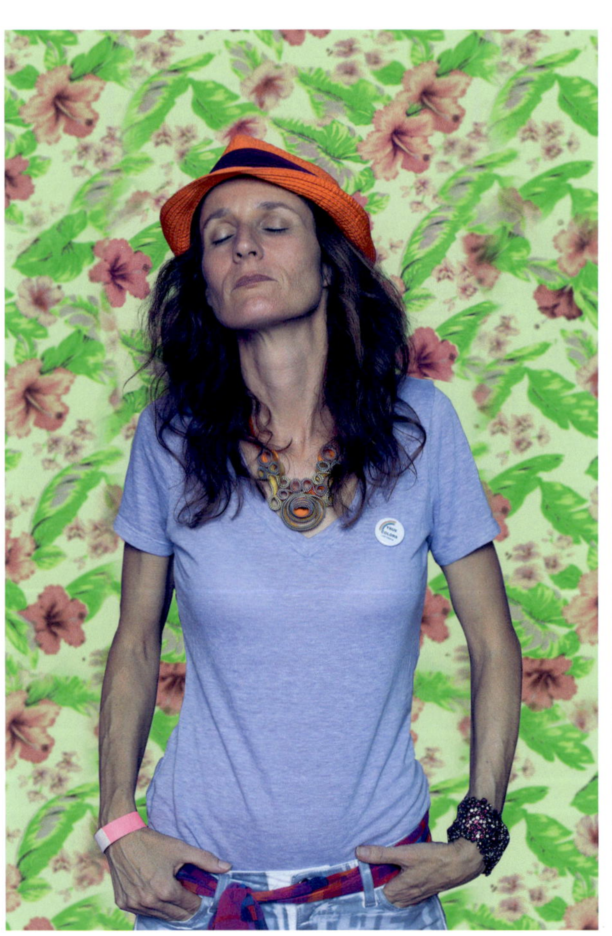

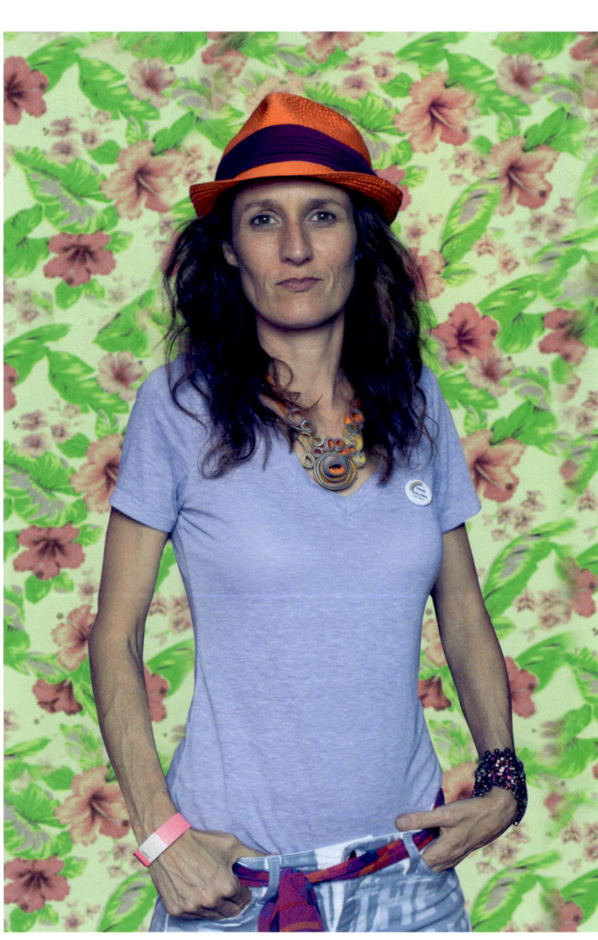

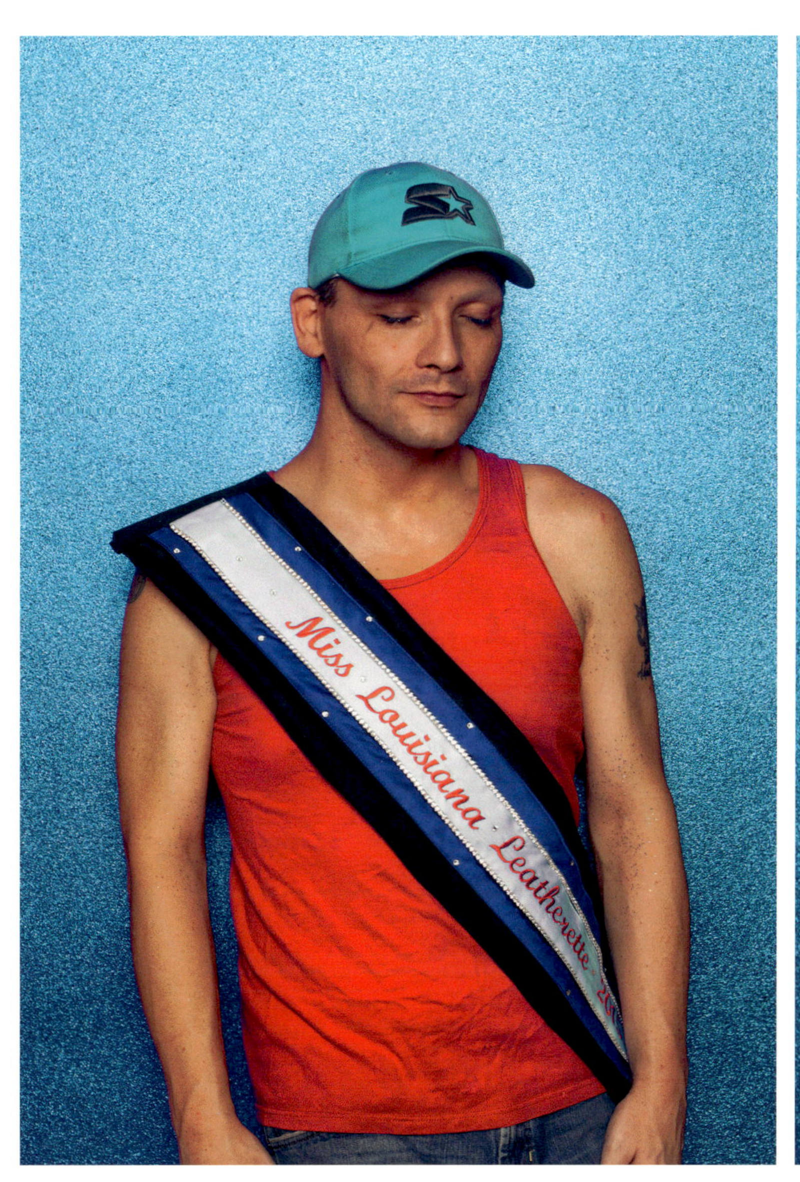

Miss Louisiana Leatherette

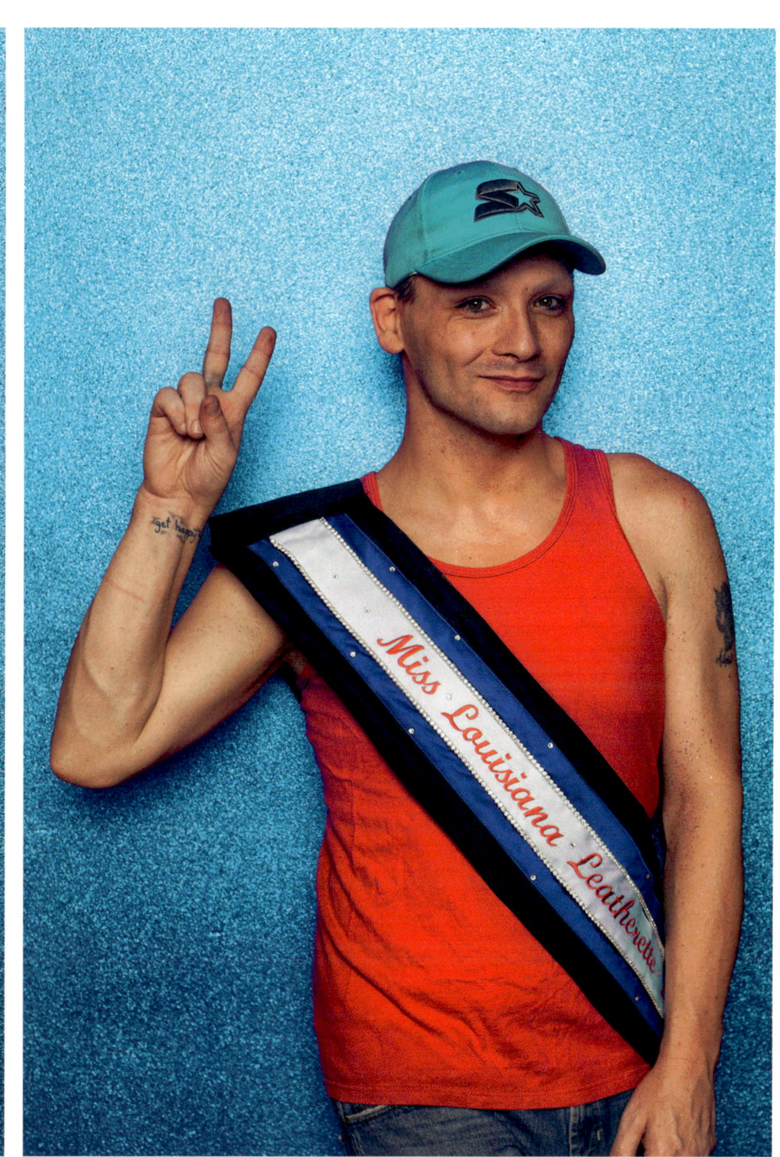

Miss Louisiana Leatherette

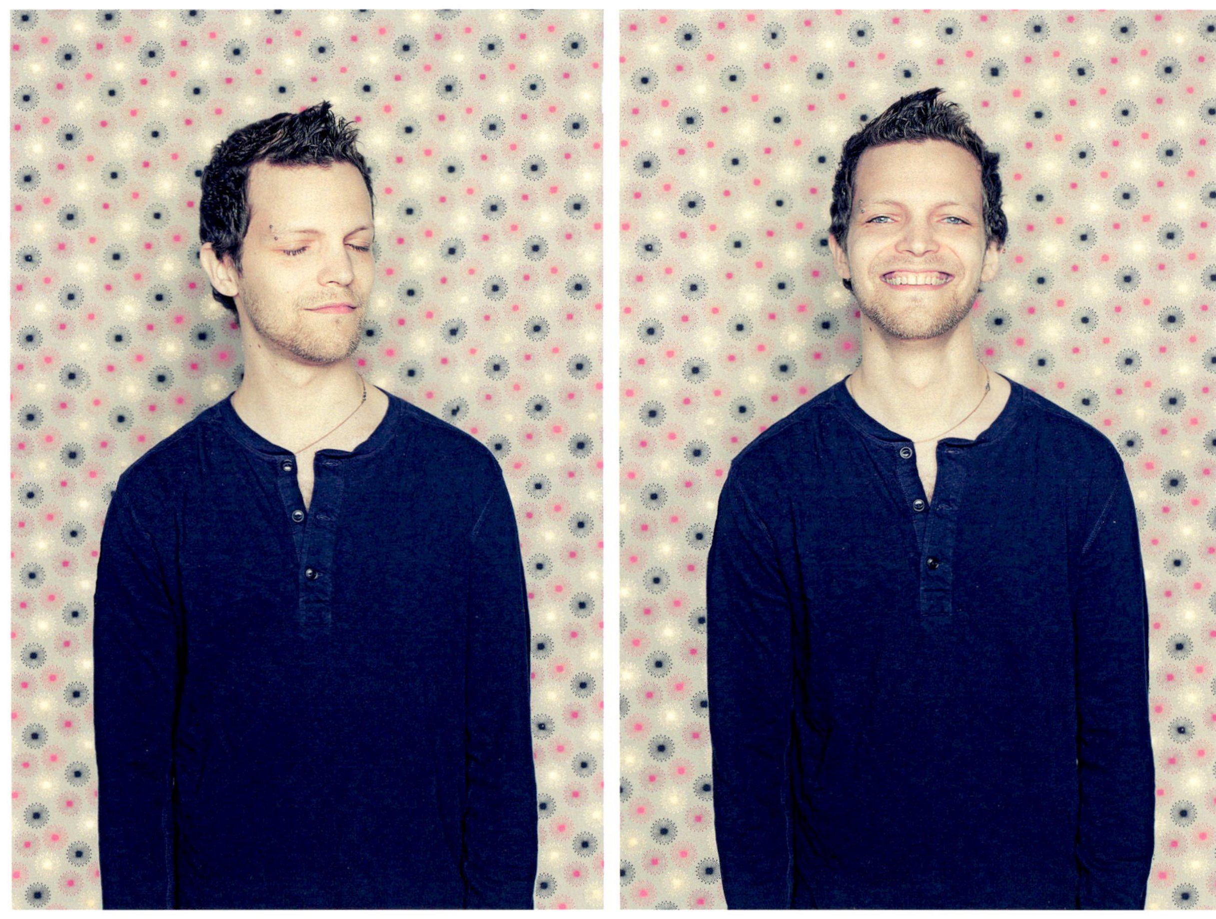

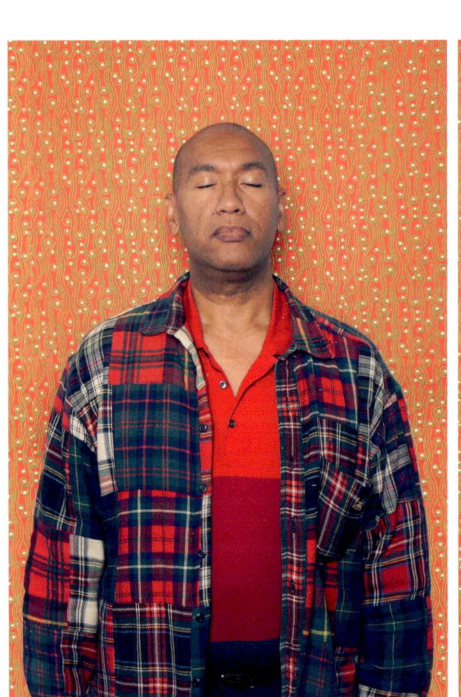

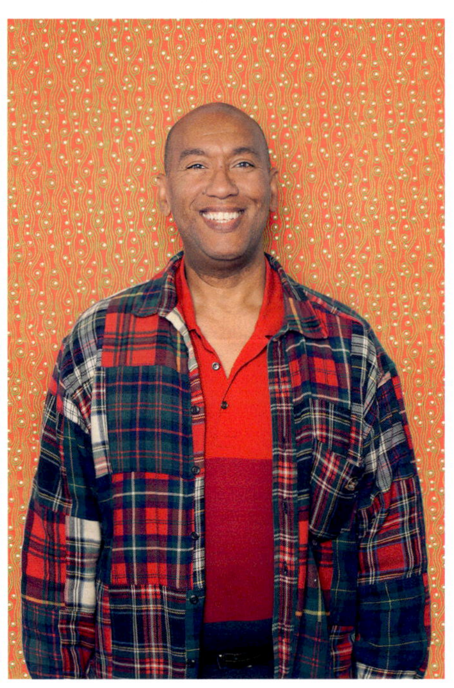

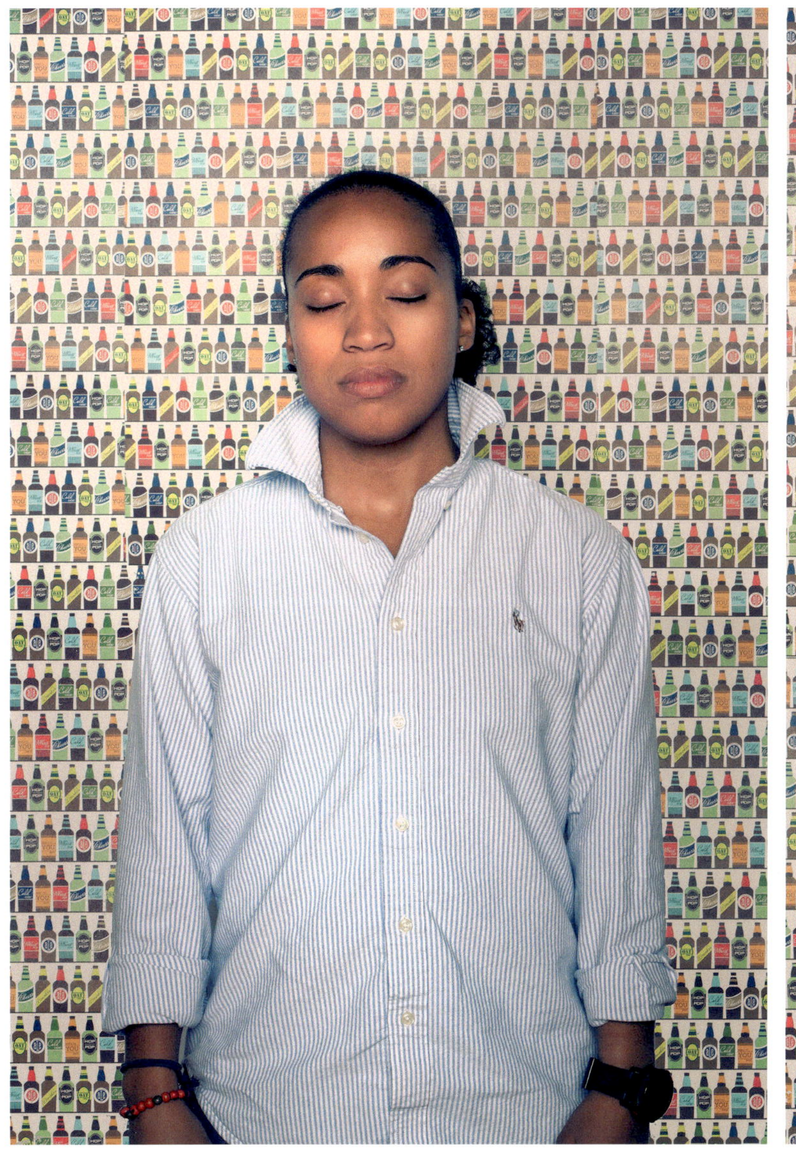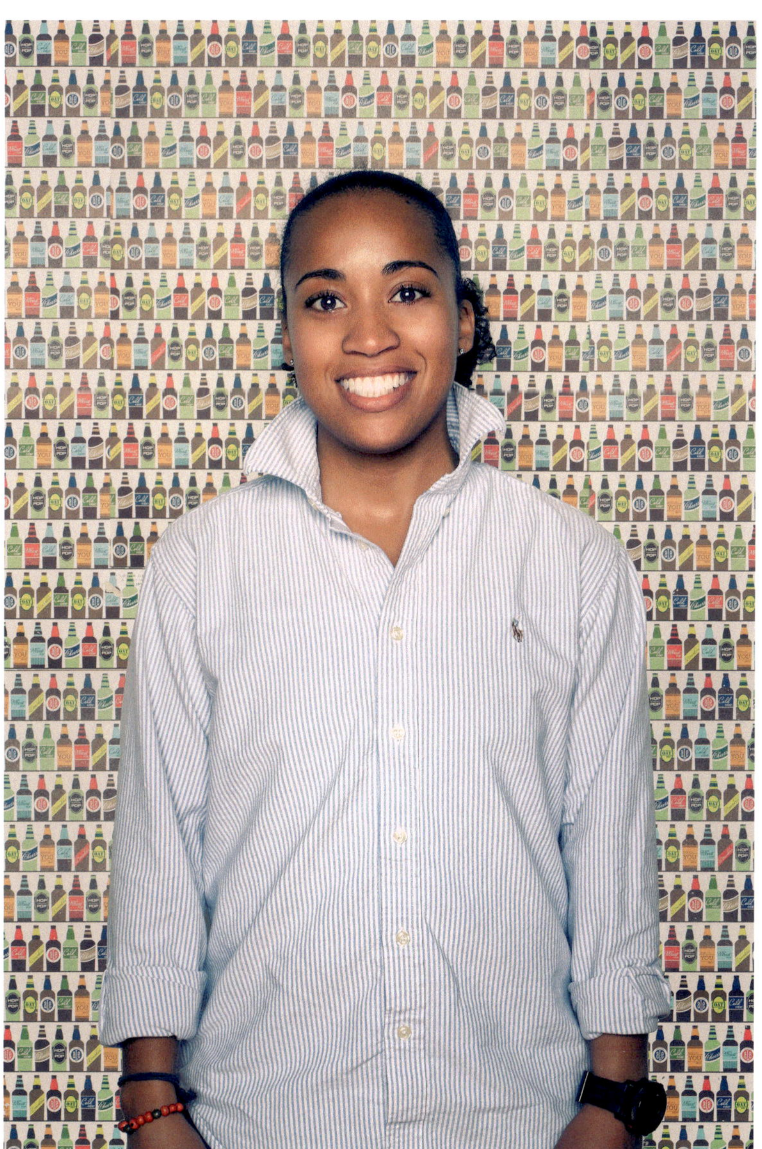

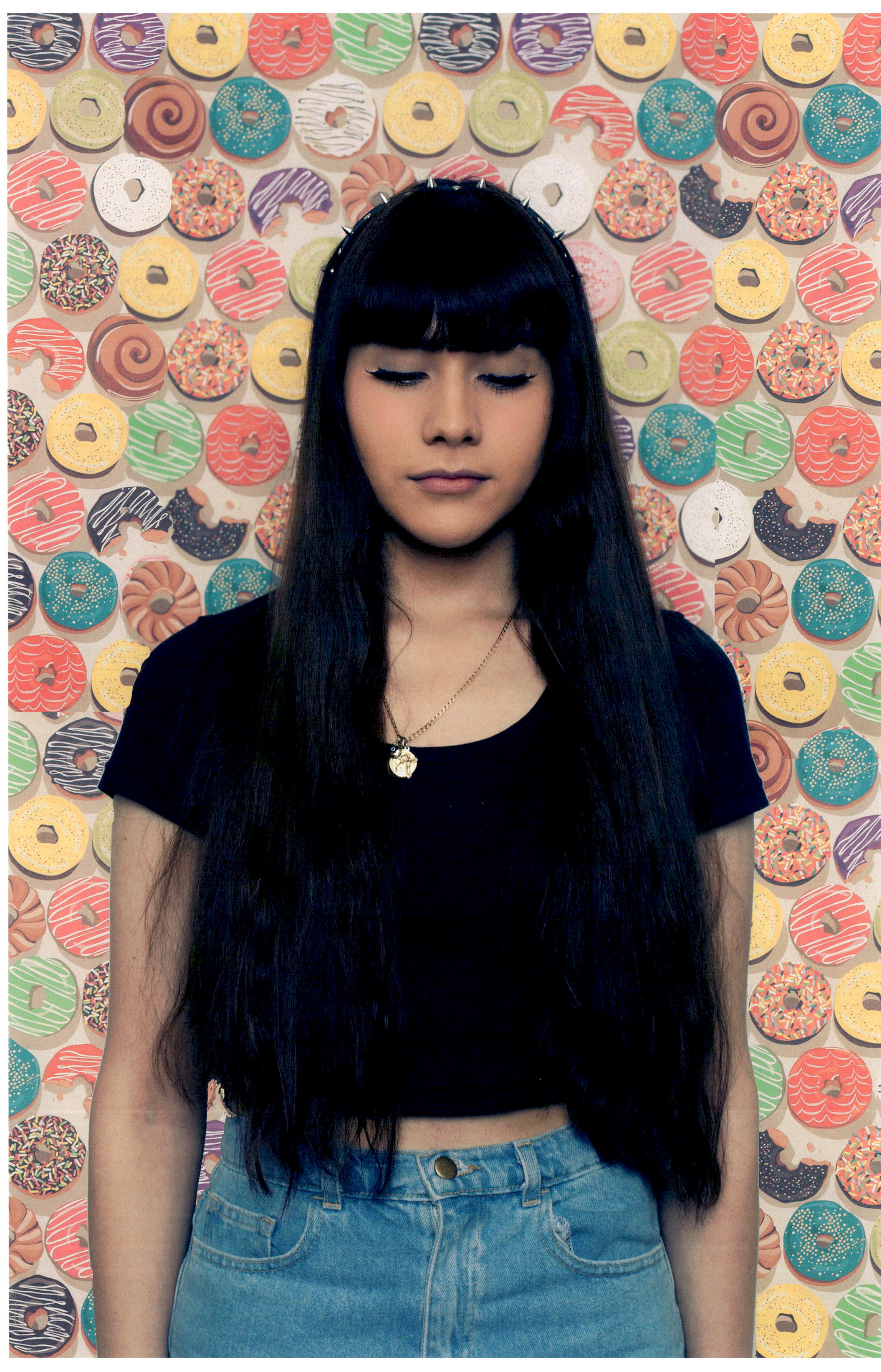

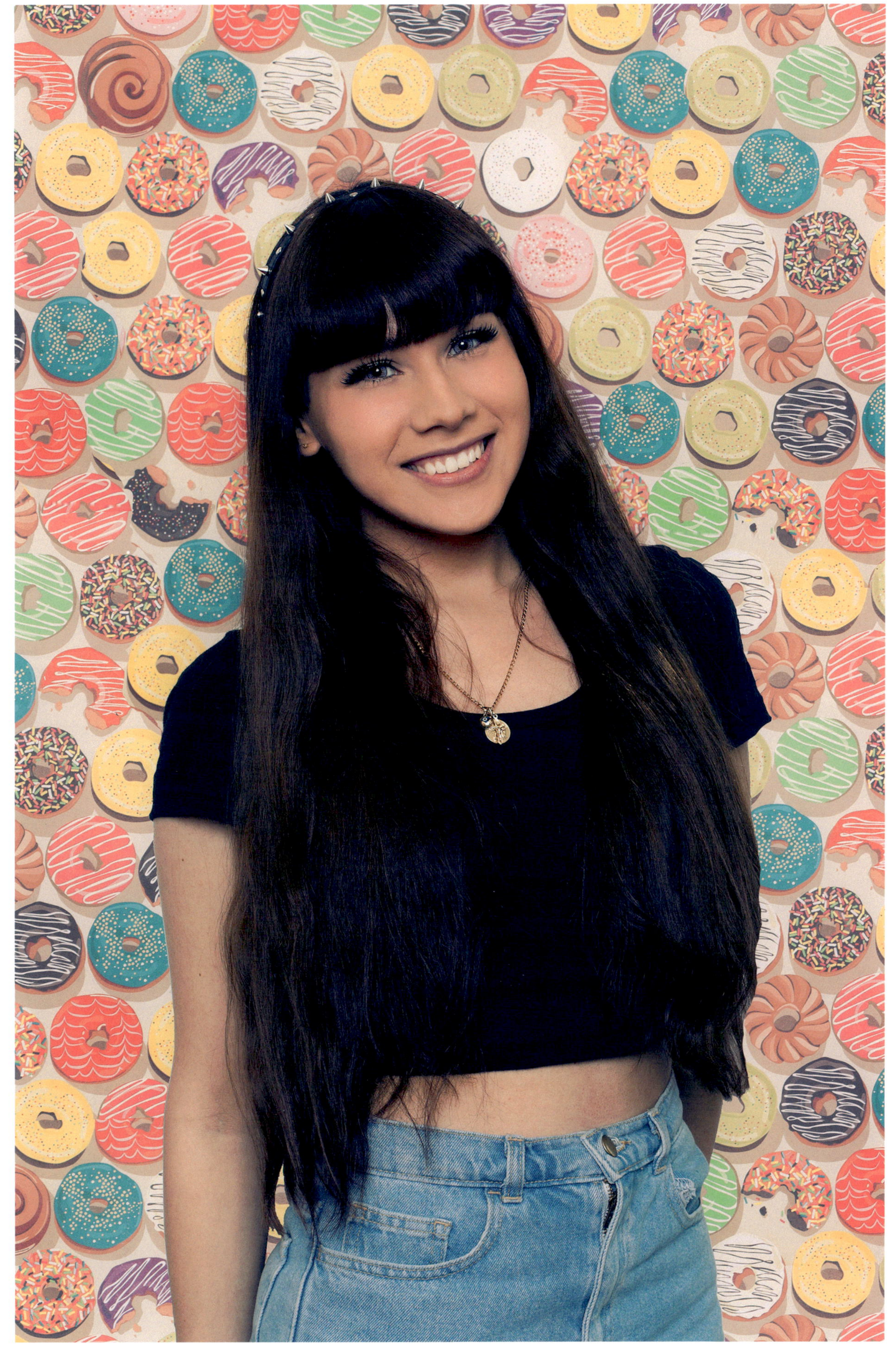

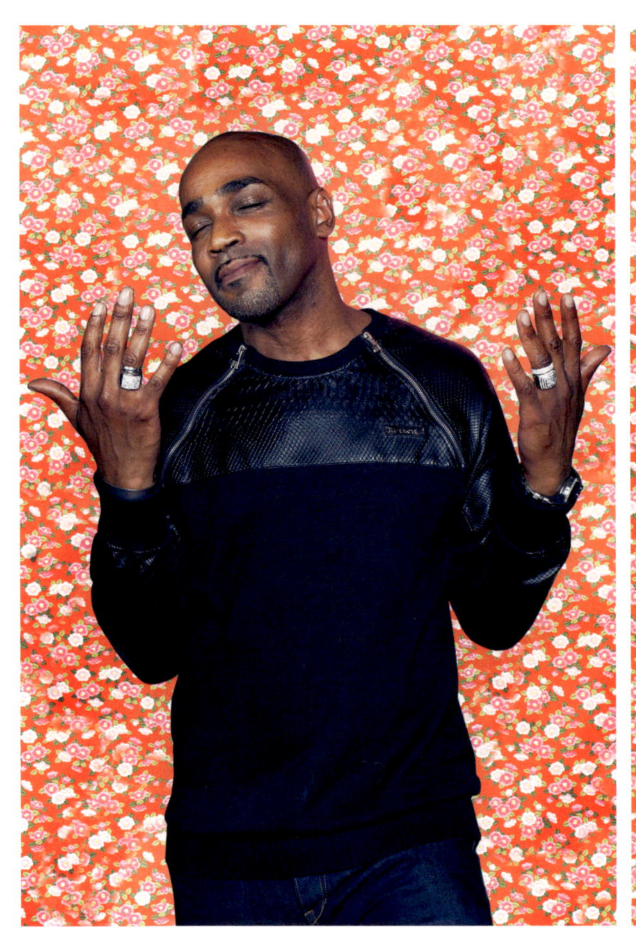
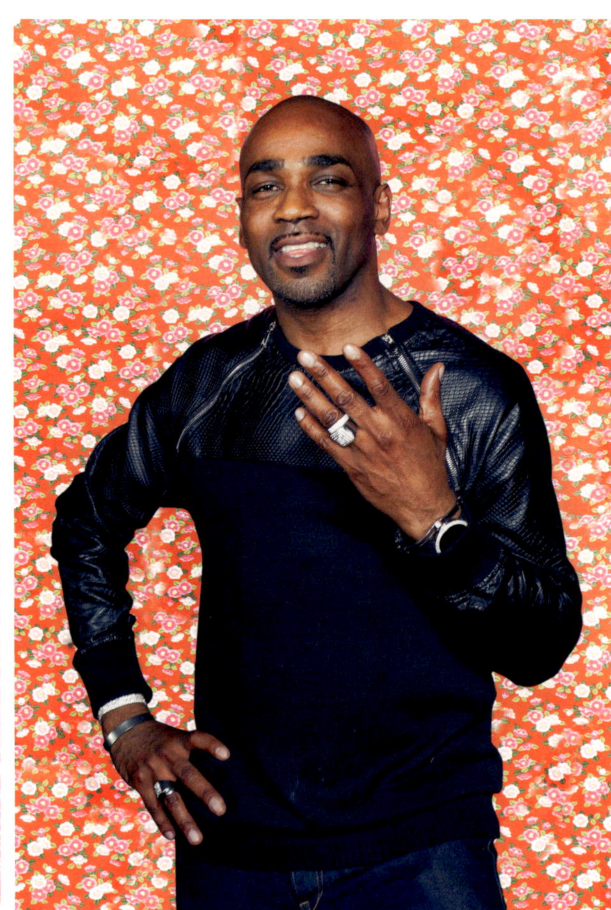
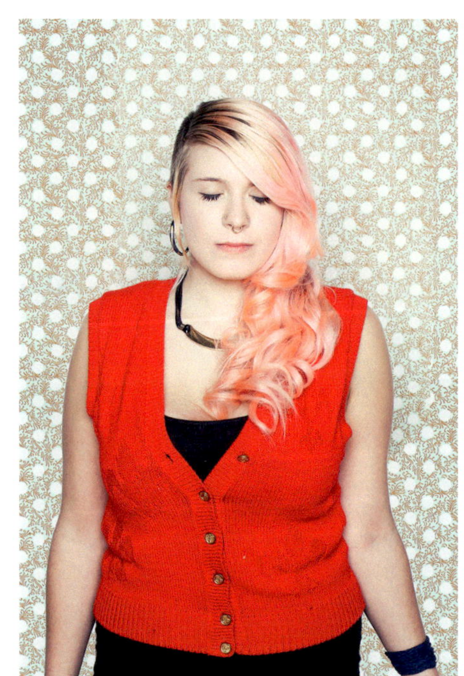
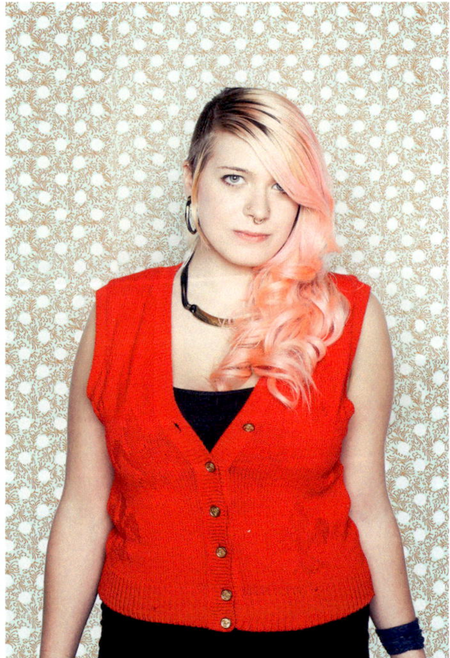

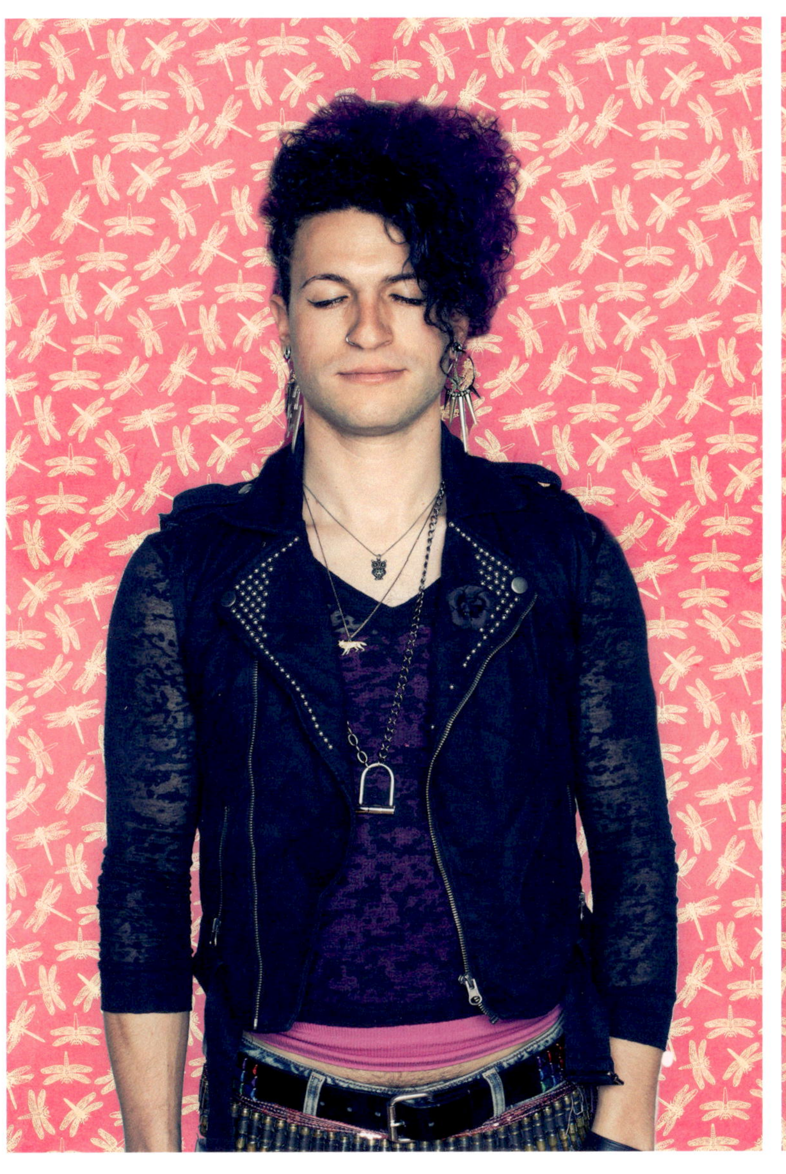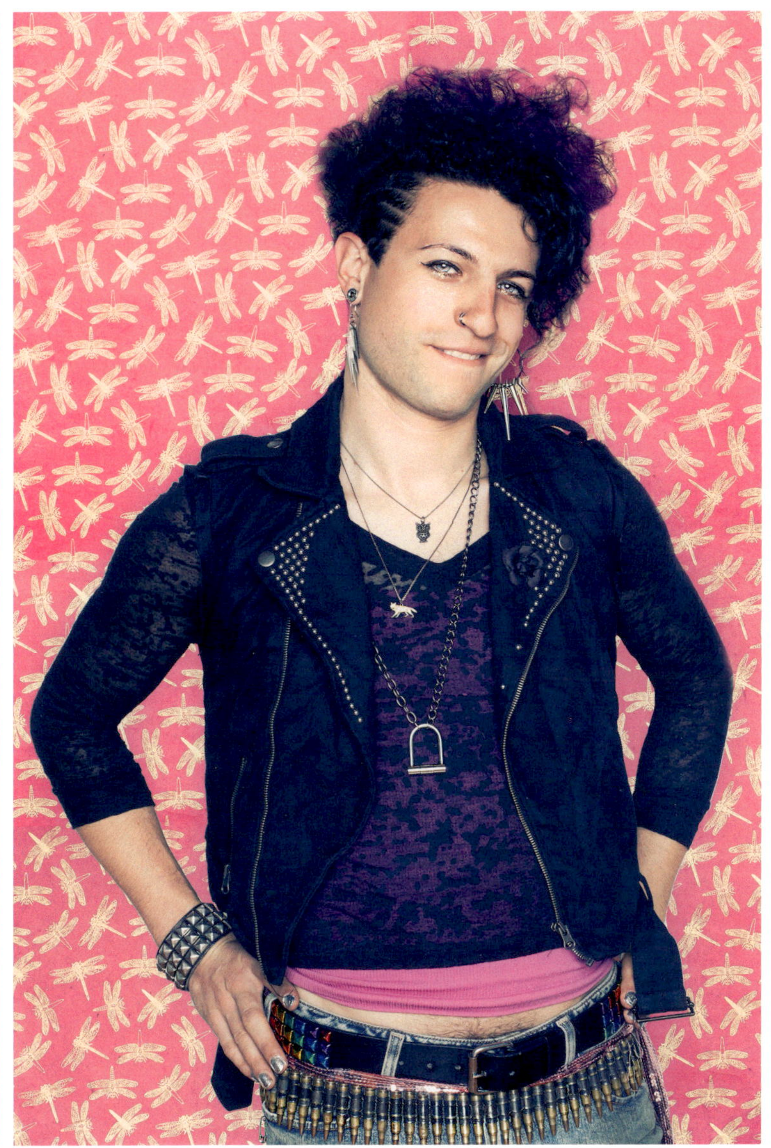

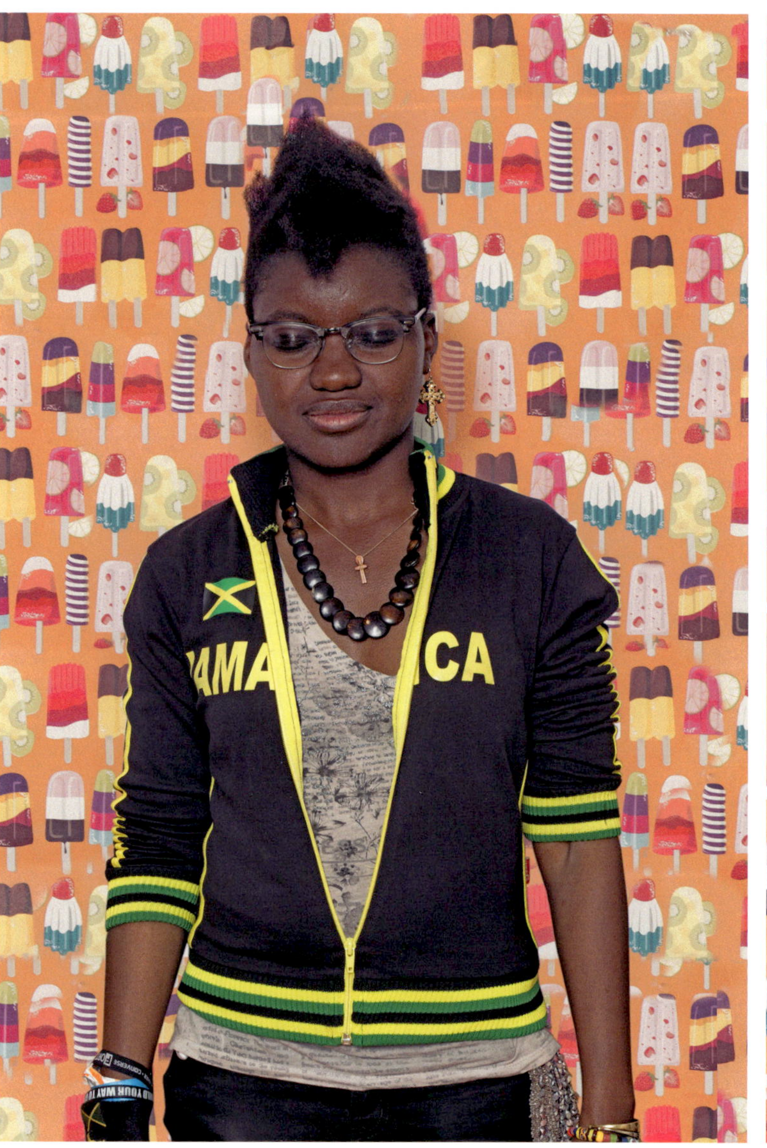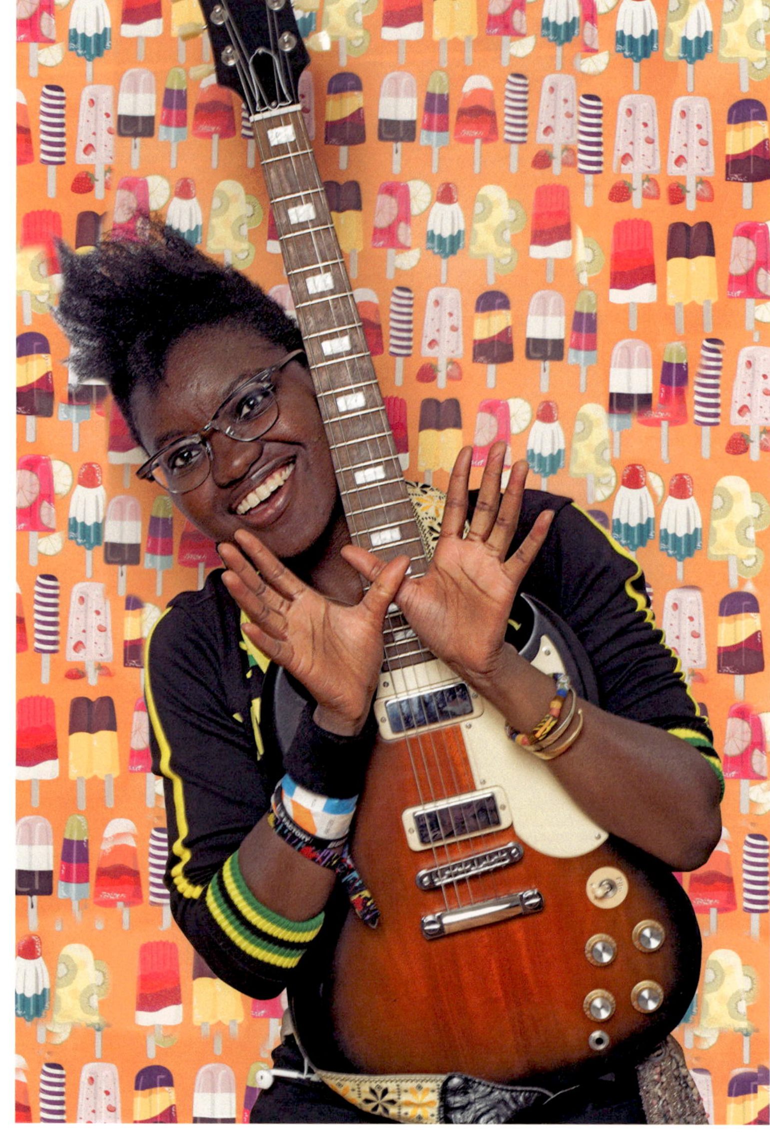

Julie O.
DAKAR, SENEGAL

How would you identify your sexuality?
Queer.

Why did you choose to be a part of this project?
I like that there is a range of LGBTQ+ individuals represented, which shows how we're such a huge spectrum of human expression.

What do you think of your portrait?
It was a fun experience and the portrait is very different portrait from others I've taken. It shows a lot of who I was at the time the photo was taken.

Describe your coming out. Are you coming out in some way by participating in this project?
My coming out is—and continues to be—complicated. I think I'm still coming out, whether it's to new people or recognizing new aspects of my identity and the community around me. Mainstream society tends to box you in, so if you don't fit into that box, your coming out is probably ongoing. At least that's how I feel about my coming out experiences.

If you could change one thing about mainstream society to improve the lives of LGBTQ+ people, what would it be?
Breaking down the stereotypes that being gay is just a "choice" or a "lifestyle," and understanding that even though we're a community, we're all very different.

Describe how this project has effected you, both personally and as a member of the LGBTQ+ community as a whole.
This project is a really impressive and unique biography of a huge community. Sometimes this community can be hidden and underrepresented, so it's inspiring to see so many different LGBTQ+ people in one project.

What advice have you been given by another LGBTQ+ person, or that you might offer someone?
The advice I would offer to someone else is to live your life as openly as you feel comfortable with. There is no timeline for when or how "out" you have to be; who you have to tell about yourself, or how you have to act or present. Express yourself in ways that feel true and authentic to yourself. Labels can be constricting. Queerness is like living in the future: you might have to create things for yourself that are not already there.

Who are your LGBTQ+ role models?
Janelle Monáe.

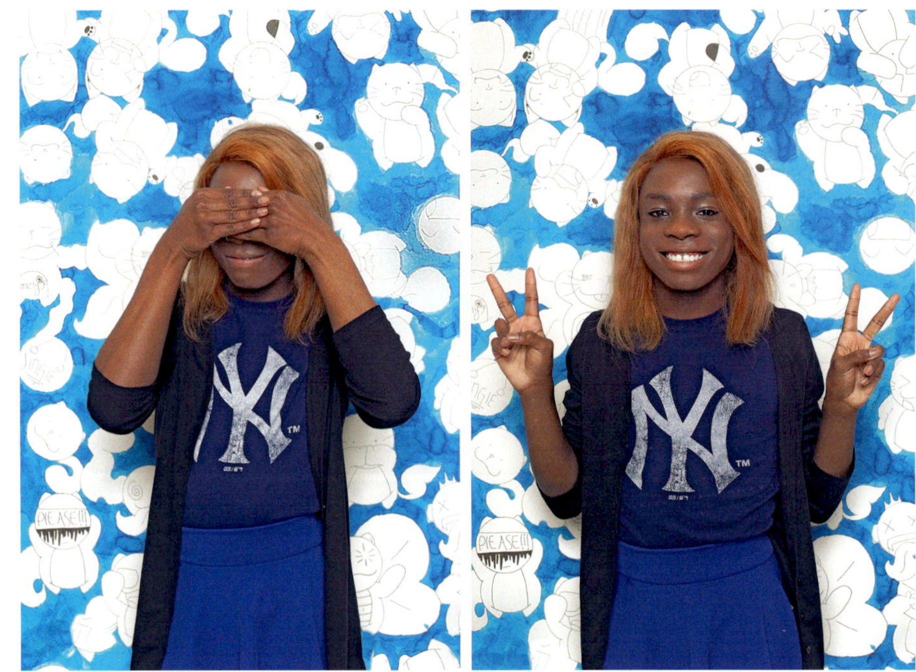

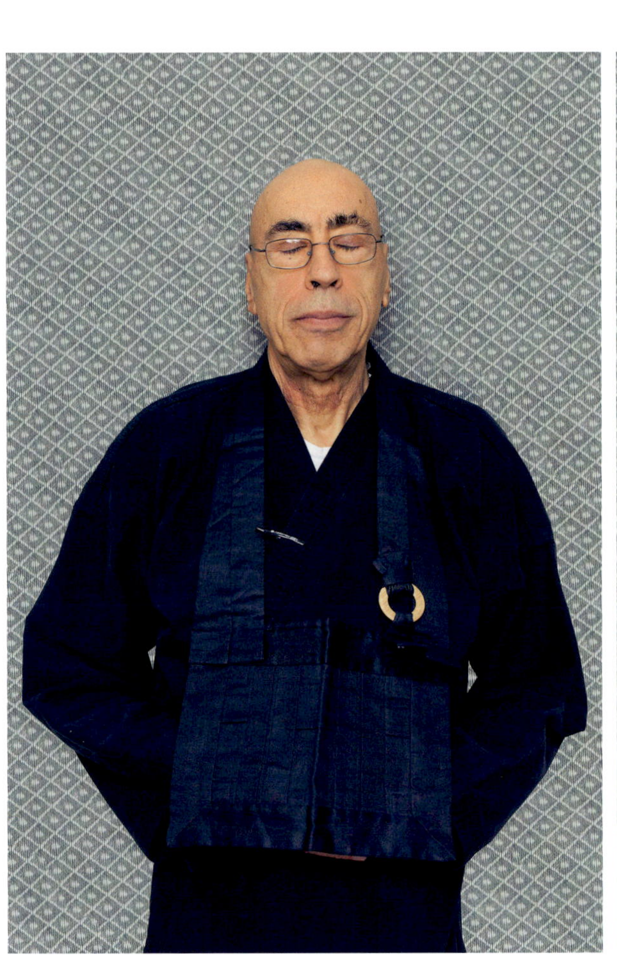

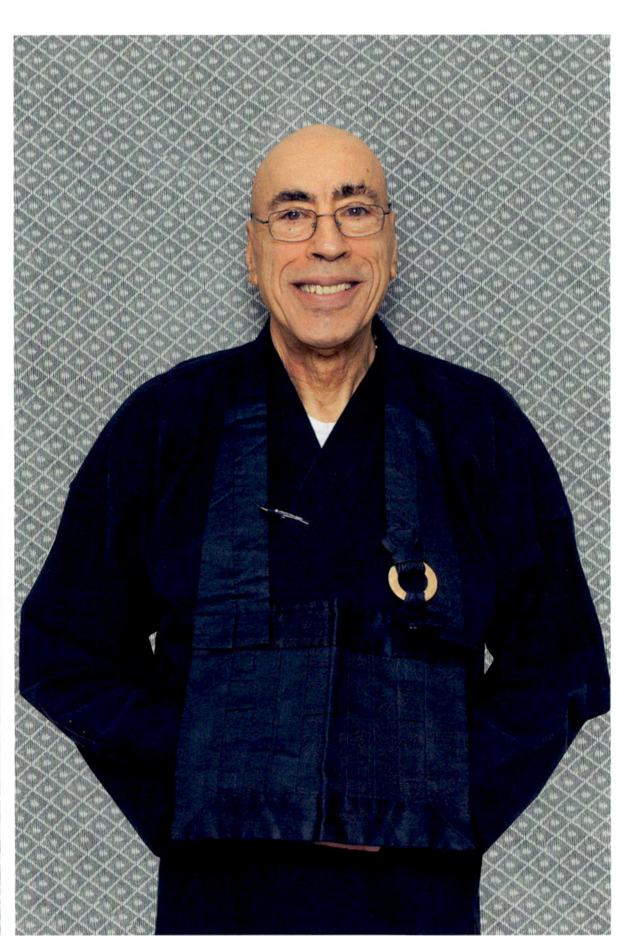

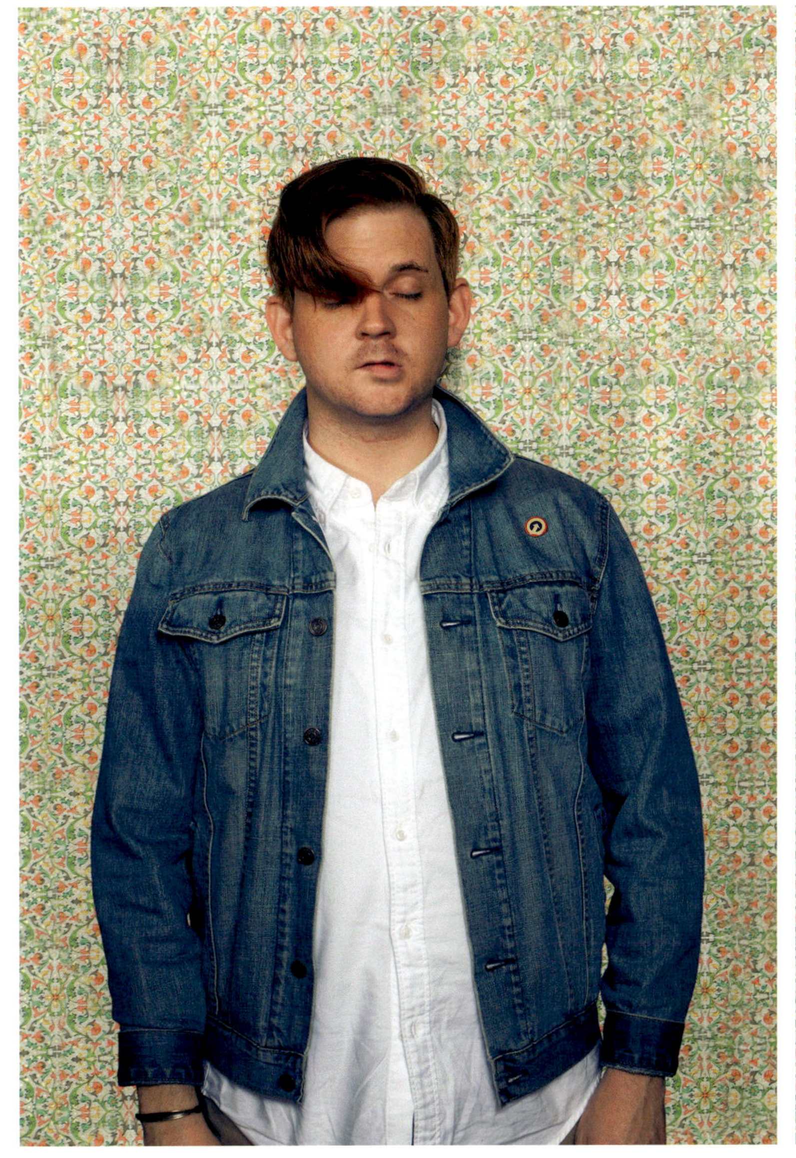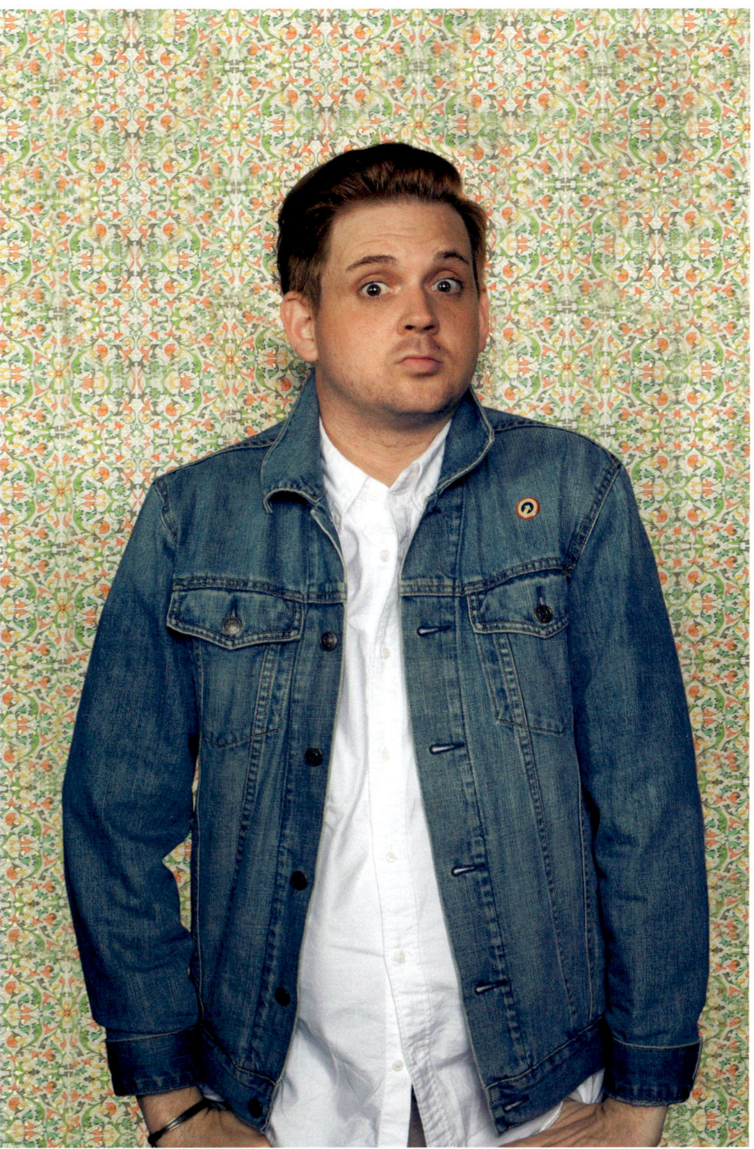

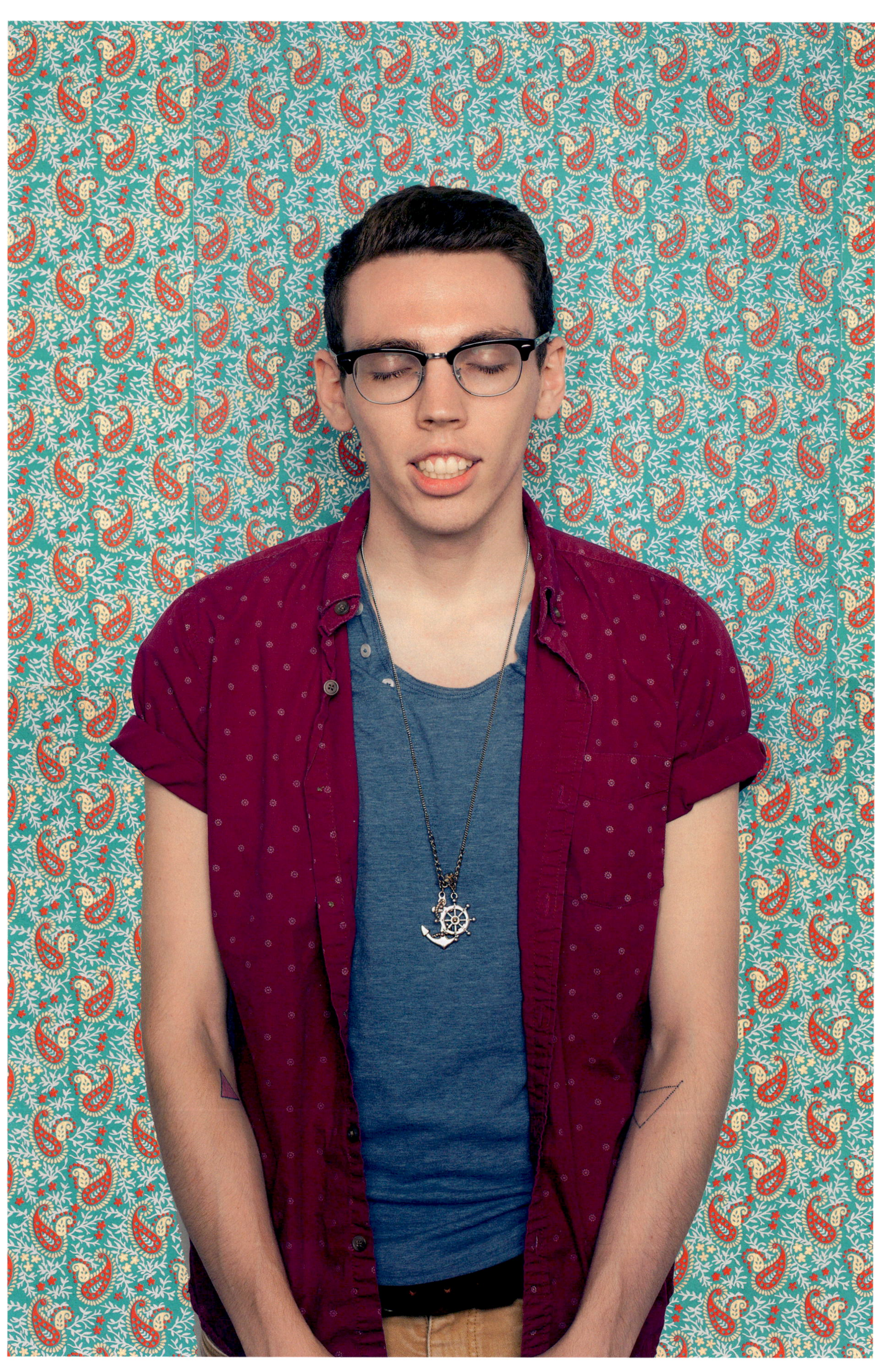

GAY | FACE

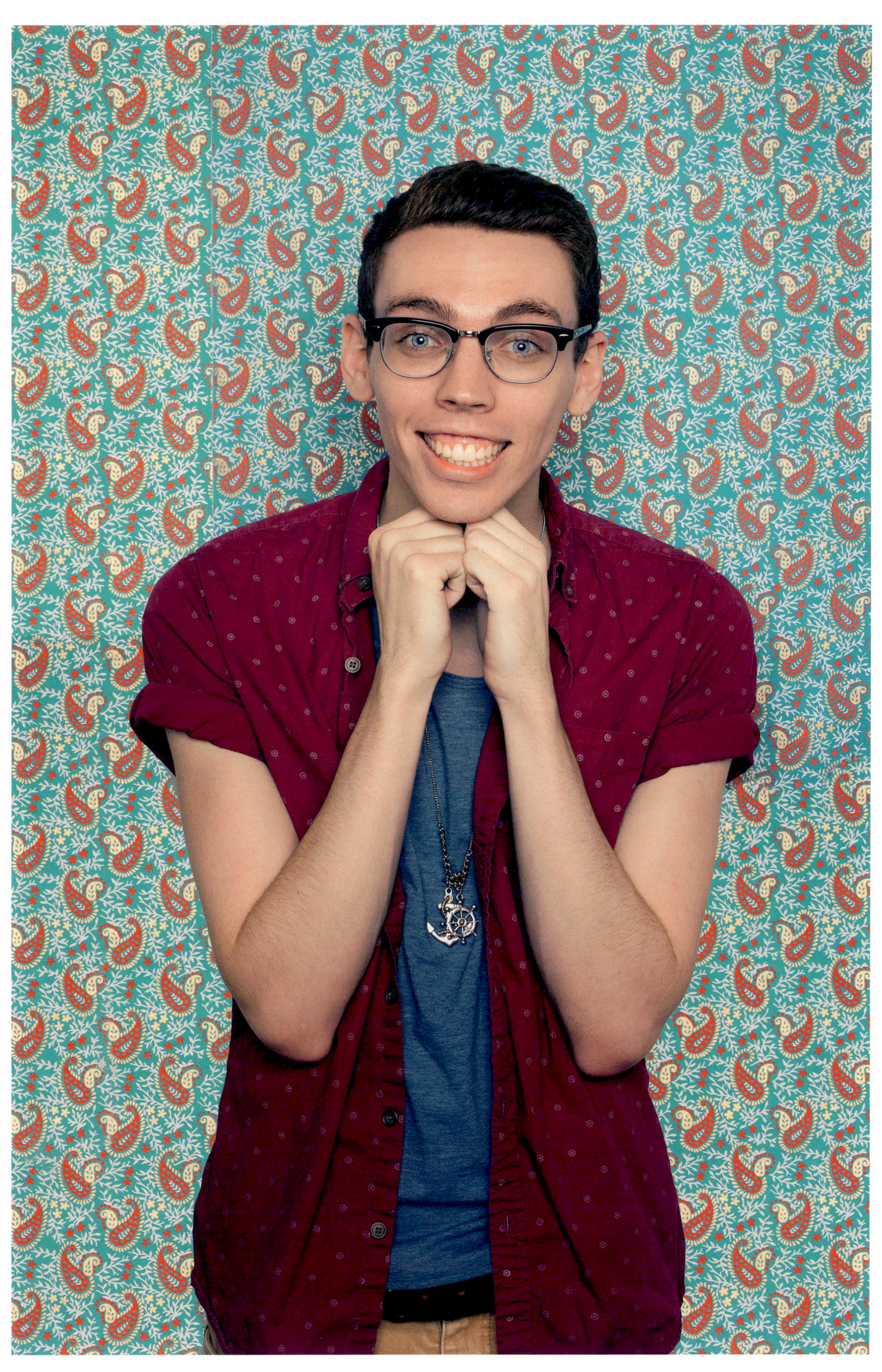

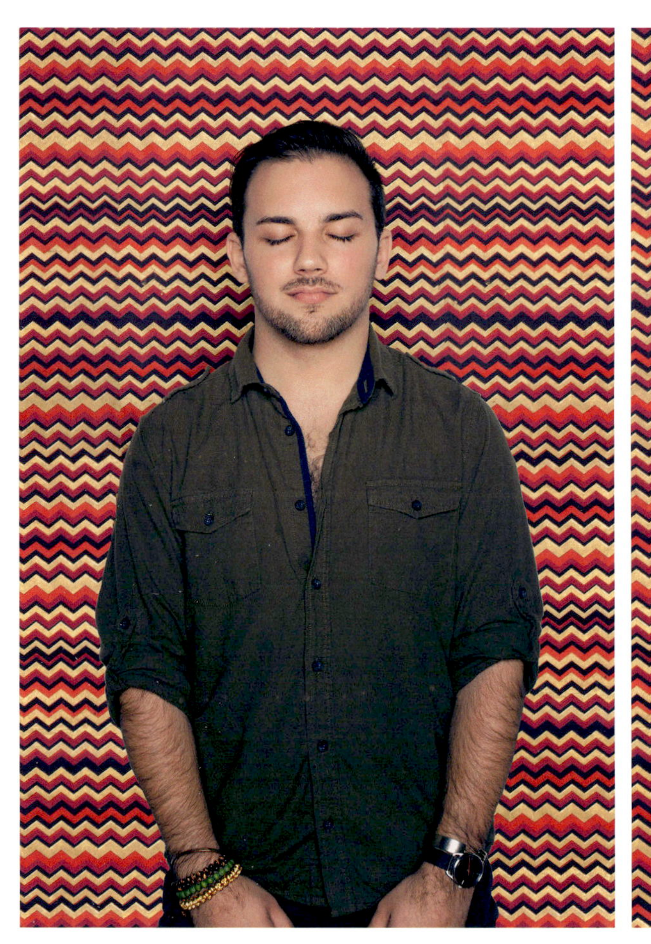
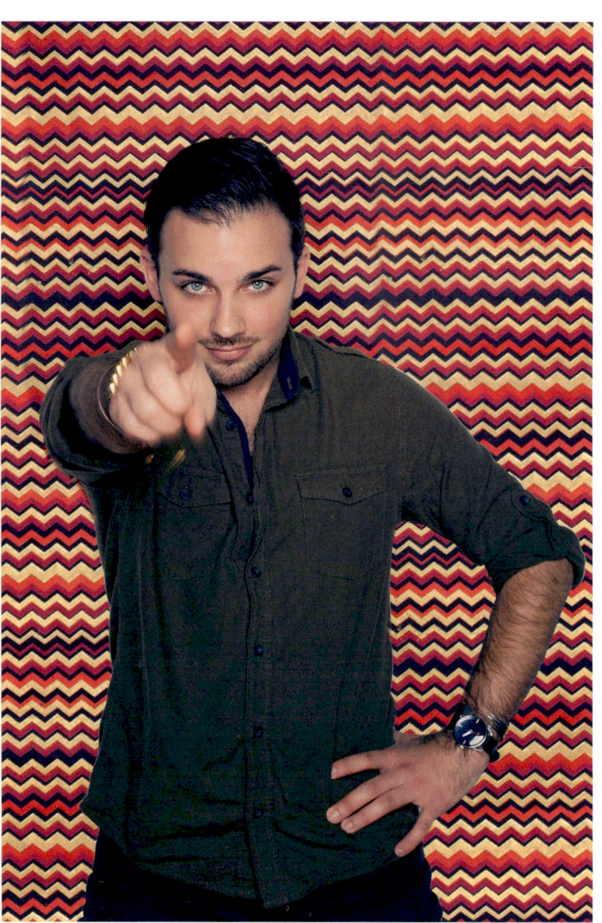
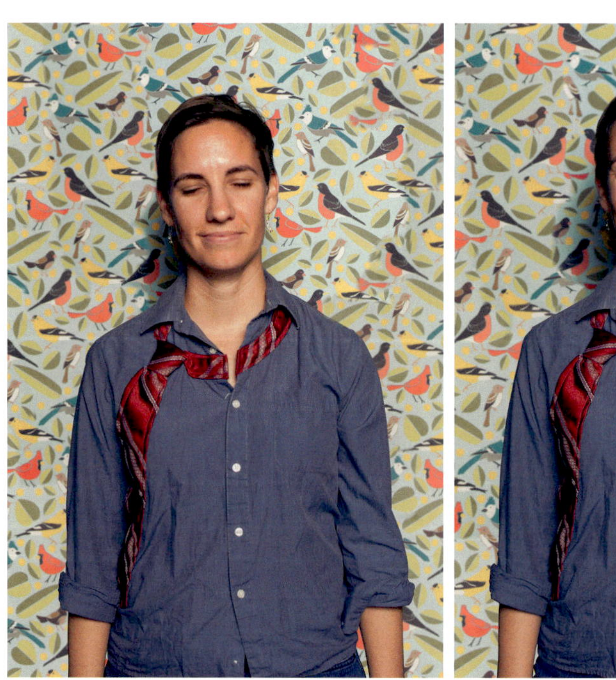

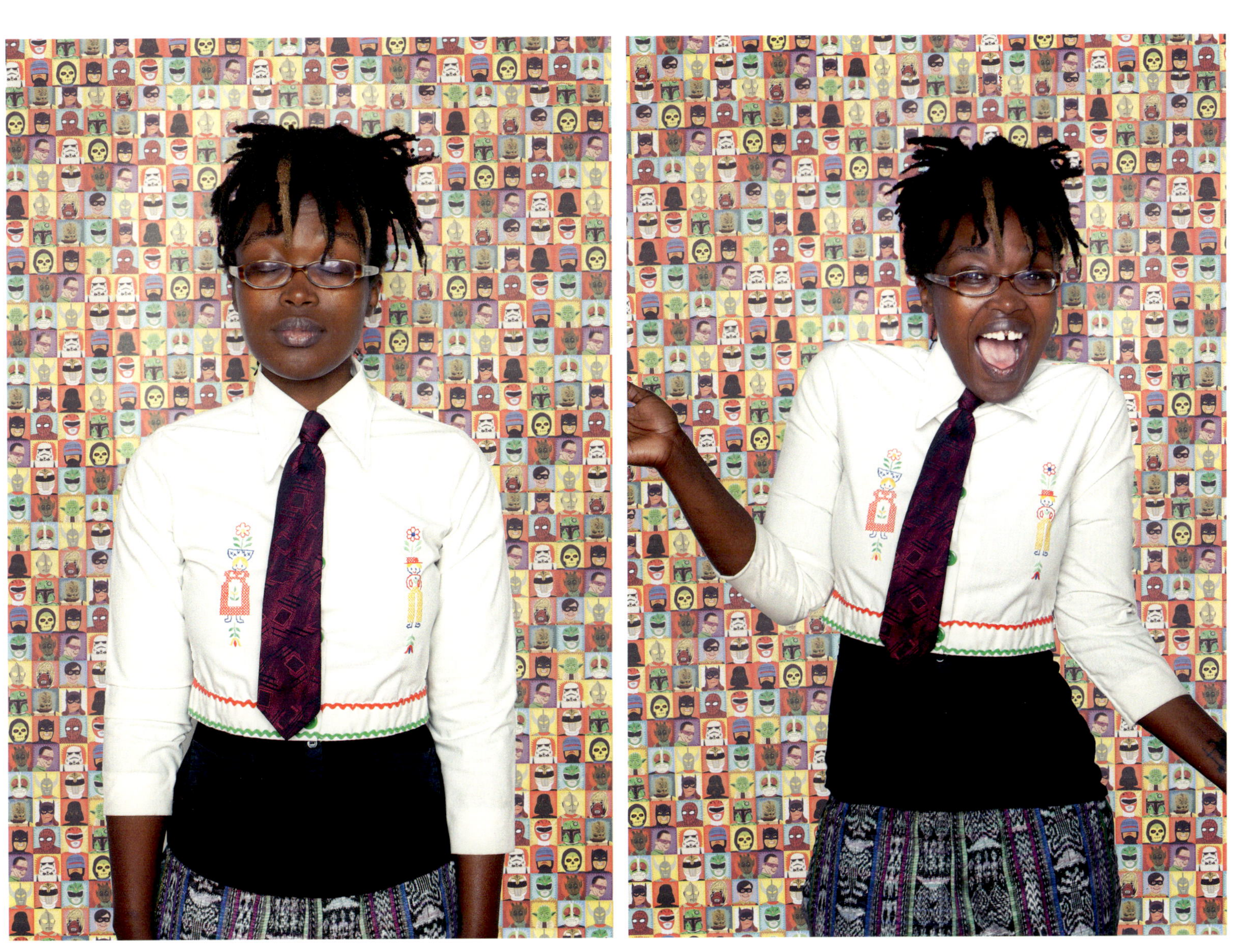

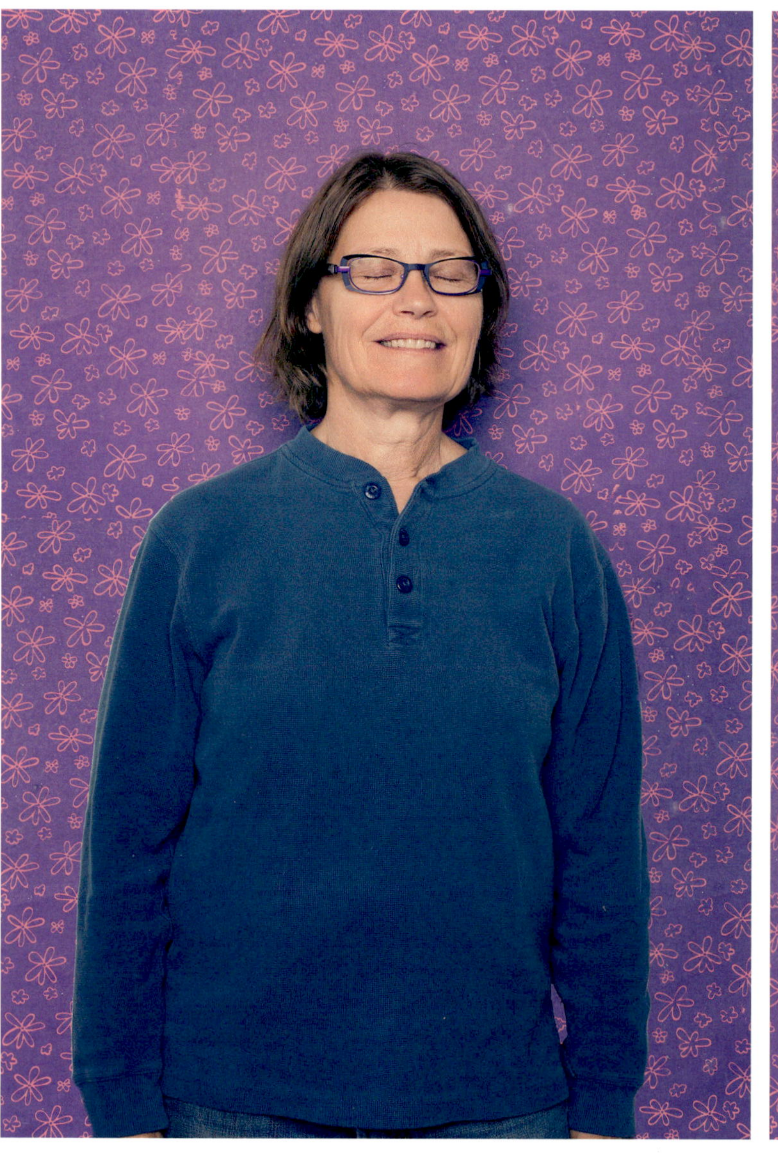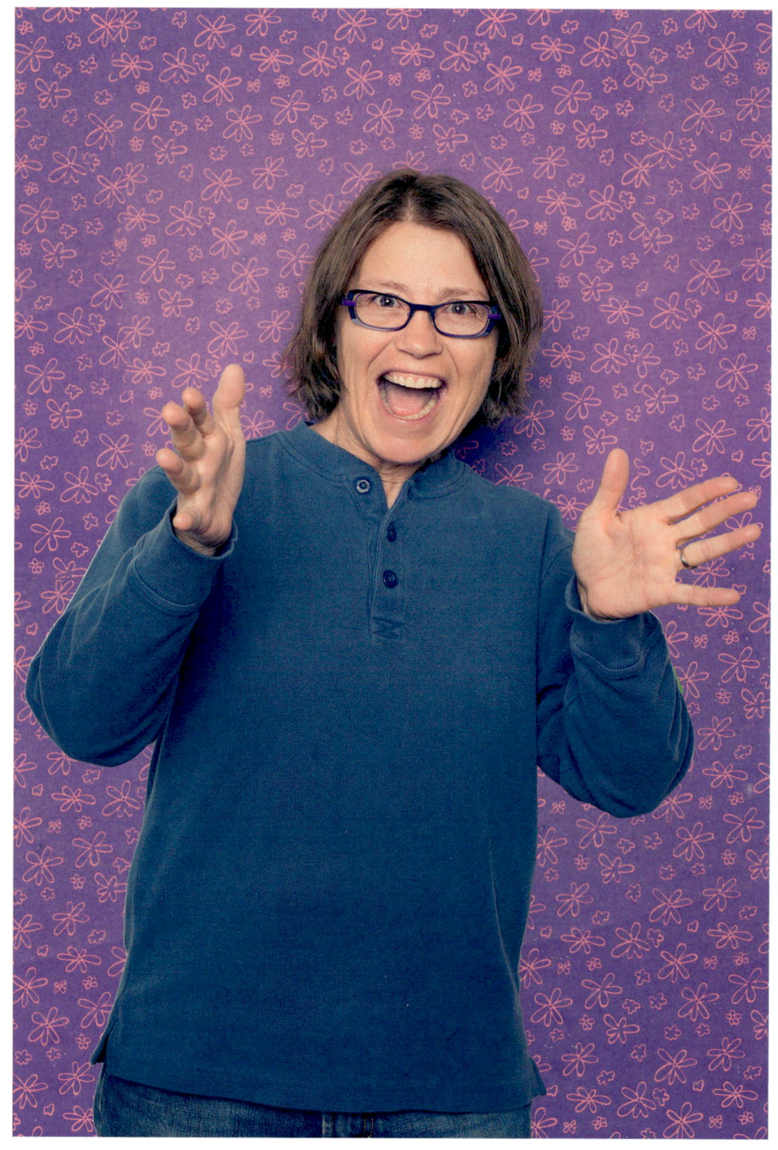

GAY | FACE

Cathy H.
EDMONTON, ALBERTA, CANADA

How would you identify your sexuality?
Lesbian with a slant toward nonbinary.

What pronouns do you prefer?
She/her/hers.

Why did you choose to be a part of this project?
I support the LGBTQ+ community at large, and anything I can do to help others is important for me to pay forward.

Describe your coming out. Are you coming out in some way by participating in this project?
I came out at a time when gays were being beaten up, bars and other gatherings were being raided, and most families shunned anyone who spoke about being gay. I once lost a job that was very important to me when people found out I was gay. Therefore advocating for equality has been important to me for my entire life.

Have you ever experienced discrimination based on your gender or sexual orientation?
Not as often as in the past—fortunately—but my fear has increased given the current state of affairs here in the US. My fear has subsided significantly over the years, living in New York City within a buoyant LGBTQ+ community, with marriage equality legislation, and the passing of GENDA [the Gender Expression Non-Discrimination Act]. Still, I am cautious in public, and even more so outside of the relative safety of New York City. I would not travel to Tennessee, Alabama, and other such states, which is really unfortunate because I love to travel.

If you could change one thing about mainstream society to improve the lives of LGBTQ+ people, what would it be?
Equality. All people should have the right to enjoy life freely, engage in work and other activities freely, without the fear of retribution for simply being who they are.

Describe how this project has affected you, both personally and as a member of the LGBTQ+ community as a whole.
From years of working with various LGBTQ+ organizations, I know that research and knowledge are fundamental to help change minds, validate our communities, and gain rightful access to city, state, and federal support.

What advice have you been given by another LGBTQ+ person, or that you might offer someone?
Open your heart. As Edie Windsor once said, "Love wins!" Allow yourself to be you. Avoid conflict, but don't negate one's self.

Who are your LGBTQ+ role models?
Edie Windsor, without doubt. She was a dear and great friend who was overflowing with spirit, compassion, and truth. She broke many glass ceilings in her life, being true to who she was. I love and miss her every day. And Billie Jean King—she beat that asshole Bobby Riggs! She showed me that nothing stops a woman who wants something bad enough. I should also mention Renée Richards and Martina Navratilova. Laverne Cox and Janet Mock are the most gracious and outspoken public leaders in trans rights. Andy Marra and AC Dumlao of the Transgender Legal Defense and Education Fund are two powerhouses whose work will affect the community for decades to come. And they are just getting started.

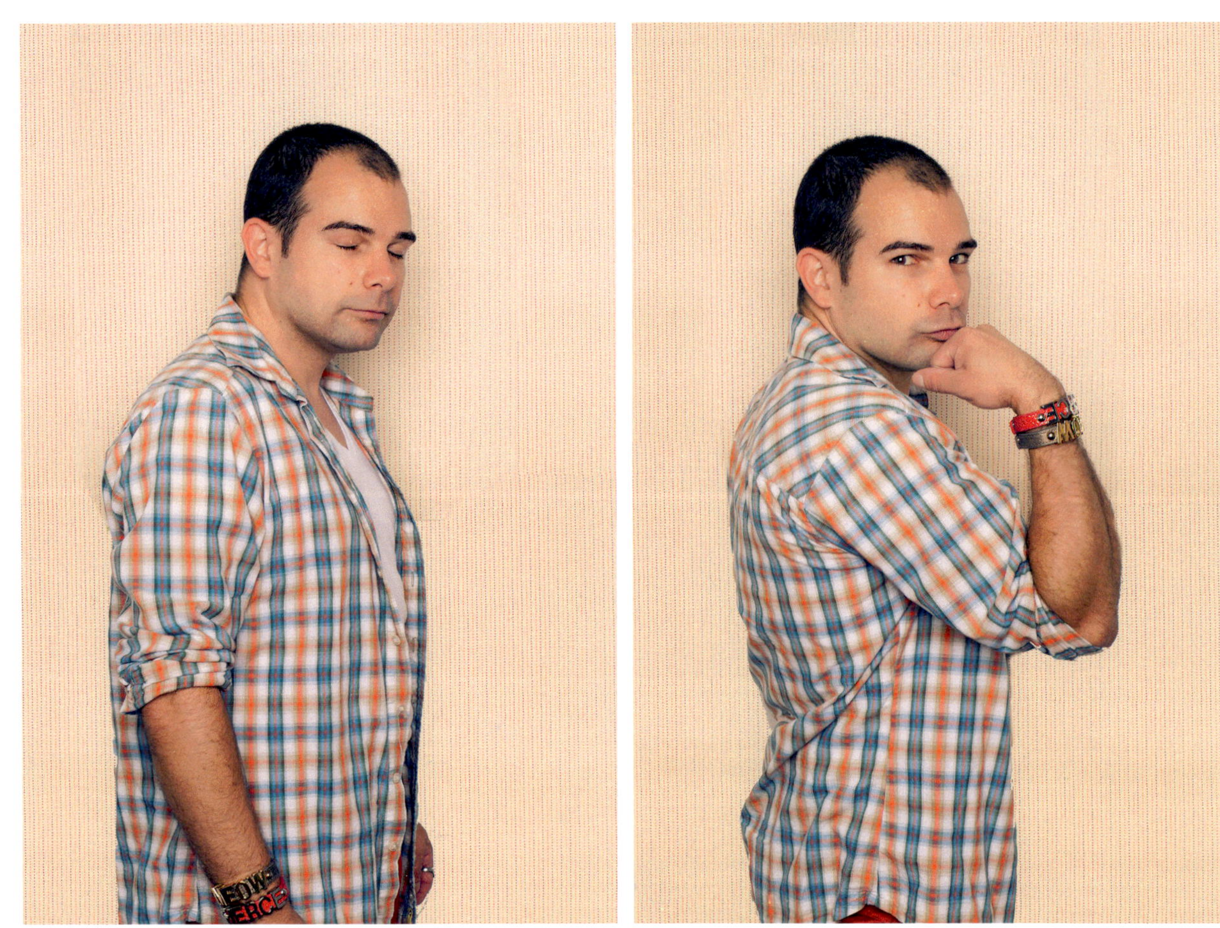

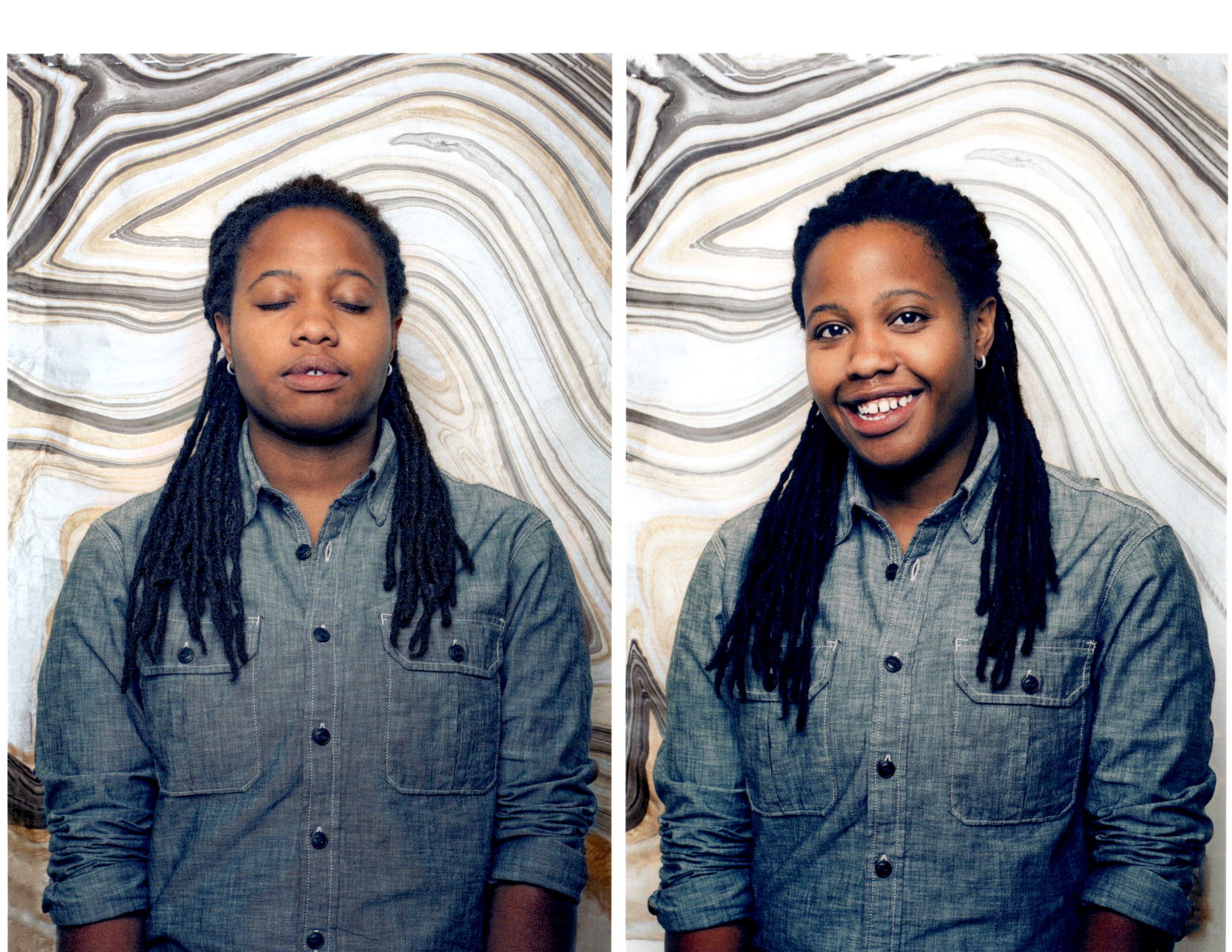

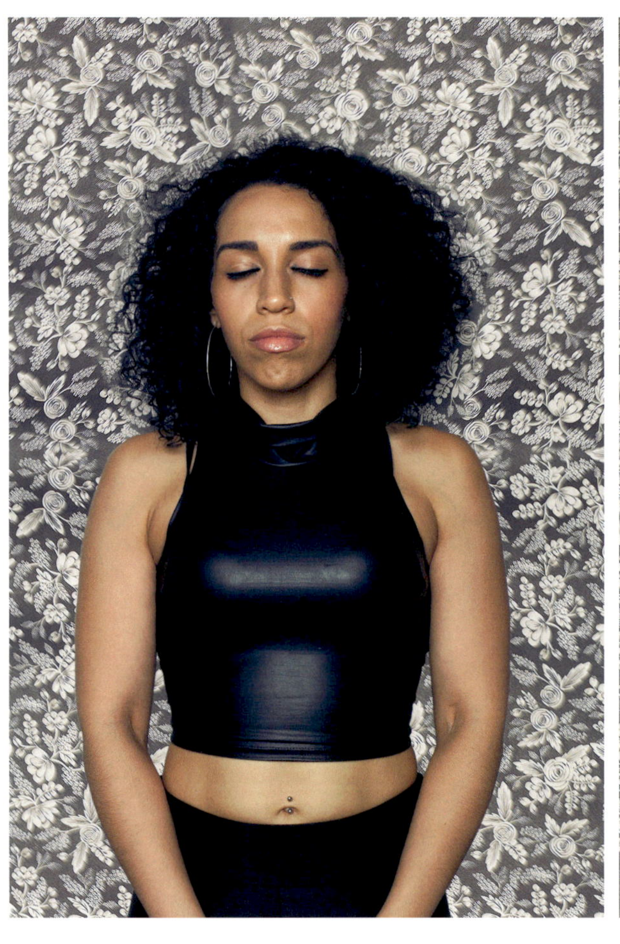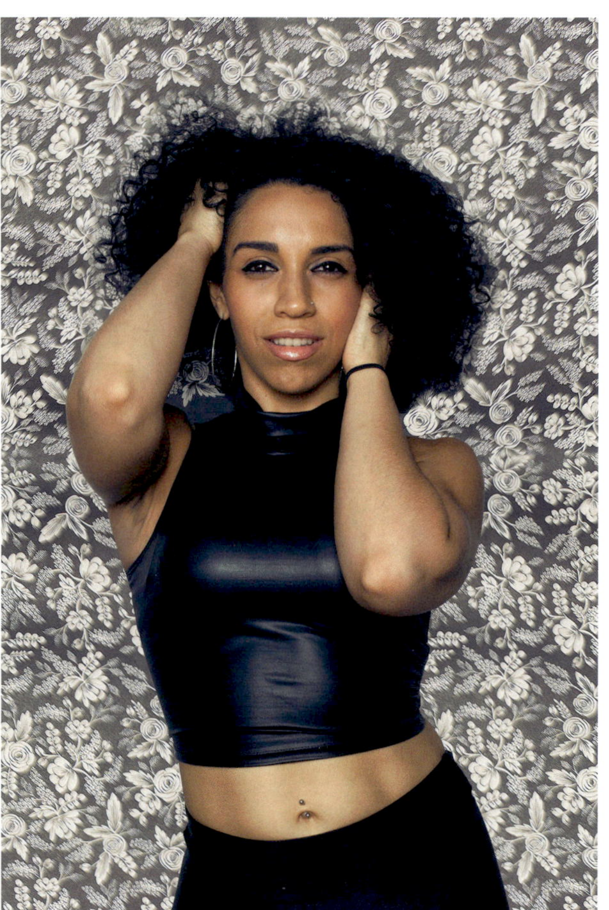

GAY | FACE

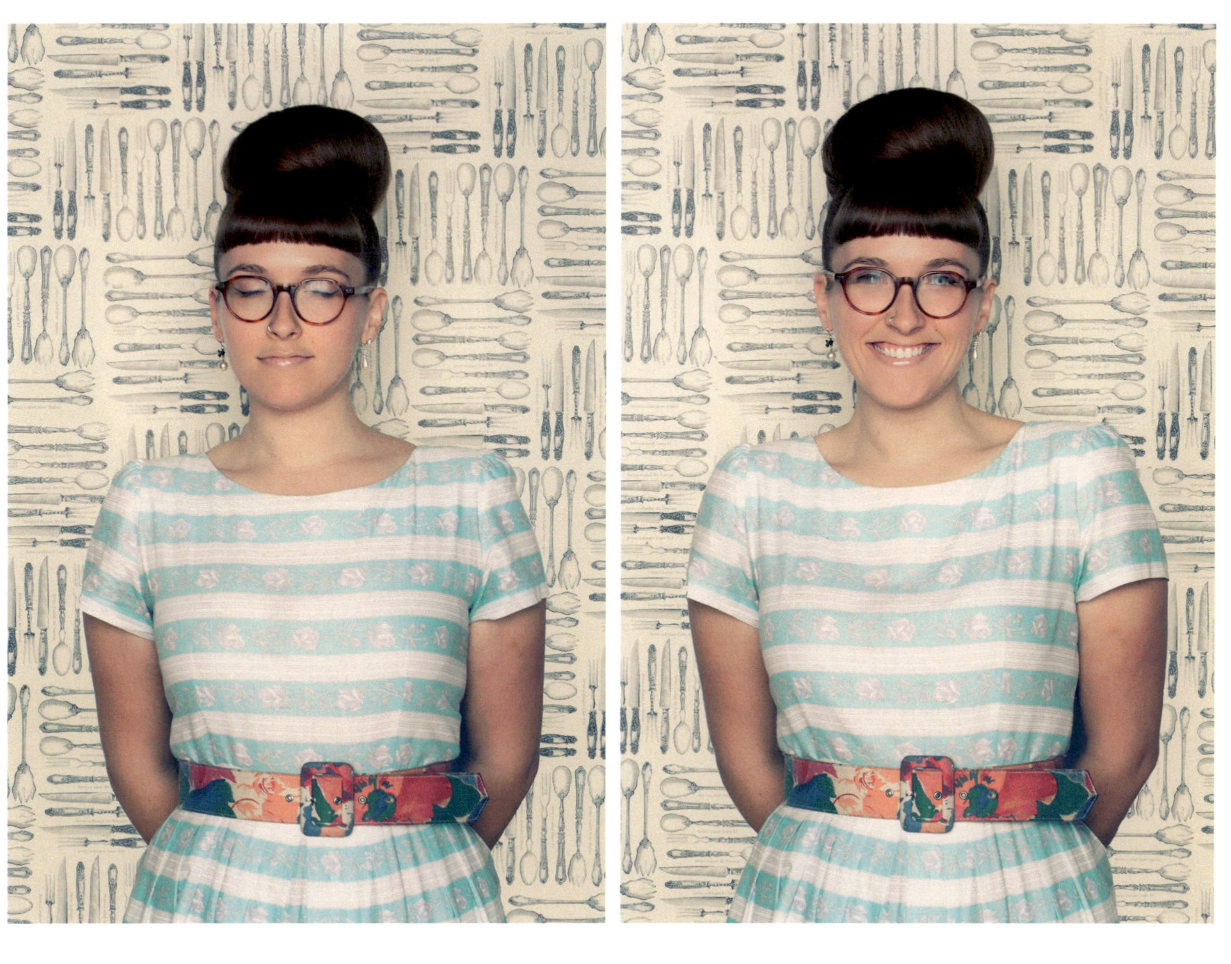

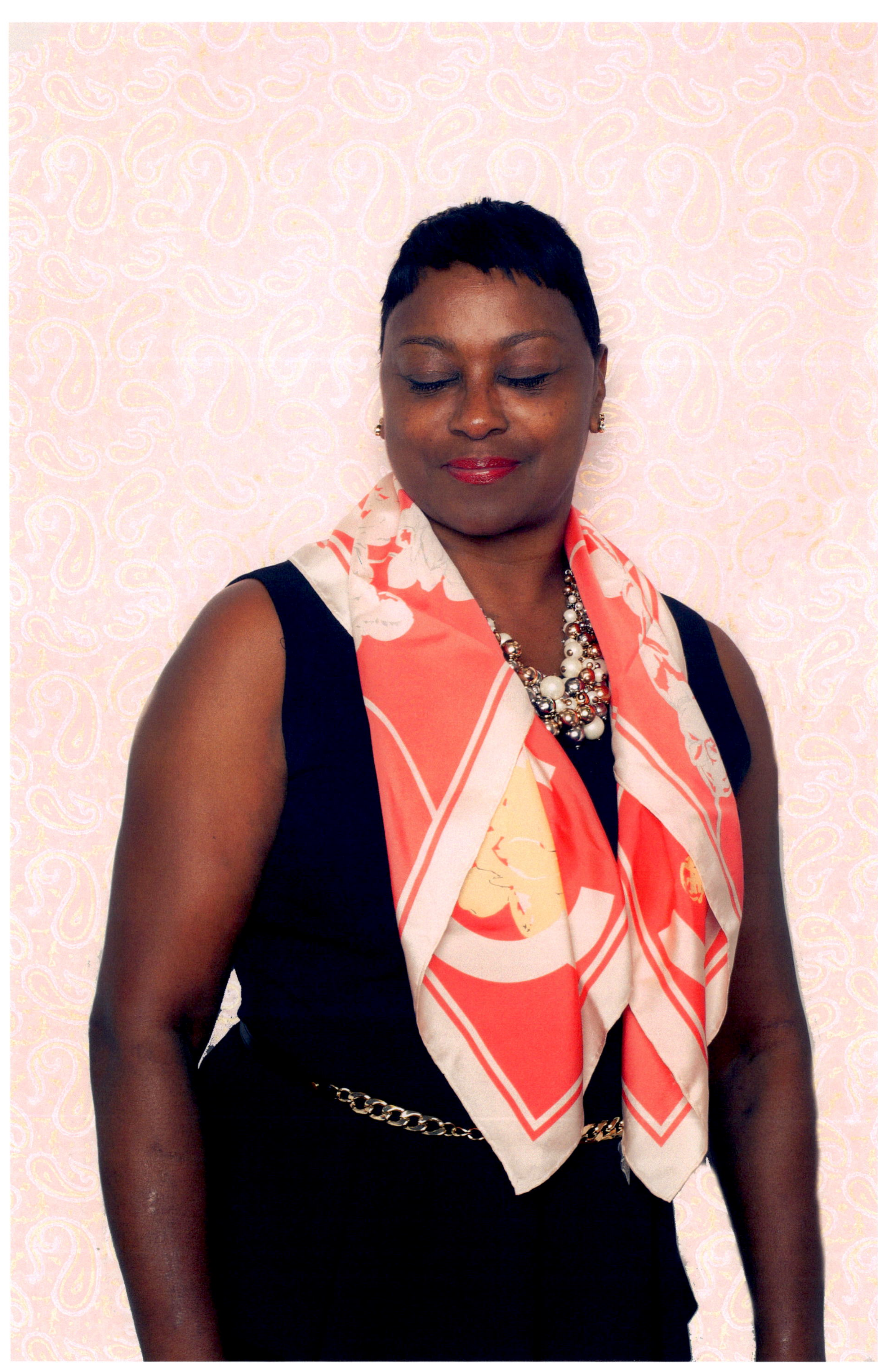

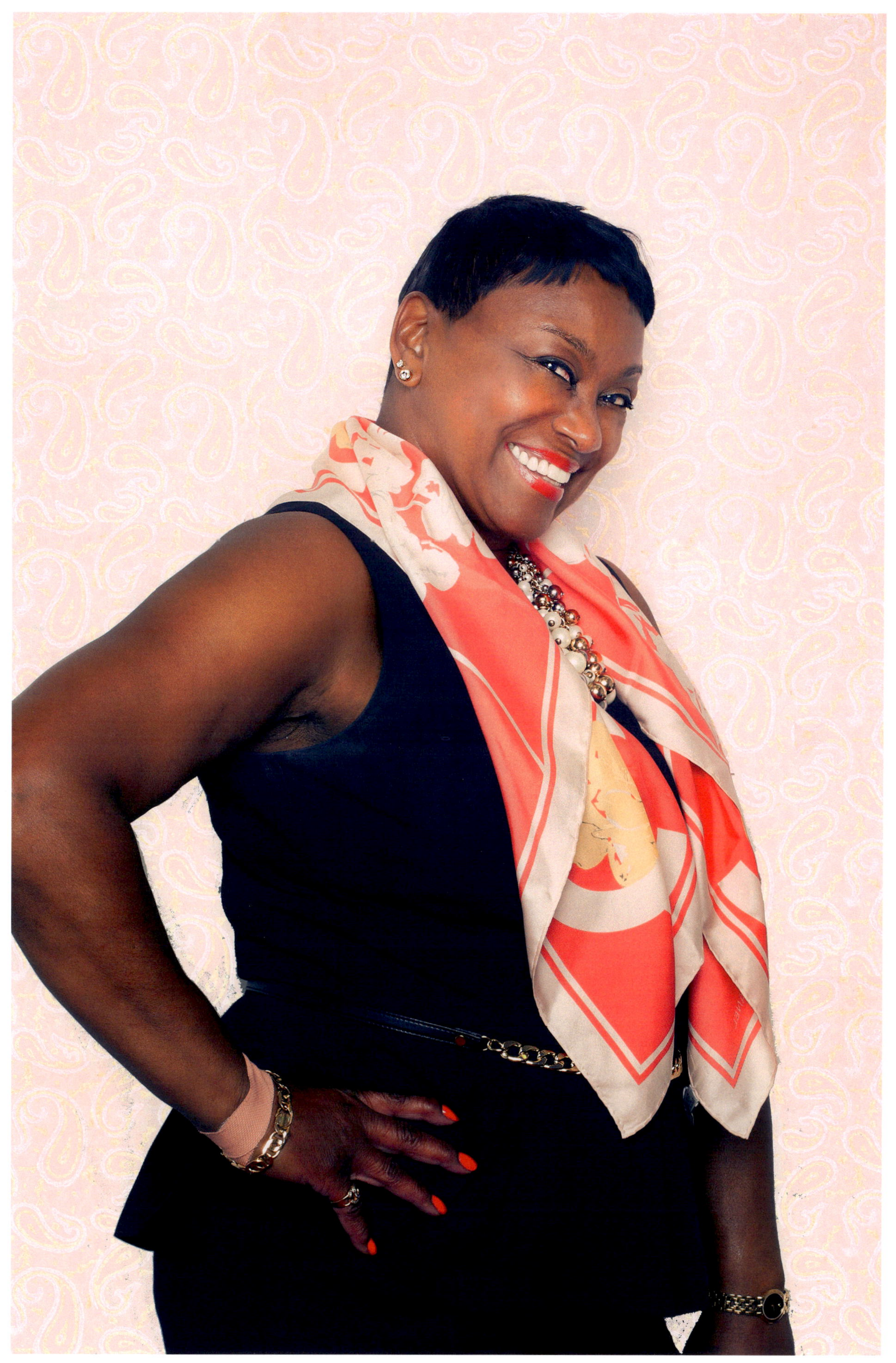

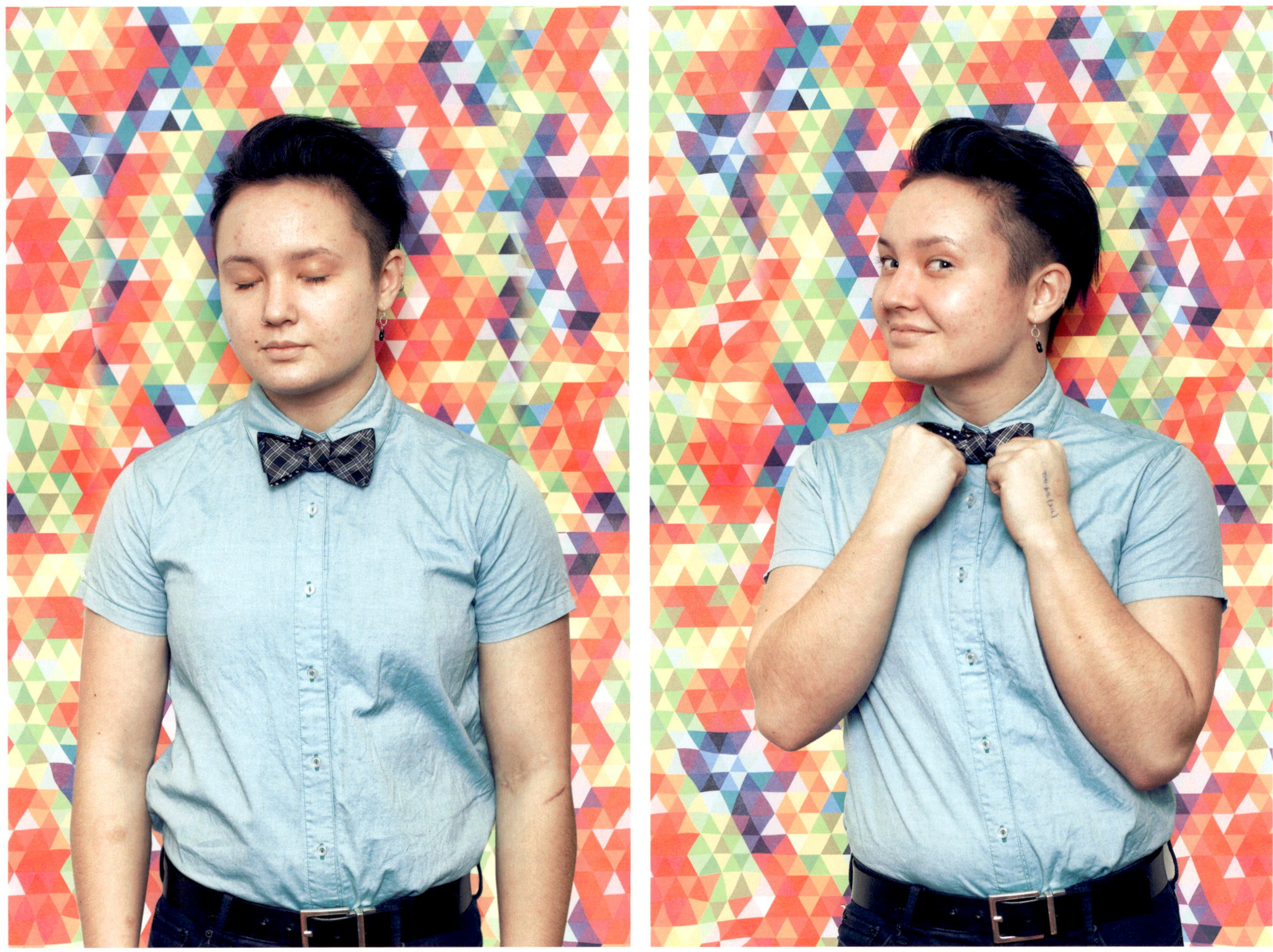
GAY | FACE

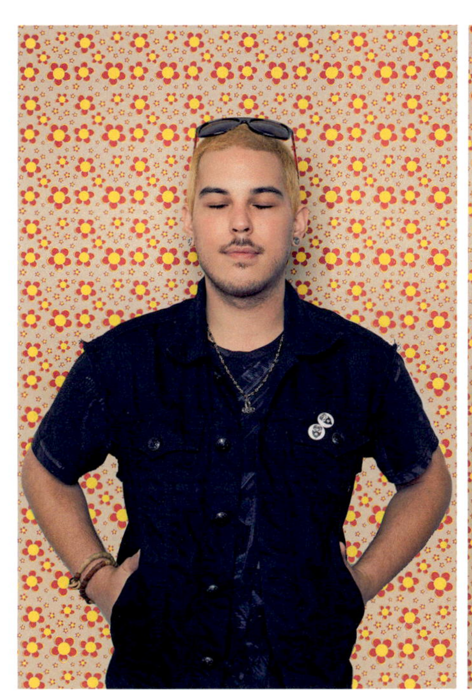
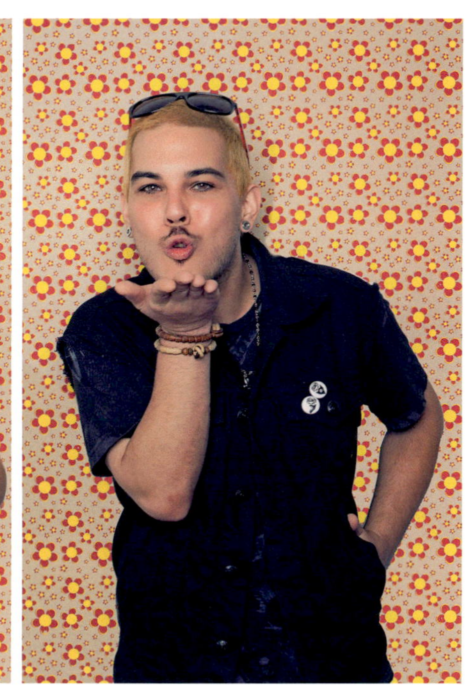

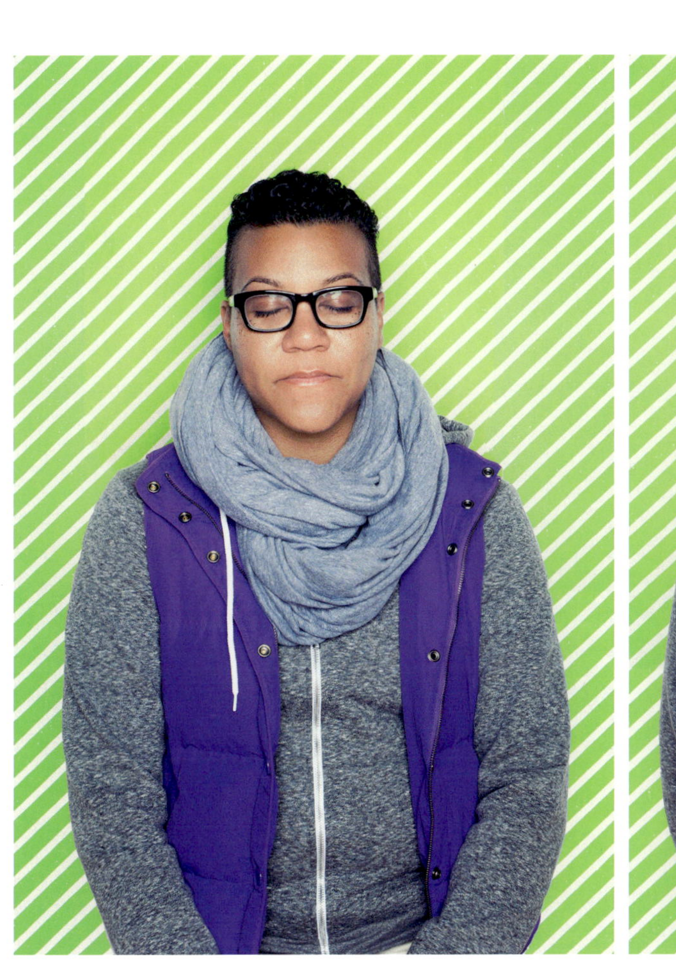
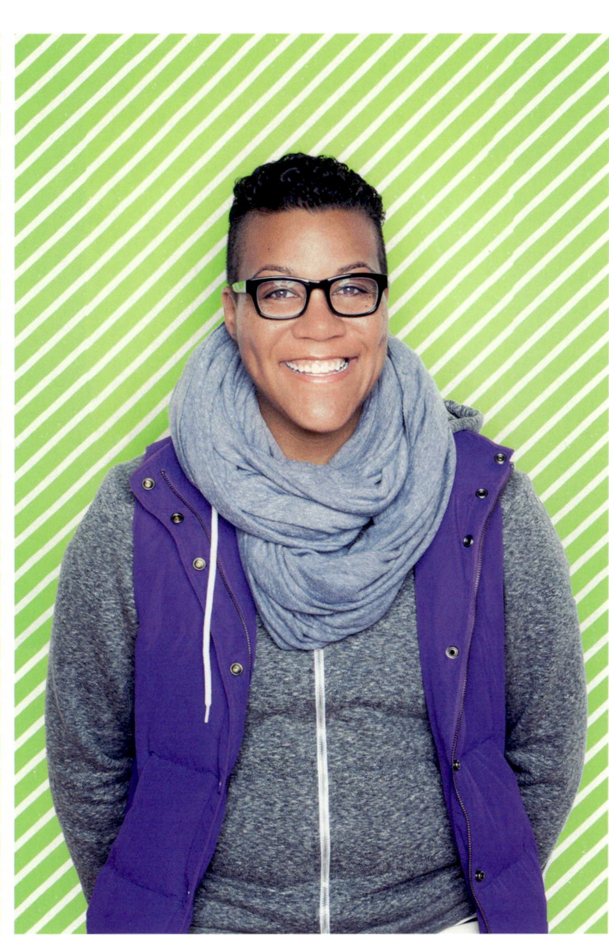

GAY | FACE

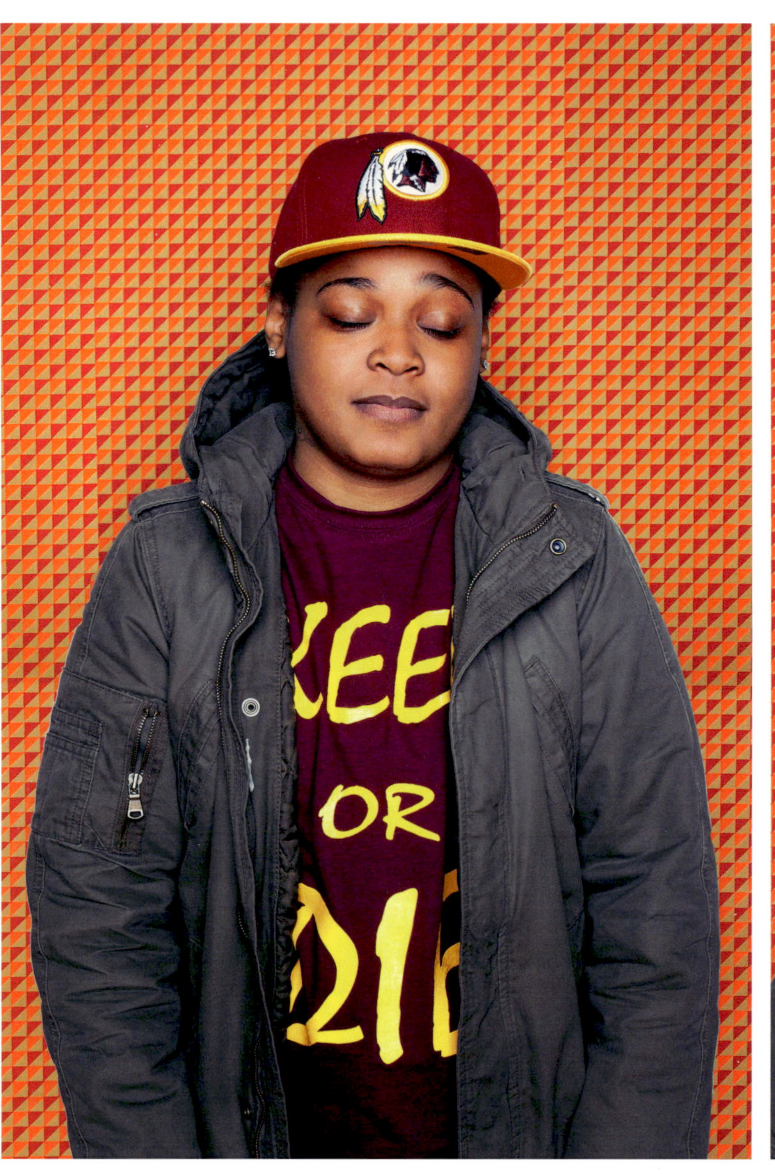
KEE
OR
DIE

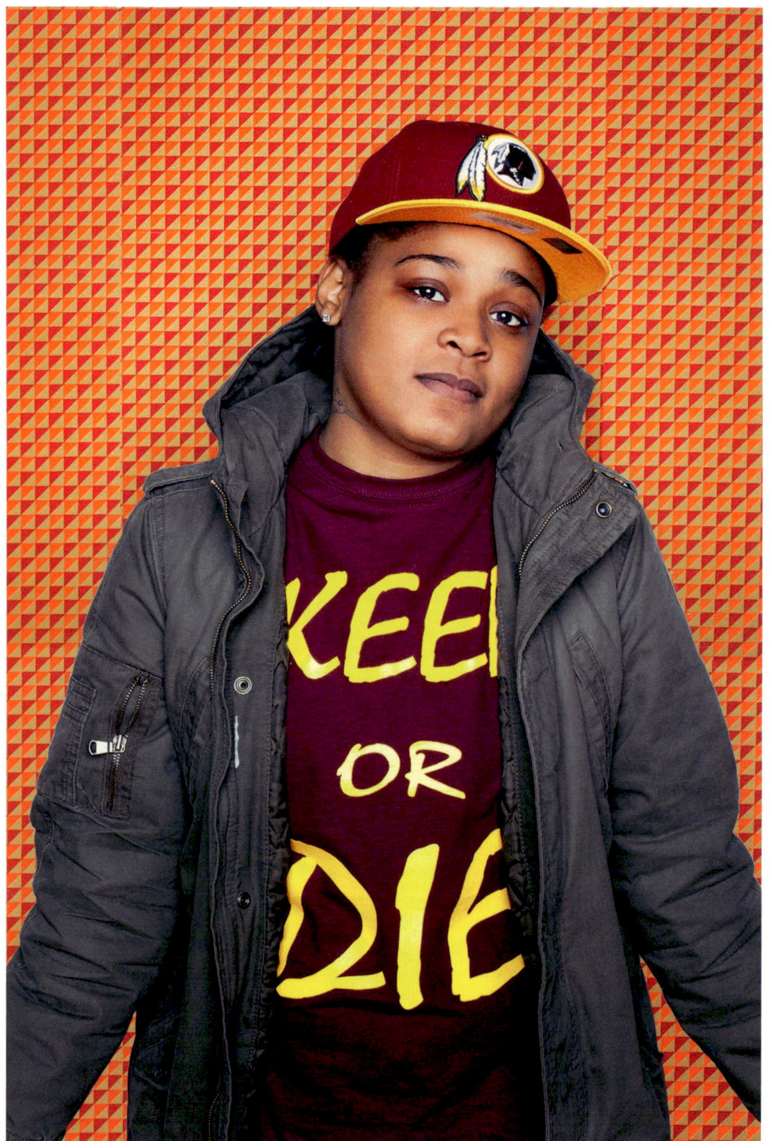
KEE
OR
DIE

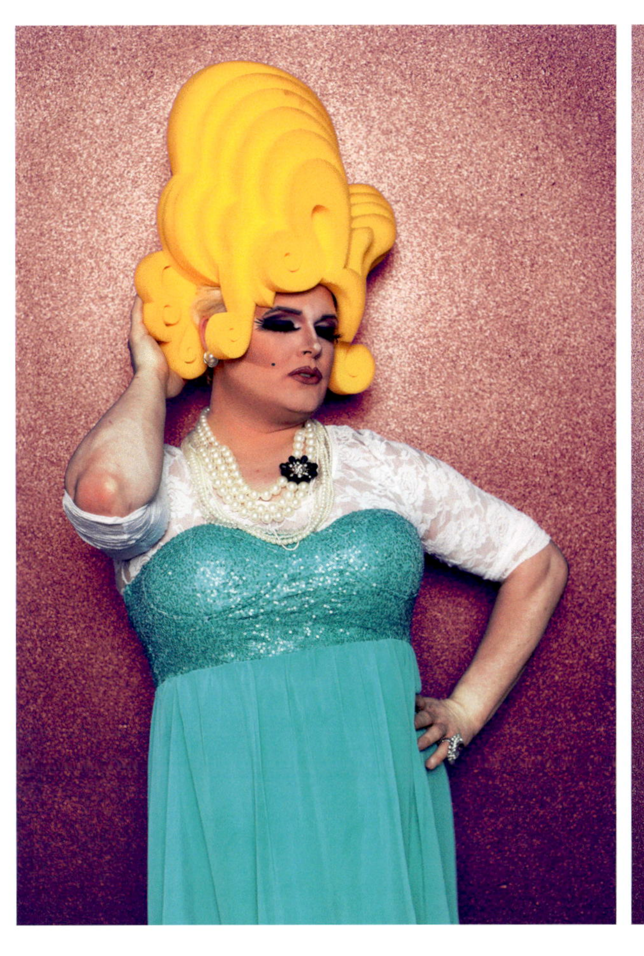
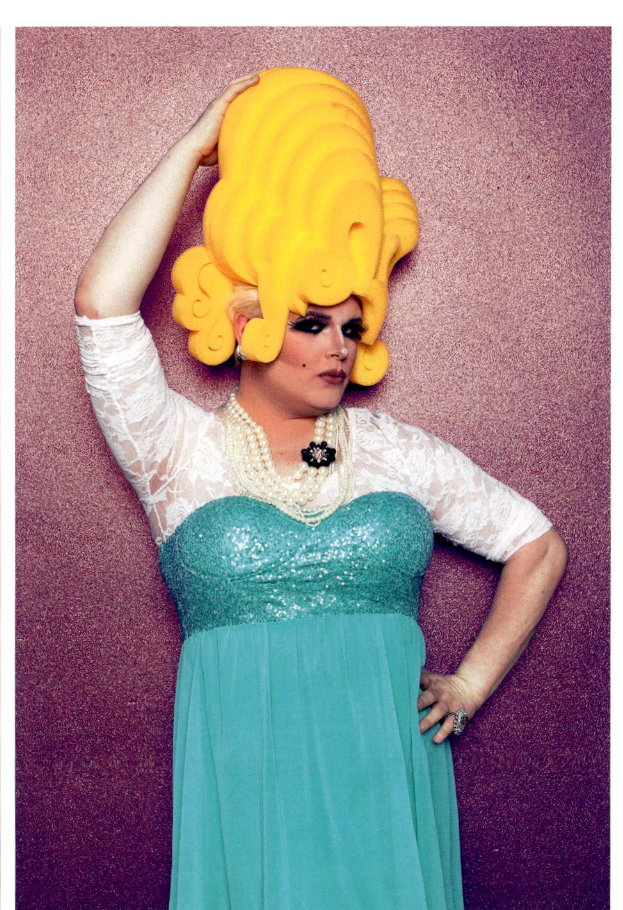

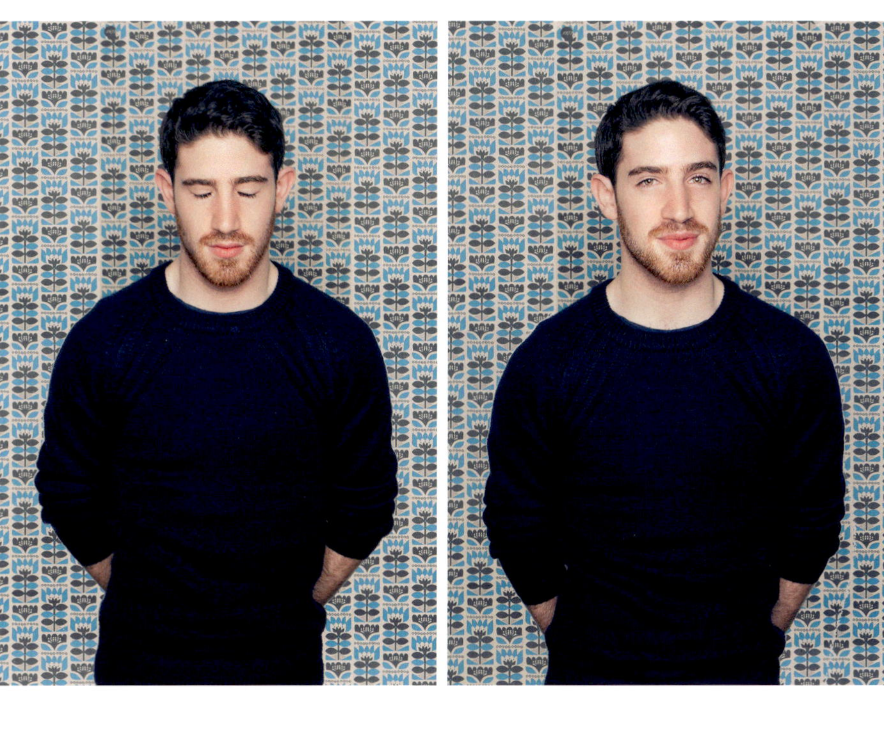

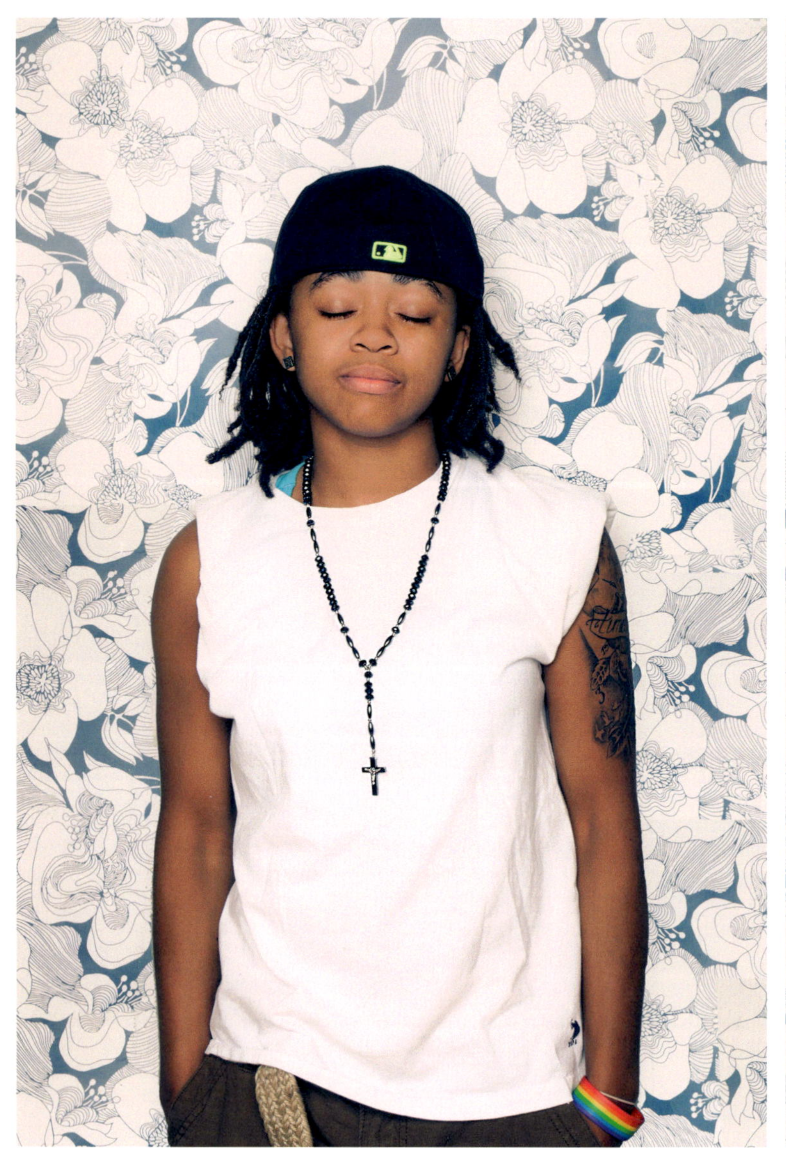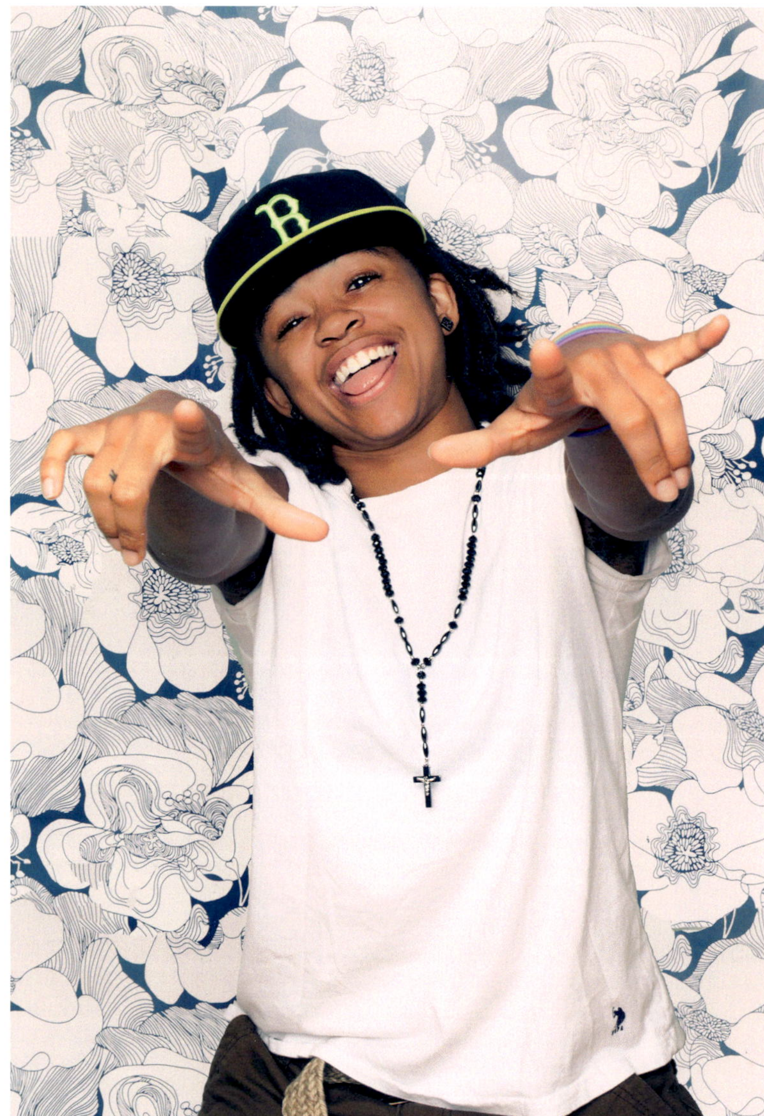

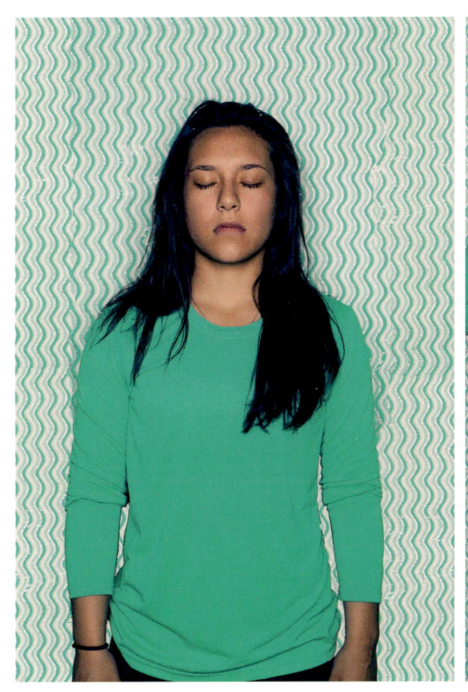
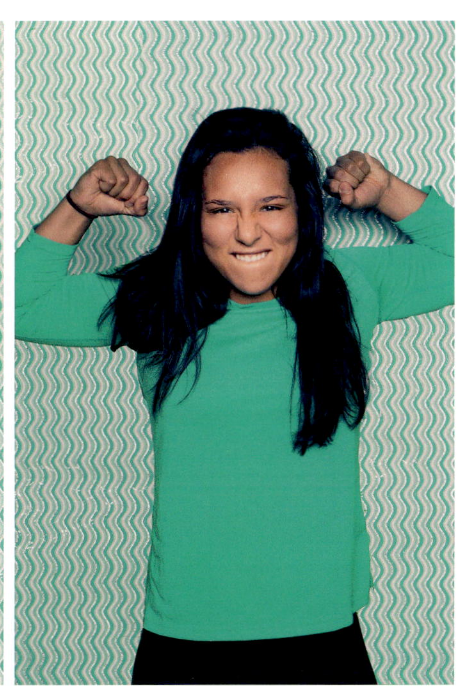

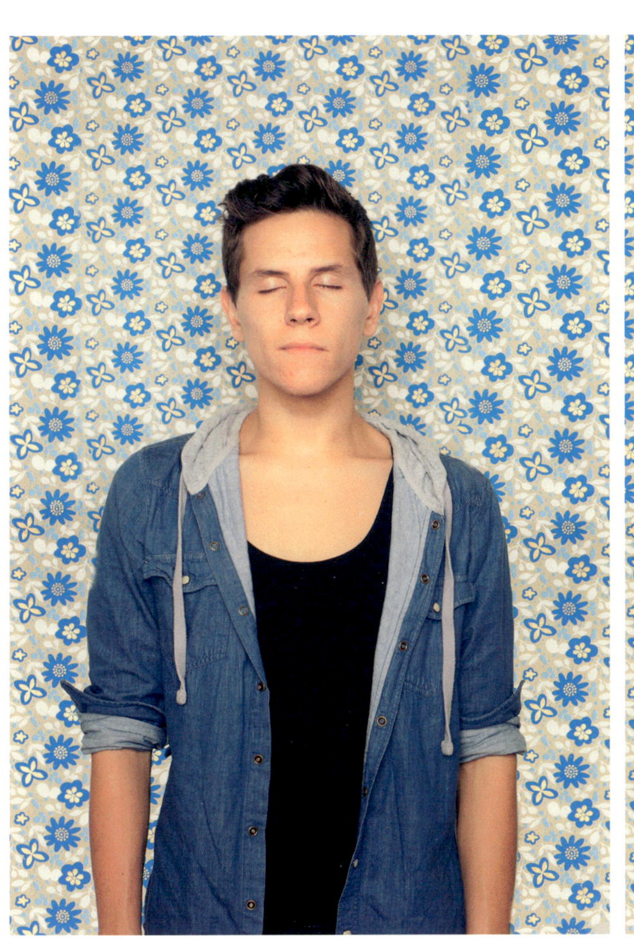
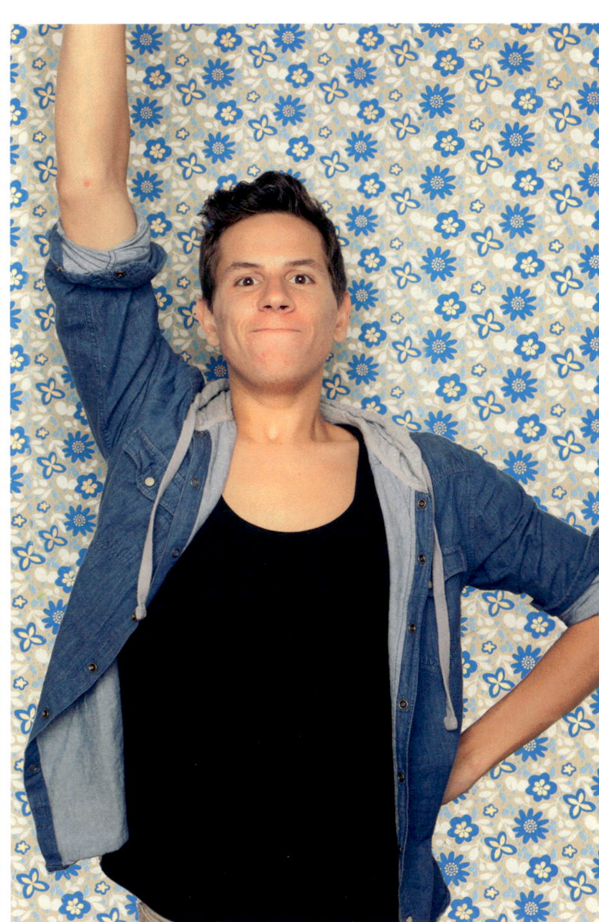

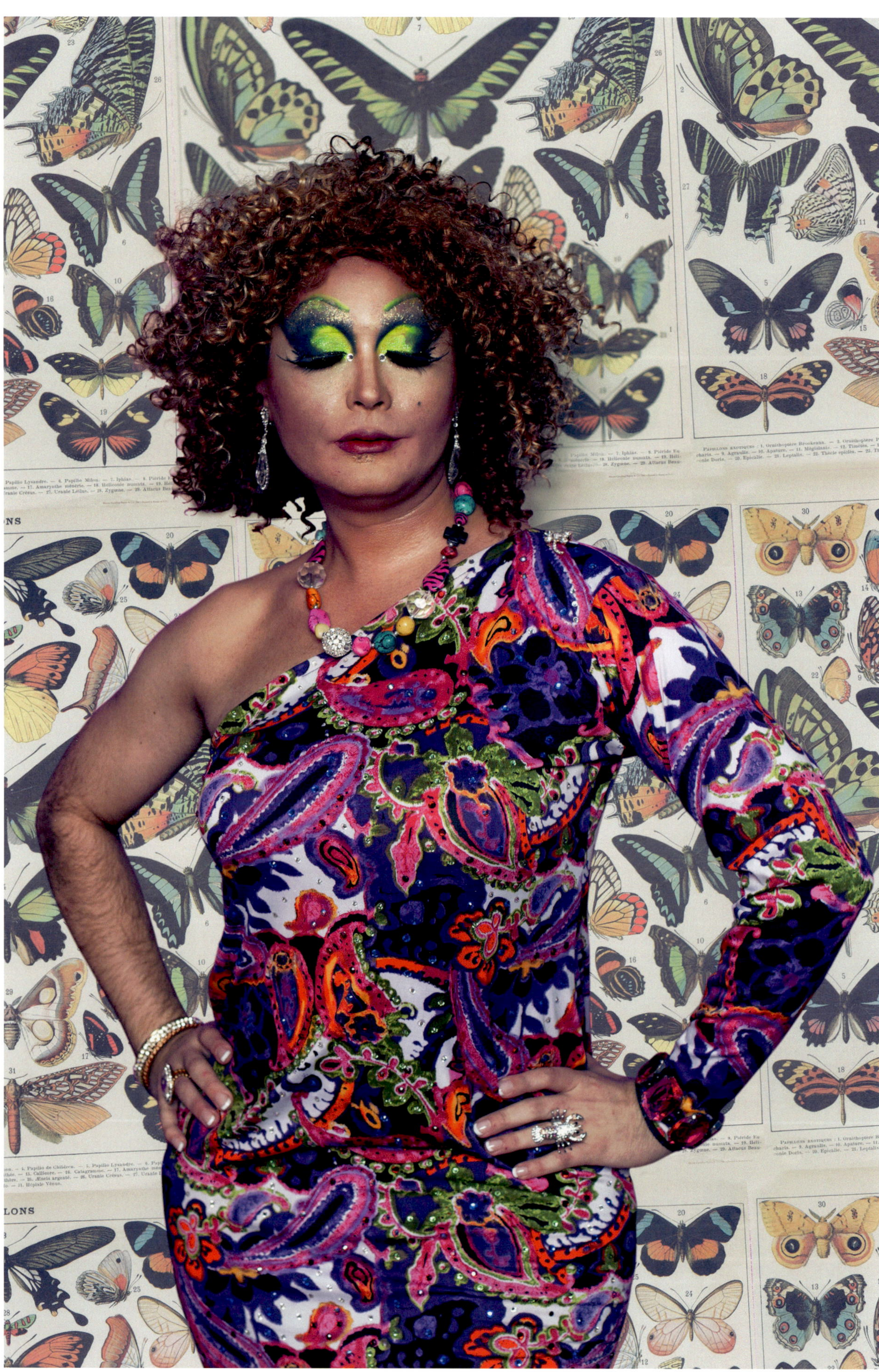

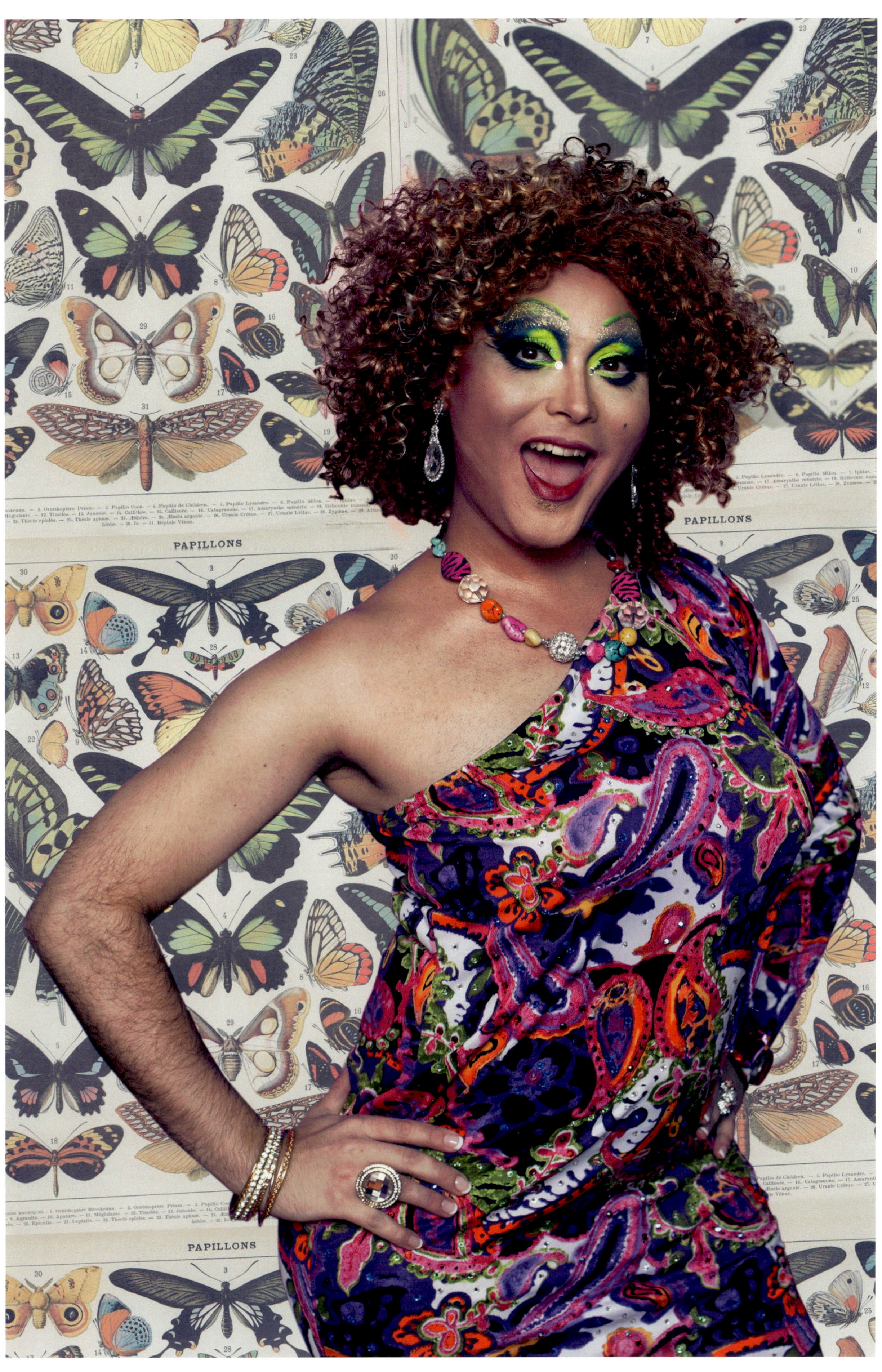

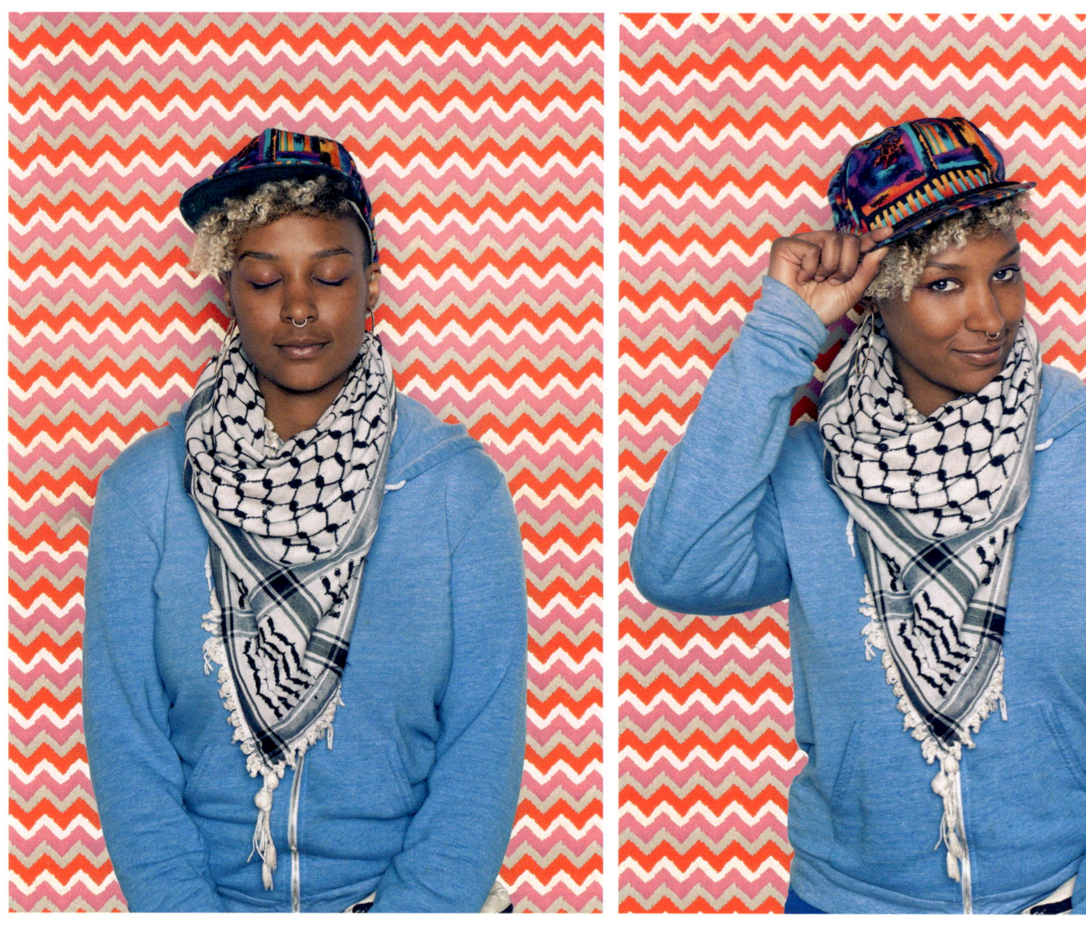

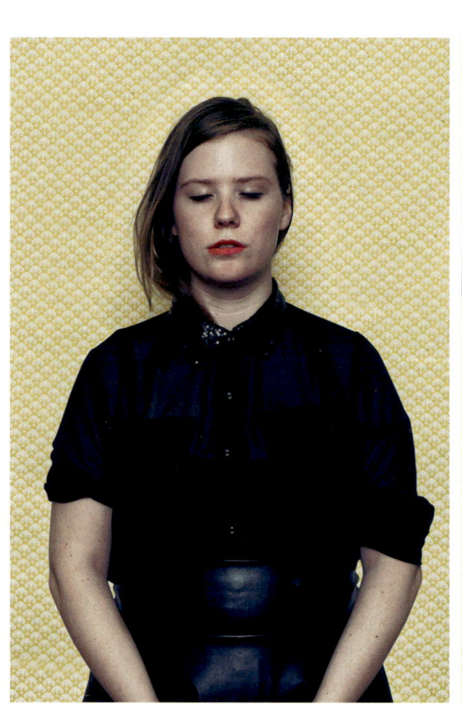

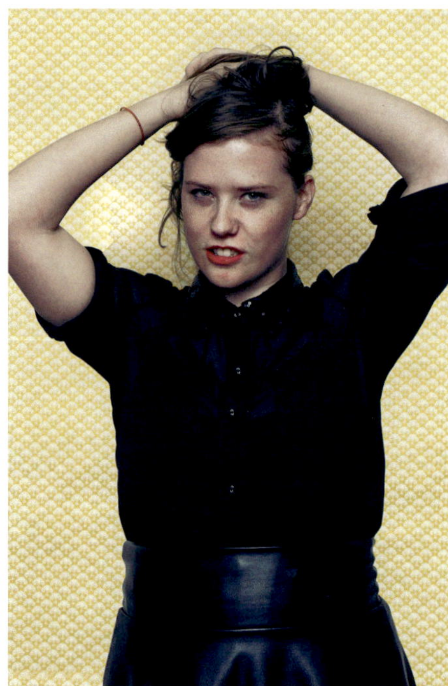

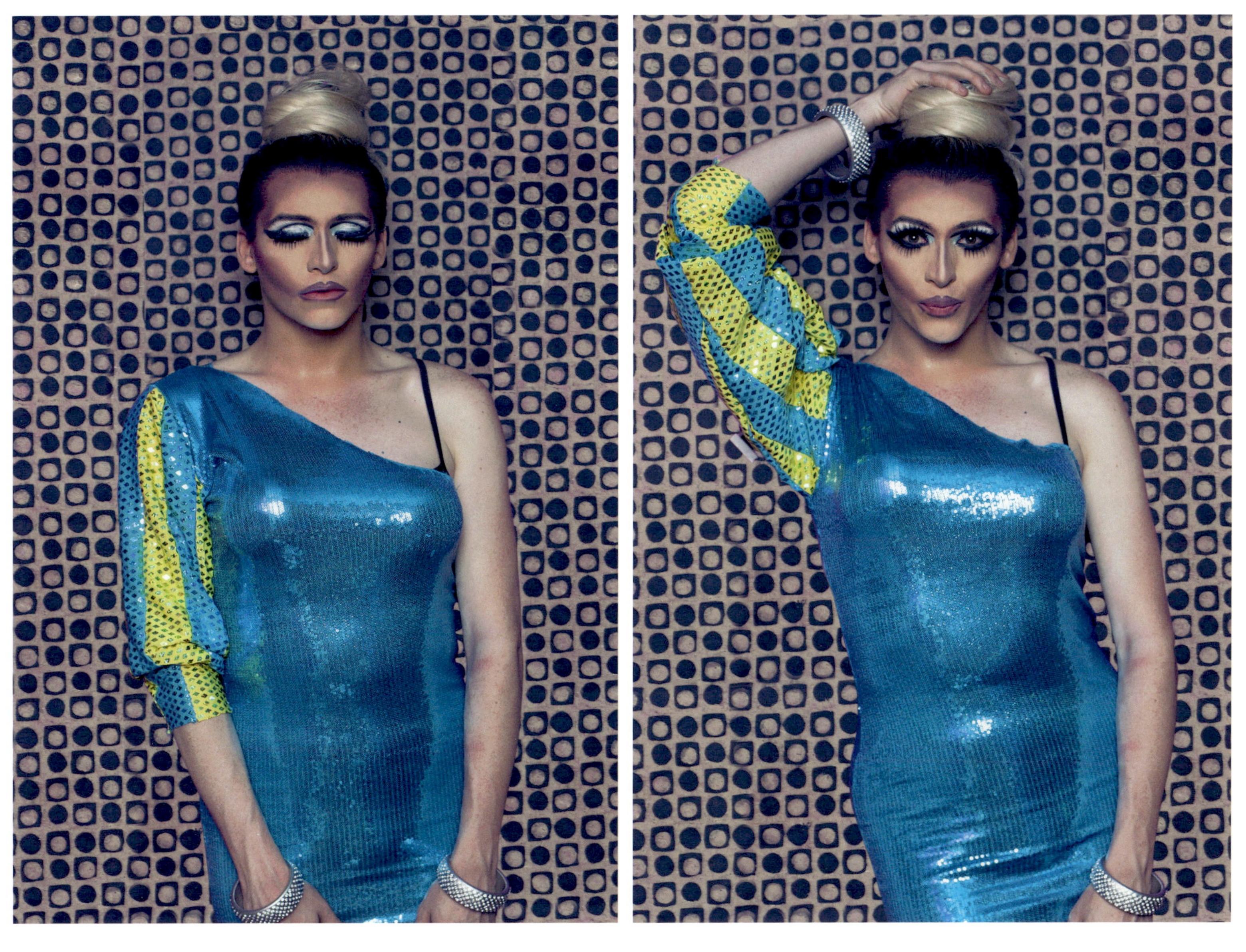

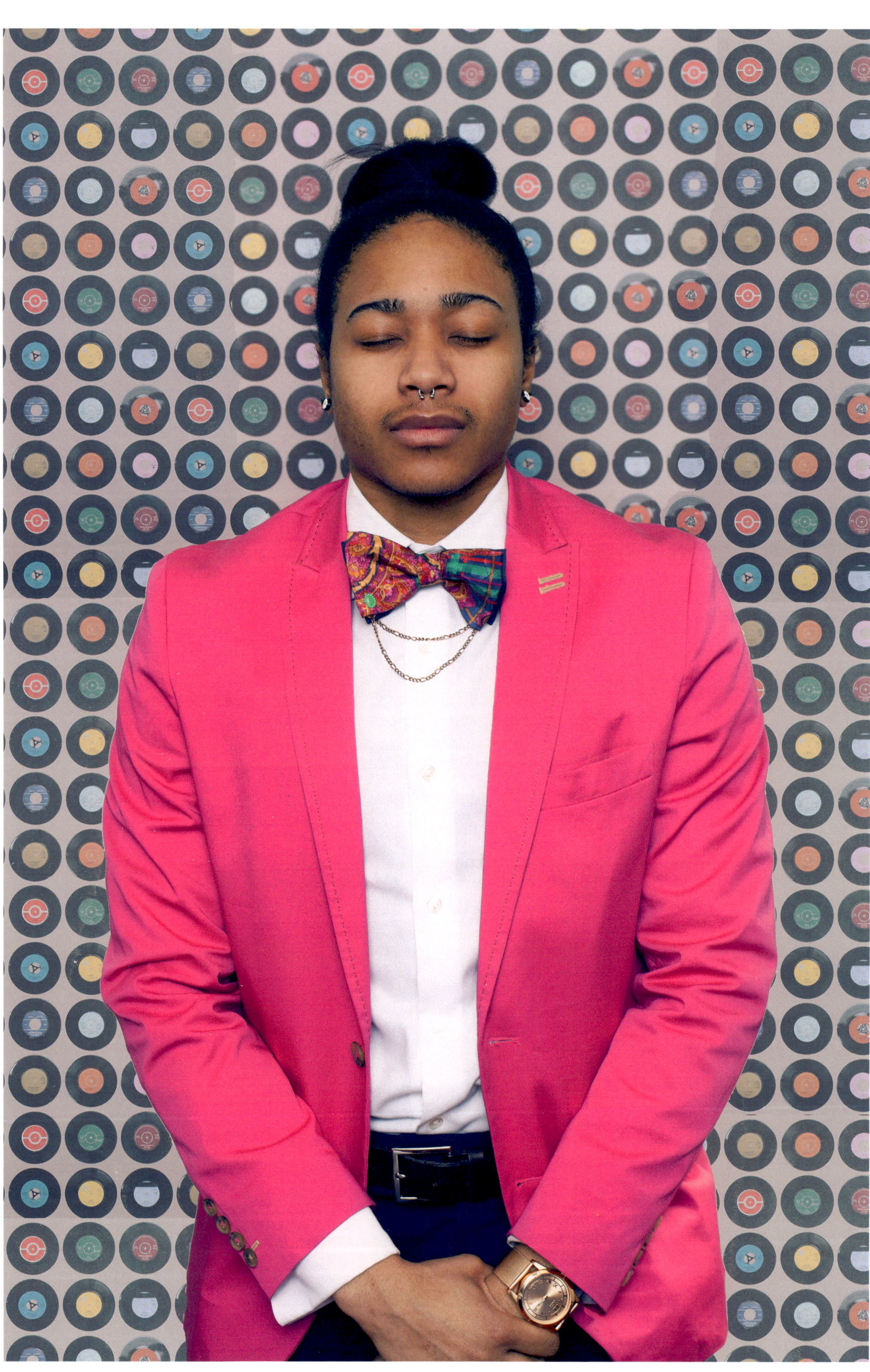

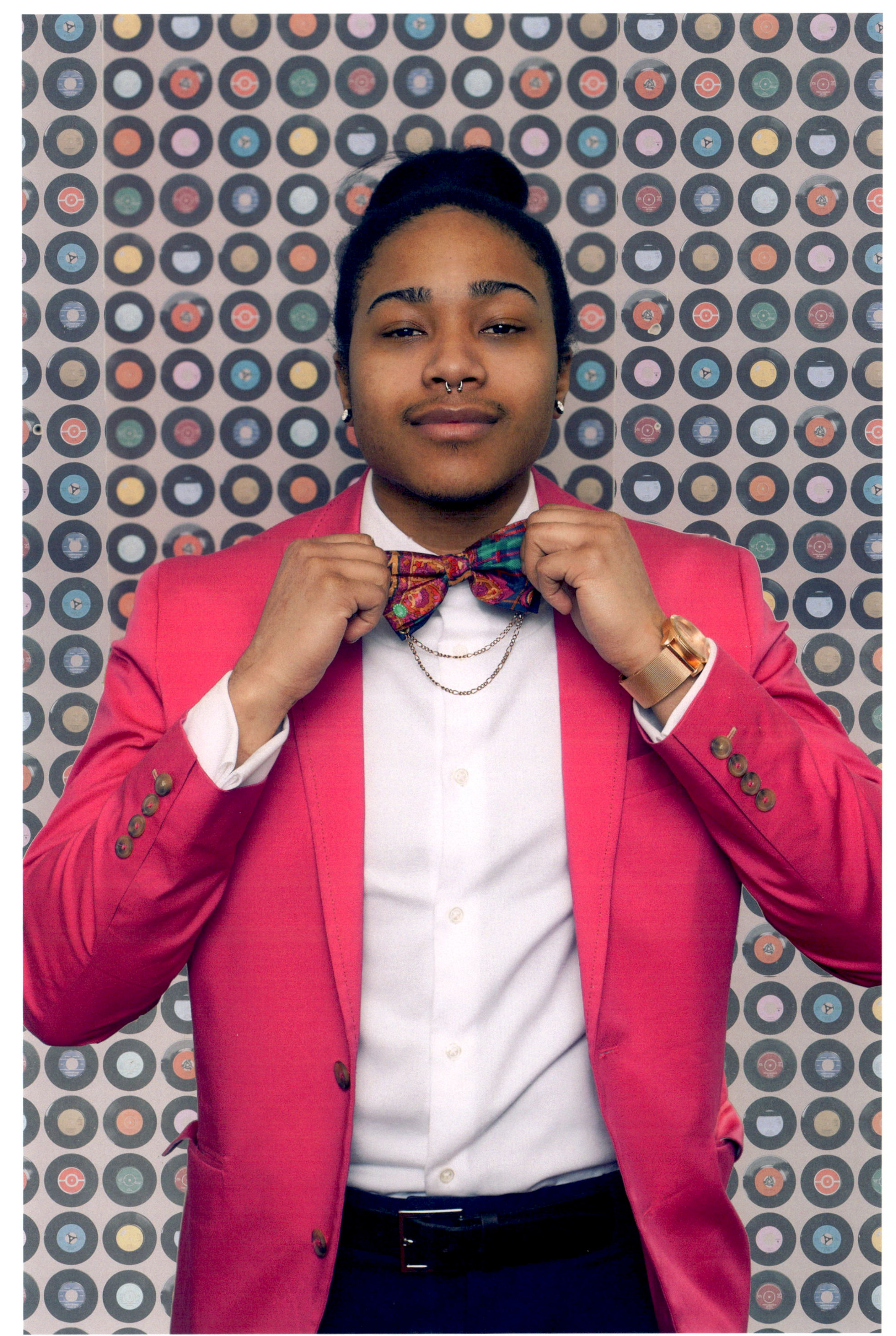

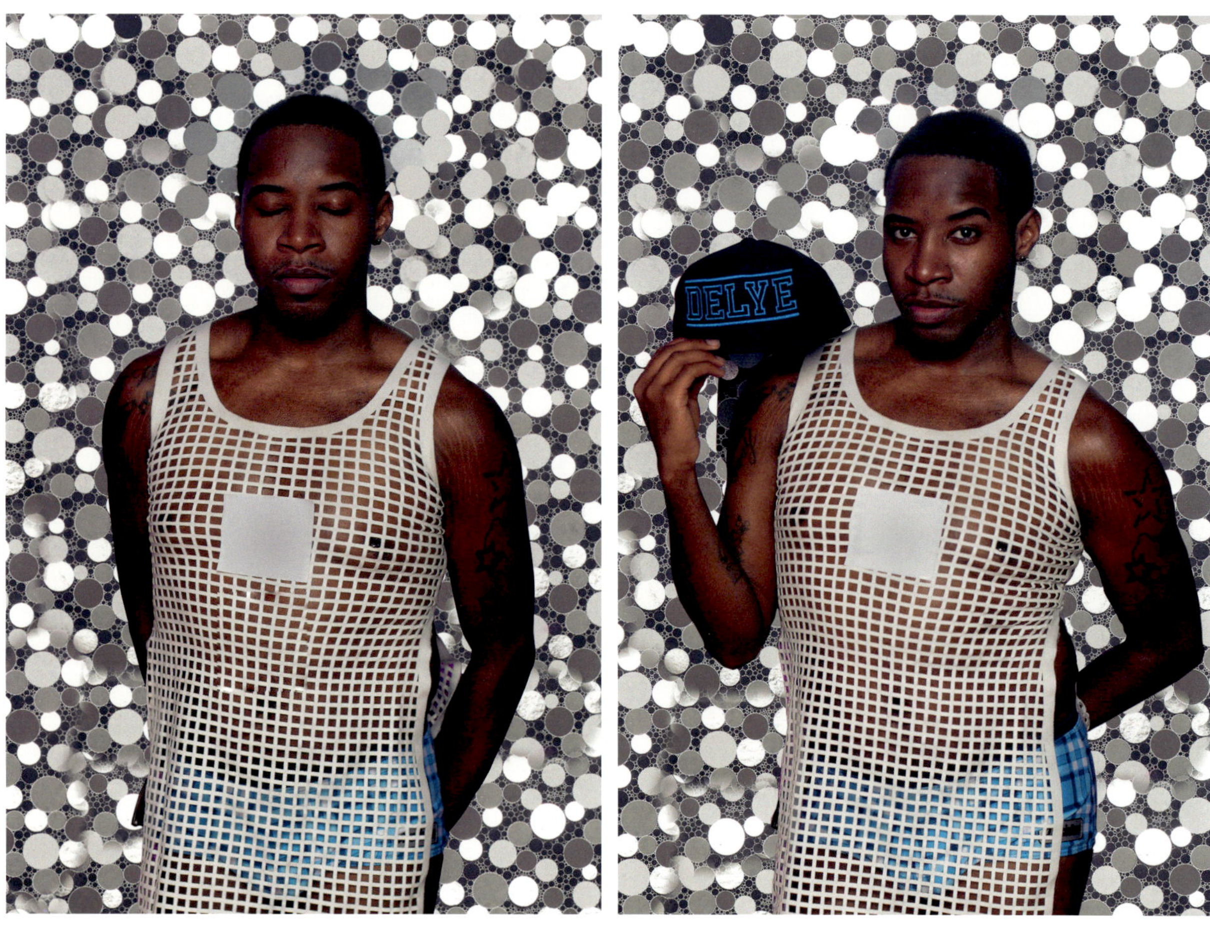
DELYE

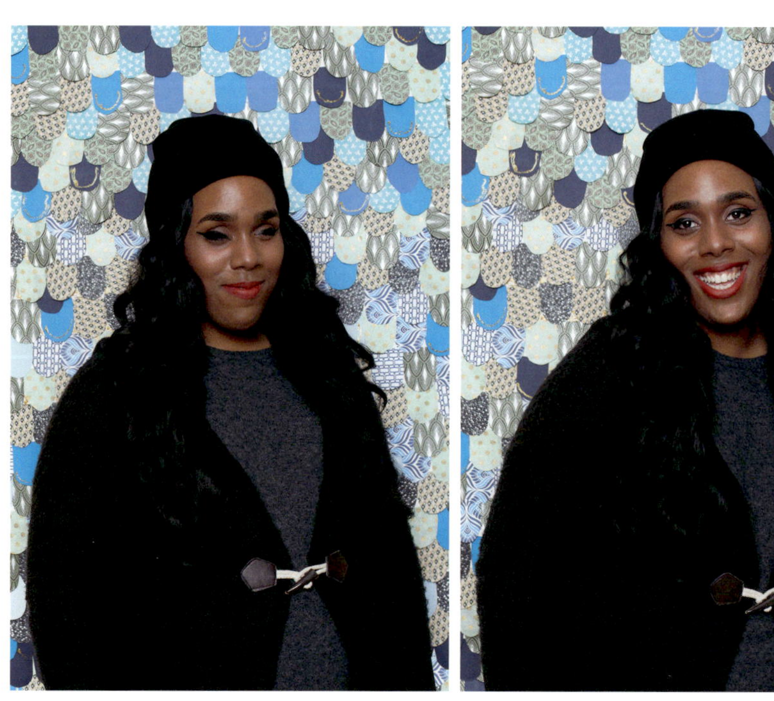

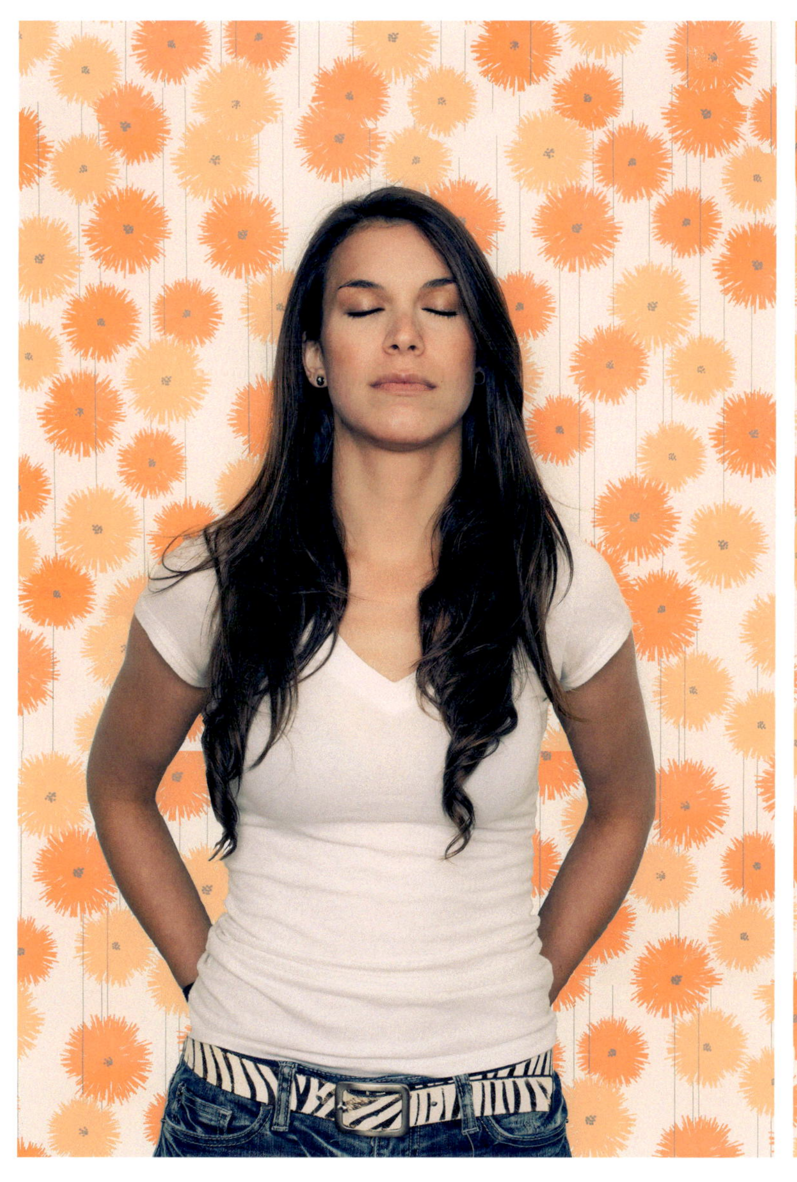
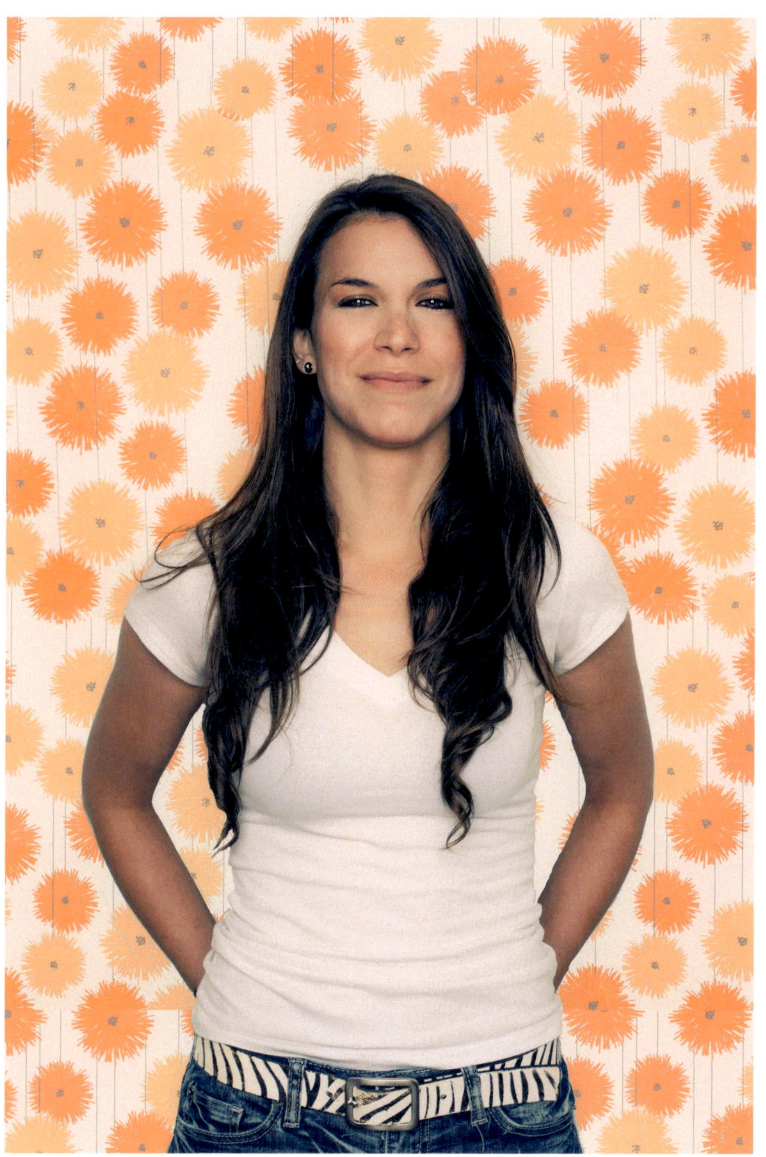

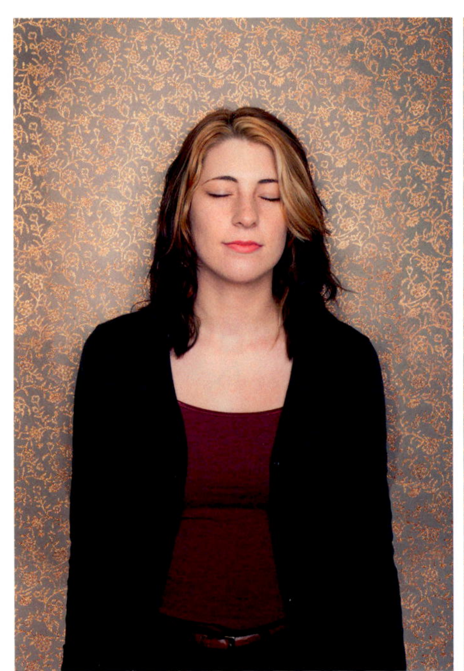
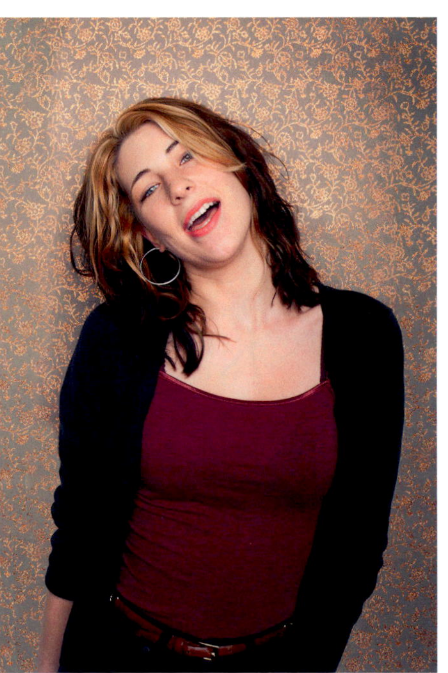
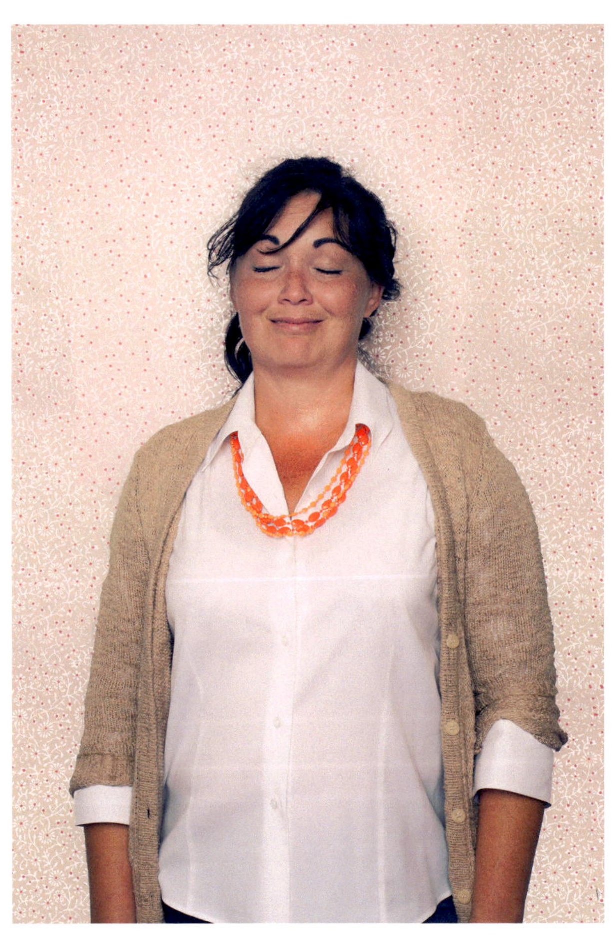
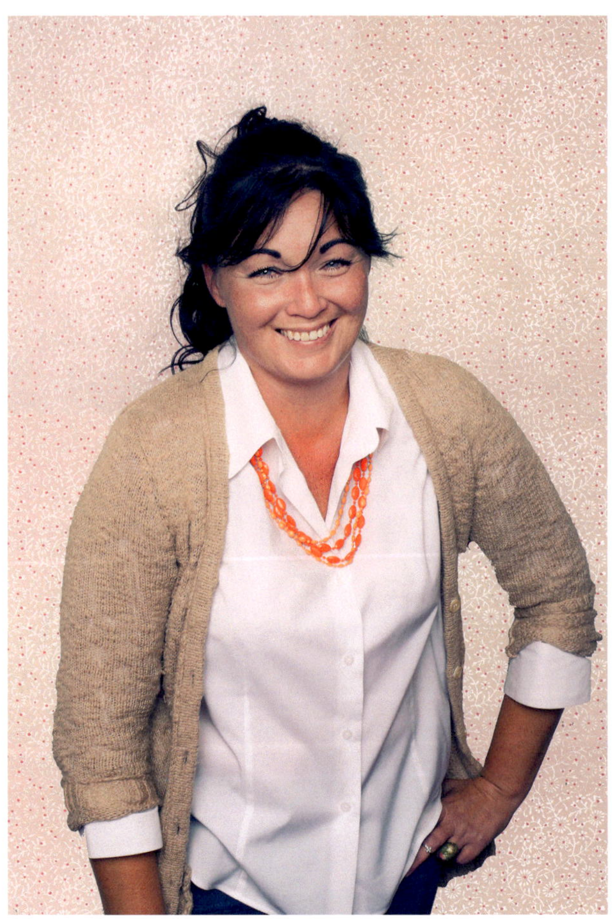

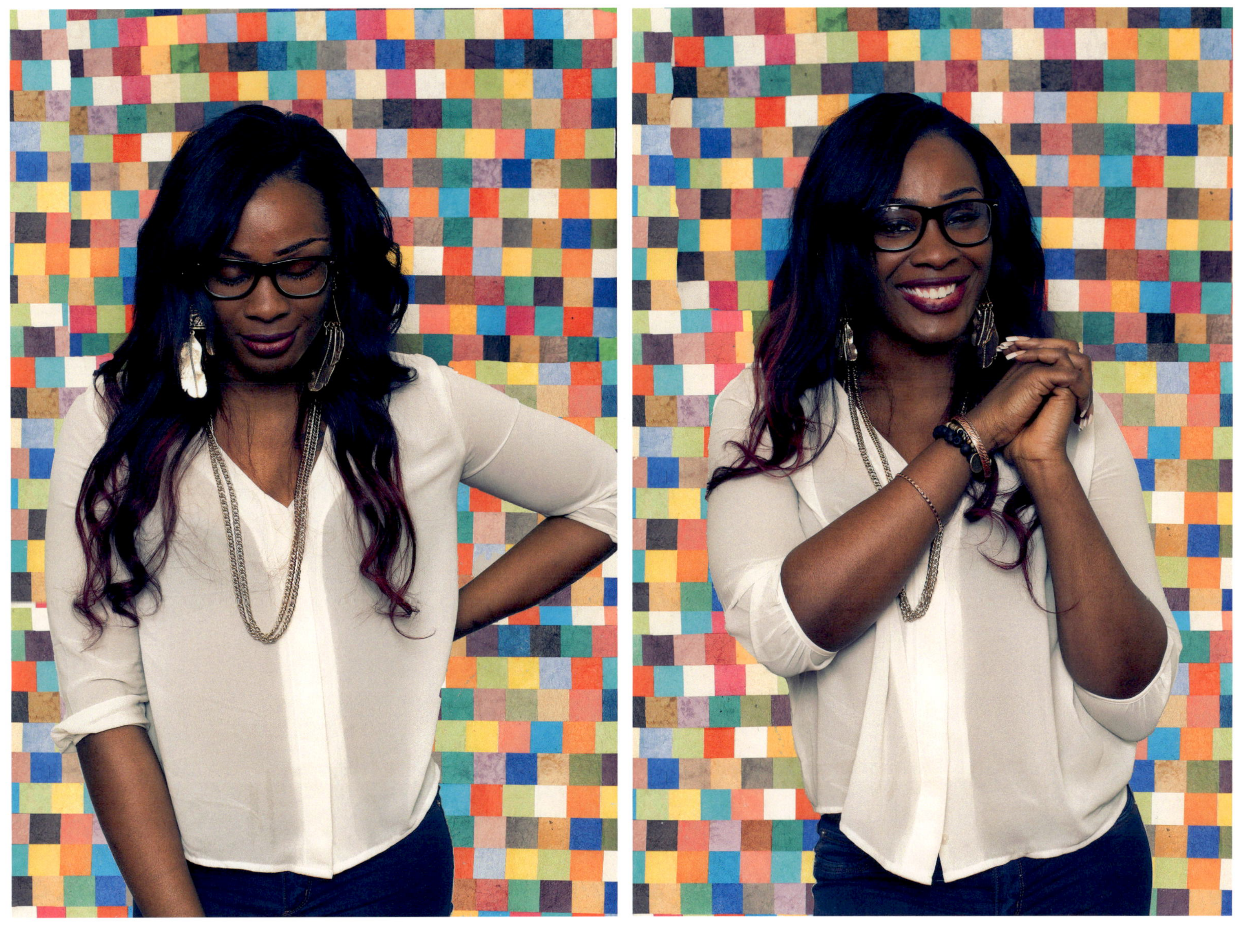

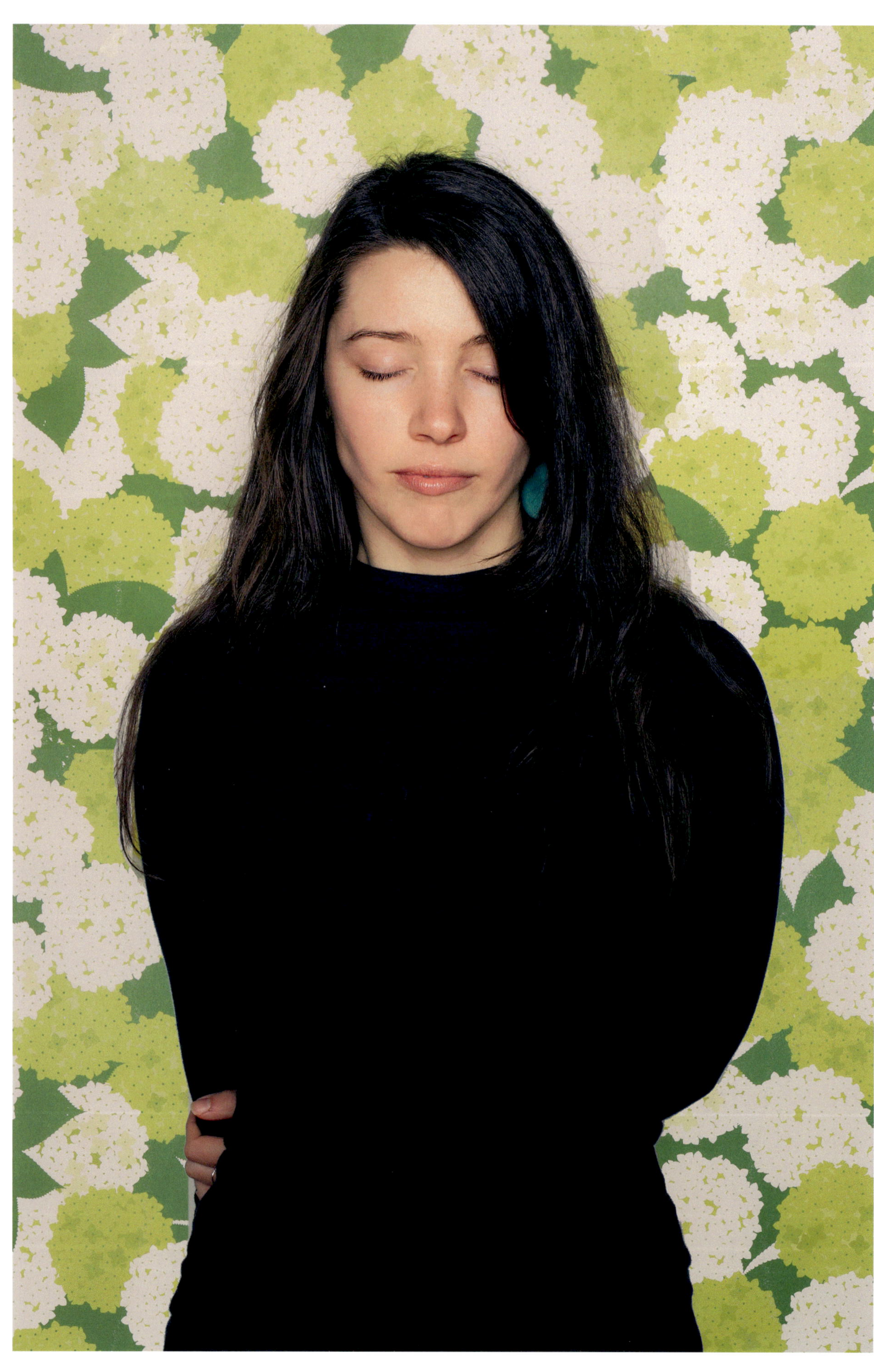

GAY | FACE

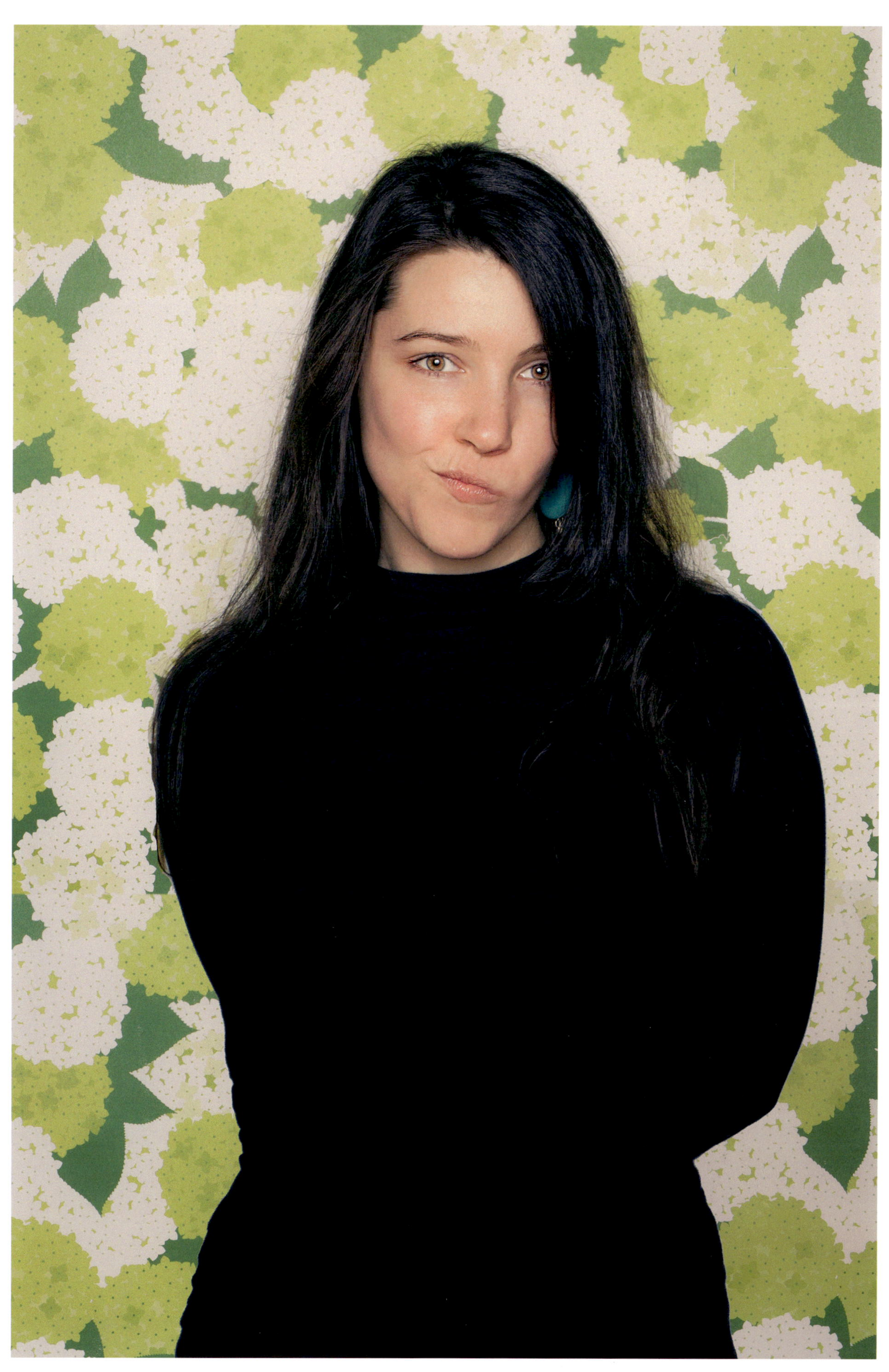

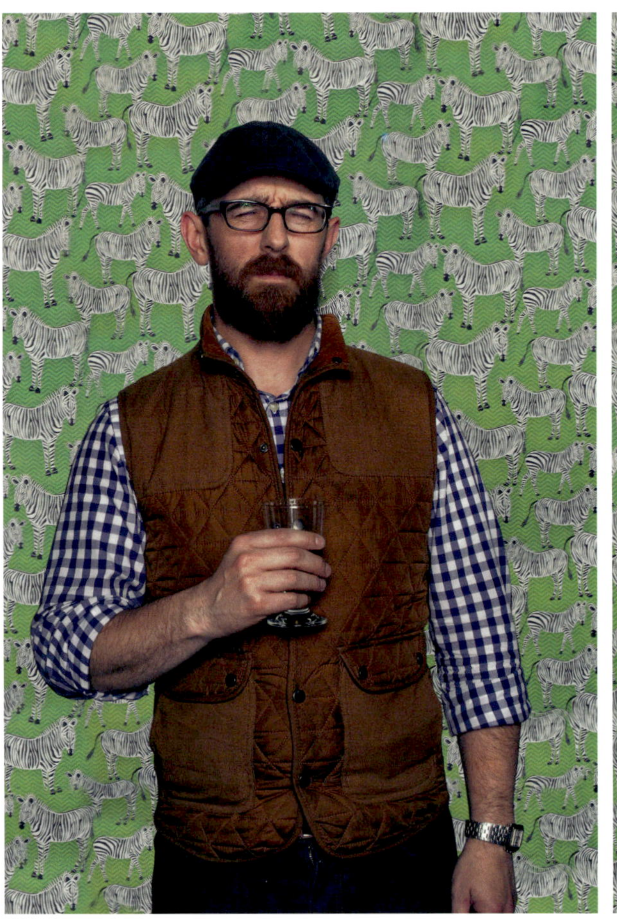
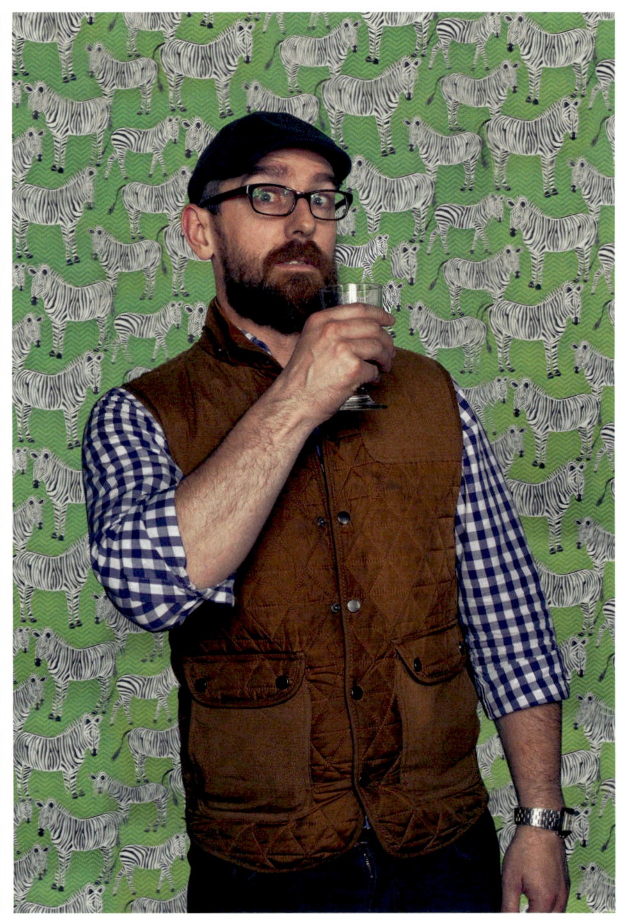
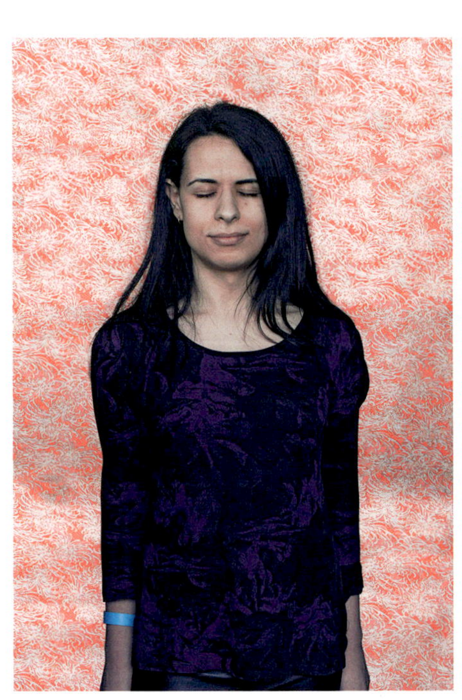
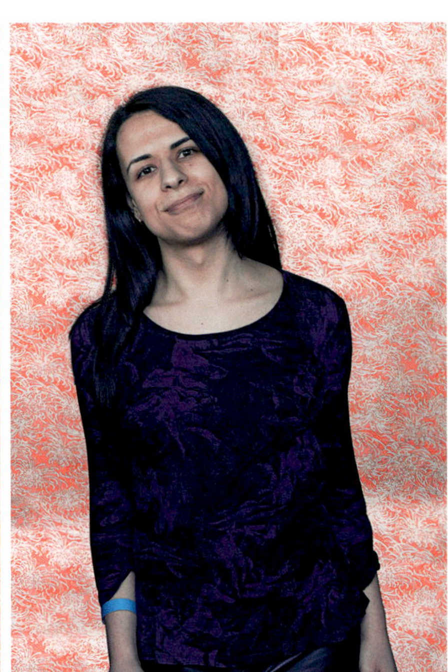

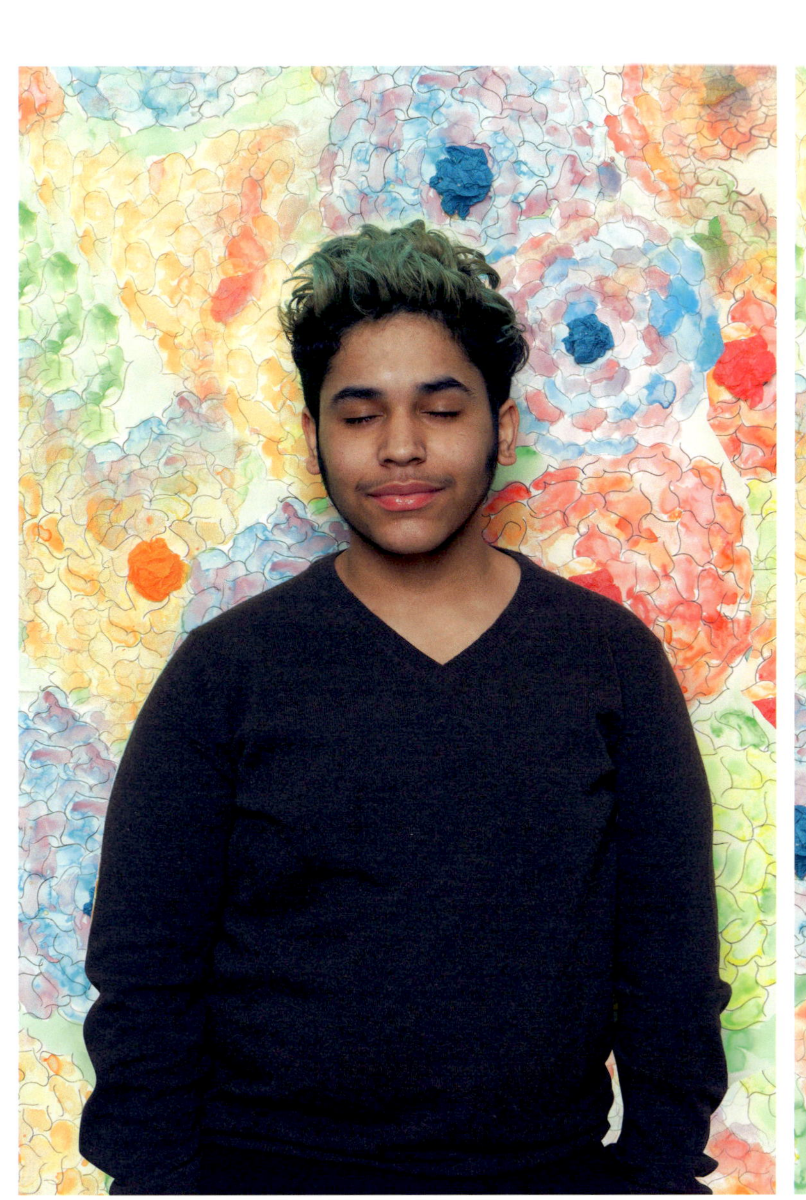

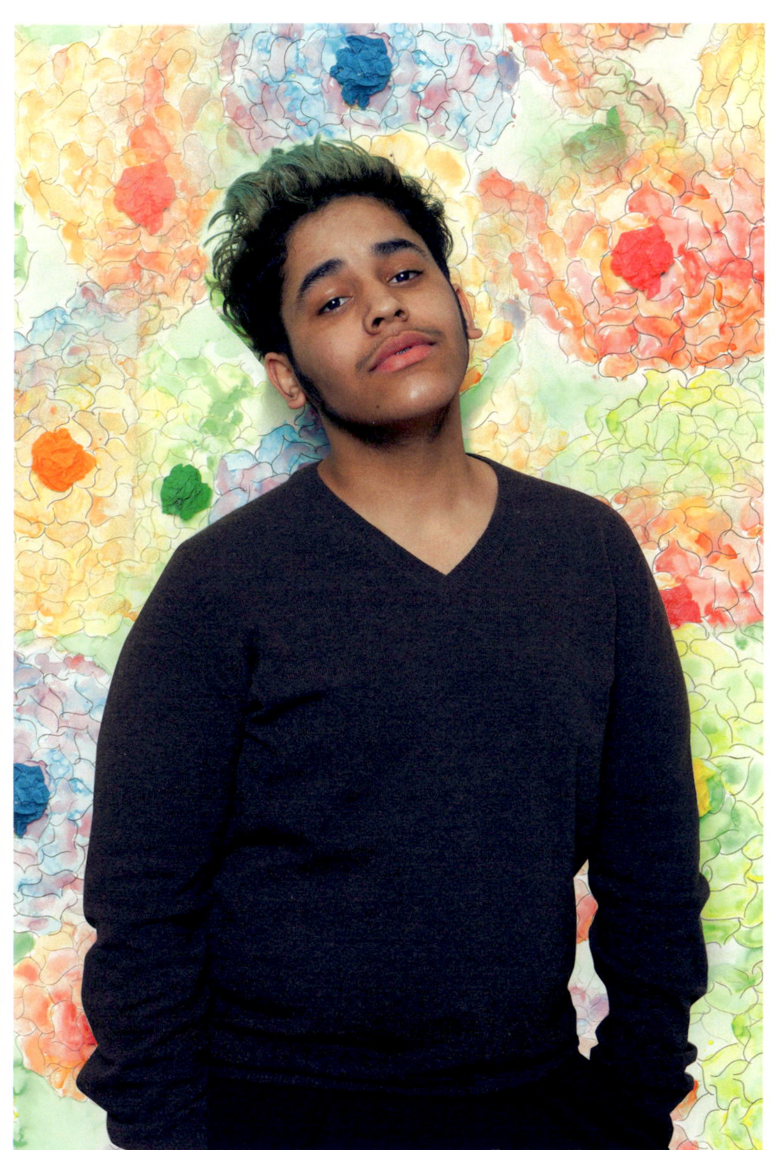

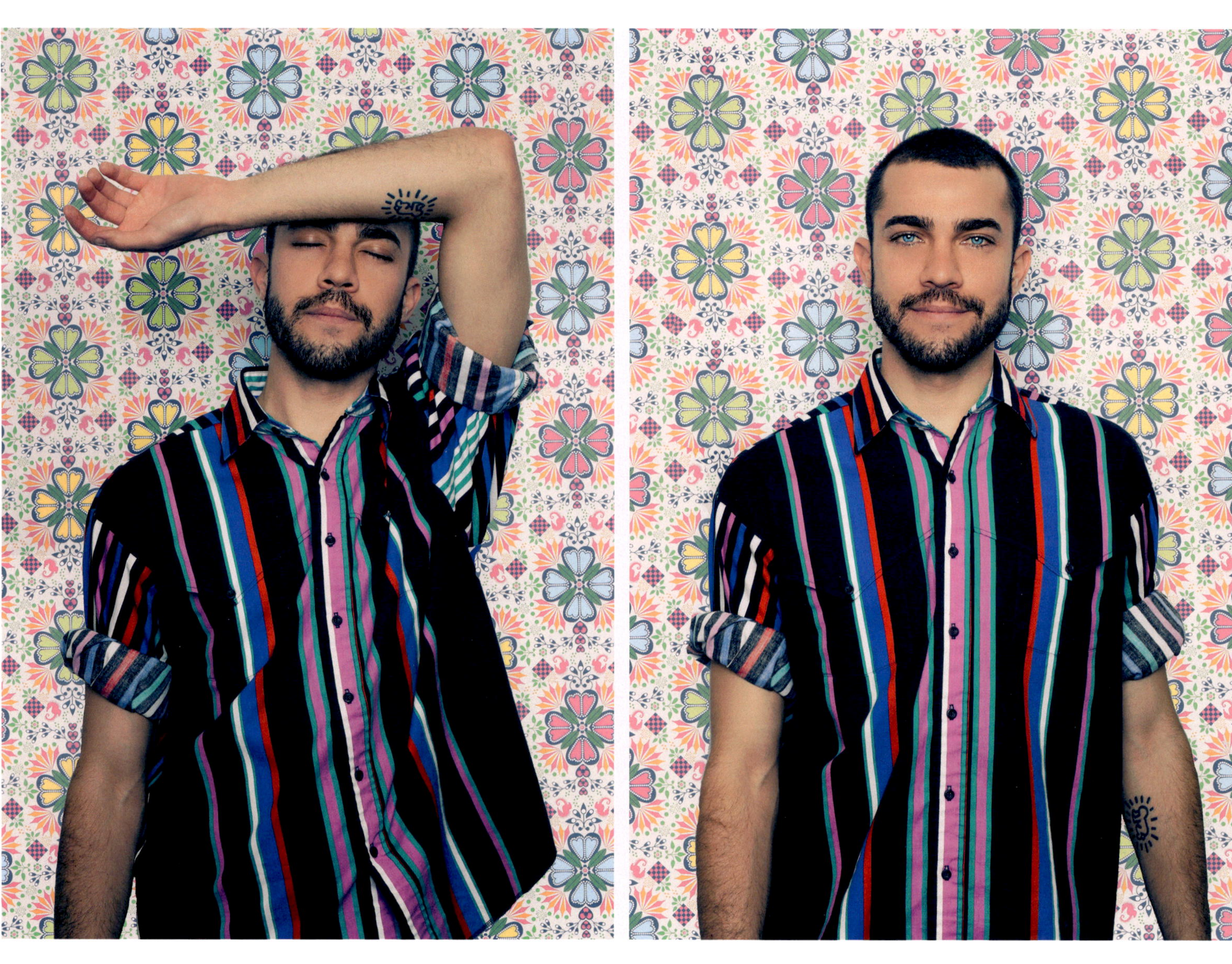
GAY | FACE

Alex F.

SAN DIEGO, CALIFORNIA

How would you identify your sexuality?
Queer/gay.

What do you think of your portrait?
I was and continue to be thrilled with my portrait. I have used it on many occasions as my headshot—so often that a friend once commented that I needed to take another picture because I had worn that one out! In response, I recently asked Ash for another series of portraits.

I love the colorful background that I selected, and I still have the paper hanging in my living room.

Describe your coming out. Are you coming out in some way by participating in this project?
I came out to my family and friends after I graduated from high school. I had some hiccups with family and friends around acceptance, but I generally experienced a sincere and appreciated response to coming out.

It's pretty widely known that I am gay—my Instagram handle is @fagalho, after all, queering my last name, Fialho—so this project wasn't too much of a coming out, other than to people who don't know me.

Have you ever experienced discrimination based on your gender or sexual orientation?
Personally, my parents supported me in countless ways for the first eighteen years of my life; although when I told my mom that I was gay, she cried, fearing for my safety and probably mourning some of her lost dreams. My father and I didn't speak for weeks after I came out to him. They are both very supportive now. I bring this all up to say that the fight required to love who we want—to be gay—is a *process*, at times immensely painful.

If you could change one thing about mainstream society to improve the lives of LGBTQ+ people, what would it be?
I think I would change how LGBTQ+ people often feel the need to perform, or overcompensate as a result of the trauma from growing up in a heteronormative society.

Describe how this project has affected you, both personally and as a member of the LGBTQ+ community as a whole.
I love the title *Gayface*. It's a word that I've heard in the world, and it implies that there is some identifiable marker, phenotype, or facial expression that relates to sexual identity that can be read as gay. (Admittedly, I often think a man with a well-moisturized—or even a little Botoxed-face—might be the closest thing to a "gayface!") Jokes aside, taking part in the project meant claiming my identity in a powerful and straightforward way for an audience outside of the one I know.

Who are your LGBTQ+ role models?
Rather than a typical celebrity as role model, I think the queer people I've celebrated in my life as friends, mentors and creative inspirations mean the most. For example, Buzz Bense (1949–2016), an ardent activist, seasoned performer, and sex-positive force in San Francisco throughout the ongoing AIDS crisis.

My dear friend and mentor Dan Cooney has meant a lot to me in recent years.

Queer authors and artists—too many to list definitively—have also been incredibly influential: Keith Haring, Richard Meyer, Lyle Ashton Harris, Kia LaBeija, Douglas Crimp, Gregg Bordowitz, Chloe Dzubilo, Viva Ruiz, Félix González-Torres, and David Wojnarowicz come to mind, among so many others.

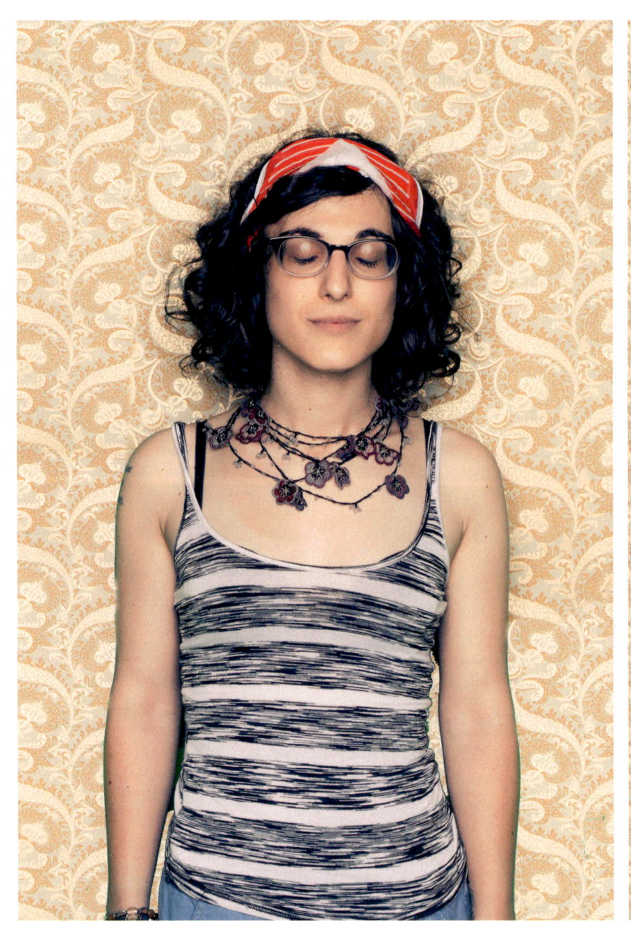
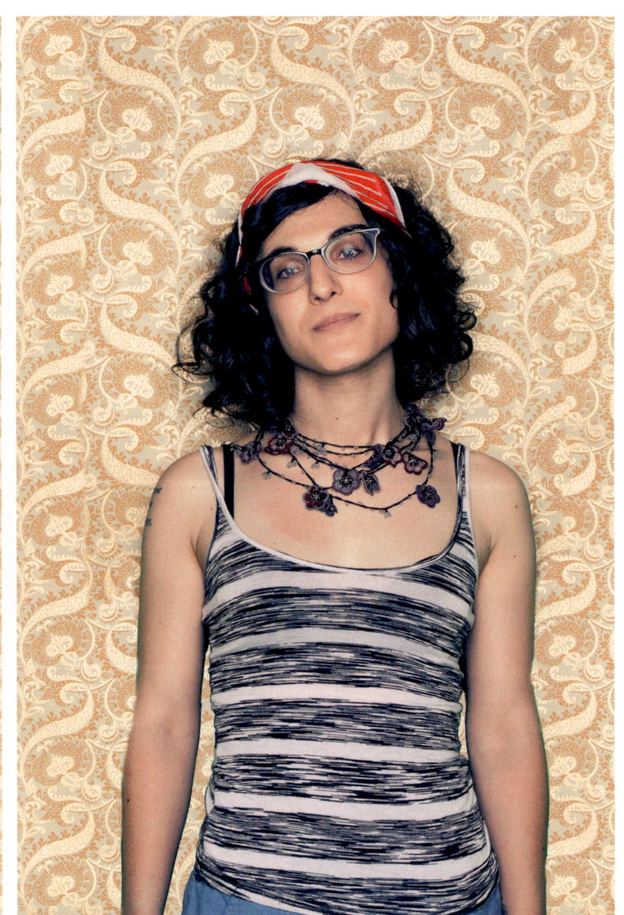
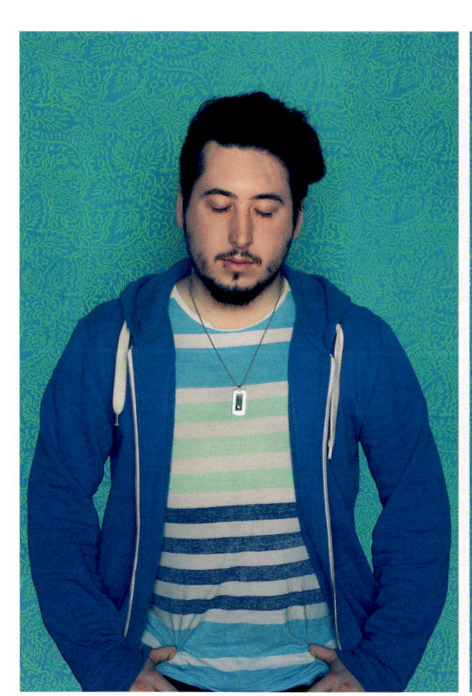
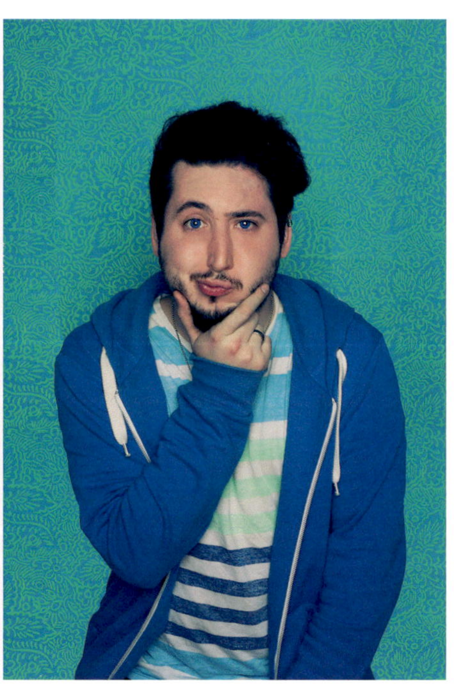

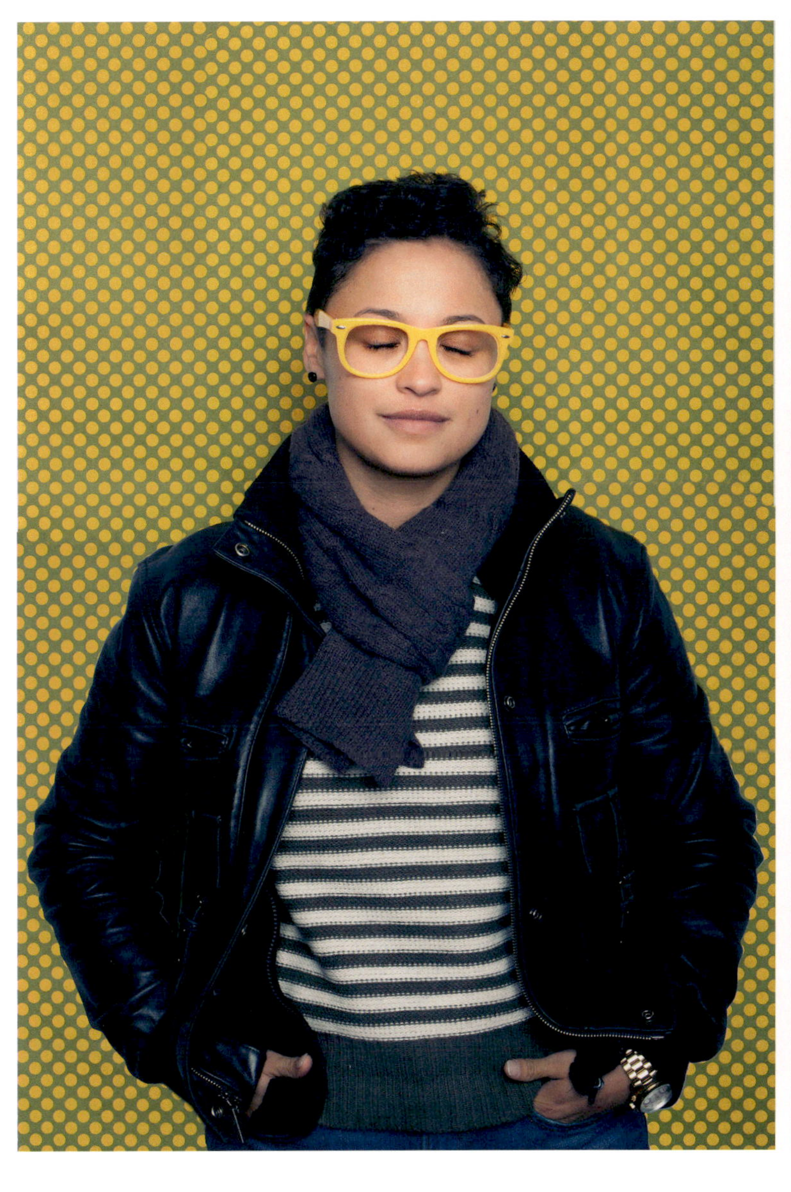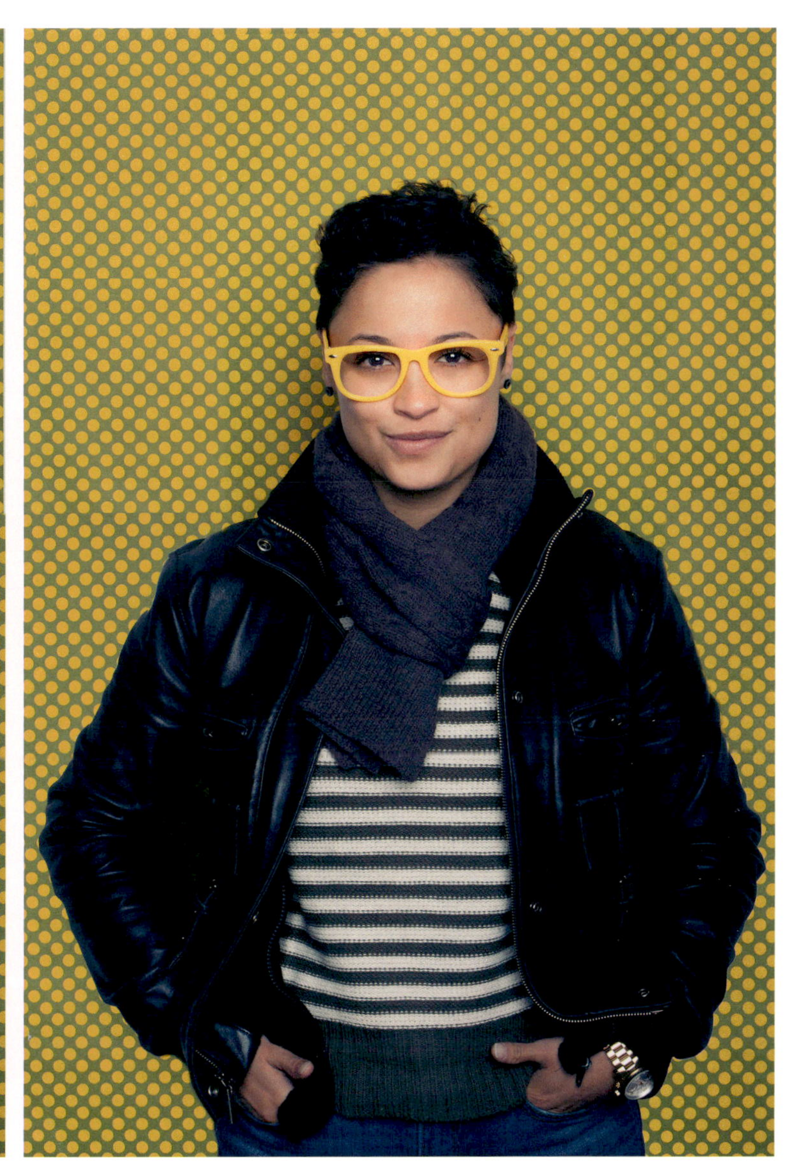

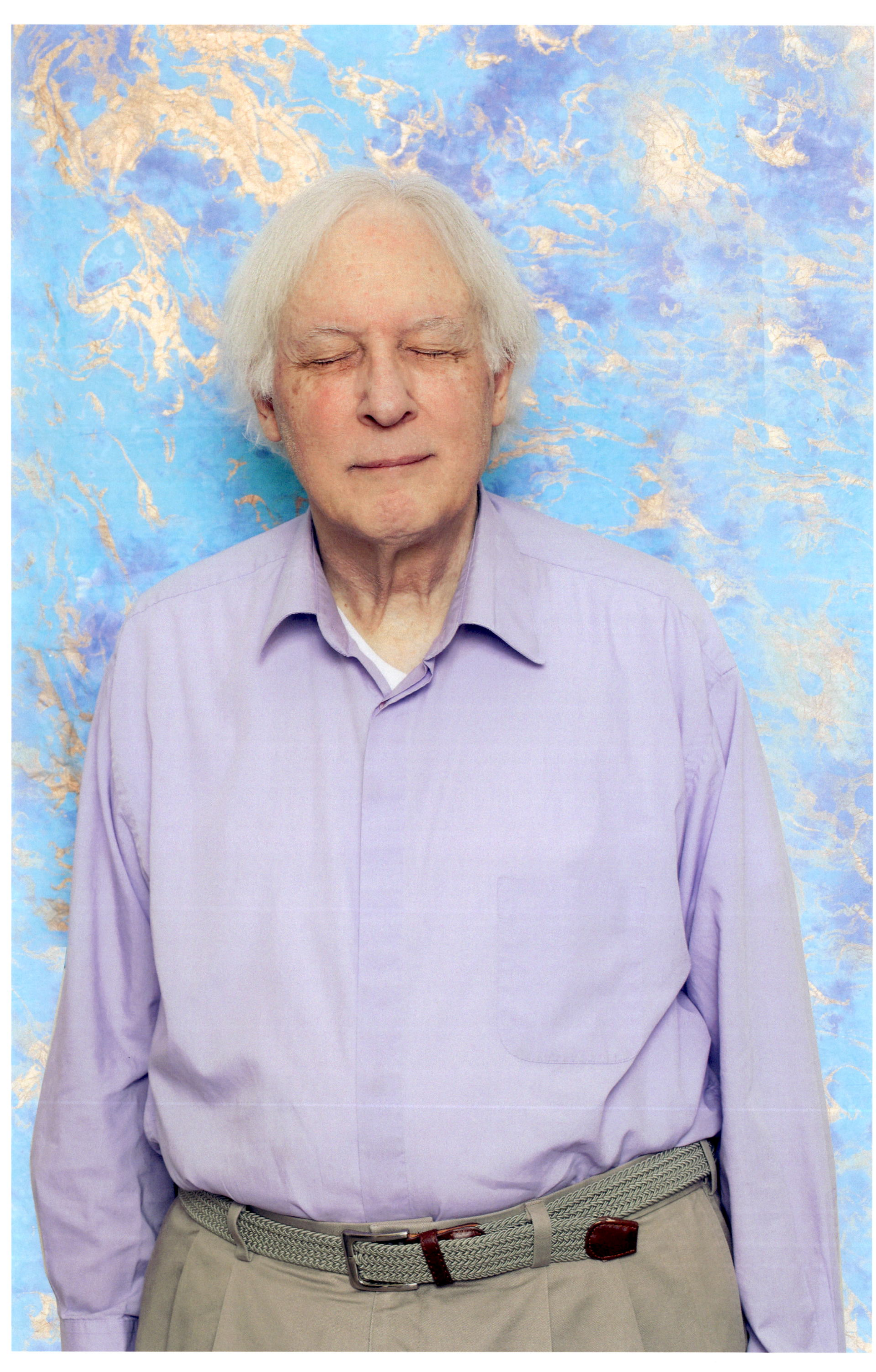

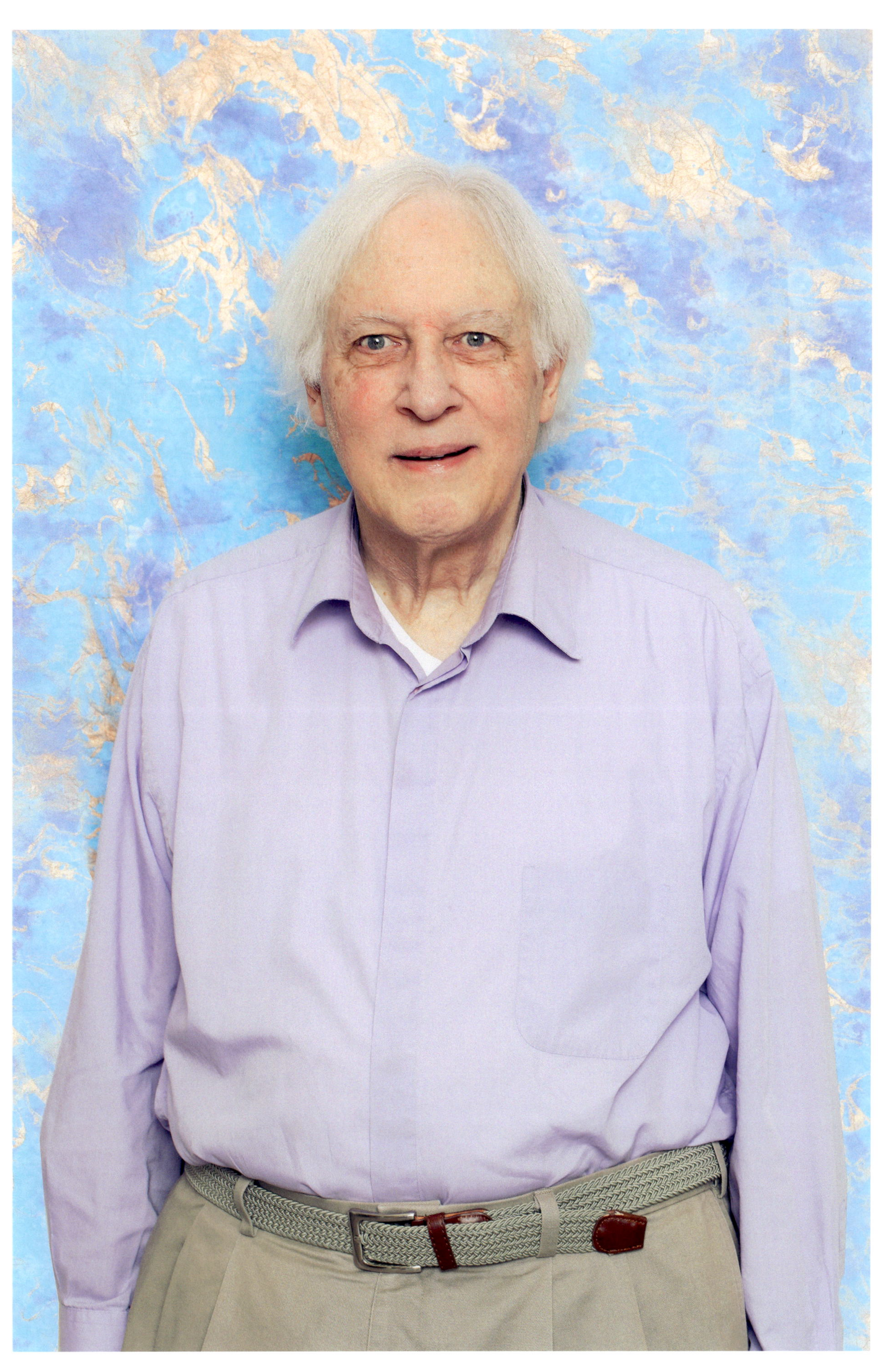

GAY | FACE

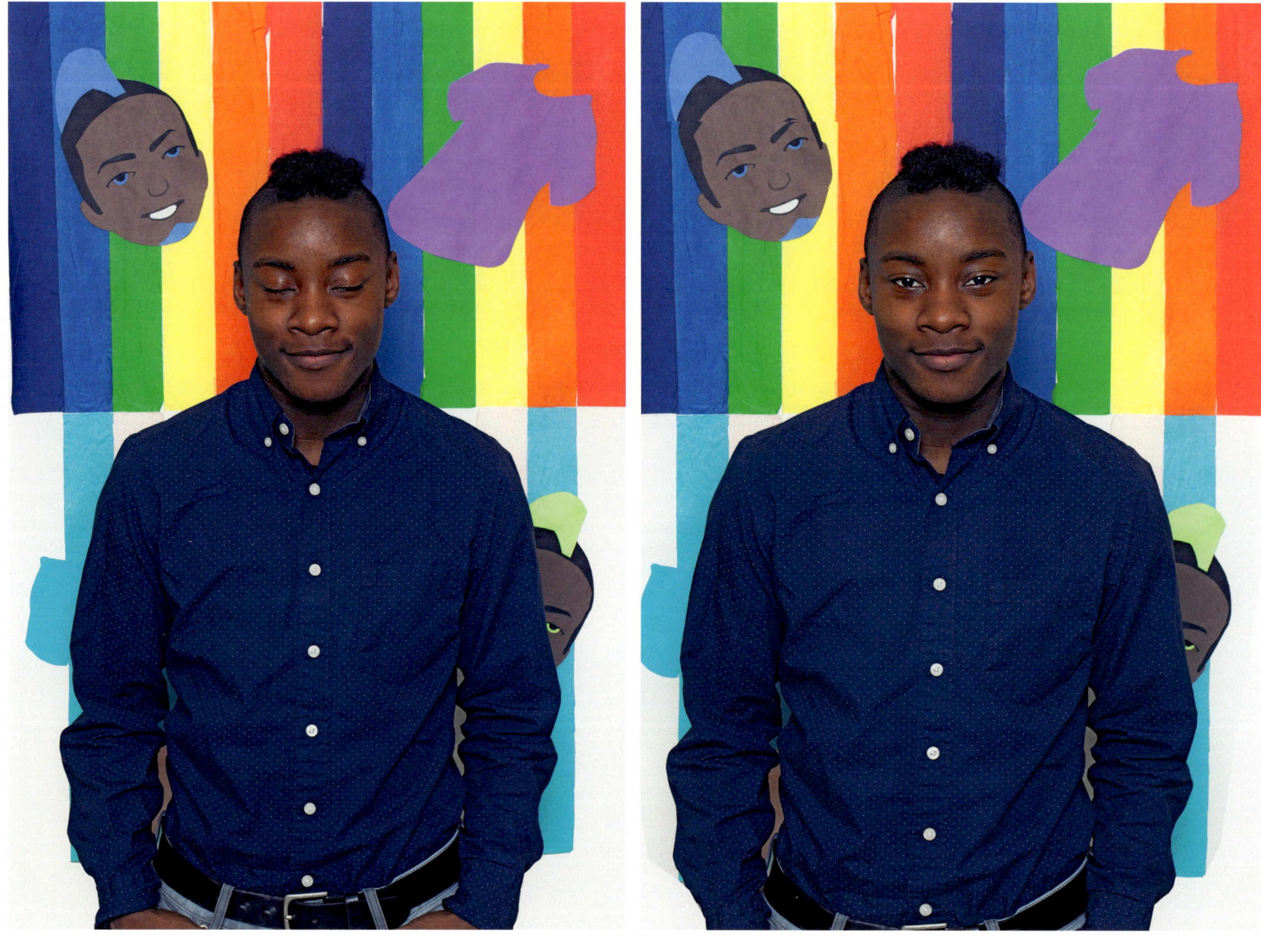

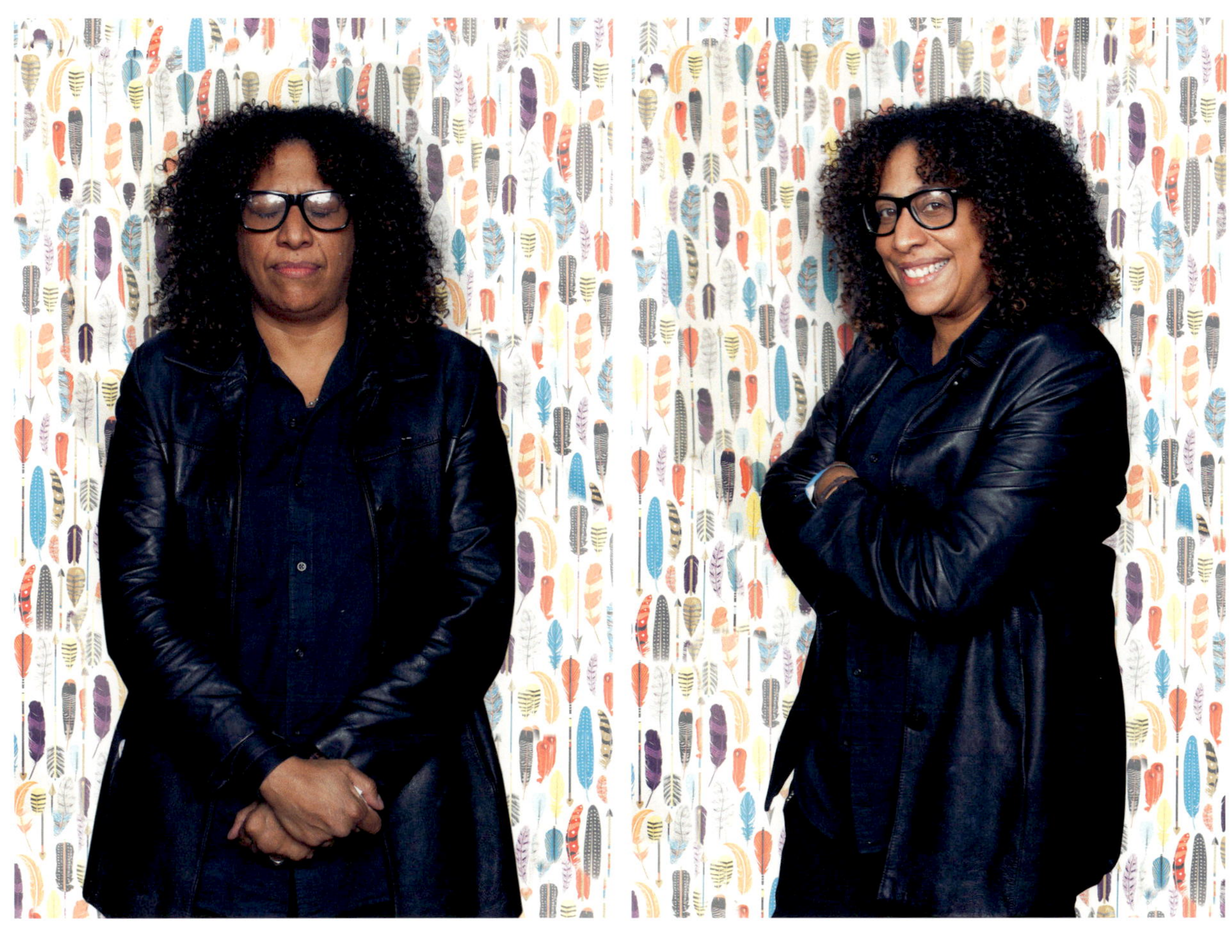

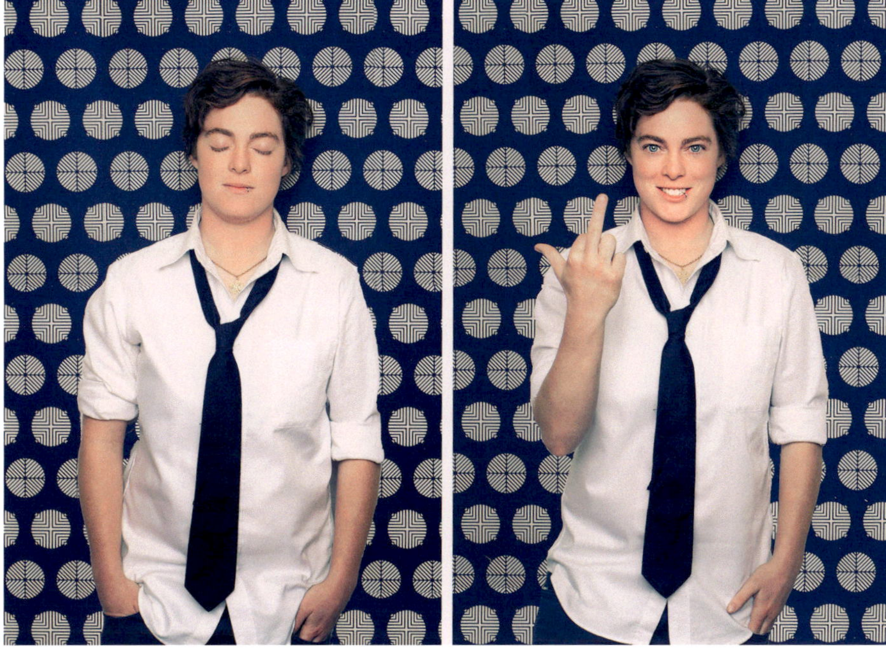

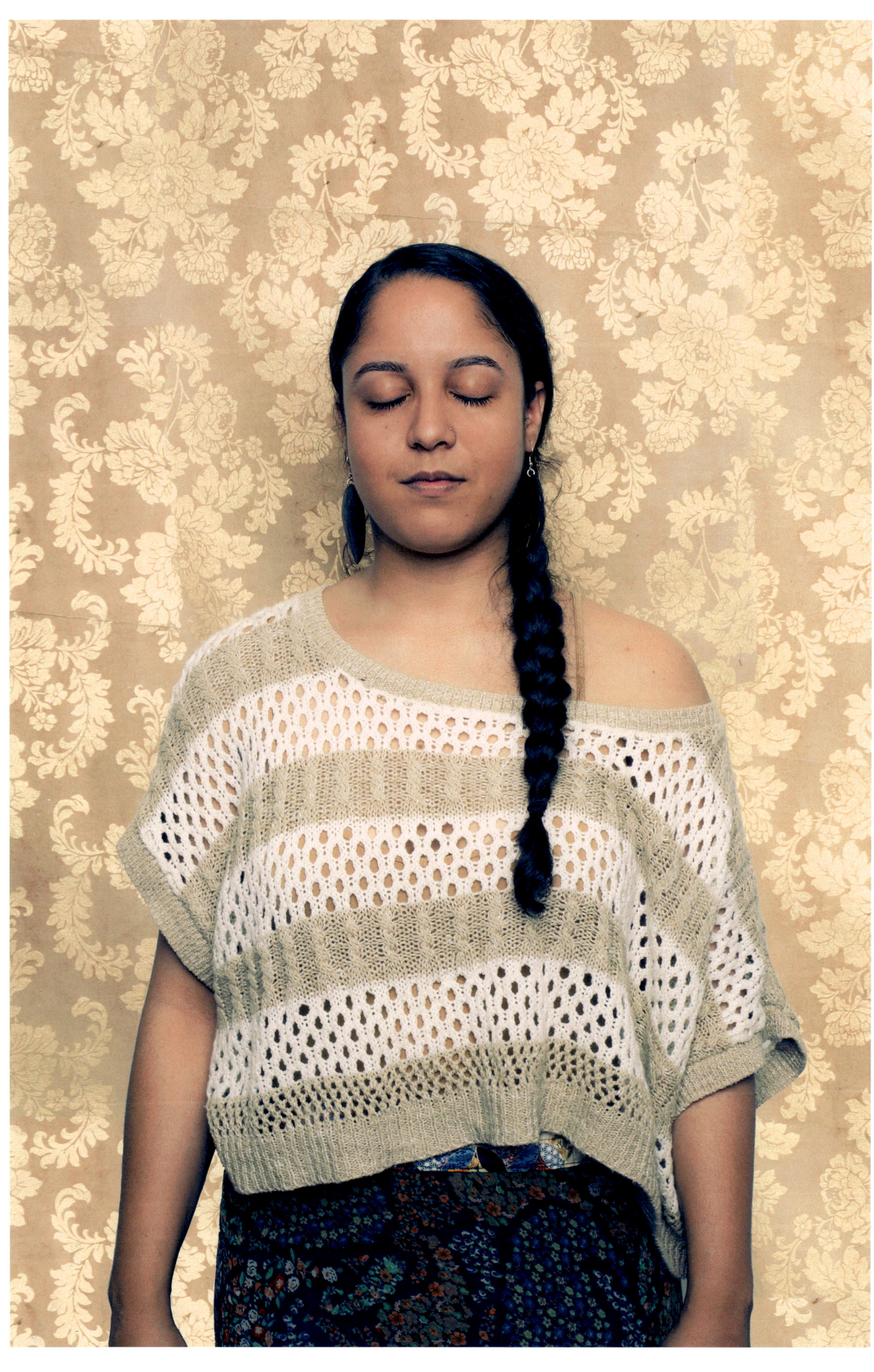

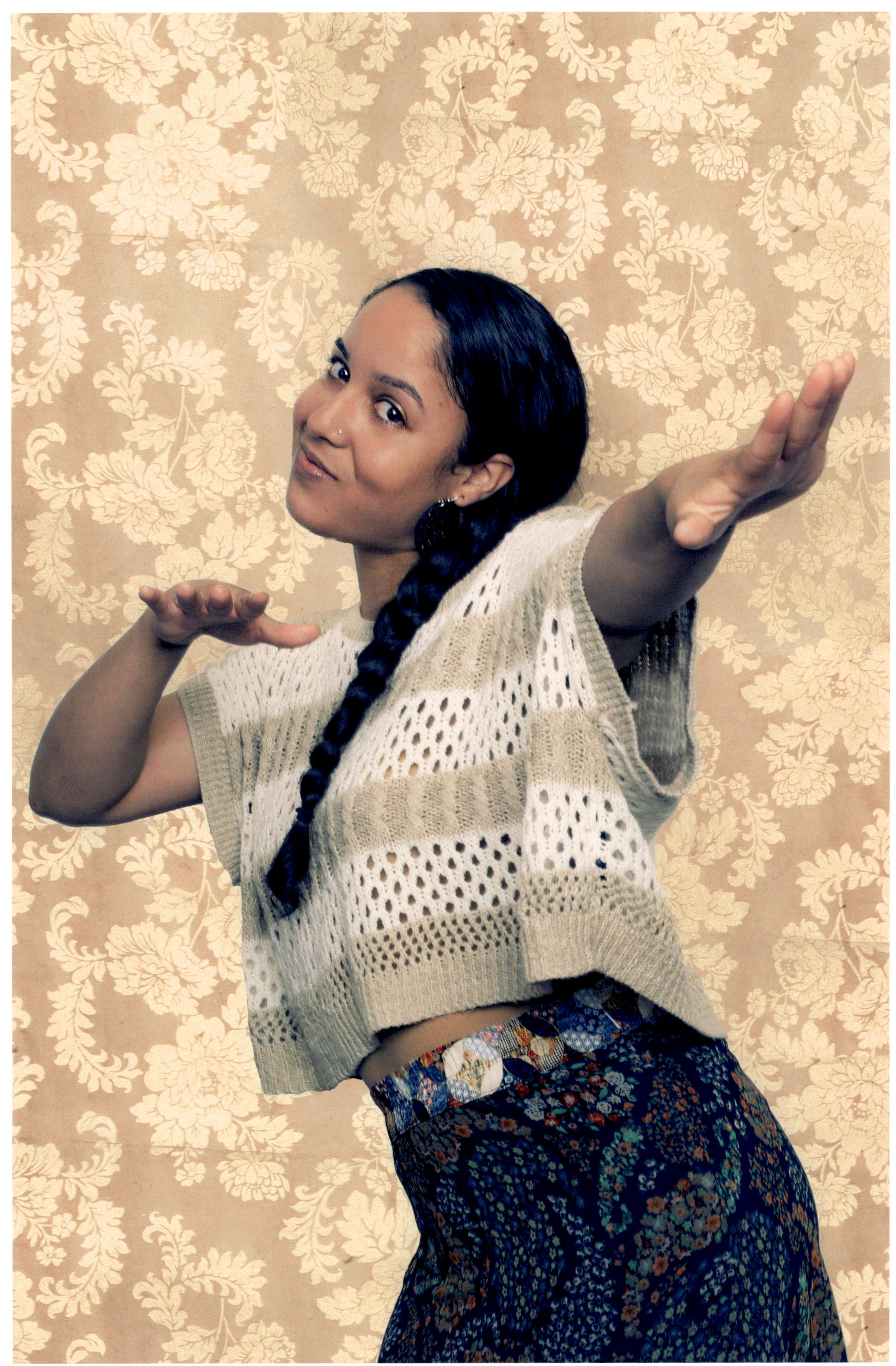

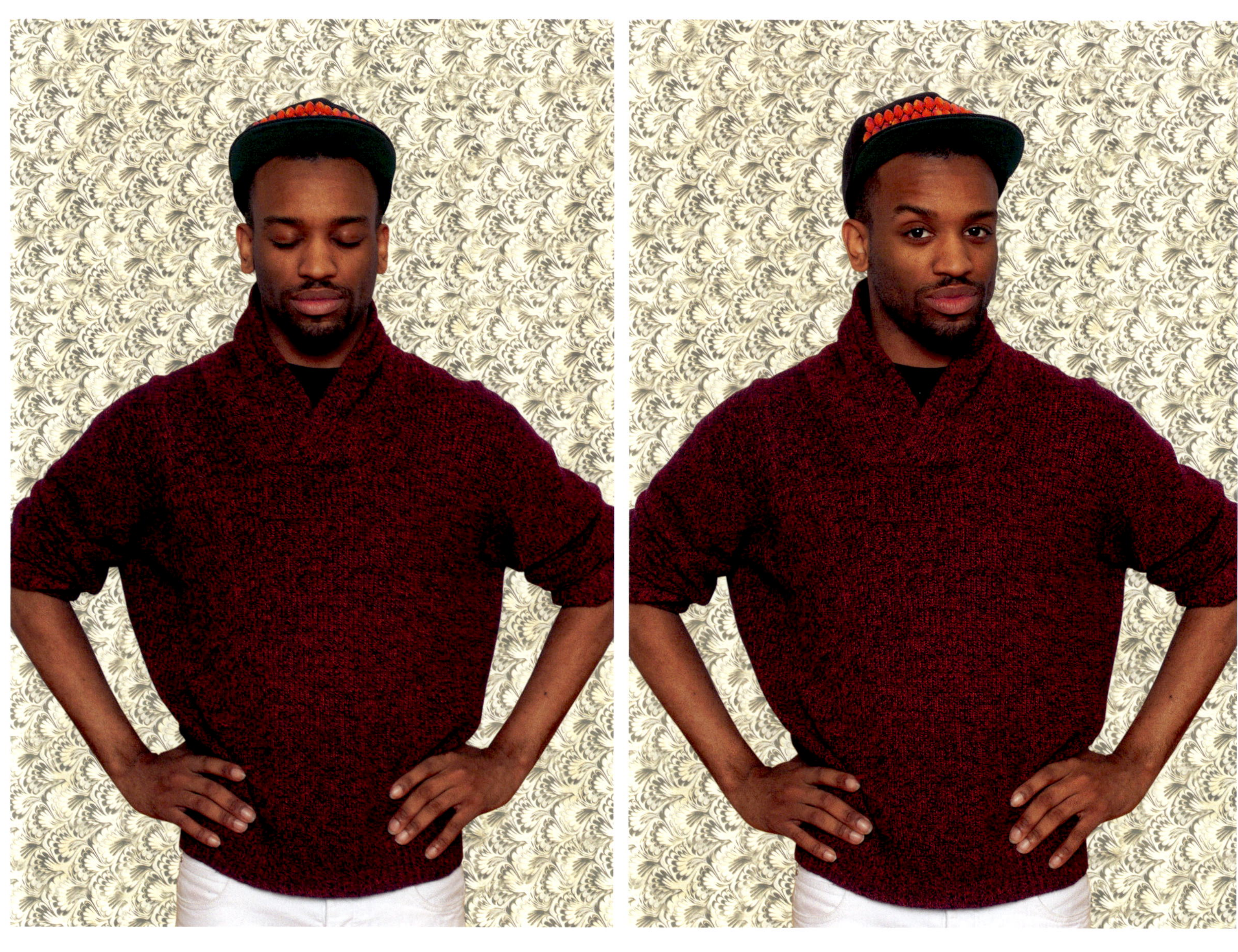

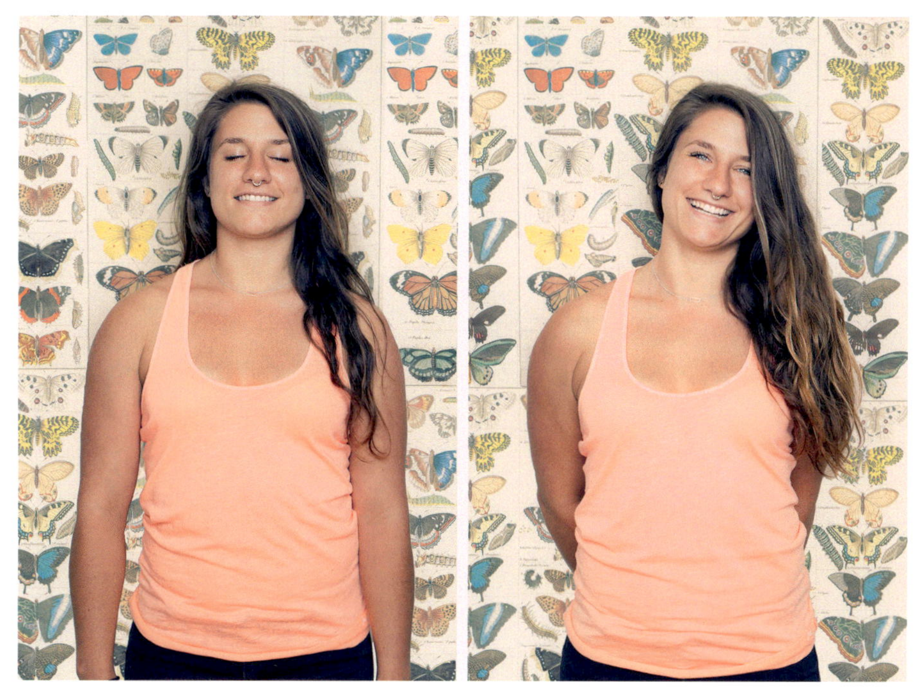

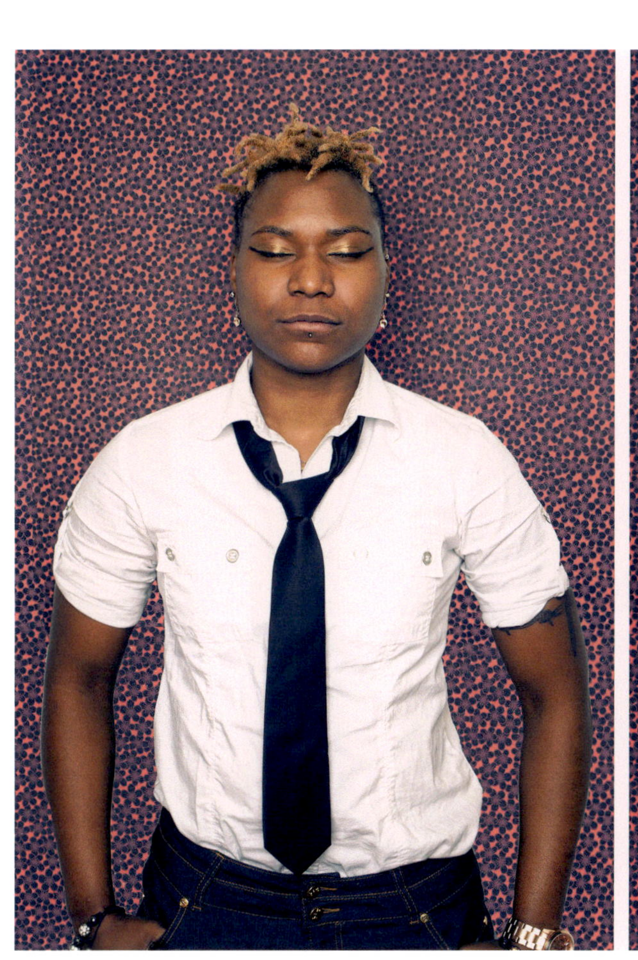

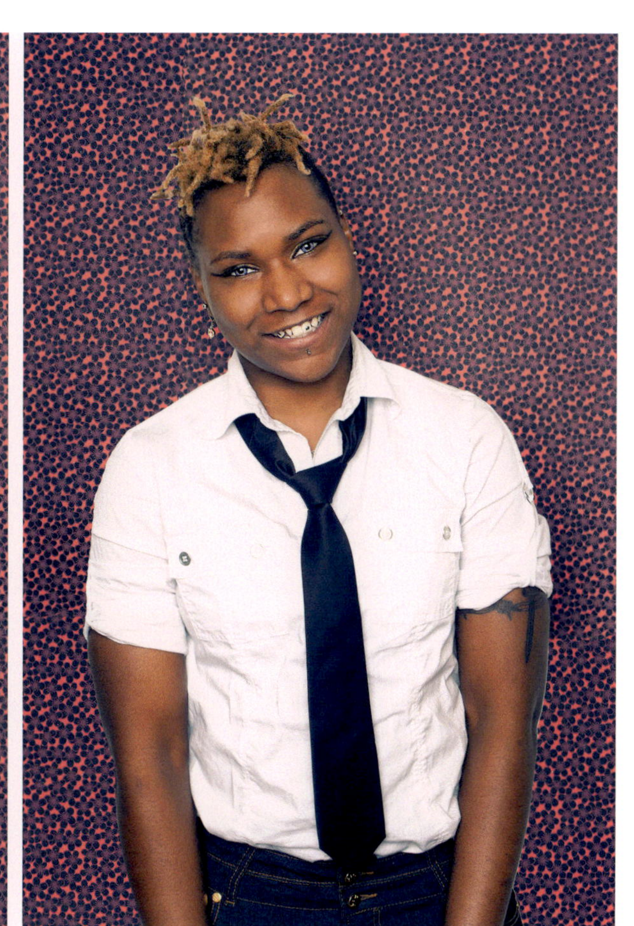

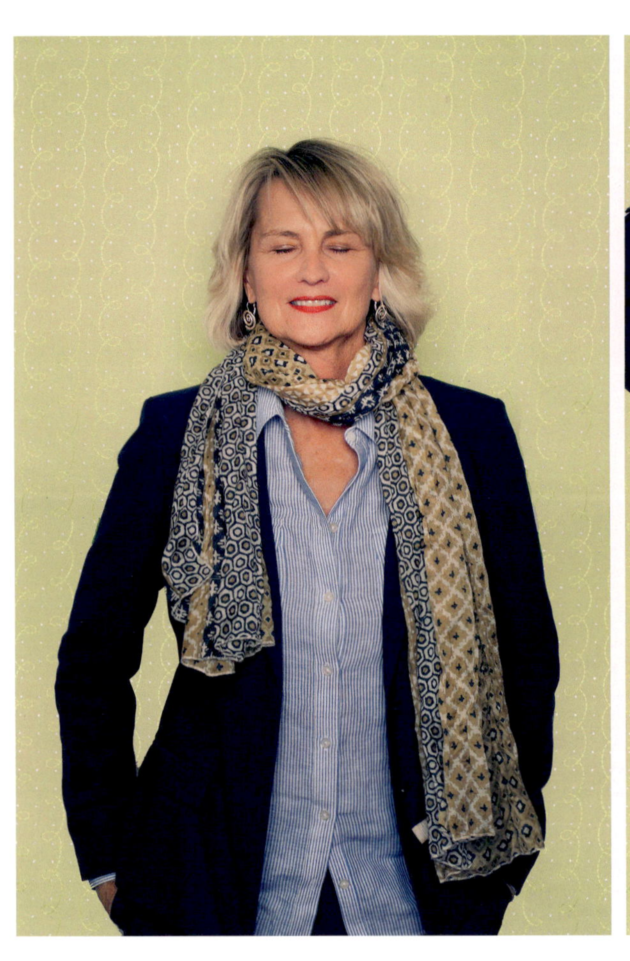 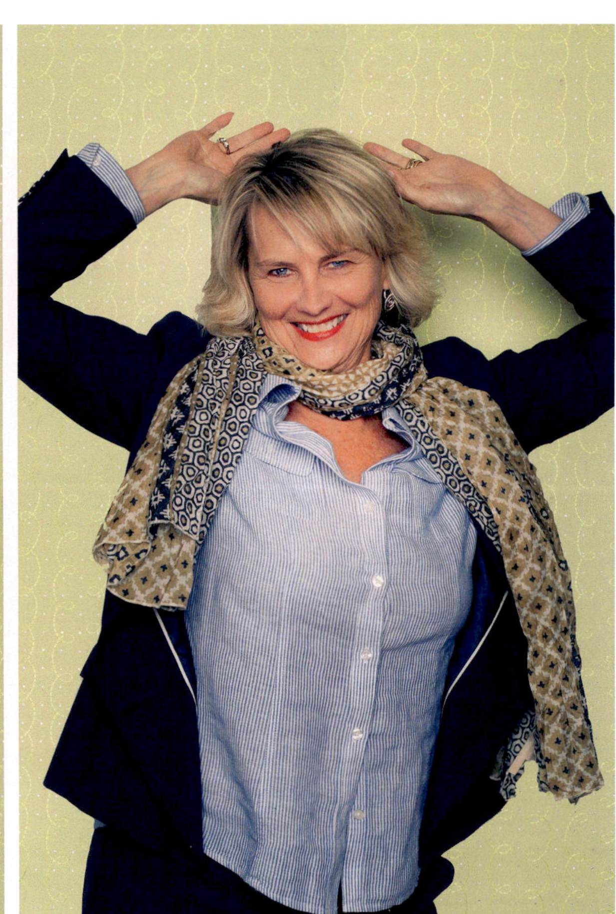

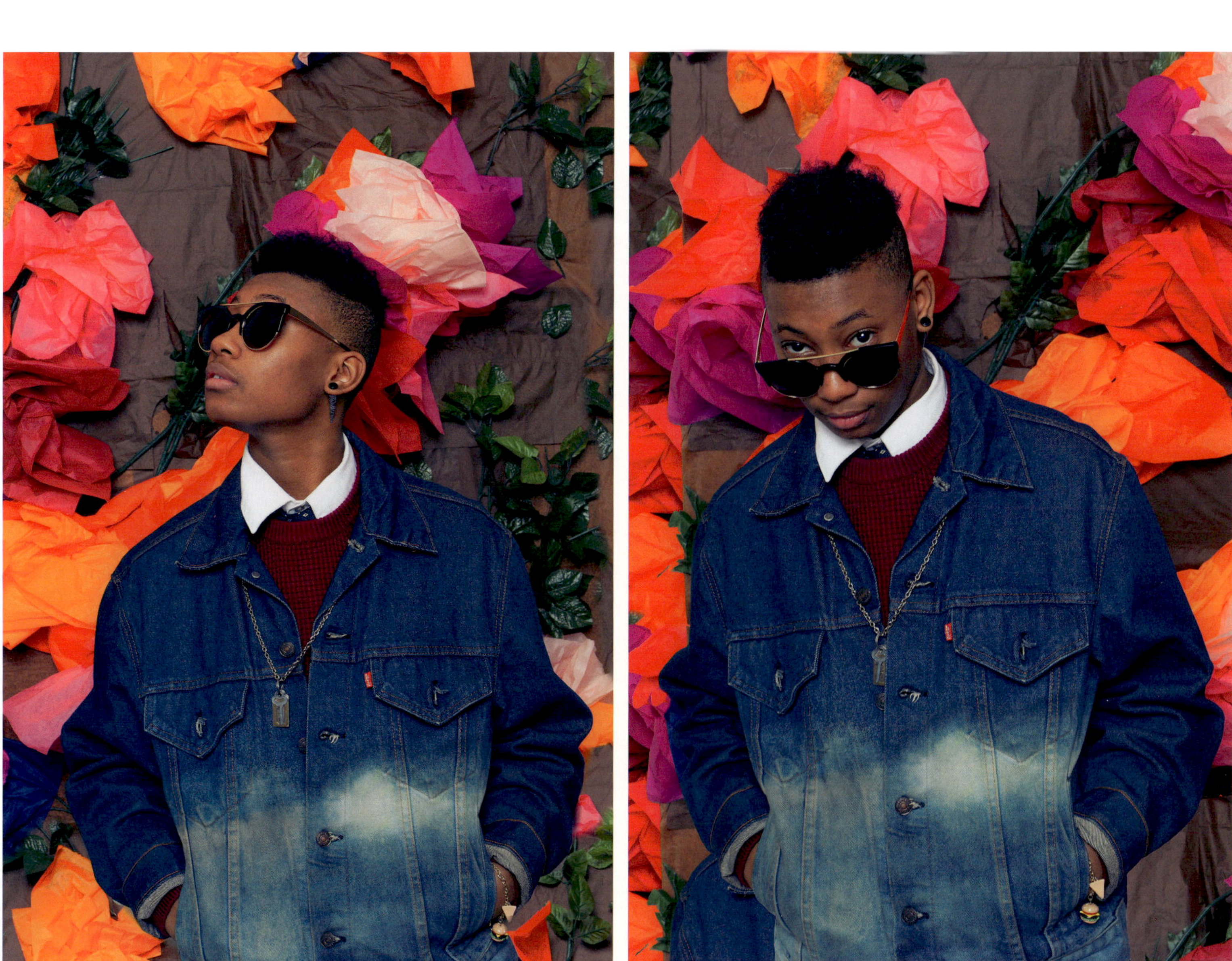

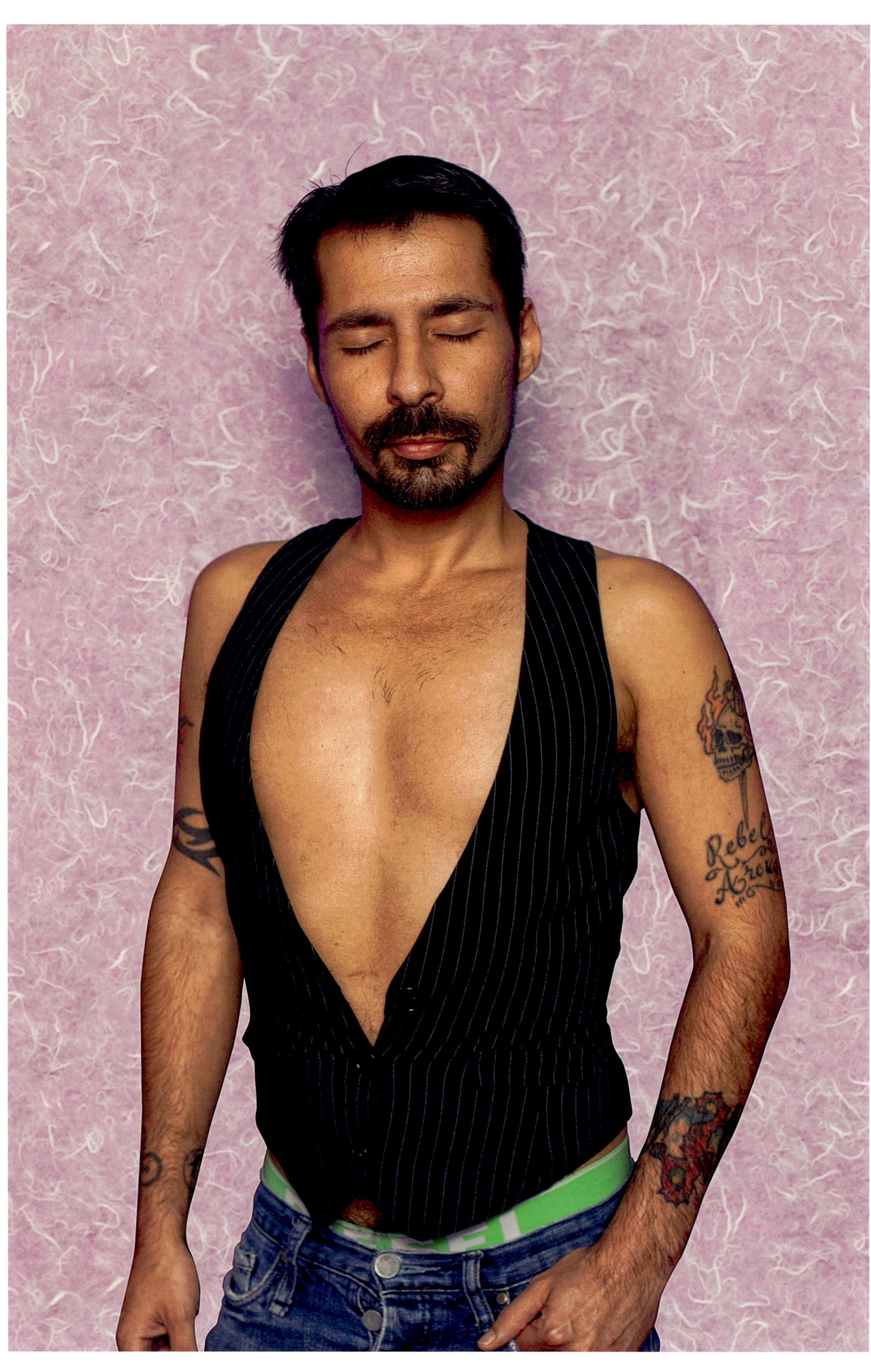

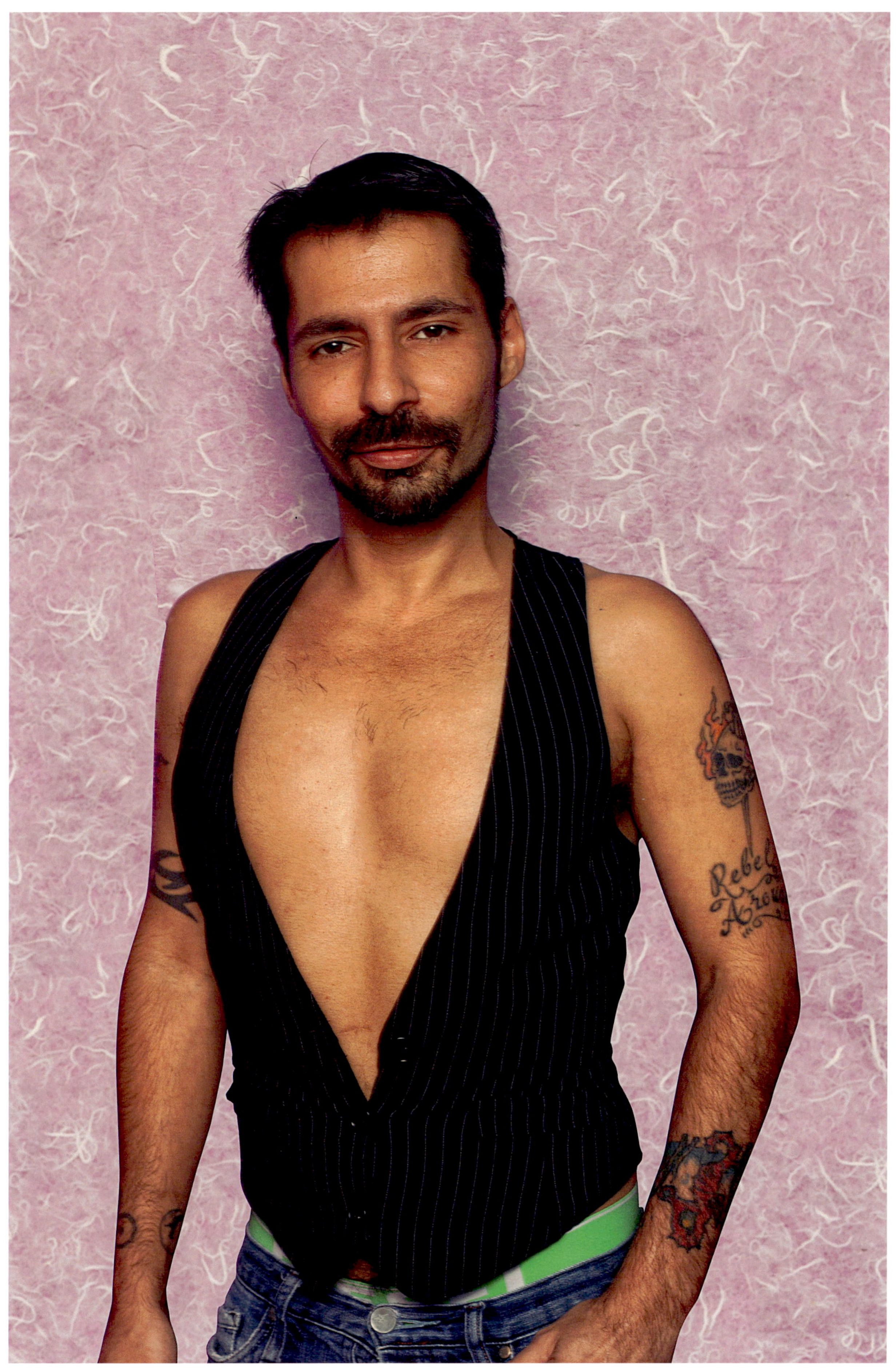

GAY | FACE

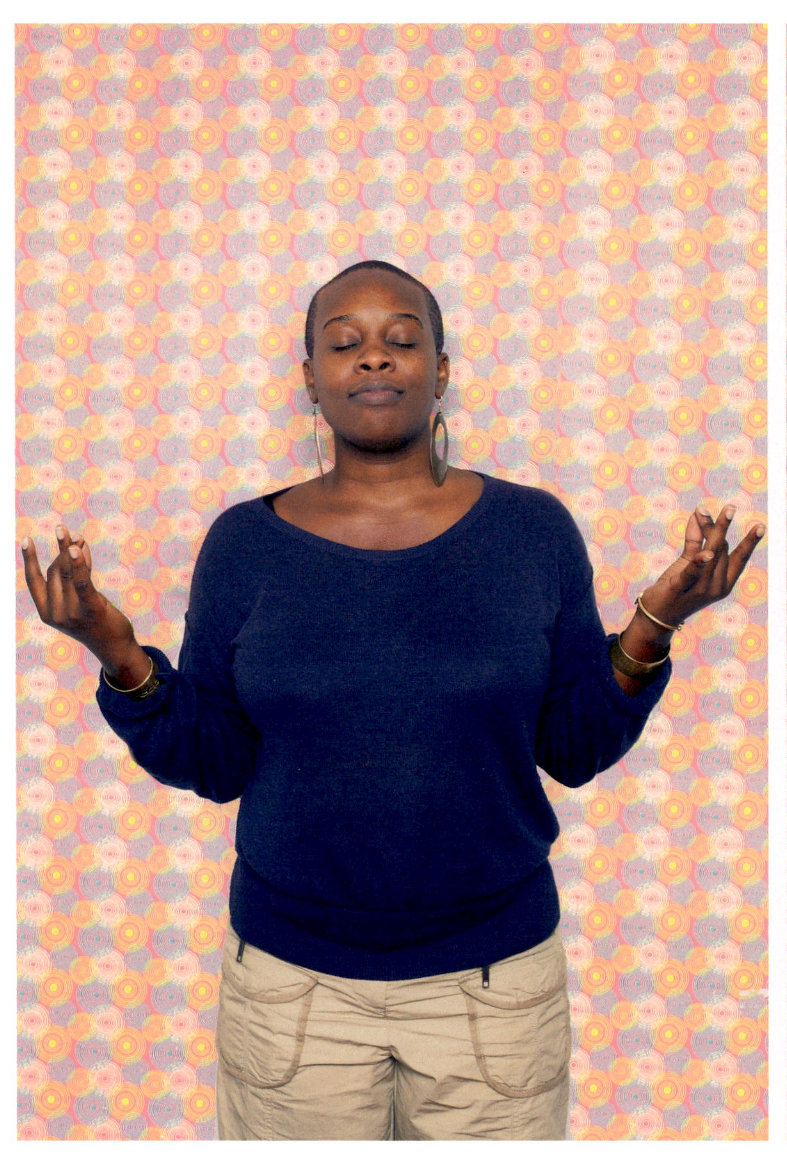 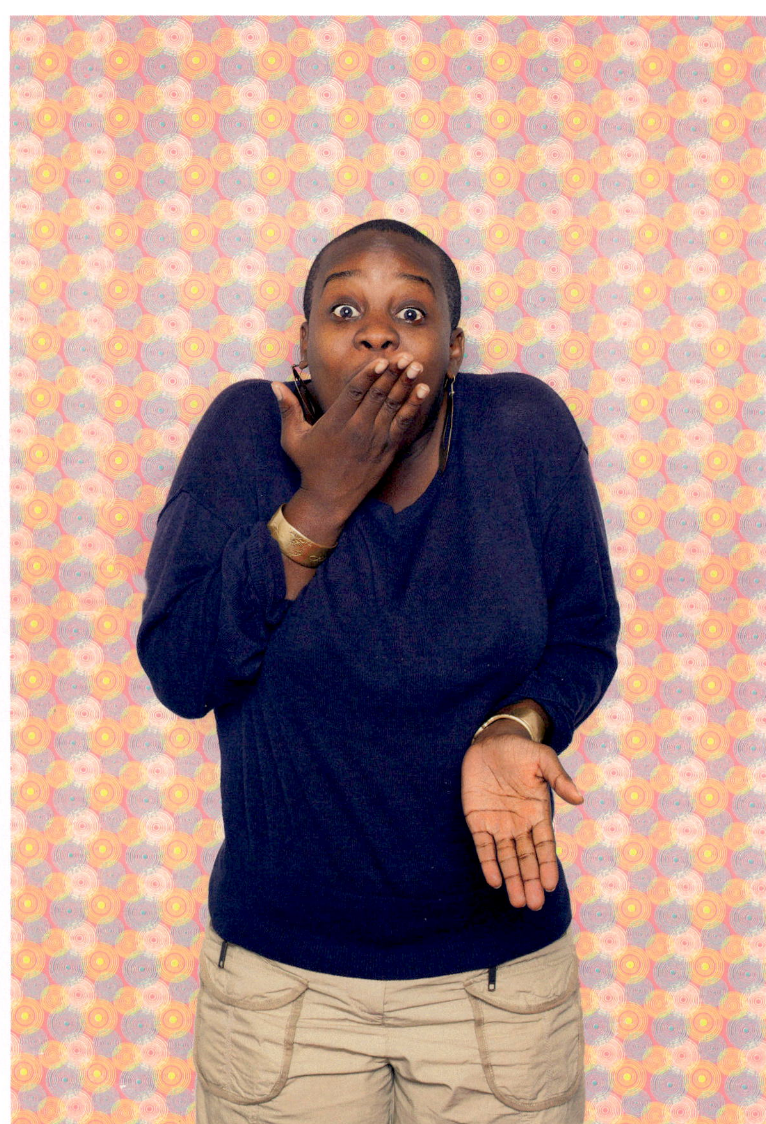

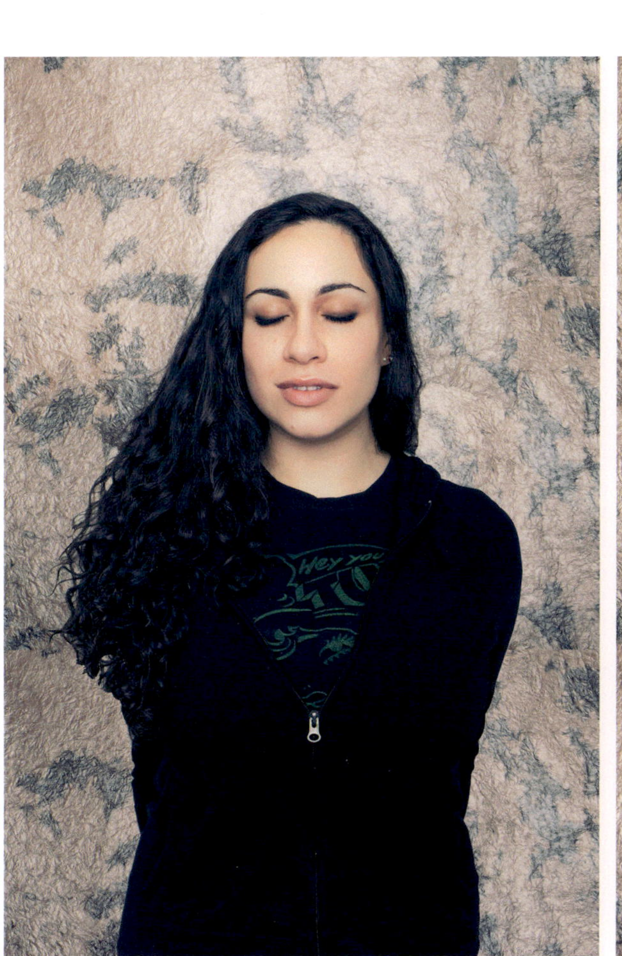 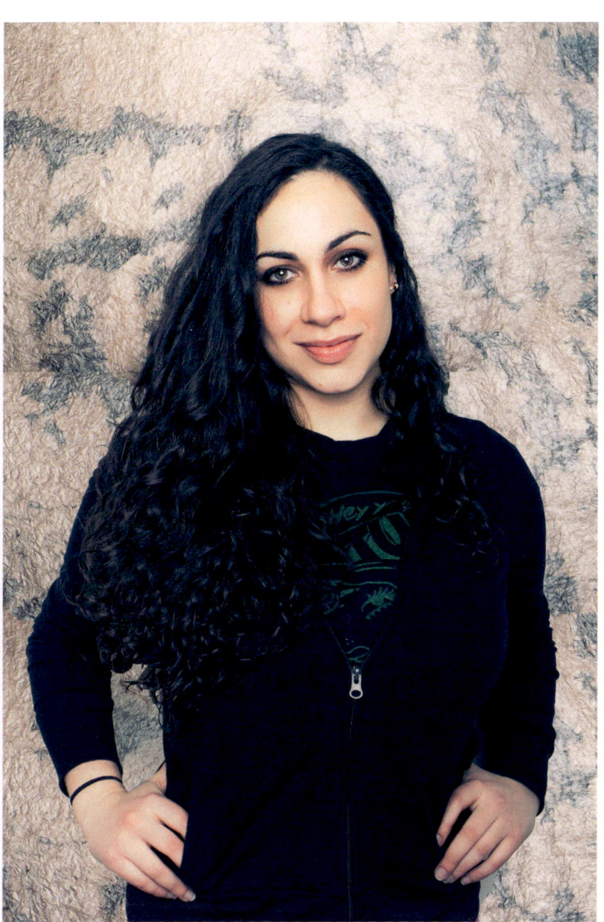

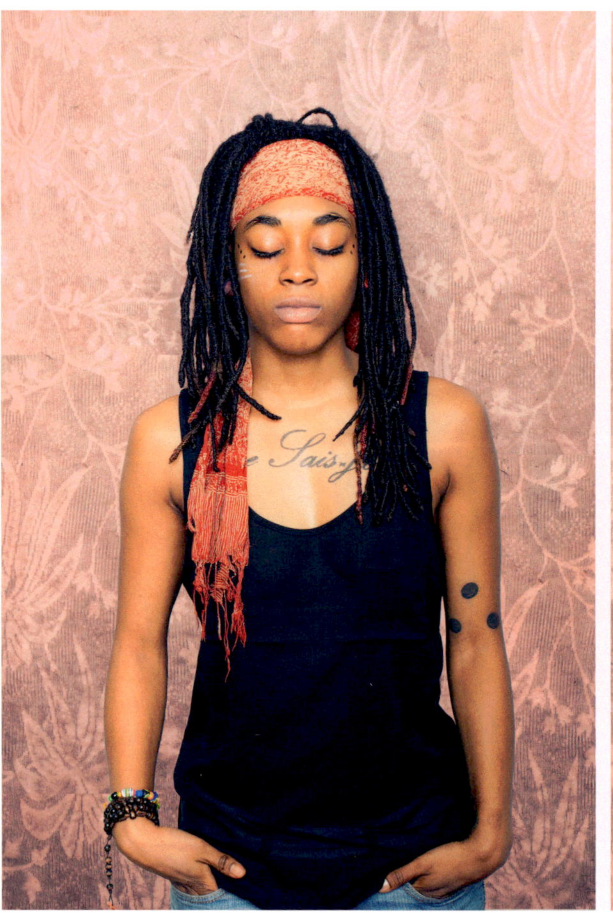
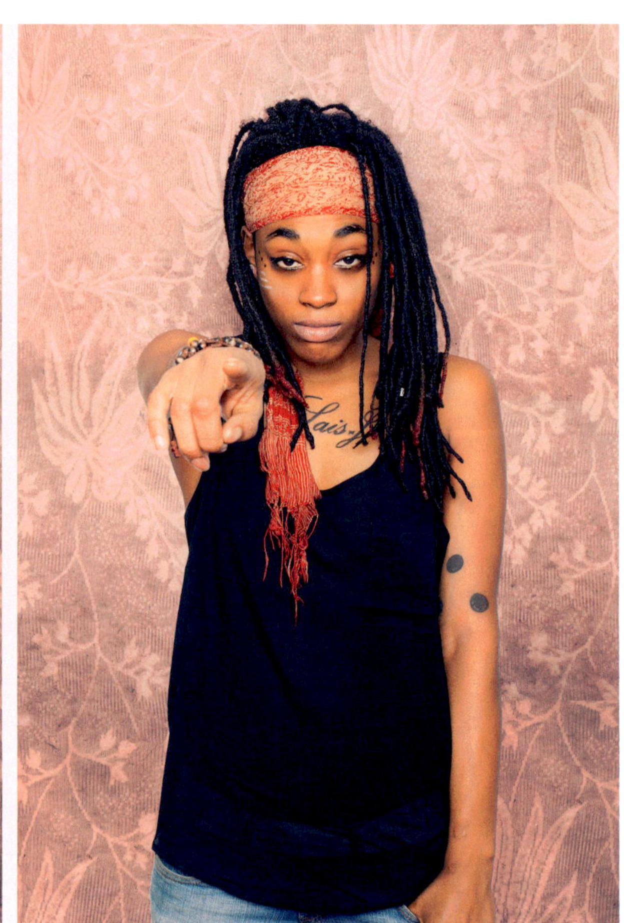
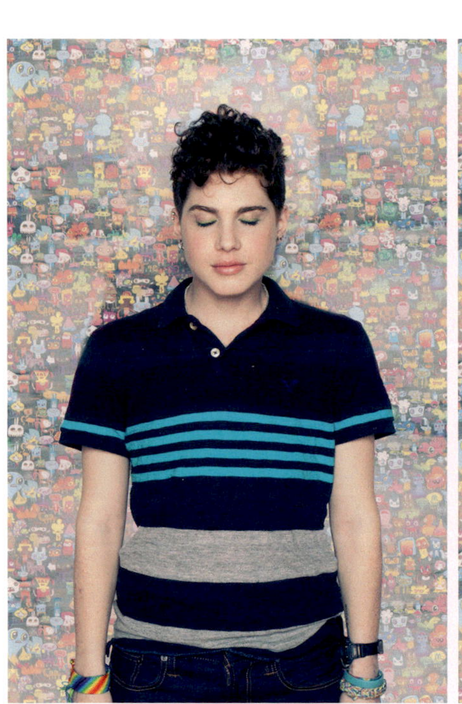
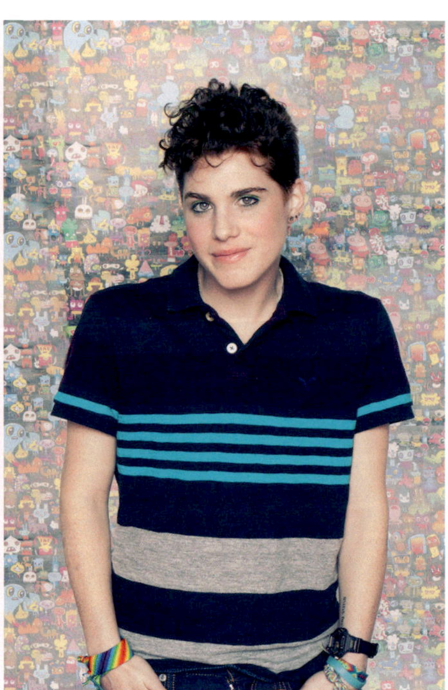

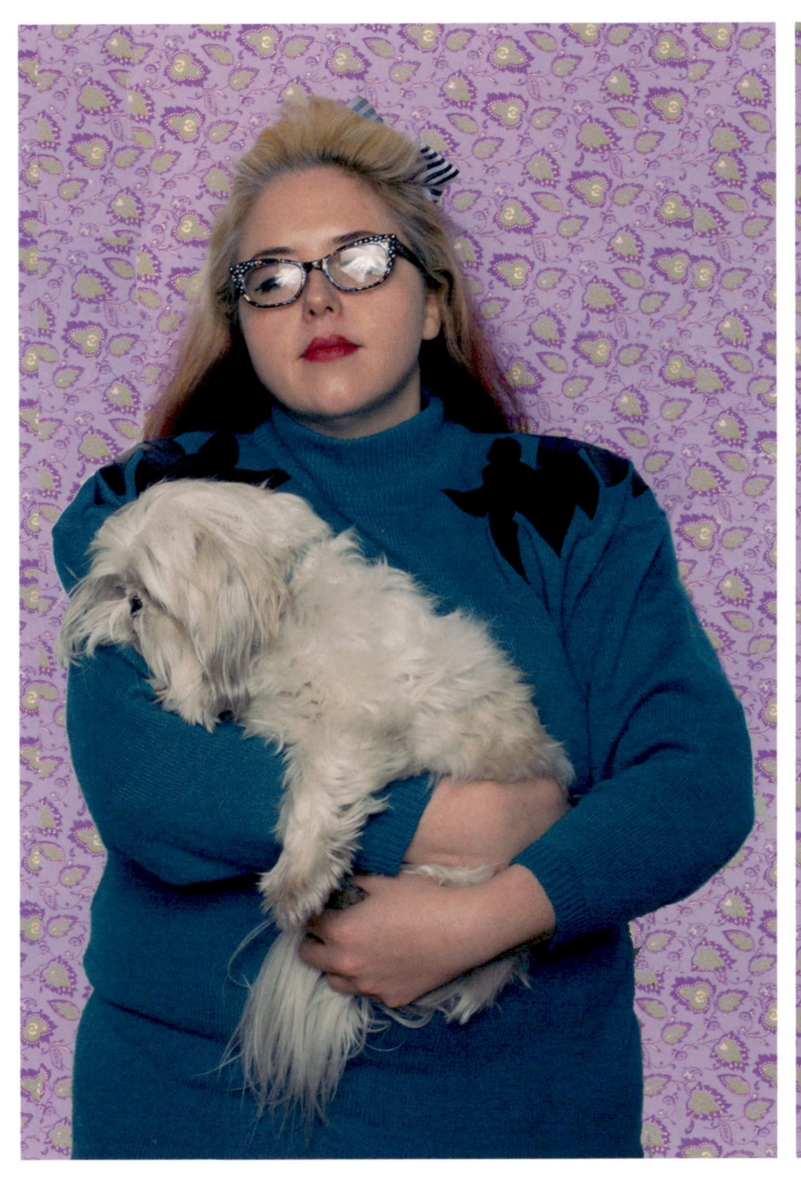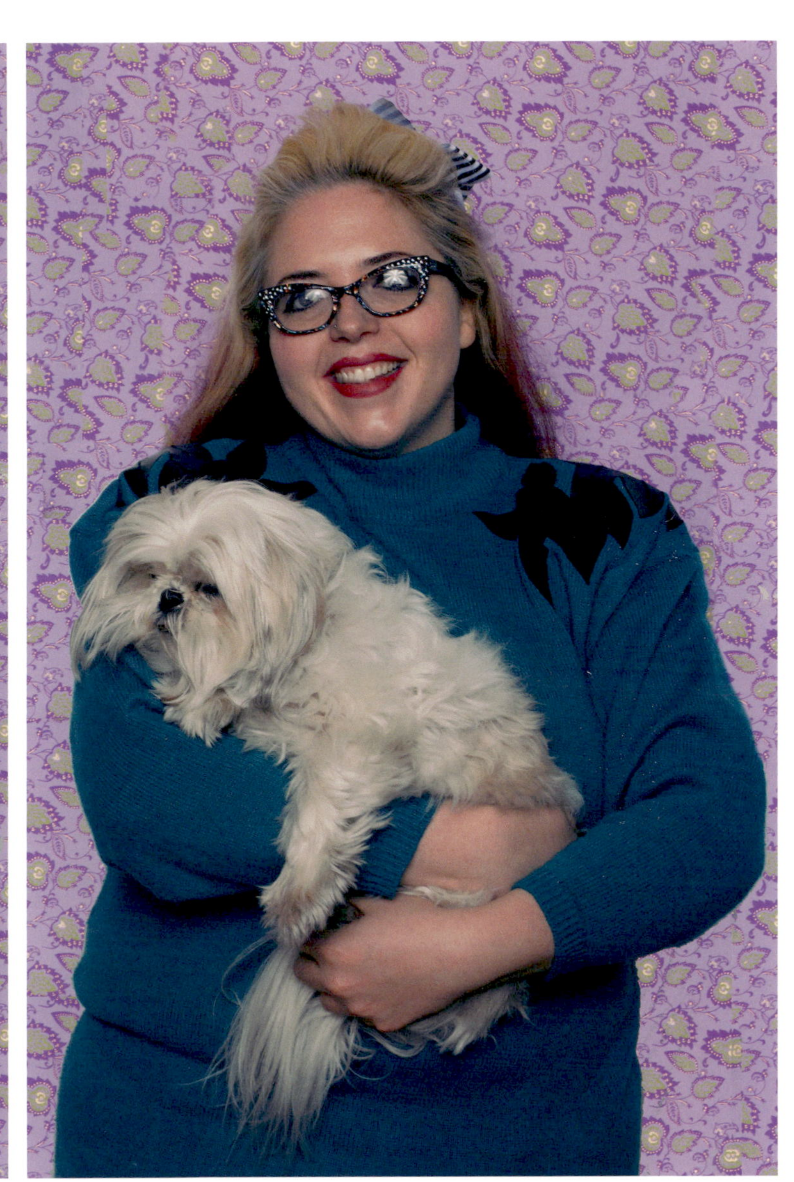

GAY | FACE

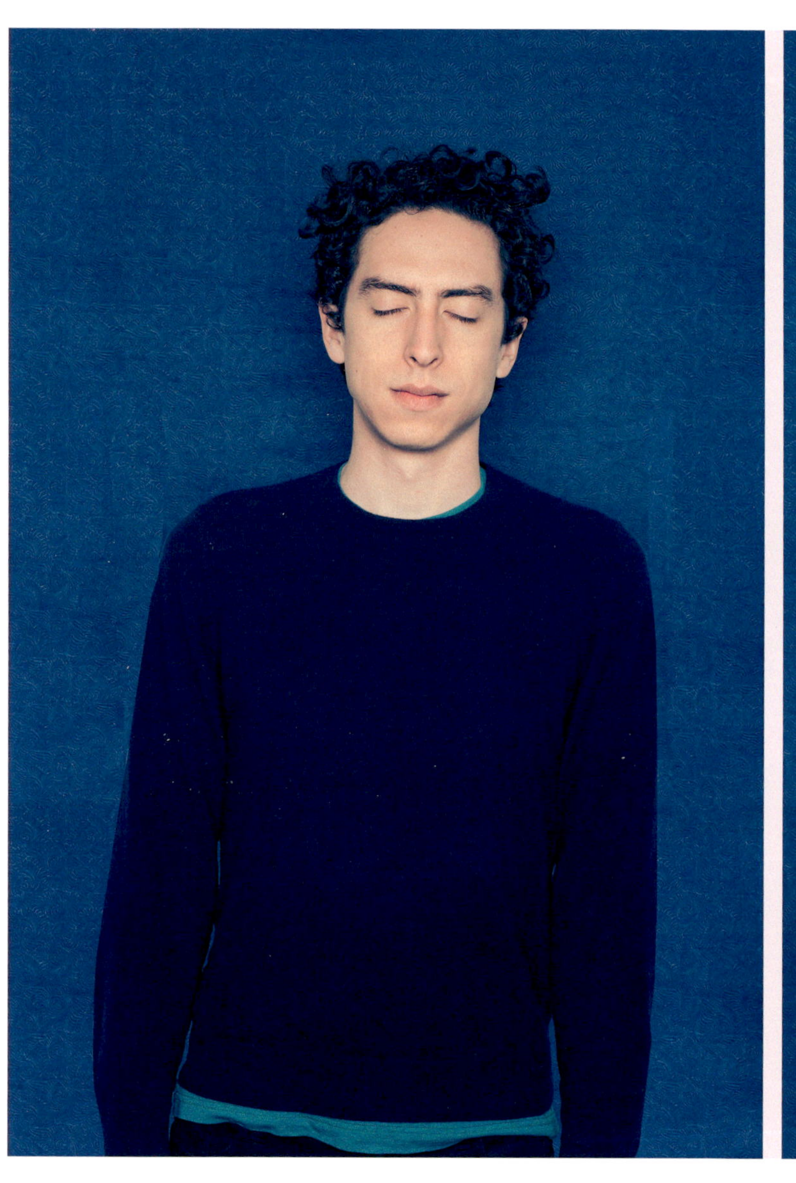 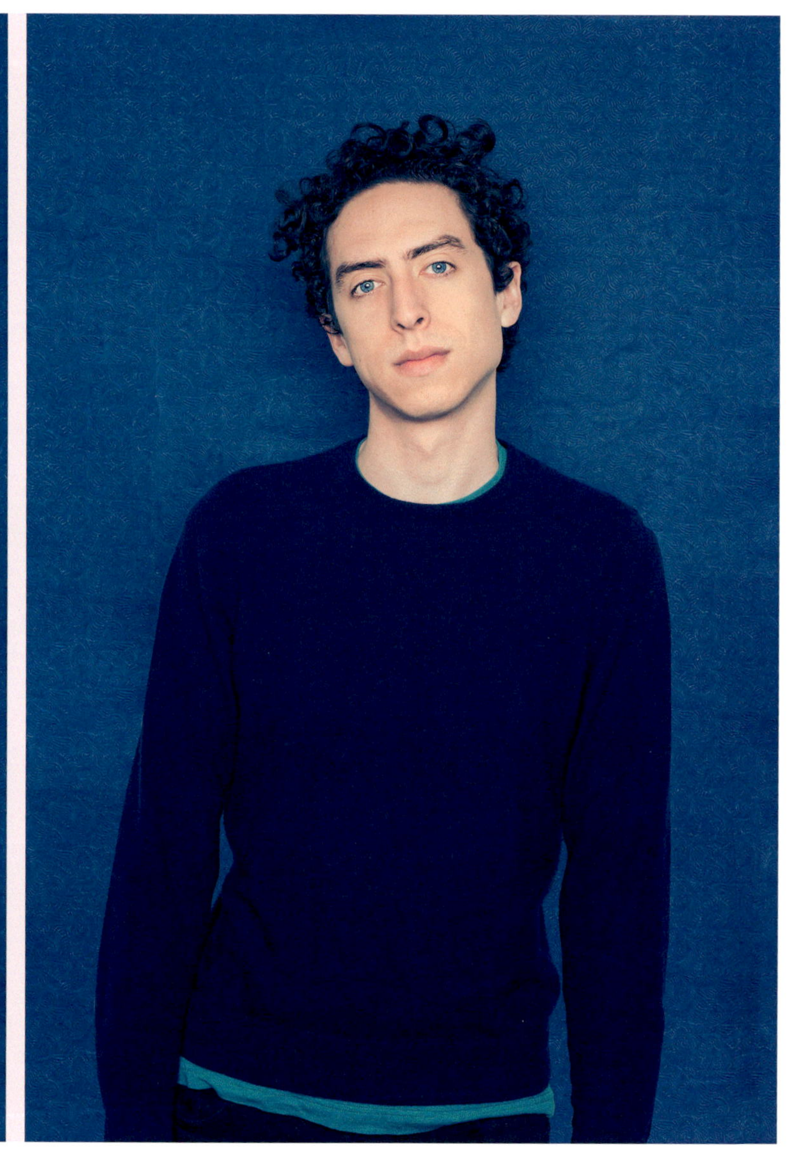

Daniel D.

CHEVY CHASE, MARYLAND

How would you identify your sexuality?
Gay/queer.

What pronouns do you prefer?
He/him/his.

Why did you choose to be a part of this project?
I've known Ash since we were eleven or twelve. Seeing their work develop and grow over the last twenty years has been a treat. I was excited to be a part of such a big project executed by someone I've known for so long.

What do you think of your portrait?
What surprised me the most is how different I read my face when my eyes are closed versus when they're open. I didn't expect that.

Describe your coming out. Are you coming out in some way by participating in this project?
My sister came out before me, so in a lot of ways my coming out was made easier by knowing that my parents were encouraging and supportive of her.

Still, it is nerve-wracking to speak out loud something you've known inside for a long time. Telling friends in high school was natural. Finally coming out to my parents in my junior-year of high school was scary, but they responded with compassion and love.

I still find myself coming out to people. Being a white, cis-male, Jewish-looking person living in New York, there are a lot of other parts of my identity that present before my queerness. Even though I run a queer apparel company, I definitely find myself having to confirm my queerness in professional settings.

I didn't think of the photography session itself as a coming out experience, but thinking about the culmination of the project as a book definitely feels like a large public statement of how I define my sexual identity.

Have you ever experienced discrimination based on your gender or sexual orientation?
No . . . which I know is an incredible privilege.

If you could change one thing about mainstream society to improve the lives of LGBTQ+ people, what would it be?
Mainstream society needs to pay attention to violence against trans people of color. Even within our community, we don't invest enough resources to combat this violence.

Describe how this project has affected you, both personally and as a member of the LGBTQ+ community as a whole.
More than anything, it is exciting to see a friend create meaningful work. It will be exciting to see the full project together.

What advice have you been given by another LGBTQ+ person, or that you might offer someone?
Gay cisgender white men in our community have an added amount of responsibility. We operate with an incredible amount of freedom and many of us feel that being gay doesn't mean that we have responsibilities to the larger LGBTQ+ community. But it's actually the opposite: because of our freedom, we have the responsibility to speak out when we see injustice, to metaphorically and sometimes physically create safe places, and to put our money where our mouths are. Being a gay man is more than a party on the beach.

GAY | FACE

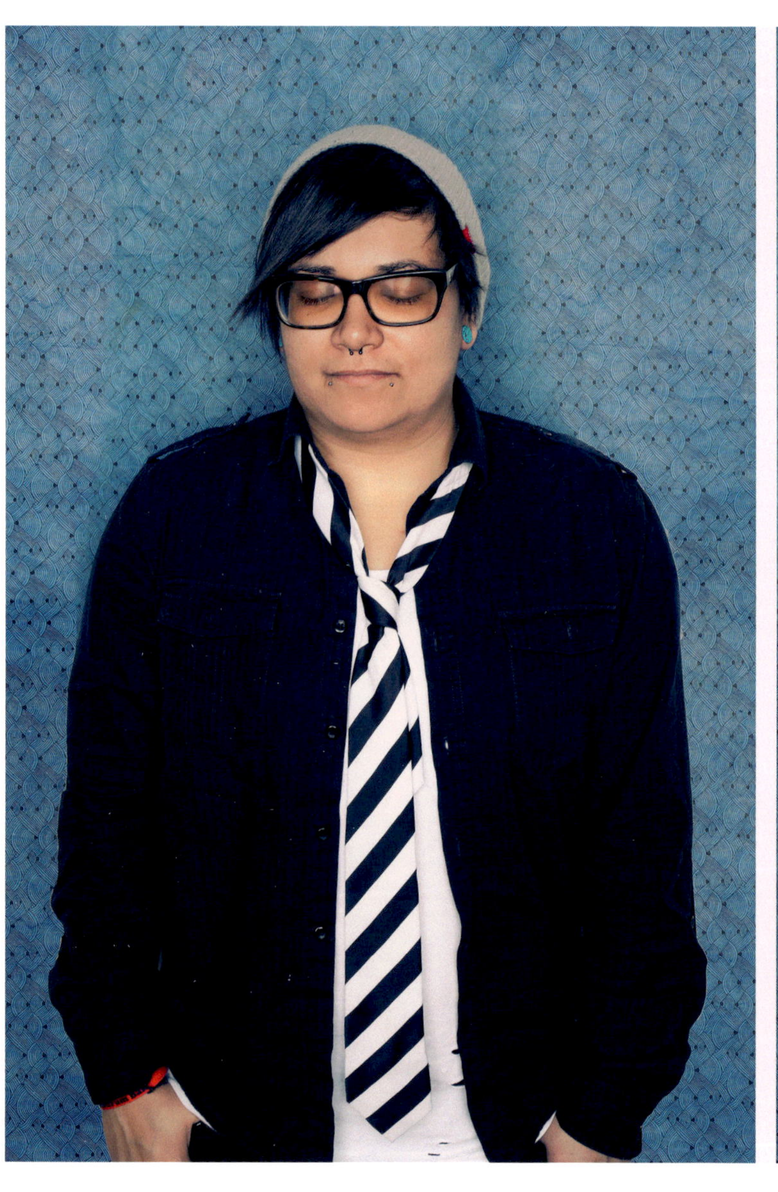
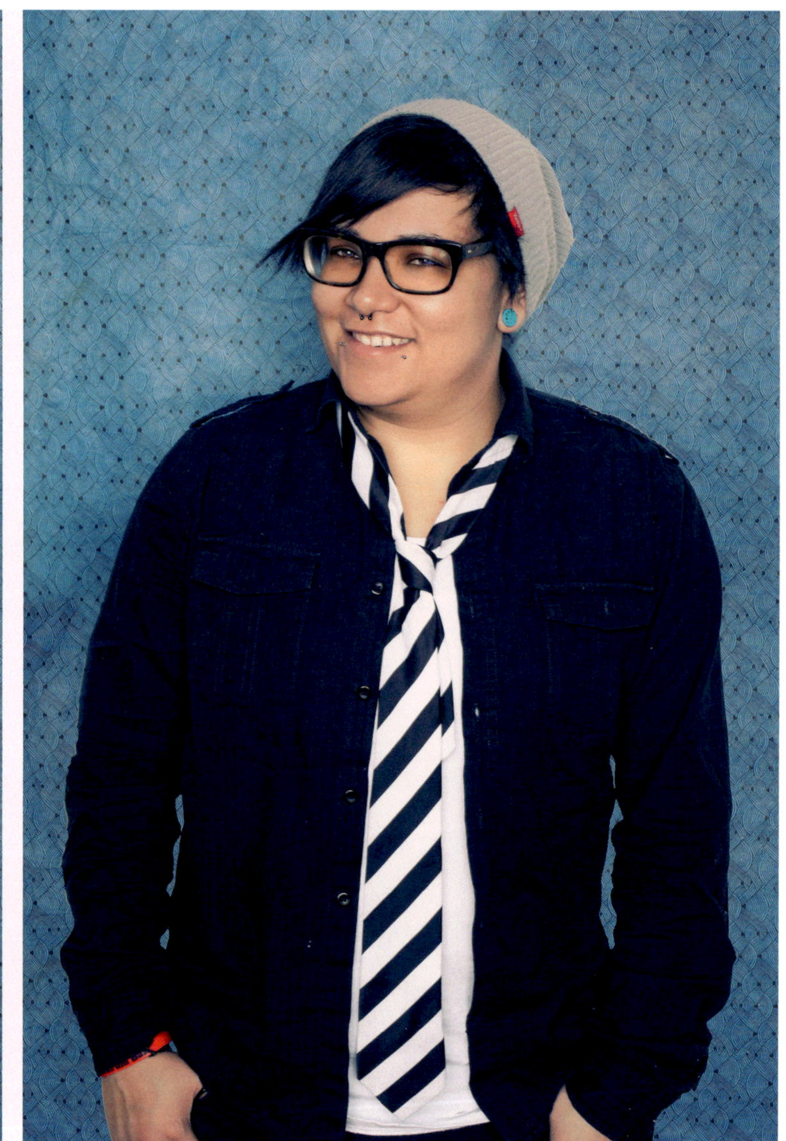

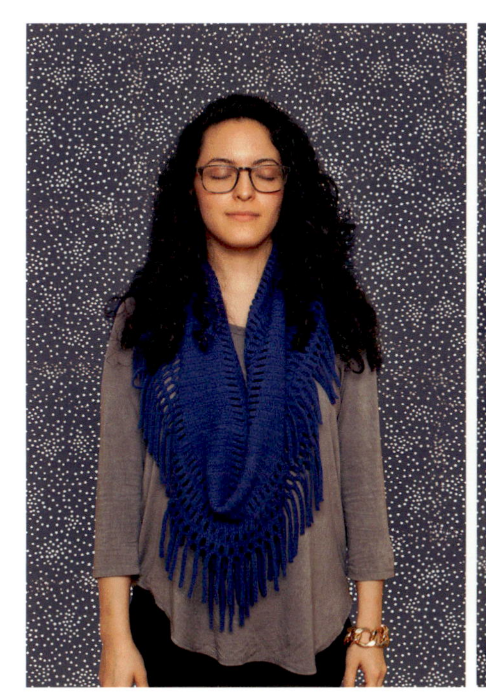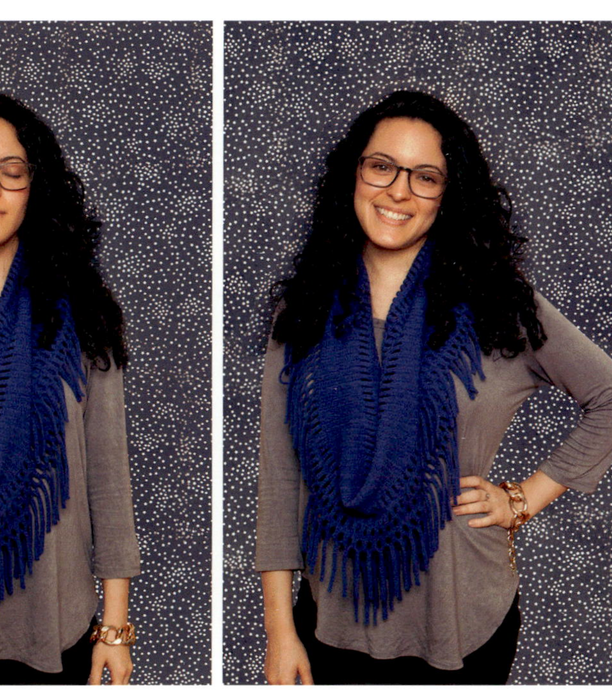

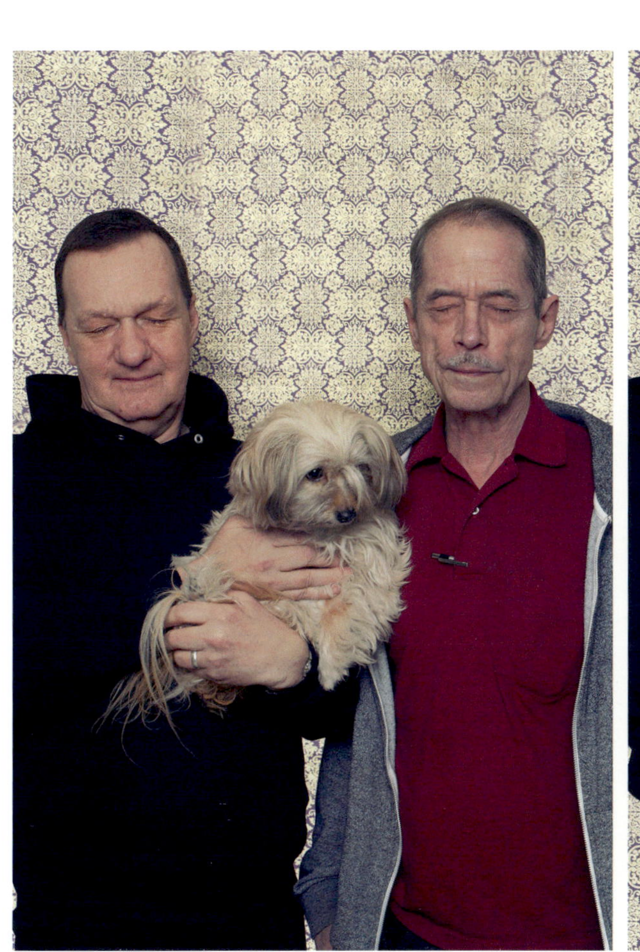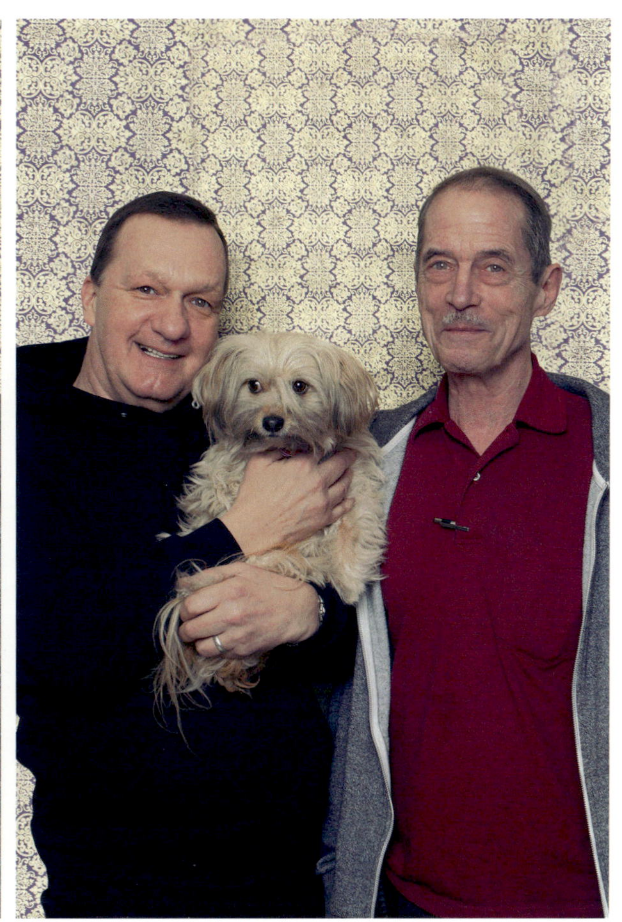

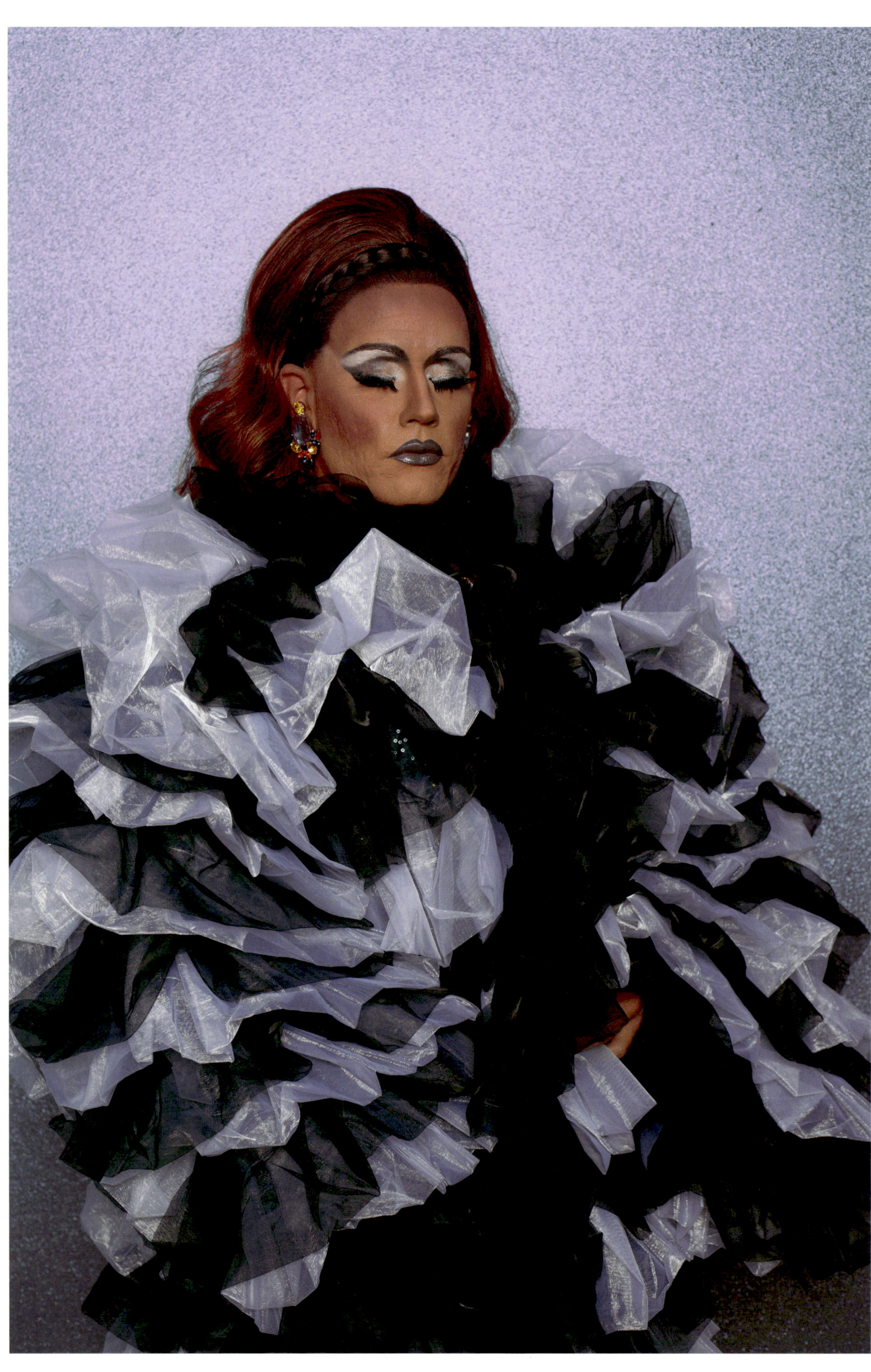

GAY | FACE

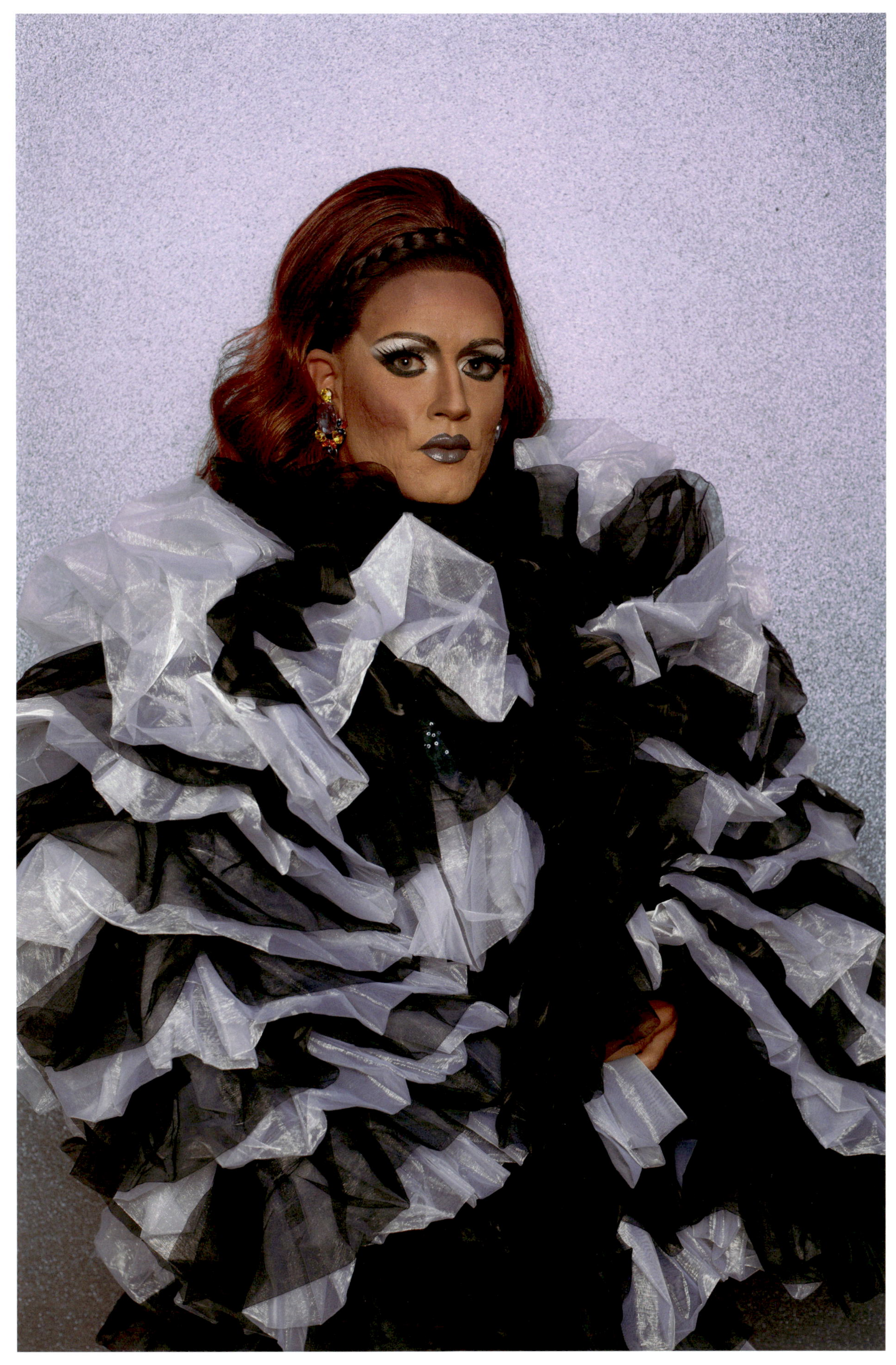

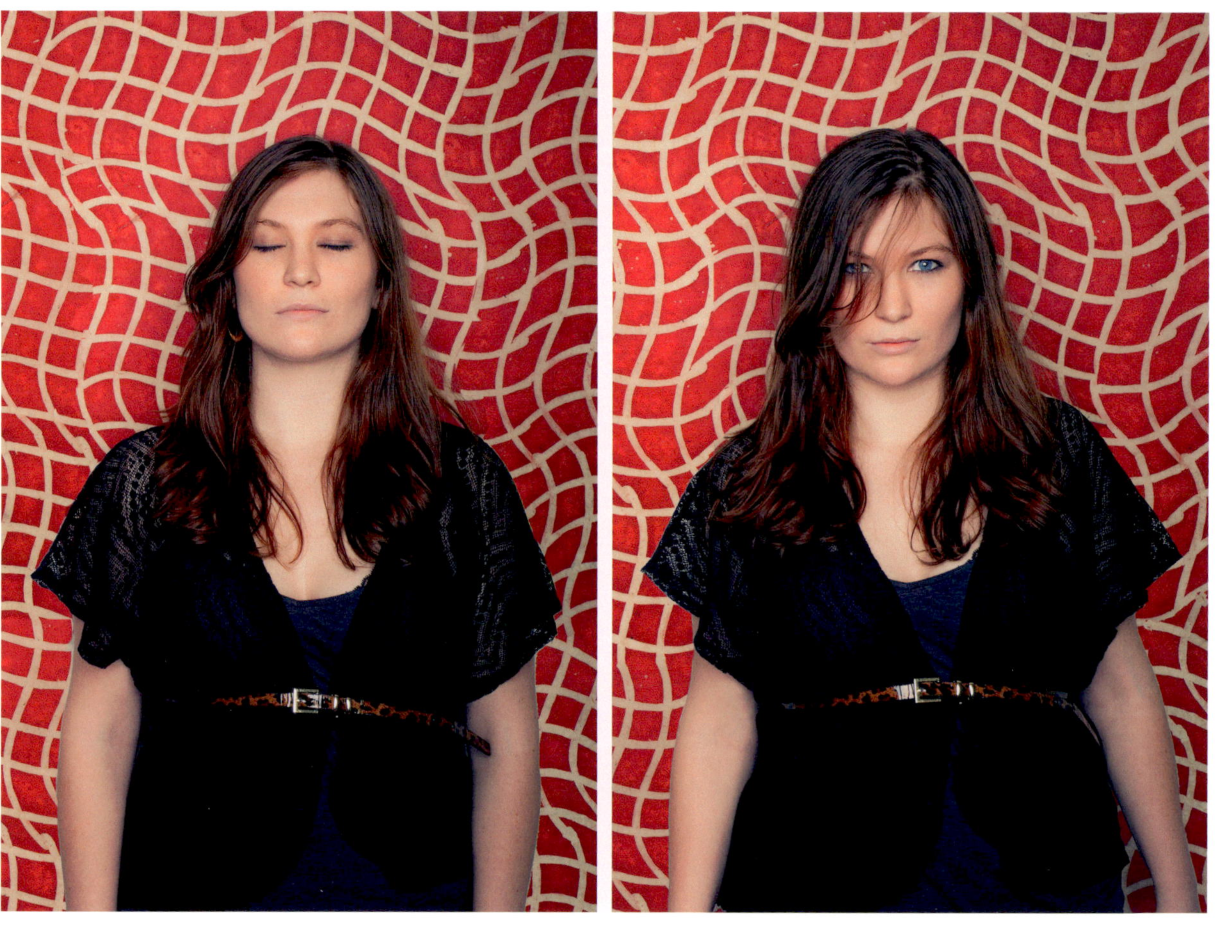

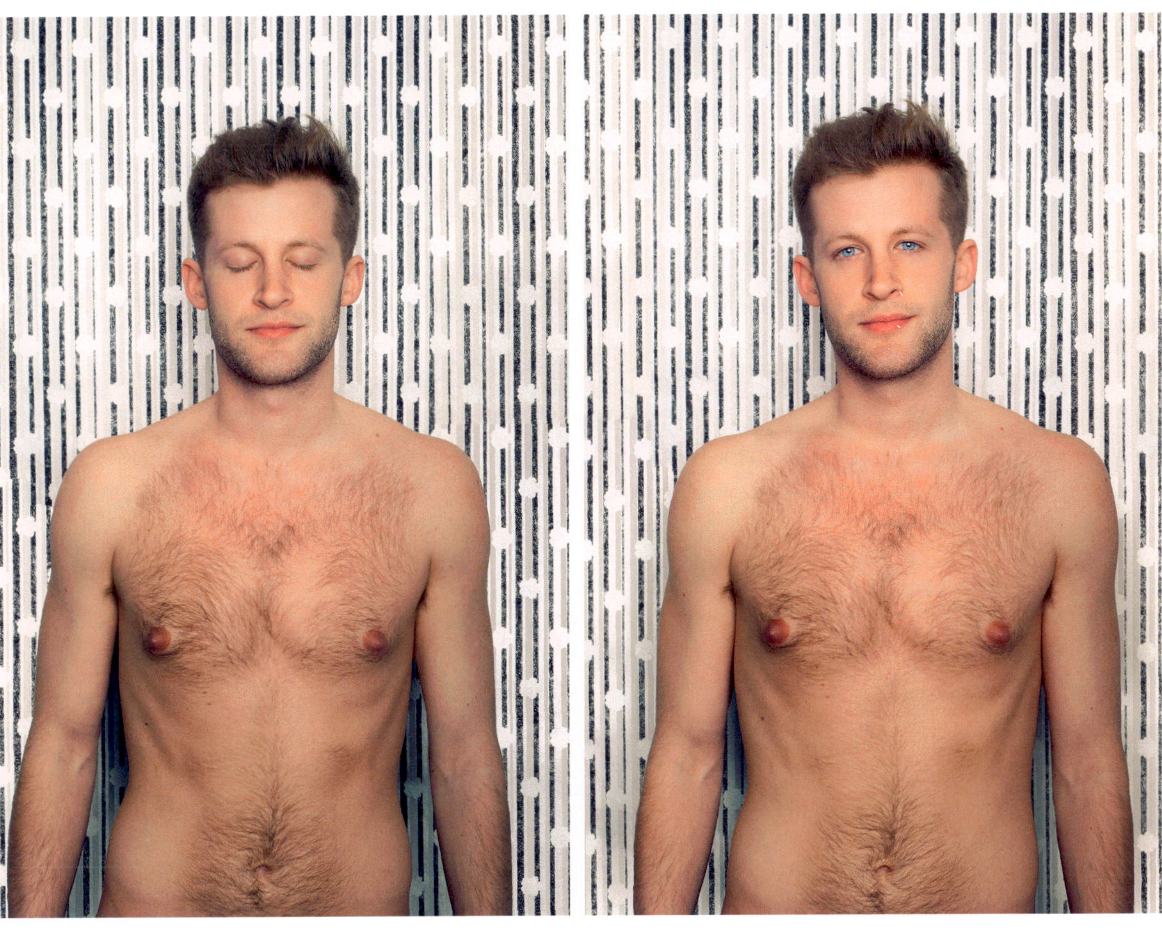

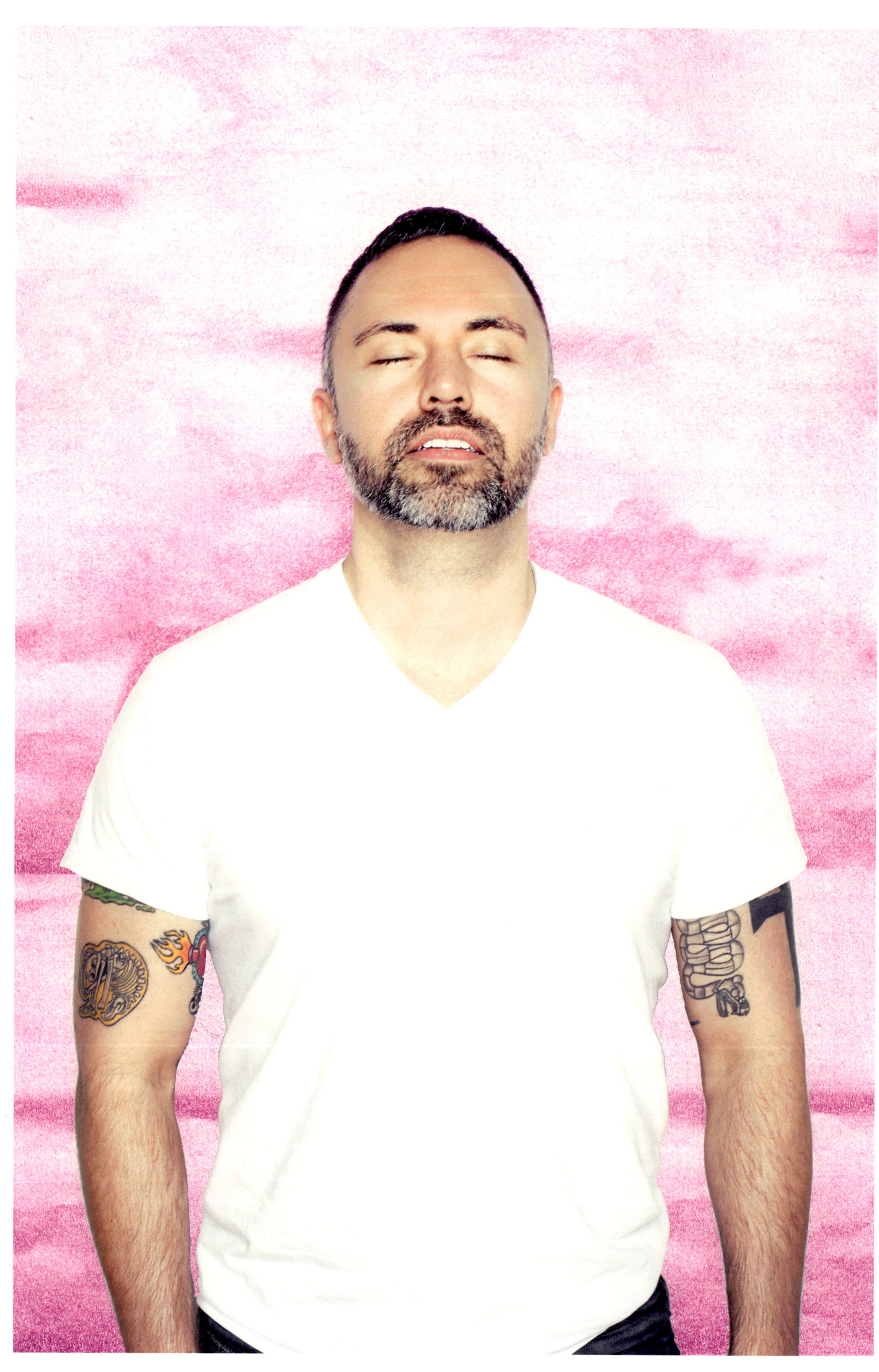

GAY | FACE

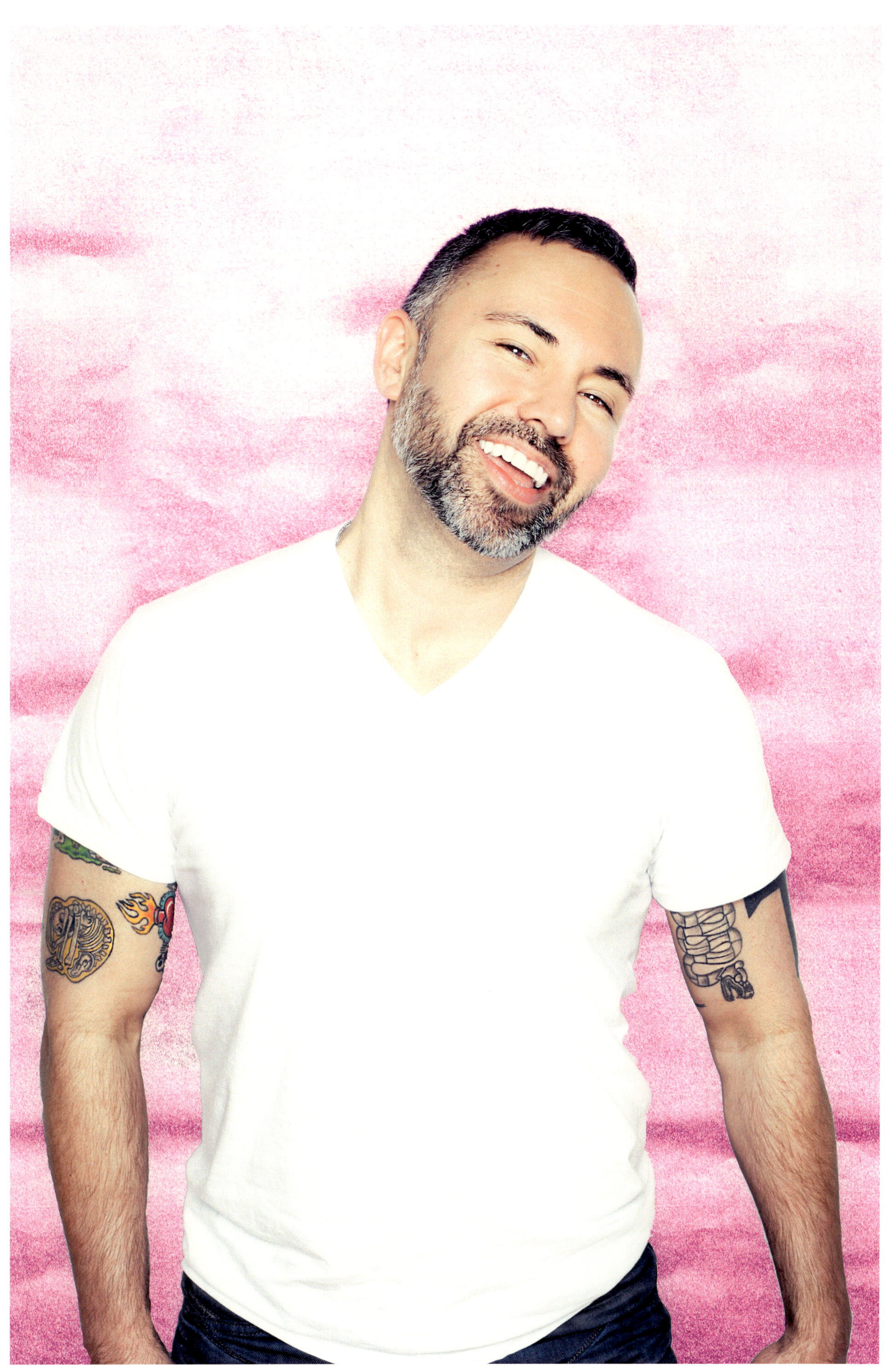

GAY | FACE

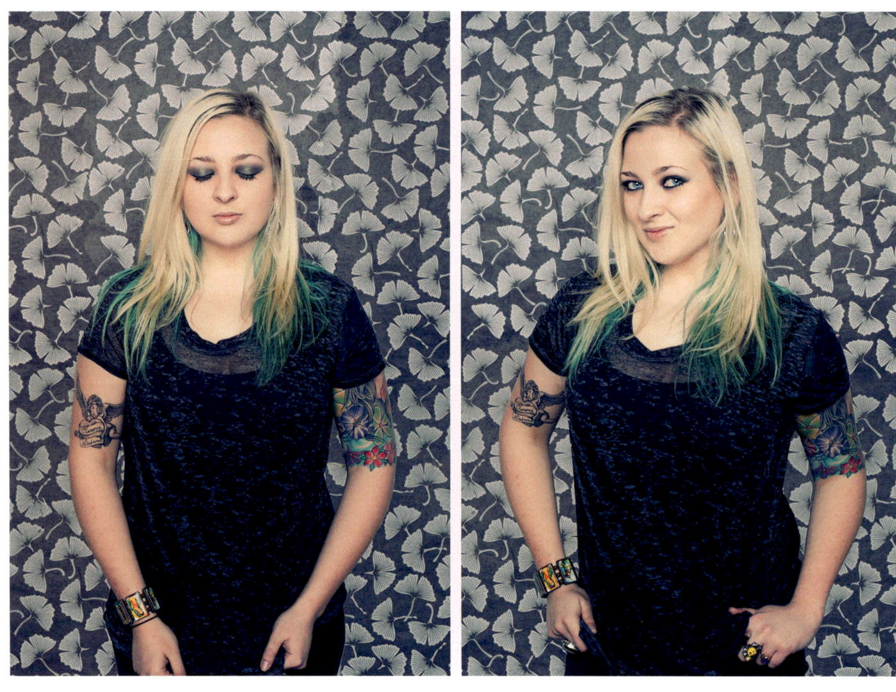

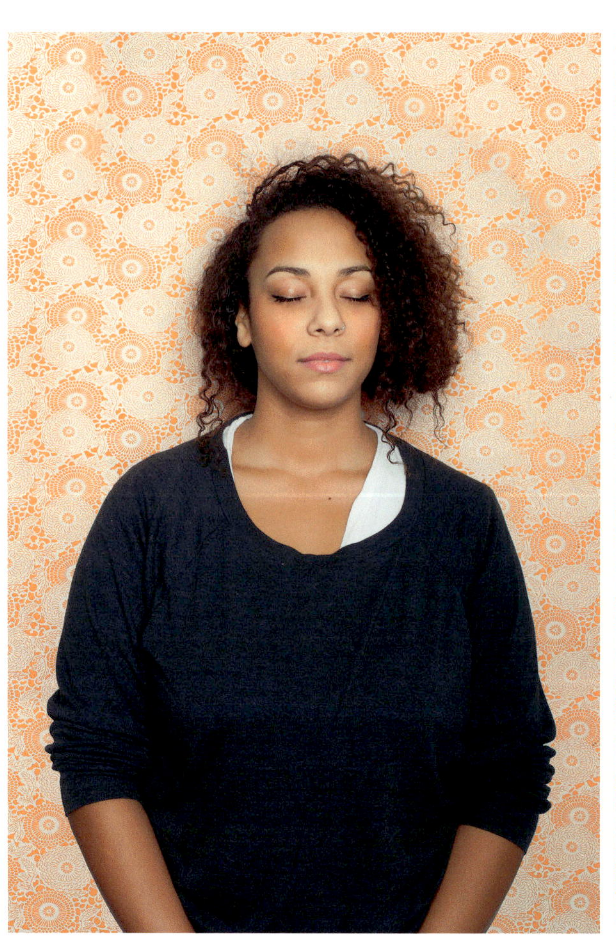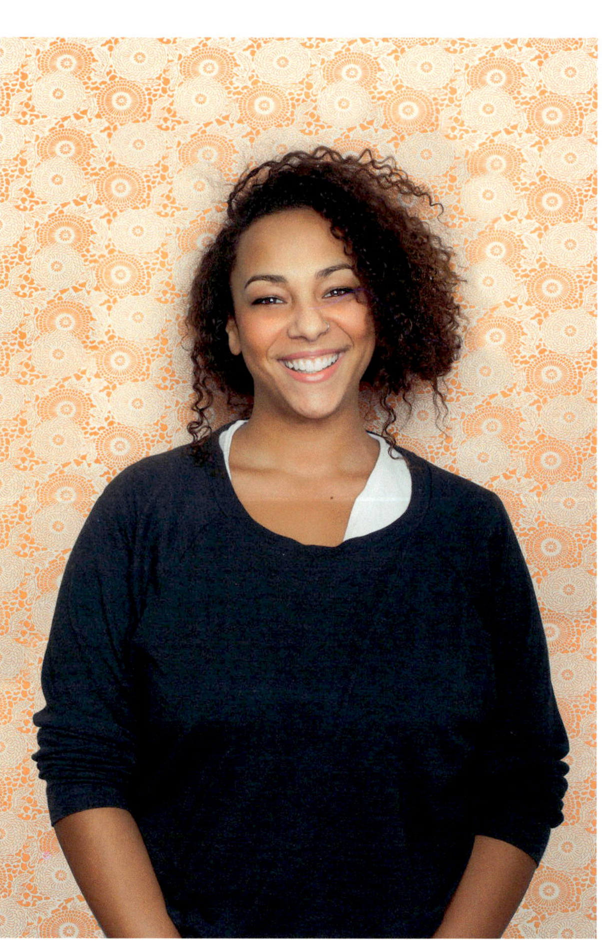

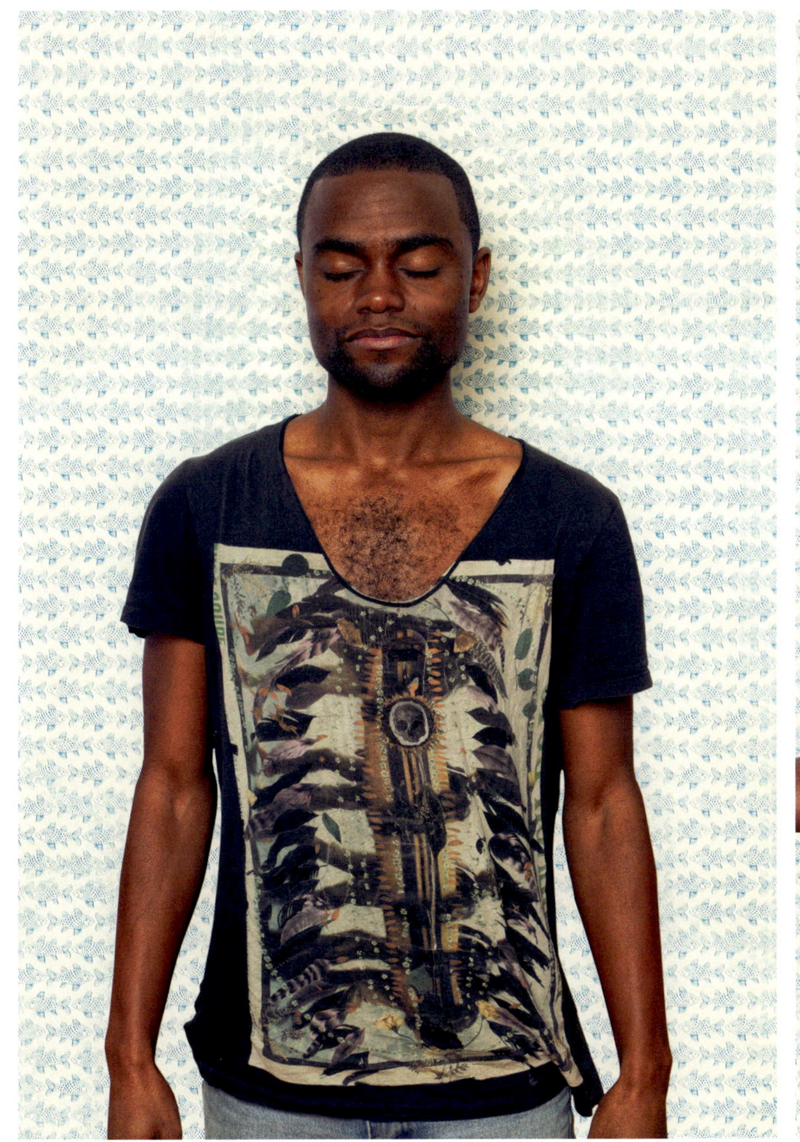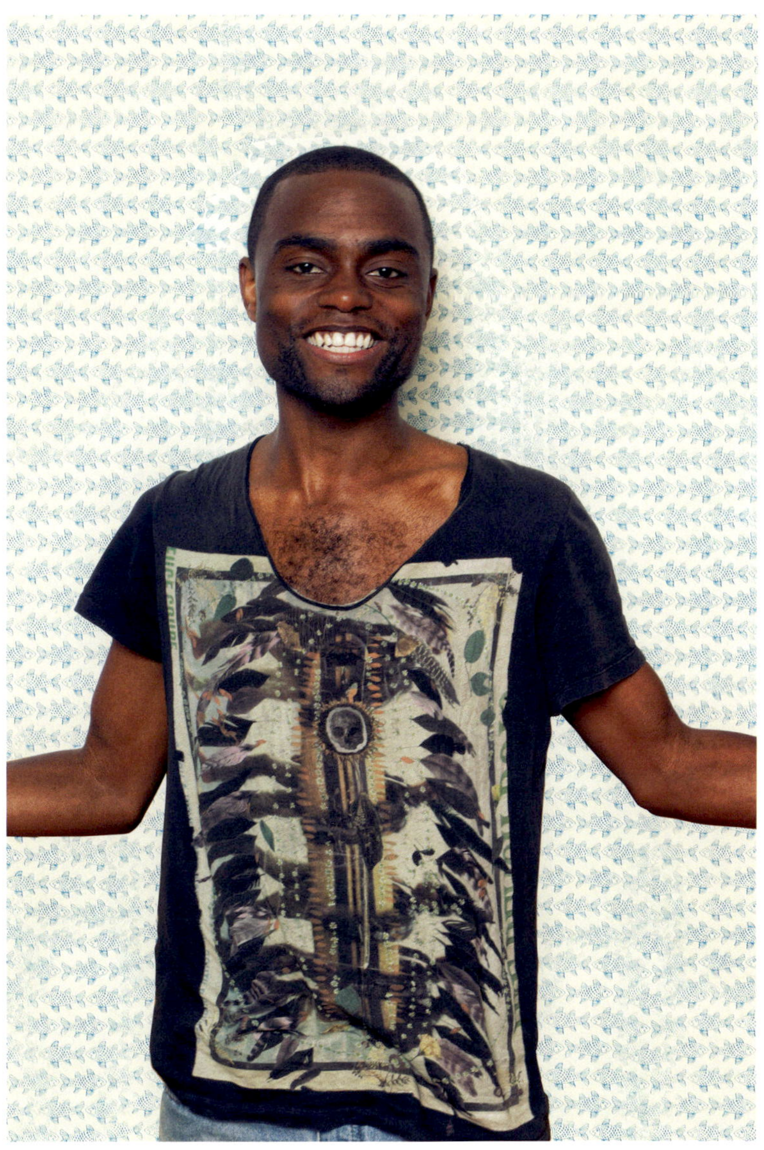

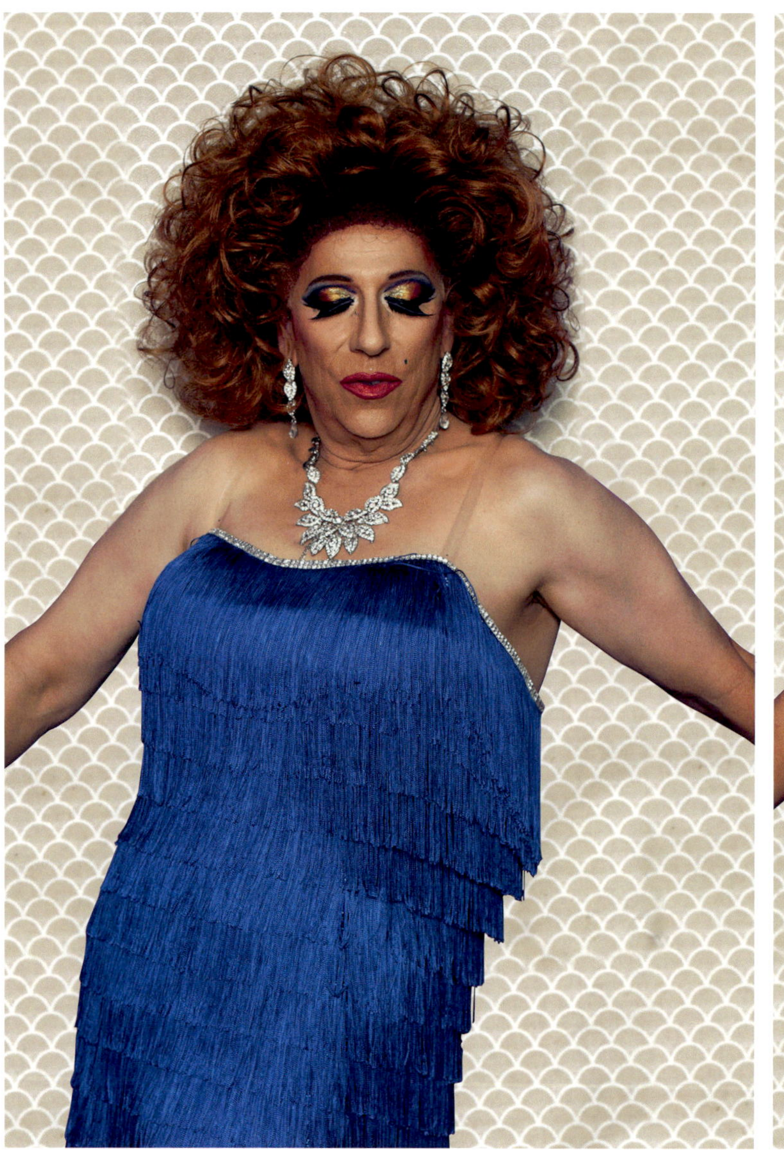

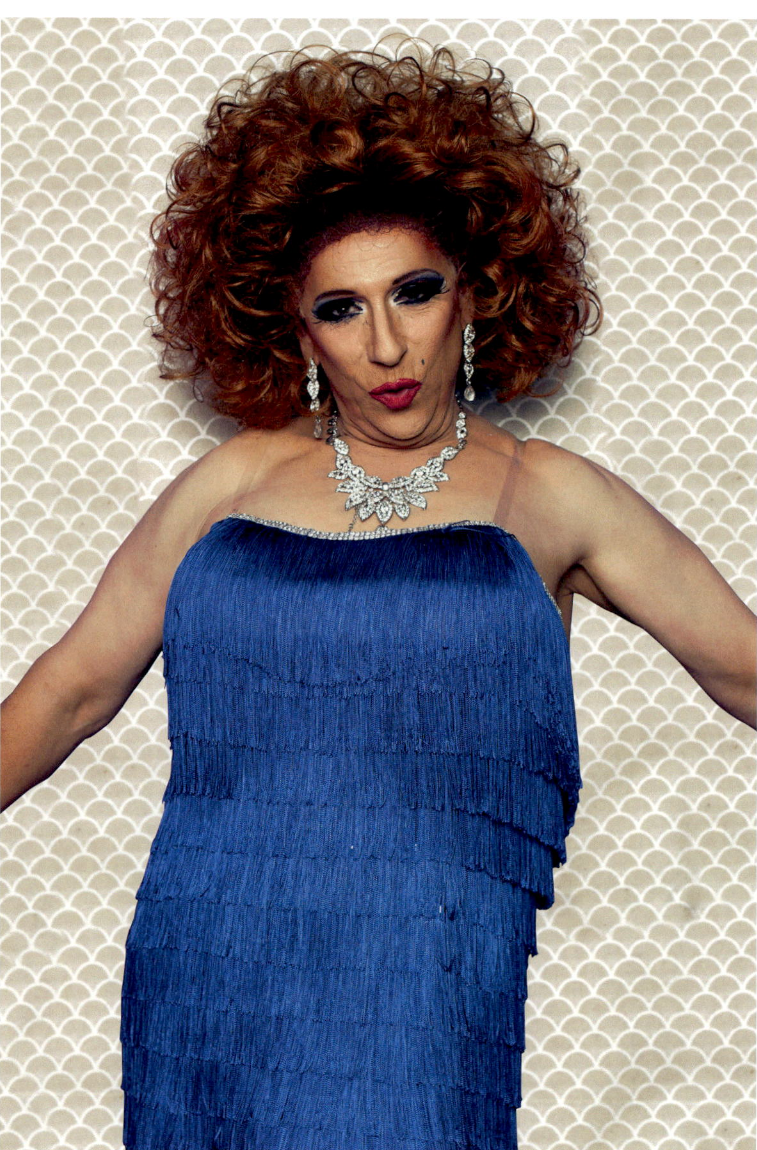

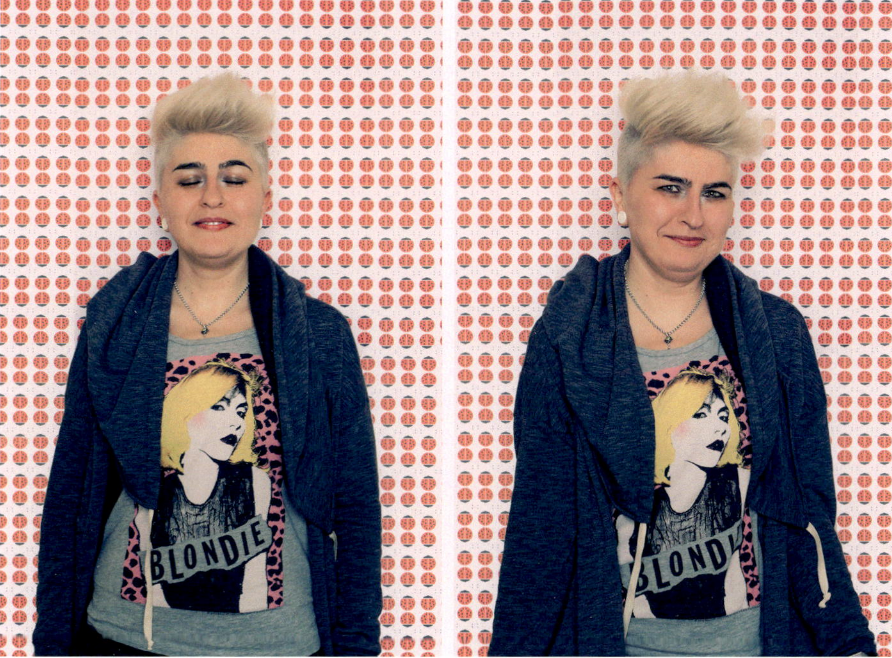

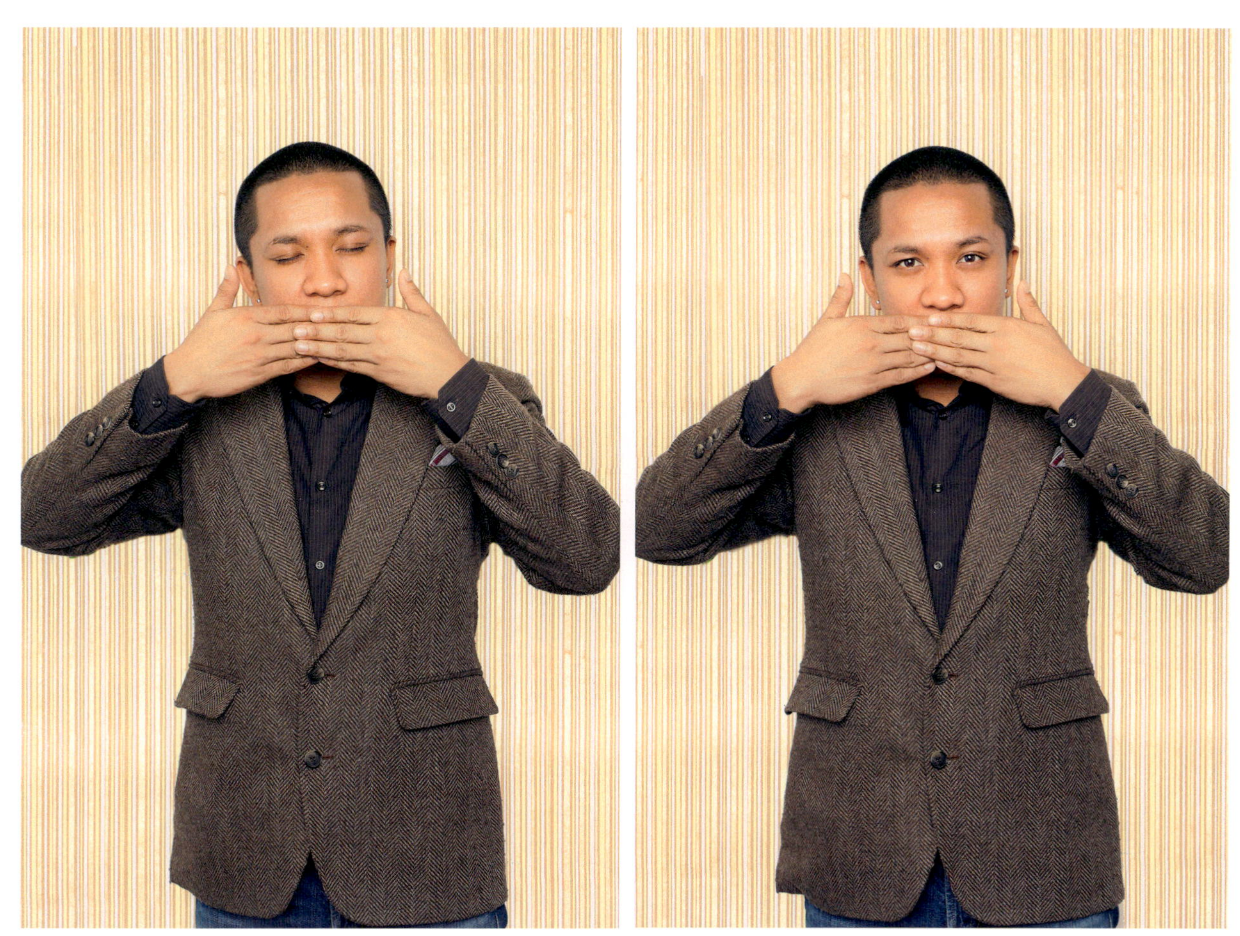

GAY | FACE

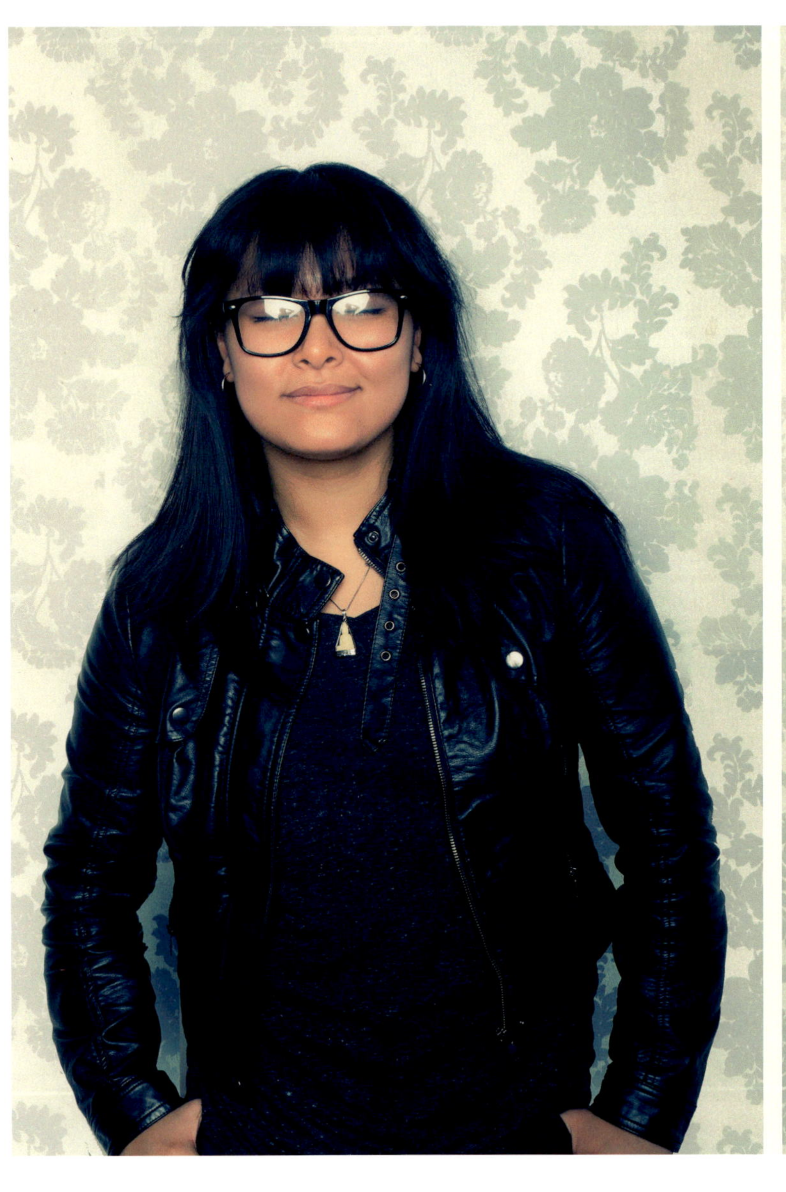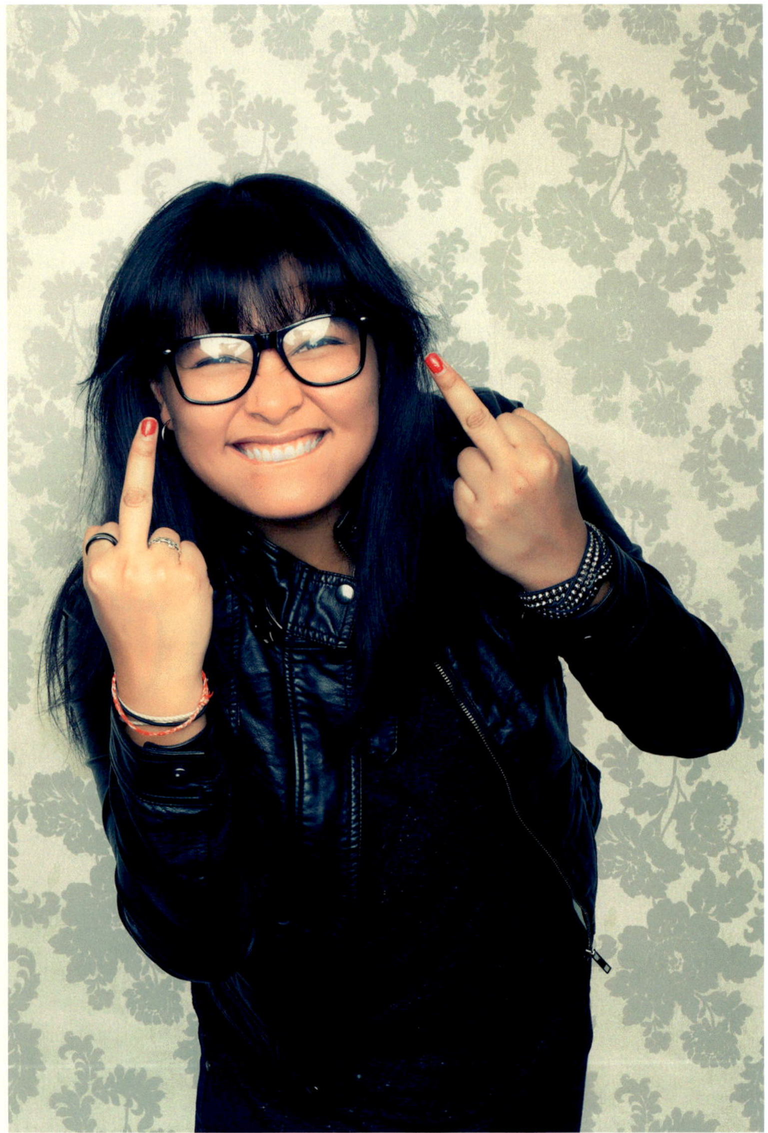

Tia O.

BRONX, NEW YORK

How would you identify your sexuality?
Lesbian.

Describe your coming out.
I knew that I was a lesbian in middle school but didn't acknowledge it until after high school. I didn't want to come out to my family because they had no experience with the LGBTQ+ community because they do not have any friends who are gay.

And then I met this girl last summer—she was great, smart, and beautiful, but as with many relationships, there were some problems and I didn't quite know what to do. My older sister is great with advice and I really needed some. So one day she was in the kitchen cooking, I went up to her and told her flat out, "Hey sis, I'm gay." It took her a while to realize that I was not joking. In the end, after some yelling and tears from both sides, she did give me the advice I needed. Coming out to her ultimately went okay because we're so close.

With my brother, who's a former Marine, it was different. He's more conservative than me and my sister and since our dad passed away when I was fifteen he's also been a real father figure to us. About a month ago, a friend told me she had been coming out to her family members, one by one. She suggested I give my brother the benefit of the doubt. When he came over to my place about a week later, I was really apprehensive—my heart was pounding and I was sweating from fear. I took him into my room and told him I'm gay. There was a long moment of silence and I asked, "So, what do you think?" He said, "I don't know what to think," then left my room without even looking at me. It was hard for the both of us. We have not spoken since. I miss my brother. I miss spending time with him.

I have yet to come out to my mother.

If you could change one thing about mainstream society to improve the lives of LGBTQ+ people, what would it be?
The media plays an important role in how humans think. With more shows and movies that feature gay people and subject matter, it can open up all those closed-minded people they'll be watching this show/movie, fall in love with a character, and then all of a sudden, it's "oh shit, gay?! But I love him/her and he/she is gay/lesbian." Yes, you do, and now you know, they're human, just like everyone else, so stop it. Stop your ignorance.

Why should people support same-sex marriage?
Not allowing LGBTQ+ people to get married is as ridiculous as when interracial marriage was illegal. Shit, if you want to get married to a toaster oven because that toaster oven makes you happy and a better person, then fucking go for it. Because WE ARE NOT HURTING ANYONE!

Has this project helped you or changed your life in any-way? Are you coming out in some way by participating in this project?
Gayface has helped me "come out of the closet" more to a group of people who I have not seen since high school (and earlier) without me really saying anything. For example, Ash tagged me on my Gayface photo so it's on my wall for everyone to see. I loved it. I left it alone so it can be a way to communicate to those people I have not seen in years: "Hey, this is *Gayface*, I'm in it because I'm gay!"

Is there anything else you would like to add?
Just one thing: HI, MOM!

GAY | FACE

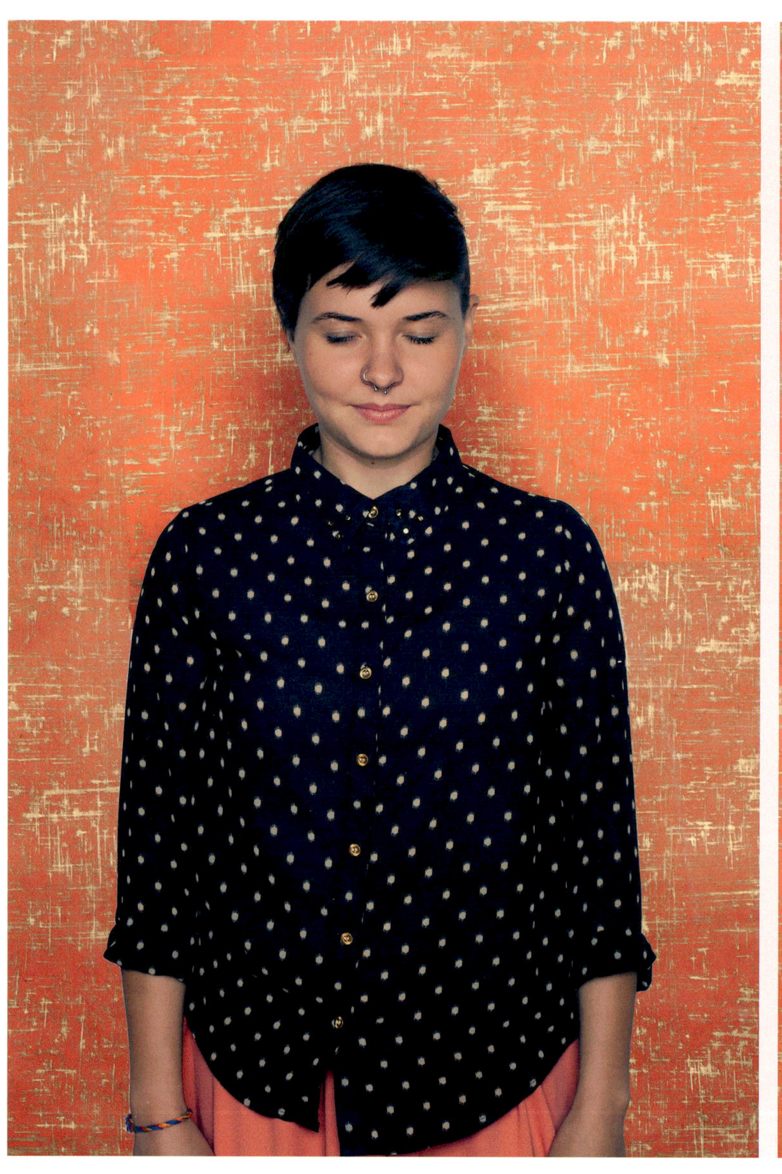
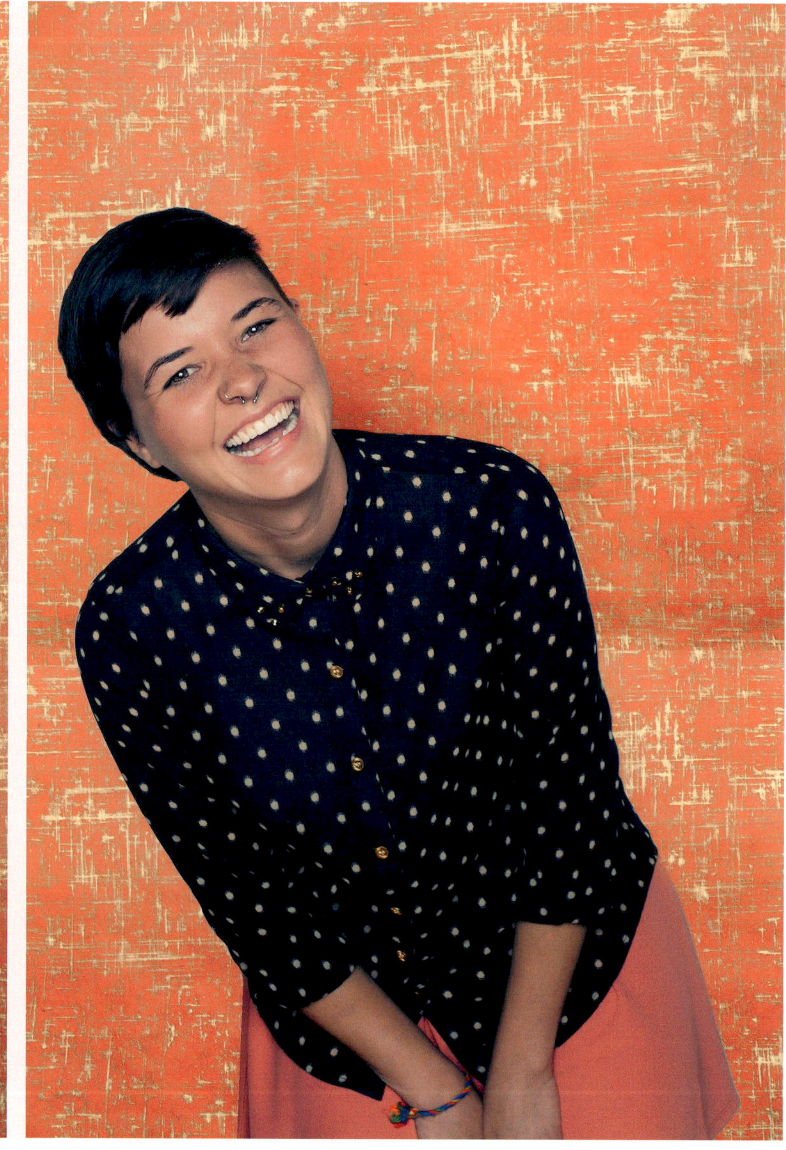

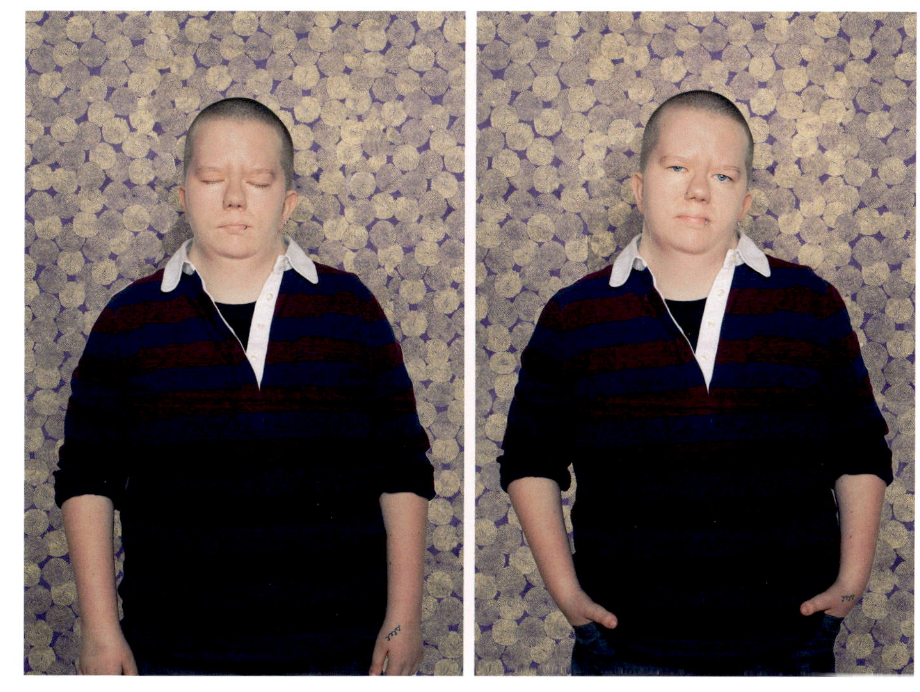

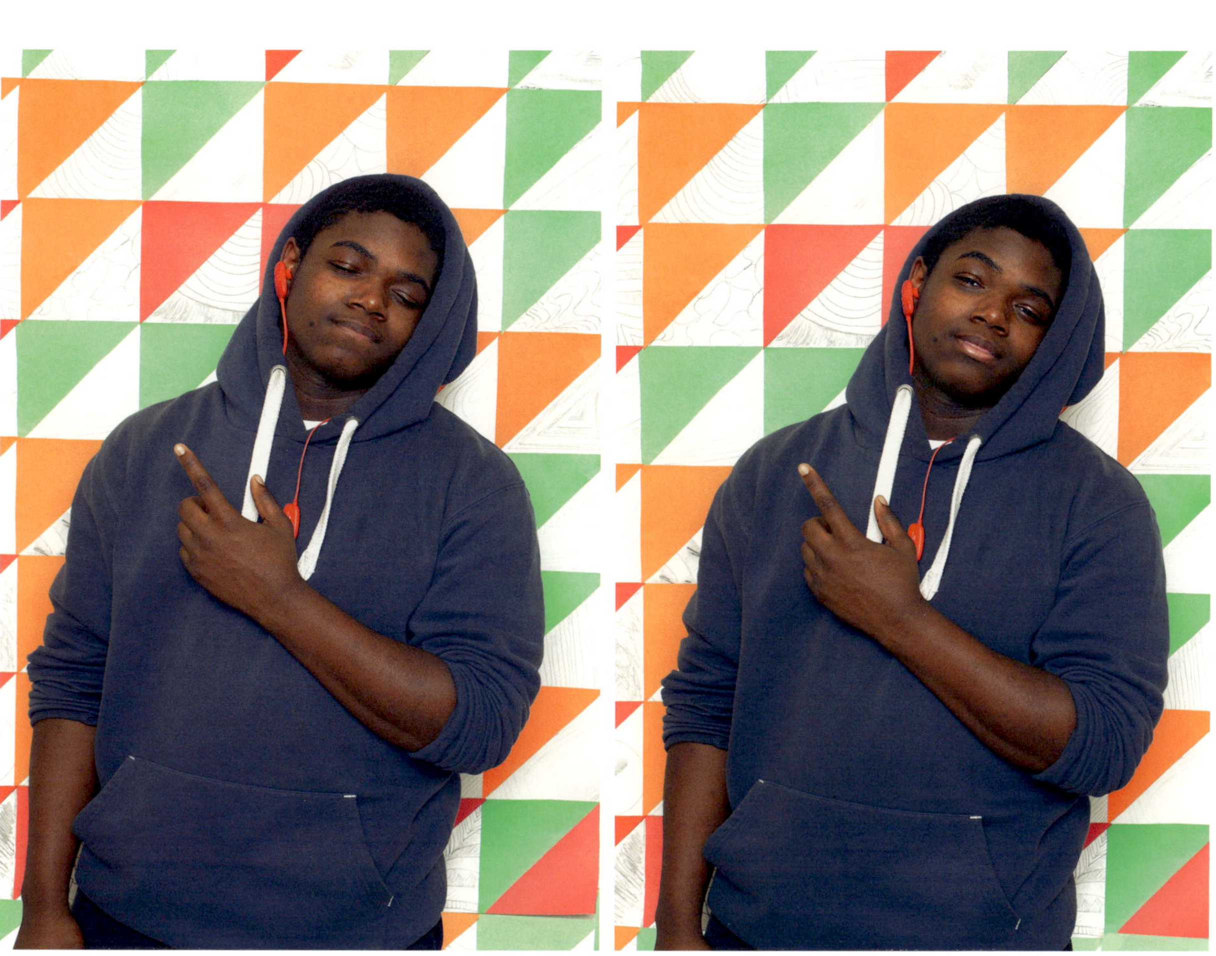

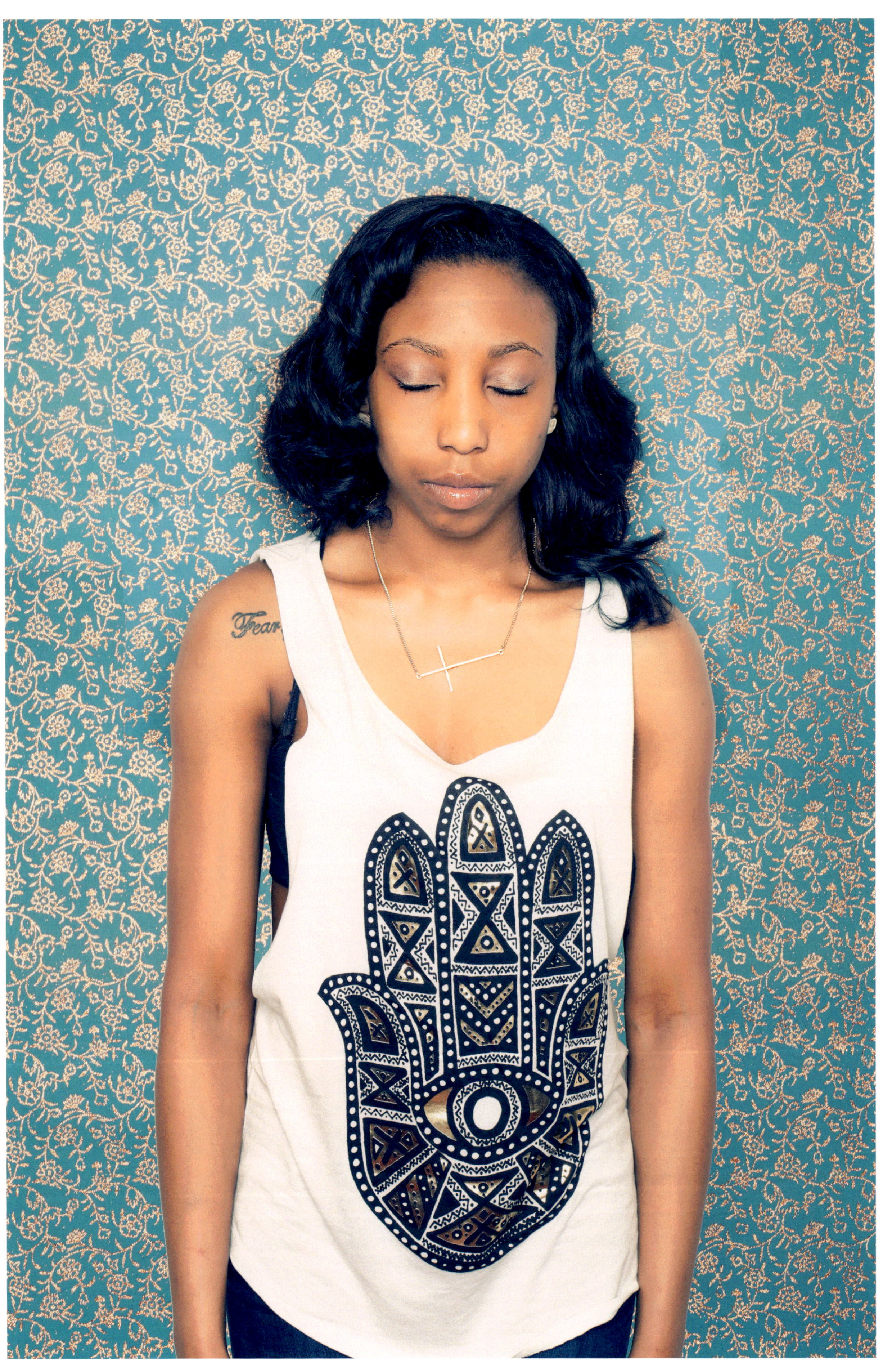

GAY | FACE

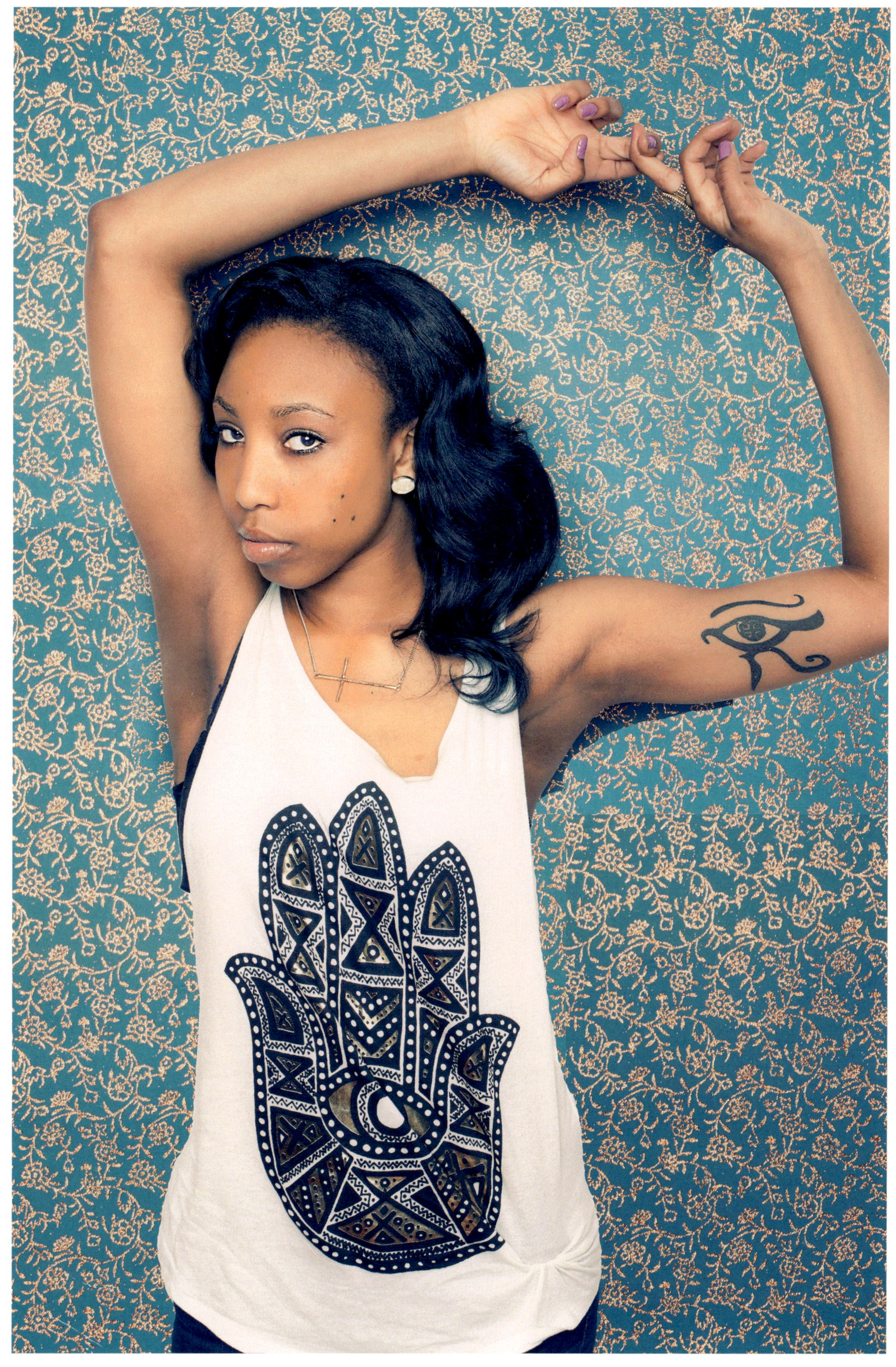

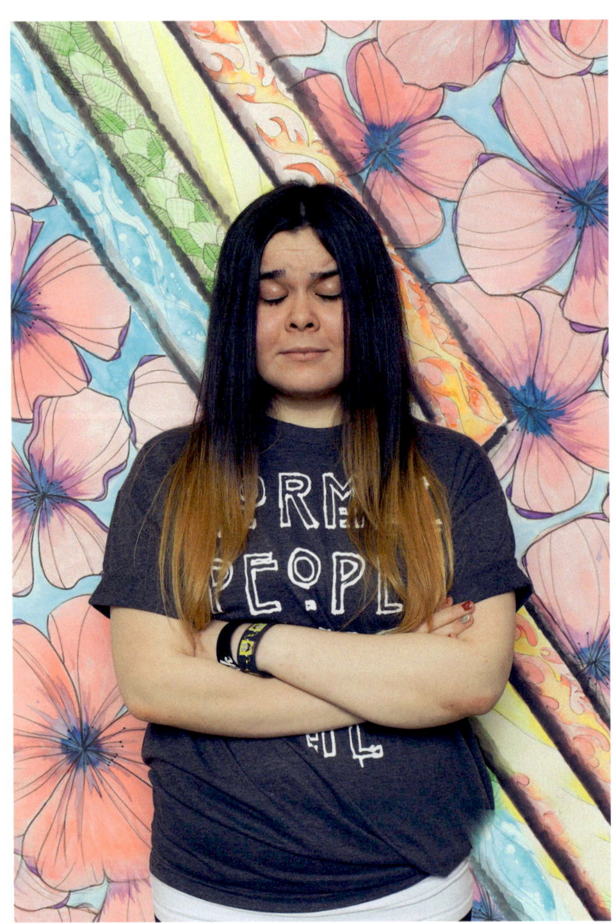
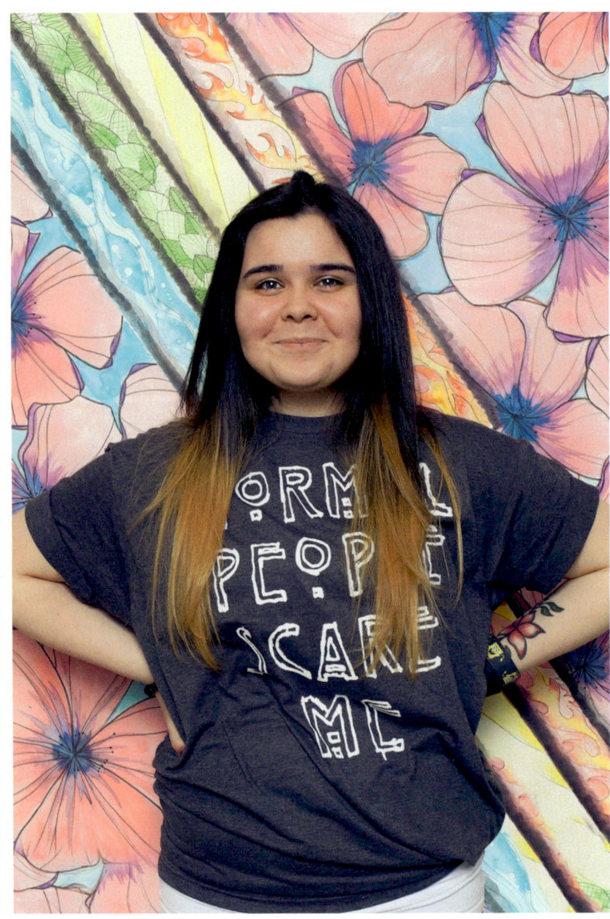

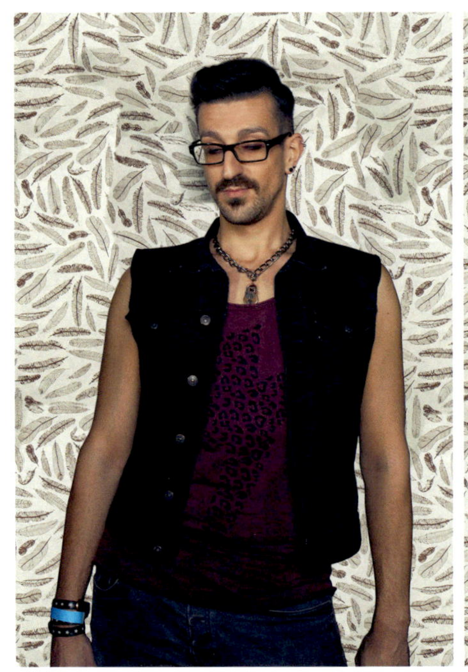
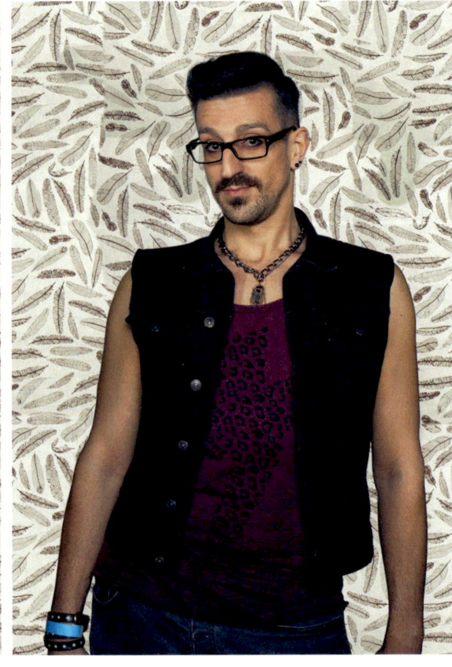

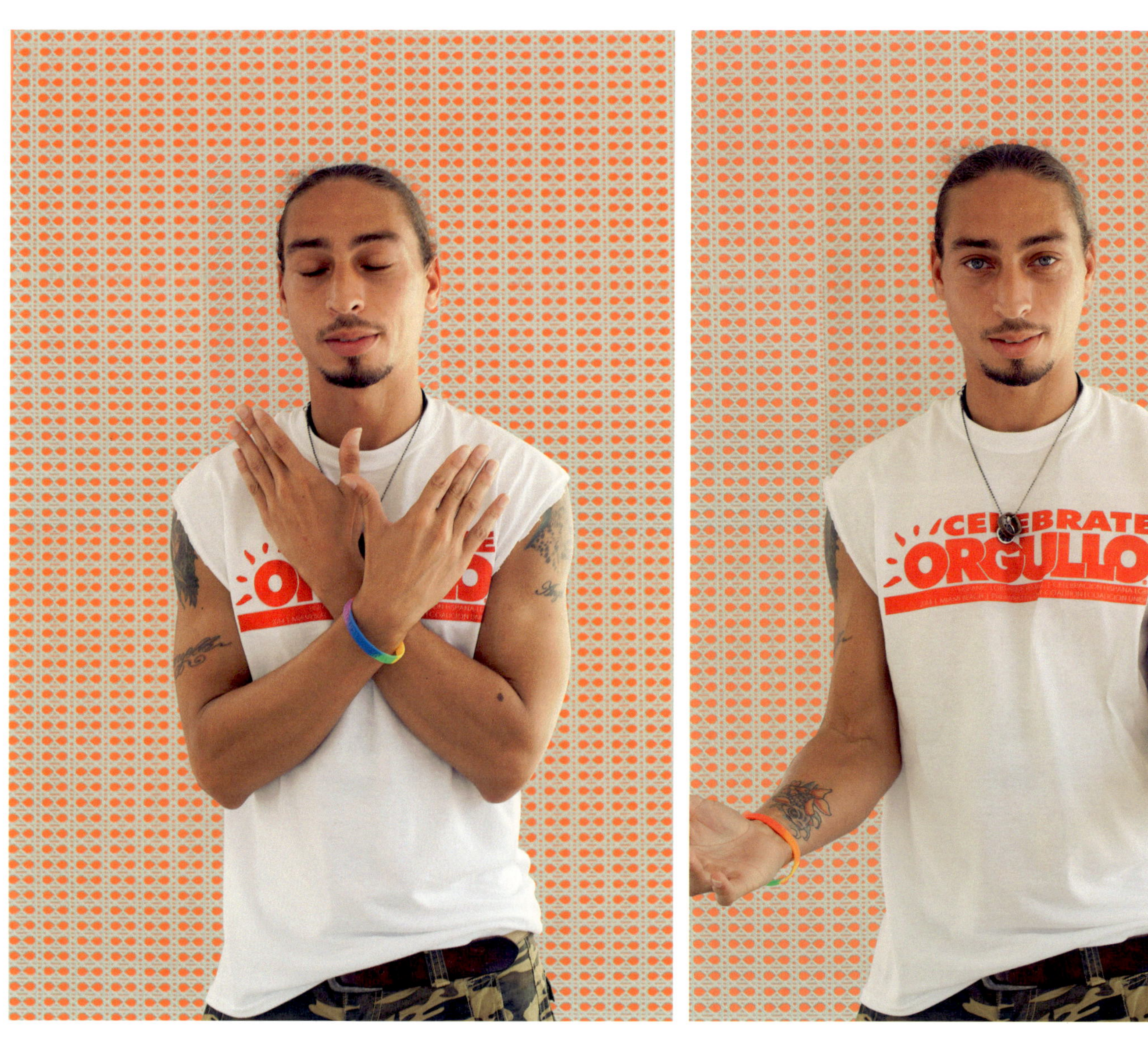

CELEBRATE
ORGULLO

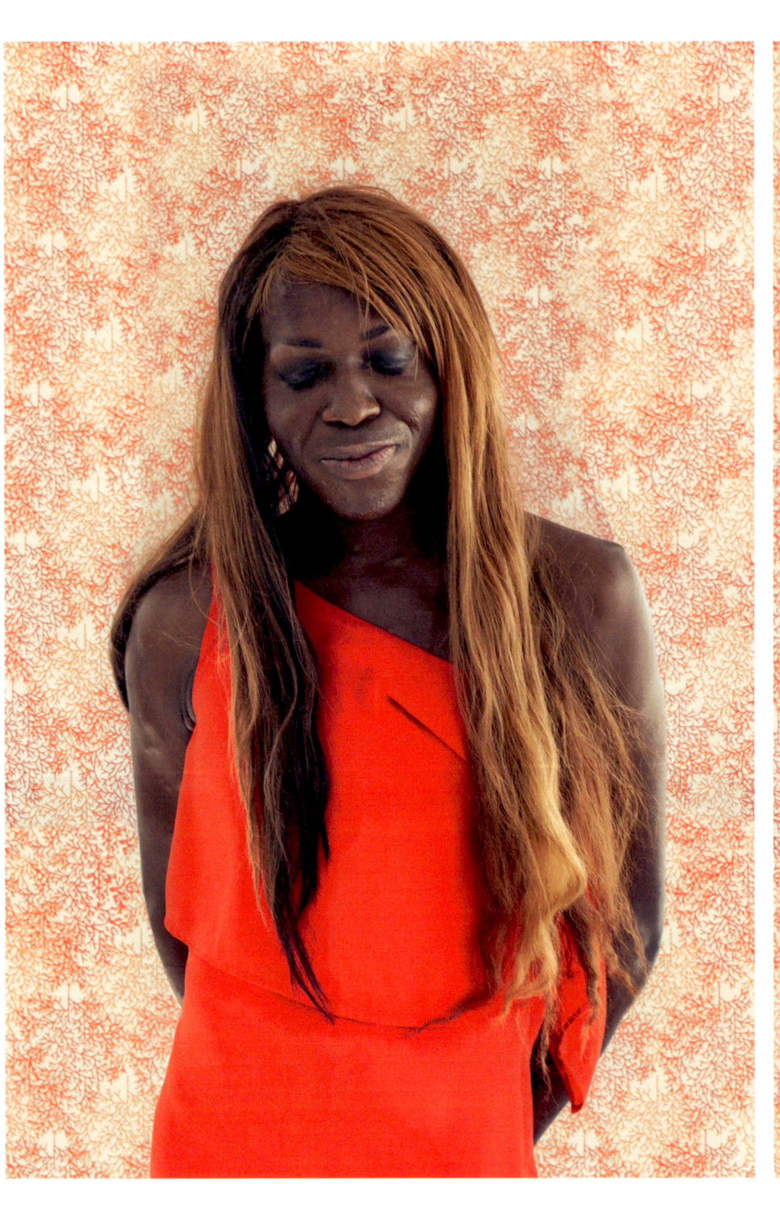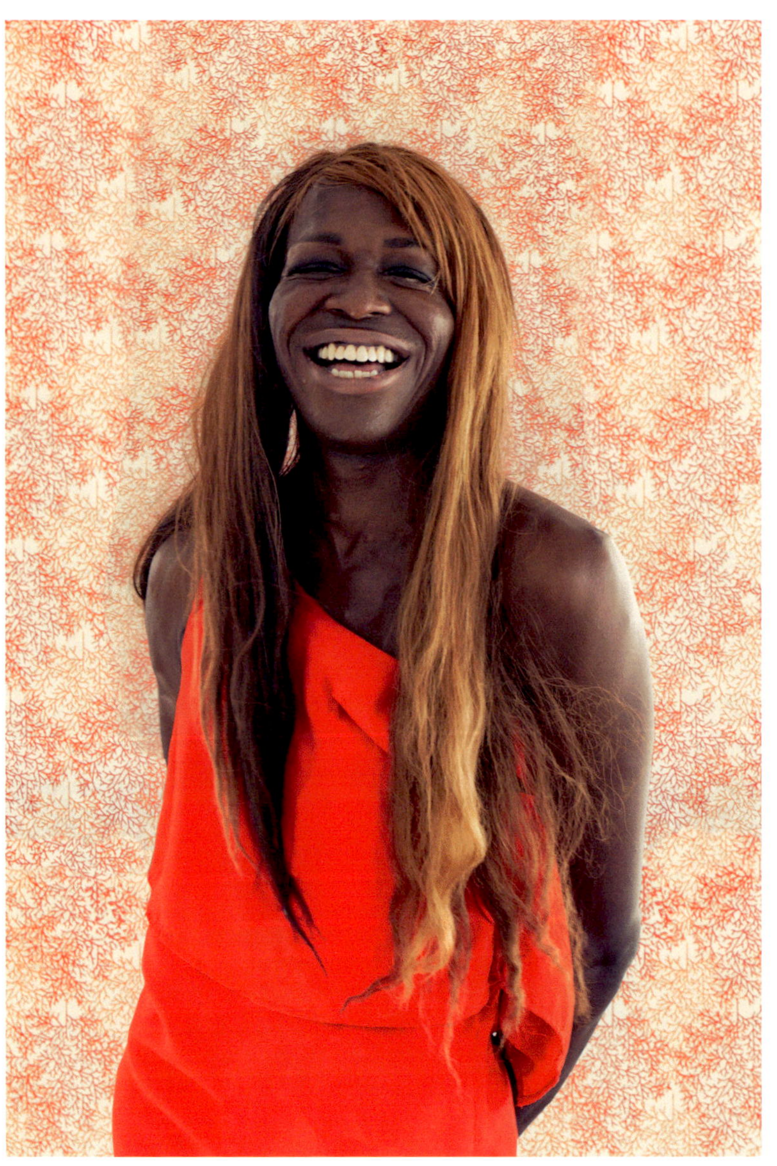

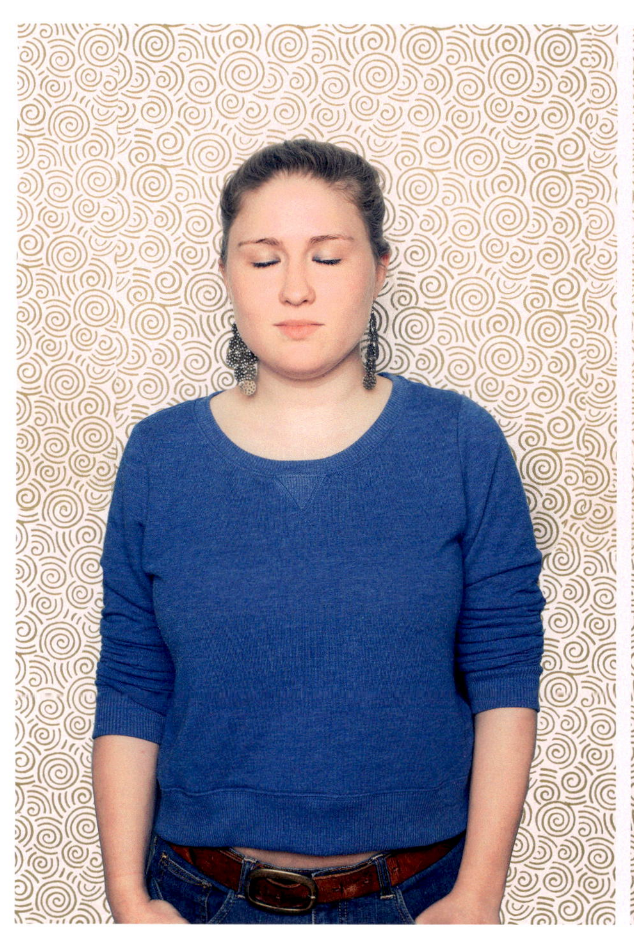
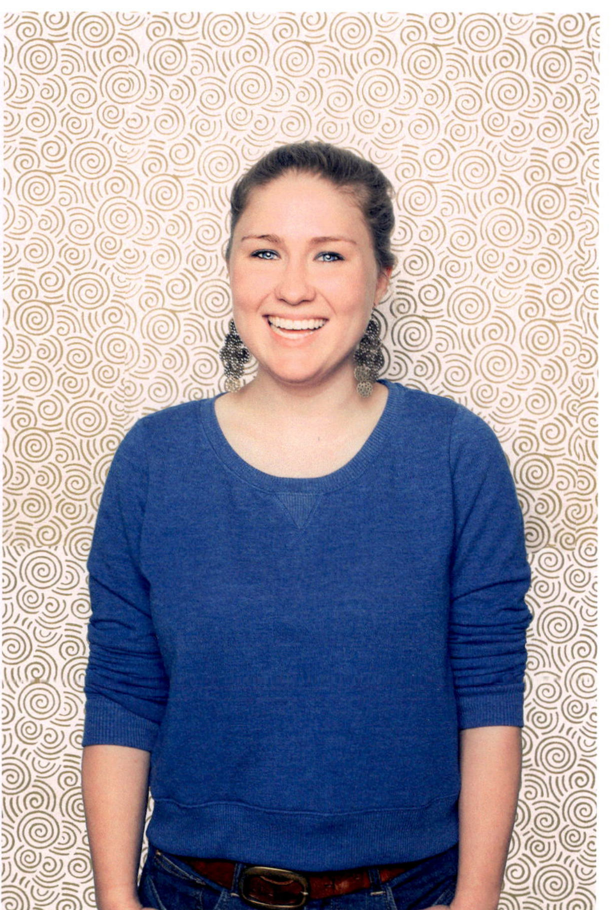

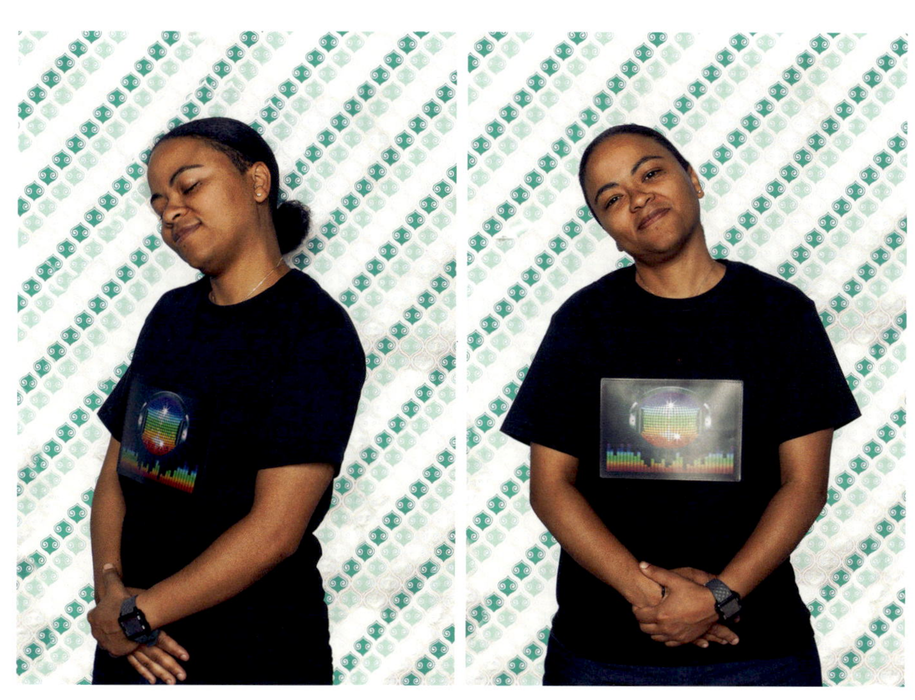

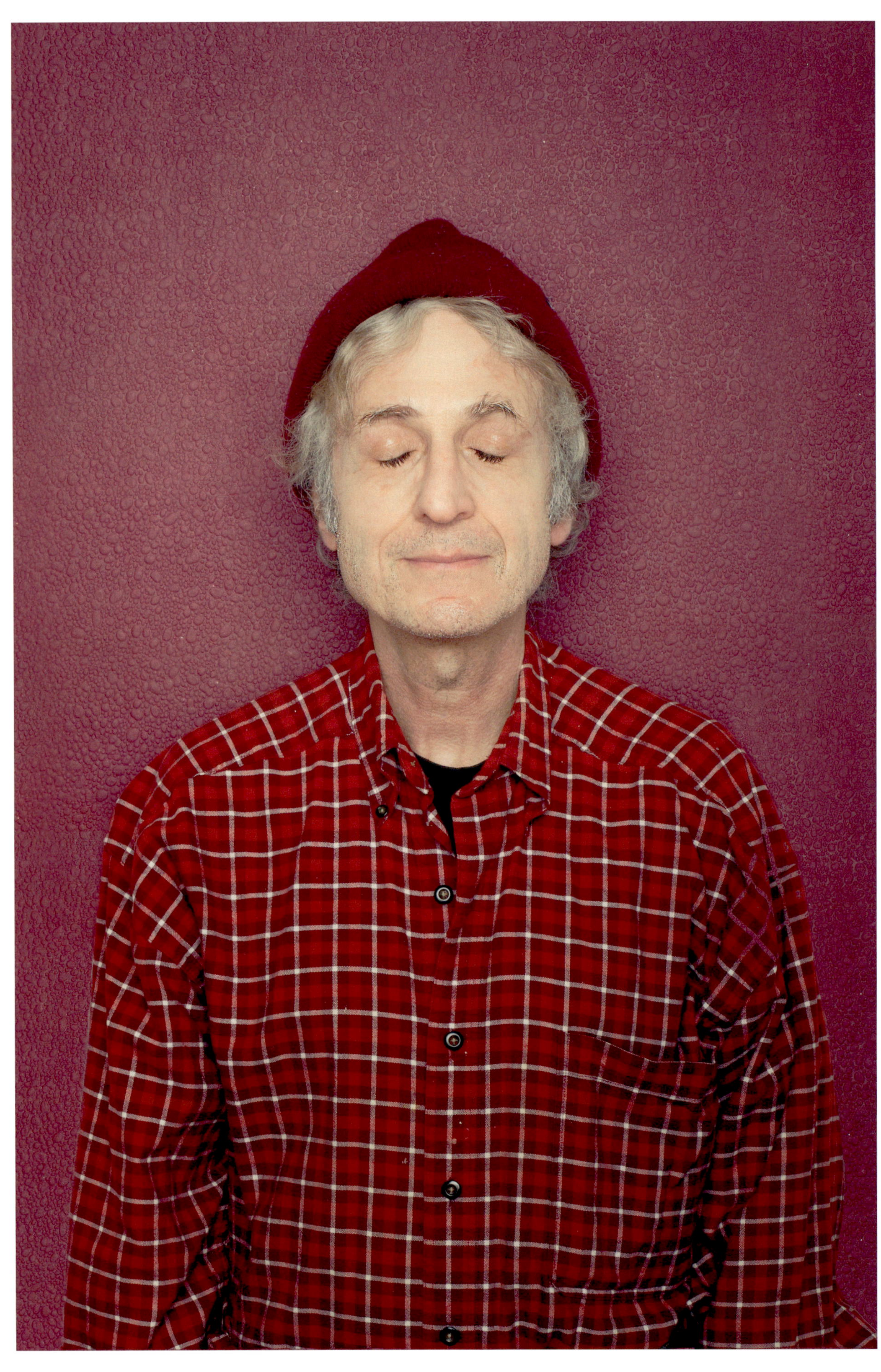
GAY | FACE

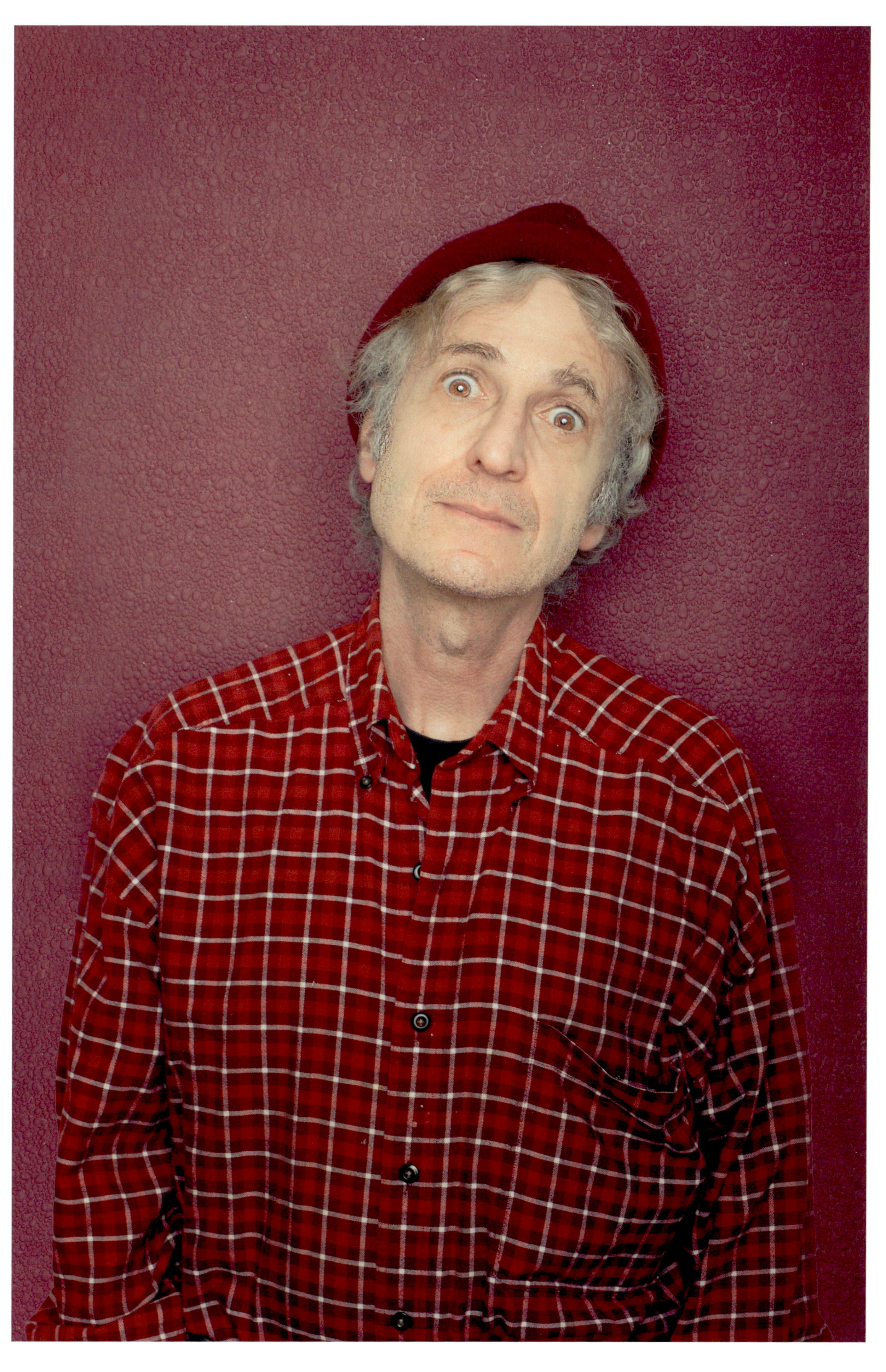

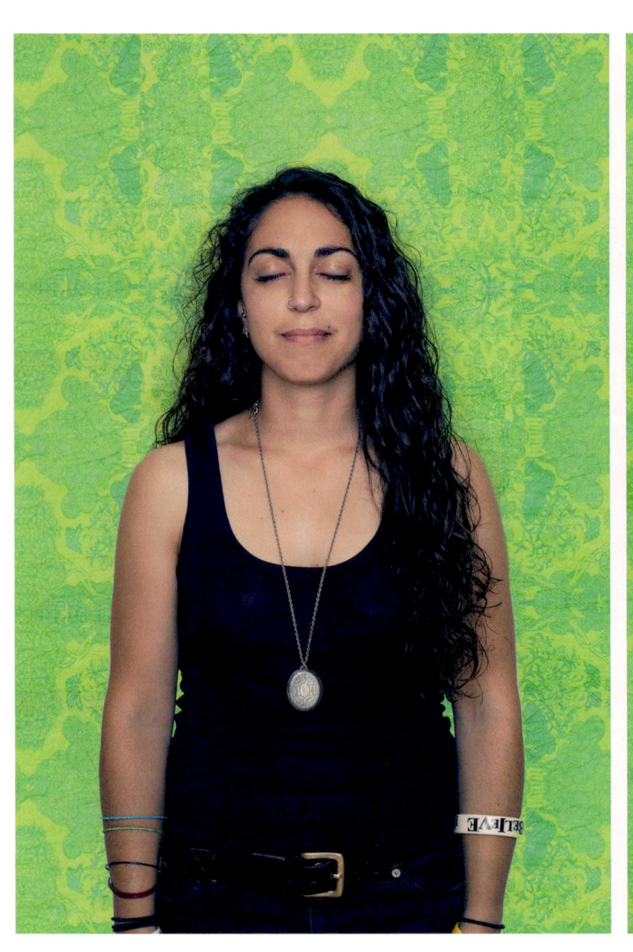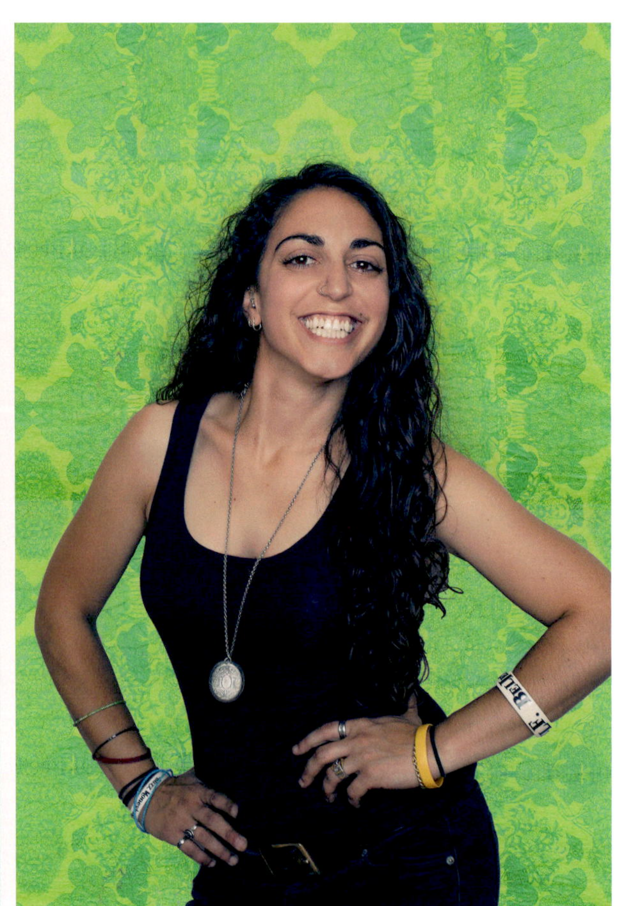

GAY | FACE

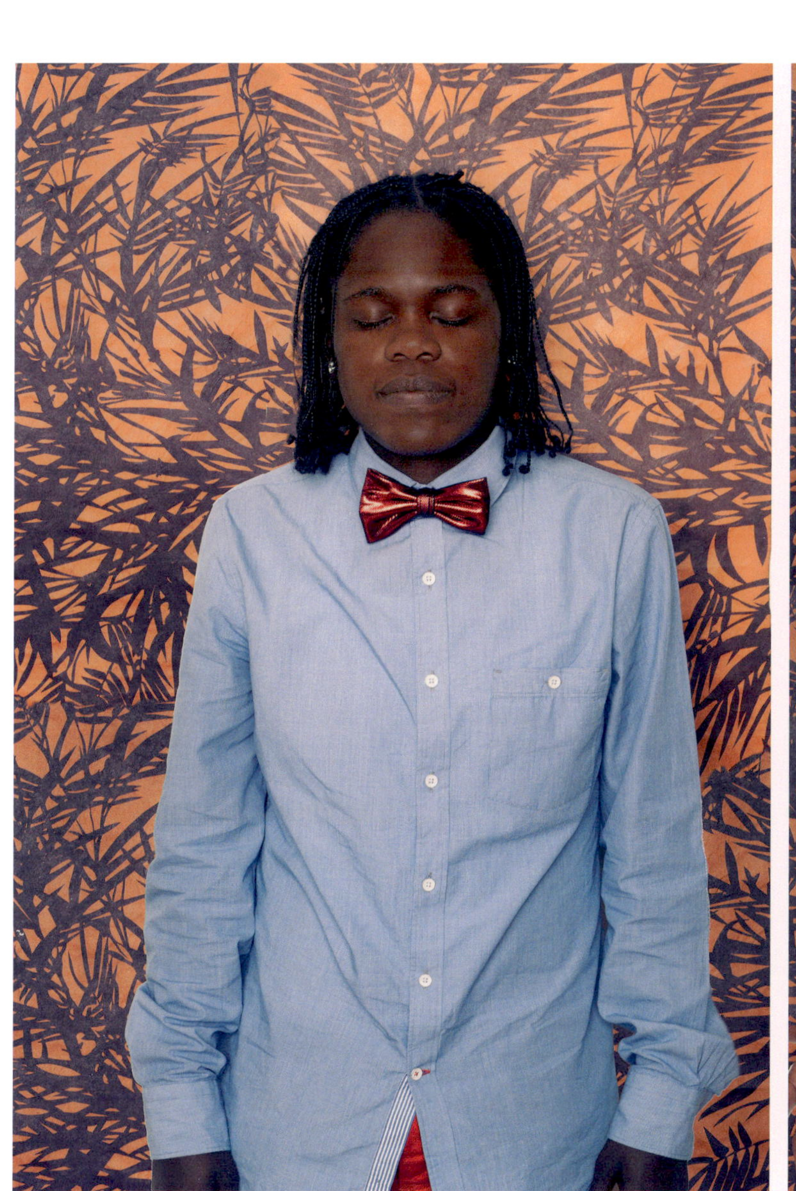
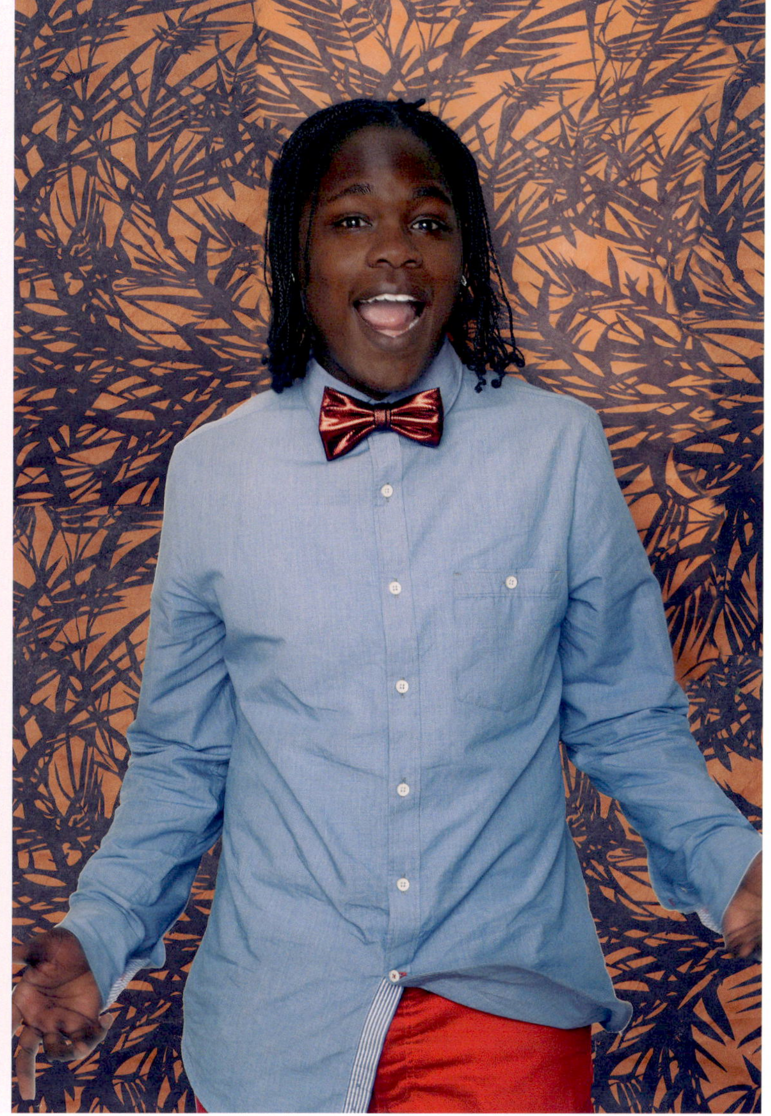

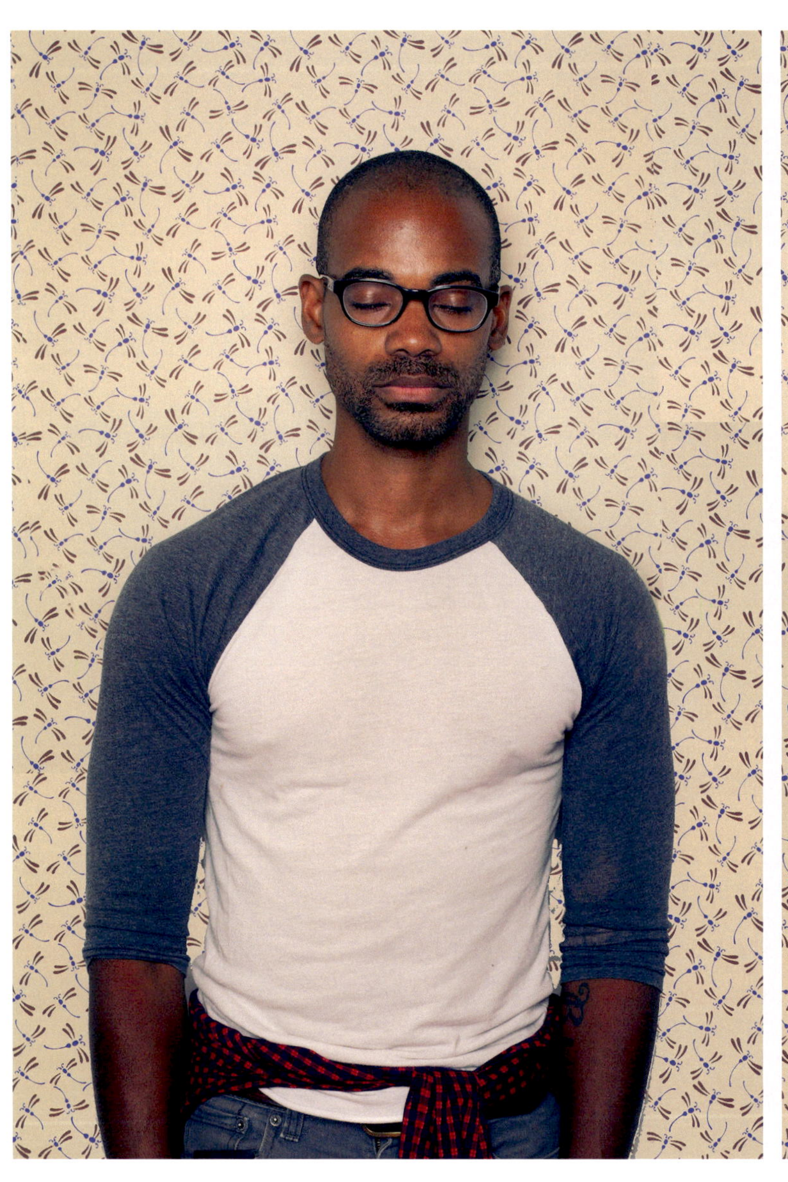
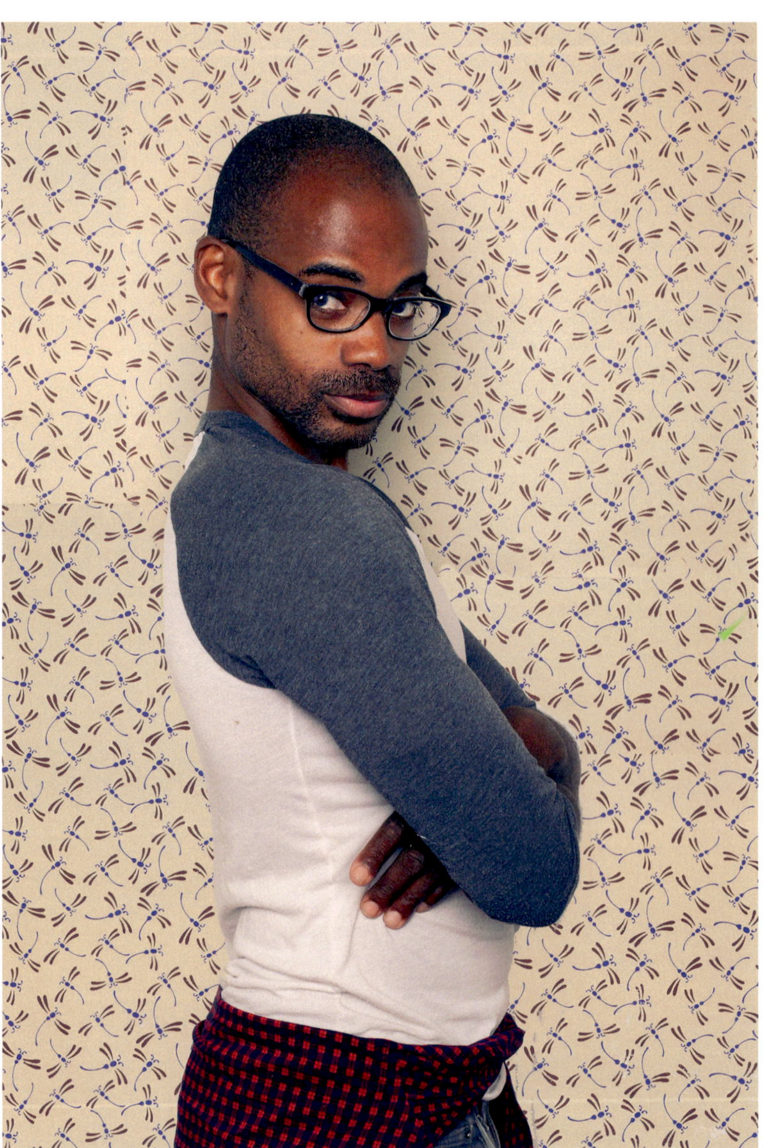

GAY | FACE

Guillermo B.
GREAT BARRINGTON, MASSACHUSETTS

How would you identify your sexuality?
Queer.

What pronouns do you prefer?
He/him/his.

Why did you choose to be a part of this project?
It was at the Brooklyn Pride Center that I heard about it; I immediately said yes.

What do you think of your portrait?
I LOVE it. I have always had a difficult relationship with photographs, and even mirrors, but seeing myself with eyes closed made me smile. I look peaceful and at ease in my own skin. I also love the second photograph, in which I'm striking a campy pose. In the past I might have thought that I look too gay, but I embraced it in this portrait—it reflects my childhood struggle of being a quiet, shy bookworm, but also wanting to be seen, even if I had to adopt a new persona to make people see me.

Describe your coming out. Are you coming out in some way by participating in this project?
I'd always thought of myself as "out," but it took me a long time to understand the difference between assuming people know about my queerness and being vocal about it. I was able to see how internalized homophobia was still keeping me in a fear-based box. I no longer think of coming out as one definitive moment, but a continual process. That internalized homophobia goes very deep and is overcome in big ways—marching for queer rights and recognition—but also in very small, intimate ways, like this project.

If you could change one thing about mainstream society to improve the lives of LGBTQ+ people, what would it be?
I'd say that the lives of LGBTQ+ people would be improved when we stop caring what mainstream society thinks of us.

Describe how this project has affected you, both personally and as a member of the LGBTQ+ community as a whole.
When a friend texted me to say he saw my portrait on a subway entrance wall in Williamsburg, I was completely floored. I went over to see it and was so moved to see myself on public display. The face that used to have so much shame and shyness was up where everyone could see it. I was super happy.

What advice have you been given by another LGBTQ+ person, or that you might offer someone?
I wish someone would have said to me: Don't compare yourself to the dominant images you see of queer people in the media, and don't feel like you don't belong because you don't have the same income, body type, appearance, race, gender, etc. Embrace your quirkiness and everything that makes you distinctly unique. Walk with your head high and never feel that you are beneath any other person on this earth. Find your tribe, but don't let your tribe define you.

Who are your LGBTQ+ role models?
DeRay McKesson, James Baldwin, Bayard Rustin, Marsha P. Johnson, Kehinde Wiley, David Wojnarowicz, and Glenn Ligon.

GAY | FACE

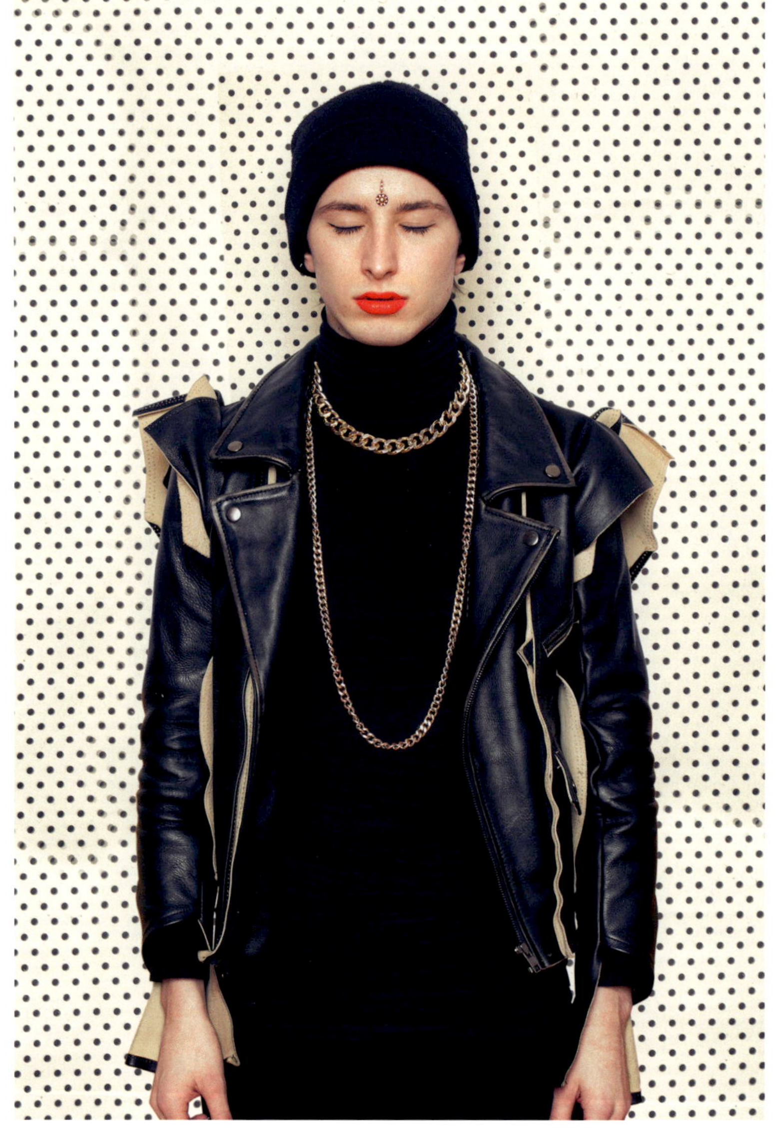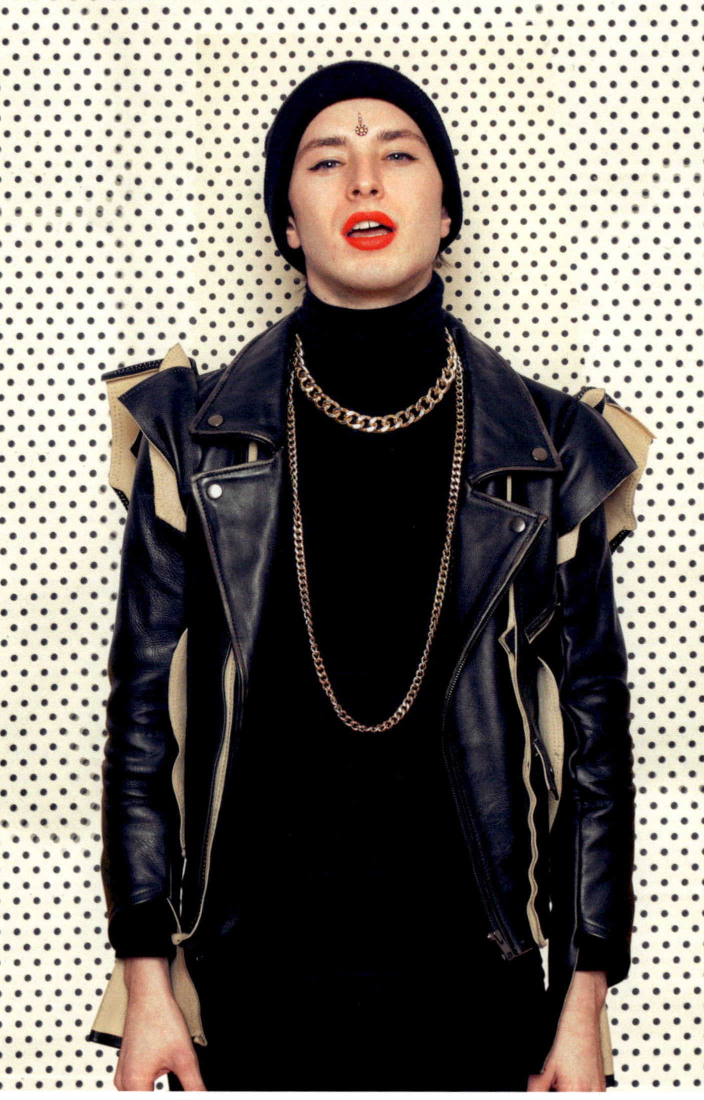

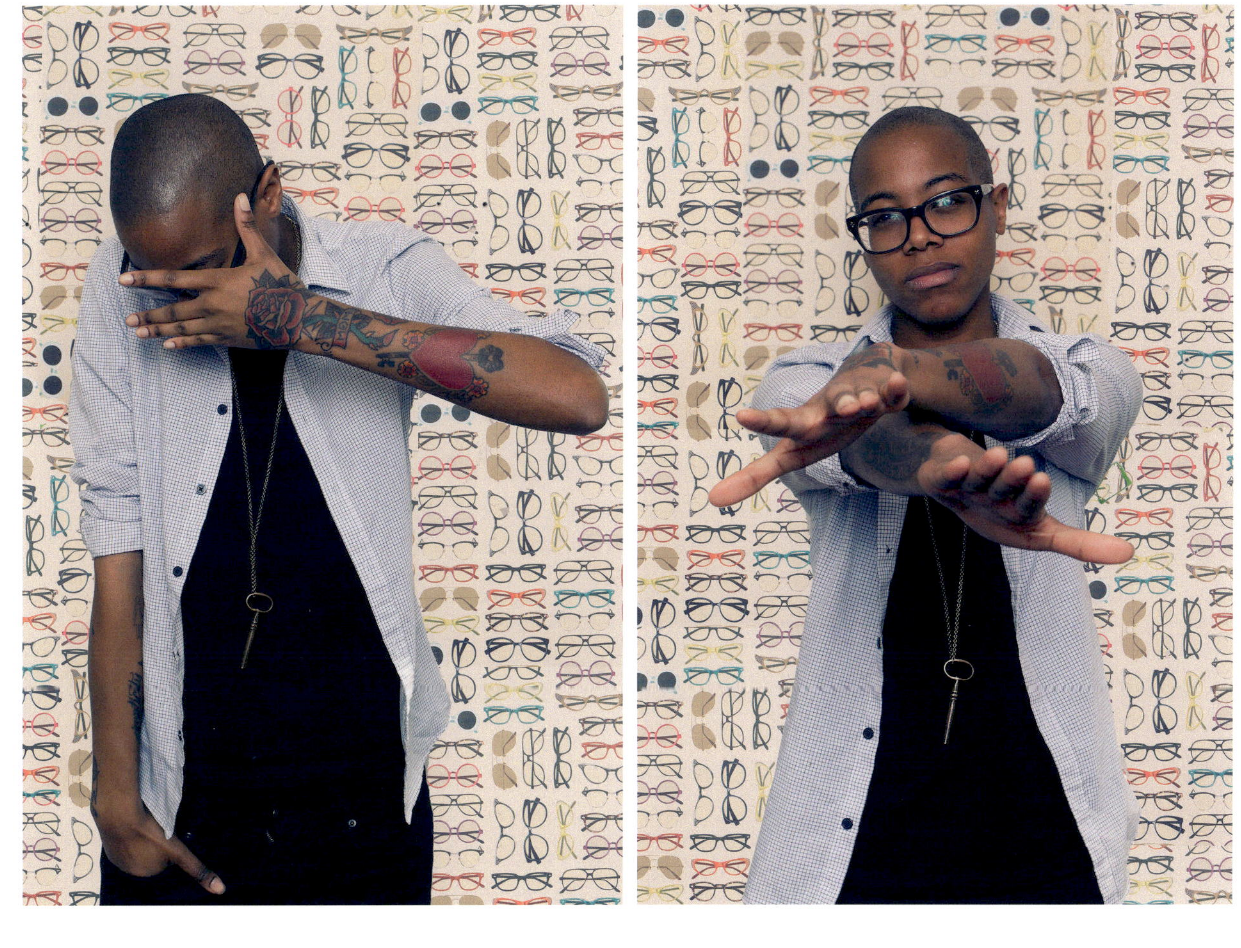

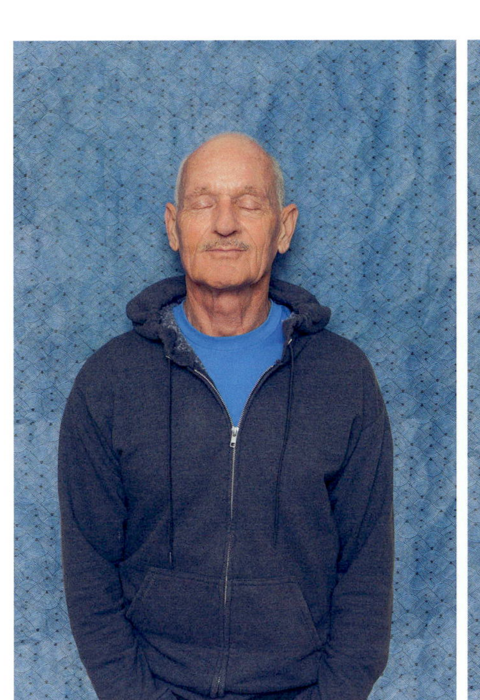
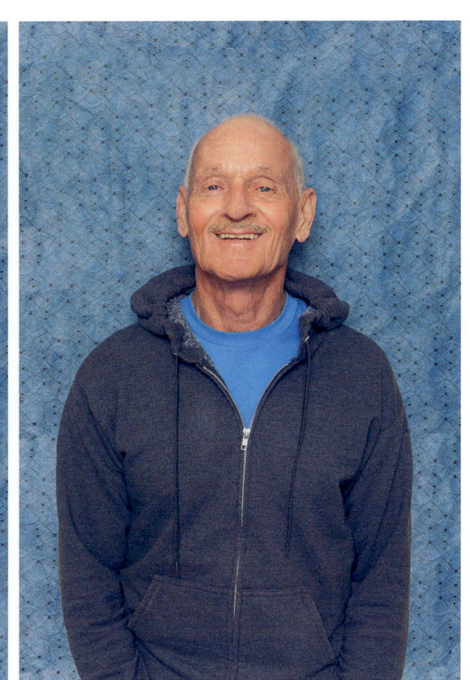

GAY | FACE

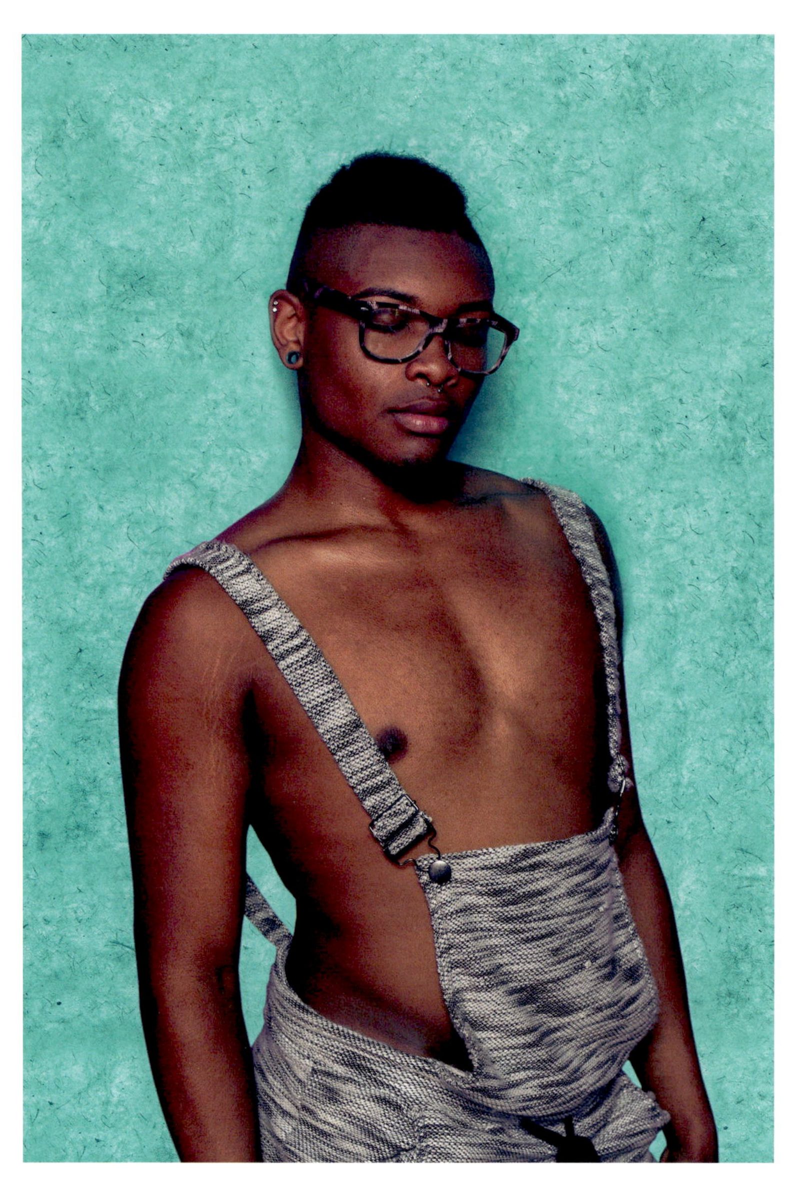 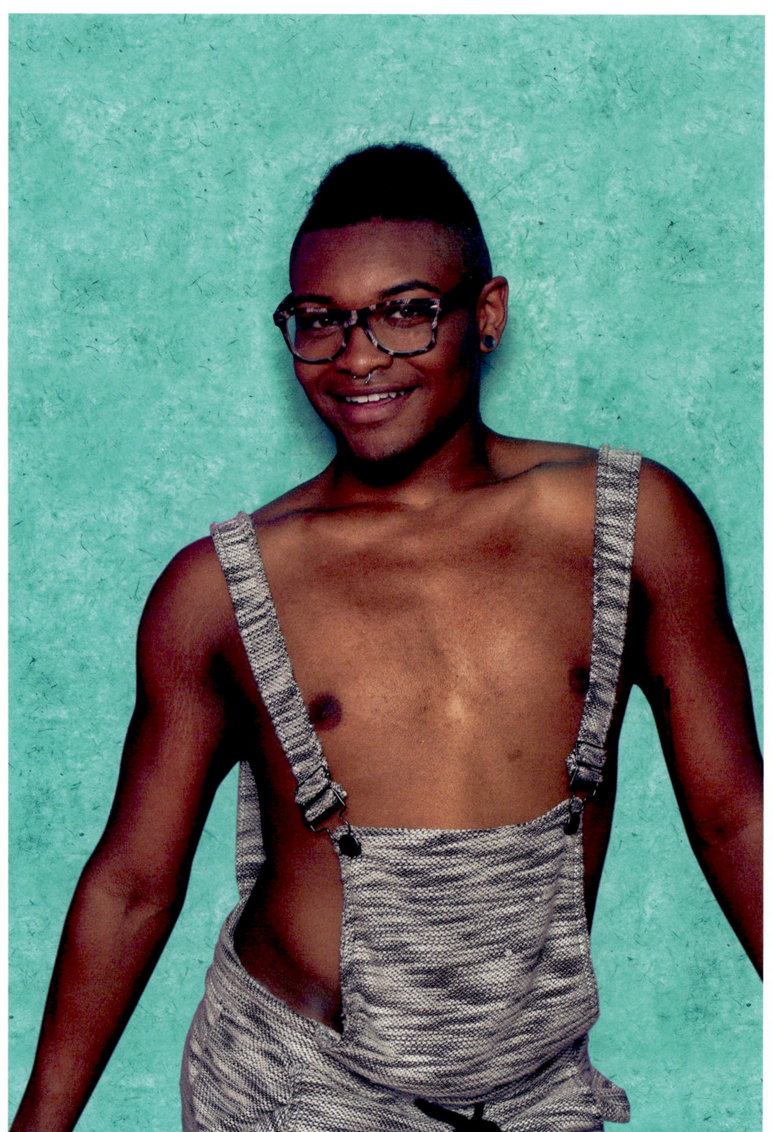

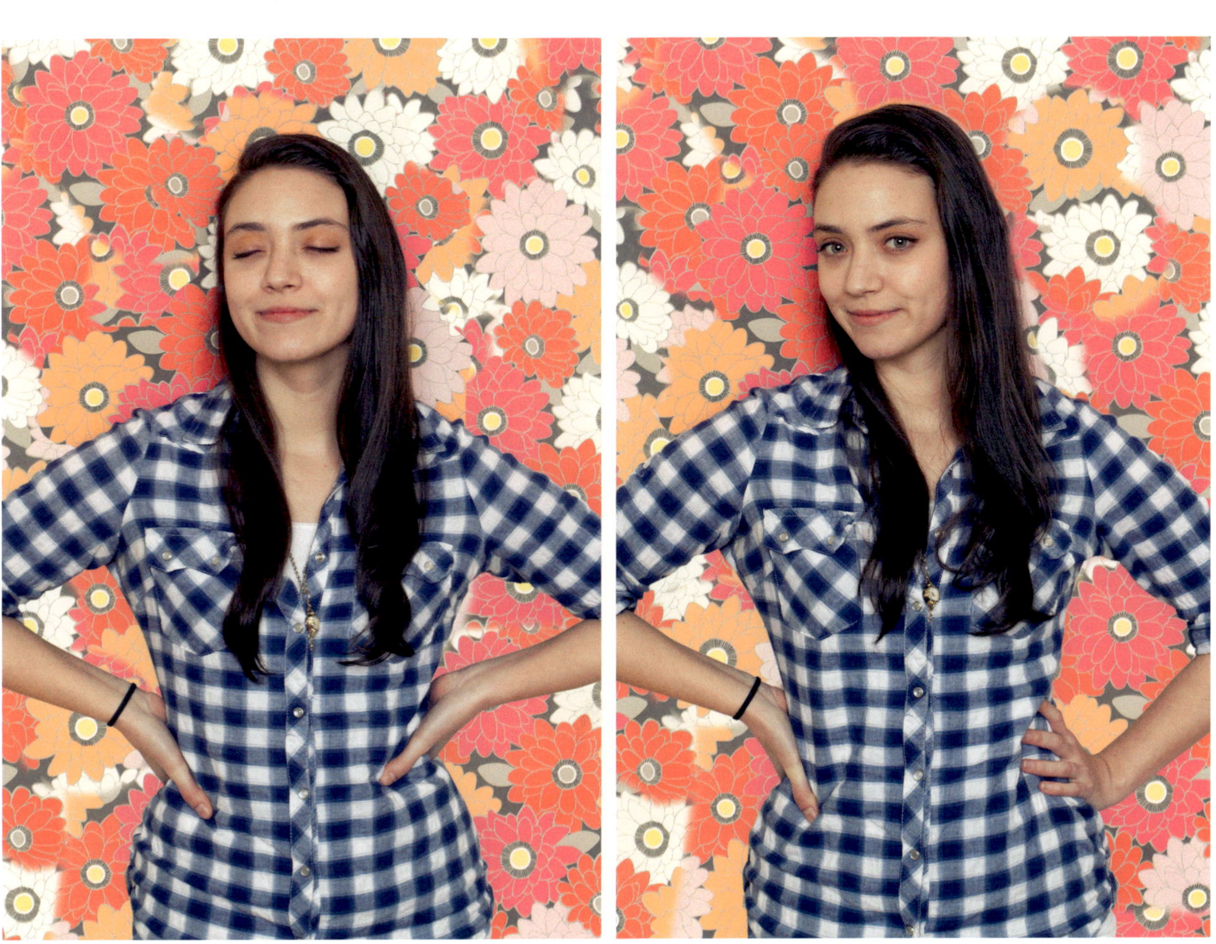

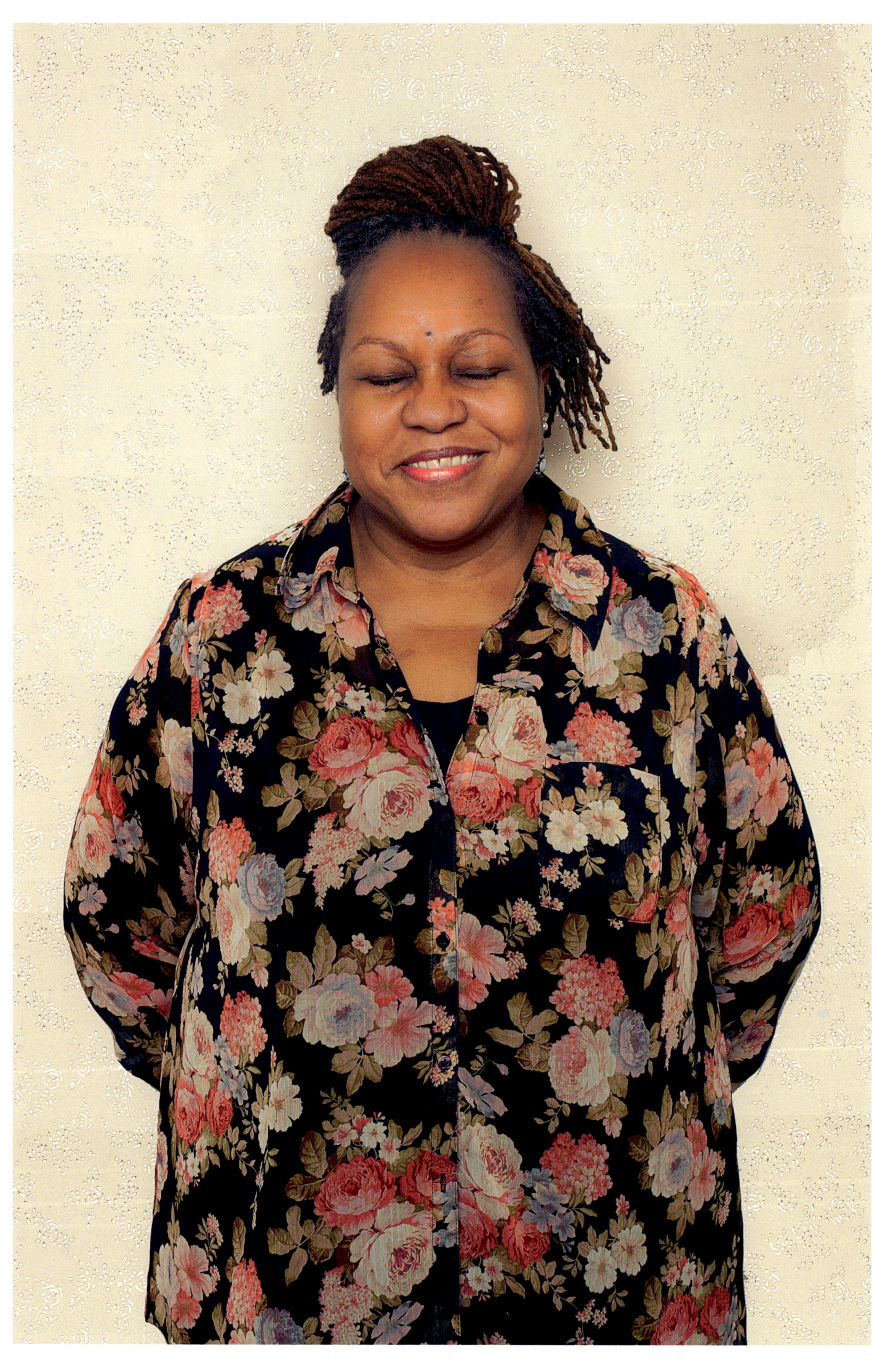

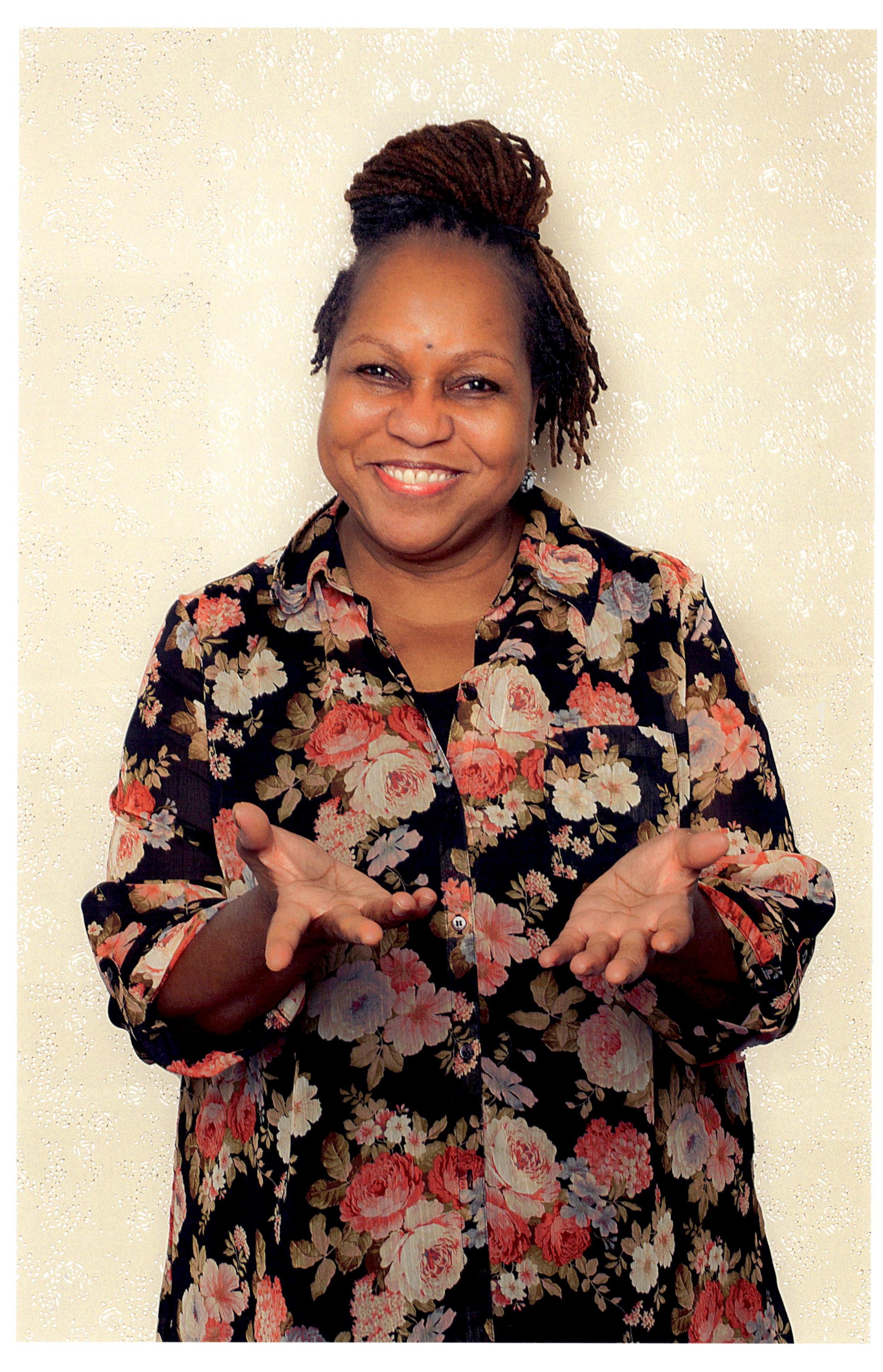

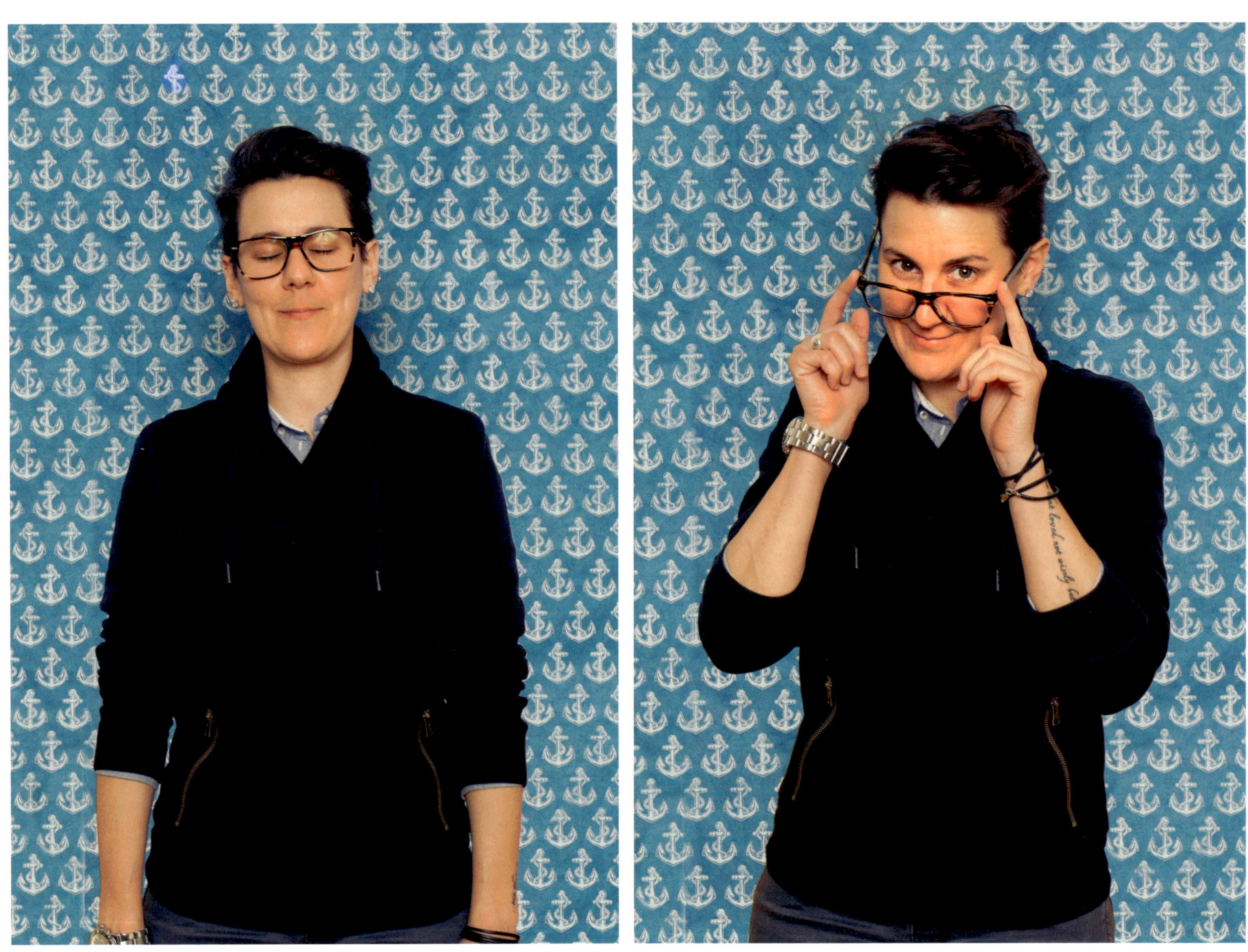

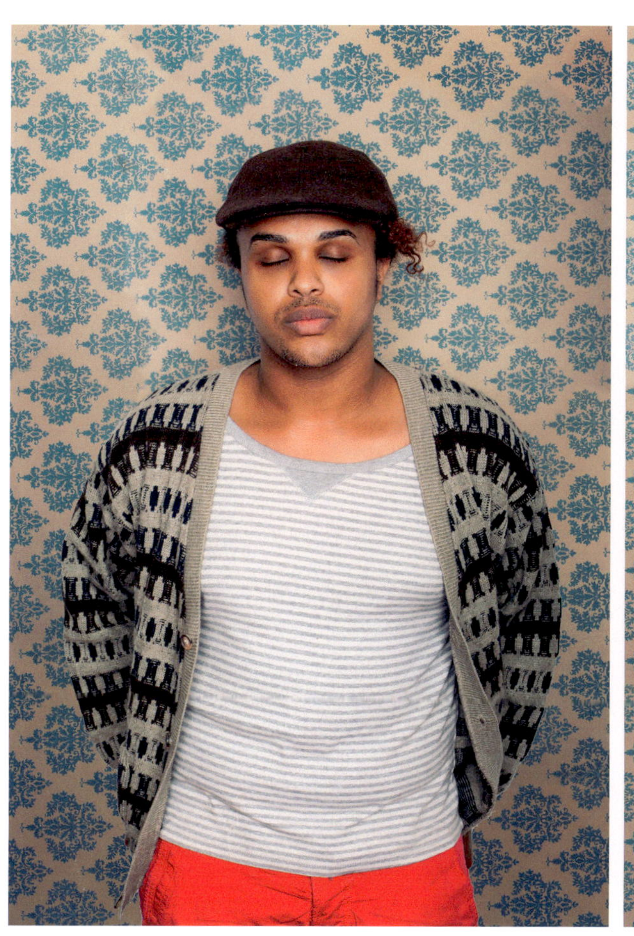
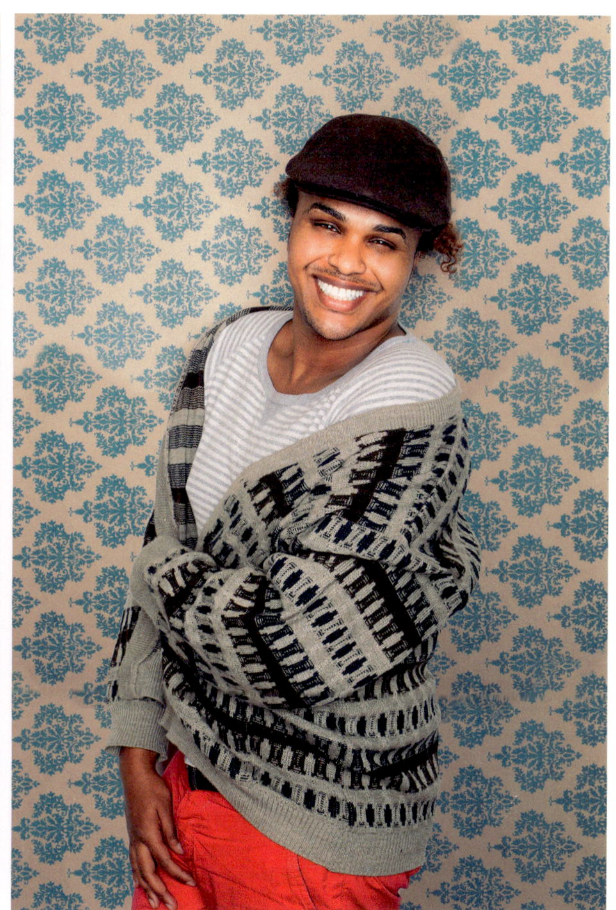

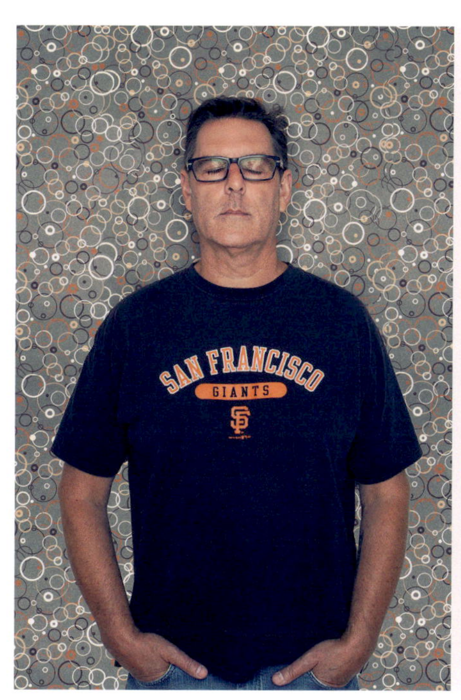
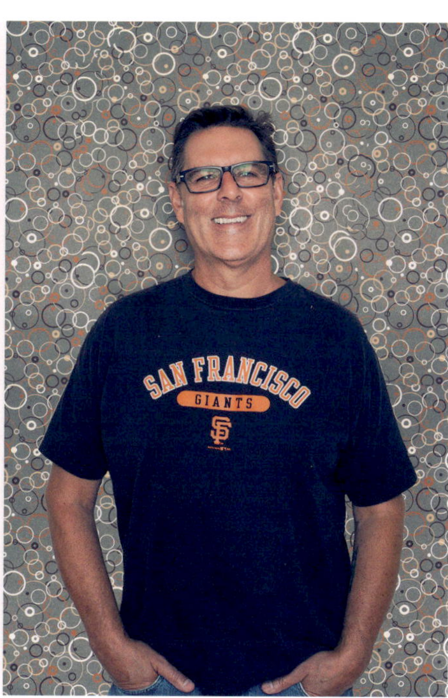

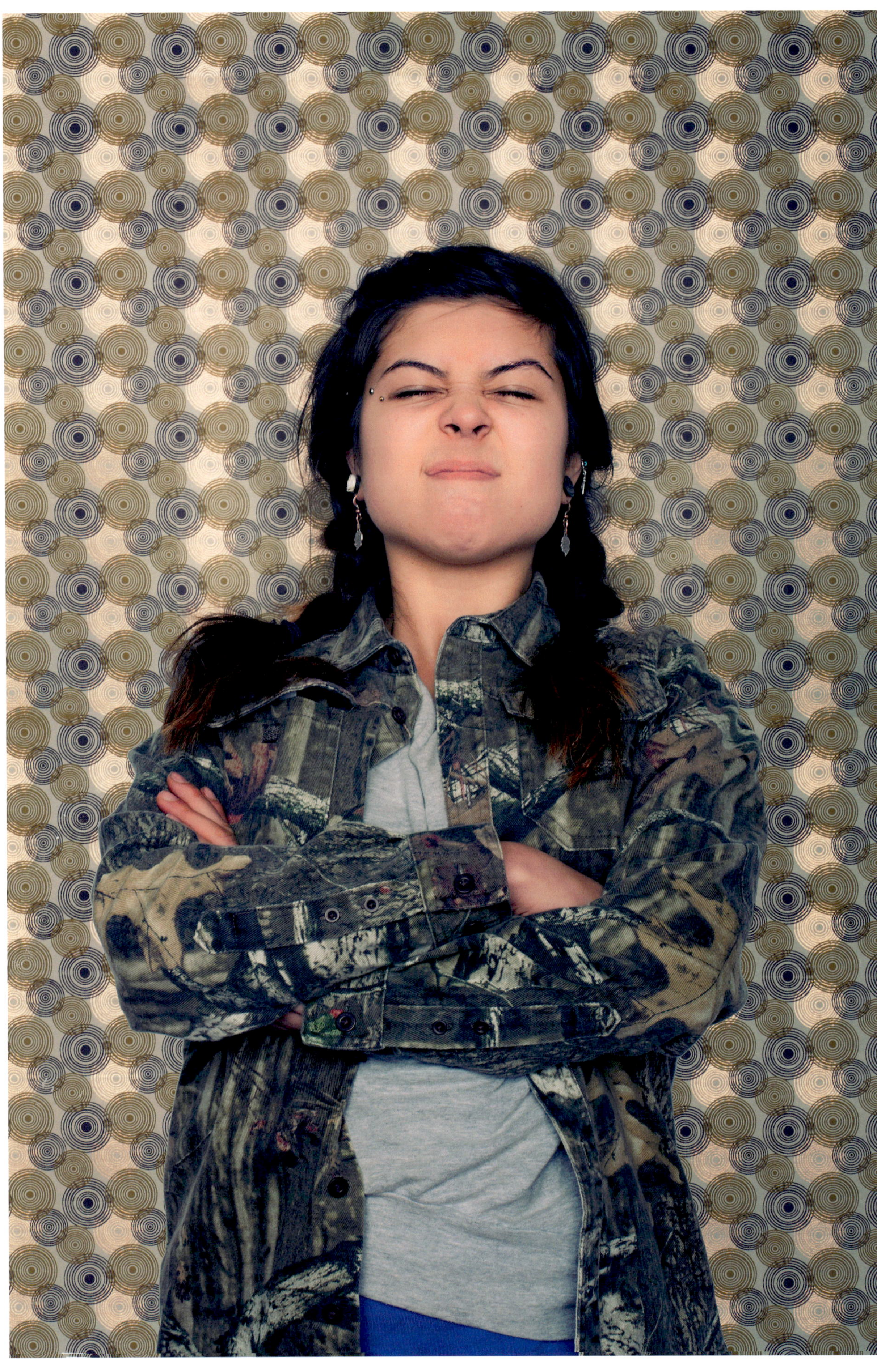

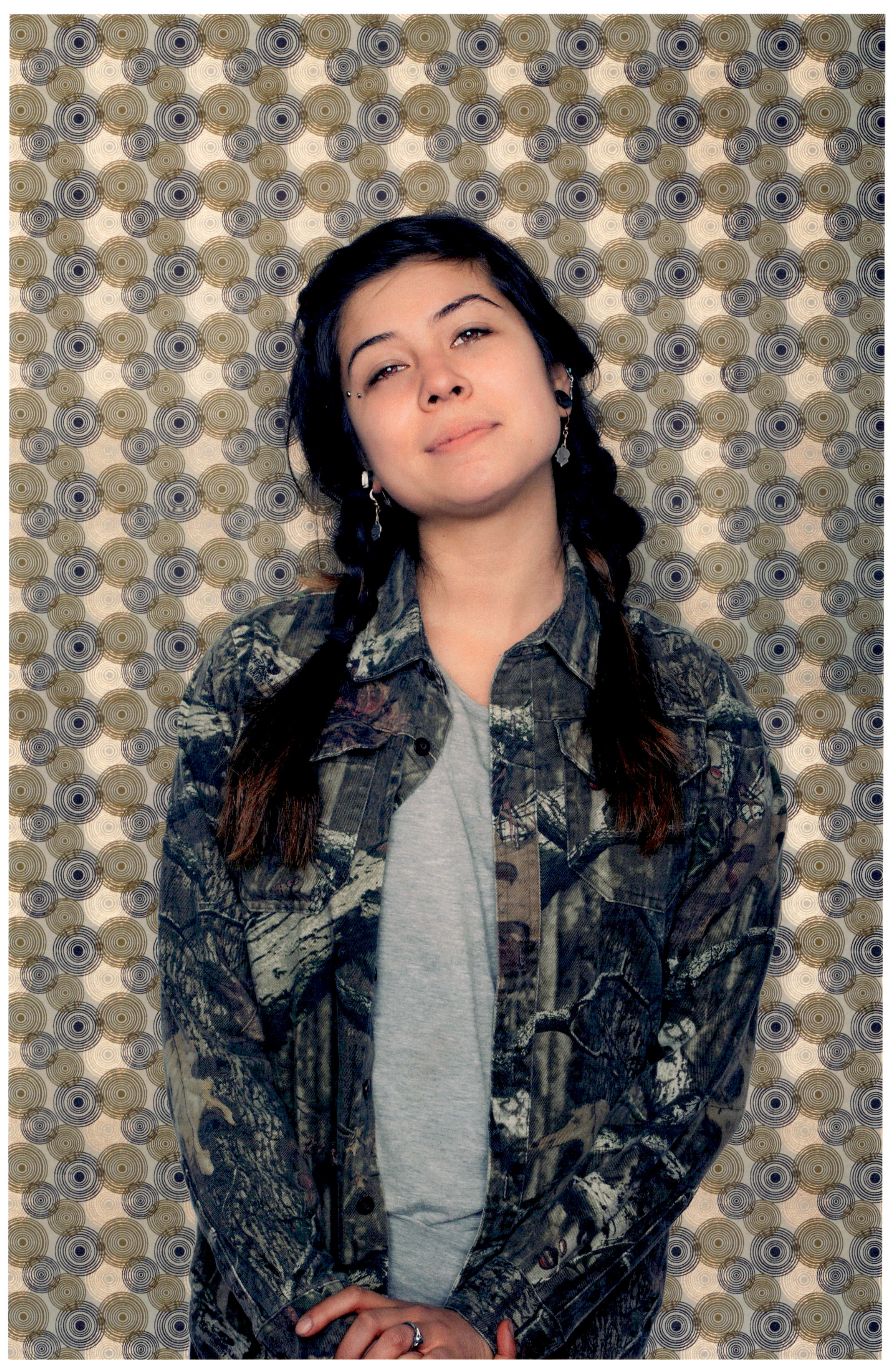

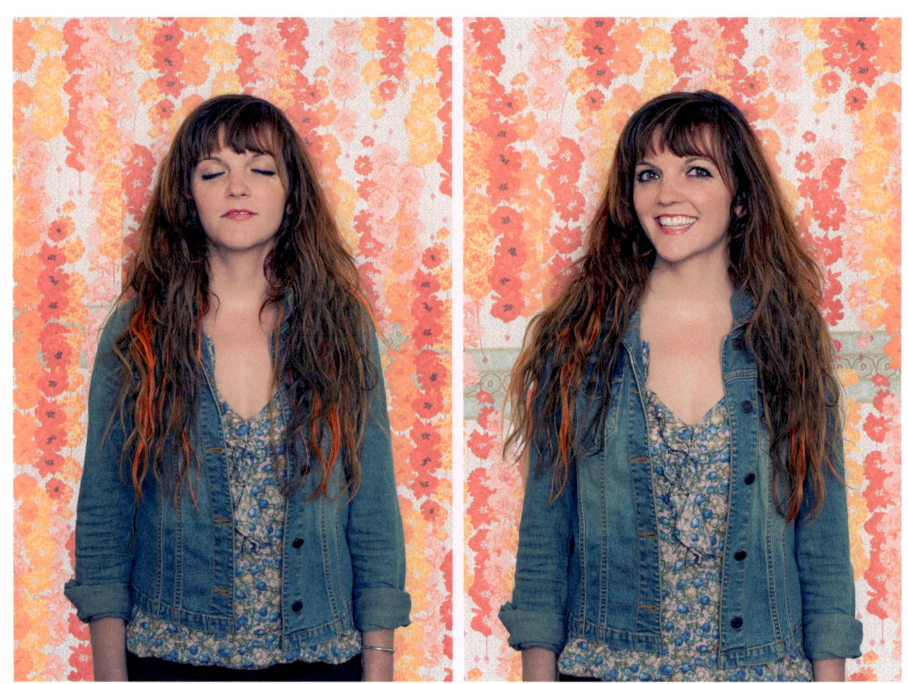

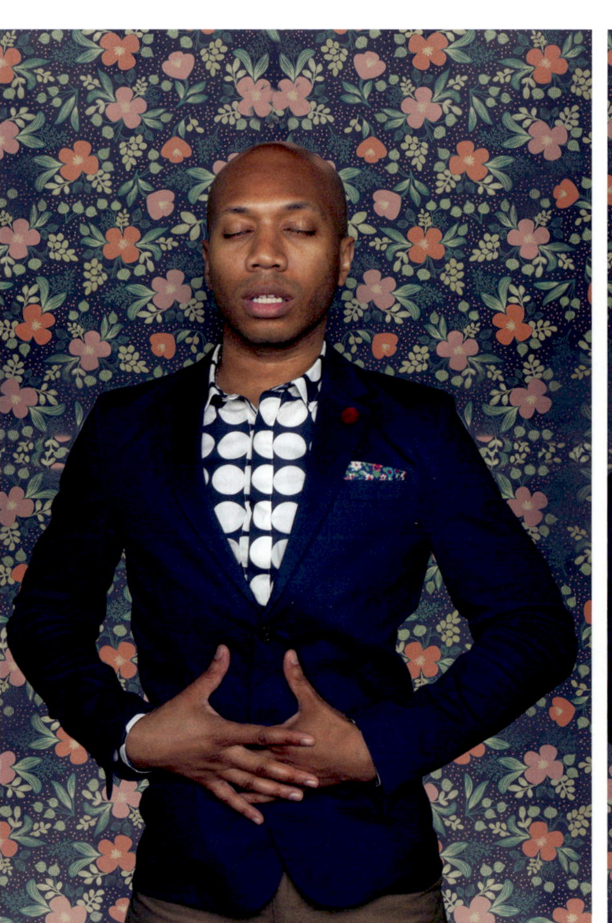

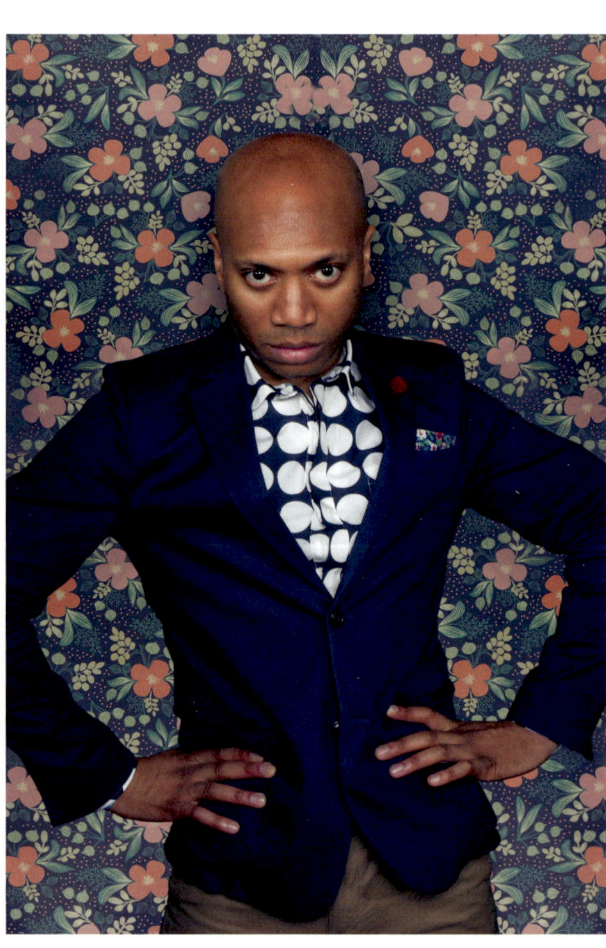

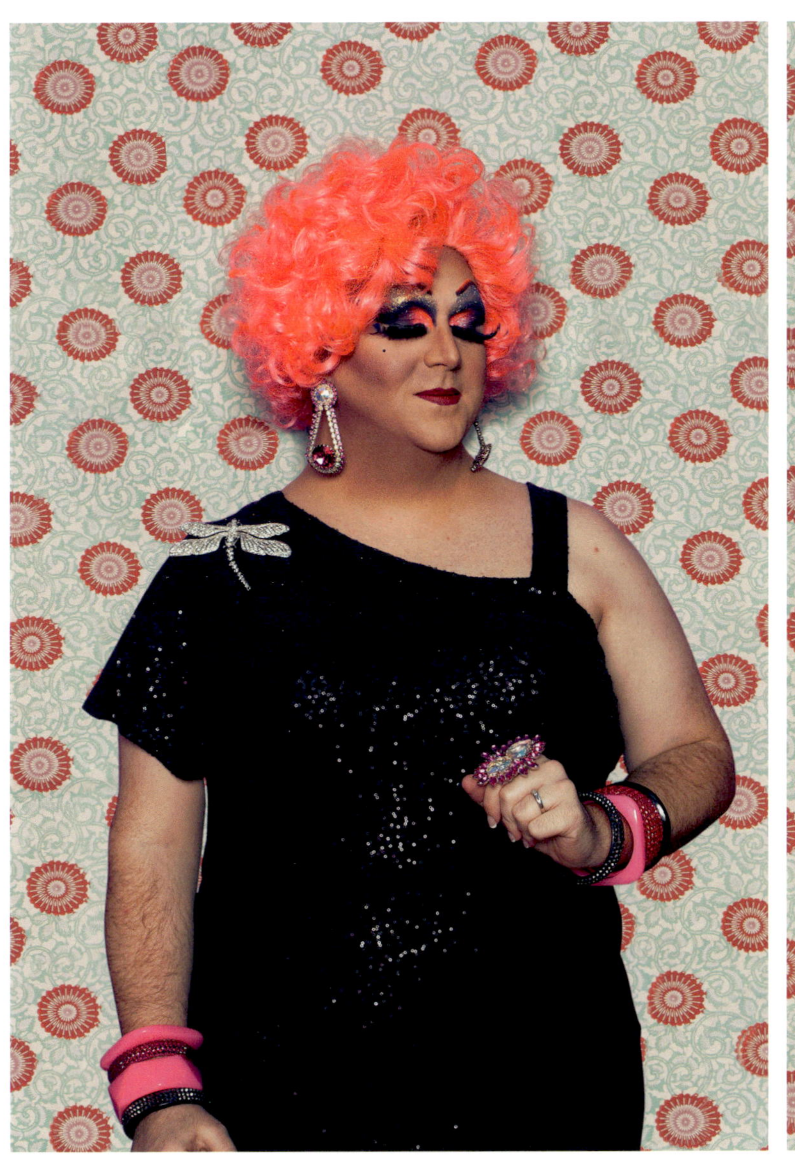
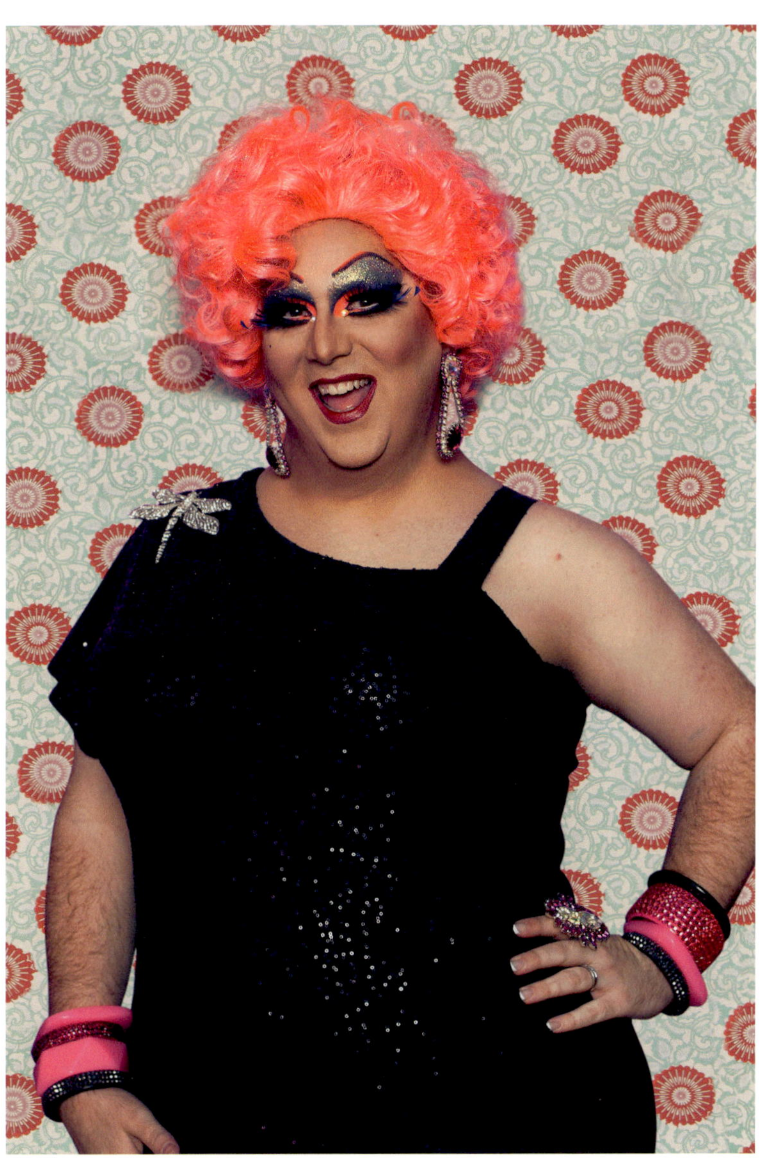

GAY | FACE

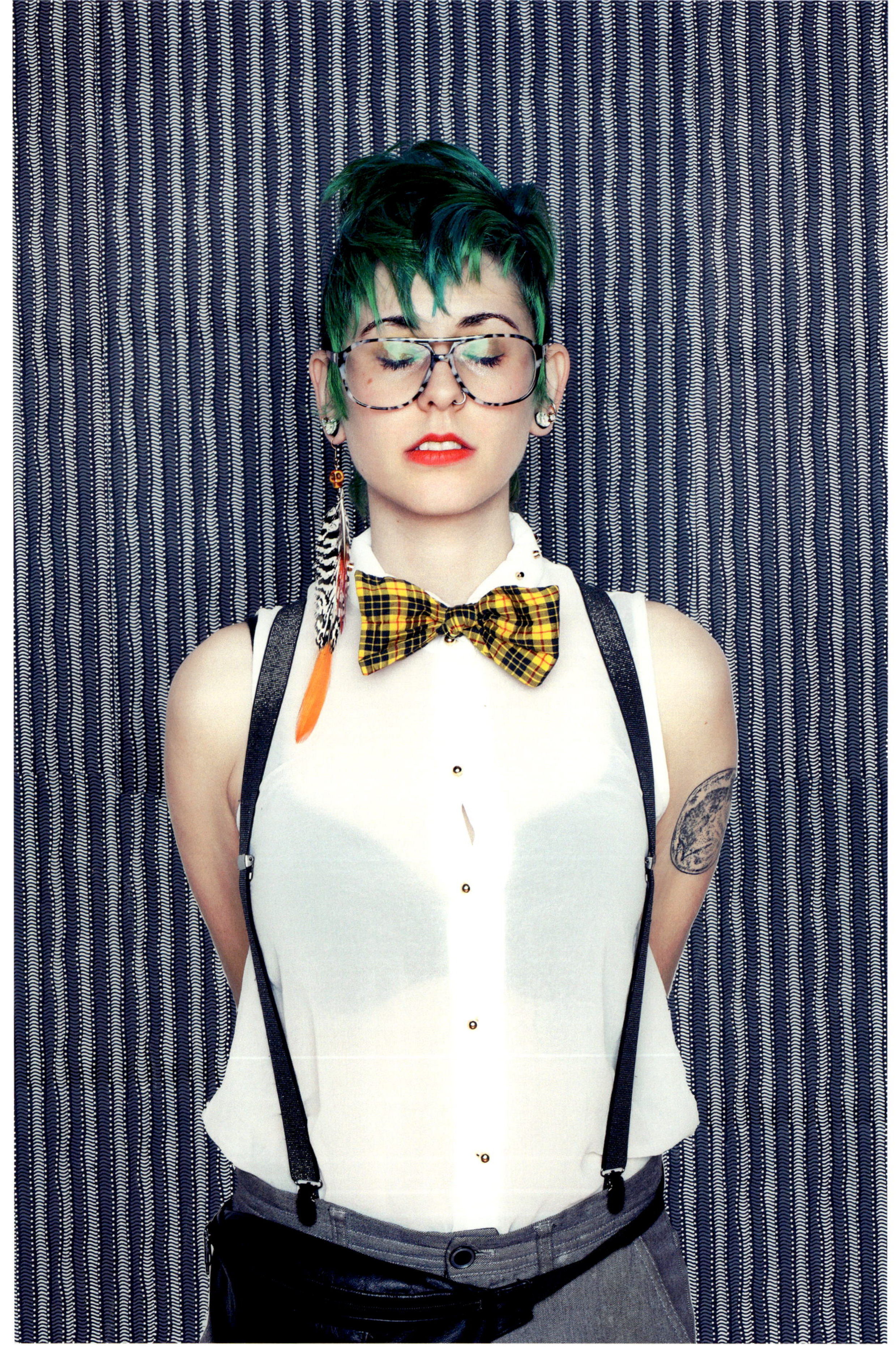

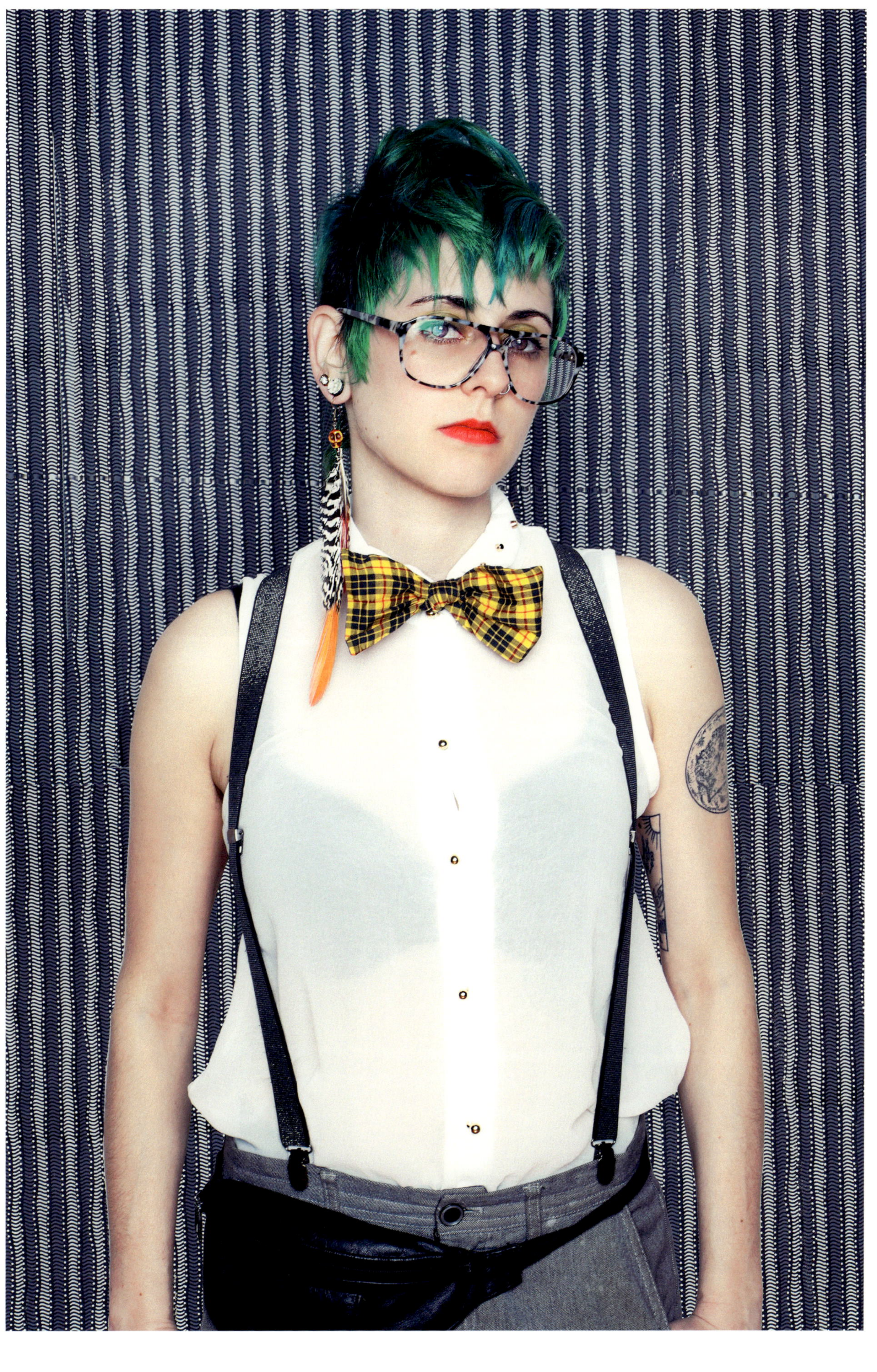

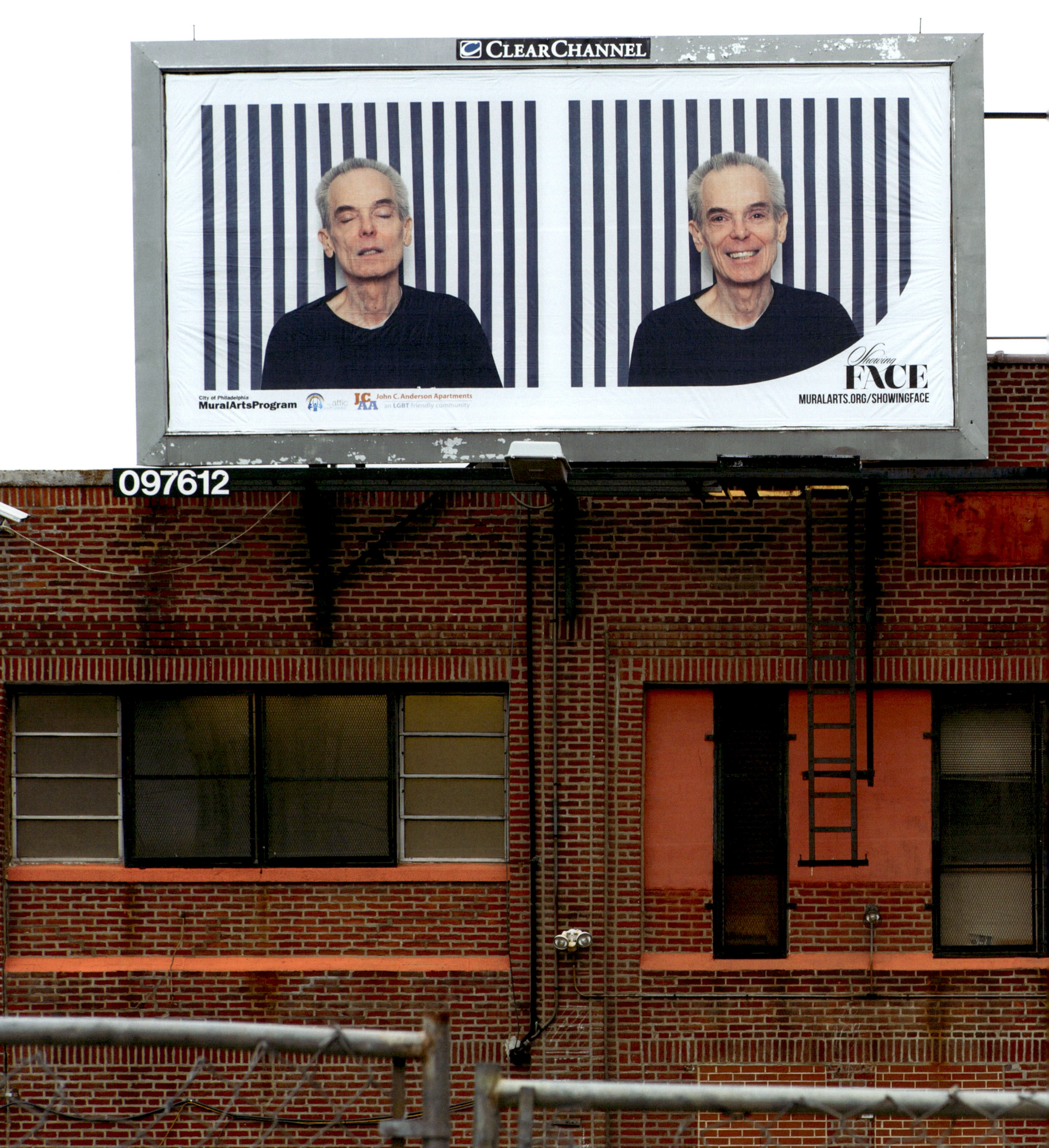

CLEARCHANNEL
City of Philadelphia
MuralArtsProgram
John C. Anderson Apartments
an LGBT friendly community
Showing
FACE
MURALARTS.ORG/SHOWINGFACE
097612

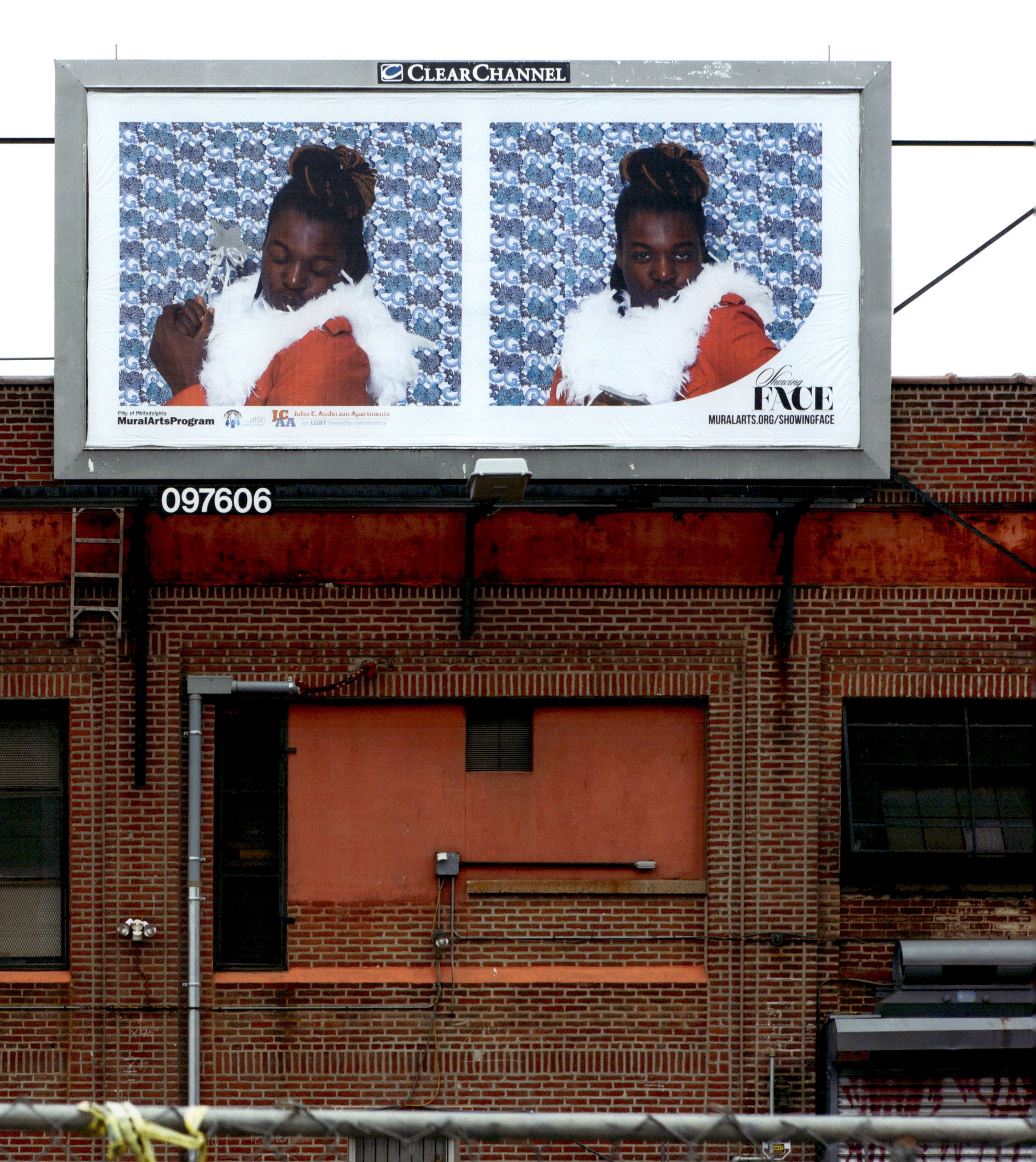
CLEARCHANNEL
City of Philadelphia
MuralArtsProgram
attic
JC AA John C. Anderson Apartments
an LGBT friendly community
Showing
FACE
MURALARTS.ORG/SHOWINGFACE
097606

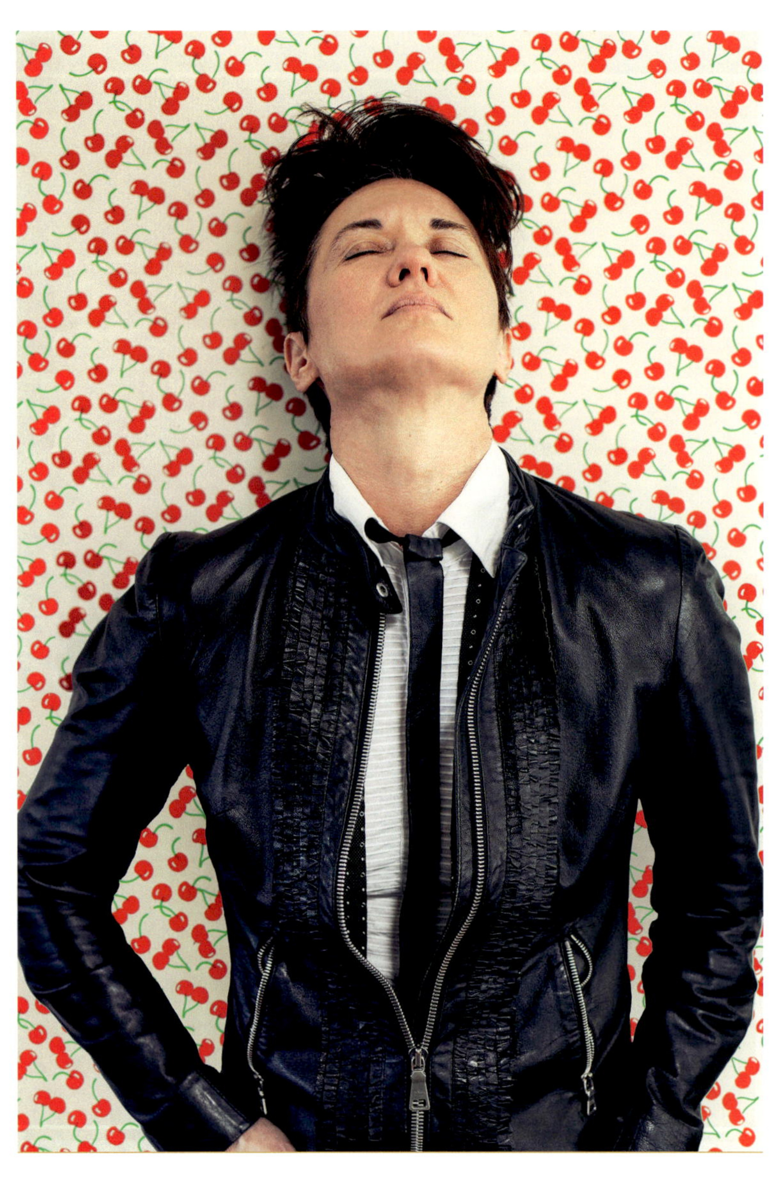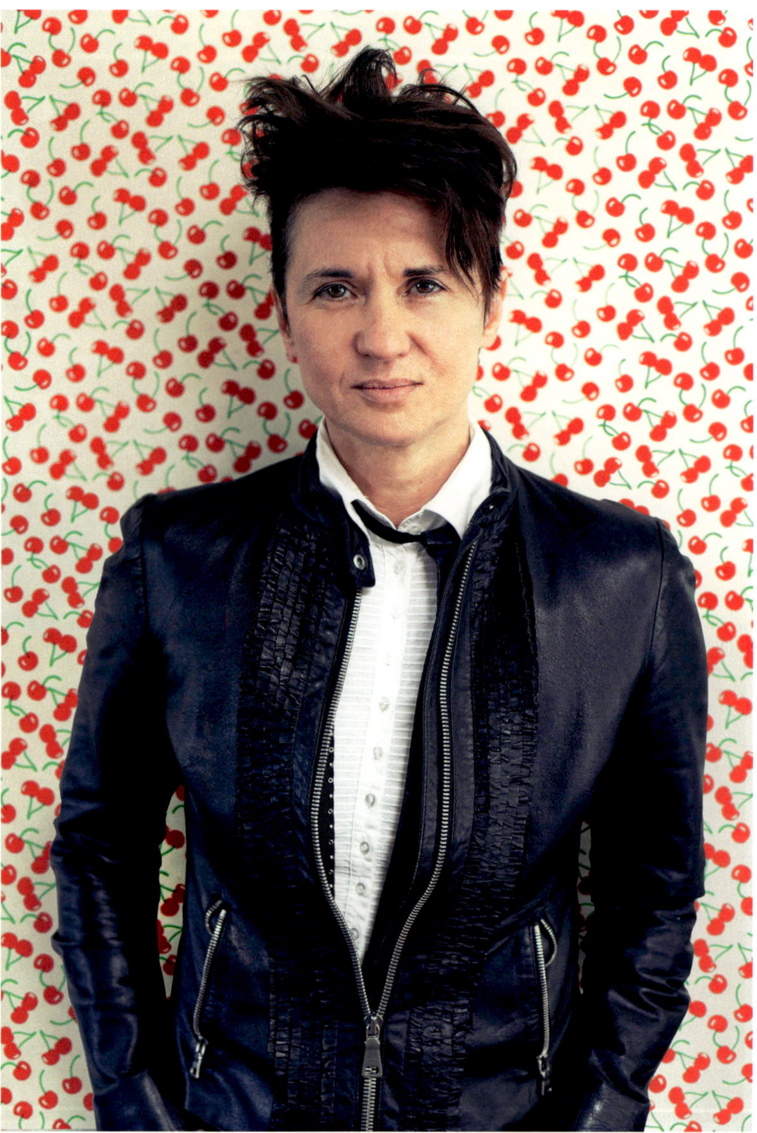

IN CONVERSATION

KIMBERLY PEIRCE AND

ASH KOLODNER

ASH *Boys Don't Cry* was one of the first films to introduce mainstream audiences to a transgender character at a time when transgender and queer characters were rarely represented on screen, much less as the central figure. I recently saw it again at the twentieth-anniversary screening at Columbia University and it hit me just as hard as—or even harder than—when I first saw it. I sobbed, which I think was as much for the tragedy of Brandon's story as it was for the way in which you portrayed the senselessness and cruelty of the people around him. I think what struck me most was how Brandon's adversaries, people he believed cared about him, could carry such hatred. It's just so heartbreaking to feel it, in 2020—after we've come so far—the hatred, based on such profound fear, being as alive today as it's ever been, amplified even more so now because of the "connections" provided by the internet and social media. I'd love to hear how you first came across Brandon's story, and what made you feel like you needed to make your film of it. What was that journey like for you?

KIM Thinking back, I'm amazed that I even heard about the story when I did. On April 14, 1994, I was working the midnight shift in midtown Manhattan at the law firm Latham & Watkins, trying to stay up all night to do my job, then make it through class back at Columbia grad film school the next morning. Around 2:00 a.m., my buddy Huong Duong ran down to get the *Village Voice* as the news trucks dropped off batches on Thirty-Ninth Street. He dropped it on my desk, opened to the cover story about Teena Brandon, a Nebraska teenager who had transformed himself into Brandon Teena, and lived and loved as a man. I immediately fell in love with this wild

and wonderful person, fell in love with the power of Brandon's desire to live and love as he wanted with few examples of any kind to guide him; and I was devastated that he was raped and murdered by people he trusted.

Early that morning when I walked out of work, I felt like I had adopted a child and it was my job to bring Brandon and his story to life. To do that, I knew I had to figure out who Brandon was, how he saw himself, how he lived and loved, and how and why he made it down to Falls City and fell in with Lana, Tom, and John, and then how the events between all of them unfolded. It was my fantasy for years to make the film *Boys Don't Cry* but I didn't imagine, in my wildest dreams, that it could ever really happen. I honestly thought that if we did manage to shoot the film and release it, we'd be lucky if it played at the Two Boots Cinema on Second Avenue in the East Village—a place where you came for a slice of pizza and a movie was playing, projected against the wall.

To understand what *Boys Don't Cry* is and what an extraordinary feat it was to make it, I have to take you back to where we were culturally and the enormous odds we were up against, making and releasing a feature film about and sympathetic to a trans person—it just hadn't ever been done.

Growing up, I didn't have any role models for my queer, trans-ish identity, my desire for women, or my desire to inhabit and explore various aspects of my gender that were not the norm—being a tomboy, dressing like a boy, having fun like a boy. So I became adept at transmogrifying my own desire onto certain characters I had some kind of affinity for that I saw in TV, movies, and art—cartoon characters, like Spiderman, Speed Racer, and Superman, hidden queers like Jodie Foster in *Foxes*, guys in movies who did things, were active and charismatic and got the girl.

Then, I saw Fellini's *8 ½*, originally titled, *The Beautiful Confusion*, and a door was blown open—it was the first time I saw desire expressed in ways I knew and yearned to express. I wanted to love women as Marcello Mastroianni did; I wanted to move through the world as this elegant 1960s Italian male—with his sweeping, silver fox hair, in his Martini slim-fit black suit, thin black tie, crisp white shirt and overcoat. He became my avatar.

So, immediately after reading the *Village Voice* piece, I got onto LexisNexis legal research and got ahold of everything ever written or filmed on the case, and started researching and interviewing trans people and butch lesbians about Brandon. During this time, I discovered a self-named trans activist group "Transsexual Menace," founded by Rikki Anne Wilchins. She and members of this group were meeting up in Lincoln, Nebraska, where Brandon was from, then travelling together to Falls City, to be a presence at the murder trial and hold a vigil for Brandon. Rikki said somebody had dropped out and needed to get rid of their ticket. I immediately bought it, took a few weeks off work, flew to Lincoln, stayed in the house with Rikki and the other members, including Kate Bornstein, Nancy Nangeroni, Tony Barettonetto, Kim Iwamoto, and others. We connected immediately about Brandon, and worked together to imagine who he was and how he might have lived. Everyone was extraordinarily generous, sharing with me, on video, their early histories, and journeys through their own desire, queerness, and identity. After a while Kate Bornstein turned the tables on me, referring to me as "he." She said, "You like that. You perked up." I did. I was open. I have always been pretty fluid in my sexuality and gender, felt "trans-ish" and masculine of center. I just didn't know where I fell on the spectrum. Still figuring it out.

Because of how Brandon identified and lived, I always assumed we would cast a trans person to play him. I looked for years, auditioning every trans person, every drag king, every butch lesbian, and every straight-identified person I could, to find someone who could bring this extraordinary person to life. A lot of great people tried out. After three long years of looking, we were greenlit and didn't have our Brandon, so I asked Kerry Barden, our casting agent

to "pull out all the stops" and bring me everybody he could find to play the role. Tapes came in, one after another. No one was getting it. Then late one night as I was lying on the couch watching the hundredth or so tape, a person came onscreen, with a wonderful energy and enthusiasm, a bit masculine, wonderfully androgynous, gorgeous, huge brown eyes, a strong jaw, a warmth and a smile. Sometimes people who had auditioned performed masculinity by sacrificing their sense of play, wonder, warmth, and their smile—aspects I knew Brandon must have had, and the Brandon in our story needed them to open the many doors he opened, to friends, family and lovers. This person's name was Hilary Swank. Hilary brought Brandon to life in a way I would never have expected and had never seen. In fact, I got an email just the other day, as I do so often, from a young trans man who wanted to let me know how much Hilary's portrayal of Brandon had impacted him.

I'm amazed that we got any money to shoot the film; amazed that when we ran out of money two weeks into shooting, my producer Christine Vachon said Independent Film Channel was going to film me directing the sex scene because they were giving us a million bucks. I thought we were rich. It turns out the studio was going to shut us down if we hadn't found that money. I was amazed that when we ran out of money again, Fox Searchlight, a major studio, bought the film based on our twenty-minute trailer from Sundance; this had never been done before. I was amazed after we got an X rating because the movie showed things that our culture represses—female desire, female pleasure, and female sexuality, as well as an authentic look at rape. I was amazed that we got a ten-minute standing ovation on our first screening, at the Venice International Film Festival. People kept saying, "We love Brandon!" "We love Brandon!" I was so deeply stunned and appreciative. But we couldn't release the movie with an X rating because the studio couldn't advertise it. I'm amazed that I was able to work with the ratings board to transform our X rating to an R. The movie sustained its audience and stayed in theaters for eight months and is still streamed and screened all over the world.

The film's reach over these last twenty years has helped introduce Brandon Teena to a lot of people who otherwise wouldn't have met or known someone like him. I think it also helped a lot of queers at

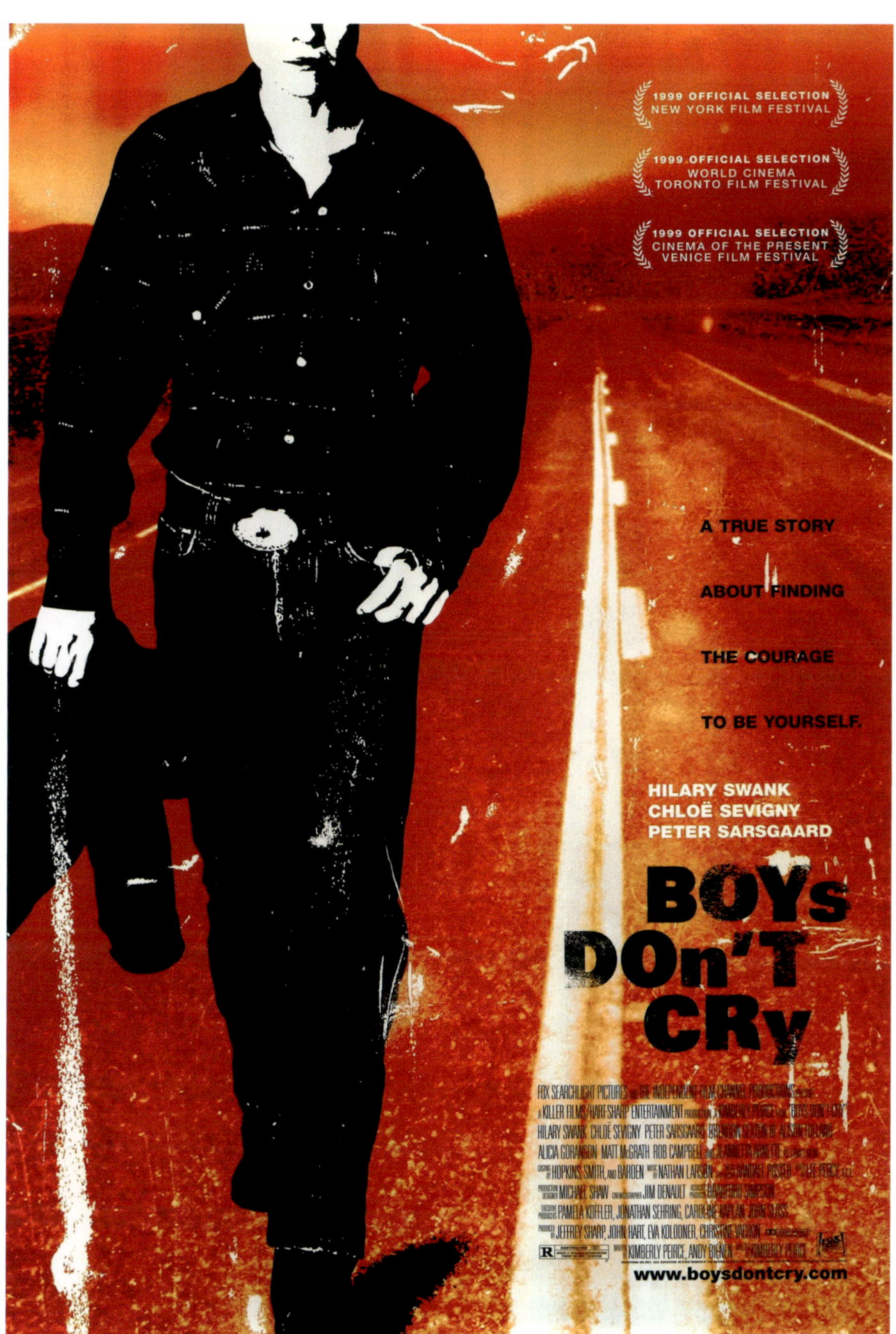

Official movie poster for *Boys Don't Cry*, the award-winning 1999 autobiographical film about Brandon Teena, a transgender young man living in rural Nebraska, directed by Kimberly Peirce.

the time "see" themselves. When it came out, and since, many people said, "I didn't know 'what I was' until I saw *Boys*," or they thanked me for making a movie that "helped me know myself." Parents would say to me, "I didn't know what my child was going through, and this helped me understand." One of my professors at Columbia told me that his child was like Brandon. I am still amazed by all of the success that followed, the world's embrace of Brandon, the awards, Chloe's nomination; Hilary's Oscar; the movie's legacy—now in the Library of Congress as a "national treasure." Bringing a version of Brandon Teena and his story to life has been the greatest journey of my life. I believe that *Boys Don't Cry*, and everything that has followed, exists because of Brandon: the power of who he was, and the power of his desire to live and love as he needed and wanted.

August 2020

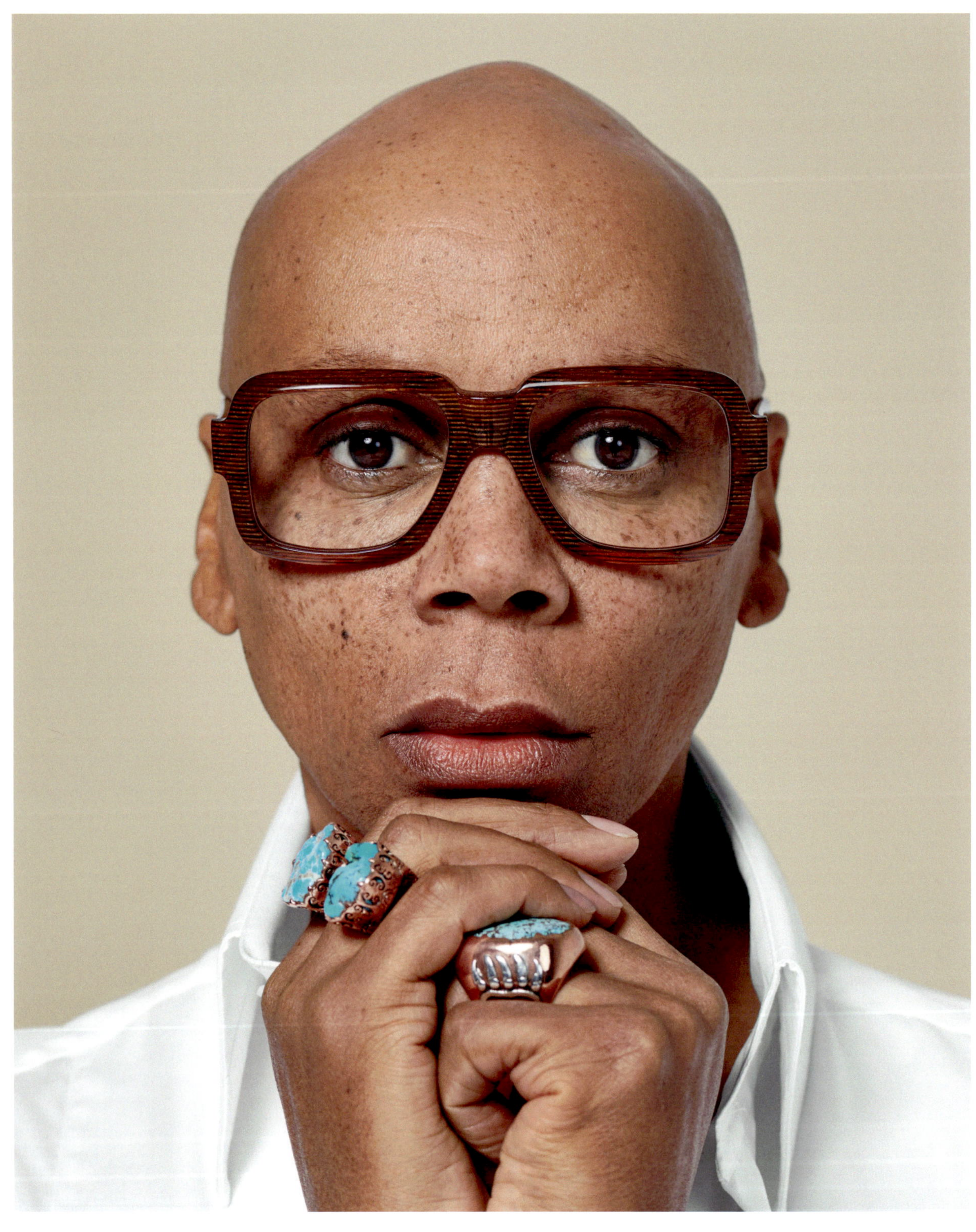

© Dylan Coulter

Q&A
RUPAUL

Of all your accomplishments, what are you most proud of and why?

I take credit for having the resilience to stay in the game long enough to reap the rewards. Life is hard, period. No matter if you're in show business or in no business, life will challenge you to accept, evolve, rethink or retreat. Ask anyone who's been around for longer than a minute and they'll tell you about their bouts with questioning the relevancy of getting out of bed in the morning. "Stickwithitness," flexibility and adaptability are your greatest strengths. In the end, the last player standing wins the prize.

Gayface is so much about one's identity in relation to visibility and "being seen." What did identity mean to you as a young person growing up and coming out? What does it mean to you today? How has that defini-tion of identity changed or evolved for you?

From as far back as I can remember, I've always felt like an alien playing "dress-up" as a human. I've never limited myself to just one or two looks. I want to try ALL the looks. That's why David Bowie reso-nated so deeply with me. Ultimately, time has taught me that the only person I truly need to be "seen" by is me.

When I came across this quote of yours, it resonated so deeply and meaningfully with me that I had to include it as the epigraph to this book: "When you become the image of your own imagination, it's the most powerful thing you could ever do." Why do you believe it's the most powerful thing someone could ever do? What was your path to "becoming the image of your own imagination"?

The word "God" is used to describe that which cannot be described. You are an extension of God expressing itself in human form. In stillness, your intuition will guide your co-creation.

You once said in an interview with *Time* magazine, "When it gets down to survival, you have to pick your battles, and you don't pick battles with your allies." Today, at a moment when the world feels so divided, allyship feels more important than ever. How do you think we can get better at not just being allies to one another, but accomplices?

We need to start by recognizing there is only one of us here. We are not separate from one another. The sole purpose of the Ego is to create enemies and separate you from the rest of the world so it can ulti-mately kill you. The solution is to remain diligently conscious of sole purpose of the Ego. From there, we move from a place of shared humanity.

If you could write a letter to your younger self, what would you say to him?

You are loved.

XO, Ru

ACKNOWLEDGMENTS

Sincere gratitude to all who participated in the project.
These names are those who were photographed but do not appear in the book.

Aaliyah V. • Aaron D. • Abbey W. • Abigail G. • Adam I. • Adam P. • Aidan W. Aishah M. • Akeno Y. • Alek S. • Alex P. • Alex R. • Alexis F. • Alice R. • Alicia M. Alissa P. • Allison B. • Allison V. • Alyssa O. • Amanda K. • Amanda T. Amber J. • Ameila O. • Amore' N. • Amy T. • Ana H. • Andre W. • Andrea T. Andrew L • Andrew S. • Angel C. • Angel M. • Angela C. • Anita V. • Anjali D. Anna H. • Anna L. • Anna R. • Anthony J. • Anthony L. • April W. • Aria U. Ashley D. • Asia D. • Atanga M. • Ava B. • Avery W. • Awah L. • Barbara M. Beckford E. • Bekie C. • Bekkah K. • Ben H. • Betty D. • Bianca M. • Bihe J. Billy O. • Bourey D. • Brad T. • Bradley E. • Bradley W. • Brandon T. Brenda S. • Brett K. • Brian L. • Brian P. • Brianna E. • Brittany C. • Bruno D. Bryan E. • Caitlin N. • Caleb E. • Carl A. • Carla W. • Carlos V. • Carly C. Carly I. • Carmello C. • Carol L. • Carol P. • Carrie J. • Carter M. • Casey T. Catalina L. • Chan M. • Charle D. • Charlotte B. • Charlotte R. • Cheveale M. Chiara J. • China A. • Chloe C. • Chris T. • Christina I. • Christina T Christophe M. • Christopher E. • Claire D. • Claire S. • Clarice R. • Cody W. Cole S. • Conner J. • Corey B. • Cory H. • Courtney H. • Courtney N. • Craig S. Crosby E. • Crystal G. • Dakota R. • Daniel B. • Danielle M. • Darnell O. Davey I. • David C. • David L. • David M. • Daychia S. • Deb J. • Deborah H. Debra P. • Deja P. • Demetrius B. • Denny S. • Denzel T. • Derek J. • Derek P. Derrick T. • DeShawn W. • Desiree C. • Deszio M. • Deylin S. • Diamond S. Dominique S. • Donald C. • Donna D. • Doug W. • Drew G. • Dustin D. Dustin V. • Dwight N. • Dylan E. • Dylan K. • Ebony R. • Eleanor K. • Elijah B. Elison O. • Elizabeth A. • Elizabeth G. • Ella D. • Emani H. • Emily R. • Emma P. Eric B. • Erica B. • Erin D. • Erin P. • Erin T. • Ethan C. • Evan R. • Evelyn S. Felipe L. • Fernado A. • Franko I. • Gardette H. • Garret R. • George M. George N. • Glen T. • Glenda S. • Grace C. • Graham B. • Grayson K. Greeny V. • Greg J. • Greg M. • Hailey M. • Harper S. • Hazel B. • Heather T. Heidi C. • Helene M. • Henry B. • Hoka P. • Holly W. • Hyacynth P. • Ian L. Imani S. • Irene S. • Isaac N. • Isabella J. • Isobel H. • J. G. • Jack I. • Jack K.

Jack T. • Jackie A. • Jackson W. • Jacob N. • Jada S. • Jamal K. • James C.
James D. • James H. • James M. • James M. • Jameson P. • Jamie D.
Janna R. • Jared D. • Jasmin H. • Jason F. • Jaydin N. • Jazmine R.
Jen D. • Jen S. • Jena H. • Jenna B. • Jenny A. • Jeremy R. • Jerry K.
Jesse A. • Jessica B. • Jessica R. • Jill Z. • Jimmy D. • John B. • John M.
John R. • Jon R. • Jonathan A. • Jordan R. • Jorge M. • Jose G. • Jose T.
Joseph B. • Joseph L. • Josh R. • Joshua S. • Juamla E. • Juan T. • Judith C.
Junior F. • Justin S. • Kaitlin R. • Karen E. • Karen K. • Karen M. • Karen M.
Katelyn V. • Kateryna K. • Kathleen D. • Kathrine L. • Kathrine M. • Katie K.
Katy M. • Ken D. • Ken D. • Ken S. • Ken W. • Kerbira W. • Kevin C. • Kiara T.
Kiersten S. • Kim R. • Kiri M. • Kristin H. • Kristina R. • Kyle L. • Lani B.
Lauren M. • Layla N. • Leah F. • Lee G. • Lee W. • Leo W. • Leonardo C.
Levi J. • Liam S. • Lillian G. • Lina G. • Lincoln W. • Linda L. • Linda M.
Lindsey N. • Lisa K. • Lisa M. • Logan L. • Logan R. • Logan S. • Lola S.
Lonnie C. • Louise P. • Lucas M. • Luke A. • Luke T. • Maddy T. • Madeline O.
Madison E. • Madison Q. • Malik M. • Marcus P. • Margaret M. • Maria H.
Maria N. • Maria S. • Mario R. • Mark P. • Mark R. • Mark S. • Marquis P.
Mary F. • Mary H. • Mary L. • Mary V. • Mason F. • Mateo M. • Mathew C.
Matthew N. • Maurice R. • Maxwell D. • Maxx S. • May K. • Maya H. • Megan C.
Megan L. • Melanie A. • Melanie D. • Melinda B. • Melinda F. • Melissa M.
Meredith D. • Mia S. • Michael D. • Michael D. • Micheal D. • Michelle A.
Michelle M. • Ming F. • Molly M. • Nancy B. • Nathan B. • Nia F. • Nick L.
Nicol P. • Nicole K. • Nicole R. • Noah B. • Nora S. • Oleksil C. • Oliver V.
Olivier B. • Owen R. • Pablo C. • Paisley A • Panos M. • Patricia B. • Patricia D.
Patricia L. • Paula R. • Paulina V. • Pedro H. • Penelope C. • Penno G.
Peter T. • Phillip L • Rachael W. • Rachel J. • Rachell R. • Rae B. • Rae K.
Rafael C. • Raheim R. • Randy A. • Rasheem F. • Rebeca P. • Rebecca S.
Rebekah C. • Reinna A. • Remy S. • Richard H. • Richard M. • Richard N.
Richard W. • Richard W. • Robby J. • Robert J. • Romina C. • Ronald B.
Ronald D. • Ryan C. • Ryan L. • Ryan N. • Sal V. • Salador D. • Sam A.
Sandra G. • Sara B. • Sara L. • Sarah G. • Sarah H. • Sarah L. • Scarlott K.
Scott K. • Sean P. • Sebastian T. • Senka F. • Sera V. • Sergio M. • Shane D.
Shanice S. • Shea A. • Shipla J. • Simon J. • Sonia A. • Sophia E. • Star S.
Stephanie A. • Steven E. • Steven F. • Steven H. • Steven P. • Susan A.
Susan L. • Tabitha P. • Tammy B. • Tara R. • Theo B. • Thomas R. • Tierra W.
Tiffanie Y. • Tiffany B. • Tom R. • Tomas V. • Travis W. • Tyler W. • Tyrone N.
Tyrone W. • Vainela T. • Valerie P. • Vanessa G. • Vanessa Z. • Victoria S.
Victoria T. • Vincente C. • Violet L. • Walter G. • Weslee I. • William B.
Willian Y. • Willie H. • Wyatt T. • Xavier B. • Xenia S. • Yunna L. • Zoe C. • Zoey F.

GLOSSARY

Each of these terms and their definitions has been thoughtfully conceived and closely reviewed by teachers, scholars, friends, and others within the LGBTQ+ community. Together, we have done our best to be as sensitive and inclusive as possible. This glossary is by no means comprehensive, nor perfect; definitions may vary depending on one's context and perspective.

And, dear readers, please remember that our use of these terms is just as unique as each of us is. We humans are ever evolving, as is the language we use for communicating. When we are unsure about how to use a term, or the context in which another person is using it, perhaps this is an opportunity to connect and communicate with mindfulness, care, and especially love.

—Ash Kolodner

ally   A person outside the LGBTQ+ community who actively supports its interests and seeks to advance the LGBTQ+ cause. An ally may show support through advocating for the rights and safety of LGBTQ+ people, publicly challenging heteronormativity, and questioning their own prejudices.

androgynous   Possessing a combination of—or lacking—characteristics traditionally viewed as masculine or feminine within a heteronormative framework.

asexual   Experiencing little to no sexual attraction to others; lacking interest in sex. Asexuality occurs on a spectrum, characterized at one end by a total lack of desire and at the other by low levels of desire, or by desire fueled by specific conditions. It should not be confused with celibacy, which refers to the intentional abstention from sex. Those who identify as asexual ("ace") may prefer to self-label as belonging to one of a variety of subcategories (*see*, for example, **demisexual**).

bi-curious   Not necessarily identifying as LGBTQ+ but interested in pursuing flirtations, relationships, or sexual encounters that would not be considered heterosexual.

biphobia   Fear of bisexuality and/or hatred of bisexual people, often based on incorrect assumptions about fidelity, promiscuity, and commitment. Those who are biphobic may take the view that bisexuality is an invalid or "false" expression of sexuality. Biphobia is prevalent in the LGBTQ+ community as well as in heterosexual society.

bisexual   One who is sexually and romantically attracted to more than one gender (*see also* **pansexual**). Bisexuality, while considered by some to be a temporary condition or "phase" (*see* **biphobia**), is also, like homosexuality or heterosexuality, a stable identity. It is not necessary for one to have had sex with more than one gender to identify as bisexual.

butch   A word used throughout the LGBTQ+ community to describe a person or thing considered traditionally masculine in quality or spirit. Within the lesbian, queer, and trans communities, the term butch is commonly attributed to a vast and varied spectrum of masculine-leaning presentations or self-identifications.

cisgender   A word describing a person whose gender identity conforms to the sex they were assigned at birth (for example, someone assigned female at birth who identifies as a woman). Meaning "on the side of," *cis* is used to call attention to the privilege of those whose identity matches the sex they were assigned at birth.

closeted   A person who is not openly living their LGBTQ+ identity.

coming out   The act of declaring one's identity as a member of the LGBTQ+ community, not be confused with outing, which is involuntary. The process of coming out is ongoing throughout one's life and is often not linear, as one may choose when and with whom the information is shared.

cross-dresser   A person whose manner of gender expression implies a subversion of traditional gender norms through dress. The term often refers to a person who dons the clothes of what might be considered the "opposite" gender. It is used as a self-identifier by individuals both within and without the LGBTQ+ community and does not connote a specific gender identity or sexual orientation. It is also incorrectly and pejoratively directed at various members of the LGBTQ+ community and can be considered an act of aggression. Cross-dressing should not be confused or conflated with drag.

dead naming The act of calling someone by the name they were given at birth rather than their chosen name.

demisexual A person who has little to no interest in sex outside a relationship involving a strong emotional romantic attachment. Demisexuals are considered to be on the asexuality spectrum.

down low A term that arose in the late '90s when young urban Black men living in a hypermasculine culture were expected to comport themselves according to prescribed social mores and thus discouraged from identifying openly as gay or bisexual for fear of violence and/or rejection from their communities. Typically used to describe the activities of a man who presents as straight but engages in covert sexual activity with other men.

drag The art of performing gender in an inherently subversive manner, often as entertainment, and often through the use of visual caricature and exaggerated mannerisms and affectations.

dyke Originally a derogatory term for a masculine-presenting, butch, or androgynous lesbian woman, the word *dyke* has since been reclaimed by some as a positive self-identifier within the lesbian, queer, and trans communities. *Dyke* is still often used as a derogatory term by non-allies.

fag/faggot A derogatory term for a gay person, most frequently used in reference to gay and bisexual men. The word's roots are in the medieval English *faggot*, meaning a "bundle of twigs"; these bundles were commonly used in the burning of those accused of witchcraft and homosexuality. The term has since been reclaimed as a subversive and provocative self-identifier; however, as with *dyke*, the word *faggot* is still used by some as a slur.

femme A word used throughout the LGBTQ+ community to describe a person that could be considered traditionally feminine in physical appearance and/or spirit. Within the lesbian, queer, and trans communities, the term femme is used across a varied spectrum of feminine-presenting individuals of any gender.

gay Sexually and romantically (and often solely) attracted to the same gender as one's self. The term can be used as a self-identifier by any person whose sexual and romantic lives exist outside the bounds of heterosexuality.

gender A set of cultural identities, expressions, and roles that people claim or that are assigned to them. In heteronormative culture, the genders are assumed to be either male or female and are based on the interpretation of bodies, specifically, their sexual and reproductive anatomy. Since gender is a social construct, it is possible to reject or modify the assignment made, and develop something that feels truer and just to oneself.

gender affirming surgery A general term for a number of different surgical procedures that enable trans people to treat their physical dysphoria and align their anatomy with their sense of self. Not everyone who undergoes gender affirmation surgery considers themselves trans, and not every trans person feels the need to undergo or has access to gender affirmation surgery.

gender binary The concept, considered oppressive by many, that there are only two genders, male and female, and that all individuals must fall into one of the two categories.

gender dysphoria The dissatisfaction or discomfort felt when one's assigned gender—that is, one's birth gender—does not match up with one's true gender. A person who experiences gender dysphoria does not necessarily experience physical dysphoria (the feeling that one's emotional and mental self does not align with one's physical self) and vice versa. Many, but not all, people who experience gender dysphoria identify as trans.

gender expression   The way in which a person communicates their gender to the outside world, through clothing, mannerisms, behavior, etc.

gender-fluid   A term that describes those whose gender identity is not fixed but may vary among two or several genders, and can shift within an individual from day to day, moment to moment, or throughout their lifetime.

gender identity   A person's deeply held inner sense of their own gender, which may correspond to or differ from the sex they were assigned at birth, and may or may not correlate with a person's gender expression.

gender nonconforming   Not conforming to society's gender norms. Often abbreviated "GNC," this term is used as a self-identifier to describe individuals whose gender (or lack thereof) does not correlate with what would be traditionally expected of them based on the gender that was assigned to them at birth.

genderqueer   A term used to describe one whose gender does not fit into heteronormative constructs. Those who are genderqueer may identify as genderfluid, androgynous, on the trans spectrum, or as a combination of these and other identities.

heteronormative   That which assumes heterosexuality and its attendant practices—monogamy, reproductive sex —as the structuring standard, or norm; of or related to a straight-centric ideology. Heteronormativity aligns with society's gender-based expectations, marginalizes other sexual practices, and stigmatizes queer people.

heterosexism   The assumption that all people are straight and that those who are not are "outside" and thus "less." Heterosexism discriminates against lesbian, gay, bisexual, and queer people, as well as against those whose desires and beliefs fall outside heteronormativity:

for example, the woman who does not desire children.

heterosexual   A person who is sexually and romantically attracted to members of what is considered "the opposite gender" within a heteronormative framework.

homophobia   Fear of LGBTQ+ people. Homophobia often manifests in discriminatory attitudes and actions against behaviors, appearances and situations that are considered outside the hetero norm.

homosexual   A person who is sexually and romantically attracted to members of their own gender. The term *homosexual* is increasingly being replaced with **gay**, **lesbian**, or **queer**.

hormone replacement therapy (HRT)   Physician-monitored administration of "sex" hormones such as estrogen, progesterone, and testosterone as medical treatment for physical dysphoria felt by GNC, trans, non-binary, and other queer people, as well as many other individuals within and without the LGBTQ+ community for birth control, as treatment for menopause, growth delays, etc.

intersex   A general term referring to individuals born with the biological, cis-specific male and female attributes of two sexes. Historically, and to this day, intersex people experienced non-consensual HRT and genital mutilation as babies, and throughout their lives, at the hands of their families and medical professionals. This umbrella term has replaced the dated and derogatory *hermaphrodite*.

lesbian   A woman-identified person who is physically and romantically attracted to other women-identified people. The term's roots are in the name of the Greek island of Lesbos, home to the poet Sappho, who herself was a lover of women.

LGBTQ+   Acronym standing for "lesbian, gay, bisexual, trans, and queer." The + refers the a vast number of other identities,

such as *I* for **intersex**, *A* for **asexual**, *Q* for **questioning**, etc.

living openly/being out   Living comfortably and freely in the world as an LQBTQ+ person. The phrase is generally associated with those who are vocal about their orientation, as the conditions suit them (*see* **coming out**).

misgendering   Attributing to a person the incorrect gender. This may take the form of an incorrect pronoun, gendered language, or the assigning of gender to someone without knowledge of how they identify.

Mx.   Pronounced variously "Məks," "Miks," and "Em-eks," this primarily written gender-neutral honorific has evolved to take the place of the gendered *Miss, Ms., Mrs.*, and *Mr.*

non-binary   A person whose gender exists outside of the gender binary. It is important to remember that not all nonbinary people identify as trans, and that not all trans people identify as nonbinary. Some nonbinary people identify as genderqueer or gender nonconforming.

orientation   A person's sexual identity or attraction, which may be fluid or not.

outing   The act of non-consensually revealing a person's sexual orientation, gender identity, intersex status, or membership in the LGBTQ+ community without that person's knowledge and/ or against that person's wishes. Whether done maliciously or out of ignorance, outing can result in dire emotional, financial and physical consequences for the person being outed.

pansexual   Attracted to people of multiple gender identities and expressions.

passing   Assumed to be straight and/ or cis-gender in general society, based on physical traits, dress, mannerisms, and so on. Passing may be done intentionally or not.

pronoun   A word standing in for a noun or noun phrase. In English, third-person pronouns referring to people have long been typically gendered (*he/she, him/her*). In recent years, a plethora of new gender-neutral pronouns has arrived (for example, *ze/zir* and variants thereof), with *they/them* being perhaps the most prevalent and reflecting the adoption of the plural as standing in for the singular where binary gender need not be or should not be expressed.

queer   A broad term describing those who don't identify as straight and/or cisgender. Historically used as a slur, the word was reclaimed by LGBTQ+ community in the late 1980s as embodying a radical and anti-assimilationist stance. Though today it is commonly employed as a positive term, the word is still used in a pejorative way by some.

questioning   Exploring one's gender expression or sexual identity.

same-gender-loving   This positive term arose in the African American community in the early 1990s as a non-Eurocentric term standing in for, variously, **gay**, **lesbian**, and the now-dated **homosexual**.

sex (sex assigned at birth; biological sex)   A medical categorization based on a person's chromosomal and hormonal makeup and anatomical appearance (i.e., genitalia) at birth, which has no correlation with or relationship to gender. Also referred to as *anatomical sex* or *physical sex*.

sexual attraction   The desire for physical sexual intimacy (for example, touching, kissing, intercourse), typically with others but also with oneself. Not to be confused or conflated with emotional, spiritual, or romantic attraction.

sexual orientation   A person's physical, emotional, and romantic attraction to members of the same and/or opposite sex. Though sexual orientation is considered inherent and thus immutable, it can also be fluid. Sexual orientation is not necessarily revealed in behavior but in feelings of attraction. One does not need to have any sexual experience to have a sexual orientation. (*See also* **orientation**.)

sexual preference   Refers to one's choice of partner and to one's partiality to particular types of sexual stimulation. Often incorrectly used in place of **sexual orientation**, this term implies conscious decision.

sex reassignment surgery (SRS)   Antiquated and offensive. See entry under **gender affirming surgery**

trans   An umbrella term that covers a variety of genderfluid, non-binary and genderqueer identities

transgender   A term that describes one whose gender or gender identity is in opposition to that which they were assigned at birth.

transition   The process of moving away from a socially-prescribed gender presentation based on the sex a person was assigned at birth, aligning one's gender expression with one's gender identity. This may involve changing one's name, pronouns, manner of dress, as well as accessing **HRT**, **gender affirming surgery**, or none of the above.

transphobia   Fear or hatred of trans people. Transphobia occurs within the queer community as well as within the straight community, and is frequently characterized by a refusal to accept trans people's gender identity.

transsexual   A largely outdated, and sometimes pejorative, term referring to those individuals whose gender identity does not match the sex they were assigned at birth. **Transgender** or **trans** are often preferred.

two-spirit   A term coined in the 1990s among North American Native communities as an English phrase representing different "third gender" roles, which have specific social and ceremonial significance among Native tribes. The term is specific to Native culture and should not be used interchangeably with other terms to describe members of the LGBTQ+ community at large.

To my children, Luna and Xolo, who constantly have
me re-looking at the world through many lenses.
I hope you forever feel loved, supported, and
free to be whoever you are your entire life.

I love you.

Copyright © 2023
All rights reserved. No part of this publication may be reproduced
or transmitted in any form or by any means, electronic or mechan-
ical, including photocopy, recording, or any information storage or
retrieval system, without permission in writing from the publisher.

Library of Congress Control Number: 2022941515
ISBN 978-1-64657-004-1

Published by Lucia|Marquand, Seattle
www.luciamarquand.com

Available through ARTBOOK|D.A.P.
75 Broad Street, Suite 630
New York, NY 10004
www.artbook.com

Jacket: Felli M., Brooklyn, NY

Edited by Donna Wingate
Designed by Thomas Eykemans
Typeset in Chronicle Text and Knockout by Maggie Lee
Proofread by Bruno George
Color management by I/O Color, Seattle
Printed and bound in China by Artron Art Group

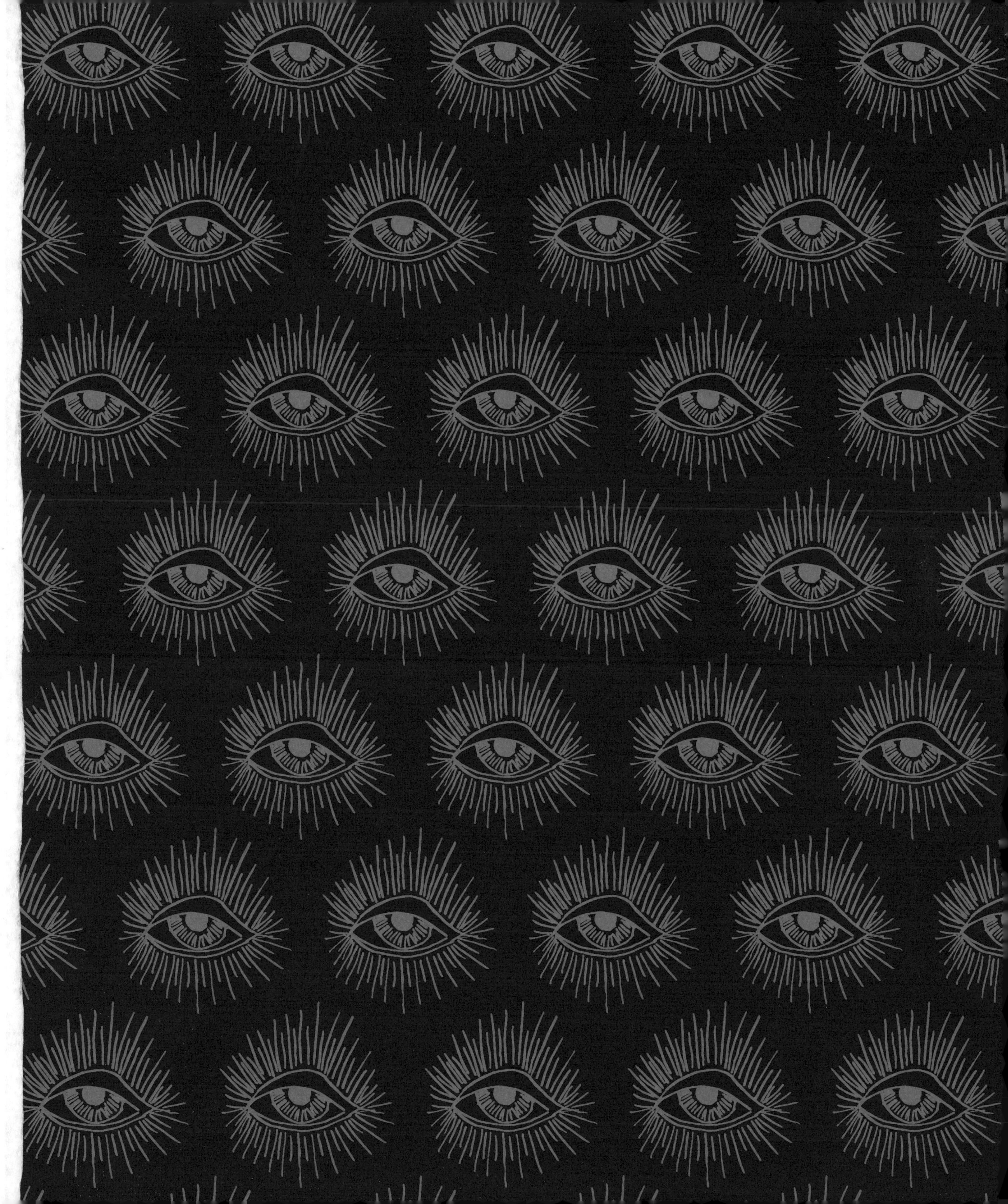

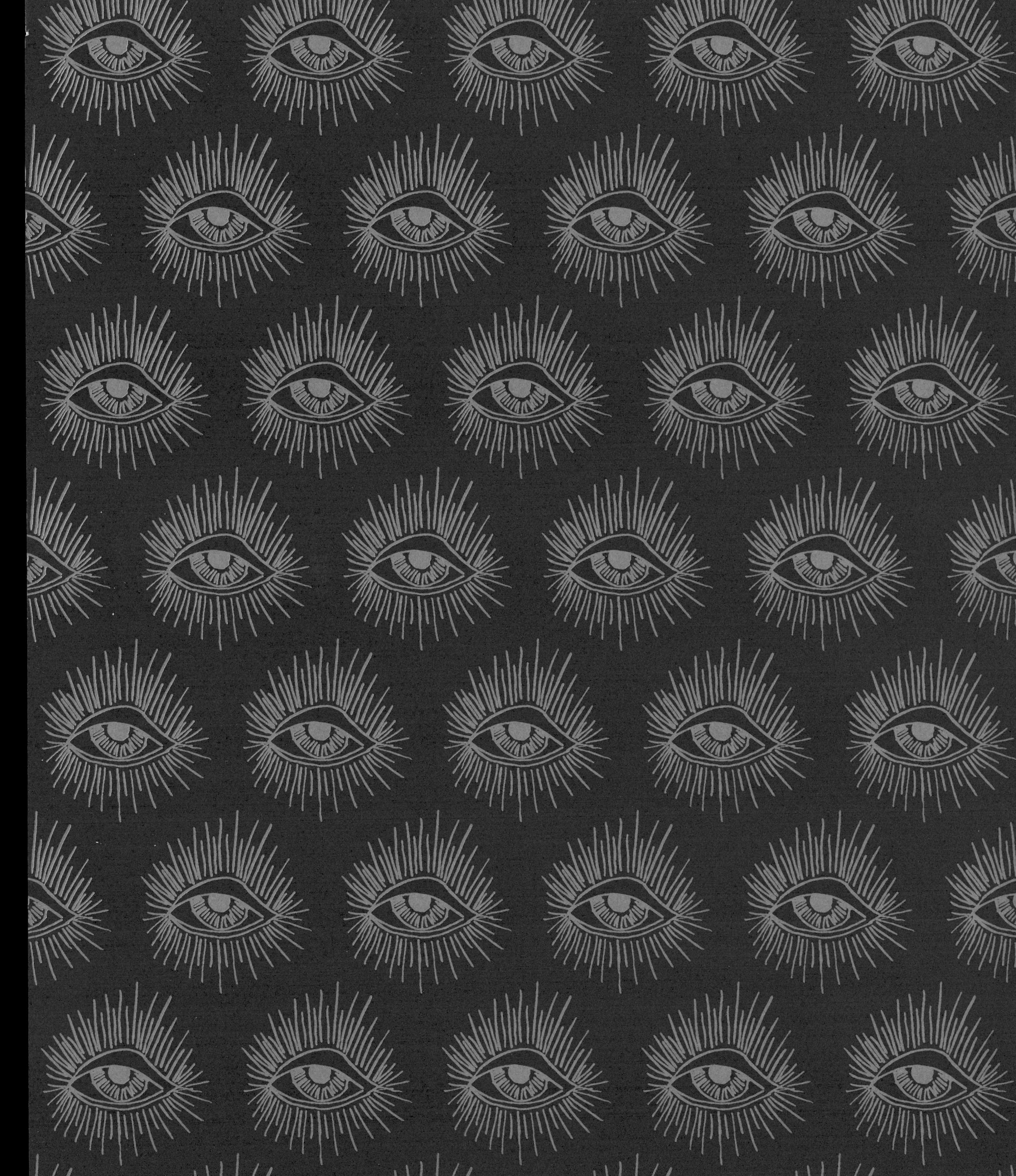